MANAGEMENT CRISIS & BUSINESS REVOLUTION

JOHN HARTE

MANAGEMENT CRISIS & BUSINESS REVOLUTION

Transaction Publishers
New Brunswick (U.S.A) and London (U.K.)

HD
30.17
.H37
1997
June 1998

Library of Congress Catalog Number: 96-47504
ISBN: 1-56000-305-7
Printed in the United States of America

Library of Congress Cataloging-in-Publication Data

Harte, John, 1925–
Management crisis and business revolution / John Harte.
    p.   cm.
Includes bibliographical references and index.
ISBN 1-56000-305-7 (alk. paper)
    1. Industrial management.   2. Organizational behavior.   3. Organizational effectiveness.   I. Title.
HD30.17.H37   1996
658—dc21   96-47504
                                                                              CIP

Contents

Foreword

That marketing has proved itself to be a successful management philosophy and methodology is demonstrated by the vigor and enthusiasm with which prominent national and multinational market leaders continue to practice it. "Marketing is now well and truly out of its proverbial back room and back seat. It is most evidently coming to be recognized as both the business of the future and the future of the business," asserted Sir Colin Marshall in 1995. He is chairman of British Airways and a fellow of the Chartered Institute of Marketing in the UK.

This is not a textbook, but it encompasses all the practical areas in which a marketing executive functions, and also those of a business manager. The following criteria that were used as the foundation for one of the best of textbooks on marketing are all explored in this book. They are business and management concepts, the business and economic environment, opportunities and information, developing strategies, sociological aspects of buyer behavior, psychological aspects that influence consumption of goods and use of services, strategic tools and tactics, market segmentation, marketing research, the marketing mix, product life cycles and categories, commercialization, pricing, distribution, promotion, communications, selling, advertising and the marketing plan, organization, analysis, and program integration, the marketplace, international marketing, ideas, services, special problems, social and ethical issues, and much more.[1]

In addition, most of the business aspects addressed by one of the finest textbooks on business management are used as a structure to establish leading subjects for most chapters of this book.[2] But practical management of the workplace and management in the marketplace have changed in the decade or more since those textbooks were written, whereas this book addresses changes brought about by a business revolution. Perhaps the most significant one, apart from the introduction of new technologies and company downsizing, is that each of those two business philosophies and practices—management and marketing—has merged with the other. Management, which was once oriented to administering the status quo, has been obliged to consider customer wants and public needs as its primary objective, instead of being purely self-serving; and marketing has become more of a general management discipline.

This book's attitude reflects the foibles and follies of the workplace and the uncertainties of the marketplace. By emphasizing workplace realities, it complements those textbooks on management and marketing principles and theories, as it does the CIM Diploma in Marketing.

While CEOs are being blamed for not producing profits or providing dividends, marketing managers are being criticized by CEOs for not delivering. "Marketing lacks direction" and "Costly brand advertising often dwells on seemingly irrelevant points of difference" are the types of remarks we hear almost daily.[3] Apparently, marketing people have become unimaginative, generate few original ideas, and are afraid to take risks in a dramatically changing and far more competitive business environment. A top management consultant recently warned that "now marketing departments are in top management's sights and marketers are going to have to smarten up their act to give value for money."[4]

All of that may be true, but it is illogical for top management to be judgemental about marketing's effectiveness without establishing what went wrong with management to cause it. Flawed marketing is, after all, merely a symptom of an irrelevant management style or inferior management standards.

Those vociferous CEOs are likely to be ones who failed to encourage and support the highest possible standards of marketing and management in their own companies. And their attitude suggests that they are the ones who would have established separate marketing departments in the first place. It is often they who have been found to be short on ideas, resistant to change, and lacking in a rational sense of direction. Those who have not already been fired by angry shareholders for choosing the wrong managers and failing to provide leadership, are even likely not to be able to define what management or marketing are or what they should be doing.

Two decades ago, Robert Heller signalled the symptoms of a management malaise that would result in a business revolution. He described how half of the five hundred largest U.S. companies had annual earnings per share of growth of less than 5 percent between 1969 and 1970. He wrote, "[A]ny company that couldn't double its earnings in an inflationary era, in which all manner of juggles for the painless boosting of earnings per share were invented, has no claim to any managerial skills, even low cunning."[5] And, back in 1960, Theodore Levitt wrote, "The problem is at the top."[6]

Is it? We cannot blame western management for technological changes, or frictions caused by deficit spending, or the economic rise of Pacific Asian economies. On the other hand, signs of impending change were made manifest for two decades. Surely that was sufficient lead time to respond to new challenges? But management hardly changed its attitude or its style at all. Some would say that top management simply lacked vision. That is only part of the problem.

That advertising standards have declined since the 1950s or 1960s is undeniable—Britain's Institute of Practitioners in Advertising held a conference at the end of 1992 to discuss whether advertising agencies were history.

And top management of some national brands went into shock when their main retail distributors began to decimate their market shares and force down their margins by competing with their own store brands. Finally, more sophisticated domestic competition and aggressive marketing from Pacific Asian countries awakened some western market leaders from their complacency. They are pursuing potential new markets in developing and undeveloped countries, and taking advantage of lower Third World costs. It is those who lack vision, entrepreneurial ideas, or innovative marketing skills who are looking around for scapegoats to blame for their own shortcomings, instead.

This book was written at a time when the business world began to change dramatically. Giant corporations like IBM, General Motors, Sears, Royal Trustco, Westinghouse, and American Express were tumbling or downsizing, restructuring or discarding their chief executive after suffering huge financial losses. New, more sophisticated or intellectual companies like Dell, Wal-Mart, Newbridge, Intel, Corel, Microsoft, and Nortel were demonstrating how to be hugely successful, at the same time. Banks, which had mismanaged their traditional services, were gearing up for an onslaught on the Mutual Funds market. Property developers like Olympia & York floundered because of a drop in demand for commercial and industrial real estate, while residential home builders struggled with the aging life cycle in the West and home buyers' reduced disposable incomes. Even the management of military forces and intelligence services was undergoing public scrutiny through a form of *consumerism*. Caught between human rights issues and having to fight wars effectively, their every action was being scrutinised by TV audiences watching the killing fields from the comfort of their own living rooms.

A view of how our managerial times differ from that of two generations ago can be gleaned from *The Managerial Revolution*.[7] Its author pointed out that "we are now in a period of social transition...a period characterized, that is, by an unusually rapid rate of change of the most important economic, social, political, and cultural institutions of society." That was from a capitalist or bourgeois society to a managerial one—whereas we are now moving from a middle-class society to a society consisting of knowledge workers at the upper level and a new proletariat at the lower one. Both largely consist of service sector executives and workers, but income disparity divides them between the haves and the have-nots.

"What is occurring in this transition is a drive for social dominance, for power, for the position of ruling class, by the social group or class of the *managers*" wrote Burnham. "At the conclusion of the transition period the managers will, in fact, have achieved social dominance." They finally did so with the help of the Harvard MBA.[8] Although Burnham's view in 1939/40 was influenced by totalitarian political regimes in fascist and communist nations, top executives became an élite class in the 1980s and 1990s by a democratic process in a capitalist system.

Harvard Business School spawned the Master of Business Administration. It arrived in the UK in the 1960s, but only two MBA courses were available by 1965. By 1995, there were 103 different business schools, colleges, and universities offering 10,000 new places in Britain, compared with 4,500 places seven years previously. The MBA was defined as "a post-graduate, post-experience course in a number of subjects that together can be said to constitute the science of management."[9] (Can it really be called a science?) But in a transitional phase with tremendous management downsizing and companies humbled or failing, are we now witnessing the triumph or the folly of investing such confidence and such large sums of money in MBA graduates?

According to Professor Drucker in 1993, "So far, no country has the educational system which the knowledge society needs."[10]

By now, ideological struggles in and around the workplaces of the 1930s seem quaint and old-fashioned. Even the idea of blue-collar workers or their trade unions struggling to make bad situations even worse, amazes, by comparison with the democratic workplace in countries like Britain today, when party politics have been neutered. Ideological partisanship barely existed prior to Britain's General Election in 1992. What most voters were concerned about was equal opportunity prevailing over the remnants of class privilege. And soon after the Labor party lost, they quietly removed the word "socialist" from their manifesto because it had become obsolete.

The greatest demographic change was illustrated by the replacement of the old paradigm of the pyramid with a small élite class at the summit and layers of impoverished working classes lying along the broad base. Gradual changes over the years turned the diagram into a barrel with its bulging waistline representing the middle classes. By now, the bulge is being slimmed down by heavier and heavier tax burdens. Some of the middle classes have become *déclassé* and are slipping downwards, while some successful entrepreneurs are moving up.

Management is undergoing a revolution in pursuit of perfection that failed to develop by an orderly evolutionary process. Its catalysts were intensive competition from the East, a global economic recession, the silicon computer chip, huge accumulated national debts, and the thrust of Third World countries with lower labor costs and lower environmental standards. The result is company downsizing and restructuring to reduce overhead costs and optimize efficiency through new technologies. The introduction of high technology is revolutionizing the way that management operates and is also creating large-scale unemployment in the West. Payment of interest on the extraordinary budget deficits—due largely to government mismanagement of funds in the 1980s—is preventing western economies from accelerating their slow rise out of a slump, and making the cost of doing business too high. That is encouraging the movement of factories and warehouses to Third World countries.

Managers who are still fortunate to be employed after company downsizing in the last three economic recessions are often so overworked that they can barely cope with routine operational functions. They have neither the time nor the attitude to undertake the very intellectual and creative responsibilities for which managers are normally hired. Often they do not possess the skills, because the era of shirtsleeves management in the past two decades emphasized cost cutting rather than marketing, innovation, or even profitable growth. But now that Japan has caught up with the West, Korea is catching up with Japan, and Germany dominates the European Union, western management is forced to improve itself if it wants to compete in order for its economies to survive.

One means that many companies used to stay in business after downsizing to survive the recessions was to hire younger and less experienced managers or temporary staff, afterwards, to limit payroll costs. Since those were short-term tactics, new personnel were often not trained adequately to understand what business is all about, and how their activities integrate with those of other departments. As well as lowering management standards and customer service, it failed to give young executives a yardstick against which they could measure their own performance. Many genuinely believe that they are good managers because they do not know what good management is—they have never seen it. When their turn comes to hire staff, standards drop still further, because managers hire people with less competence than themselves to avoid any possible threat of competition. Then they become inferior role models for inferior managers.

Without managers who can excel there can be no excellent companies. Until now it was the multinational market leaders who attracted the best managers, because they were recognized as being the most professional business organizations. Only there, it seemed, would they be trained in properly structured management and marketing methodologies similar to those described in this book. Their intention was to maximize a manager's contributions and also encourage him or her to remain in that company by developing a progressive career path.

"When globalization became a cliche," wrote *The Economist*, "businessmen assumed that big firms would gain the most from lower trade barriers and converging tastes. Global markets, it seemed, would call for global brands from global companies managed globally. Firms big enough to spend lavishly on automated factories and computerized offices would be able to exploit glittering new technologies faster than smaller, poorer, rivals. Increasingly sophisticated and deregulated capital markets would enable big firms (but only big firms) to scour the world for the cheapest money. Many pundits confidently forecast that a handful of giant firms would dominate car making, electronics, banking, entertainment, publishing and advertising, to name only a few.... The great surprise of the past decade has been that the changes which were supposed to make bigger even better have had the opposite effect."[11]

In fact the falling of international barriers is easing the way for exports from smaller enterprises; computer technology enables smaller manufacturers to produce smaller volumes at lower unit costs, instead of having to expand to emulate corporate giants who relied on mass production with its economies of scale to perform that function; overproduction in the electronics industry resulted in plummeting prices that made computer techniques available to smaller firms, and they became more sophisticated in managing materials and margins; universal attention to product quality has eroded the power of national brands that achieved premium prices in the past; and smaller entrepreneurs with the flexibility to turn around and address new challenges wherever they arise are innovating their products and the ways they market them.

But experienced managers continue to be discouraged by the chaos or inertia each day in their own organization, or by the second-rate service they receive from suppliers. They reason that there must be a better way to manage but don't know what it is. The following insights into western and Japanese corporate cultures should make it clear. And there is an ironic parallel between western failings and the inflexible ideology of former communist countries that protected management mediocrity for three generations. Those that are struggling with the concept of a free market economy will find new role models for their managers and for their business enterprises in the following pages.

Most business people believe they merely have to provide the means of production, administration, and sales. The failure rate would not be nearly as high if it were as elementary as that. Those are simply three of the numerous skills that need to be learned to provide a starting off point for an enterprise. The essential skills of commercialization and marketing cannot be imposed on a business from the outside, afterwards. Marketing is the catalyst that molds the structure; and that dictates the choice of personnel. It is the integrating force that welds an enterprise together through internal relationship marketing. It provides the dynamism that initiates momentum in a marketplace, and controls it by means of strategic planning; then maintains it with appropriate tactics. It is the force that propels an enterprise into the future, by advertising, promotions, public relations, database marketing, and sales management—all of them based soundly on the results of professional marketing research, benchmarking, and total quality management.

The aim of this book is to disclose the motives and mechanisms of modern corporate society as it is developing and changing at the turn of the century. And management culture cannot be described intelligently without exploring some fundamental features and problems of society as a whole.

That many managers in small and medium-size business enterprises are either directionless, like a boat without a rudder, or are drowning beneath waves of management theories that pass over their heads, and others that persist in spite of the fact that they remain unproven, may well be a reflection of the drift of western societies. They too lack strong leadership and are uncertain of their objectives or of how to reach a selection of conflicting ones.

Despite a sardonic note when comparing a number of academic theories on motivation that contradict each other, the following chapters pay homage to those imaginative professors in business schools and marketing faculties who manage to escape from the classroom to create new worldviews and elaborate new theories of business cycles or the effects of surplus populations on society and the economy, or develop a management "knowledge base."

Over a quarter of a century ago, I began to consider whether claims about providing executives with "an appropriate body of knowledge" were honest or capable of being fulfilled. In the intervening years I was able to observe management behavior among my colleagues, my staff, and my clients. With the exception of superior performances of managers in the major multinational market leaders I was fortunate to work with, I found several deleterious features common to many of them. What seemed remarkable was that it made little difference whether those executives were newcomers to the company and their job or long-established managers. Nor, in those cases, did it appear to make any difference whether they had previously earned a diploma or a business degree, or entered the business world by other means. It was a lack of personal effort or a broad enough focus to comprehend what the business was all about. That omission might be described as not possessing "a prepared state of mind" or a vision of the company, of its industry, and of the breadth and depth of their responsibilities in it and their commitment to it. *Few knew the parameters of their own job, let alone those of their colleagues.*

It was some years before I realized that whereas knowledge and understanding of the span of their job was directly related to a lack of operational experience in a variety of functions on the factory floor—its assembly lines, workshops, warehouses, regional showrooms, and the marketplace—the failure to understand its depth was due to an absence of knowledge about the origins and development of trade and industry as an impetus to their own civilization. *They did not know their own history.* Consequently, they continually demonstrated Cicero's contention that, "He who does not know history is destined to remain a child."

Immaturity, unworldliness, naivety, or inexperience, result in taking too much on trust, instead of developing suitable skepticism and learning to question everything. It takes time to gain experience of and in the world, and some people remain immature, provincial, or narrow focused, regardless.

Traumas of adolescence arise from a realization that what had been taken for granted about the world as *facts,* in childhood, are actually *ambiguities.* That discovery often causes confusion, which shows itself in multiple means of trying to come to terms with one ambiguity after another. The ascent from immaturity to maturity is marked by an assumption of objectivity and reasonableness. Understanding that we can make reasonable choices in our lives is a hallmark of reaching maturity.

That is why an effective substitute was developed over two thousand years ago to broaden a person's narrow perspective and sharpen his or her depth of focus. It was a thorough grounding in the classical liberal arts.

Unfortunately, the gradual democratization of education to fit people for routine jobs, instead of developing their character and ability to teach themselves, led to a rejection of the humanities in favour of such administration or accounting credentials as might be considered acceptable by an average employer. Recognition of individualism and character dropped out of fashion in preference to possession of a business diploma. Since the formation of character and all it implies may be the most important determinant for success, that trend created enormous gaps.

Those gaps or emptiness hinder the development of *phronēsis*—a word Aristotle used to denote *wisdom in action* or an ability to make wise decisions.

I have attempted to fill those gaps by means of a broader-ranging narrative—so that a business graduate, a newly appointed executive, or a business manager may obtain a more holistic sense of what a business enterprise is really about. Hopefully, a fuller knowledge of what makes it happen will add to their enjoyment of *making* it all happen, instead of being a mere time server or just going after "the big bucks."

But nobody can gather together all knowledge and spread it out for us to consider, like a dummy hand in a game of bridge. One option was for me to write a separate book on each management topic, but that could be a lifetime's work. Instead, I chose to create a perception of the whole by describing a series of scenarios, each one represented by a different chapter, and each chapter devoted to a different aspect of business management.

What you see may stimulate thought and challenge erroneous beliefs. It certainly reveals the enormity of the gap between the ideal and the reality.

Ottawa, October 1996.

Introduction: The Management Jungle

Looking back on 1993 we can see it as a crucial year. While economists informed a weary and anxious public that the longest post-war recession had ended, they and the business sector took a skeptical view of management disasters in the private and public sectors of the economy. Investors and taxpayers were equally outraged at the mismanagement and waste of their funds. The list of financial failures in the West so embarrassed the Japanese that they felt obliged to apologize humbly for having achieved a record trade surplus when major western economies were saddled with huge debts through their own ineptitude.

IBM's announcement of a loss of $4.96 billion broke all records, until GM admitted to a loss of $23.5 billion. O&Y were restructured with debts of $9.4 billion. Sears announced it would cut 50,000 jobs, close 150 retail stores and 91 catalogue outlets, and terminate the catalogue that had put them in business. Macy's had already declared bankruptcy. Ford lost $4.7 billion. Chief executives of several North American banks expressed regret at their own losses and admitted to poor judgement and a number of blunders. The chairman of The Royal Bank of Canada promised investors that it wouldn't happen again.

Typical of the time was Terence Corcoran's column in the *Globe and Mail,* in which he wrote, "As some of North America's biggest corporate monarchs are mowed down, sending CEOs flying in all directions, nobody for a minute should lose sight of the primary cause—profits, profits and more profits— and the executives who have been toppled in recent months have a common trait; an uncanny inability to deliver profits to their shareholders.... For the most part, however, the almost daily purge of CEOs represents the continuation of a trend that began a decade ago—the reordering of corporate North America."

With the hindsight of other disasters over the following years—the bankruptcy of Confederation Life in Canada and the collapse of Barings Bank in Britain in 1995—we can more easily realize how the cause of all those failures was quite simply bad management. And what we were all enduring was the passing of the old ways of managing a company or a government department, to make way for new disciplines and accountabilities and management styles. Revolutions do not take place in an orderly fashion; they slash and burn to provide new foundations for regeneration and economic growth.

By 1993 the United States had run up a gross accumulated debt of over $4 trillion. Canada's national debt was $471.7 billion. Britain was in the red by $441.3 billion. At the same time, Japan had achieved a record surplus of $209.7 billion. Calculated as per capita debt, Canada—with a population only one tenth of the size of the United States—was the worst off of the three. Britain, with twice Canada's population, stood somewhere between the two, with a national debt representing 1.4 percent of 1992 GDP, compared with 4.5 percent of GDP for Canada.[1]

Japan's massive trade surplus was viewed with envy. Notwithstanding its economic and political problems the following year, we should ask ourselves how Japanese management continued to show tangible evidence that it was doing something right, while European and Canadian managers stumbled along as ineffectively as before?

German management ranked only fourteenth in the World Competitiveness Report of 1995; the UK was twentieth, and France came twenty-first. We would be justified in asking whether a nation's poor economic performance resulted from poor management or bad government, and whether there is a correlation between the two. But before we can answer those questions convincingly, we must define what we mean by "management." Then perhaps we will be able to understand what exactly is *mismanagement*. Is it those management styles that lead to failures of business organizations or economic recessions? Not necessarily, since macroeconomic factors may have played a significant role. Moreover, there are many different management styles and management theories that we need to review.

Management Theories

Professor Harold Koontz wrote a paper for the *Academy of Management Journal* in 1961, in which he complained of "the management theory jungle." In it, he tried to make sense of six quite different approaches to management. Each theorist seems to have been viewing business organizations through a different window, so that they appear to have been observing quite different activities. Koontz was then Professor of Management at the University of California.

Since his descriptions are more detailed than is necessary for us here, his definitions are condensed. They are:

1. *Traditionalists*. Managing, for them, is a process that can be dissected intellectually by analyzing its functions. Because it stemmed from an era of mass production that glorified the assembly line, its emphasis was on production capacities and time and motion studies; exemplified by Henri Fayol, and Frederick Taylor who wrote *Scientific Management*.
2. *Empiricists*. They study and analyze case histories as precedents on how to manage. But—as Koontz remarked—unlike law, management is not a sci-

ence based on precedent. Situations in the future are rarely exactly comparable to those in the past. As an example, he quotes Ernest Dale's comparative approach, *The Great Organizers*.

3. Behaviorists. Since management involves getting things done by and through people, they believe the study of management must be centered on interpersonal relations. Some examples are Maslow, Graves, and McGregor.

4. Sociologists. Their approach is that management is a social system consisting of cultural relationships. An example is Chester Barnard's *The Functions of the Executive*. But Koontz advises that they are merely attaching the term "management" to the field of Social Psychology.

5. Decision Makers. They emphasize a rational approach to decision making, by selecting from a number of possible alternatives. They are concerned with such economic problems and analyses as utility maximization, indifference curves, marginal utility, and economic behavior under risks and uncertainties.

6. Mathematicians. They use a system of mathematical models and processes, symbols and relationships. They include operations researchers or analysts who sometimes call themselves "management scientists." Koontz took the view that mathematics is no more management than it is astronomy.

Professors Koontz, O'Donnell, and Weihrich outline eleven approaches to the analysis of management. They say that until the early 1950s, writing on management came largely from practitioners. But once academics began thinking up all sorts of theories, there has been "a veritable deluge." Academic approaches, research, and analysis, and a welter of views "have resulted in much confusion as to what management is, what management theory and science are, and how management events should be analyzed...the developments of management science and theory still have the characteristics of a jungle."[2]

Since manufacturing developed into a process separate from the marketplace, there has been an anomaly—even an apparent contradiction—between F. W. Taylor's Scientific Management (or the manufacturing-cum-engineering approach) and the Human Resources perspective of the first properly organized marketers like Sears-Roebuck and Unilever. It could be described as a conflict between man and machine. Knowledge-oriented companies that knew they were marketers were conscious of the paradox when they chose to make marketing initiate, dominate, and permeate the manufacturing and distribution process. As Lever Brothers, Lipton, or Jergens might say, "We tell the factories to make what our customers want."

Manufacturing and marketing began to be brought together by the concept of Statistical Quality Control. For all practical purposes, SQC is a facet or responsibility of marketing; since poorly designed products or poor quality ones or uncompetitive ones will be rejected by the marketplace. But it seems that this responsibility was undertaken, in most cases, by marketing executives in those national or multinational market leaders who are often described as being "excellent" companies. Since the majority of businesses do not possess experienced and knowledgeable marketing people of such a calibre to undertake the necessary responsibilities for quality management—as well as innovation, which is their core responsibility—it is understandable that the gap would be filled by others from different disciplines or with other skills.

To avoid undue emphasis on product and processes, TQM's core concept is that every department in an organization is a customer of other departments and also supplier. And the external customer is brought into the center to be satisfied as the prime consideration. By comparison, marketing's yardstick is that it begins and ends with the customer. Or, as marketer Matsushita said, "The customer is god." Marketing's internal responsibilities are addressed by "relationship marketing."

The first half of the 1990s was a period when many businesses turned desperately to the latest management theory or fad, hoping for a quick fix, rather than taking time and effort to study marketing. In quick succession came TQM, Process Re-engineering, Reshaped Organization Charts, Competing Teams, Lateral Thinking, and some others like Empowered Workers or Bottom-Up Management.

TQM misleads if it claims to be the elixir of life, and can even persuade top management that none of the other links in the marketing chain are necessary and that quality is everything. But quality alone cannot guarantee the success of a product or service in the marketplace. Indeed, most new products and services are launched by the very multinationals who specialize in invention and innovation and are renowned for their outstanding quality management. So it could be said that most products that failed in the marketplace exemplified remarkably high standards. And yet, neither the quality of their design or materials, machine tools or production, assembly or handling, helped them when it came to the new product launch. On the contrary, it could have deceived them into being too complacent.

Of Business or Process Re-engineering it could be said that without a top-down marketing philosophy and the establishment of marketing principles and practices, a company naive enough not to possess them would be likely to re-engineer in the wrong direction. The London Business School in the UK warned in its advertisements against re-engineering business processes. It also warned against discarding vertical organizational charts. It did not take long for one of the authors of *Re-engineering The Corporation* to admit openly that "re-engineering is in trouble." According to James Champy, the reason for poor results was that managers continued to behave in the same old-fashioned way as before: "The obstacle is management."[3]

Confusion about what should be the ideal shape for an organization chart stems from not knowing the type of company or industry it is intended for. Knowledge or creative industries are likely to differ from an automobile manufacturer or a brass foundry. Using the same mold for all organizations would be as inappropriate as using the same business strategy for all of them.

There is nothing new about teamwork. Sales teams have competed for generations. Sometimes they work, sometimes they don't. But anyone with shirtsleeves experience in the workplace can envision how it might turn out to be like playing games instead of producing useful outputs. A survey showed that nearly seven out of ten teams failed to produce the desired result, and was remarked on by *The Economist*. Some workers prefer to be told what to do, rather than have the burden of decision making thrust upon them. And those who enjoy responsibility "sometimes found it hard to discipline their wayward colleagues." Worse still, "members of supposedly 'self managing' teams start wondering how to manage. This gives birth to an epidemic of woolly courses on 'conflict management' and 'stress relations.' Meetings swallow time as 'empowered' workers break off from the tedium of making things and chat endlessly instead about 'process improvement' or 'product imperfections.'"

When management researcher Meredith Belbin experimented with teams to measure the effects of intelligence and creativity at Henley Management College in the UK, he chose members of one team for their outstanding IQs and another team with high degrees of creativity. But in a series of business games that required those qualities, both teams repeatedly came in last or close to last. The reasons were that executives with high IQs were brilliant as critics and evaluators and tore other people's ideas to shreds, while the creative members produced masses of ideas but no one else would pick them up and elaborate on them. The conclusion is that brilliant individuals can be collectively sterile.[4]

As for lateral thinking, Arthur Koestler described "thinking aside" as the typical way that creative people ideate, solve problems, invent, and innovate. Like some other processes, it is one of many links in the marketing chain. But to take just one link and promote it as a sure-fire business methodology is naive and misleading.

Small business managers, in particular, are likely to seek quick fixes to save time and money, instead of elaborating on the most effective ways and means of achieving sound long-term objectives and setting realistic and measurable goals. There is therefore "a constant market for doctrines that play to popular prejudices, whether they make sense or not. In times of economic distress, the search for politically useful economic ideas—which often means ideas that are demonstrably wrong, but that appeal to those impatient with hard thinking—takes on a special intensity."[5]

Some new management theories are actually *products* designed by large management consultancy firms as their brochure aimed at drumming up new clients. Such management books are sometimes capitalized or promoted and marketed by the consultancy. It may even buy up thousands of copies to get the book on the best-seller lists. Their objective is not only to obtain new business by arranging for their theories to be serialized in magazines, endorsed by business celebrities, or publicized on TV talk shows and other media, but also—if possible—to own the theory or management methodology featured in their book. *The Economist* described it as "a scam."[6]

With all those ingenious theories being created by academics, journalists, consultants, and others, it is puzzling why the calibre of management has failed to improve in the UK or on the continent of Europe, in Australia, Canada, and elsewhere, when it advanced so dramatically in Singapore and in some other Pacific Asian economies.

Another puzzle is why so many businesses are biased toward hiring inexperienced executives when the success or failure of a business depends so much on the knowledge, skills, and performance of its managers.

"In every business the manager is the dynamic, life-giving element," wrote Peter Drucker in 1954. "Without his leadership, the resources of production remain resources and never become production."[7]

The importance of superior management has been shoved carelessly aside and replaced by other considerations at a time when managing an enterprise—or a government department—has become far more complex than ever before, in a fast-changing world that is more competitive than it ever was. And yet it is the calibre and achievements of managers that determine whether a business survives, and how successful it will be if it does. Innovative management performance is the only really effective ingredient to turn an ordinary business enterprise into a superior one.

But what exactly is it? What does it do? And how does it do it?

There is as much vagueness in business as there is in government as to how a business organization or an institution functions from day to day and year to year. What type of inputs and outputs are desirable for them to perform sufficiently well to be considered successful? One reason why our perception may be clouded is because western management has lost itself in myriad diversions through such aspects as academic niceties, the confusing hand of bureaucracy, short-termism, or ego, greed, incompetence, indifference to the public, or even a deliberate choice of mediocrity, rather than basing decisions on a sound business philosophy.

We know that a business enterprise is an organization that supplies goods and services economically. In order to do so, it is obliged by market pressures to offer products or services that the public wants and is willing and able to purchase. Its marketplace is a specially selected sphere to which its products and services are directed. It owes its very survival to the fact that it must provide them economically to its special constituents. And to do so it requires managers to make specific decisions, initiate, perform, or monitor essential functions, and to facilitate activities that are required to produce and make available to the public those goods and services—or to commerce, industry, or institutions. It can therefore be seen that every idea, every judgement, every decision and action of a manager is directed by economic motives.

It is always important to define terms and avoid ambiguities. Most business people would glibly claim to know what management is and what marketing does, until they are asked to define them. Is one "administration" and the other "selling"? Or is one "managing the bottom line" and the other "putting an advertisement in the newspaper"? Those are the most frequent descriptions to expect, and they are both superficial and misleading. To encapsulate the spheres in which management is required, we should take another hard look at the Total Quality Management-cum-Marketing paradox.

Notwithstanding TQM's ingenuity in borrowing the "links in a chain" concept from marketing methodology and depicting each link as a customer of the other, and despite Deming's insistence that everything is being done on the customer's behalf, his concept cannot help but be product and process oriented—as compared with the marketing concept, which is always focused on addressing marketplace needs and opportunities. But, understandably, proponents of TQM do not wish to see it as a flawed concept, any more than advocates of marketing would be willing to accept that the philosophy they practice can fail them.

In fact both can; because the potential for failure is built into the human condition. But what each fails to acknowledge to themselves or each other is that marketing and TQM are two sides of the same coin, and that one will fail if the other is not properly addressed.

Marketing is aimed primarily at the birth of an idea—in beginnings that will influence results—and also in the end result itself. But that result spontaneously generates new ideas and a new beginning, which requires further innovations to tackle newly created objectives and goals. TQM, on the other hand, puts things together. It involves workmanship, performance, achievement, or production—but not completion. It is like a bridge that takes us from beginnings and *toward* end results. All of those beginnings and bridges and results—and their regenerations—require management. Managers manage a business by managing other managers, other employees, and work.

Drucker contended that by breaking down management functions into smaller components and analyzing each one, we could discover how a manager performs those tasks, in order to determine what management is.

Further examination would show that every judgement a manager makes to solve today's problems may influence all of those management spheres, not only today but also tomorrow and next year and thereafter. That is just one way that the complications of managing a business develop and mount up. The responsibilities of management are prodigious. Just how far-reaching they can be is often not realized until a business organization is in crisis through faulty management decisions or ones that may have been correct at the time but were not changed or adapted to changing circumstances.

On the other hand, we have also to bear in mind when we judge with hindsight a company's decisions that it is equally possible that their failures could not have been anticipated. There are frequently moments when choices have to be made between several possible options for which no-one can know how the future will turn out. Unlike the law, where there are historic precedents, managers sometimes follow trails that lead into dense jungle where there are no signposts, and the path they just took provides no clues to signpost future directions with certainty. Knowledge born out of experience may help to form judgements, as does informed analysis, but—as every experienced entrepreneur knows—there are times when we also have to rely on our own good luck. Some managers are good at taking risks while others are not. Ike Eisenhower once remarked, "I'd rather have a lucky general than a good one."

Managing a Business Enterprise

Management is not a science because it does not operate in isolated and clinical laboratory conditions—but a manager's work can be analyzed and categorized systematically, and even measured and evaluated. It does not therefore have to be solely a province of seat-of-the-pants managers. It can be learned. Although there is an important place for intuition or gut feelings in business, it is not here with the awesome responsibility of managing a business organization.

Not only can intelligent and self-disciplined executives learn how to manage, but those entrepreneurs who feel they are born managers, and often act instinctively, can improve their performance. They should have no difficulty in developing corporate management skills through the systematic study of principles, the acquisition of organized knowledge, and the systematic analysis and evaluation of their own performance.

The importance to society—as well as to a company—of a manager who excels, is so great as to require of him or her the self-discipline and effort to develop a capacity to become knowledgeable and to assume the high standards of service expected of any professional person of integrity. But since management is defined as a practice rather than a profession or a science, the ultimate test of a manager's caliber is essentially performance, not theory. Evidence of high standards of management can therefore be found only in business achievement. While experience is of course valuable, as Aldous Huxley wrote, "Experience is not what happens to you, but what you make of what happens to you."

Management is not merely routine or adaptive behavior, but involves a determined responsibility for taking creative actions that add value to an enterprise. A manager is a prime mover who controls and shapes activities for the purpose of translating them into achievements by meeting predetermined goals. In that way, he shapes his environment. He plans, initiates, and undertakes changes in the workplace that can change the marketplace. In short, a manager's job is to make things happen that he or she has *planned* to happen. To do so, managers must master their circumstances and change them to meet their objectives. To manage a business enterprise therefore means "to manage by objectives."

Those seemingly innocent four words of Drucker's, which a previous generation of management trainees would have read, started a new style of management that became known as Management By Objectives, or MBO. It is a dynamic system that can help a company to identify and achieve its growth and profit goals through a manager's desire to contribute and to achieve, and also develop himself. It is a professional style of managing a business or a department of a business.

The earliest type of business practice we know of was, simply, trading. Merchants were viewed with tolerance but some contempt in many ancient societies like Greece, Rome, China, and Japan. In one sense, they were little more than storekeepers, middlemen, or factors. Their contribution to an economy merely involved moving goods from one place where there were prodigious supplies to other places where there was abundant demand. Success in business resulted from quick and smart adaptation to events immediately they were known to have occurred. Neither the forces of demand nor the forces of supply were shaped or controlled by the merchant in those societies—nor were they even influenced by him, because the big money came from owning slaves who were productive.

As local markets became established and competitive, opportunities for business were sought in more distant places where premium prices could be obtained, to cover additional costs of transport and risks. The most important skills required of traders then were not business skills but knowledge and experience in transporting goods. Those skills might involve handling a span of oxen to pull a wagonload of merchandise into the interior where no proper roads existed. Or they might be the skills of a mariner crossing dangerous seas. Trading was quite different from being a storekeeper in a moderately civilized urban or rural community. It required considerable courage to enter lawless territory alone, and only the extent of the economic rewards would make it worthwhile.

That type of trading ultimately became associated also with making, growing, or excavating the goods to be transported and sold. And the means of transport gave way to bigger or safer or quicker vehicles, each of which needed to be mastered in turn. They involved, for example, the introduction of the "clipper"—a sleek sailing ship designed for speed. It brought goods, like tea, from India and Ceylon, to Europe. Lipton's tea clippers were famous for bringing their commodities to markets faster than those of their competitors could travel, to obtain the best prices while demand was high and supplies short. The invention of the steamship made clippers obsolete.

By that time, business risks had become something more than the dangers of travelling alone through lawless or hostile territories, where piracy or climatic hazards could wipe out entire inventories. There were now also three other specific risks, to which John Maynard Keynes referred in *The Inducement to Invest:*

(1) the entrepreneur's or borrower's risk...as to the probability of his actually earning the prospective yield for which he hopes; (2) the lender's risk...due either to...voluntary default or other means of escape, possibly lawful, from the fulfillment of the obligation...or...involuntary default due to the disappointment of expectation; and (3) a possible adverse change in the value of the monetary standard which renders a money-loan to this extent less secure than a real asset; though all or most of this should be already reflected, and therefore absorbed, in the price of durable real assets.

Perhaps that was the time that a transition took place from trader to modern businessman.

Of course, there is another type of businessman who is an investor. He merely speculates in order to maximize his return on capital investments. But he does not *manage* a business. He does not produce wealth by supplying added value to material or human resources. What he does do is produce wealth by creating employment through investing in business enterprises. Employment creates consumption, which triggers production, which creates more employment and more consumption and production, and so on. In return for his investment, he skims off some of the surplus.

As well as financial risks that require astuteness, the complexities of modern business practices today (and of economics and marketing)—arising from intense competition in the global village—require far more of managers than ever before. They must manage imaginatively as well as competently. The success or failure of a business enterprise now depends more than ever on original ideas, or the inability to provide them. Managing has become both an intellectual and a creative pursuit. That is the added value that a business organization has a right to expect of its managers. Ideas have become the essence of the performance of good managers, and the operational logistics, while being as important as ever, have become less important than the introduction of new concepts and ideas. And if one were to analyze each aspect of the infrastructure of typical market leaders today, one would be obliged to conclude that the edge they possess over the rest is the calibre of their managers.

A market leader will naturally take great pride in the excellence of its products, but product excellence is no longer enough. Intense competition ensures that customers will no longer "beat a path to his door." And a company could be forgiven for feeling a glow of pride at the establishment of its brands and its creation of consumer loyalty to them—but the public is fickle. It is ready and willing to try other brands too, and switch loyalties if it likes them.

A business enterprise can never afford to be complacent, even about its well-established distribution channels. There is no exclusivity on supermarket shelves or on the showroom floor of a retail appliance chain store. Products, packaging, brands, distribution, pricing strategies, economies of scale, robotics, organizational structures, and strategic plans—none of them is good enough without the input of effective managers. Even Henry Ford, who was obsessed with his assembly lines, declared, "You can take away my factories, burn up my buildings, but give me my people and I'll build the business right back again."

But we are also obliged to recognize that the best managers are naturally attracted to the best companies. That is where greater experience can be obtained and sophisticated skills learned, where a manager can develop by emulating the very best marketers, receive training, and be provided with a progressive career path that could lead to the top. Those are obviously ideal companies for any ambitious executive to join. But they are comparatively few in number. Most business organizations are only as good as the poorer calibre of managers that they attract. And since most average companies and awful companies, are far less sophisticated in management and marketing methods than the successful market leaders, their managers are generally used merely as hired hands for an overworked chief executive who thinks of himself as the entrepreneur. Those managers are unable to add value to the business enterprise because of their lack of valuable on-the-job experience, their own lack of marketing sophistication, and also the lack of leadership sophistication of many of those chief executives.

Faulty management judgements appeared to be exemplified in 1992 by the unfortunate situations of both IBM and Olympia & York. IBM announced a further cut of 25,000 jobs at the end of that year, after previous cutbacks of 40,000 employees. Many were highly skilled white-collar workers. IBM is bigger than all the other U.S. computer manufacturers combined. Consequently, when their turn came to downsize the operation, they did so in their usual monumental fashion. It came as a particular shock to President-elect Clinton—as he then was—who had been openly discussing the possibility of encouraging industry to invest in research and development in order to assist the United States to recover from its economic doldrums. Instead, IBM announced it would cut its R&D budgets by one billion dollars.

Some critics claimed this was due to bad management decisions in the past. And it is true that IBM's objective had been to command a premium price for its core products—mainframe computers—when quite different trends were taking place in the market. They also believed that, with their muscle, they could be a dominating force in all their markets, and had evidently geared themselves up for it. But what they had planned for did not happen.

There is some comparison with O&Y, which was the biggest property development company in the world before declaring bankruptcy in 1992. Although the damage to both companies may have appeared to have been self-inflicted, O&Y's Reichmanns were generally given the benefit of the doubt. But in both cases, no doubt management made their judgements with the best of intentions. Both organizations had enjoyed excellent reputations and were respected throughout the world—except by some of IBM's most vociferous detractors.

Timing was certainly not on their side. Both had allowed their infrastructures to grow too big and their overhead costs too high, in anticipation of future profits that did not materialize. Both underestimated the length and extent of the recession, and their debt loads grew too big as a result. In the case of O&Y, even the interest on bank borrowings was too high to repay without sufficient revenues from Canary Wharf, their commercial rental subdivision on the bank of the River Thames in London. Consumer demand shrank with the onset of the recession, and competition increased in both cases. Property developers in London began constructing other high-rise office buildings in the city, which provided better transport facilities for tenants and workers, while the Jubilee Line planned to bring them in to Canary Wharf was still under discussion and still not capitalized.

IBM's management decisions made in the past enabled its suppliers to sell identical parts to competitors, which built them up to pose a threat. And IBM should have anticipated the decline of mainframes and the trend toward cut-rate personal computer clones.

The cause of both faulty management judgements could be described quite simply as delusions of grandeur. That implies emotional content to their decisions instead of cool and analytical or rational appraisals. It requires no stretch of imagination to perceive the Reichmanns as totally captivated by a grandiose and commendable plan to restore that area of London that the Luftwaffe had bombed relentlessly until it lay in ruins. Goering had attempted to force the British to sue for peace by setting London ablaze with wave after wave of bombers flying up the Thames to drop clusters of incendiary bombs on working-class residential areas. If Olympia & York had succeeded in building a new and modern city center in London and created employment, a grateful British government might well have granted them an accolade for their gallantry.

But gallantry is not a sound business reason for making major decisions. That is probably why it failed.

IBM's sheer size and power seemed to have overwhelmed their sensibilities instead of the marketplace. While it is true that they made impressive use of that power to become the market leader in PCs in the 1980s—as described in a later chapter—their perception of competition, market activities, and objectives evidently became clouded. Greed for premium prices charged for their mainframes and a compulsion to be the most powerful can trigger the adrenaline glands and become as addictive as a drug. Reason deteriorates or is tossed aside as irrelevant. It has a corrupting influence—as Maxwell and Campeau discovered to their great cost. Delusions of such proportions end in *hubris*. But biggest is never best when the bottom line is endangered. It cannot even be said that it may be better to strive for than to reach. A desire to be the biggest is an entirely misleading objective for the channelling of resources. Illusions are, after all, simply a loss of control over reality. Business managers perform best with their feet firmly on the ground, even when their intellectual creativity may soar into the realms of discovery and innovation, so that they can master ideas instead of being mastered by them.

In *On War,* von Clausewitz wrote of the longing for honor and renown that inspired people in battle. "None is so powerful and so constant." But he also added that those passions are "unjustly tarnished" by associations with "Greed for honor" (*Ehrgeiz*) and "Hankering after glory" (*Rumsucht*). Such qualities often misdirect property developers, whose city centers and suburban shopping malls take on even bigger dimensions than classical sculptures depicting victory, or triumphal arches, or even those monuments built to create immortality for ancient Egyptian and Assyrian rulers.

Even if the Reichmanns never recover their financial losses, they can at least sustain themselves by attributing their failure to noble ambitions.

That could hardly be said of IBM. Siliconization and integration of the transistor into small chips, and compatibility with other systems were recommended by their chief designer, Dr. Gene Amdahl, as early as the 1960s. But IBM chose to ignore his advice and closed down his laboratory in 1969. Their reaction "set the company on the road to its present, possibly terminal situation," according to Kevin Cahill, who wrote, "That meeting may rank as the foremost example of corporate stupidity ever recorded."[8]

Instead, Amdahl's chips and boards, that were lighter, faster and cheaper than IBM's machines, were adopted by major Japanese manufacturers like Hitachi, Fujitsu, NEC, and Mitsubishi. Japanese competitors' machines were air-cooled, whereas IBM's were still water-cooled in 1983. That is how IBM became the world's largest plumbing company by accident. Ron Condon compared its disaster to that of the Titanic: "IBM hit the iceberg a long time ago, perhaps as long ago as the mid-seventies. It's just taken an age for the message to reach the bridge." And Richard DeLamarter—author of *Big Blue*—wrote in the 1980s, "Like its competitors, IBM is at times poorly managed, its products inferior, its customers unhappy, and its actions ruthless, if not illegal." Bill Gates of Microsoft even went so far as to predict in 1990, that "IBM wouldn't exist in ten years' time." But IBM subsequently changed its CEO, turned to the marketing philosophy, and had its top managers trained by The Chartered Institute of Marketing in the UK—all of which succeeded in reversing its downward trend.

Of those two market leaders, one directed its attention to opportunities in Mexico, while attempting to buy back Canary Wharf through a newly structured partnership, and the other was big enough to bury its mistakes and successfully undertake damage controls. But what qualities do most or all market leaders have in common? What factors contribute to the success of some companies while others fail? What is it that stimulates some managers to contribute to the success of a business enterprise in a dynamic way, while others become stumbling blocks that hold a company back and create problems for it? What leadership criteria in a CEO contain a bias for success, and which personality characteristics lead almost inevitably to failure? Those are some of the questions this book seeks to answer.

There is no doubt that emotions and ego frequently enter into business judgements and warp them, when they shouldn't. And there are always willing financial controllers and accountants to provide proforma accounts and cash-flow projections to prove their masters' judgements are sound. But they are almost certain to be flawed when there is an equation missing. That is the people factor, which accountants do not consider to be their concern. And in the final analysis, management generally chooses to believe financial spreadsheets that support their opinions. Their pragmatic approach clouds the fact that projected figures are fictitious by definition, because management cannot predict the future with certainty. Apart from cataclysmic events, it arises from interactions between people, and no one can know for sure how each one of them will act. There is also the matter of discontinuous change. Nevertheless, an important factor in being a successful or even a "lucky" general or CEO is that good executives can usually identify small and seemingly insignificant changes that might precede major ones. And one way of doing so is by managing a team of top managers in such a way that inputs are continually provided from every facet of the organization.

That some chief executives feel more comfortable with one business discipline rather than with another, raises the question as to which management function should take precedence—managing the business, managing its managers, managing other employees, or managing work? Their relative importance may be ranked differently according to the personality, background, or leadership style of a president or a divisional or general manager.

A pragmatic manager, or one trained in accountancy, may firmly believe that managing the bottom line is his or her priority, rather than motivating people. Is he or she not accountable, after all, to the shareholders, for profitability? That CEO might be convinced that future profits can best be assured by manufacturing products or providing services that can command premium prices—as IBM once felt about mainframe computers. But a persuasive marketing vice-president should feel free to convince the top management team of the difference between "paper profits," which can be illusory, and the realities of the marketplace at that point in time; since marketing research might reveal that consumer demand for such products or services is too small for sufficient profits to accrue. It is important to emphasize that it is the dynamics of a marketplace that drive productivity, and not production that motivates the marketplace to buy—as some classical economists once thought and *Say's Law* wrongly insisted.

A CEO who is more of a people person might choose for his priority those management functions that focus on people. He would know that it is people who run organizations. And people are as much concerned with democratic rights as with balance sheets or the factory floor. A reality of the workplace is that employees can withhold their labor. And a business organization can thrive in a democracy only if people's basic social values and rights are recognized and catered to. That CEO's decisions may rather take into account keeping his management team and his workforce skills intact and continually improving their knowledge and skills. By contributing to their development and their career goals, such a company would be likely to benefit from greater productivity, higher work quality, and an abundance of useful new ideas from its employees.

A more analytical type of chief executive with an engineering background, or R&D, or production, or time and motion studies at the factory level, might consider his priorities to be production and assembly lines and workplace economies, rather than people.

There used to be a breed of older CEOs who had worked their way to the top through sales. Their priority was simply to increase revenues by selling more and more goods. They did not understand the refinements of marketing or economics. Nor did they understand finance or production. They came into their own when there was less competition in developed countries, and considerable opportunity in developing countries where their goods were in short supply and demand for them was continually growing. Most have retired long since, but there is still room for them in South and Central America and on the African continent, and in the Middle East. But with accelerating competition and sophistication in the West, the need is for CEOs who are general managers. Their priority is to inspire a top management team of specialists. And the priorities of their business organizations are marketing and innovation.

In fact, neither one of management's four major jobs is a priority, because they are inseparable. Whatever priorities a CEO may think he has, a reality of management is that there will be no business if managers and workers and work are *mis*managed. If they are, increased costs can result from management apathy or worker slowdowns, the necessity of replacing demoralized or inefficient employees, work losses from lack of continuity and the induction and training of new staff, increased time off the job from real or imagined sickness (which occurs in mismanaged companies), and the hidden cost of inertia. Any of those can raise unit costs to a point where an enterprise ceases to be competitive.

Or, by creating adversarial relationships between departments or between managers and workers, systems and procedures may slow down, and management may find itself continually involved in new problem areas which reduce productivity. Such cases are typical of organizations that become bankruptcy statistics during economic recessions. But the worst of them simply lose business when they lose sight of consumer needs, and fall apart as a final result of self-inflicted wounds that erode their infrastructure or their constituency, or both.

Managing Other Managers

The function of managing managers is intended to create a business enterprise out of human as well as material and financial resources. That means managers must be hired and directed so that they add value to the enterprise's bottom line and also to its future prospects. The goal of managing managers is to produce something more valuable from an enterprise than merely the sum of all its resources. It is not enough to invest capital in consignments of raw materials, equipment and staff, and manufacture goods. Someone of value is needed to turn those resources into some thing of value. That person is a manager. And, similarly, another manager is required to turn him or her into a valuable resource.

A superior manager has been compared to an outstanding conductor of a symphony orchestra, in that he is able to produce far greater quality output than the inputs of each individual, however talented all of them may be. The same is true of an ideal chief executive or of a divisional or general manager with his own managers and staff.

Material resources are improved economically by adding the value of ideas. It is those ideas that turn them into desirable products that are needed and can be sold at a reasonable profit. Developing managers may seem to be altogether different in that their objective is to acquire practical knowledge that would make them desirable to their employer. But there are parallels, one of which is that—like material resources—human resources can be enhanced. They can also deteriorate and depreciate in value.

Managers can easily forget their real objectives, and often do. They can lose their skills by failing to keep abreast of new trends or otherwise being complacent. They can shrink in stature through character defects. Their resolve can be worn down by the friction of day-to-day problems and stresses. They may even crack under constant pressures of work. Their attitudes can become warped by internal politics or cynicism within an organization. They can lose their way through not being informed of the parameters of their job, of what is expected of them. Or they can be lost to other organizations after time and money has been spent in training them. The skill of managing managers is in ensuring that none of those things happen and that human resources are continually improved. That requires direction, development, rewards, and charismatic leadership.

"There has been a deep change in the temper of science in the last twenty years: the focus of attention has shifted from the physical to the life sciences. As a result, science is drawn more and more to the study of individuality. But the interested spectator is hardly aware yet how far-reaching the effect is in changing the image of man that science moulds."[9]

All of that is elaborated on in the following chapters describing what motivates people, management methodology, leadership and management styles.

But in order to manage other managers, they must be made clear about what fundamental things they are responsible for managing. They need to know the essential ingredients on which a company culture is built, and the key results areas for which they will be held accountable.

In search for the salient elements of a business organization, two management consultants working for McKinsey International—Pascale and Athos—wrote a book entitled *The Art of Japanese Management,* which was published in 1982. In it, they categorized criteria that they considered were essential for success in business, as revealed to them from studying some of the very best Japanese organizations and comparing them with some multinational American and British ones. The seven elements they chose were strategy, structure, system, staff, style, skills, and superordinate goals.

That all organizations, including institutions, need some type of structure is self-evident. The type of structure would be likely to depend on its industry, size, mission, and strategy. Systems and procedures would be needed for it to be operational. Staff would be required to operate the systems. Style develops in a company even without a properly planned corporate philosophy and culture, although it might be an unsuitable style. And employees would add little value to a company if they did not possess skills. So much is clear. But the seventh criterion evinces an intellectual struggle, even if only because—as the final one—it would have to represent anything or everything else. It therefore compels one to question it. For example, is it intended to convey the principal goals of the company? Or is it simply a commitment to achieve specific goals? Then again, if we were obliged to consider alternatives, what would *we* choose in preference?

Peters and Waterman chose something different in another paradigm, also attributed to McKinsey, when they wrote their later book, *In Search of Excellence.* They replaced it with shared values. Since both books were written over a decade ago and a great deal has changed since then, more questions are in order. In the light of the massive downsizings and restructuring of so many companies during and after two significant economic recessions since then, what model has been used mostly? Indeed, what model is appropriate for the high-technology revolution that heralds the twenty-first century?

Those questions and many others resulted in considerable thinking through of the essential needs in an ideal business organization facing challenges from highly developed and sophisticated economies, on one hand, and also labor-intensive Third World ones on the other. A turn-of-the-century paradigm appears to be needed. But before designing one, we need to examine the cultural differences between Japanese and American approaches, or western ones and Pacific Asian ones, to the same business problems and opportunities.

It was, after all, the four people-driven elements in their paradigm that catapulted numerous Japanese companies into world leadership. That obliges us to reexamine the traditional western approach to human resource management. Whereas the Japanese manage to establish harmony in the workplace, that does not appear to be a characteristic of the West. What we see almost daily in western cultures is segmentation, separation, alienation, and even isolation, as an antidote to prevalent confrontation, conflict, and violence. *Wa,* or harmony, has long been considered a prized characteristic of both the Japanese home and the workplace. The only western characteristic that might be mistaken for it is a studied uniformity. It is a management preference for hiring executives who look, act, think, and even dress alike, and who possess the same bundle of values. That look-alike syndrome has resulted in excluding the very diversity that is required to develop a dynamic business enterprise. It causes sterility. Not so for the Japanese, although we see them in identical suits and ties and glasses. We need to find out why that is.

Before we can do so, we have to ask ourselves the question: If it is so difficult to define what management is and does, how can a manager manage other managers? Management guru Henry Mintzberg wrote, "Like thousands of other students at the time, I took an MBA, a degree ostensibly designed to train managers, without questioning the fact that no one ever discussed in a serious way what managers really did. Imagine a program in medicine without ever a comment on the work of the doctor."[10]

French industrialist Henri Fayol described what managers do as "plan, organize, coordinate, and control." But Mintzberg considered that as merely "some vague objectives." His own description of what he had observed in the workplace was interpreted by the *New York Times* as "calculated chaos" or "controlled disorder." He shared four facts with us about how managers really work:

> (1) Study after study has shown that managers work at an unrelenting pace, that their activities are characterized by brevity, variety, and discontinuity, and that they are strongly oriented to action and dislike reflective activities; (2) In addition to handling exceptions, managerial work involves performing a number of regular duties, including ritual and ceremony, negotiations, and processing of soft information that links the organization with its environment; (3) The senior manager needs aggregated information, which a formal management information system best provides; (4) The manager's programs—to schedule time, process information, make decisions, and so on—remain locked deep inside his brains. Thus, to describe those programs, we rely on words like *judgement* and *intuition*, seldom stopping to realize that they are merely labels for our ignorance.

Since most management training involves logical approaches to contrived situations in a regulated environment, as opposed to Mintzberg's descriptions of disorder or chaos in the workplace, and most business people don't really understand what managers should do or what they actually do, it has become commonplace to see look-alike managers being shuffled around like playing cards, as if the two of clubs possesses the same value as the king of diamonds or the joker.

Managing Workers

Despite the interchangeability of managers, it is obvious to management that workers have to be chosen for their diversity. There is no escaping the fact that each must provide different skills and some who are unskilled are better at performing different functions in a division of labor. They may be laborers, packers, drivers, warehouse staff, assemblers, toolmakers, engineers, quality inspectors; they may drive forklift trucks or be foremen or women, secretaries, bookkeepers, commercial artists, sales people, or after-sales administrators. Just like artisans before them, consideration must be shown for their particular expertise. They are also human beings who have been recognized as business resources. They must be addressed as human beings if management does not wish to be confronted by them as union members.

A manager's job is to assist and support employees in a variety of ways, to enable them to work most effectively and enjoy solving day-to-day problems. That means not only more productively, but also with a greater degree of skill and precision. Attention to quality as well as output will result in minimizing wastage of time and materials, reducing the number of rejects, undertaking fewer remakes, better handling and packing, and all those other aspects that may be described as part of quality management leading to customer satisfaction.

Outstanding end results require outstanding working conditions and human resource relationships. Drucker listed eight essential requirements to meet the needs of employees. There has been no reason to change any of them or add to them in the four decades since he gave the matter due consideration, despite considerable changes in the workplace in recent years. They are motivation, participation, satisfaction, incentives, rewards, leadership, status, and function. All of those criteria are examined in the following pages. Also examined are social and industrial cultures and management and leadership styles. And an attempt has been made to summarize the often confusing workplace and economic theories on capital and labor by Karl Marx.

A manager does not have to believe any of those theories—even ones developed by genuine experts. They are, after all, only theories, and most of them have not been proven. What is important is that a manager knows and understands them. There will be ample time for him or her to observe whether or not they work in day-to-day workplace conditions. The intention of this book is to cover all possible bases that may be necessary in order for a manager to function most effectively. Those aspects are particularly worthwhile exploring and mastering if a manager wishes to work his or her way up the corporate ladder to become a chief executive.

Although the four fundamental functions of a manager—managing a business, managing other managers, managing employees, and managing work—

are inseparable, one or other of those functions may take precedence at a critical stage in the growth of a business enterprise, or according to environmental factors.

Managing different types of work is covered extensively in the following chapters, but some effects of the passing of time, and of the importance of timing, require some general comment at this stage.

Time

Due attention must be paid to time; "For the importance of money essentially flows from its being a link between the present and the future," wrote John Maynard Keynes. Changing one's views on the future can influence present situations.

Time can result in unforeseen costs. It too is a resource that must be managed. In fact, it is even more perishable than all the other resources under review. And apart from the relationship of time to financial costs and time-deposits, an extraordinary amount of time is wasted in organizations, through its mismanagement and through disorganization resulting from poor planning.

That is why effective managers prioritize activities to maximize the use of their most productive abilities for their company's most urgent needs. It also means avoiding wastage on management functions that could be delegated. And it may involve setting up systems for one's own management team in order to make the best use of their special skills, too.

Planning is vitally important for calm management at an even tenor—but not slavishly following plans without due regard to changes taking place. Cool, level-headed management is the mark of efficiency through careful planning. And one reason why it is so essential is that managers always live simultaneously on three time planes. A company's business plan is invariably divided into short-term, medium-range, and long-term plans with objectives. A manager must consider all three.

Unfortunately, a most common attitudinal error of entrepreneurs managing smaller businesses, and chief executives of many medium size ones, is an overriding concern for immediate profits at the expense of a company's future. Their business philosophy is "Take the money and run!" A business enterprise, to them, is quite simply a cash-cow always ready to be milked. But what they frequently skim off is the surplus capital required for a company to grow.

When nomadic communities settled and farmed the land, about five thousand or more years ago, they discovered that they could create a surplus over and above their immediate needs, which could be stored for the future. Today we call it profit. But Marx argued so vehemently that profit is a surplus stolen from the workers, that the word "profit" became associated with dishonesty just as the word "capitalist" became a pejorative epithet in the mouths of communists. But profit is quite simply a surplus required for replacements, obsolescence, expansion, market risks, and economic and political uncertainties.

In short, profit is a cost of staying in business and the foundation for a company's survival in the future. Economist Schumpeter asserted that profit is the only job creator.[11] The collapse of industries in communist economies seemed to prove his point—if proof were needed in the face of continual empirical evidence. That not enough manufacturers were achieving acceptable levels of profits in the West is evidenced by the drop in employment by manufacturers in the U.S. from 24.6 percent to 15.4 percent since 1970. Employment in Canadian manufacturing companies fell from 22.3 percent to 15.9 percent in the same period.

In profit terms, Hong Kong is a prime example of capitalism at its best, with an unemployment rate of less than 2 percent. It reaped the advantages of wealth creation through modest personal and corporate income taxes. That, together with a traditional work ethic, provided ample seed capital for the growth of its economy. And Japan is the prime example of a country that raised itself to become the second largest economy in the world, and a high-technology leader, through an imaginative economic strategy based on full and lifetime employment. Japanese management recognizes that every employee is a consumer of goods and services.

"Consumption," wrote Keynes, "is the sole end and object of all economic activity."

On the other hand, western governments slow down domestic consumption by imposing heavy taxes on potential consumers, while businesses fail to realize that massive staff downsizing reduces the consumption of their goods and services, and government discourages wealth creation.

Business managers need to understand the inherent dangers of taking out immediate surplus at the expense of long-term profitability. Nor should they risk their company's future survival—as public service managers have done in the West—nor gamble this year's surplus on illusory prospects for the future. It is not easy for a manager to balance the present with the future, but it is necessary just the same. Failure to balance an annual budget may result in a deficit, but failure to balance present circumstances against the future can lead to bankruptcy.

The same thing applies to government, whose imprudent spending can result in economic decline, job losses, social disruption, and even the crumbling of a culture. The time to prepare future opportunities is the present, so that we can avoid the possibility of being forced to address threats at the very last minute when it may be too late to remedy them. The inevitability of time is that it catches up with us all.

Time is of particular importance to a manager, because cost is always related to it and affected by it. For a property developer, a new high-rise office building that takes longer to complete will cost more. And the current rents that the market allows may not help to recover its costs for many years. At that breakeven point in time the construction company, the syndication, or the landlord may have been forced into bankruptcy. Costs of R&D too have to be recovered in the shortest possible time frame, before competitors who merely copy products without incurring such costs, saturate the market with their own me-too products and inhibit an entrepreneur's sales. A newly formed sales force or a newly designed assembly line will take time to pay off. And the payoff period for capital investments will take longer and cost more when the central bank's prime lending rate is raised.

Capital itself is another resource that can deteriorate in the course of time, according to a country's inflation rate, or fluctuations in the bank's interest rate, erosion of the currency, or changes in foreign exchange rates. That is why management always has to maximize its investments; whether in its own real estate, capital equipment, material resources, inventories, human resources, or the investment of its capital reserves.

When we come to consider management systems and procedures, we find that management is always reviewing a number of factors on an ongoing basis. It continually makes a number of judgements and a variety of decisions that will affect the company regarding increased costs of essential raw materials, a fluctuating bank rate, the extent of bank borrowings and their current cost, frozen lines of credit, higher than normal inventory levels that may require renting additional warehouse space, production capacities and whether to lay off staff because of reduced customer demand, labor disputes, shrinking returns on investments, wastage, quality control, reduced profit margins, unreliable suppliers who hold up production and increase costs, over-extended customer credit, ineffective managers, increased competition, returned damaged goods, and so forth.

A business is like a living organism that needs constant nurturing in order to survive. It is the responsibility of managers to make the business enterprise successful and keep it alive. It must be made continually profitable in order to remain viable in the future, with its infrastructure and its skilled workforce intact. But—as we have seen with IBM and O&Y—that ideal is continually at risk and often prevented from being fulfilled.

However proud we may be of our superiority over other forms of life, as *homo sapiens,* it is now acknowledged that human nature is flawed. Studies of the human condition in specific chapters that follow describe the evolutionary gap that may be the cause of so much irrationality, leading to the destruction of so many of our resources, and often to business enterprises.

John Maynard Keynes described a recurring situation: "We are merely reminding ourselves that human decisions affecting the future, whether personal or political or economic, cannot depend on strict mathematical expectations, since the basis for making such calculations does not exist; and that it is our innate urge to activity which makes the wheels go round, our rational selves choosing between the alternatives as best we are able, calculating where we can, but often falling back for our motive on whim or sentiment or chance."[12]

Therein lies the source of most business losses and failures, as we shall see. But there are other reasons for management lapses—such as vanity, arrogance, complacency, fear of change, lazy-mindedness, and a dedication to cheapness and the second-rate.

Not many years before this book was in the planning stage, W. Edwards Deming wrote, "The problem is where to find good management. It would be a mistake to export American management to a friendly country."

Having enjoyed little success in preaching quality management in the United States by the 1950s, his became a significant voice in directing the attention of Japanese big business toward economic recovery and market ascension to the global summit. American big business had begun to take Deming seriously by the 1980s, when books on Japanese management abounded and Japan was ranked first in the World Competitiveness Report for nine consecutive years.

The United States was ranked fifth in 1994, when Japan's domestic problems had already become the focus of international news. The decline of consumer spending by the West, as well as a strong yen, had eroded Japan's export trade. They lost world leadership in management to the U.S. and slipped to fourth place by 1995. America's revival must also have been influenced by Hong Kong's decline from fourth to eighth ranking, rather than from any sudden improvement in American management capabilities. Global rankings continually fluctuate.[13] And, however much American management or marketing may have improved as a consequence of challenges from Pacific Asian economies, remaining on top will require constant vigilance and continual improvements in management skills.

I

Principles

"Our 'Age of Anxiety' is, in great part, the result of trying to do today's job with yesterday's tools—with yesterday's concepts."

—Marshall McLuhan

1

The Marketing Evolution

The public's perception of a business executive has long been influenced by the fictions of Hollywood's dream factory. The suave man in the grey flannel suit mixed easily with those glib hucksters talking customers into buying things they didn't need, and cynical admen increasing their bank balances at the expense of naive clients. More recently, TV and movies regaled us with ruthless entrepreneurs propelled to the top by single-minded greed. Whenever such larger-than-life individuals do become prominent in the world of business or finance, the media is quick to spotlight them as stereotypical characters with whom we have already become familiar through show-biz. But that is very far from being a true picture of business managers in the real world.

Popular books on business management, of the self-improvement genre, have lent credibility to those distortions by describing success stories of what have become known as "excellent companies." But how many really excel? Statistics show that 80 percent of North America's workforce is now employed in small companies. We also know that between 97 percent and 99 percent of businesses are small (depending on whether we use statistics from the UK, Canada, or the U.S.). But the number of truly outstanding performers must remain a matter of conjecture, since "excellence" is a purely subjective designation unless we use clear definitions like annual growth, profits, or assets, or R&D in the pipeline, which can be measured. But we don't have to be that exact when less that 3 percent of companies can be described as "big." If we generously praised a quarter of those as being excellent, then over 99 percent of all business enterprises would differ vastly from the media's and the public's misconception of them.

That would most likely include erroneous perceptions of university and college graduates in business administration who continually study case histories about companies like Bell, General Motors, IBM, 3M, HP, Matsushita, Texas Instruments, P&G, Eastman Kodak, and other such market leaders. Big performers are news. The ordinary, smaller enterprise is unlikely to be spotlit by the media unless it performs so well that it becomes *extra*ordinary. Such businesses have become known as GSMEs, or Growing Small and Medium-size Enterprises. The outstanding performers among them probably rep-

27

resent less than 3.33 percent of the total, and we rarely hear about them. But when we do, the chances of their demise within ten years is considered to be 50 percent.

Nor do we hear much about the absurdities or ineptitude of top managers in the average successful big companies, unless they have been previously praised and saluted as "excellent" ones for some time. Then, when poor judgement tarnishes their reputation and their shares drop in value or they declare huge financial losses, the media pounce on them. Such are the ups and downs of companies in the media spotlight that we might well wonder if *any* company can succeed just from upward momentum of an economy. But if that were the case, then, similarly, we should expect to see most of them failing during economic recessions. In essence, there are only well-managed companies and badly managed ones. Or if we wish to focus more closely on their marketing skills, we might place them in three categories, as follows: (1) those that are propelled by a top-down marketing philosophy—like Unilever companies, General Foods, Matsushita, or P&G; (2) those that possess marketing *departments* instead of top management and staff motivated by marketing principles and practices; and (3) those that do not practice or even understand what marketing is or what it can do to improve their balance sheet.

The first type appear to be always successful over the long haul. The second appear to have been successful in a limited way until intense competition began to humble or tumble them during the past two decades. And the third kind suffer from an extraordinarily high failure rate, year after year.

Size is not all that material as far as success is concerned, since success is relative—except in the case of new SMEs, whose failure rate is far higher than that of GSMEs or the major multinationals. The major reasons for their failure have been found to be inexperience in marketing and management skills, and those same risks that are inherent in the launch of new products. Most new products don't even get off the ground. But some new SMEs are fuelled by capital that should never have been provided for them: they become airborne for a fleeting moment before crashing. In most cases of new SME failures, start-up capital derives from personal savings of a former corporate executive who has become unemployed through company downsizing and restructuring. His or her motivation is usually either desperation or delusion. The odds on failure seem to be about 90 percent.[1]

Does management style play a significant role in success or failure? Clearly styles will differ according to the size or complexity of an organization, where requirements and skills differ. There are industry differences too. But perhaps the biggest differences in management style are found where cultures and values differ. As a general rule, in the West, corporate executives tend to be more disciplined because their organizations are more structured, while entrepreneurs tend to flexibility. But in Germany there is little difference between the style of entrepreneurs and corporate managers: both tend to be organization persons in accordance with rigid systems and structures on which they prefer to depend. In Latin countries, on the other hand, corporate executives seem more like entrepreneurs.

The dichotomy might be described loosely as a difference between Northern and Mediterranean characteristics; as between Paris and the Midi, Barcelona and Madrid, Milan and Rome. But the style differs in Munich from Hanover. And anyone who has taken a business trip to Johannesburg, on the highveld, knows how different it is from coastal cities like Cape Town or Durban, or from government cities like Pretoria or Bloemfontein. And top executives in India find it hard to delegate authority and spend too much time on minor details. That forces business people to deal only with the highest ranking executive. Despite a North American propensity for believing or wanting to believe that everyone is the same, attitudes and style differ because cultures and, therefore, values are different. American CEOs and VIPs were to discover that fact with some bemusement on meeting their Japanese counterparts for the first time. American management appears to be as perplexed today as at that first encounter, because that other industrial culture works very well, and perhaps the North American one does not work well enough.

Cultural characteristics appear to confuse because of the different uses of communications, different bundle of values, different approaches to economics, different interpretations of customs, different organizational structures, and different priorities of management. While northerners tend to be more methodical, technological, or skilful, southerners lean more toward subtlety and ambiguity, flexibility or impulsiveness. It is no wonder that the West has been bewildered and confounded by the Japanese. They are quite different again, because they respect another set of values and customs than those of the West. The paradox is that they immediately understood and realized the need for a management philosophy exported from the United States by Drucker, Juran, and Deming in the 1950s, that is only now beginning to be emulated in North America. Meanwhile, other Pacific Rim countries like Taiwan, Hong Kong, and Singapore found that Total Quality Management combined well with their own natural tendency to the marketing philosophy and their own work ethic.

But the business style of Third World economies differs again, although they too are environments where purposeful vagueness and ambiguity minimize the effects of confrontations that are part of the political and religious fabric of those regions. Mexico, Central and South America, and southern Africa's attitudes are related to the low living standards of their mass populations, over 50 percent of whom are likely to be under the age of fifteen; hence an acceptable hourly wage of forty-five cents for unskilled labor in El Salvador in 1992.

Similar demographics illustrate the Third World economy of part of South Africa's society with an unemployment rate of over 45 percent. But it can tap the resources and infrastructure of the developed industrial part of that dichotomy and is doing so. Having seen what the white middle classes used to earn, they are holding out for something better for themselves. But the pie is smaller and has to be shared between many more people. Nevertheless, the management culture is still marketing oriented and poised for growth. Its style can be described as "modest, despite achievements." That assessment is equally applicable to establishment conglomerates like SA Breweries or Dr. Anton Rupert's Rembrandt/Remgro (second biggest company on the Johannesburg Stock Exchange after Anglo-American De Beers), or new entrepreneurs like Herman Mashaba (a former door-to-door salesman who is now managing director of his own multi-million rand cosmetics enterprise called Black Like Me). He was chosen as Marketing Person of the Year in 1994, Rupert in 1962. In this new "rainbow society," as Nelson Mandela describes it, the dichotomies of old money versus new money possess none of the old connotations that once existed in Europe and in North America, because of the widespread opportunities for new black entrepreneurs in a largely untapped market of some 30 million blacks.

Conflicts between management and labor in developing economies resemble nineteenth century ones in the U.S., when an abundance of poor immigrant labor was forced to work for low wages in undesirable factories and the sweatshops of the garment industry, with their environmental hazards.

If we accept the fact that the excellent companies naturally attract the best managers, then the converse would be true of the majority of companies that are obliged to take whatever personnel they can get. That includes many who never bother to study management principles, or even borrow books on management from a public library. If they are so little interested in developing themselves to provide value to an employer, they are really no more than hired hands, and not managers at all. They just do whatever the boss tells them to—just like other employees in the packing department, the warehouse, loading bays, accounts receivables, or the sales floor. And since they are treated as labor for the boss to order around, they never learn how to manage. Even those who might have some potential would be unlikely to be given an opportunity to take initiatives, to show responsibility, or to provide added value to the company—because the problem is often at the top.

But that is not the only reason for inferior management.

Said a manager in a company that went from one crisis to another and spent most of his time putting out fires, "We have a union problem."

"No," said the shop steward, "We have a management problem."

Said a lawyer at the 1985 annual convention of the Retail Council of Canada, "The reason that employees join a union is because of poor management."

He elaborated as follows; "Employees join unions because management fails to respond to employee concerns, or because management makes rash decisions with which employees strongly disagree."[2]

That lawyer specialized in advising management on solving trade union problems. He listed eight fundamental reasons why employees join unions.

1. Unfair treatment (favoritism, discrimination, inequities in discipline);
2. Failure of management to respect employees' contributions to the business;
3. Failure to listen to employees' suggestions and complaints (lack of two-way communications);
4. Failure to keep employees informed of important decisions or trends that affect the company and, therefore, their work;
5. Insecurity from lack of information, or from management aloofness;
6. The feeling of not being in control of their own destinies;
7. Dissatisfaction with their physical surroundings (while management creates a pleasing atmosphere for customers at reception, or the front of the showroom, or in the executive suite, the back of the store or workshops or the factory are often neglected);
8. Frustrations because of incompetent or lazy managers (who are responsible for all of those things).

Despite a recent fashion of empowerment, many employees need and want direction, so that they can at least understand their company's attitude to particular situations, and what is expected of them. In spite of academic theories to the contrary, even superior creative people in knowledge industries want to know that at every step of the creative process, because they wish to know the parameters in which they can work. It is one of the hallmarks of the best employees that they want clear answers to those types of questions. And having their needs addressed by top management without having to ask is a mark of recognition, as opposed to commonplace symptoms of indifference. And yet the most common lapses encountered in business organizations are lack of leadership, an absence of formalized planning, and poor communications.

A consequence of those omissions is that managing in many organizations is an unsatisfactory and unsatisfying round of confrontations. Management is continually confronted by unnecessary problems and mistakes, frustrations and argument, disorganization and waste. All of that results in loss of time, cancelled orders, lost contracts, and lost opportunities. That is neither a constructive nor a creative way to manage a business enterprise.

Several meetings took place between elected employees and top management, but workers' problems were left unsolved again and again. In fact, they did not start off as problems, but only as questions. They became problems when the questions were left unanswered. The result of such indifference by management was that the Teamsters were invited in and the company was unionized.

Employees who are genuinely involved with their work often have real contributions to make, in the form of suggestions, fresh ideas, new proposals, and constructive improvements. If management makes important decisions that involve them, they want to be involved before the decisions are finalized. They do not want to be dragged along against their will, kicking and protesting. They would rather be invited to the decision-making process, and go along willingly with the final decision. Obviously it is also to the advantage of management for that to happen.

It boils down to a matter of trust. If management trusts its staff, it can only benefit from inviting them to participate. And if it does not trust them, it should not have employed them.

Procrastination is a valid and fairly common management style. And sometimes when there is serious doubt, it *is* better to do nothing. But problems rarely disappear of their own accord—more often they breed further problems. And even a decision to do nothing is a decision. It affects the management of a business as much as a positive decision, but it affects it negatively. It can create frustration now, and frustration can lead to impulsiveness in the future.

A manager, like a doctor having diagnosed the cause of an illness, should never wait until complications develop before taking remedial action. And just as a responsible and conscientious doctor will make every attempt to ensure that he has all the facts before diagnosing and curing an illness, so a manager finds himself in similar situations almost daily.

The best way for a manager to sense problems, before they become serious, is by keeping physically in touch with every facet of a business organization. Management By Walking Around has become known as MBWA. It is the best way for a manager to feel the pulse of every employee and every activity, from time to time—and even every machine in the plant.

A manager cannot know what is going on in a business enterprise if his time is spent behind the closed door of his office. Old family department stores used to employ someone called a floor walker who was the eyes and ears of the owner. Since other employees looked upon him as a spy, his existence created a continual adversarial relationship between management and labor. The use of such an intermediary by management is a cop-out. It is a poor substitute for leadership by a CEO who does not possess leadership skills.

Management by walking around involves intermittent reviews of all aspects of a business enterprise by watching, asking questions, listening, and analyzing. Good managers develop a sixth sense, as it were, by using all their other senses as they walk around offices, warehouses, factories, workshops, assembly lines, quality control, receiving and shipping bays, customer service departments, and the like. For example, a manager of a furniture factory will instinctively run his hand over panels of wood to check their quality and ensure that sanding machines are working properly, knots have been filled in, or cracked and warped timber has been rejected. An experienced factory manager will know from a change in sounds emanating from the machines that one or two are not in operation. He will identify which ones from the new sound. In plants where industrial gases are used, or in a food processing plant, a manager's sense of smell can become as sensitive as a hunting dog's. Very experienced and knowledgeable managers develop a visceral feeling that something is about to go wrong before it actually does. There is nothing mystical about it—it is intuitive. Some managers call it gut-feel. And it is simply a situation in which a number of different factors in a work environment—which may appear to be meaningless in themselves—start to form a meaningful pattern in the unconscious mind. Illumination comes suddenly—in the brain or in the gut.

The existence of gut-feel is substantiated by medical evidence. The enteric nervous system in the human gut is located in sheaths of tissue lining the oesophagus, the stomach, small intestine, and the colon. It is packed with neurons, support cells, and complex circuitry that enables it to act independently, to learn, remember, and produce gut-feel. The gut has even been described as a second "brain." It is also interconnected with the real brain, so that one gets upset when the other does. And symptoms from either of them get confused with the other—so that when the brain becomes consciously or unconsciously aware of particular clues, a person may feel a warning sensation in the gut.[3]

For example, a manager may know in an instant that an engineer is about to make a wrong judgement that could lead to manufacturing faulty products, because of delays in the arrival of the right components. Or he may become aware that a sales manager has been avoiding giving him direct answers about a regular contract for which documentation has not arrived but production is scheduled imminently. Or he may realize that the purchasing officer of essential raw materials, or a warehouse manager, has been distracting him from making a decision to build up seasonal inventories. When all the meaningful signs slip into place, he becomes suddenly alerted to a situation that can still be saved before it creates costly problems—through latent knowledge.

Four Case Histories

The following case histories are not fictitious. They were chosen not because they were unusual but because their problems are typical of what management consultants encounter all the time. Each failed in one way or another through poor judgement by inferior managers. They also had in common chief executives who did not possess the capacity to rise to challenges.

Different company names have been substituted for the real ones, and in some cases their industry sector has been altered to something similar, since each one was well-known at the time.

The most important single factor common to all of them is the failing of human nature. Time and time again it is the human factor that makes or breaks a business organization. That is why some knowledge of psychology and motivation is useful for managers, and why the subject of personnel management is necessary for students of marketing and management. Readers of Balzac's *Human Comedy* or the writings of Joseph Conrad may recognize the missing or weak characteristics that a leader needs to develop. It is an author's knowledge of human frailty that often produces timeless classics. One such classic is *Buddenbrooks* by Thomas Mann. In it we recognize the human forces that shape a business enterprise, the personal temperaments that prevent it from developing, and the deleterious effects of domestic distractions and social ambitions. We also encounter personal unsuitability for a particular industry or for business in general, through lack of suitable skills or complacency. Although it is not a subject normally dealt with in books on business management, the fact is clearly evident that people are the most important ingredient in the success or failure of a business enterprise.

What we miss when we read two-dimensional books on management or watch videos to learn our craft are the essentials. They are what literary critic Walter Allen described when he praised novelist Sir Walter Scott's grasp of "the organic relationships between man and man, man and place, man and society, and man and his past, the impersonal past of history." [4]

Fashioncorp was ultimately reduced to a much smaller, leaner, and more efficient company after the entire board of directors was fired. Anderson & Sons was obliged to pay its bills and close its doors after three generations. Trump Imports quietly disappeared in a similar fashion. Admirable Manufacturing was the overseas division of a major multinational conglomerate that finally sold off that operation when they lost patience with it. Mandrake was allowed to go bankrupt.

Fashioncorp, Inc.

This well-respected national organization was the market leader in its industry. It manufactured all its own products in five separate factories, each located in a different coastal city. Each factory had been purchased one at a time to create a comprehensive product range, since each plant specialized in its own particular market segment. For the sake of simplicity those segments could be described as men's top-of-the-line products; men's bottom-of-the-line products; men's middle-market products; children's middle-market lines; and women's middle-market lines. Products from each factory bore its own well-established brand name.

Fashioncorp also owned and operated the five biggest wholesale outlets in the country. Each one served the needs of independent retailers in each of the five sales regions. They too retained their different names and images which they had possessed when each individual family business was acquired, because the reputation of each one was considered to be an asset in its own special community.

In addition, Fashioncorp owned several hundred retail stores nationwide. Approximately half operated under the name of Katz and catered to the lower-priced mass market, while the rest traded as Palmers and aimed at the huge middle-market segment.

In that way, Fashioncorp controlled all but the very small, exclusive women's fashion niche, which was catered for by more expensive imports sold through independent boutiques. It was a fine organization and a highly successful one. It enjoyed an excellent reputation with both the trade and the public. Its strength was in the proliferation of its products, segmented under successful brands that were sold to major chain stores and department stores and had achieved a high degree of brand loyalty. Those established branded goods, sold also through their own chain stores, represented 80 percent of their sales. The remaining 20 percent was achieved through their regional wholesale warehouses. The head office was located in the main commercial and industrial city. Each division controlled its own separate warehouse.

No doubt the reason that the parent company had hired the new CEO was because he possessed considerable experience from having devoted his entire career to this industry. Moreover, the manufacturer and distributor with which he had worked in a different country, enjoyed a reputation as highly regarded as was Fashioncorp's. But apart from that, the core reasons for the success of each of the two companies differed in every possible regard.

The parent company was reputed to include several brilliant economists, strategic planners, chartered accountants, and financial wizards in its top management team. Whether it was they who developed a synergistic cost-cutting program or the newly appointed CEO is open to question. Certainly his appointment would have required ample discussion and agreement between them. On paper, there would have seemed to be too many warehouses and office buildings, and a great deal of duplication and triplication of effort, and therefore staff, in most operational spheres—as might be concluded from the following chart. It is also true that there was a passing fashion at that time for a strategy of centralization, with all the savings claimed for it. If the program was not the actual creation of the new CEO, his was the responsibility either for undertaking it or rejecting it. In the event, he chose to implement a centralization program.

When we examine the chart below, we can immediately see the significant differences between the narrow experience of the new chief executive, and a much broader vision now required of him in his new role. But to understand his own view of his new challenge, we must cover up the entire right hand column, because he was totally blind to the salient factors that had shaped the destiny of Fashioncorp up until his appointment as its head. It was beyond his experience.

CEO's Experience versus **Fashioncorp's Dynamics**

Marketplace:

Shorter distances with
lower transport costs.

• Huge distances for deliveries of goods.

Products:

Focused on standardization.

• Different requirements in each sales region.

Product Design:

Very slow design changes
geared to mass market needs.

• Designs geared to both seasonal and regional
fashion differences.

Inventories:

Regular even stock rotation.

• Seasonal sales driven by new fashions that
make slow-moving inventories obsolete and
valueless.

Brands:

All products marketed
under one brand name
and image.

• Five separate brand names and images.

Retail Trading:

Retail operation traded
under same name as brand.

• Two separate retail operations aimed at different market segments, offering some of the
five different brands.

Cash Flow:

Steady cash flow from
national sales.

• Largely driven by cash sales from five separate regional wholesalers.

Marketing:

One national marketing
department.

• Five separate marketing VPs and five regional wholesale branch managers.

Research:

Simplified according to
mass market requirements

• Complex consumer and market research
needs for different market segments, and
seasonal fashion changes provided by separate VP.

Advertising:

Simplistic and standardized.

• Complex and subtle brand advertising driven
by seasonal fashion changes, created by three
major advertising agencies.

Organization Structure:

Essentially hierarchial.

• Round Table approach required by creative
knowledge workers.

Management Style:

Autocratic.

* Participative and consultative style essential to accommodate diversity of elements and subjective viewpoints of managers in manufacturing, major sales, wholesaling, retail outlets, and marketing divisions.

Customer Base:

One central trade showroom of minor significance because of long-lived standardized products.

* Five trade showrooms required by seasonal fashion changes, for major chain and department store buyers; plus five regional wholesale showrooms for small, independent neighborhood retail stores and boutiques.

That comparison between the experience of the new company head and the far more complex marketing environment in which Fashioncorp had so far been eminently successful, indicated a need for a more creative entrepreneur with skills in managing an enterprise geared to continually changing and diversified fashion needs. Even without such a background, the marketing needs of Fashioncorp could have been learned very quickly by any intelligent and able marketing person. But the CEO was not a marketing man. Even so, the senior marketing VP, who was, had assiduously built up a valuable fund of information, which was placed at the CEO's disposal. A CEO with marketing experience would have considered himself most fortunate that the special strengths of the marketing and research VP were analyzing internal data and interpreting meaningful market and consumer research.

Perhaps the new CEO would have changed his entire approach if the research had been summarized for him on one sheet of paper in this simplified form, but it is doubtful. He had already enjoyed the advantage of feedback from forty-five experienced and mature sales people who knew their customers' requirements, five very senior sales managers with an abundance of experience of each market segment and sales region, five factory managers who were probably the best in the country, and five wholesale branch managers who had grown up in each of the sales regions and were closely involved with their own community. All were adamantly against the implementation of the centralization plan. He chose to disregard their advice.

It is easy to see why accountants, economists, or administrators who do not understand management or marketing would believe that considerable savings could be made by centralizing all administrative, sales, and marketing personnel in one building with a central warehouse attached to it. The warehouse would incorporate all inventories previously held by each of the regional wholesalers, who had also held stocks for the company's own chain stores in their area. It would also carry inventories formerly held by each factory. Fully automated state-of-the-art technology would facilitate the movement of this highly diversified fashion merchandise, in and out of the vast central warehouse. In theory at least, access, storage, and egress could be controlled by only one warehouseman, by means of an operational panel.

The five manufacturing plants were left to continue producing goods on the coast, as before, since supplies of raw materials and equipment were shipped to local ports from overseas. But each factory was now isolated from its own administrative, sales, and marketing people. They were located, virtually out of touch, far away in another city. The five regional wholesalers also remained where they were, but they had been emasculated. They no longer possessed any stocks of merchandise, which were stored, instead, a considerable distance away at the head office.

The brand new head office complex contained only one central trade showroom. Five new marketing directors were responsible for its merchandise displays, which represented the products of the five factories. Since they had replaced the marketing people who did not wish to uproot their families from homes and schools on the coast, they were obliged to accept the revolutionary changes on trust. For the same reason, most of the administration, accountancy, and secretarial staff were new too. That in itself resulted in a slowdown.

It is possible that by the time all the moves had been made, the major 20 percent of department store and chain store buyers—who represented 80 percent of purchases—had already begun to obtain alternative sources for some of their supplies elsewhere.[5] Their buyers needed the reassurance of continuity and back-up stocks to avoid any possibility of losing sales. Certainly the flow of new orders had slowed down and was causing some concern in the factories. Meanwhile, managers of wholesale branches saw their worst dreams realized before their eyes, just as they had warned the CEO it would happen. Their retail customers now bought from local competitors because they picked up their own orders immediately they needed them. The very reason why those small neighborhood stores had always bought from them was to avoid the capital outlay and overhead costs of purchasing and holding stocks for themselves. Wholesale cash sales therefore diminished too—and with them the company's source of a ready cash flow.

Meanwhile, the technology of the new warehouse suffered from teething problems. Even when the warehouse manager knew he had the inventory that some major chain store wanted, he couldn't find it. The proliferation of types of fashion merchandise made its difficult to select on demand, while trucks waited. The system seemed not to have been designed to access all the different sizes, models, genders, colors, materials, styles, patterns, price ranges, or other variables. Nor could warehouse clerks easily identify appropriate customer orders to pair them of with the relevant consignment notes. Further complications were caused by the number of incomplete consignments being despatched as a consequence of not being able to find goods. And more confusion was created whenever customers cancelled orders or parts of orders because they could not wait any longer and bought elsewhere.

Transport costs were heavy because merchandise was being shipped back and forth, from coastal factories inland to the warehouse, and often back again to customers in the same city as the factories. Additional costs accumulated from trucks or containers being three parts empty because complete orders had not been located, and had to be despatched separately afterwards. Antics in the technological warehouse resembled the film of *Modern Times* by Charlie Chaplin. But no one was laughing. Customer service had fallen apart.

The CEO had begun to isolate himself in his office to escape from the chaos seeping through each department and every division of the company, which he was helpless to stop. His resignation was accepted at the point when the monthly balance sheet showed that the fast erosion of profits had resulted in the first month with a net loss.

Orders from major buyers declined still further. Diminished factory production led to workers being laid off. And the slowdown in administration and accounts in the open-plan offices, resulted in cash flow problems. But the biggest problem with crisis management is that companies always leave it too late to be dealt with effectively. The result is a panic-stricken working environment, and a necessity to work fast as monthly balance sheets reveal greater and greater losses. And the reality is a demoralized workforce that stands around gossiping and planning for their future, while consignment notes and orders pile up on their desks and invoices fail to go out to customers for payment.

J. Anderson & Sons (PTY) Ltd.

The founder of this family enterprise, Jacob Anderson, could be regarded as another Johann Buddenbrooks. It was he who saw a need he could fill in the paper and board, packaging and printing industry. He established a business first as a paper merchant in London in 1894. On his death, a going concern equipped with rows of modern machinery and approximately one hundred workers and staff passed into the hands of his two sons. They had learned the business as boys instead of continuing their education. One opened new accounts and obtained repeat orders, while the other manufactured the goods for the customers. The company grew in time to become a well-respected enterprise supplying wholesalers and other middlemen.

Attention to customers' needs resulted in considerable goodwill and customer preference. But the needs of the marketplace changed after the director of sales died. And since he had been an "outside" man, and therefore the "window on the world," the remaining owner lost touch with the marketplace. He carried on doing what he had done before, and a salesman was hired to maintain customer contact and take orders.

After the owner's death, the management of the company passed to the third-generation offsprings of each of the two brothers. They became joint directors. Since there were now two separate factories—each in a different section of the city—each partner was a director of operations or factory manager. That is to say, each was responsible for purchasing, production, administration, warehousing, and transport.

Sales were maintained at a fairly constant level because of goodwill until the practice of buying from wholesalers and middlemen declined. Customer orders became smaller and smaller. Had the partners continued to isolate themselves from the changing business environment, they would have lost one customer after another without replacing them, and been obliged to close down.

The reason why their market was being gradually whittled away was the growth of chain stores and the continual takeover of department stores into powerful buying groups; also the introduction of supermarkets and the prepackaging of goods. Major buying groups did not buy through wholesalers because their own combined purchasing power was greater than any number of wholesale companies. That enabled them to buy direct from manufacturers at much lower prices than any wholesaler could. Wholesaling virtually ceased to exist in their particular industry.

But neither director addressed the changes taking place in the outside world beyond their own factory walls. Each had been trained as a boy to manage a factory, and neither had learned anything new about the industry or the marketplace. Without an educated perspective on the future of the industry or its markets, they had no reason other than to believe that what had worked for them in the past would carry them into the future.

There was an obvious need to change the customer base, but the symptoms—which were a decline in sales—were attributed to inferior salesmanship or a need for more salespeople. That was evidenced by a large number of competitors who sold the same products. All that was required, it was felt, was to take some sales away from them. Ultimately, a better class of salesperson was found who negotiated large contracts with powerful buying groups and gradually changed the customer base. By standardizing those products and undertaking longer production runs with fewer machine changes, their factories were kept continually busy with more cost-effective production. Then, by replacing both outdated and uneconomical factories with one large and modern plant on one floor, and installing much faster machines, they were able to increase their production capabilities while also reducing overhead costs.

Had they continued to grow and innovate from their new premises there is no reason to suppose that they might not still be running a cost-effective and profitable business. But they did not do so. Consumer trends and trade practices changed again and eventually made their technology almost obsolete. In the meantime, more competitors had entered their industry because of the simple-to-handle technology and a need for relatively low capitalization, while they themselves had not progressed to more sophisticated technologies. They could not grasp the fact that management requires constant improvements and business organizations need continual innovations. They had only administered the *status quo*.

The demand for paper products declined still further. Smaller competitors cut their prices to compete and stay in business. Bigger ones installed more sophisticated technologies. As they were squeezed from both sides simultaneously, more and more of their machines stood idle for longer and longer periods, until finally it was unprofitable to continue in business. They had driven themselves into a dead-end and run out of ideas and commitment. All that remained—as with Buddenbrooks—was to close the doors and find a buyer for the real estate.

The case of Trump Imports demonstrates a similar situation played out even more dramatically in the retail trade, where a sufficient number of new customers must be attracted to a store, daily, for it to succeed. This entrepreneur on another continent had founded a successful discount store when young. Although it provided him with a comfortable living for many years filled with hard work, it failed to last for even one generation. Its emphasis was on affordable clothing and other soft goods for the family. His success was due to his skills as a merchandise buyer in sourcing low-cost items and negotiating favorable terms. But his pride and power as a store buyer became an overwhelming compulsion like an addiction. He would not let the job out of his control. Instead of delegating that function so that he could manage his business and renew his aging constituency, he remained isolated from the outside world, bargaining with manufacturers' and importers' reps, and endlessly bickering with constantly changing staff in the buying department.

His business declined remarkably quickly, and so suddenly that he panicked. Self-imprisoned in his buying office, he phoned frantically to all his friends and business associates for help.

"I used to have two thousand customers in my store every day," he would explain; "last year the numbers dropped to a thousand. Six months ago they dropped to only five hundred. Now my store is nearly empty!"

His customers had aged to that point in their life-cycle when they bought very little except food. Some of his old customers had left town. Others had died. And the next generation bought quite different products from "younger" and smarter boutiques. Had he attended to the marketplace and innovated his store and his products, he could have acquired a new customer base. He left it too late. It is extraordinary how quickly a customer base can be eroded by neglect. Markets change all the time. That is why businesses need marketing people.

But that will not automatically turn them into marketers: only a CEO can do that. The speed of change is quickening and the duration in which a business can collapse is shortening. It is partly due to increasing competition, but also to the interdependence of national economies. We live in a global village where the struggle for markets is ever more intense. Consequently, a manager who does not continually improve his business and his performance will lose the battle for customers and maybe his entire enterprise as well.

Admirable Manufacturing Corp., Ltd.

This large manufacturer and distributor with five plants had been known by the industry to be a sick company for over fifteen years, but somehow it had survived. Regular downsizing of top marketing executives and their staffs, and restructuring to meet entirely different corporate strategies every three or more years demonstrated lack of leadership and absence of long-term planning. Its continual restructuring was not a matter of flexibility to address changing market situations, because it habitually shed its productive marketing, advertising and sales managers, and R&D and strategic planners, when favorable economic cycles provided ample opportunity for growth. It left itself hollow, without skilled staff to exploit the boom, while its competitors were geared up for it. Since it was a subsidiary of an internationally visible American conglomerate, local marketers assumed that U.S. top management were out of touch with overseas market conditions that were evidently alien to them.

A previous cycle of stop-go management had been exemplified by the appointment of a dynamic marketing-oriented individual who had done his best to develop new product ranges. He had appointed a new marketing VP, established a new market research department, hired additional product managers, new R&D staff, and advertising and public relations managers; with all the necessary back-up staff, office accommodation, and equipment to make them effective. The result was that sales soon soared and there had been a sense of reassurance and a feeling of confidence in future prospects. But approximately three years later, it appeared that head office management in the United States had studied their balance sheets and decided that costs had crept up and were encroaching on profit margins. They replaced the CEO with one whose background was financial controls. His mandate was to implement a cost-cutting exercise to restore profit margins.

The first stage was the closure of those marketing departments that had been responsible for creating additional revenues and increasing their share of the market. Sales stopped almost immediately and factory staff had to be reduced. New or innovated products planned for the future were abandoned.

When far-distant American management reviewed the situation in its overseas subsidiary several years later, they naturally discovered that although overhead costs had been cut, revenues too were down, and profits had been eroded. Now head office appointed a new CEO with marketing experience and skills and a solid reputation for creating accelerated growth. He immediately hired the best R&D, marketing, advertising, strategic planners, and brand managers he could find.

Wrote psychologist Carl Jung, "The pendulum of the mind oscillates between sense and nonsense."

Although this subsidiary company had been treated in the past as a separate cost and profit center, there was little doubt that its minimal averaged margins did not make it an attractive proposition for the U.S. holding company; that is why they had been generally indifferent to it. It had survived largely as a consequence of the established global brand name. Admirable became semi-autonomous through lack of interest by the United States. Its own local CEO had been a chartered accountant rather than an engineer, a marketing vice-president or a general manager. Despite that, there were no signs of the old-time cyclical cost cutting. Its own top management complement was relatively large now, and included several strategic planners with specialized staffs and the latest information technology. The CEO spent considerable time isolated from his other managers, the business organization, and the marketplace, to concentrate single-mindedly on planning, instead.

Rather than discuss planning with his marketing people, he preferred direct access to each planner. Both were directly responsible to him. As a consequence, the marketing VP was anxious to break his contract and leave rather than lose control of the marketing responsibility; the senior marketing manager was suffering from a nervous breakdown that would soon result in his departure; and other marketing managers were confused and indecisive because of lack of direction.

It was abundantly clear that the old sickness persisted, although in a somewhat different form, and it seemed to be far worse than ever before. But the reason was the same—lack of inspired leadership.

National and regional sales arenas were explosive with more than usual emotionalism, and with good reason. The national sales manager and his area branch managers showed classic signs of paranoia because they were being prevented from making sales and earning their living. Admirable was a diversified furniture manufacturer. Although they had obtained an accumulation of orders from their customers, they could not procure sufficient supplies of merchandise to meet those orders and obtain their sales commission. That also prevented them from seeking repeat orders. They were discontented and frustrated.

Meanwhile, chain store buyers periodically cancelled their orders when they could wait no longer and had to obtain supplies from other manufacturers.

The pressures that declining sales figures placed on branch managers had already driven one to drink. Others continually threatened to leave but were restrained by old loyalties to the company they had served for so long. Everyone in sales and marketing knew what was wrong with the company, but no one at the head office would listen to them. Although they had lost confidence in top management, they restrained themselves from being confrontational because of the risk of losing their jobs. Meanwhile, the branch managers' courageous attempts to continue to motivate their regional sales teams were met with cynicism. The sales people felt no loyalty to a company that prevented them from earning a living.

The reason for all the tensions in every one of the trade showrooms in each major city across the country was displayed around the walls of store rooms in each regional warehouse. They were damaged and unsalable items of merchandise, each one of which would otherwise be sold for between $600 and $1,500 at today's prices. Beside every one was the undamaged cardboard container in which it had arrived from one of the factories, to show that none had been damaged by handling but had left the assembly lines in that flawed condition. No one from the factories came down to see the displays, despite repeated invitations. They didn't need to: they knew what was wrong. Meanwhile, sales people were too embarrassed to face their customers and tell them why they couldn't deliver their goods. And they were afraid to lose future business.

The reason that supplies of merchandise had dried up was twofold. Those assembly lines producing goods were sending them out in damaged condition and they had to be concealed from customers. And other assembly lines were not in production because they had been closed down by the president. He had chosen the peak period of demand to redesign and shorten them. He claimed that they would produce more goods at less cost. But by that time, according to the sales managers, they might not have any customers left to sell them to. Meanwhile, the company was confronted with losses in the sales departments that would far exceed any possible production savings.

The president evidently had grandiose plans that he was keeping to himself, but he lacked both the experience and the ability to put them into practice. And his sense of priorities was clearly misguided, to judge from his destruction of the production lines. His lack of operational management experience evinced itself in the chaos that prevented progress. He could not lead his management team, nor was he capable of delegating to them. He was not even communicating with them. The reason was that his top management team had disagreed with his priorities. He seemed to feel that he was punishing them by withdrawing from them. He had even taken the extraordinary step of briefing recruitment companies to replace his outgoing marketing vice-president with someone who did not possess any marketing experience at all. When they realized that all he wanted was a yes-man to shield him from his own top managers, the executive placement consultants shrugged him off.

Somehow Admirable had been able to keep its brand alive for over three decades, despite misguided or inconsistent management. And because of the strength of the brand, distributors had been obliged to stock its products.

Customers had demanded, and they were proud to display, products bearing the respected logo with its elegant, international "A" symbol. Now those same stores wore losing sales because of gaps in their ranges of merchandise, due to the failure of their supplier to deliver the goods. As they lost confidence in their supplier, they began to fill those gaps with merchandise carrying other brand names. And their store salespeople found ways to switch customers to those competitors' brands. Admirable's trade franchise gradually disappeared as better managed companies benefited.

The president suddenly left his long-range strategic planning and became aware that he had a national sales manager, and perhaps he should start visiting the presidents of the major chain stores with him. But by that time they had lost interest in Admirable's problems. What had once been a highly desirable premier brand name disappeared altogether from nationwide retail stores.

Mandrake Wholesale Textiles Plc.

It can be instructive to consider a much smaller company where the problems, or their symptoms, can be easily seen by an outsider, even though they are not apparent to its manager.

Mandrake had been situated in a good location in the textile area of a major city for a good many years. But instead of gathering momentum by the expansion of its customer base, as might be expected, it now showed disappointing financial results. In response to its shareholders' questions, its managing director had presented them with a proposal that required more capital for reorganization.

According to the shareholders the wholesale premises always looked deserted and no one ever came forward to serve them when they entered. According to the manager, most of the sales were made over the phone, and the salesmen had clerical duties to perform, which pinned them, head down, to their desks and phones.

The manager's office was hidden away at the rear of the warehouse, accessed through the showroom and past shelving and an area where broadloom carpeting could be spread out and measured, and in which a forklift truck usually stood.

The shareholders uneasily reviewed the spreadsheets. Despite what they had been told, the lack of dynamism in the showroom concerned them. And although they knew little about the textile industry, they did know that most store managers want to know what is going on in the showroom. They frequently have two-way mirror glass installed in the partition wall between them and the customer sales area. They normally have an obsession about keeping in close personal touch with potential customers. Managers responsible for several stores generally have updated sales figures phoned to them throughout each day from every branch.

Although he had worked in the industry all his life, it appeared from their conversations with him that he had no perception of customer trends and changes within the textile industry. They considered ways to motivate him, but came to the conclusion that he was a loser. If he had ever possessed enthusiasm it had long since waned. He had no conception of how to hire or train his sales people, and made the paramount error of burdening them with paperwork and using them as administrative drudges. If he had ever known what were his business goals or his company mission, it had since completely escaped him. Had he possessed any initiative or even common sense, he would have sent them out to look for sales instead of preventing him and them from being effective. And in making contact with the outside world, they would surely have reported to him that the wholesale textile industry was suffering a death. Then he would have been forced to plan some other way to continue in business—perhaps by becoming an agent for several textile mills.

He had grown up in an era when textile wholesalers served a useful purpose and there was very little competition. When chain stores obtained better prices from mills than wholesalers did, because they bought in far bigger quantities, the wholesale trade had declined. The struggle for business became more intense. But he had refused to acknowledge to himself that the industry was changing, because he didn't know what to do about it. So he deceived himself that sales would begin to pick up again soon. Meanwhile he continued to do what he had always done as a matter of routine: he sat in his showroom in the center of town and waited for business to come to him.

Across the street from him stood a very large and successful textile showroom that offered a far bigger range and variety of merchandise than he did, to both the trade *and* the public. Its business strategy in changing times had been to change its tactics altogether. It rightly deduced that smaller trade customers would be prepared to pay cost plus 2.5 percent more for the convenience of being able to pick up merchandise from its warehouse when they themselves were out of stock. And just as its sales had dropped when it had originally tried to maintain its traditional profit margins, so when it reduced its margins to the limit it increased its sales. That qualified it for special discounts and rebates from the mills. And to offset its lower profit margins, it also imported exclusive fabrics which it sold at premium prices. It sold direct to the public too, at full retail prices. Its three-way strategy resulted in averaging its total profit margin at much the same level as it had always done before.

There was nothing to stop the managing director of Mandrake from crossing the street and finding out what his major competitor was doing that was right, but he lacked initiative and no longer possessed any commitment. After a short investigation by an independent management consultant, they accepted his verdict that what they were witnessing was tenth-rate management. After one final review of the balance sheet, Mandrake was closed down.

Chief executives are hired to manage change to the advantage of the firm. Those failed to do so for a variety of reasons. The prime mover in the centralization program was conditioned from having previously spent his entire career *resisting* change. So that, although he chose to embrace it on this occasion it was a novelty and he failed to understand that change has to be relevant and competitive. The executive who ruined his brand daydreamed of the future to shield himself from acting in the present, probably because he suspected he possessed neither the experience nor the ability to manage such a large organization. Anderson and Trump were simply unaware that competitive improvements must be initiated continually. The manager of Mandrake was blind to changes taking place around him and evidently possessed no management skills at all.

Firms stay in business only when they find new ways to compete or to improve on old ways of doing things. Survival cannot be guaranteed, but it can be prolonged by continuous improvements of products and processes.

Yet the need for continuous innovation runs counter to organizational norms in most companies. Firms would rather not change. Particularly in a successful firm, powerful forces work against modifying strategy. Past approaches become institutionalized in procedures and management controls. Specialized facilities are created. Personnel are trained in one mode of behaviour. Self-selection attracts new employees who believe in the existing way of doing things and are particularly suited to implementing them. The strategy becomes almost like a religion, and questioning any aspect is regarded as bordering on heresy. Information that would challenge current approaches is screened out or dismissed. Individuals who challenge established wisdom are expelled or isolated. As an organization matures, its need for stability and security seems to rise. It takes strong pressures to counteract these forces.[6]

But the price of stability is stagnation.

Despite the fact that those four case histories were chosen at random to represent typical problems in entirely different types of business organizations, the major failings that caused the demise of all of them were exactly the same. Their dynamics lacked four vital ingredients: direction, purpose, curiosity, and vision.

Only in the case of Admirable Manufacturing could lack of Total Quality Management be cited in fifth place. What is usually at fault is the quality of marketing, the quality of management, the quality of strategic planning for the future (or the absence of it), and an inability to provide innovations and practice ongoing R&D.

The paradox is that if professional marketing and management is practiced, total quality is practiced too—by definition. On the other hand, Fashioncorp's five factories benefited from excellent managers practicing very high standards of TQM as a normal part of factory management. Design and manufacture of their products were outstanding. Nevertheless, they were inundated with destructive problems.

Good management addresses those four major weaknesses as follows:

A *sense of direction:* That is provided by professional marketing.

A *sense of purpose:* That is created by inspired and charismatic leadership.

A *sense of curiosity:* That and the resultant initiatives are sparked by intellectual and creative management.

Vision: This requires planning for the future and continually innovating to achieve a company's mission.

Companies without vision merely "wing it" to overcome one problem at a time. They have no time to explore or exploit opportunities.

As we have seen, chief executive officers are human. They are, therefore, prone to failings like everyone else. But in their position, one big failing or a multitude of little ones may cause considerable damage to an organization and even throw everyone out of work as a consequence. But it can be lonely at the top. A chief executive needs someone to whom he can turn for genuine and worthwhile advice when special problems materialize and conflict with his plans. If he is a parsimonious owner who hired cheap labor instead of choosing creative managers, he would hardly respect their opinions. Even if he were a president of a large organization and enjoyed all the advantages of an excellent top management team, each of his managers would be a specialist—when what he needs is a generalist like himself. It is also objective opinions that are needed. What is required is a devil's advocate.

It is no wonder that chief executives often withdraw and become uncommunicative when they are aware of special problems that only they can deal with but don't yet know how to. Nor would they choose to show signs of personal confusion to their top management team or the chairman. Every chief executive needs a management consultant who will take a fresh and vital interest in his business. And he must be someone who has experienced bottom-line accountability himself. Only then could he understand the full implications of the problems.

The skill of a management consultant is often in knowing the right questions to ask, and sometimes even knowing the right answers. But when the appropriate questions are posed after an investigation of the problems, it is frequently the chief executive who is illuminated and comes up with the most suitable option. Then the consultant provides the new strategic plans.

The Marketing Mystique

Those four case histories introduce the mystique of marketing. It is a mystique only because so few business people seem to understand what it is and its implications for a business enterprise. It has a unique capacity not only to develop markets, but also to create the most suitable products for those markets. It is holistic, just as management is, in that it permeates every activity in an enterprise. Despite that, one continually hears stories of managing directors introducing a young assistant who clearly could not have accumulated professional marketing experience, and describing him as the person who "does all our marketing." What they really meant was he answered customer enquiries on the phone or at a trade counter. And one often hears of a corporate president saying the same type of thing of a Girl-Friday who is actually responsible for coordinating advertising material from graphic artists or PMTs from typesetters.

There are also managements who have been led to believe that marketing has been replaced by Total Quality Management, or TQM. No suggestion could be more of a distortion of facts, since TQM is really one of many marketing tools, although designated by a fashionable new name.

W. Edwards Deming is the person most often associated with TQM. He pioneered the technique of Quality Circles in Japan in the 1950s with Joseph Juran. TQM was initiated by the earlier practice of Statistical Quality Control.

Deming's description of the flow of quality throughout all phases of management is synonymous with modern marketing thought—although rarely with its practice. A product manager is responsible for the quality of his products, but marketers tend to concentrate their attention more on beginnings and ends like consumer research and the conception and design of products; also on product distribution and customer satisfaction. Whatever happens in between is most often left to the judgements and skills of engineers and production managers. They are: negotiating with suppliers of essential materials and equipment, procurement, receiving and testing materials, production and assembly, and quality control inspections. Although Deming's perspective of the circle of built-in or applied quality may seem to be directed at the sequences in the middle—and TQM adherents are often accused of a bias toward the process—he is in fact acutely conscious that "the consumer will from now on be the most important part of the production line."[7]

Any marketing manager who has been involved in regular meetings with engineers and production teams, to establish agreement on product quality, pricing, and production volumes and schedules, will recognize Deming's concerns and acknowledge his approach to many of the problems of assembly lines. But despite that, it is marketing and innovation that are the two special functions of a business organization. Some people believe that marketing is the business. Others, to their detriment, believe that the business is production, or administration, or sales. In practice, every department of every business organization is another instrument for a marketer to use tactically, to facilitate profitability and growth by satisfying customers' needs.

Marketing orientation is not easy to adopt for managers whose disciplines did not include some knowledge of it. But it is vital for *all* managers to understand the principles of marketing and innovation, because their main function is to support the marketing program. And each manager's special function is innovation.

It is easier to understand its significance to a business organization if one considers how people sold or bought goods before the Industrial Revolution in England. Suppliers were craftsmen or weavers making things in their homes, or blacksmiths in their forges, or they grew produce on their lands. Merchants made nothing, but acted as middlemen in a community or travelled abroad and brought back goods made in other countries. Those goods might be taken by a packman with his horse, to villages, outlying hamlets, and farms. In bigger or less developed countries, a smous might transport goods by oxwagon, to sell them to farmers hundreds of miles from each other. In towns that were economically worthwhile, hawkers would sell from door to door, or bring goods into a marketplace on the outskirts, and villagers and farmers would come in and buy on specific days of the week. Regular market days developed in bigger European towns and cities. Sundays became customary market days because populations had habitually converged on the towns to worship the sun in pre-Christian Rome. But permanent markets might be established in densely populated places, like African or Indian bazaars.

Wares are still brought to permanent markets on the Mediterranean coast, or in Balkan countries, or rural French or Italian communities, or German market towns. From a smallholding at five o'clock in the morning, a teenager might load her barrow with fruit and vegetables and wheel it to the nearest town with a permanent marketplace. She would plan to reach her destination early, to choose a good location out of the glare of the sun, and she would spread out her produce on a trestle table or a permanent concrete platform, and sit and wait for customers.

The late Lord Cohen, who founded Tesco Stores in Britain, never forgot the marketplace concept, because he started his career in management as a barrow-boy. He too arrived at the fruit and vegetable market early, in London, to choose the best location he could get. He described how he had to fight off other traders who would tip over his barrow and spoil his produce.

The advantage of such beginnings is that competitors are visible all around the marketer. He can therefore know from the assortment of goods and their prices what is in demand and what prices are acceptable to customers. All he has to do is keep his eyes and ears attuned to market activity and talk to customers to find out what is going on, and also what he will have to do to compete successfully. It is easy to see from that scenario that the specific function of a business is marketing.

So many corporate managers have not been closely in touch with a marketplace, or cannot equate it with their own business enterprise. Owners of small or medium-size businesses who were once closely in touch with their marketplace easily lose that personal touch and become isolated from customers and involved, instead, with administration. Financial controllers, production managers, warehouse and transport managers, R&D managers, and human resource managers are likely not to understand its significance to the enterprise and to their own jobs, because they are in-house managers. Perhaps they need a framed picture on the wall of their office as a continual reminder of where and how products and services fill customers' needs, and that without customers they could not exist. It might be the fish market near Lake Chapala in north Mexico, the flower and fruit market in Zagreb, the meat market in the center of Munich, the crafts market near Guadalajara or in the capital of Swaziland. They are not a custom that belongs solely to the past. They exist, as do the markets of more sophisticated business organizations that may not be visible from the windows of top managers' offices. A picture might remind them of that place where customers come to buy and marketers go to sell.

> Dealers in goods from around the country came to Osaka with information about conditions in their respective regions. From Wakayama came news of forest and fishery products, and from Shiga and Hyogo up-to-date lines of farm products. People from Kyoto and Nara, meanwhile, were a reliable source of information on traditional handcrafted goods and, most important, trends in consumer demand in these advanced and highly populated cities.
>
> This is how the Osaka merchants kept track of such important matters as where large quantities of particular items were being produced, methods of transportation and preservation, processing techniques, and sources of information. The people who had the best grasp of all this were the wholesalers and brokers. From their ranks came the entrepreneurs who would use this ability to make detailed, competent analyses and judgements from the information at hand to set up their own processing or manufacturing businesses.[8]

As productivity grew through bigger and better handlooms and mechanization took place in the eighteenth century, marketers and managers concentrated more on production methods and, in effect, turned away from customers, so that by the twentieth century the business arena had become the workplace, and the marketplace was a territory to be shunned as fit only for commercial travellers.

Long before that, a technological transformation had taken place in the textile industry, in mining, and for iron foundries. It was the invention of the steam engine that mechanized what had been hand work. Britain pioneered the miracle of industrialization, which was later copied by America, Western Europe, Russia, and Japan; and with it, the mass enjoyment of more affordable consumer goods.

Investment in industry in eighteenth-century England created higher living standards for the working classes and for everyone else. And those standards would have been higher had it not been for the threat of the French Revolution and the cost of armed forces to resist Napoleon's conquests from expanding, by keeping his troops at bay.

Living standards in England rose until 1795, when war led to a decline. Recovery was slow but steadily increased after the 1840s. Then the growth of industry prevented massive starvation from occurring in England, as was being suffered in Scotland, Ireland, and on the continent of Europe. It was industry that made mass immigration possible from Ireland, because England was able to feed and absorb immigrants. The size of the British working classes increased by 400 percent. Between the turn of the nineteenth century and the turn of the twentieth, real wages doubled and then doubled again.

Despite agitation by Marx and Engels—whose special sphere of study was working-class areas in Manchester—the Industrial Revolution was responsible for providing better housing and a better quality of life even in the slums of industrial cities, than had been the case in rural areas. The romantic picture of rural England, as depicted in the novels of Thomas Hardy, bears little resemblance to the squalor, cruelty, impoverishment, and degradation of farm laborers and their families, and even tenant farmers. And conditions were far worse in the remote countryside on the continent of Europe. Industrialization actually improved living standards, but its drawbacks were more visible to writers like Zola and Dickens.

What Japan seems to have learned from Britain's Industrial Revolution and its own is that real wealth comes from the creation of full employment by progressive capitalism; that the primary objective of government should be the wealth of individuals who make up a community. What Hong Kong learned was that low taxation must be coupled with low interest rates; that as long as government takes most of the surplus, economic development will be discouraged—because the impetus to invent, to innovate, to take out patents, and to create business enterprises that can provide employment is discouraged in the absence of inducements. Invention and entrepreneurship are largely economic activities pursued for gain. One reason that England took the lead in the Industrial Revolution instead of Holland, which was in a better position to do so, was that the Dutch were taxed two and a half times more than the English, and were therefore not motivated to compete.

In a successful capitalist society like Hong Kong, government is merely an organization to provide the protection of law, order, and justice, in return for the payment of modest taxes. Given a secure environment, entrepreneurs can amass capital for investments and feel free to create growth by solving economic problems and seizing opportunities. Britain came close to that ideal in the eighteenth century. After the Acts of Union, the United Kingdom became the biggest single market in the world. There was sufficient labor, and a dynamic economy was enabled to grow through the technology of the steam engine.

Market Forces

Most manufacturers and suppliers of services suffer from two repetitive nightmares. The first is competition. But the worst is fear of market saturation. That is what took place in Britain around 1830—primarily because real incomes had declined for the first time in one hundred years. We find ourselves in the same position today. The result then was that warehouses were jammed with mass-produced goods designed for a mass market when the masses could no longer afford to buy them or already had them.

The theory of capitalism involves the concept that manufacturers who are motivated to start up new business enterprises will provide more and more employment so that employees can afford to purchase goods and services— and consequently create a viable market for other manufacturers, who in turn will be able to provide even more jobs, and so on. But there emerged from that situation three interesting questions, which are still continually being asked by manufacturers and other suppliers today:

1. What should a manufacturer do when everyone possesses the type of goods it manufactures?
2. How can a business enterprise survive when its competitors are reducing prices just to maintain production runs?
3. What should they do when customers can no longer afford to buy their products?

Those three market forces combined—market saturation, over-production, and diminution of disposable incomes—began to stop one machine after another. Fortunately for Britain, it possessed an empire with enormous populations. Now, creating overseas markets for surplus production and selling off inventories became the priority. Overseas agents were the answer. The single-minded obsession of industrialists with their machines and their factories began to turn into a compulsion to sell.

Manufacturers hired more commission salesmen in later years. Work opportunities expanded for men with little education who were neither craftsmen, artisans, or qualified to be professionals. What brought better educated men into selling was the enormous unemployment at the end of the first world war when conscripts and volunteers for the armed forces returned to civilian life. That situation was soon followed by the Depression from 1929. Those who had once travelled from town to town in bygone days, like the packman with his horse, were now commercial travellers out looking to make sales.

Apart from a few innovators like Henry Ford with his Model-T, which was the first affordable people's automobile designed for the mass market, most manufacturers continued to turn out the same products they had made in the past. They believed stolidly in long production runs and short assembly lines with fewer changes, as did Ford. It was his success with that formula that persuaded most manufacturers in the United States that his was the *only* formula to follow. But some did invent new products or innovated to make better ones, or were able to reduce prices through design innovations, or innovations in materials, manufacturing, distribution, or marketing.

Most manufacturers, converters, and other suppliers continued to be conservative in business because they thought they had achieved the right formula for success. If it had worked so far, why change it? And when a commercial traveller returned to his office at the end of the week without having made any sales, his manager would inevitably say, "What have you been doing all week?" It was a rhetorical question; more of an implied threat. When a salesman attempted to describe pricing problems, better competing products, or better service, the boss would reply, "Don't make excuses—get out and sell! That's what I pay you for." That scenario was performed daily in hundreds of thousands of businesses in the West. That adversarial relationship bred contempt on both sides, but each needed the other. The manufacturer's attitude arose from a conviction that all salesmen were idle and had to be bullied. After all, he was making exactly the same products as he always had, and they had *always* sold.

Successful marketers nowadays use their sales forces to provide helpful feedback from the marketplace, as well as making use of other forms of market and consumer research. And they have learned to react instantly to any changes in a market. But market research was little known then, or barely considered as being of any importance. By that time, industrialists seemed to have forgotten, or never knew, that their more entrepreneurial predecessors *always* knew precisely what was happening in their market. That was where they sold their goods—personally. They knew immediately what their competitors were offering the public. They could hear what prices were being paid, and see customer resistance to buying. They saw new products as they entered the market. They could examine innovations to familiar products. And they had the opportunity to take immediate actions to ensure they could always compete. In short, success in business depended on adaptability.

The sales, as opposed to the market approach, dominated business in Europe and the U.S. right up until World War II. The West struggled to pull itself out of a slump, which in America, followed the Wall Street Crash. The answer to mass unemployment in Germany and Italy was recruitment in the armed forces, the manufacture of armaments, and the wholesale theft of other people's property that terrorism and invasion provides. Those were primarily military economies. Meanwhile, the peace-time economy of the United States still benefited from its capture of international markets during and immediately after the Great War. And the decade from the mid-1930s to the mid-1940s was an era of get-rich-quick salesmen in the U.S. Some of the best, like Frank Bettger, became immortalized through best-selling books like *How I Raised Myself From Failure To Success In Selling*. And Dale Carnegie sales courses became famous when instant financial success seemed to be assured just by learning how to sell.

It is tempting to search for "firsts" in any sphere or any country. Did Machiavelli write the first strategic plans in the fifteenth century, when he wrote *The Prince* or *The Art Of War* for the Medicis? Could Benjamin Franklin be cited as the first marketer to introduce and promote innovation in the eighteenth century in America? McCormick and Obed Hussey independently but simultaneously invented the reaper in the middle of the nineteenth century. And the main difference between them was that Hussey was concerned solely with its invention and manufacture. McCormick was, arguably, the first to use a marketing approach to create sales of his invention. He analyzed and researched the market, concerned himself with market standing, offered service with his sales, provided parts and servicing, and also a credit plan for payments on easy instalments. But all that initiated no marketing trend.

It was not for another hundred years—after the second world war, in the 1950s—that managers and business enterprises began to take an interest in the possibilities of better organized and better trained management. Until then, books on business management had not been profitable to publish. Most likely that was because most had described factory production, and were devoted to time and motion studies and quantitative measurements of work on assembly lines. It might therefore be said that Drucker's books about management pioneered a whole *genre* of such books on management and marketing. Certainly the 1950s seems to have been a period of intellectual curiosity by business organizations. But—just as in today's business climate—only the top 5 or 10 percent of companies in the West acted on new management theories or findings. However, a quiet industrial revolution was taking place in Germany and Japan.

As for the two decades between world wars—while Britain floundered with its national debt and its loss of markets to the United States, and its labor problems—it was finally the mass production of munitions, army uniforms, canned rations, gun sights, aerial cameras, submarines, tanks, and aircraft that pulled the U.S. out of its Depression.

A half-century later—despite the multitude of popular books on business management that have been written—most western manufacturers today still do not understand the marketing concept; or they practice it half-heartedly and subordinate it to other departments. Some build up such an administrative bureaucracy as a priority that it is impossible to practice effective marketing in their organizations.

How can we convince the average type of business to convert to marketing? It should be significant that those companies that do understand and do practice effective marketing and management are mostly national or multinational market leaders in their particular industries. They consider marketing to be of prime importance to their companies. And they ensure, by enshrining it in their methodology, that it is always practiced as a priority by their managers. They acknowledge that it was primarily marketing or customer orientation that propelled them into leadership positions in the first place. It is they who became known as "the excellent companies." Unilever, Rembrandt,

Colgate-Palmolive, Eastman Kodak, Pfizer, Toyota, Honda, Matsushita, SA Breweries, 3M, Proctor & Gamble—those are some of the fine companies that know how to practice a properly planned management methodology that is marketing oriented. They also benefit from the talents of top managers who encourage creative management and marketing, because they themselves moved up the ladder in progressive career paths within the company, instead of moving around. That means there is continuity, constancy of purpose, and commitment.

The Unilever group of companies, for example, does not describe itself as a manufacturer, although it manufactures cosmetics, laundry detergent, toilet soap, and margarine. It does not call itself a food processor, a tea blender, or a coffee packer. Nor does it describe itself as a sales organization. It knows that marketing comes first and last and in the middle. Since all its activities are driven by marketing, it knows itself to be a marketer. It was probably the very first manufacturing organization to recognize and formally adopt marketing principles. Sears Roebuck was probably the first retail organization to do so.

But most business organizations were not marketing oriented in the postwar world of the 1950s. There had been such an enormous pent-up demand for goods after wartime shortages and postwar austerity, that it was comparatively easy to sell them. Dealers were busy building up war-depleted inventories, and consumers enjoyed the pleasure of earning money and buying goods with it again. That and the fact that the public was uncritical, resulted in a belief that the key to supplying the mass market was to make a standard product to be sold in large volumes, with economies of scale that would automatically lower prices.

What happened was the market became saturated with goods. Customers became more discriminating about their purchases, and more fastidious about what they were willing to pay for them. The word "consumerism" had not yet begun to be heard, but advertising agencies were warning their clients that "the customer is king."

To overcome market saturation, some of the more innovative marketers developed a strategy of market segmentation. It was sometimes known also as fragmentation of the market. Market leaders spent more money on research and began to separate markets according to demographic segments. They designed products and priced them to appeal to specific needs and wants of different types of consumers. No doubt it was initiated by the recognition of a postwar baby boom. Its first stage was an inordinant demand for diapers, baby oil, and carrycots. Companies targeting that market—like Johnson & Johnson—showed considerable growth. That stage of the cycle was replaced a few years later by increased demand for infants and children's clothing and shoes, nursery books, and toys. Then the teenage market suddenly bloomed in the 1960s. It was of a proportion hitherto unknown in the West. And it became preeminent because that largest of all demographic consumer groups enjoyed a considerable disposable income. In fact, most or all of a teenager's income was disposable. The age of the miniskirt had dawned, Carnaby Street was invented to cater for the era of "the swinging sixties," and so were the Beatles and the Rolling Stones.

Not only did that stage of the life cycle of the baby-boom generation create new and innovated products, it also revolutionized the ways in which they were sold.

Teenagers are iconoclasts because they look at formerly established things through new eyes. There was no way they could enjoy shopping at fusty old department stores that were autocratic and intimidating. Nor did they want to shop at chain stores, which had been successful for generations by catering to families. They used old-fashioned slogans; "Like father, like son," and their staff were patronizing to teenagers. Moreover, fathers and mothers were often looked upon by that generation as tiresome old bores. No—they wanted to do their own thing and shop at boutiques that were friendly, sold their kind of clothes, played their type of music—loudly—and hired staff who were their kind of people. What's more, this miniskirt and blue jeans generation had the power to revolutionize marketing because it had the money.

Department stores that had been famous all over the world since Victorian times—like The Army And Navy Store and Selfridges in London, Bon Marché in Paris, and Greaterman's in South Africa—all suffered from a decline in sales. Some department stores were bought out by groups like Great Universal Stores, which had in any case been buying up old-fashioned family department stores since the 1950s. Some finally closed down, like Whiteleys. Others innovated their marketing, like Macy's in New York. But even they were only buying time: they filed for bankruptcy in the first half of 1992.

In the course of time, the teenagers of the 1960s grew into flower children, or rioting students, or beach bums, and sales of marijuana and LSD soared. By then, marketers had begun to realize that marketing by demographics was not as precise at they had once thought, because everything changes so fast. What counted more was different consumer needs that were dictated by their changed position in their life cycle. Young revolutionaries of the 1970s grew up. Some married and even had children in the 1980s, when they became known as *yuppies*. They enjoyed high disposable incomes. Housing markets boomed as a consequence, and so did the sales of domestic furniture and appliances. As their incomes increased, they bought tax-sheltered real estate as well as their own homes. By now the yuppy generation are around the age of fifty. Many are wealthy; some own their own high-tech companies, while others are in software. And just as that baby-boom generation drove new markets at each stage of their life cycle, so they have grown to influence politics, too.

Meanwhile, statistics continue to show that families in developed economies in the West are having fewer children or none at all. That too affects markets. Notwithstanding a lower birthrate, populations now live longer because of improved diets, exercise, and health care. The result of those factors is that as the average age of western populations is increasing, so is their life expectancy. It has been described as the greying of North America, but the same is happening in Western Europe. Many are still buying home computers, and the market grows through lower prices and innovations. New models that fit into a briefcase are increasing the demand and it still has a long way to go. But condominiums are a very soft market in North America because of overbuilding. The tourist market declined with the recession and its demographics are changing: German tourists give way to new-rich Japanese, and will probably change with the rate of development of other nations' economies. Canadians who own maintenance-free condominiums can lock them up to retire to their Florida holiday home for the winter months. And there are settled retirement communities strung along the east and west coasts of Florida, segmented into Francophone or Anglophone ones. And yuppies planning ahead for retirement bought mutual funds in the 1990s.

If the typical demographics of developed economies show an aging population, the reverse is true of undeveloped countries. Most African, Central American, and South American countries have a predominantly young population, with something like over 50 percent under the age of fourteen. In general, they have a very high birth rate and also a high mortality rate. South Africa is unique in that its demographics show both patterns. It has a First World infrastructure, while simultaneously suffering from some—but not all—the disadvantages of a Third-World economy.

Because of its aging economy, North America is obliged to gear its economic strategies to finding new young populations to provide a skilled workforce and also the professionals it will need. "Immigration or copulation" was once a slogan of former Canadian prime minister Macdonald. It is now fashionable again. But higher living costs have reduced the size of the average family, and immigration has already resulted in race riots. Although western Germany should have benefited from the influx of young skilled workers from the east, unification led instead to unemployment, lower wages, and a higher cost of living. The results were street riots, intimidation of immigrants, murders, and the reemergence of several neo-Nazi street gangs claiming political rights through threats of unrest.

Undeveloped countries, on the other hand, are in the classic situation described by Malthus, where population increases faster than the food supply. Despite a very high mortality rate at birth, they still show an extremely high birth rate and insufficient resources to meet the needs of a growing population—not enough food, housing, health services, schools, raw materials, jobs, and so forth. Even the severe spread of AIDS—reputed to affect one-third of the population of some countries in Africa, like Uganda—does not seem to affect the ratio between demand and supply of food.

In South Africa, however, there is a functioning industrial and economic infrastructure that could provide those services to the whole of Southern Africa providing there is an injection of capital from the West. From the marketing point of view, there is a growing middle class emerging as consumers in many developing economies like Latin America, India, Malaysia, Thailand, and other nations. Their new wealth will buy more goods and services, as well as provide taxes for the creation of more modern infrastructures. That, in turn, will provide more employment and still more disposable income for more goods and services.

All of those life cycles will be addressed by commerce and industry, and personal lifestyles will continue to be catered to by marketers. But about ten years ago, marketers were introduced to yet another way to segment populations in order to fulfil their needs. This method was described as "psychographics."

It had become increasingly evident to marketers for some time that some personal tastes cut across demographic factors and also life cycles. Even in 1921, Jung had been studying different personality types. He wrote that "every judgement made by an individual is conditioned by his personality type and...every point of view is necessarily relative."

Populations began to be broken down by market research organizations, according to different groups that have similar psychological attitudes. For example, two quite different consumer groups were shown to have purchased two brands of major domestic appliances in South Africa. The research was undertaken in 1980, and the two brands were GE and Defy. Both companies had recently merged and their goods were now manufactured in the same factories. But it was found that purchasers of the Defy brand of electric stoves, refrigerators, and freezers preferred their chosen brand because they considered its products to be more dependable. That consumer segment had a somewhat older profile than the other one, lived in rural communities or small towns, and belonged to traditional institutions like the church. Some were farmers while others were schoolteachers. Many spoke Afrikaans. They were described in psychographic terminology as "the responsible we." They generally held conservative opinions. Research also showed that the Defy brand name was still associated in the minds of consumers who bought its products, with much older electric stoves still in use, which appeared to be more sturdy and durable. They might have been made in Defy's iron foundry in Newcastle, with baked enamel on cast iron—instead of spray-painted pressed steel. Buyers of the GE brand, on the other hand, were younger, better educated, largely English speaking, with higher incomes, and tended to be more liberal in their views. They were the yuppy generation, or young new-rich. They were devoted to material possessions. In particular, they were that segment of the population that was compulsively attracted to anything high-tech—and the main visible difference between the two branded product ranges at that time, was that the GE brand offered more electronic features.

That consumer study influenced the direction of advertising and marketing toward the two separate and different groups of buyers who showed a decided preference for one brand over the other.

In 1995, two separate teams of researchers reported their discovery of "a partial genetic explanation for a personality trait called *novelty-seeking*." Individuals with a high novelty-seeking quotient tend to be extroverted, impulsive, extravagant, quick-tempered, excitable, and exploratory. Novelty seekers possess a slightly longer version of the D4 dopamine receptor than that of more reserved and deliberate people. Dopamine is the chemical most strongly linked to pleasure and sensation seeking.[9]

What was named "novelty-seeking" by Dr. C. Robert Cloninger of Washington University's School of Medicine, appears to equate with the first of eight psychographic categories that were established in the 1980s. The following percentage breakdown represented ratios of South Africa's whites at that time. Since psychographics differ according to a multiplicity of cultural groups, those of the black population are shown in chapter 8. These are: Achievers (19 percent); Contenteds (19 percent); Aspirers (15 percent); Hedonists (8 percent); Introverts (15 percent); Socialites (11 percent); Pessimists (7 percent); Strugglers (6 percent).[10]

A marketer might segment a particular target market by combining two or more similar psychographic categories, if consumer research showed that all would be likely to want the same product or service. Achievers and Aspirers together, for example, could deliver a potential market segment of 34 percent of that population. And if Socialites too were found to have the same wants or needs, the marketer might conceivably enlarge the prospective market segment to 45 percent.

It would, of course, be of paramount importance to undertake consumer research and survey the market first.

Market and consumer research are essential tools required for accurate marketing, since, if it is neither accurate nor complete it is not worth having, because it would only be misleading. But they are only links in a circular chain that begins and ends with interfacing with customers—first to find out what they need or want; then to find out if what you have produced meets their wants, and to test packaging, advertising, merchandising, shelf offtake, innovations, and so forth. It is a mistake to imagine that any link is more important than any other, because the marketing performance will be as weak as its weakest link. They include—but are by no means limited to—conception and design, formulation, testing, packaging, product development, research, pricing, sourcing raw materials, financing, budgeting and forecasting, production scheduling, test runs, distribution, trade advertising, promotions, selling-in to dealers, consumer advertising, advertisement research, test-marketing, machinery, assembly-lines, procurement, warehousing, and after-sales service. Both marketing thought and practice must pervade every activity in the marketing chain, because each is concerned only with getting and keeping customers.

General Electric Company's 1952 annual report defined that company's culture as building customer and market appeal into the product from the design stage on. They considered the physical act of selling to be merely the last step in a selling strategy that began before the first engineer prepared the first blueprint. The marketing manager was introduced at the very beginning, and would orient every phase of the business toward the marketplace.

1. Marketing research would establish what the customer wanted from a specific product, what price he or she was willing to pay, and where or when it was wanted;

2. The designer, the engineer, and the manufacturer would do what marketing management recommended they should do;

3. Marketing would authorize production planning, phasing, and inventory control, sales, distribution, and servicing.

The attitude of most of the leading fast-moving packaged consumer goods manufacturers and marketers today is that their job is to market direct to consumers—over the heads of their own sales people and their retail distributors. In that way, dealers are obliged to buy their products because the public demands them.

But that progressive philosophy is certainly not practiced by every manufacturer. And many of those that acknowledged or even practiced it in the 1950s and 1960s became misdirected in time, or lost their commitment to it because of other pressures.

If a marketing group has done its job effectively, it will have influenced buying decisions favorably by means of brand image, advertising, product, packaging, store display, and pricing, toward creating a hierarchy of effects on consumers who want that type of product or service: First—Brand Awareness; Second—Brand Preference; Third—Brand Loyalty.

Twelve years after General Electric Company's marketing-oriented annual report, the president of Alberto Culver Co. answered a provocative question; "Which comes first—product or marketing?" His answer was not what General Electric had in mind: "Sometimes one, sometimes the other. We *have* created a product and gone in search of the customer who might use it. We have also deliberately created a product we thought the consumer would prefer over others."

Creating a product and *then* looking for a customer is not customer orientation, but product orientation. And it takes us several steps backwards in time. That they also created products they *thought* a consumer would prefer over others, is an ominous reminder of the disastrous launch of the Ford Edsel. And it points to the era of 1952–1964 as a possible watershed. It seems that—like the invention of the wheel—marketing was discovered sooner by some business organizations than by others.

But, to give that president the benefit of any doubt, perhaps Alberto Culver had already established, through research, that a product already in the marketplace was not entirely what the public wanted. Perhaps the public knew how they wanted it improved. And if Alberto Culver came out with a new improved product—based on in-depth consumer research that revealed *what* and *how*—then that would have been innovation. If that is what happened, then they did build their marketing into the new, improved product at the very beginning.

In fact, the situations referred to may not have been product orientation at all, but serendipity—a situation in which a search for one thing leads instead to a discovery of another. Fleming's discovery of penicillin is an example. Another laboratory example took place in Durban in the 1960s, when a cosmetics manufacturer was experimenting in order to develop a face powder. Arriving at the laboratory one morning, the researcher found a ring of dead insects around the powder left on the table the evening before. The result was an insecticide that was marketed under the name of Peu-Beau.

Marketing and innovation are both entrepreneurial functions. An entrepreneur takes risks in running a business enterprise. To do so, he uses imagination, flexibility, opportunism, innovation, and change. A corporate manager, on the other hand, does not take the same type of risks, unless he is also the chief executive. If so, then he performs the entrepreneurial function, too.

Of course, a marketing vice-president, a marketing manager, or any other manager takes risks on a daily operational basis. But he or she does so within an agreed management framework to meet established goals and objectives with approved budgets. If there is an element of unplanned or unexpected risk in any major activity, the degree of which might not be considered acceptable to a president or a top management team, it is his responsibility to apprise the CEO of all available options. He states his case, explains the risks, and seeks approval. The decision to be made by the CEO is a matter of company policy.

Whenever someone attempts to describe succinctly what marketing is and does, there is no shortage of definitions. In 1957 the American Marketing Association stated, "Marketing implies integration of all functions in moving any type of goods or services from production to the final user." But that seems to suggest that marketing commences only at or after the production stage, whereas it actually starts at the conceptual or design stage before a prototype is even made. In 1964 Charles St. Thomas wrote in an introduction to an excellent book on marketing, "Marketing is a way of managing a business so that each critical business decision...is made with a full and prior knowledge of the impact of that decision on the customer."[11]

Trying to define precisely what marketing is and what it can do to improve a business became something of a word game at a time when most enterprises were either bewildered, bothered, or bewitched by the marketing concept. With poor management standards today in the West and intense global competition, which is changing marketing to become more of a general management function and leading to the entire business becoming a marketing department, it is even more important to understand this all-embracing management philosophy.

Following the definition by the Chartered Institute of Marketing in the UK, the Canadian Institute of Marketing states, "Marketing is the management process responsible for identifying, anticipating and satisfying customer requirements profitably." It elaborates by saying, "That includes all functions of development of products and services, including Research, Planning, Design, Quality, Pricing, Packaging, Advertising, Promotions, Public Relations, Sales, Distribution, and After-Sales Services." But it is by no means limited only to those marketing facets, since it includes less tangible functions such as ideation, invention, innovation, Q-Circles, and every aspect of managing a business.

Some definitions are incomplete, while others are so unwieldy that they can be confusing. Although minimalism can bring with it a danger of emasculation, perhaps the simplest way to define it, without resorting to appendages, is: "Marketing is finding out what customers want and providing it profitably."

In order to do that, a marketing manager or vice-president is involved with myriad responsibilities and therefore needs to possess a variety of interests and skills. As we develop more and more of an understanding of how marketing embraces every sphere of managing a business, we become aware that some of his or her activities represent a balancing act on a high wire, while others are like acrobatics. Instead of the perception that many people have of a manager performing routine functions each day in an office, then returning home with a clear desk and an empty mind, the image changes. Self-perception must change too, because bureaucratic management, or administration, is ineffective against aggressive global competition. They are defensive in combative times. Today's manager must be both the prime mover and the final cause.

2

Innovation—The Key to the Future

The other special function of management is innovation. To innovate means to introduce something new. And it is innovation that is the answer to those earlier questions arising out of market saturation. *Innovation is introducing something new that benefits customers and provides a unique and persuasive concept.*

From that definition, innovation is clearly part of the marketing orbit. But it is also a separate function that should be practiced by *all* managers in a business organization. For example, a credit controller innovates by creating a new credit plan that may increase company sales. A financial controller may design a new financial or merchandise program that could result in quicker stock turn and greater return on investment. It is not uncommon for a production manager or an engineer to innovate the design of assembly lines to increase the quality of products, or the volume, or both. He might reduce the number of staff required, by his innovation, or reduce costs to lower prices and sell more goods. Scheduling for customer deliveries—particularly in the retail trade, which involved myriad small shipments—might be innovated by a transport manager or a shipping clerk. An innovated inventory control system may improve the effectiveness of customer service, and reduce the time frame for moving merchandise out of a warehouse, resulting in lower costs or quicker cash flow.

What makes innovation a *special* function of a manager is that instead of a company being confounded by change, it treats change as an opportunity and exploits it fully to its own advantage. And when there is no change—only inertia—it *creates* change advantageously for a business enterprise.

But innovation is not only a management function—it is a special function of *all* employees, by means of Quality Circles, which are described later on.

In the minds of many marketers, innovation is the key to success. And some organizations—like 3M for example—owe a great part of their success to new products marketing. Their paramount strategy is to get something new into the market first. The preferred strategy of the majority of businesses, however, is to wait for a competitor to launch a new product after spending years on research, formulation, product development, and even test marketing—then decide whether or not to imitate that product, without having to bear the burden of all the development costs. They are me-too products. But the advantage to the innovator is that he has an opportunity to establish his brand in the marketplace first, and obtain consumer loyalty before competitors jump in with me-too and no-name products and store brands.

Innovation could therefore result in any or all of the following improvements: a new or improved product or service, a more competitively priced product, the creation of a need for a product where a need did not previously exist, a more convenient product or service, innovating and establishing new uses for an otherwise obsolete product, improving the design of an existing product, designing a novel and improved package for an existing product, an improved marketing technique for an existing product or service, an improved decentralization plan for a large organization, improved methods or systems, a new financing plan, an improved way to handle materials, an improved distribution network, innovating a chemical formula with ingredients that are more easily sourced or less costly, improving a formulation to offer additional consumer benefits, improving assembly lines, an improved method of quality control, an innovative way of manufacturing or converting, the creation of a new advertising medium to reach a specific market-niche, a more cost-effective way to advertise or promote to consumers—or a more persuasive one, new selling techniques, improved sales aids, a new recruitment method to improve standards of personnel, an improved executive training program, and so on. The list of possible innovations is endless.

That short list of possible improvements aimed at creating a competitive edge for a business enterprise through innovation indicates a need for a new management position in companies that are large enough to benefit from it. A vice-president in charge of innovation could stimulate all departmental and staff managers to create innovations. He or she would analyze and develop innovative ideas from any department. He would relate to Quality Circles, through which innovations could be provided by all other employees. And he himself would be responsible for continually studying all possible ways and means to provide innovations to benefit his company.

Comparisons are frequently made between the practice of management and the practice of warfare—with some justifications. Military aggression and business have been the main occupations of most tribes, principalities, and nations. Budgets are allocated by governments for research and development of arms and armaments for defensive or aggressive strategies, while business organizations too, invest in R&D. Both have similar problems in recruiting and training personnel straight from schools or from rural communities. Both use hierarchical organization structures to facilitate management or leadership, communications, and supplies. Their strategies and tactics are remarkably similar. On a more superficial level, marketers use military terminology like advertising *campaigns,* price *wars,* and *battles* for markets.

The military may not market goods, but it does buy them for its own use. That initiates innovations by armament manufacturers to improve the effectiveness of their products. An improved anti-tank shell that penetrates armor initiates innovation to provide better armor to withstand the antitank missiles. An aircraft that can be intercepted electronically requires innovation to enable it to evade detection. That is probably the main justification for comparing business management with military management—because it was the innovation of new weapons technology that most often weighed the balance of victory in favor of the innovator.

We can look back on two and a half thousand years of history, if we wish, to find that innovations in weapons technology, or their tactical use, led to success after success in defeating an enemy or plundering a rich city-state. The parallel with technology being continually improved through innovations in our own times is self-evident. But instead of their innovations producing new or improved weapons to protect or expand into new territories, manufacturers and service companies use innovations to protect their own markets and to expand their market shares. The real value of management in our combative society is therefore its aggressive creation and support of relevant new ideas, and not the purely defensive posture of bookkeeping or administration, which have always been subservient to innovation or entrepreneurship.

The following is a short list of inventions, innovations, and discoveries that illustrate the broad range of original ideas, and the ingenuity of scientists, mathematicians, engineers, entrepreneurs, and marketers:

1876 Bell speaks on his first telephone—U.S.

1877 Edison invents phonograph.

1884 Eastman mass-produces the Kodak box camera.

1885 Burroughs builds the first adding machine.

1888 Herz discovers photo-electric tube.

1888 Dunlop invents pneumatic tyre.

1889 Dial telephone system patented.

1890 First gas-operated machine-gun—Austria.

1892 Ford builds first gas-operated automobile.

X-rays discovered by Roentgen.

1891 First incubator for premature babies—Dr. Lion, France.

1892 Crown bottle top & opener.

1954 Texas Instruments develop transistors using silicon as the heart of the chip.

1959 U.S. scientist Hoeni invents process for creating transistors on a wafer of silicon and triggers the age of microelectronics.

1961 First computer to be designed by another computer—Bell, U.S.

1976 First male contraceptive pill—Baroux, France.

1977 Artificial pancreas—W J Tze, Canada.

2-inch pocket TV—Sinclair Radionics, UK.

1978 First test-tube baby—Steptoe & Edwards UK.

1979 Artificial blood—Naito, Japan.

Rubik's Cube—Rubik, Hungary.

1893 First dry breakfast cereal.

1895 Marconi applies for wireless telegraph patent—Italy.

Canned baked beans in tomato sauce—Heinz, U.S.

Fish-paste in jars—Shipham UK.

1896 Ice-cream cones—Marcioni U.S.

1897 First wildlife game park— Umfolozi, RSA.

1898 Parabellum automatic pistol— Luger, Germany.

1899 Aspirin—Hoffman & Bayer, Germany.

1900 Paper clip—Vaaler (Norway).

Quantum Theory—Planck, Germany.

Airship—Zeppelin, Germany.

1901 Double-edged safety razor— Gillette, U.S.

1902 Overhead camshaft—Maudslay & Craig, UK.

Radium—Curie, France.

Teddy Bear—Mitchum (U.S.) & Steiff (Swabia).

1903 Aeroplane—Wright brothers, U.S.

Barbiturate drugs—Fischer & Behring, Germany.

Seamless bust support—Morgan, UK.

V-8 Motor car engine—Ader, France.

1904 Double-sided gramophone disc— International Talking Machines, Germany.

1907 "Persil" household detergent— Henkel, Germany.

1908 Automatic typewriter—McCall, U.S.

Firearm silencer—Maxim, UK.

1909 IUD (intra-uterine contraceptive)—Richter, Germany.

1947 Sargrove's electronic circuit-making equipment automates production of printed circuits in Britain.

1952 Pfann develops techniques with silicon and germanium on which micro-electronics will depend.

Nuclear-powered Mega-submarine "Ohio" with 24 Trident-1 missiles—U.S.

"Walkman" personal carrying stereo tape replayer—Sony, Japan.

1980 High-quality Underwater Video Camera—Sony Broadcast Ltd, UK.

Solar-powered aircraft

1982 Artificial heart—Jarvik, U.S.

Computer-controlled production line—Oita-Canon Inc., Japan

Computer floppy-disc pen— Berol Ltd, UK

"Voice-advice" motor car— Peugeot, France.

1983 Robotic manufacture of robots— Yamazaki, Japan.

"Voice-advice" still camera— Minolta, Japan.

1984 Computerized translation machine—Fujitsu, Japan.

Hologram-illustrated magazine cover—National Geographic, U.S.

1,048,576-bit computer memory chip—IBM, U.S.

Credit-Card operated parking meter—GEC, UK.

Wristwatch TV—Sony, Seiko, & Casio, Japan.

Robotic electronic component assembler (High-speed)—Asea, Sweden.

1985 Cellular Radiophone—Racal-Vodaphone Ltd, UK.

Computerized submarine-hunting detection device—Gresham-CAP, UK.

"Jumbotron" 40m x 25m TV screen—Tsukuba, Japan.

Laser-disc electronic filing system—Philips, Holland.

3mm-thick Miniature Radio— Sony, Japan.

Omnigripper robotic hand device—Imperial College, UK.

Solar-powered pay-phone— Plessey, UK.

Even before the turn of the twentieth century, we see the successful commercialization of innovations by America, as they imitated the British industrial revolution. By the time Henry Ford was successfully selling the innovated products of his assembly lines, German industry had followed suit and began to compete in small market niches, and then for world markets against Britain. Closer to our own times, we see Japan emerging, learning, growing, catching up, and finally surpassing the United States with an abundance of innovations, patents, and commercialization.

Number of Patents Filed in 1993

Japan:	208,347
United States:	57,890
Germany:	42,922
France:	11,187
Britain:	9,333
China:	5,566
Italy:	3,726
Australia:	3,315
Czechoslovakia (former):	2,528
Sweden:	2,389
Brazil:	2,371
Canada:	2,127

Adjusted to avoid double-counting.
Source: Orbit Online Service.

The invention and continual improvements of the silicon chip alone has resulted in the acceleration of a variety of inventions, developments, and innovations in the past four decades.

Computers reduced the numbers of staff in banks by about half, and computerized robots have eliminated almost entire labor forces in the past decade. CAD/CAM has revolutionized design and manufacturing, even medical diagnosis. By 1982 General Motors used T3 robots in the U.S. to spot weld car bodies at the rate of 200 welds per car and forty-eight cars an hour. Robots are not disturbed by a continuous deafening noise, and work on two or three shifts every twenty-four hours. They do not suffer from fatigue or take time off for sickness. Their brains are microprocessors made on silicon chips.

It is not uncommon now to enter a factory at night-time, which continues to operate in almost total darkness for seven days a week. Only pilot lights are needed for one person to operate an entire plant by supervising control panels.

Product Life Cycles

It is not only populations that go through life cycles. Economies do, business organizations do, and their products do. But just as the average age of populations in developed countries has been extended by innovations (like diets, regular exercising, medicare and artificial body parts), so can those other life cycles be extended by innovations.

Figure 2.1 shows the traditional life cycle of a typical new product from its launch to maturity and obsolescence. The objective is to decide if and when the product should be innovated.

This typical but fictitious product is a laundry detergent. Apart from the fact that it washes laundry clean, it offers three consumer benefits: it does not need hot water for machine washing; it is chemically formulated to be kind to delicate fabrics and to hands—so that it can be used also for hand-washing woollens; and it makes laundry smell "fresh as a daisy." Its brand name is Daisy, and it has a picture of a giant daisy on the front of the box. Otherwise the box is printed in pastel shades with a preponderance of yellow, and has feminine appeal. The original package was tested for impulse buying, and its shelf offtake was found to be satisfactory. Its launch campaign conveyed the message, "Now Daisy gets clothes clean and fresh-smelling." A subcaption repeated the statement on the box; "Kind to hands and delicate fabrics."

The new product's sales increased gradually in year one and accelerated in year two. Research showed that women who bought it the first time became repeat buyers because it kept its promise. And the marketer ensured that its price was always in line with other brands in its product category. As the years went by, the manufacturer gradually reduced advertising and promotional budgets, because sales created their own momentum as most new purchasers continued to buy it. The extra net yield, coupled with savings from bulk material purchases and economies of scale from increased production runs, contributed to meeting its planned profit targets for the following few years.

Meanwhile, several changes had taken place in the market. Many users had switched to Daisy and stayed with it. But all its competing brands had addressed the product launch, and each had reacted in a different way. Part of the reason for Daisy's initial success was that the major competing brand did not live up to its consumer promise—"Exclusive wash for exclusive hands." In fact it was harsh to hands because they had been unable to replicate the overseas formulation, where it had sold successfully for years. One ingredient was not available locally and another was too expensive. They had therefore decided to substitute others. That also made it unreliable in warm or cold water. Daisy's manufacturer had simply taken its competitor's unsatisfactory product and improved it under a different brand name. The market leader was now forced to improve its own products, and found ways to obtain better ingredients to do so. It also added a pleasant scent and what its manufacturer called a skin lotion, in order to dramatize the re-launch.

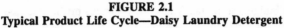

FIGURE 2.1
Typical Product Life Cycle—Daisy Laundry Detergent

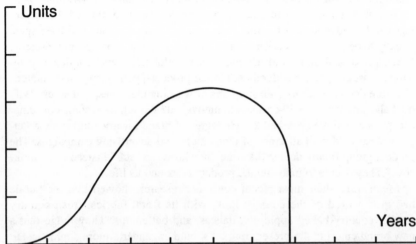

Although Daisy's market share came largely from its competitor—whose new sales slowly eroded that share—it had also picked up a few percentage points from each of the other competing brands. The cheapest of them, named No-Frills, finally decided to change the color of its detergent to yellow, added a scent, and innovated its name to Buttercup—Without Frills. Other brands had innovated in a variety of ways. One designed a new yellow pack with a nosegay of daisies and buttercups on the front. Another began to give away a different plastic flower with each pack, so that a collection of artificial flowers could be made. Another brand called Softie had added yellow beads and put a picture of a lemon on the pack. It was re-launched with the name of Lemon Softie.

The result of all the activity on supermarket shelves, and increased advertising and promotional budgets, was that buyers tended to switch brands to try each one in turn. Daisy's sales continued to grow, but at a slower and slower rate. Its sales had barely been affected at first, because the market for the branded products had grown at the expense of the store brands and no-name products. Its manufacturer was satisfied as it followed the traditional life cycle. Over the next few years its sales began to plateau out, as had been anticipated. And in the normal course of events, Daisy's sales would fall more and more sharply until the product was considered to be obsolete because all the other brands offered more consumer benefits. And, except for the "top-of-the-line" brand, they also offered lower prices. Most consumers therefore considered them to be better value than Daisy. But some of Daisy's buyers were still loyal, even if only because they couldn't be bothered to change.

Many marketers have long accepted that situation as normal. They "milk" the product before it reaches maturity, by gradually reducing advertising and promotional budgets in its last years. Any surplus profit obtained in that way could be used for R&D to create a new product to replace the obsolete one.

Top management met to discuss its progress. They considered the advantages and disadvantages of letting it die. A great deal of money had been spent already to penetrate the market—on attitudinal research, motivational research, R&D, package designs and testing, a small pilot test market, a dealer campaign, cross couponing with others of their products, point of purchase materials, store demonstrations with suppliers of washing machines, and so on. Why do it all again when it will cost less to innovate it? We still have some consumer acceptance, and we once had a high degree of brand loyalty, until the marketplace went wild with all kinds of innovations and advertising campaigns. The product group finally decide that what they have is a "star" instead of a "milkcow." They decide to innovate the product to extend its life.

Meanwhile, their most recent consumer research showed that the public had grown tired of the country look, with its floral fabrics, fresh country smells, country-baked apple pie, daisies, and buttercups. They judge that a new brand entering the present market should engender a more sophisticated image. And if it can do what the other brands do, little innovation would be required to switch purchasers from the other brands to their own.

Fashions have changed since the original launch of Daisy. Clothing, furnishing fabrics, and even some of the more elegant automobiles have introduced jade green as the smart color. Perfumes have moved away from fresh scents to more exotic ones. A new perfume branded Lady Di is already in such demand that its marketers are introducing other toiletries and cosmetics to the brand range. Products, bottles, and packages are jade green. Their fragrance is like sandlewood.

A pattern emerges for innovating Daisy:

1. The product will contain soluble jade green beads which provide a scent like sandlewood;
2. It will also include pink beads as a promotional device to remind consumers that it protects the skin and delicate fabrics;
3. The package will appear even more feminine because it will suggest women's sophisticated fashions;
4. Its name will be innovated to Lady Daisy;
5. Its basic product formulation will remain unchanged except for the addition of the colored soluble beads, because the detergent always was superior;
6. The price will be increased slightly; partly to offset some costs of improvements, but also to convince consumers that this is a superior product for discerning people who care;
7. A tune is commissioned for radio and TV, to suggest a fashion show in progress; but the jingle will be about hand protection from the pink beads, and the delightful fragrance from the green beads—in new, improved, and fashionable Lady Daisy.

If all that can succeed in renewing and extending the life span of this laundry detergent, its life cycle should change when the innovations begin to influence consumer buying habits, favorably, in the marketplace.

FIGURE 2.2
Innovated Life Cycle—Lady Daisy

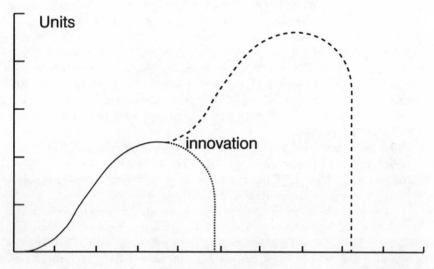

Figure 2.2 shows the point in the product's life cycle when it requires innovation. The broken lines show the anticipated extension of its life. However, there is no reason why that process should not be innovated again, and successfully extend the product's life even further, from the center of the arc of the broken line, upwards. Some manufacturers have repeatedly innovated their products, time after time after time. On each occasion, they thoroughly researched the market and consumer trends to decide what changes were needed and would be beneficial to regenerate a successful product's life. Each time they did what they felt changing conditions required.

Despite the fact that the decade of the 1990s is one of accelerating and unpredictable changes, with apparently impermanent markets, business carries on. It continues through innovation, but also because of attention to basics instead of misdirection into scores of popular management or marketing fashions that are likely to be forgotten soon. Management and markets have been disorganized for most of the twentieth century. New products have been coming and going since the beginning of time. And change is always taking place—most of it unpredictable.

Said Charles Mortimer of General Foods, "The very moment you put a new product on the supermarket shelf it is out of date—and you should already be thinking of developing the next one."

Said James V. Bassett of Borden Foods, "A fine product isn't necessarily a successful one from a marketing standpoint."

Wrote Theodore Levitt, "The fact is most new products don't have any sort of classical life cycle curve at all. They have instead from the outset an infinitely descending curve. The product not only doesn't get off the ground; it goes quickly under ground—six feet under."

Commenting on Campbell Soup's R&D investment of six million dollars in 1962, president William B. Murphy remarked, "Even if our sales were to stay level, without these stimuli, our profits would drop from the last fiscal year's 7.7% of net sales to about 3.8% five years hence—and, in ten years, to a net loss, because of the expected rising costs and other factors that work attrition in our business."

How many new products fail? No one can say with certainty. President Cross of 3M was reported as saying, "As a rule of thumb, out of every 100 laboratory starts there will be an average of 33 technical successes—but only three of these will be commercial successes."

Since 3M is renowned for its expertise in new product development, it is most likely that 3 percent is higher than the average percent of commercial successes. That is why the objective is to bring managers back to basics and direct their attention to key elements that can make things happen in their favor, if they know how to handle them effectively.

What applies to extending the life of a successful product may also apply to prolonging the life of a business organization. "Clogs to clogs" was an old North Country cliché in Britain. In North America, one hears "shirtsleeves to shirtsleeves" instead. It had long been observed that the springboard from which a new family enterprise was launched was usually the hard work, skills, and long hours of a founder who was committed to overcoming deprivation, or improving his economic or social status. The result of his success was that his children were brought up in comfort and security. They therefore lacked the necessary motivation or drive to take the company much further. Often a modernization program would be implemented while father still lived; with new technology, more cost-effective premises, and more modern methods. The business would expand as a consequence—but there it would stay, because of an absence of dedication. Decline would take place in the third generation, when profits would be milked and no improvements would be made. Markets would have changed, but the third generation would be indifferent to changes. That generation would be more preoccupied with social activities or a profession. No commitment would be made to the business enterprise, which would become uncompetitive, or its products would become obsolete.

We have observed the decline of a number of companies due mostly to lack of interest, lack of drive, lack of direction, or lack of competence. Each one was a tragedy unfolding. And yet, with the right management at the right time, every one of them could have been saved for at least another generation.

We shall see how chaos or inertia, which result in obsolescence, arise from out of the human condition—not out of an organization, a product, a market, or a system. A business organization is born out of an innovative idea. Some entrepreneur turns that concept into reality by creating a product for which there is a need in a market. After that, an enterprise will succeed because of the quality and skills of managers, or the system will fail because managers are no longer productive.

Most major businesses were started by technical inventors specializing in optics or electronics, engineering, chemistry, biotechnology, or some other science. In time they fall into the hands of acquisitors, asset strippers, financial controllers, or bureaucrats who are far more interested in inflating their own incomes or in the company's value to another conglomerate, according to the TSE or the New York Stock Exchange. It must be frustrating for shareholders who invested in a brilliant innovation, and for managers who worked in the new company that successfully manufactured and marketed it, to see a scientist-founder retire and accountants take over the management of the company. Inevitably the excitement, the dynamism, and the creativity must go. The fun of responding to challenge goes with it. And if a company fails to hire creative people who can innovate continually, the company is unlikely to last for very long. Failure to manage a business organization with the same spirit that the founder injected into it can result in the end to unemployment for managers and workers, and losses for shareholders. But often the originator of the company, who was a technician, proves to be the wrong person to run the company after it is set up. His skill was as an originator, not as an administrator.

One example of this was Mitel Corporation. It was founded in Ottawa in 1979 by Michael Cowpland from Britain. Legend has it that he obtained his finance by pounding the pavements of the residential neighborhood where he lived, knocking on doors, and selling shares. By the end of 1991, Mitel had become the world leader in cumulative systems and had sold 163,000 PBX systems. It was the second biggest in telecommunications in Canada, the second biggest in the UK, and the fifth biggest in the United States. But Cowpland had left Mitel by then. Remarks by his colleagues indicated that there were disagreements about how the company should be run. Cowpland started a new company—Corel—which is now the biggest of its kind in CAD, in the world.

Where do original ideas come from? What motivates them? How can they be stimulated? What type of environment is necessary for creativity? Who originates ideas? Why should they illuminate one person rather than another?

How is it that one company originates an idea rather than some other? And why should it happen in one country rather than in another one? The answers to those questions will gradually unfold. It is sufficient to say here that it is a function of management to encourage productive ideas. That is what defines a marketing organization. And it is this that induces managers to excel and become part of an élite and dynamic force.

Executives should possess a deep reservoir of ideas—in proportion to their reading habits, their personal experience, and probably also their maturity. They should be compulsive readers of a variety of different subjects, devouring several books simultaneously. They should possess a diversity of interests, and be avid habitués of reference libraries, theaters, concerts, museums, art galleries, original movies, and intellectual and social groups. They should be like squirrels, incessantly chasing after sustenance—facts and theories, figures and new attitudes, new approaches and discoveries, ideas and trends—to store away for future use. They should possess a need to assuage their curiosity about the society in which they live and work.

Author Saul wrote, "Voltaire used to ridicule the elite of his day by pointing out that, apart from their titles and their money, they were pitifully ignorant. They simply bought knowledge and advice—whether financial, architectural, ministerial, artistic or military. The elite's ignorance was so profound that it made them incapable of leading."

"The technocrats of our day make the old aristocratic leaders seem profound and civilized by comparison. The technocrat has been actively—indeed, intensely—trained. But by any standard comprehensible within the tradition of western civilization, he is virtually illiterate. One of the reasons that he is unable to recognize the necessary relationship between power and morality is that moral traditions are the product of civilization and he has little knowledge of his own civilization."[1]

In the course of time erudite and cultivated managers with natural curiosity may turn themselves into computers, with every piece of information they encountered cross-indexed. Then, whenever they leave an executive meeting with major problems unresolved, and consider the circumstances and needs which beg for an appropriate solution, they can delve deep into their unconscious minds. Data, information, theories, opinions, and concepts will be stored there in preparation for such occasions, and be ready to be attached—sometimes randomly—to other items; not unlike the trial and error of scientific experiments. Again and again, a new or innovated formula will rise to the surface, and be recognized instantly as the right one.

That is how acts of creation occur. Management is not a function of accidents, but of orderly preparation. Ideas do not appear from out of the air, but from a reservoir where they have been carefully stored in readiness over time.

Pythagoras, with his mathematical experiments and theorems, is an ideal example of what it takes to be a successful intellectual and creative person. Of course he was dedicated. Not only was he a reservoir of practical, effective, and valuable ideas that could be demonstrated, but they were original ideas. He was an innovator. He also introduced precision into his work.

With all the skills required to create and implement marketing concepts, for example, a marketing person must use precision to coordinate each and every function to meet essential deadlines. He must have a natural feeling for timing and urgency. However sound the idea, it can be eroded or altogether wasted if implemented too soon or too late or undertaken half-heartedly or without finesse.

Philosophers like Pythagoras, Socrates, Aristotle, and Confucius were also excellent teachers who inspired both respect and enthusiasm in their students. Managers, too need the ability to involve other managers and staff in the excitement of discovery and achievement, for which all of them are needed to play a part. For, although it is true that after every executive meeting, only one person is capable of solving the problem under discussion, the implementation of its solution can best be achieved by the properly coordinated input of specialists.

A manager can create innovative ideas on his own, but he cannot implement them unless he has the support of a chief executive who is committed to ensuring that all managers understand and practice the marketing and innovation process. They have to understand fully its importance to company growth and profitability, and to the security of their own jobs. And he must also ensure that they support the innovator, and provide innovations of their own. Every manager should be held accountable for contributing to company growth and profits by continually considering new ways in which their specialized services could be innovated to the benefit of the business enterprise. Despite the fact that they may have been appointed as support departments for managers who produce marketing information, products, or sales, support departments too must be productive. What they must produce are innovated services, systems, or procedures to assist in increasing the wealth of the enterprise, and therefore the wealth of the community.

Perhaps the best example to show the importance of innovation in 1993 is the silicon micro-processor chip. Silicon chips were invented in the United States. But by the mid-1980s, U.S. manufacturers were losing ground fast to the Japanese, who were producing them better and cheaper. A number of manufacturers in California's Silicon Valley were closing their doors. The main reason for their inability to compete was that they had not kept up with innovation. But to support Japan's innovations, the Japanese government funded and subsidized its companies.

The first retaliatory measures by the Reagan government were to impose tariffs on Japanese imports and to force the Japanese to open up their local market to U.S. suppliers. Since then, U.S. companies like Intel, Sematech, Advanced Micro Devices, and Cypress Semiconductors have concentrated on innovations to recapture lost markets. The balance of the world market at the beginning of 1993 was as follows:

United States: 44 percent

Japan: 43 percent

The battle for the silicon chip market will be fought on innovation in 1993. And through the example of the U.S. high-tech industry—which is headed up by skilled entrepreneurs who have learned the lessons of devastating competition from some of the best Japanese entrepreneurs—it is likely that many other North American business organizations will make innovation the core of their business strategies.

There are likely to be millions of business enterprises all over the world that have reached a stage like some of those U.S. companies in the mid-1980s, who thought they were ahead of the game and could sit back for a while and watch the profits flow in. But management can never relax—there is always some company out there who can do better through innovation. Business organizations must innovate in order to survive. Innovation goes on forever.

In 1981, while some high-tech companies were congratulating themselves on their success and enjoying its rewards, Intel introduced a mini computer with the capacity of a mainframe model. The iAPX-432 used three silicon chips the equivalent to 225,000 transistors that performed functions at speeds that would make a mainframe overheat and use too much power. Much of the software was built directly into the chips.

Other such discoveries, inventions, or innovations are taking place all the time in some competing organization, either in North America, Europe, or Japan. Any of them could revolutionize the industry you are in by making your products obsolete. There is never a moment for complacency, in the high-technology industry in particular. The very nature of the industry has shortened the normal product life cycle considerably. Whereas laundry detergents were once a marketing challenge because of their simplicity, high-technological products are even more challenging because of their complexity and their novelty. Electronic consumer products are novelties in much the same way as clockwork toys once were. And novelties are bought on a whim, because consumers allow themselves to be persuaded to buy them for benefits that turn out to be only marginal or even illusory. How many people who purchased a personal computer really needed one? How many offices with word processors could have continued to manage perfectly well with an ordinary electronic typewriter?

Novelties wear off very soon, and demand for high-technology products designed for the public can fall very fast. Moreover, high-ticket durable goods cannot be easily tossed aside as can an old packet of laundry detergent, so that a buyer may purchase an innovated product next time she visits the supermarket. Nor is it so easy for a manufacturer to innovate. But they are compelled to innovate non-stop and fast. And managers and workers in that industry have to learn to live and work at a much faster pace just to maintain their market position.

Economist Schumpeter showed that only an innovator makes a real profit; but that it is always short-lived because innovation is creative destruction."[2] It makes yesterday's capital and equipment obsolete, as well as yesterday's products.

The process of innovation dominated management thinking in 1996 and is now at the forefront of eastern and western business minds, because Asia is forecast to account for one-third of global economic activity by the year 2000. Even without Japan's global share of markets, Asia's economy would be the equal of the European Union's. While Japan's superior performance has slowed to something above that of leading western industrial nations, the rest of Asia is likely to grow at an extraordinary 8 percent.[3] And in order to compete globally, Asian economies are turning from imitation to innovation.

At present, 82 percent of all research and development is undertaken by the United States, Japan, Germany, France, and the UK. Only 2 percent is undertaken by nations outside of western Europe, Japan, and the U.S. And Asia and the United States are expected to gain market shares at the expense of Europe. The rate of innovation is therefore likely to continue to increase, because, for them, innovation is the key to the future.

The need to innovate is strongly felt in Britain. Seventy-one percent of respondents in a recent survey considered innovation to be more important than existing products and services. It also showed that as many as 96 percent think innovation is the key to the survival of British business. But only one-third believed that their own companies were truly committed to innovation. The most innovative country was considered to be Japan. The U.S. came a somewhat distant second, and Britain an even more distant third, with only 10 percent of the opinion poll.

Richard Branson was considered to personify innovative thinking in the UK. Others mentioned were Peter Wood, Bill Gates, and Ian McLaurin of Tesco Stores. It is significant that each of the companies mentioned possesses an innovative CEO.

Categories most influenced by innovative thinking were considered to be product and service development (60 percent); marketing (55 percent); and management (28 percent). While examples of innovation provided by respondents focused largely on marketing and promotions, one-third concerned improvements to internal processes and systems. Over 70 percent had worked with external facilitators for help with innovation. Marketing consultancies came first on their list, followed by design consultancies, then management consultants. Advertising consultants were least popular in helping with innovation. Successes resulted mostly from using marketing and design consultants, whereas results from advertising and management consultants were much less successful in that sphere.

Seventy-one percent said that the key to having their companies driven by innovation was management initiatives and the need for a risk-taking culture and better communications.[4] But the main problem in developing an innovative management culture was expressed as being in the transition from showing interest to becoming committed.

The need for innovation is felt particularly in the high technology sector. When we consider the destructive forces attendant on the technology revolution—the highly competitive nature of the business, resulting in incredibly short product life cycles and narrowing profit margins, with overproduction leading to market saturation, which in turn results in large-scale downsizing and unemployment—it is sobering to realize that such a scenario was anticipated with foreboding by such eminent economists as Ricardo and Thorstein Veblen. Ricardo was as aware as Malthus that ours is a world engaged in a continual struggle for survival. He saw only continuous decline and gloom. John Kenneth Galbraith summed up Veblen's attitude toward poverty and other misfortunes of American society, as follows:

> [B]oth the moral and material debasement of man, was part of the system and would become worse with progress. There is an inescapable conflict between industry and business—between the "excessive prevalence and efficiency of the machine industry" and its "deplorable" tendency to overproduce and thus to threaten the basic goal of a business which is to make money.[5]

An example of this occurred in the personal computer market, where Apple Computer Inc. of Cupertino, California, announced they had lost $188.3 million in the third quarter of their fiscal year ending 15 June 1993, compared with a profit in the previous year of $131.7 million. Much of the loss was attributable to pressures from price cutting in the PC industry and a weaker than expected European economy. Said Scott McNealy, president of Sun Microsystems, "There are two or three times too many people in the computer industry."[6] What he meant was that industry overproduction was two or three times greater than the market requirement.

> This is fairly typical in new industries of assembled products: a pioneering firm gets the ball rolling with its initial product, a growing market begins to take shape around that product, and new competitors are inspired to enter and either expand the market further or take a chunk of it with their own product versions. At this embryonic stage, no firm has a "lock" on the market. No one's product is really perfected. No single firm has mastered the processes of manufacturing, or achieved unassailable control of the distribution channels. Customers have not yet developed their own sense of the ideal product design or what they want in terms of features or functions. The market and the industry are in a fluid stage of development. Everyone—producers and customers—is learning as they move along.

Within this rich mixture of experimentation and competition some center of gravity eventually forms in the shape of a *dominant product design*. Once the dominant design emerges, the basis of competition changes radically, and firms are put to tests that very few will pass. Before long, the ecology of competing firms changes from one characterized by many firms and many unique designs, to one of few firms with similar product designs.[7]

Beneath the seeming equanimity of normally reasonable people, a seething rage is rising against the *hubris* of high technology engineers and entrepreneurs who appear, more and more, to be crossing the boundaries imposed by our human nature, and destroying our society by creating mass unemployment and marginalizing unskilled and semi-skilled workers. Said Ludwig von Bertalanffy, "Much can be said for this view of man as sorcerer's apprentice, frivolously liberating forces that far surpass control by his intellectual and moral capacities. Nevertheless, this is romanticism no less than the romanticism of necessary continuous progress by science and technology. Mankind was expert in making themselves miserable long before there was any science to speak of.... The reason for our predicament, it seems, is not man's scientific and technological *hubris* defying divine or human law—it is man's nature itself, split into animal and something more than animal.... *Science has conquered the universe but forgotten or even actively suppressed human nature.*"

Now that technological innovation has surpassed human beings in particular skills, the time has come for the innovation of people; otherwise they will be excluded from the grand design of the global village in the twenty-first century.

While our political and social systems are stuck in the rut of nineteenth-century liberalism, and our civil service and other staff practice nineteenth-century trade unionism, our managerial class is ill-equipped with nineteenth-century colonial administration to cope with the pressing realities of increasing new cycles of dramatic changes in technology, in the workplace, and in the marketplace. It is no wonder that we inhabit an age of discontent because of betrayed expectations. A question that often rises to the surface of our discontents is whether the movers and shakers who cause our business and social revolution possess the *nous* or the morality to make people central to their designs, or whether the quality of life in the twenty-first century is designed solely for their own account.

Professor von Bertalanffy was able to view those concerns with a wry and self-deprecating humor, but time has shown them to be as justified as was Marshall McLuhan's vision of the future. Wrote Bertalanffy, "Once more, we have to find a new conception for man. There is something basically wrong; and we must find out what it is or perish."[8]

3

The Killing Fields

Strategies

All forms of life compete in a continual battle of wits for possession of limited resources, and there is a constant need to overcome adversities in the environment. In our conceit, we once believed that societies developed through freedom of choice to alter their destinies, while the behavior of animals and less developed cultures was predestined. But—as Darwin discovered—animals possess an ability to change their shapes, their colors, and their habits in order to survive in continually changing circumstances. But the majority of people resist change. Change challenges attitudes, skills, and customs. Those who resist it are usually defeated in the great conflicts between new ideas and old habits. The silicon chip has already changed our lives, whether we like it or not. And the superinformation highway could revolutionize the way we live. While we want to take control of our lives, we seem always to reach a crossroad, with the uncertainty of which path to take.

On the other hand, there are always a few movers and shakers with competitive ideas or skills who are eager to respond to challenges and confront adversities to their own advantage. Ambitious entrepreneurial spirits who choose a path that may lead to success or failure in business take their own destinies into their hands. Since their business enterprise becomes an extension of themselves, it will suffer the same kinds of dilemmas and be faced with similar challenges, hardships, and crises as most of us are confronted with as individuals. Entrepreneurs and business executives need to *anticipate* them in order to be in control of every situation that may arise, or run the risk of losing the battle to survive.

If we cannot use our ingenuity to anticipate change, or at least to react immediately to it, we will be no better off than simple forms of animal life that were forced to change as a result of the extinction of many millions of their kind. *Their* ability to change in the face of failure was imposed on them by a series of errors, according to John Gribbin. He wrote, "The point is that nothing *wants* to evolve. The basic process of life is replication.... Nor do mutations happen in response to environmental changes—the soft-bellied animals of the late Precambrian did not 'know' that it was getting colder, or that there were more predators about, and grow their shells in self-defense. Rather, they must have carried an allele (a competing gene that offers different ways of doing the same particular bit of body building) for a thicker skin, competing with an allele for thinner skin. When the climate changed or predators spread across the seas, the thin-skinned individuals were killed, and only the possessors of the thick-skin allele survived. Repetition of this process over many generations produced creatures with hard shells."[1]

Perhaps human beings will evolve into a more reasonable form in a similar way. Meanwhile, we have to grapple with whatever means are at our disposal to prevent ourselves from being destroyed by our own kind. The same is true of business enterprises.

Managing a company as if it were a military organization is not new. But only now that competition is so intense that it requires a combative approach is it beginning to be stated openly. The former chairman of Saatchi & Saatchi recently astounded the media by describing marketplace challenges in martial terminology. And IBM's CEO, Louis V. Gerstner, Jr., flashes a picture of arch-rival Microsoft's Bill Gates onto a screen and talks tough, along the lines that "business is war and in war one has enemies. Enemies must be conquered."[2] Back in 1959, when Harry L. Hansen spoke at the Boston Conference on Distribution, his subject was Creative Marketing Strategy, but he used metaphors from strategic principles in warfare to illustrate the points he wished to make. He said:

> Over two millennium ago the Chinese Sun Tzu set down 13 principles of strategy. Napoleon had 115 maxims for warfare; General N.B. Forrest in our own Civil War had one: "Get there fustest with the mostest." Today the United States is said to have 9 principles; Great Britain and Russia, 10. More or less common to these last three lists are principles involving the objective, the offensive, cooperation or units of command, mass or concentration of force, economy of force, manoeuvre, surprise, security, and simplicity....
>
> Those who have studied war...know that the secret of a successful campaign is attack, not defence. It is true that history gives us examples of how strategies of retreat or containment have exhausted an enemy, but these are the exceptions to the general rule. And the recent history of distribution in the United States has shown how traditional distribution forms have ultimately had to take the offensive to survive. For instance, the supermarket and the discount house were first fought defensively and unimaginatively and on a limited scale by the chains and the department stores. Ultimately it was necessary to move aggressively and adopt the very tactics of these new competitors that were once decried.

The struggle for markets is much like a military engagement to defend or acquire territory and the political struggle to defend or acquire a constituency. Both activities require a planned strategy with effective tactics.

The very essence of marketing is preparation of a strategic plan with clearly defined tactics and goals. But situations change constantly in the marketplace, just as they do on a battlefield. To be prepared for change, therefore, requires the formulation also of *alternative* strategies and tactics. Just as Field Marshall Montgomery pinned a photograph of General Rommel to the wall of his quarters at El Alamein to study his adversary, so must a marketing manager study the management style of his competitors. He must also be aware, on an ongoing basis, of every strategic and tactical move made by each one of his competitors and their brands.

Carl von Clausewitz, the great expert on warfare whose strategies and tactics are still taught at such military academies as St-Cyr, Sandhurst, West Point, and the Frunze Academy, wrote, "Tactics is the art of using troops in battle; strategy is the art of using battles to win wars."

It is significant that von Clausewitz described warfare as an art, in much the same way as Drucker described management as a practice—not a science or a profession. In 1924 Leon Trotsky—who became commander-in-chief of the Red Army after the Russian revolution—wrote, "There is no science of war and there never will be any. There are many sciences war is concerned with. But war itself is not a science; war is practical art and skill."

Business cannot be described as a science either; because there are no natural laws that direct a marketing strategy—or a battle—toward absolutely certain ends, like a scientific experiment under laboratory conditions. Nor can a business be described as a profession, because there are no clearly defined professional standards of conduct or performance, and no redress for shareholders whose return on investment might fall below an acceptable level. And in cases of incompetence, investors cannot turn to an official organization like a Law Society or a Medical and Dental Association, to impeach the chief executive officer.

But although management must continually address crucial problems in the marketplace—where it is marketing knowledge and skills that are essential—other types of problems are also encountered with managers' judgements and decisions in the workplace, because they are fallible. They present unacceptable risks, whereas an important part of their job is to minimize risks. That is why a carefully planned organizational structure and established methodologies, systems, and controls are essentially in every business enterprise. And the foundation of all of that is a strategic plan with clear objectives, tactics, and goals.

In the economic recession of the early 1970s (which was worsened and became prolonged by the OPEC oil crisis of 1973), return on investment and market share objectives were abandoned altogether and replaced by a more fundamental objective—survival. The goal of many companies was just to keep the infrastructure intact, so that they could aim at profitability objectives some other time. It was a strategy of preparedness for siege or engagement.

Some idea of flexibility—and even subtlety—in the use of tactics can be learned from the principles of General Sun Tzu.

- When an enemy is resting, harass him;
- If comfortably encamped, force him to move;
- If well supplied with food, starve him out;
- Appear at points he must hasten to defend;
- March swiftly to where you are unexpected.

Sun Tzu appears to have been always in control of every possible situation on a battlefield. His strategy was to keep the enemy guessing and unnerve him by manoeuvres until he pushed him into making a fatal mistake, which Sun Tzu was prepared to exploit to his own advantage. His was a strategy of manoeuvre. As he wrote, "The opportunity to defeat an enemy is provided by the enemy himself. After putting oneself beyond any possibility of defeat, a good fighter waits for such an opportunity."[3]

Those principles, which were written over 2,500 years ago, are as valid today as they were then. It is interesting to compare them with one of Mao Tse Tung's, immortalized in the Little Red Book which, we were informed, all his guerilla forces were obliged to carry with them like a military training manual. Since he had only relatively small forces at his disposal at that time, he was obliged to use less aggressive tactics. They were more defensive in nature, because he could not take the risk that they might be decimated each time he provoked the enemy. On one hand, his objective was to wear down the enemy by a strategy of attrition.[4] Alternatively, he could render them ineffective by a strategy of containment.[5] His overall strategy was to take initiatives that would shape the eventual outcome of the total war in his own favor.

- The enemy advances, we retreat.
- The enemy makes camp, we harass.
- The enemy retreats, we pursue.

Those tactics seem to have emerged naturally from out of Sun Tzu's principles of warfare. And they have been used by countless guerilla forces whose manpower and arms were limited. General Louis Botha used them against conventional British forces with considerable effect in the Boer War. They led General Kitchener to protest rather plaintively, "The Boers are not like the Sudanese who stood up to a fair fight. They are always running away on their little ponies."

Effective guerilla warfare of that type can be likened to small and imaginative business entrepreneurs who are mobile, flexible, deadly, and fast.

If we compare military forces in wartime—whether conventional or guerilla—with entrepreneurial business forces in peacetime, there are obvious fundamental differences. There are also remarkable similarities. Business organizations have to fight on two distinctively different fronts—in the microcosm and in the macrocosm. The former is the struggle for markets. The latter is the more frustrating struggle against factors that combine periodically to wipe them out—like abnormally high interest rates, levels of inflation, high taxes, monopolies, cartels, tariffs, embargoes, sanctions, bureaucratic government interference, technological changes, political unrest, and so forth. An apt comparison might be a military force embarking on an invasion, but never reaching its destination because it is wiped out by storms at sea. The fate of the Spanish Armada comes to mind.

Generals are obliged to take the elements into consideration in their military strategies. But business management seldom does, because management of economic, diplomatic, and political elements is supposed to be a function of government. Indeed, government's main job is to create a suitable environment in which the real income of a community increases, so that consumption of goods and services can increase.

We see from the following summary how the economic recessions of the 1970s, 1980s, and 1990s differed in what business enterprises could and could not do in the face of destructive forces beyond their power to influence.

The real effect of the 1973 OPEC oil crisis, which increased the price of oil by 300 percent, was to increase the cost of production and distribution of goods. It also increased individual travelling costs. It made big cars too expensive to run. Oil heating became too costly. And it influenced a move of populations from rural areas closer to urban workplaces. The accumulation of costs reduced the ability of consumers to spend money on goods and services. But despite the havoc it wrought on business enterprises, the prime consideration when implementing staff layoffs was keeping a company's skills intact.

In the economic recession of the 1980s, however, as thousands of corporate bankruptcies piled up again each month, many organizations began to throw management and staff to the wolves, in a desperate attempt to keep their own bankruptcy at bay. Talk of trying to save the structure and skills of a company was muted. Managers eyed each other and wondered who would be next, and some were instrumental in jettisoning others in order to save themselves. This recession could not be blamed on a political situation like the power of the Middle East oil cartels to bring the West to a standstill. Bank rates shot up and mortgage interest rates catapulted to over 21 percent in some countries. Those industries most sensitive to high interest rates on borrowings began to tumble. Property developers with huge debt loads tried frantically to unload raw land holdings and real estate onto anyone who would buy. Some managed to dispose of their entire residential land banks before the carrying costs could destroy them. The household furniture and major domestic appliance industries suffered from loss of sales. Some manufacturers went out of business, and some retail stores followed suit. Auto makers, and their distributors with large inventories and heavy lines of credit to support them, embarked on mass staff firings or closed down factories or outlets.

And—as always when the public stops buying—advertising and promotion industries, media, printers, and graphic artists were hit immediately by a sudden halt in business. A holding operation was no longer enough. Industry and commerce were demoralized by having only recently survived the nightmares of an oil crisis, before being plunged into another recession. This one required a strategy of elimination. Capital assets, which were draining a company's liquidity, were expeditiously unloaded as well as personnel. Even so, many thousands of businesses filed for bankruptcy, and about six times that number of individuals declared personal bankruptcies each month that layoffs continued.

Those who were fortunate enough still to have jobs—including civil servants, who can generally rely on job stability—postponed financial commitments in case their security turned out to be short-lived. And in business organizations still in operation after considerable staff cutbacks, managers learned about shirtsleeves management in a hurry. They soon undertook work normally delegated to middle managers, assistants, and secretaries, as well as their own jobs. The days of excessive staffing seemed to be over.

But with insufficient demand for their goods or services, competition changed to assault on whatever markets still operated. Being merely competitive was no longer enough in such a desperate situation—business now had to be *combative* in order to survive.

Meanwhile, the domino principle had begun to take effect. As overextended retailers began to close their doors, their wholesale suppliers were unable to obtain payment for goods they had sold; and many of those too were forced into bankruptcy. Next in line were manufacturers who—without positive cash flow from their failed customers—were unable to pay suppliers of raw materials. Those suppliers also suffered losses. In Canada, where the recession had commenced in 1979, over one thousand business enterprises were still being pushed into bankruptcy every month in 1983. And about six and a half thousand personal bankruptcies were still being declared monthly. The marketplaces had become killing fields.

By the time the economic recession of 1990 took place, organizations that still survived in the private sector were much leaner and faster to react. Many had also enjoyed a period of prosperity provided by the unbridled spending of the public service on one hand and the baby-boom generation on the other. Grandiose government construction projects, government and private sector spending on high-technology, the growth of demand for personal computers, and a booming housing industry all provided funds. Spending on domestic furniture, appliances, and automobiles grew. And many of the forty-plus age group that benefited from the economic boom of 1984–1989 bought tax-sheltered real estate investments as a hedge against inflation. That investment initiated a spate of residential and commercial development that provided work for all those industries tied to building and construction.

On the down side, governments soon scrambled to recover some of their deficit spending by increasing taxes and imposing other taxes and levies and development charges on industry and the public. By 1990, the public and industry were over-taxed again. Again the end result was a shortage of disposable income and consequently a reduction in the consumption of goods. And once again, the drop in consumption led to staff layoffs and bankruptcies.

Although most destruction was triggered by macroeconomic factors, the question arises as to whether "intelligent" or "experienced" or "skilled" management, or entrepreneurial management with "street-smarts" could have— and perhaps did—escape much of the damage inflicted on other companies. It is the genius of great military leaders to avoid such catastrophes or carry on regardless of them, that makes them great. General Patton and Marshall Zhukov succeeded by always being on the offensive, and Wellesley assessed and planned all the details beforehand with considerable care to his own advantage. There is no substitute for tacit knowledge born out of considerable hands-on experience. It can bring into play visions of what might happen "if," and of how to avoid failure by any number of ways and means. In business terms, perhaps Onassis was the best example of planning in advance for every possible eventuality. The lesson to be learned is to choose the right leaders.

In Edinburgh, a feature writer for the *Scotsman* wrote an article extolling the virtues of bankruptcy, on the grounds that poorly managed businesses which cannot accommodate change deserve to go under.

It is true that an inert economy with insufficient consumer demand to support it requires innovation. But unlike the microcosm of a business where management is responsible for its own destiny, only government can attempt to influence a country's economy in order to provide an environment conducive to increased employment, consumption, and growth. All that a business organization can do is be lean, aggressive, innovative, creatively managed, and alert to opportunities in the marketplace and dangers in the political and economic environment.

Inflation remained at a low level because unemployment and high taxation inhibited consumption and restrained prices. Continual reductions of interest rates did not prime the pump of the economy. The economic rituals practiced by most western governments were loosely based on theories on money, interest, and employment that Keynes developed in the 1930s, but a great deal has changed since then. Moreover, governments with huge deficits seemed to have purposely misread Keynesian economic theories by assuming that low rates of interest and inflation would of themselves restore the economy. What they should have done was reduce taxes to trigger consumer spending.

If the recession of the 1970s was characterized by the effects of the OPEC oil crisis and the 1980s recession by the panic with which business enterprises unburdened themselves of costly assets, including throwing top executives to the wolves, that of the 1990s bore a remarkable similarity to the Depression of the 1930s.

Wrote Galbraith, "After the Great Crash came the Great Depression which lasted, with varying severity, for ten years.... In 1933, nearly thirteen million were out of work, or about one in every four in the labor force. In 1938, one person in five was still out of work."[6]

The recession of the 1990s, too, continued to take a heavy toll. Some began to call it a slump, while others named it a depression. Seemingly, the words were interchangeable. Continual attempts to induce recovery by reducing the bank rate further and further showed no more success after five or six years than it had done in the 1930s. In neither case were consumers encouraged to spend—those who were unemployed or bankrupt had no surplus to spend, and those still working went in fear of losing their jobs.

But it was not only lack of employment or lack of confidence in the economy or in government that prevented recovery. The size of the previously affluent middle classes was shrinking as a consequence of heavy taxation. And nearly one-third of the North American population was over the age of fifty-five and losing about two-thirds of their investment income, because of steadily diminishing bank rates. Rates, which had been abnormally high only a few years earlier—around 12 percent—dropped to about 4 percent. Since that demographic group normally spends over half of all discretionary income, their substantial loss of spending power resulted in considerable decline in their shopping, travelling, and leisure pursuits. That factor alone could have been the biggest single reason for an unusually slow economic recovery in Canada and Europe. Few causes are more destructive than an inability of the public to afford to buy goods or services, since recovery needs to be consumer driven.

In the previous century, Jean Baptiste Say had theorized that "supply creates its own demand." And Alfred Marshall's economic theories appeared to validate "Say's Law," in that they claimed the economy was automatically self-regulating and tended toward full employment. His *Principles of Economics* had assumed there would be enough consumer demand, in normal circumstances, to employ the factors of production. But the 1930s economy was not normal; nor was the economy of the 1990s.

His concerns had been matters of value, distribution, and efficient allocation of resources. Permanent unemployment was considered to be impossible.

Malthus, Marx, and others did not believe that. And apparently Marshall recognized the flaws in his own theory, as did Marx and Keynes. He admitted that when business confidence is shaken during times of commercial disorganization, "though men have the power to purchase, they may not choose to use it."[7] But in the 1930s and the 1990s it was not a matter of choice, since fewer and fewer people possessed "the power to purchase."

Lack of confidence in government and a feeling of insecurity from being out of control of their lives were more the effects of depression at the realization of their declining quality of life. In turn, it led to frustration and the Ross Perot phenomenon in the United States, the loss of office of the Republican party, riots in Germany, a change of government in Japan, and a landslide victory for the Liberal Opposition in Canada's Federal Election.

Most business management skills normally marshalled to create or respond to opportunities in the marketplace were rejected in favor of reducing business costs and sharpening accountancy skills to weather the economic storm. But as military strategist Frunze said, "Those who are merely defensive are doomed to defeat." That is why those manufacturers in California's Silicon Valley are not just passively sitting out the storms. Instead they are busy innovating their products and perfecting new strategic plans and tactics.

Intel and Microsoft are both preparing to introduce new technologies likely to erode IBMs market still further. In 1993, Intel will market a new microprocessor—the Pentium chip—that can run typical programs twice as fast as its present successful chip. It contains over 3 million transistors. And Microsoft is expected to introduce a new operating system—Windows NT—that builds on its presently successful Windows program. Those new technologies are likely to consolidate their authority in the personal computer market.

Both companies became key suppliers to IBM in the 1980s. By the end of 1992, IBM's stock price had fallen to its lowest level in eleven years, while Intel's and Microsoft's stocks rose sharply. Their combined capitalization surpassed IBM's market value by nearly 50 percent.

There is tremendous economic energy in the high-technology industry at least. Personal computer maker Compaq Computer expects to compete with Sun Microsystems and Hewlett Packard in workstations, and also with minicomputer makers like Digital Equipment. At the same time, competitors like IBM and Apple Computer will be preparing to counter-attack.

Sun Tzu established five essential criteria for victory: *timing; skills; commitment; preparation;* and *autonomy.*

Management in the West is generally weak on all counts. Those dynamic, high-tech companies just mentioned are exceptional by any standards. But even they became complacent when successful, and failed to continue innovating while Japanese companies were doing so. Most western business organizations have a poor sense of timing because of a lack of management urgency, and they are unprepared for economic recessions because they do not plan. Those that do, generally look no further than a time-frame of five years. But economies nowadays tend to seven- to ten-year cycles, and need to be integrated into business plans. Most western business management is unskilled in business and in management.

Where it is skilled—such as in highly technical industries—its skills are those of the industry rather than those of management or marketing. And the introduction of new technologies has created a shortage of staff who know how to use it most effectively. Western businesses are now spending large sums of money on technology that they may not even need, but are penny pinching when it comes to training their managers and staff. As for commitment, we have to admit that it is no longer so easily found in the West, except in knowledge industries, where people enjoy novelty and accomplishment. But the word *commitment* is only a substitute for what Sun Tzu actually wrote in full; "His army must be animated by the same Spirit throughout all its ranks."[8] That is even more difficult to find than individual commitment, because of changed attitudes to employers and careers, and poor management and indifferent leadership. The West is generally weak on preparation because it is so poor at planning and timing. And neither the very big organizations nor medium-size manufacturers in the West are very good on granting autonomy to small splinter groups, because there is a lack of trust—although IBM has recently declared that as its intention.

When we observe management in a typical business organization, we generally find a lack of planned purposefulness and a vagueness about corporate strategy or departmental tactics—because there is no carefully thought out business plan with a clearly defined company mission. And yet, in real-life situations of a more military nature, tactics are often clear-cut. We see how they often almost present themselves to a pragmatic leader with unarguable logic. The following is an example of an extraordinary victory. It therefore provides an opportunity to test the five criteria of Sun Tzu. It is the conquest of the Incas in 1532 by only 150 Spaniards under the leadership of Francisco Pizarro. They were outnumbered by a force of possibly 80,000 warriors.

They considered what were the most appropriate tactics to conquer the Incas, along the following lines:

1. They could exploit the element of surprise, by attacking without provocation, and taking advantage of their strange appearance, the discipline of their horses, and the novelty of their military methods.
2. They could kidnap the Inca, as Hernan Cortés had done in 1519 with the leader of the Aztec Empire in Mexico.
3. They might exploit the internal feuds in the Inca Empire, which was divided, by fighting first with one side, and then turning and killing their Indian allies.

The Spaniards chose the second option because the South American Indians were unarmed. After their victory, the Inca admitted that his tactics had been aimed at capturing Pizzaro, then sacrificing some of the Spaniards to the sun. He would castrate others to act as eunuchs in guarding his womenfolk. Instead, he had been carried on a litter in a procession of five to six thousand unarmed men straight into the Spanish ambush, where most of the Indians were butchered.

The Inca had underestimated the strangers as a result of faulty intelligence from his envoy, who had told the Inca that the Spaniards were not fighting men—they were disorganized; two hundred Indians could capture them. The Inca's men went unarmed because he could not believe that the Spaniards would attack against such heavy odds. Nor did he imagine that an attack would come before he had first held a formal meeting with Pizzaro.

Despite the fact that the Spaniards had acted out of fear and desperation, they had followed a plan. Pizzaro's successful military tactic was a preemptive strike. Had they not chosen the right moment when the Inca's warriors were unarmed, the end would have been quite different.[9] As it was, they fulfilled every one of Sun Tzu's five criteria for victory, while the Inca did not fulfil any of them.

As well as understanding the value of all five of Sun Tzu's principles, a manager can benefit from viewing the situation from the perspective of his or her competitor—or "the enemy." A manager would then know never to underestimate a competitor, however small—as IBM apparently did with Intel Corp and Microsoft. Top management can never afford to be complacent, however big or successful its company—as were all three of those organizations at different times. They should never place their company or their product at the mercy of another—as the Inca did by parading his troops without arms, and as IBM did in assisting suppliers to become competitors who posed a threat. Incomplete intelligence cannot be relied upon. Diplomacy is useless without strength to back it up. A preemptive strike is one of the most useful tactics. Paranoia can be an excellent life saver.

Useful lessons of a different kind can be learned from Desert Storm—despite the fact that Kuwait was freed. The errors and omissions by the U.S. Army have a familiar sound, and demonstrate that there is little difference nowadays between managing an army or a business organization.

The Iraqi War commenced after unusual preparations by U.S. and United Nations forces, which were overwhelming; so was their state-of-the-art technology. And Israel had taken the initiative to destroy Iraq's nuclear plant several years earlier.

The plan to drive the Iraqis out of Kuwait soon ground to a standstill when the Iraqi army fled. And President Bush, as Commander-in-Chief, decided not to follow, harass, or destroy the retreating army. According to General Schwartzkopf's subsequent autobiography, there was never any intention of destroying Saddam Hussein's military strength, only to drive his forces out of Kuwait. And that was accomplished. But despite the victory, the campaign revealed many of the same lapses commonly suffered by business organizations.

- *Lack of Resolution*—to exploit the opportunity to destroy an adversary. Army high command failed to take advantage of the situation in which the allied forces had destroyed the enemy's air force on the ground and made the allies virtually invulnerable.

- *Poor Communications*—between General Schwartzkopf (who appeared to want to destroy the Iraqi army); General Powell, who wanted to stop and get out; and the Commander-in-Chief, President Bush (who seemed to be diverted at the moment of decision by how best to use the moment for a TV opportunity so that the media could describe the operation as "The Hundred Days War").

- *Weak Leadership*—which (according to *Newsweek* magazine) left America's allies amazed and speechless at the lack of military savvy and lack of commitment to follow through.

- *Faulty Intelligence:* Russia's explanation for the "adoption of incorrect decisions," was overreliance on technology and lack of human intelligence. The U.S. overestimated the size and ability of Iraqi forces, underestimated its nuclear program and never knew how many Scud missiles they had. Overlapping agencies feuded and information was slow getting to the front: Said an air force captain, "They kept hoarding the satellite photos and I kept asking, "What are you saving this for, the next war?"

- *Poor Coordination*—of technological and other resources. (The M-1A1 tank was so fast that field artillery units could not keep up with it to provide support. It strained supplies of gas because it travelled only half a mile to a gallon. And "because of incompatible computer links, the Air Force had to send daily bombing-target orders to Navy pilots by courier.")

- *Failure to React to a Trend*: The whole world seems to know that American Presidents are apt to put on a show for the elections, but seldom take it into consideration. The next Presidential election was due when the Iraqi war was being planned. That should have raised the possibility of a political agenda taking precedence over a military decision.

- *Failure to Follow Through* generally costs more in the end, because losers learn more than winners.

- *Inadequate Quality Control:* The 24th Mechanized Infantry "arrived with tired 10-year-old M1 tanks and threadbare Bradley Infantry Fighting Vehicles that had to be replaced before fighting began" (*Newsweek*).

- *Shortage of Spare Parts:* "When a detachment from the Army's Tiger Brigade went to the port of Jubail looking for spare tank parts, a duty officer pointed to a mile-long line of cargo crates and asked, 'Do you know what container they're in?'" No one had a list of their contents, and the soldiers did not get their parts. "By the end, some units found critical shortages of fuel and munitions."

Most of those lapses are fairly typical of what happens in many business organizations. It pays to use the latest technology, but people run businesses and win wars. "It was tough realistic training of a highly motivated (force) that made the real difference." Iraqi troops were unwilling to fight after the first encounter with overwhelming forces and superior technology. The fact that the allied troops did not pursue, harass, or attempt to destroy the retreating army was a political agenda, not a military decision. General Sun Tzu knew that a general in the field must have autonomy to act without interference by the ruler. We know what he would have done. He would have viewed Desert Storm as a strategy of recision that merely returned the Iraqi players back to where they were before their military adventure. It leaves them in a position to re-form, re-arm, and watch for the next opportunity—having learned their opponents' strengths and weaknesses, and reactions of other nations. They can then continue to test the resolution of the American public, and the power of the President and the United Nations again and again.

That defines Desert Storm as a purely defensive strategy. Von Clausewitz's attitude to defensive strategies was that they are undertaken either to inflict losses on an attacker so that he will retreat, or to provide defending forces with a suitable opportunity to counter-attack. The opportunity was provided but ignored. "In war," wrote M. V. Frunze, "victory belongs to those who find in themselves the resolution to attack."

We tend to picture an "attack" or a "counter-attack" as a *frontal* attack. Even when we talk of assaulting a competitor's markets, our tendency is to visualize a direct attack against his products or his distribution. But in fact, direct assault of a fortification or frontal attack on a well-defended position are the least attractive options for an experienced general. Paid mercenary armies in fifteenth-century Italy always avoided attacking well-organized defense systems because their goal was to leave the battlefield alive and intact. Experienced marketers have the same goal.

The classic tragedy of a frontal attack was one made famous as "The Charge of the Light Brigade." Five hundred British officers and troopers out of a total force of 673 were slaughtered because they galloped straight into the barrels of Russian cannons. The blunder has been attributed to faulty communications in the field. Balaclava is therefore a prime example of inferior leadership and poor communications—both commonplaces of many business organizations. That heroic charge is also an example of a *Pyrrhic victory,* meaning one gained at too great a cost. The moral for a manager is that it is folly to risk the resources of an organization in order to gamble on winning a battle for a market. No company can afford to gamble 75 percent of its resources, human or otherwise, in order to compete against another company.

Proctor & Gamble offer an interesting example of a business organization facing a similar marketing situation. Its defensive strategy in the U.S. to prevent powerful companies like Unilever from assaulting their consumer franchise is to allocate an unusually large budget to maintain its own market position. A figure of $500 million was quoted for 1981. In Britain, on the other hand, P&G allocate a similarly large sum for its *offensive* strategy against Unilever and Colgate-Palmolive. The result of the use of such large budgets in both countries could be described as a standoff.[10] But there is another country that P&G has never yet properly attempted to penetrate, in which both Unilever and Colgate are both strong. Those traditional competitors are firmly entrenched in southern Africa, with excellent distribution, admirable market shares, and enviable consumer loyalty to their brands. Even if P&G managed to penetrate that marketplace successfully it would be likely to be a Pyrrhic victory.

Before we move right out of the military arena and into the marketplace, it is useful to emphasize the relevance of Sun Tzu's criteria for victory one final time—this time with two examples of excellent leadership.

Fortunately for Britain, and for Europe, there were more brilliant British generals than stupid or ignorant ones. Two that immediately come to mind are Marlborough and Wellington. Both planned every campaign meticulously in advance. Their timing was invariably perfect. Their military skills and attention to details were such that they never lost a single battle. The spirit that both imbued in their troops was legendary. And such was the respect in which they were held because of their authority, that no one would dare to interfere with their autonomy in the field. In that way, each fulfilled to perfection the five criteria for victory that the highly experienced and skeptical General Sun Tzu practiced over two thousand years before them.

Marlborough was one of the greatest generals of all time. Each one of his military campaigns is still studied in military colleges. In them we find many examples of imagination, innovation, and excellent management. He was always in total control of every situation. The smallest details of each battle were planned with care and often implemented in total secrecy. After a long march at the head of his army, they would arrive at their destination in the dead of night. Even his officers would sometimes be amazed to find fortifications already constructed, cover arranged according to the best location for a battle, food and water provided for troops and horses, and cannons and other equipment ready at the most appropriate time and the most suitable place. In addition—like Sun Tzu—he used to the full his remarkable talent for spreading disinformation, so that an enemy rarely knew where or when the British troops would arrive. The enemy was generally unprepared as a consequence, while Marlborough's army was in control of the terrain, and he was in control of the ensuing battle, which always ended in victory.[11]

Business strategies, too should aim at controlling a marketplace. That is what market leaders do; and it is the reason why they become market leaders. Like most powerful leaders they earned their position by the legitimacy of power. And the likelihood is that they achieved their success by concentrating their efforts on a competitor's weakness and avoiding its strengths.[12]

4

Disposition of Forces

Tactics

Strategy is everything that happens before and after a battle takes place in the killing fields. Tactics are the means used to influence the outcome of a battle in one's own favor. The following major factors that can favorably influence the battle for market shares are key links among others in a marketing chain. Each of them is a tactical weapon or tool for a marketer to use skillfully in a marketplace that might otherwise become a killing ground in which his brand franchise is destroyed. They are the main armor and armaments at the disposal of the officers and staff of such market leaders as Proctor & Gamble, Colgate Palmolive, Matsushita, 3M, Eastman Kodak, and others who dominate their own particular market segments. They are: dependability, technological innovation, customer service, value and pricing, design innovation, brand image, quality management, durability, distribution, exclusivity, packaging, communications, merchandising, and selling.

Each would be used according to an overall strategic plan; either singly, or more likely in concerted tactics where each could reinforce another or several others.

Utilizing all of those forces in the same campaign would be a strategy of total force. A company's overall product or brand campaign would clearly define which one should be used for more aggressive tactics and which for support. And in each case, as in communications, for example, major media would benefit in undertaking its special function by having support media to perform its own tasks that would be synchronized with it, thereby increasing the effectiveness of the whole campaign. The marketing plan would also define how each of them should be used, as well as where, when, and by whom, and what immediate goals and ultimate strategic objectives they are planned to achieve. As a field marshall would be closely involved in planning the strategy and leaving the tactics to his generals in the field, so a chief executive would step back after approving the marketing plan and leave the conduct of the battle to the marketing vice-president. And as a general might gather all his chosen resources for a united effort, so a vice-president of marketing would ensure a properly balanced campaign. His aim would be to achieve greater output than the individual input of each marketing instrument, by integrating them most effectively.

A close scrutiny of each one of those instruments of marketing management emphasizes the importance of the contribution it makes to the grand marketing strategy.

Dependability

Retail chain stores and discount houses continue to buy from suppliers they know and trust. In the case of fast-moving packaged consumer goods—where a marketer has created brand loyalty—they are obliged to stock products that their *customers* know and trust. That is the essential difference between brand management and product management.

Well-established brands of durable goods also create consumer preference for specific makes of domestic appliances or furniture. The same type of brand preference applies in the soft goods market with known brands of shirts, suits, ties, woollen goods, dresses, or pantyhose. The highly successful *St Michaels* brand of Marks & Spencer, or *Maytag* laundry appliances, Matsushita's *Panasonic, Sulka,* or *EMI* are examples. Brands that gain popularity are successful because the public finds them dependable. It is therefore a responsibility of a brand manager to ensure that they always live up to their reputation, by completely fulfilling the promises that each brand makes when advertising its goods. That means superior quality control is essential to ensure dependability of the product, its packaging, and also its handling and shipping to dealers.

The situation is different for nonbranded goods or a dealer's own brand, both of which are me-too products. Shoppers generally accept the implied trade-off that if goods are cheaper, their quality might not be as good as a similar branded product, and the packaging is likely to be inferior. A lower price often induces some prudent shoppers to select them from supermarket shelves in preference to more expensive brands. Manufacturers are happy to dispose of surplus production in that way. But a manufacturer might offer a dealer a quantity discount or rebate to induce him to stock and display those items at the same price as branded products, or for only a few cents less.

If a supplier has a long-standing relationship with a dealer, and its products and service are sufficiently dependable to satisfy its customers and provide the dealer with profitable volume sales, it is unlikely that the dealer would consider replacing those products with another supplier's. Established brands could therefore be said to be part of a strategy to deter competition. Launching a new brand would be an offensive strategy. Providing a nonbranded product might also be a strategy of deterrence, to fill a supermarket's shelves so that there is less room for competing products—unless the dealer's category management preempts that goal.

Dependability means not only a consistently dependable quality of formulation, product, and packaging, but also the dependability of continuous supplies, dependability of competitive pricing, dependability of shelf offtake resulting from dependable advertising and promotions that work, and the dependability of substantial budgets placed behind them. The only type of dependability of value is all-round dependability.

Technological Innovation

Having the best technology once provided a business organization with time to enjoy its dominance of an industry or a market. But technological advances have accelerated in the second half of the twentieth century to such a rate that no company can afford to rest with complacency any more. Profits need to be ploughed back into R&D, which must be committed to a program of continual innovations. The danger of relying solely on technological superiority is illustrated by the situation of a textile group named Feltex Ltd.

The brand name of its excellent broadloom carpeting is Van Dyck. Its top-of-the-line brand is Crossley—which was once a multinational company in Britain, Australia, and South Africa. The combined market share of all of its brands in South Africa was reputed to be around 90 percent at a time when wall-to-wall carpet was considered to be a luxury. Fine quality Wilton, with its 80 percent wool mixture, and Axminster, with its range of magnificent patterns, required a considerable investment in technology. And since less than a million homes in South Africa could afford to buy it in those days, it was most unlikely that competition would be created. Feltex had the technology and the skills to go with it, and their brands enjoyed a fine reputation. Evidently they felt that they did not need either an offensive or a defensive strategy, because the considerable cost of technology would act as a deterrent to any competitor. Their's was therefore a strategy of deterrence.

But the unexpected can always be expected to happen.

What happened was an innovation in the manufacture of broadloom carpeting. It arose out of a tufting process used to make Candlewick bedspreads. That manufacturing process produced rows of loops in raised patterns. It was only a matter of time before someone realized that the same process using carpet materials could make rows of nylon loops. Some loops could be sheared to create cut-pile carpeting. It was an easy and a cheap process. Small manufacturers could afford to buy one machine, which could be set up in a shed and operated with a minimum of labor and skill. There was no problem in marketing the carpet, because the price was so much lower than Wilton or Axminster.

Feltex's deterrent was no deterrent at all. Although their technology did not become obsolete immediately, its use was limited to a very small luxury market niche for the Wilton, and a commercial niche—like hotels—for the Axminster.

Small tufting manufacturers sprang up all over the country. Now Feltex was compelled to change to an offensive strategy. First of all, they bought out the best and most successful of their competitors, Constantia Carpets, which had been growing fast. But when it became clear that there would be a proliferation of tufted carpet manufacturers, and buying more would only encourage others to set themselves up to be bought out, they turned to quite a different strategy to defend their dwindling market share.

Their new defensive strategy was to buy controlling interest in twenty-eight retail chain store groups, department stores, and regional wholesalers. Most were in the furniture and furnishing trade, some included major domestic appliances, while others sold soft goods. What each had in common was a carpet department. Feltex Ltd. formed a new company named Tapsa Limited. They could now defend their production capacities with the possession of some 200 tied retail and wholesale carpet outlets nationwide. That would depend on the twenty-eight managing directors, who would be obliged to buy a minimum of 60 percent of their carpeting from Feltex.

The small tufted carpet manufacturers were now faced with a problem of logistics. They had no intention of losing orders from those outlets. They did what marketers of nonbranded merchandise have always done—they offered attractive discounts and rebates to the dealers to keep *their* machines running.

A conflict of interests developed. Since the managing directors of the outlets were pushed by head office to meet profitability targets, they felt they had justification for buying all the carpeting they could get with the best possible discounts and the highest possible quantity rebates. The reason why they chose that option, rather than complying with head office's target of 60 percent of merchandise, was that their contractual agreement made it inevitable. In order to encourage each of them to build up their profits, they had been given a buy-out clause whereby they could sell their remaining shares at market value if they wished.

The impasse was resolved only when Feltex became illiquid and the Tapsa Group was bought out by a local conglomerate.

It is not only in high technology that new discoveries are being made all the time. The same applies to ethical drugs, optics, photographic film, textiles, biology, surgery, entertainment, and space. Fashions change much faster, too. And it is technology that drives most of that change. A company that is afraid to change and continue changing should not be in business today—because management today must continually search for ways to change, and embrace those changes.

Customer Service

Service was once a part of the quality offered to shoppers and trade customers. It is fast disappearing because of downsizing of organizations and the introduction of new technologies. Ironically, that is happening at a time when more and more business enterprises desperately need to make sales but do not have the capability to do so—nor do their staff appear to care. Suppliers in smaller cities and towns depend for their livelihood on repeat business and referrals. That comes only with good service. And in bigger mass markets where more competitors are hunting like predators, no business can afford to neglect customer service.

Pitney-Bowes is a business organization quoted as an example by James[1] as enjoying 92 percent share of the U.S. postage meter market. A market share so unusually large might in itself appear to deter competition. In fact, it normally attracts a multitude of "rats and mice" who all want to nibble at it, as happened with Feltex. But Pitney-Bowes left nothing to chance—it used 7,500 sales and service personnel to protect its market share in the United States. The service they gave their customers was so consistently good that they wouldn't want to take the risk of changing suppliers. And potential competitors are smart enough to know that it would cost too much to attempt to compete in such a complex product and service sector.

But they are an exception. Service is neglected in the West today. Money and attention has been focused on new technologies and taken away from customers. About one-third of western populations is now over the age of fifty-five, and about a quarter over age sixty-five. They were accustomed to service; now they have become merely computer numbers. Perhaps a younger generation will become accustomed to being depersonalized, but that will neither deter competition nor create new business. Distraction by inventory controls, computer data, operational costs, cash flows, administration, and the rub-off effects of government bureaucracy are no substitutes for customer service. And there will be no cash flow without customers. Computer printouts will not supply it—only service will. That means hiring customer-oriented personnel and training them to understand that just saying "Have a nice day!" or "Howya doin'?" has nothing to do with it.

Value and Pricing

It is impossible to separate value from price. Price is the yardstick by which the value of most products is measured. It is part of a formula in which "x" equals something of benefit to a consumer. Price + x = Value. The character of "x" differs from product to product and manufacturer to manufacturer. A product without a price tag therefore cannot be perceived to have a value.

A market leader in oriental rugs in a major city hit a ceiling in its sales volumes. Like its competitors, its window displays never featured price tags because common wisdom declared that customers would be obliged to enter the store to ask. They had never thought to question the practice. In fact, this company's major problem was that they were not obtaining new customers.

Their old ones, who had been created by a previous generation of entrepreneurs, had either saturated their homes with oriental rugs, moved out of town, or died. Meanwhile, pedestrians passing the showroom rarely gave much of a glance into the display windows, because they could not evaluate the products on display. They too made an assumption—that if the company was afraid to reveal the prices, then they couldn't afford to buy them.

A new generation of entrepreneurs was forced to come to terms with a bundle of new tactics to create new markets for their goods.

The moment that readable price tickets were displayed in the windows, occasional pedestrians would stop to examine the rugs more carefully. Those who liked them began to enter the showroom. Sales increased. Advertising was similarly changed to show affordable rugs and feature their prices. The result was that store traffic and sales increased still further.

Since the new customer base that was being developed consisted of younger buyers, the merchandizing policy was innovated to provide color combinations and designs that younger buyers preferred, and more products that they could afford to buy.

Pricing, advertising, merchandizing, promotions, and store selling all became part of an offensive strategy.

The word *value* on its own means little. A customer considering whether to buy a specific product will evaluate it according to several factors. Even something as simple as a plastic tub of margarine offers a bundle of benefits that a consumer might consider. The pack itself is obviously designed to appeal. Then there is the taste, which a customer won't know unless it has already been tried. There is the appeal or lack of appeal of its color. There is its smell, consistency, and ingredients. There is the question of its fat content; one tub states 25 percent less fat, while another claims half the fat and shows the number of kilojoules. Some declare the percentage of polyunsaturates and others don't. There is the salt content. And of the additives, some might be beneficial—like vitamins A and D—but others are more questionable, like preservatives, flavorants, and colorants. After assessing some or all of that, a customer will check the price against that of other margarines on display in case there is a special offer in operation—before deciding which one to buy.

Pricing, apart from its relationship to value, is of vital importance on its own. A marketer who is able to reduce the price of a product is usually rewarded with an additional group of buyers who were previously undecided—either because they couldn't afford the old price or because they thought it was too high. Sales of a saleable product expand when the price is reduced. What often happens then is a form of perpetual motion. Figure 4.1 illustrates how Henry Ford viewed pricing in relation to his assembly plant.

A. Lower the price. B. Sales increase. C. More goods can be made to meet increased demand. That in turn reduces the unit cost, so that A. Prices can be reduced. B. Sales increase...and so on. Economies of scale come into play with increased production volumes:

FIGURE 4.1
Henry Ford's Paradigm

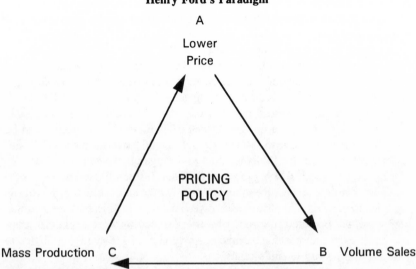

A

Lower
Price

PRICING
POLICY

Mass Production   C   B   Volume Sales

- Raw materials are cheaper when purchased in bulk;
- Packaging materials are cheaper in larger print runs;
- Bigger print runs for instruction leaflets, owner's manuals, warranties, labels, and other printed material reduce unit costs further;
- Larger production runs enable overhead costs to be distributed between more units, thereby reducing the cost of each unit;
- Output of assembly lines can often be increased without adding labor costs, but by more cost-effective use of existing under-utilized staff instead;
- Advertising and promotional costs per unit are reduced;
- Increased demand could enable advertising budgets to be reduced;
- Shipping costs per unit may be reduced by transporting full loads less frequently, instead of a multitude of half-empty trucks or containers;
- Increased consumer demand could permit a supplier to dispense with discounts and rebates.

Design Innovation

Design is dictated by fashion and the ability of new technology to change it. For example, the design of buildings was changed in 1879 when the innovation of steel beam construction enabled buildings to be constructed higher than five stories. Automobile windshields became curved only when new technology enabled them to be made that way. But in the fashion world, an established couturiére who fails to create exciting designs for several consecutive seasons can go out of favor and out of business. Design innovation, for fashion houses, is essentially an offensive strategy. The very fact that fashion is a novelty means that it is obsolete as soon as it is no longer new.

That applies equally to the material or shape or type of container for a hair shampoo, the typeface used on a carton, or its color, and the style of its advertising. They are cosmetics applied to seduce the public.

But beneath the hood or trunk of an automobile is the technological design from which the consumer product develops. The shell of the Volkswagen "Beetle" was made possible by the compact air-cooled engine and the challenge to create a low-priced people's car prior to World War II. The same limitations were imposed on the Citroen 2CV in 1948. Its success can be judged by its sales of five million by 1976. Demand for an even cheaper popular car in Europe in the 1950s resulted in a range of two-seater bubble cars like the Isetta, which BMW produced until that fashion passed in the 1960s. The mass market had become more affluent by then and could afford a Morris Mini-Minor instead. The British Mini owed its design to its transverse mounted engine, which powered the front wheels. Designed by Alec Issigonis, it appeared in 1959 and became as much of a symbol of the swinging sixties in Britain as did Mary Quant's miniskirts.

The most influential factors that contribute to design changes can therefore be said to be technology, fashion, price consideration, and consumer needs or life styles.

What Porsche's design did for Volkswagen, Terence Conran did for the furniture industry in Britain. So did an unusual furniture manufacturer named Hille. In the 1930s Mr. Hille visited his customers personally in their homes to show them his designs for custom-made reproduction furniture of a very high quality. He managed a group of craftsmen in his own workshop at a time when Maples of London were firmly established as suppliers of handmade furniture to generations of royal families all over the world. Maples displayed suites of their furniture in their impressive and massive showroom near Marylebone High Street. The well-known Heal family of furniture craftsmen possessed smaller but exclusive showrooms further south in Tottenham Court Road. Mr. Hille kept his overhead costs down and was able to compete with both of them for a smaller market share by not having to provide a showroom or hire salespeople, but by calling in person on his new-rich customers.

Hille designs and craftsmanship were outstanding. But in the course of time, one by one, his craftsmen aged and retired, and no comparable craftsmen entered the industry. And, in any case, the cost to produce fine artifacts by hand after World War II was so great that fewer customers could afford to buy them. Old customers were now burdened with higher taxes and therefore possessed far less disposable income. Those years saw the passing of an era of fine craftsmanship, and mass production of unornamented furniture produced by machinery became the norm. Hille was forced to recognize that he might have to close down, but he was concerned about the future of his daughter and son-in-law, who worked in the family business.

He was fortunate to employ a young designer with innovative ideas, who changed the direction of the enterprise from hand-made reproduction furniture to simple but well-designed modern furniture that could be produced far more cost-effectively in their workshop. Hille also moved away from the time-consuming customized retail trade into contract work for architects, showrooms, hotels, boardrooms, and office reception areas. Consequently, Hille's products, image, and name were innovated at a crucial point in its life cycle when sales would otherwise have declined to the point of obsolescence. The very name became synonymous with sleek low lines, excellent proportions, and the simple elegance of tasteful modern furniture at its commercial best. Modern advertising created awareness to specifiers and Hille furniture displayed in public areas created a referral business. New generations of furniture buyers would be unlikely to know that Hille's business enterprise was ever different.

So successful was Hille that young Terence Conran admired and envied the company so strongly that he resolved to compete and excel. He opened a modern furniture store named Habitat. And when it was successful he opened another one, and then another. Sir Terence Conran was knighted for his services in spreading good quality British modern furniture design all over the world. And he admits openly that it was Hille's example that inspired him. For him, design was an offensive strategy all along, although for Hille, modern design was initiated as a defensive strategy to stay in business.

Brand Image

Most people know what *image* is, and some even know what it does—because we are all consumers and we see the images of products advertised to us every day on TV or in magazines and newspapers. Not only do we see images of products and services, but also of movie stars, rock groups, and politicians whose images have been designed, groomed, or changed with the objective of obtaining public approval, just like a new brand of laundry detergent.

The danger to product and service marketing is to draw the erroneous conclusion that an image portrayed of an individual or a product generally has nothing whatsoever to do with that person or product; that it is like donning a mask; that perception is all.

The creation of individual images for different products arose from a need to create a consumer perception that each product possessed a personality of its own, entirely different from any other generic product. When it comes to such product categories as cigarettes, alcohol, toiletries, tea, automobiles, rock groups, and politicians, it is difficult to discern differences within each category; so that selling them relies very largely on selling different perceptions instead. What is not so clearly understood is that each product or service must comply with its image in order to fulfil its implied promise, or there may be no repeat purchases.

The Volkswagen Beetle generated a friendly, youthful, continental image. The "Mini" was young and friendly, too, but essentially British and more urbane. While a Rolls Royce is also British, it engenders an image of established success and affluence. Those three examples demonstrate that effective image building requires the creation of a persona that actually projects the salient criterion or consumer benefit of that product. Good image building is not mere cosmetic added afterwards: the strength of a properly marketed product is that its image and the product itself are one and the same thing.

The problem with generic products that were fundamentally the same as each other was that marketers and their advertising agencies could not find anything unique to say about them, so they were obliged to stamp them with a unique image instead.

Stamping an image onto a product afterwards, instead of building it into a product at the outset, presents a danger that if the image bears little relationship to it, or much the same relationship to other generic products, then it can easily be confused with any of them.

If a locally made vodka has a Russian label stuck on the bottle, for example, it should at least taste something like Russian vodka. And if three other local brands all feature different Russian labels and all taste the same, how can a marketer create consumer preference for *his* brand? If he were to rely solely on the design of his bottle or the label—all things being equal—then statistically he should obtain 25 percent share of the local vodka market. But if he were to innovate its taste and smell to resemble imported Russian vodka, the likelihood would be that he could increase his market share to more than 25 percent.

That example assumes that local buyers of vodka prefer the taste and smell of the genuine Russian article. Consumer research might show evidence to the contrary—that they prefer it to be tasteless, because they always add tomato juice, orange juice, or vermouth. That is what a marketer has to find out first. He also needs clear results from properly controlled taste tests of his product, without the label, as well as with it, before he commits himself to a brand name, image, and package design.

If the whole objective of creating a suitable brand image is to identify a product in a unique way, so that it cannot possibly be confused with others, then the name, bottle, and label should match the formulation of the vodka that consumers preferred. Perhaps it shouldn't be a Russian brand at all, but Polish, Finnish, or Israeli.

But image-building TV commercials and print advertising became popular not only because it was getting more difficult for a brand to be recalled among a proliferation of other similar products. It was much easier for an advertising agency to make a short movie with atmosphere than come up with a convincing advertisement that offered tangible consumer benefits to persuade people to buy it.

"That's all very well," say motivational researchers, "but you and I know that most people are emotional and irrational and prefer to live in a world of make-believe. Why not create one for them?"

Dr. Ernest Dichter made marketers understand that people don't make buying decisions by using logic, although they may justify their actions afterwards. They buy things for "hidden reasons"—reasons that they themselves are often unaware of.[2]

Several types of qualitative in-depth consumer research methods were developed for small groups of individuals chosen because they possess the same demographic profile as the target market to which a specific product is to be marketed. They are generally known as focus groups. They are useful for undertaking taste tests or researching different scents for a toiletry product. In the case of motivational research, in-depth studies can be undertaken to determine what it is that gives them "satisfaction," "happiness," or "pleasure" from smoking a cigarette, drinking beer, or taking tea with friends. Product criteria is one thing, but the real reason might be an excuse to meet people of the opposite sex, or an opportunity to be extrovert and have fun with friends of the same sex after a boring workday. A famous brand of cigarettes offers a promise of "after-action satisfaction."

Sexual connotations are frequently used, on the basis that young people think of little else. And they seem to work. They can get attention when well done. They can also be memorable. A refrigerator with a lever on the outside, which operated an ice-maker, advertised that special feature with a slogan; "I only use one hand." Post-advertising consumer research showed it to be a memorable claim that established the highest rate of brand recall for any refrigerator at that time. A famous hair colorant asked, "Does she or doesn't she?"

Once a researcher discovers the reason why specific people want a particular product, the objective is to build the promise into the product by means of an overriding image that tells those people that this product is different from all the others—it offers them exactly what they want to make them feel good. But the product must deliver what it promises in order to be successful.

An advertising agency will develop a communications strategy from all the consumer and product criteria that their creative team, or the film production unit, will need. It will be vitally important to emphasize the target market for the product and the image they want conveyed. The viewers they aim at must be persuaded to identify with the hero in the movie commercial. When the cowboy hero lassoes the last shorthorn in the roundup, then relaxes in the saddle and reaches for a cigarette, those viewers will identify with the cowboy if the movie is properly made. And chances are that the brand they buy next time will be that one.

The desired image for a specific market niche is so carefully associated with the brand name and the logo that, in effect, it is you and your consumer segment that become branded, like that shorthorn on which the cowboy used a red-hot branding iron, to establish who it belongs to. Heineken beer, Carlsburg lager, Chesterfield cigarettes—they don't belong to *you,* you belong to *them.* And the marketer intends you to be branded for life.

But just as cattle used to be rustled, so marketers entice customers away from competing brands and into their own corral. Brand switching goes back and forth, particularly among weaker brands and products of less quality. Loyalty is stronger with brands like Coleman, because it means mustard; Xerox is synonymous with copiers; Kodak with film; IBM with computers; Toyota with automobiles; Royal with baking powder; Lipton with tea; Coke with cola; Nestlé with chocolates, Rothmans with cigarettes; Kellog's with corn flakes, Gillette with shaving; and so on. That is why they are successful brands.

The strength of brands that have been nurtured with care, over time, can be seen in terms of hard cash, by examining the top ten most valuable brand names. They are rated in 1995 ranking order in billion dollars, according to *Financial World*: 1. Coca-Cola ($39.05); 2. Marlboro ($38.71); 3. IBM ($17.15); 4. Motorola ($15.28); 5. Hewlett-Packard ($13.17); 6. Microsoft ($11.74); 7. Kodak ($11.59); 8. Budweiser ($11.35); 9. Kellog's ($11.00); 10. Nescafé ($10.34).

It is noticeable that Marlboro's value increased by about $6 billion since 1993; that Nescafé slid from third place in the same year to tenth and dropped in value by about one billion dollars; that although Kodak increased its value by about a billion dollars, it dropped in ranking from fourth place to seventh; that IBM jumped smartly back to third place, where it was in 1992 before it plunged to 290th ranking in 1993; that Microsoft dropped from fifth to sixth place as a consequence, although its value increased by about two billion; that Budweiser and Kellog gained about two billion dollars; and that Motorola jumped from eighth position in 1993 to fourth place, by gaining approximately 64.5 percent in value in only two years. Why?

A respected marketing magazine named *Printer's Ink*—which was known for its regular comparisons of consumer pulling power for different advertisements of the same product (Starch Tests)—also published significant research findings in the mid-to-late 1960s on which common criteria were responsible for the success of sixty major multinational market leaders in different industries. Was it their distribution? The calibre of their top management? Their advertising effectiveness? The amount of dollars placed behind their advertising and promotions? Or the excellence of the product? The most important factor, by far, turned out to be what they called *momentum of image.* Each had managed to establish a unique identity, over time, which generated an image of dependability and was renown for its incomparable quality and value. Their management expertise had gradually built a fortification that was impregnable from assaults by competitors—as long as they continued to nurture existing products and introduce new or innovated ones, and undertake aggressive strategies and tactics to launch and promote them.

The answer, in short, is superior management. *Financial World* points out that brand leadership does not depend *entirely* on superior management, however; that provides "performance." But there is also the matter of where the brand started from. On the other hand, momentum of image implies momentum of superior brand management over time. They consider the best managed brand to be Microsoft. Other rankings differ too when it comes to the world's best-managed brands: Louis Vuitton (second); Coca-Cola (third); Gillette (fourth); Playtex (fifth); Braun (sixth); Levi's (seventh); Johnnie Walker Black (eighth); Jell-O (ninth); and GE (tenth).[3]

Quality Management

Without quality there is no chance for success and every possibility of failure of a company that neglects quality management, because dependability relies on it.

Quality has to be built into a product or service at the very beginning, by establishing acceptable and unacceptable standards for each component at each key stage. The importance today of the ISO 9000 International Standards registration can be seen in a recent issue of the official magazine of the Association of Zimbabwe Advertisers—*The Advertiser*—which asked its readers, "Do buyers outside Zimbabwe have the perception that your goods are not up to world standards? Do you lose money because you have to lower your prices to get a market share overseas? Why not go for ISO 9000?"

The objective is to escape from those pointless exercises that established quality control inspections at the end of each assembly line. All it did was measure the number of variations and faulty products, and which faults predominated. But few companies even took those measurements. Those that did generally kept their records for a while and then disposed of them without having taken the necessary actions to rectify the frequency of errors. They may ask why and at what stage and who caused them to occur, but orders have to be completed in the meantime. And there is a reluctance to tamper with existing systems in case new problems materialize.

If we compare such a factory assembly line with movements of customers in a service sector industry, we can see that quality control would have taken place *after* customers had already been inconvenienced by faulty service, and had probably decided never to set foot in that store, hotel, or theater again.

One market leader in consumer durables boasted that its control charts limited defects to an acceptable 4 percent. But what is "acceptable" about losing 4 percent of products or components or customers? Why spend time and labor on re-work or customer complaints? Why not aim at zero defects? In that particular case, the factory manager was told that "control charts do not limit defects, people do"; and no one had told his production manager, because their rejects actually exceeded that figure.

Statistical Quality Control, or SQC, was designed as a workable concept as long ago as 1930 by Walter Shewhart, from a theory by Sir Ronald Fisher. Its objective was mass production with zero defects. Among Shewhart's team were W. Edwards Deming and Joseph Juran. It was they who developed independently a methodology that came to be known as Q-Circles. They influenced Japanese industry during its post-war recovery and helped to ensure that Japan's economic growth was driven also by consumer or marketing orientation.

Deming was to write later, "The formalization of QC-Circles was accomplished by Dr K. Ishikawa by 1960. A QC-Circle is the natural Japanese way of working together. Dr Ishikawa brought to the attention of management the importance of making full use of the successes of small groups of workers in the elimination of special causes of variability of product, and in improvement of the system, through changes in tools, changes in design, and in scheduling and even in alterations of the production process."[4] From that statement it can be seen that his main concern was the processes that lead into, through, and out of assembly lines.

Systems analysts have known for a very long time that the quickest and most effective way to improve any systems or procedures is to invite the users to analyze and criticize the methods they use. They are generally perceptive and often imaginative in suggesting better ways to do things. Q-Circles consist of concerned users from every stage of operations, who make useful proposals to improve the quality of work—its systems, procedures, processes, and services, leading to improved product quality and customer satisfaction.

But Q-Circles offer many additional benefits: (1) they improve the effectiveness of a company; (2) they improve the quality of working, by making work more meaningful and therefore enjoyable—by removing unnecessary complications and frustrations with time-wasting and inefficient procedures; (3) they enable individual employees to show their interest in the well-being of the company; and they also develop an employee's abilities; (4) they create harmonious work relationships and also develop good labor and management relations; (5) they ensure that customers can depend on the quality of a company's products and services; and (6) they help to reduce costs while also improving production and quality.

Although several countries have organizations that offer awards for outstanding quality—like the Baldridge in the U.S. and the Canadian Awards for Excellence—most companies that realize the need for product quality are disinterested in awards, hence, the sharp decline in applications. That is only because the best single motivation for improvements in quality, now that there are recognized international standards, is profit. Branding goods and services is more effective than creating awards. As Nicole Oresme wrote in the fourteenth century of coinage, which were the first branded goods, "Who, then, would trust a prince who should diminish the weight or fineness of money bearing his own stamp?"

That was the basis of the acceptability all over the world of gold coins stamped with the portrait of the Empress Maria Therese, Napoleon, or the British sovereign. Money was a commodity and such brands as those guaranteed perfect quality, and also engender implicit and absolute confidence in their true value.

Durability

The Rover company in Britain already enjoyed an outstanding reputation for quality and dependability. And it was known for its innovations, too. Some—like its invention of the first jet-powered car in 1950—did not go into production. But its Land Rover four-wheel drive did. When introduced in 1940 it outsold all other professional cross-country vehicles on the continents of Africa, Asia, and South America, as well as the Middle East. In the course of time, competitors offered greater passenger comfort and more modern designs. But Rover knew that it was durability that was of major importance to customers, not comfort or cosmetic design changes.

Land Rover had already proved that it was durable in tough conditions over long periods, for people who worked in the bush, across deserts, in forests, and on mountain tracks. And that was exactly what was required of it.

Rover did not rely solely on its reputation. Market leaders seldom do, or they soon cease to be leaders. Their dedication is to offensive strategies. That is what keeps them on top.

Distribution

A manufacturer and marketer of products is really in partnership with dealers who provide it with retail channels of distribution. They share a common objective, which is to satisfy customers. A retailer offers a manufacturer an outlet through which its products can reach the public. A brand manufacturer offers insurance that it will move them off the dealer's shelves and quickly replenish them.

Like all relationships, it has to be continually developed to ensure the satisfaction of both parties. A dealer needs effectiveness and dependability on the part of products, brand advertising, promotions, and stock rotation, without the inconvenience of too many price changes, and without problems. A marketer needs prime shelf and other display space, a commitment on the part of the dealer to its products, and regular opportunities to replenish supermarket shelves. Only if that relationship is viewed as a partnership will it contribute to the profitable growth of both the manufacturer and the retailer.

Supermarkets have come a long way since their objective was to replace high street family grocery stores. Their range of merchandise has spread to products as varied as clothing, wristwatches, and paperback books. That development would not have been possible without customer orientation and entrepreneurial innovation by both supplier and dealer.

Perhaps one of the most quoted examples of excellent distribution strategies is that of Matsushita. Its brand names are international household words— *National, Panasonic, Technics,* and *Quasar.* Pascale and Athos described how instead of dealing through existing networks of independently owned manufacturers' representatives, Matsushita created his own distribution channels by going directly to retailers. Instead of an indirect relationship, he offered trade financing to dealers and created close and continuous partnerships. He pioneered instalment sales and point-of-purchase store displays.[5]

That may have been the case with traditional Japanese organizations, but we should not become hypnotized by the Japanese mystique: L Suzman & Company have been wholesale distributors of tobacco and confectionery to variety stores throughout South Africa for generations, and they initiated much the same type of practices. Lidchi International were market leaders in purchasing oriental rugs direct from weavers in Iran and other rug-making countries, and supplying dealers all over the world, for two generations. They too financed their customers. Both their strength and their problems arose from thinking of themselves as merchant bankers.

With consumer durables, there is an even greater need for close collaboration between a manufacturer and a dealer, because of the greater hazards with big ticket items like furniture and major domestic appliances. And those types of merchandise require *selling* to customers on a showroom floor, as opposed to impulse buying by a supermarket shopper. Motivating a dealer's sales people is a joint effort. It requires regular assessment of a dealer's inventory to ensure that the manufacturer's brands are in evidence in the showroom, and that there is also backup stock in the store room. A dealer's sales people also need thorough product training to enable them to sell a brand effectively. They should be imbued with a commitment to a manufacturer's brand, to motivate them to switch customers from products that may be asked for, to a dealer's preferred brand. That brand may be preferred because of its quality and dependability or because of quantity discounts and rebates.

Although cooperative advertising and promotions can form an integral part of a relationship between a manufacturer and its dealers, competitions between sales people or sales teams can play an important role in increasing sales at the retail level.

A manufacturer's objective is not only to sell its products into a store but also to be largely responsible for moving them out. If it does so with outstanding success, it can be assured of a long-standing relationship. It may even be able to exclude some or all of the competing brands from a store.

In the case of fast-moving packaged consumer goods, however, significant changes took place in the early 1990s with the introduction of bar codes in supermarkets. Its effect was to provide more marketing information to distributors, which had always had to rely for it on sophisticated market leaders who supplied them with national branded goods. The need to pool narrower but direct data obtained at the local retail level with information obtained by manufacturers at the broader market level created an even greater need for close cooperation between national brands and supermarkets. That led to the introduction of category management (as described in chapter 7).

One result of the development of almost universal product standards is that loyalty to brands was weakened. Special offers encouraged consumers to try different products. And often they found little if any difference between the national brands to which they had become accustomed and some retailers' own-label products. That is not surprising, since many of the me-too products were made by national manufacturers under the store's own label. Customer loyalties have switched more and more from a brand to a price advantage, particularly since the recession of the 1990s when they became more price conscious than before. The result is that many national brands lost market share to private labels. Some, like P&G, Kraft, and Philip Morris, were forced by competition to cut prices; so that, as usual, consumers benefit from the competition.

The irony is that national brands are now competing with themselves as well as with other brands, because they also make some of their products with their customers' retail labels. That has reduced profit margins.

Retailers now need private labels to survive, and they have to advertise and promote them to their customers instead of leaving their sales to impulse buying. And, by now, most national brand marketing firms no longer expect the trend to private brands to reverse itself when the economy improves. One indication of price preference is the considerable success of Wal-Mart stores, which promote their low prices to the public as the main benefit for shopping there. Wood Gundy estimated that in-house brands now account for approximately 15 percent of supermarket sales across Canada, and 20 percent in some supermarket chains in Europe. Britain leads the way, largely because of the power of large established chain stores like Sainsbury and Tesco with their umbrella claims of quality, value, and economy, and also Asda's stores. Switzerland and Germany come a close second and third to the UK.

Now retailers are using tactics formerly undertaken only by big national brand marketers, to hawk their own private label brands on TV, radio, and in magazines, as well as in newspapers and with leaflets. Prominent among them is the President's Choice line marketed by Loblaw Ltd in Canada, which is expected to double its U.S. sales in 1993 to $130 million. During a thirteen-week survey up to the end of 1992, Information Resource's InfoScan reported that private label goods accounted for 18.4 percent of all units sold in U.S. grocery stores and 14.5 percent of total supermarket dollar volume. That represents 3.2 percent growth for private-label goods over the previous year—twice the growth rate of national brands. Private-label cigarettes topped the list of fastest-growing brands. Their quarterly supermarket sales nearly tripled to $54.0 million in that quarter. Sales of private-label cold, allergy, and sinus remedies increased by 24.8 percent in the same period, to $28.2 million. And sales of private label bottled water increased by 21.6 percent to $49 million.

Exclusivity

Tim Hamilton-Russell's excellent Cape wines are in demand not only because of the care he took to develop his vineyards and his wine-making processes, but also because he deliberately chose the quality vintage market niche, and reinforced his quality claim by offering a benefit of exclusivity.

His prices are high for South African wines, to cover the cost of the added value achieved by creating quality in his vineyards. His is an example of building quality into a product right at the beginning. His production is limited, which sometimes makes it harder to find in the stores. That, and the numbered label on each bottle, are evidence that each vintage is limited. That is what makes it exclusive.

Hamilton-Russell wines like *Pinot Noir* also evince a unique taste advantage.

Other suppliers of exclusive products or services are renown by such brand names as Dunhill, Guchi, Asprey, Sulka, Sotheby, Roche-Bobois, Wildenstein, Fortnum & Mason, Dior, Yves Saint-Laurent, Rolls Royce, Veuve Cliquot, and so forth. Most have been established for a long time, and their reputations arose naturally from their acknowledged preeminence in their own special sphere. Their names and their image assure even those people who cannot afford to buy them that they are the best in their product category.

What they are acknowledged for is quality and exclusivity. It therefore follows that although quality and exclusivity are not necessarily synonymous, exclusivity, by definition, must incorporate quality.

Exclusive companies market themselves or their products on the clear understanding that there is always a wealthy class of people who do not have to settle for second best. But just like every other marketer, they can never afford to be complacent, because fashions and life styles change all the time, and those changes require product innovations to satisfy new needs and tastes.

The exclusive market niche is particularly demanding of the highest quality of both products and designs, because it is the most discriminating of all niches. But it can justify a premium price to cover the costs of providing top quality. A high profit margin is also justifiable to compensate for the relatively small size of the market. Its criteria are the opposite of a mass market product for which affordability is paramount. Not only is an affordable price unnecessary, but it could be detrimental to its sales. A very high price is a sign of superior quality and a demonstration that supplies are severely limited. That is what makes it exclusive.

Packaging

Packaging normally possesses four main functions: it protects the product; provides shelf appeal to encourage impulse buying; provides information; and it offers convenience in handling and storing and transporting.[6]

Packaging manufacturers continually innovate their products according to fashion trends, new technology, and new demands on distribution and display. The growing popularity of wine in North America provides an example. Bottles are heavy and difficult to handle, relatively costly, and they break. Some suppliers of cheaper wines for the mass market therefore introduced a separate brand to cater for it. Like fruit juice, its container is either a plastic-lined bag, a coated cardboard box with a carrying handle, or a large box with a plastic spigot at its base, like a wine cask. They display well on supermarket shelves and are easier to carry with the groceries. Wine is even sold in cans, like Coke or Pepsi.

Decorative glass jars or vases have long been used for some exclusive wines, and Japanese sake is generally marketed in delicately decorated porcelain jars. Those containers are used not only to distinguish the product, but also to provide an artifact for the home when the bottle is empty. Although the cost of the container is included in the price, it offers another attractive reason to buy that particular brand. And of course it makes an ideal gift.

As with so many innovations, the new containers are merely extensions of previous ideas. The once-cheap Italian Chianti was traditionally sold in a recognizable, individually blown glass bottle that required a woven straw base so that it could stand on a table. But the innovation of boxes, bags, and cans has done more than simply provide a cheaper, more handy, or unbreakable container that is easier to transport in bulk, and also becomes its own shelf-talker when displayed—it has elevated *vin ordinaire* from a generic, no-name product with little "class" to distinctively different products. It has extended the market for table wines in much the same way that similar containers assisted fruit juices to penetrate mass markets.

Communications

The main purpose of communications for a marketer is domination. Few can dominate a marketplace by using 7,500 trained sales and service personnel like Pitney-Bowes, but there are other ways to keep competitors off your turf. One of the most effective is to dominate the advertising media, as a first step to dominating in-store shelf space. Prime examples are marketers of household products who place as much as, or more than, 85 percent of their advertising budget into TV commercials to dominate the home. Baking powder, frozen foods, household aerosols, washing powders and liquid detergents, cooking fats, toilet soaps, food wraps, garbage bags, cake mixes, and a whole range of other household products sell themselves to you in your own home by demonstrating their usefulness and becoming indispensable.

Heavy advertising and promotional budgets successfully protect the multinational marketers from losing market share to lesser competitors. They can afford to use a continuously offensive strategy of total force that few other companies can match. By placing their branded products before the public all the time, they manage to achieve considerable top-of-the-mind awareness for when a shopper walks down the aisle of a supermarket and identifies those brands on the shelves. Shoppers can remember only so much product information, or automatically limit the input at a conscious level. What the big marketers achieve is a large share of mind that pushes out the other brands by dominating a shopper's memory. Whoever shouts the loudest often wins the argument; not necessarily by reasoning or logic, but by dominating the discussion. In the same way, smart money dominates the media. For example, Coca-Cola shouts so loud that its voice is heard all over the world.

Merchandising

To most retailers, merchandising is the traditional function of buying merchandise for the store. To a marketer it is maximizing the effectiveness of persuading customers to buy it.

A product manager or a merchandising manager might plan in-store displays of their products. And unless special merchandising staff are employed, a sales person might maintain them.

If products are well advertised and well known by the public, merchandising would include having appropriate point-of-purchase material designed, installed, and maintained. Special racks might be designed to display the products better. The packaging might be designed to act as shelf talkers to persuade shoppers to buy on impulse. Just as importantly, merchandising includes creating and maintaining inventory on continual display in a dealer's showroom, with ample reserve stocks in the dealer's store room and in the chain store's regional or central warehouse. Although smaller marketers may not be able to afford to dominate the advertising media, they might manage to dominate a shopper's mind when she or he is ready to buy. Original packaging and display material, which is designed to get attention and provide the right type of information, can persuade a shopper to buy.

When the merchandising effort is undisciplined or not properly coordinated, one frequently finds large sums of money being wasted on new product advertising when the advertised product is unavailable in the stores, or stocks of standard products have not been replenished.

The function of an alert and well-motivated merchandising manager, or a sales person trained to undertake the job, is to maximize repeat sales by ensuring a high degree of stockturn in the store. That can be done only through advance planning, which allows for adequate lead time in a properly coordinated plan aimed at providing a continuous stream of merchandise for nationwide chain stores. A marketing department, in conjunction with the retail outlets, provides customers to buy the products. But the function of a merchandising manager is to ensure that goods are moved in and out and rapidly replaced. He or she would be in complete control of a continuing program aimed at ensuring that no sales are lost through gaps in inventories.

What used to be the laborious and time-consuming chore of stocktaking has now been simplified and accelerated in companies like Kmart, through hand-held lasers that read bar codes on products on the shelves. The laser gun provides instant information on the number of each product on store shelves and in stockrooms, compared to what a store should be carrying. It also conveys information on current Kmart sales, outstanding orders, price comparisons with competitors, and what price each product should sell at. While one objective is instant stock rotation, another is measuring customer offtake to identify more effective store locations for particular products in juxtaposition with others.

The "remote maintenance unit" (or RMU) has access to all relevant inventory data. Fresh stock, when needed, is ordered by satellite to Kmart's head office in Detroit. After transmission of information to their inventory distribution center, the new stock should arrive in the stores within forty-eight hours. Kmart has the advantage also of accessing information from every transaction at sixty of its 2,300 stores, in order to analyze and maximize effective pricing and placement of all items on every store's shelves, with the end objective of increasing the number of purchases made by each customer.

Merchandising and distribution can be used in both a defensive and an offensive strategy.

Selling

What should be one of the strongest links in a marketing chain is most often the weakest. However good a product and however effective its advertising, only a sales person can control a sale. Selling appears to be so simple a task that most businesses do not understand the necessity to train their sales people in selling techniques and product knowledge. So simple does it appear that many small and medium-size enterprises do not want to spend money on sales training, or they confuse it with pep talks. Often they assume it is being undertaken by the sales manager. But if he or she were hired because of success in creating sales, rather than in management or training, the sales teams are unlikely to be well organized or properly trained or cost-effective.

Customers can be at the mercy of poor, over-aggressive, or misleading salespeople when they want to buy an automobile or a home, an electric appliance or a camera, a suite of furniture or mutual funds. And businesses can lose sales to better calibre salespeople in competing companies. Unlike the management vortex in the West, where standards keep dropping, the standard of selling and sales management has remained at an unacceptably low level. Sales people are often considered to be a menace or as simpletons who don't know their job and don't possess the capability to improve, rather than being knowledgeable, helpful, and successful. They have to be mature in order to establish relationships of mutual respect with trade buyers or repeat-buying consumers. They also have to be professional in how they approach and undertake their work. They need intelligence and application to discuss a dealer's problems and know how to solve them so that customers will come to depend on them for product or market knowledge and advice. They must know enough about the marketing process to be able to obtain important and relevant information from which their company could benefit in improving products, packaging, service, advertising, promotions, and other marketing tools likely to improve their performance. And they must have initiative to make sales instead of waiting to be given orders.

The prime objective is to increase sales profitably by excluding competitors. But most business enterprises just tell their salespeople what to do and keep their fingers crossed in the belief that salespeople know how to sell even if they themselves don't. In fact salespeople who approach their job professionally should be able to tell their employers what to do. If they are both knowledgeable and sensitive to the needs of their marketplace, salespeople should know exactly what a market needs.

The cost of hiring, inducting, training, and managing salespeople is high: competence is therefore essential. NVQs in sales were launched in October, 1993 in Britain under the government-funded National Council for Vocational Qualifications. Its objective is to improve the quality of selling, and therefore the volume of sales per salesperson, by measuring such activities as planning time and negotiating skills. NVQs embrace 500 types of industries and job functions. They are competence based instead of being solely knowledge based. In other words, salespeople are tested for what they do rather than for what they know. The concept arose out of the 1986 White Paper on *Education and Training in the 21st Century,* aimed at making Britain more competitive to survive in the global marketing era.

Each industry defines criteria according to what is expected from employers, against which an individual's skills can be measured. Assessment is made on the job. NVQs appear to have finally brought selling skills into a measurable area of training, so that national qualifications can be awarded. One awarding body is the Chartered Institute of Marketing in conjunction with City and Guilds. The standard-setting body for sales is the Sales Qualifications Board.

Command Decisions

The media made much of the idiosyncratic behavior of field commanders in World War II, but it was precisely those personality characteristics that made each of them such outstanding generals. From Patton's audacity to Montgomery's drive to perfection, McArthur's conviction that he was a man of destiny, to Zhukov's unconquerable determination to drive all German troops from Russia, and Bradley's and Rommel's quiet and confident professionalism—all were forceful leaders who possessed commanding attributes that win battles. When we get to consider leadership skills in large business organizations, later on, we will find similar attributes required of captains of industry, too. And what all those field generals shared in common was that they were the only individuals capable of making and implementing command decisions.

Timing

Linked to all fourteen of those tactical criteria is timing. A general chooses from several options as to when to initiate actions. And however excellent the plan, it may succeed or fail according to his timing in exploiting any opportunity that presents itself. Similarly, a marketer cannot afford to act too late, nor dare he or she act precipitately.

"The need to concentrate the greatest possible force and deliver a smashing blow at the decisive point will continue to clash with the need to outwit, mislead, deceive, and surprise the enemy. Victory, as always, will go to the side that best understands how to balance these two contradictory requirements, not just in the abstract but at a specific time, at a specific place, and against a specific enemy."[7]

Frontal Assault

Even when led by a brilliant general like Marlborough, a frontal assault can end in disaster. At Malplaquet in the Low Countries in 1709, he and Prince Eugène only just defeated the French, and they lost 20,500 men to the enemy's 12,500. It was not intended to be a direct assault, which is best avoided. But Marlborough was unable to find a weak spot at a decisive point, and could not manoeuvre round the flank of the French army under Villars. Enemy artillery was sited for cross-fire in a gap between wooded areas with cavalry in the rear. Marlborough's allied Dutch infantry were slaughtered in a frontal attack. Fierce cavalry charges and counter-charges ensued without results, Villars was wounded, and Boufflers ordered a withdrawal and conceded victory.

According to Frederick the Great, Villars was beaten because what he thought was a marsh protecting his flank was a dry field. In his *Discours Sur la Guerre,* he wrote of generalship:

> A profound knowledge of the country in which one is going to fight is most necessary. Something can be learnt beforehand from maps—the towns, the rivers, the roads. Always go to the nearest height, map in hand, and study the view. Never neglect an opportunity of talking to old inhabitants, especially shepherds and gamekeepers. You must know where there are fords, and which rivers or marshes dry up in summer.... Find out how many columns of troops the road can take. All this is fairly easy in the plain and much more complicated in the mountains where one must know the gorges and defiles. Never camp away from water. One can send officers to find out these things but it is far better to do it oneself. Full use should be made of the lie of the land.[8]

He urged his officers to study Turenne's last two campaigns. Frederick was the greatest military genius of his time because he left nothing to chance. He became a role model for commanders who followed him, including Napoleon. He is an example for superior managers to study, too, in getting personally involved on the spot to address particular problems and outwit competitors by planning how to exploit every possible opportunity.

Direct assault is not recommended in business any more than in battle. It will be time consuming to organize and costly to implement, because it is likely to use too many resources and the chances are against success.

Although business organization charts, with their staff and line appointments, were based on military organization, business management did not continue to follow a combative military style. Instead, it emulated the more passive or "disinterested" administrative style developed for the Victorian colonial civil service, where the responsibilities of local administrators were limited to taking instructions from London. That style seeped into both the private business sector and the military, so that inept administrators became indifferent to improper uses of taxpayers' funds and ill-informed generals sacrificed the lives of their men by "leading from behind" without personal knowledge of the terrain or the circumstances in the front line. Typical of that bloody sacrifice of resources were the commander-in-chief of the British army in 1914, Field Marshall French, and Douglas Haig, who succeeded him. General Sir John Hackett wrote of them, "Neither had the intellectual capacity to evaluate the importance of new techniques, or the imagination to break the bonds of his own experience.... Very many of those deaths were the direct consequence not only of failures in management and faults of technique but also of error in the formulation of general principles."

Total Force

Maximizing the effective use of limited forces is not an activity with which Americans feel comfortable, even today. The size of the United States and its population have accustomed it to mass action in mass markets. That is probably why IBM decided to use a strategy of total force against Apple Computers in 1981. It may have seemed entirely appropriate to make use of one of its greatest assets, which was sheer overwhelming power.

The struggle for the personal computer market has already taken a new turn in 1993, with Intel's near monopoly of microprocessors. Intel enjoys a considerable economic advantage because it can spread its fixed overhead costs over millions of units, instead of only thousands for workstation manufacturers. It now looks as if powerful PCs could erode the market for workstations. But back in 1981, IBM thought that powerful workstations would become cheaper and erode the PC market. Then it believed that its market position was threatened by the $1.4 billion U.S. personal computer market—so it mounted a massive assault against Apple, which was the market leader.

IBM launched its own product with a $40 million advertising campaign aimed at first-time buyers. It was distributed by company-owned retail outlets. And IBM also used 800 selected computer retailers. It used its own sales force to penetrate the office segment of the market. The result was that in approximately sixteen months it managed to obtain 17 percent share of the PC market. That put IBM in second place behind Apple. Then, with economies of scale, IBM was able to cut its prices by 20 percent in 1983. By then it offered higher performance at lower cost. The market activity meanwhile increased the size of the PC market by $4.2 billion. IBM secured 26 percent market share and became the market leader.

Now its position is threatened by Intel and Microsoft. Intel was able to cut the price of its Pentium chip because costs had been slashed by 60 percent since it was introduced in 1992. It expects to sell its next generation X86 chip in 1995. It has also formed an alliance with Hewlett-Packard "to develop a chip that will combine the best of RISC and X86 designs."[9]

But news leaked out at the end of 1994 that the Pentium chip was not as perfect as originally thought: "The rush to get on the market contributed to the fiasco of the flawed Pentium microprocessor chip.... And its producer, Intel—the biggest chip maker of them all—has not been the only IT manufacturer to fall down recently. In the same month that the Pentium hit the headlines, Compaq was obliged to recall tens of thousands of notebook computers which had bugs in the memories and faulty power supply units."[10] Intel shrugged off the problem at first by claiming that it would cause inaccuracies only in complex calculations and only once in every 27,000 years. But when IBM refused to accept it as a component of their own Pentium-based technology, Intel offered to replace any Pentium on request.

A major component of war is psychology. And sheer size has a psychological dynamic as well as a physical one—both for the confidence it imbues in a larger attacking force and the fear it instills in a smaller defending one. There has therefore long been a common wisdom (or bias) shared by von Clausewitz, Napoleon, the European generals in World War I, and the American forces— that all else being equal, *God is on the side of the big battalions.*[11] IBM is an example that it can work also in business; if the attacker has sufficient funds, if the company has already earned the confidence of distributors and the public, if it possesses a good enough sales force and big enough distribution, if it can afford massive advertising budgets, if its product is superior and also price competitive, and also if its product is so well-designed that it can enjoy huge cost-effective advantages from mass production.

There is even one military example of a direct assault that was successful. That was the combined invasion of German defenses behind the Normandy beaches in World War II. But it was the biggest military force ever to have been assembled, the Germans had already been worn down by British forces for five years, it was an alliance of armies, and the American forces were fresh.

Deterrence

The strategy of deterrence is intended to avoid confrontation, which is likely to lead to conflict, bloodshed, and destruction. The instrument of deterrence is generally—but not always—a technological innovation. In its simplest forms, some ancient Chinese armies once wore frightening masks and beat numerous gongs to scare their enemies into running away instead of giving battle. Greek, Roman, and other soldiers of their time wore fixtures on their helmets that made them appear much taller. Zulu impis of thousands of warriors would beat their shields with their short, stabbing spears to demoralize their enemies. Scots guard regiments struck terror into the hearts of their enemies as they marched forward to the skirl of their bagpipes, with rows of bayonets fixed at the ready.

When the British Empire was respected or feared, sending a battleship to an unstable area of the world was enough of a deterrent in most cases. It became known as "battleship diplomacy." U.S. atomic power deterred further loss of lives by ending World War II in Nagasaki; Japan sued for peace the following day. It has deterred major wars for four decades. But now that several other countries possess nuclear capability, its power as a deterrent may have been reduced. Implicit in its mass destructive force is a belief that no rational person would risk nuclear warfare. But as we shall see, human nature has a propensity for irrationality.

As trouble spots appear all over the world, it has become more clear that a strategy of total force is too dangerous and too costly to use in order to prevent minor conflicts from spreading. Economy of force may be more effective as well as less expensive.

Whatever the deterrent, a strategy that depends on the possession of a winning technology must also include the skills to use it effectively. As high technological warfare becomes more complex and more dangerous to allies, the quality of weapons and the skills of military personnel present new challenges.

A similar situation exists with new technologies in business organizations. And, as Feltex discovered with its outdated carpet looms, technology ceases to act as a deterrent when it is not continually innovated. The Maginot Line did not deter invasion, because it was flawed.

But it is not only technological dominance that deters competition. It can also be an overwhelming force of consumer loyalty to long-established brands, or massive advertising and promotional budgets in the hands of world leaders like Proctor & Gamble, or exclusive distribution channels, a monopoly (or semi-monopoly) of raw materials, the longstanding establishment of a consumer franchise like McDonalds Hamburgers, or protection of a new invention, discovery or formulation, by patents.

Economy of Force

The myth of overwhelming numbers has been disproved at least as many times as it has been successfully demonstrated. Although it is prudent to take such a precaution whenever possible, what counts is the calibre of leadership and the quality of troops or employees. A charismatic leader can imbue them with a winning spirit. The David and Goliath story of tiny Israel's victory against the combined Arab forces surrounding them has been repeated many times by individual entrepreneurs and small companies taking initiatives against big business organizations and winning. Perhaps the most notable one is that of Bill Gates, who confronted IBM—the biggest multinational computer company—with his Microsoft enterprise, because he is now alleged to be the richest man in the world. But Richard Branson's Virgin Atlantic Airlines is unforgettable too. He fought the big established airlines with a price-cutting strategy described by Robert Heller as *penetration pricing* designed to crack a big market—compared to *predatory pricing* practices of big airlines designed to smoke out the little ones.

Another "little man" who made it big was Onassis, with his oil tankers and Olympic Airlines. Then there is Michael Dell, still described as "boy billionaire", who started his mail order computer business straight from high school. Michael Cowpland's Corel is another leading company that began with one man's dream, drive, and ingenuity. A quality common to all of them is audacity coupled with entrepreneurial skills. Onassis's particular strength was an ability to close up all gaps at the planning stage. Once his plans were launched they were invulnerable. And the skill that kept them all in place, once they had achieved their market position, was the ability to keep on innovating.

"A war involves much more than mustering one's resources to build the most powerful armed forces, concentrating them at a selected spot, and delivering a smashing blow," wrote van Creveld.

The British have been obliged to use individual ingenuity and skills to maximize the effectiveness of limited resources ever since they declined as a superpower after World War I. Perhaps it is their tiny island and relatively small population, compared with the United States, that was instrumental in developing their skills in economy of force. Like Japan with its limited natural resources, or Israel with its limited population, they have had to make the best of what they have. In the Elizabethan era it was audacity and innovation. When the British Empire stretched around the world in Victorian times, it was leadership and organization.

Small British commando forces were effective in World War II. And British scientists, engineers, and entrepreneurs made their reputations then, and in the austerity years following the end of the war, for producing discoveries and inventions "on a shoestring," by improvising. In a similar way, small business enterprises are obliged to set modest objectives and achieve them by isolating small market niches. In that way, they can use limited resources to maximum effect. Tactics of manoeuvre are used to seek out opportunities in undefended territories. And the strengths of smaller companies are mobility, flexibility, and speed—all of which are highly desirable in using a flanking attack.

Von Schlieffen called it "the essence of the whole history of war." It is a matter of positioning a company's strength in innovative ways to exploit a competitor's weakness. Marketing companies do it all the time by undertaking ongoing and thorough research to determine weak points in a market area. Then they use the most appropriate technology and the most effective tactics to capture that territory.

Van Creveld described it as follows: "[W]ar is no longer simply a question of one wrestler throwing the other out of the ring. From Moltke through Schlieffen to Lidell Hart, the shining goal of strategy has been just the opposite: namely to outflank the enemy, encircle him, cut him off, deprive him of supplies, and bring about his surrender *without* actually having to fight for the ground on which he stood.... Large armed formations are regarded as having been defeated—and, equally important, regard themselves as having been defeated—as soon as they are surrounded and their lines of communication are severed." As in wargames by IBM, Intel, and others.

There are many arguments in favor of utilizing small, autonomous forces who are experienced in working closely together, and know and respect each other. Clausewitz declared that there are two great obstacles that bedevil military forces, and van Creveld added a third. They are inflexibility, friction, and uncertainty. The quality of management performance is judged largely by its ability to neutralize those destructive influences. While common philosophy, based on Clausewitz and Napoleon, asserts that "everything else being equal the biggest battalion will win," the larger an organization is, the less flexible it is. And the greater the efficiency of a campaign, the worse are the frictions arising from unexpected problems, which can create chaos and lead to disaster—particularly in larger forces.

Friction, according to Clausewitz, is "that which distinguishes war on paper from the real thing." It can arise from torrential rain and mud, blinding snowstorms and sub-zero temperatures, or it can develop among men under pressures of starvation, deprivation of boots or medical supplies, anxiety, and fear. The bigger the force, the greater the effects of hazards. Business is the same.[12] One of the few commanders who could handle the logistics of huge forces was Marshal Georgi Zhukov, who controlled the largest army in the world. In 1941 he commanded the defense of Moscow with eleven armies on a 640km front, and repelled the German attack. To defend Stalingrad, he commanded over one million men, 13,550 guns, and 900 tanks. He overwhelmed the German invasion in 1942.[13]

Van Creveld describes the effects of friction on General Rommel. "(He) repeatedly drove his forces to the breaking point and beyond. In 1941 his dash to Sollum almost ended in the destruction of his forces. In 1942 he reached Alamein with no fuel left, his ammunition a thousand miles in the rear at Tripoli, and with only nineteen tanks left in working order. To make things worse, his impossibly long lines of communication were subjected to constant sea and air attack. The Afrika Korps had clearly shot its bolt; from then on it only attempted one more half-hearted offensive at Alam Halfa. That attack having failed, all it could do was cower and wait for the enemy...to launch his counteroffensive. When the offensive came it spelled the end of the Korps."

Military experts believe that nuclear warfare has made massive conventional battles like Stalingrad obsolete. The destructive power of the first atomic bomb exploded over Hiroshima in 1945 also revealed unexpected hazards of deadly alpha and gamma radiation, which opened up a new era of deterrence. High technology weaponry in the Falkland Islands in 1982, and then in Desert Storm, made battles faster, more mobile, and deadlier than ever. It taught that wars must be won fast, and demand low-intensity forces to isolate and deal with an enemy with deadly effectiveness. Low-intensity guerrilla war is likely to continue, interspersed by periods of medium to high-intensity, non-nuclear war.

"Technology will dominate in the hands of those who are most creative in its use. In practice, this may mean the paradox of the small, mobile team regaining its importance, with the infiltration tactics used so successfully by the Japanese infantryman in World War Two returning to prominence—as long as new tactics and soldierly attributes are developed. The constant scrapping and replacement of routine procedures has to be accepted as a part of the new military doctrine. The battlefield is always changing: the fighting man must be prepared for this."[14] So must the business manager. And nowhere is this more true than in the information sector.

Compaq Computer did not even exist when IBM launched its personal computer in 1981, and yet, by spring 1993, Compaq could enjoy a bigger market share in PCs than IBM. Close on its heels is DELL Computer. In 1992, 60.5 percent of the PC market was in the hands of small clone makers like Zeos, AST, Northgate, Wyse Technology, and Blackship. The following global market shares set the scene in 1992.

Personal Computers:		Workstations:	
IBM:	12.4 percent	Sun:	32.9 percent
Apple:	11.9 percent	Hewlett-Packard:	18.1 percent
Compaq:	6.6 percent	IBM:	9.9 percent
NEC:	5.1 percent	Digital Equipment:	9.9 percent
Dell:	3.5 percent	Silicon Graphics:	8.6 percent
Others:	60.5 percent	Intergraph:	6.0 percent
		Others:	14.6 percent
TOTAL:	$46.5 billion	*TOTAL:*	$9.4 billion
Source: Dataquest		*Source:* IDC	

What IBM discovered to its cost was that big is not necessarily best. Small is now more beautiful. Shell Chemicals, ICI, BP, British Gas, BTR, and Dalgety had all recognized the importance of decentralizing into smaller, more flexible cost and profit centers as early as the 1980s. And Asea Brown Boveri segmented into 1,300 independent companies and 5,000 autonomous profit centers.[15]

Amid concerns of a possible PC slump in 1996, the worldwide market was actually growing strongly at a rate of about 18 percent, with a market of 15.95 million units in the second quarter of the year, alone, compared with 13.68 million a year ago. Five market leaders represented one-third of the global PC market. The change in their positions since 1992 shows the typical volatility of an industry in which the dominant design of a new product is still very much at issue in the marketplace.

1996 Global PC Market		1996 U.S. Market	
percent		percent	
Compaq:	9.7	Compaq:	11.8
IBM:	8.8	Packard Bell:	9.7
Apple:	5.3	IBM:	8.6
NEC:	5.1	Apple:	6.9
Hewlett Packard:	4.3	Dell:	6.2
Source: Dataquest Inc. (San Jose, Calif.)		*Source:* International Data Corp. (Framington, Mass.)	

* Preliminary: as at second quarter.

As defined by Darwin, in his theory of Natural Selection, the dominant design is that in which the "preservation of favourable variations and the rejection of injurious variations", have taken effect.

Defense

"Defense is the stronger form of war," wrote von Clausewitz. It is easier to hold onto something and requires less effort than taking it away. Defenders have more time on their side to entrench themselves firmly or create fortifications. And they defend what they already possess. Attackers have to advance, sustain themselves away from their base, enter hostile territory, and expose themselves to enemy fire from land, sea, or air—and sometimes from all three.

But the problem with a defensive strategy is that there can be no victory for the defenders—only a stand-off.

Sun Tzu—whose advice on strategy is considered to be the best book on war ever written—commented as follows; "Defensive tactics are required to provide security against defeat. The ability to defeat an enemy means taking the offensive."

Most business organizations are blissfully unaware of the need for an offensive strategy or are satisfied with mere defensive strategies. They are not marketing organizations at all, but simply factories that produce goods randomly. Since they neither plan nor follow offensive strategies, they are continually vulnerable from attacks and can be made ineffective by attrition. Even if they successfully maintain stand-off positions, they are unlikely to be able to grow. They will remain at the mercy of new technologies and economic recessions, or have their essential supplies cut off.

A defensive strategy in business is simply not a good enough business strategy, unless it is enforced by an offensive tactic.

Preemptive Strike

A tactic used to enforce a strategy of defense is the preemptive strike. It possesses the considerable advantage of surprise, and takes the initiative away from an enemy by arriving when and where least expected. As well as wreaking considerable damage to important strategic weapons or positions, it also demoralizes an enemy and prevents him from mounting an effective defense or from counter-attacking. That aspect is of particular importance since the Falkland War showed that with the destructive power of high-technology weapons, it is essential to ensure that an enemy does not have the power to retaliate.

From the inception of the new state in 1948, the skill of the Israelis has been improvisation. They are also imbued with a commitment to survive against considerable odds while encircled by Arab countries that refuse formal recognition of the State of Israel or their right to exist. They began with inferior technology from World War II and the necessity for aggressive tactics because they have so little territory of their own. In 1967 they were obliged to defend themselves from a combined onslaught of Egyptian, Jordanian, and Syrian armies. Although overwhelmingly outnumbered, they achieved victory in only six days. They did so largely by tank warfare. But that depended for its success on a preemptive strike which destroyed the entire United Arab Airforce on the ground at the outset.

Then in 1973 they were involved in the greatest armored battle since 1945. Israel was suddenly faced with a surprise attack by the forces of Egypt, Iraq, Syria, and Jordan. Fifteen thousand armored vehicles were involved, and it was the first time that antitank guided missiles were used extensively. 800 Israeli and 3,000 Arab tanks were destroyed or captured in three weeks. Only political intervention from outside prevented the Israelis from overrunning their enemies' territories.

As a result of continued threats by surrounding Arab countries, Israel was obliged to destroy the Iraqi potential of nuclear warheads and germ warfare by another lightening preemptive air strike. Neither of those strikes was offensive; both were defensive measures initiated in the certain knowledge that enemy attack was imminent.

Preemptive strikes are the products of ingenuity, often of improvisation, always of intelligence information, usually of necessity, and they always depend for their devastating effect on timing.

Many unique new inventions could be considered to be preemptive strikes—from Bell's North American monopoly of the telephone system, to Bayer's aspirin or Du Pont's nylon. A preemptive strike in today's auto industry might be the production of a practical electricity-driven automobile. One was invented as long ago as 1899 by Jenatzy in Belgium. Its highest speed was sixty-six miles an hour—quite adequate for today's congested streets. But with all the extraordinary high-technology innovations in the past two or three decades, one would imagine that some resourceful inventor would have produced a modern electric car by now. Auto makers must surely have something in reserve for the time when the oil wells begin to run dry and prices are hiked again, but panic would erupt among the oil cartels if it were to be unveiled right now.

Since neither Japan nor Israel possess their own oil wells, and South Africa is obliged to manufacture its oil from coal, perhaps a preemptive strike with a new type of electric Mini or Beetle will come from either of those countries, or an alliance between all three.

The most effective type of preemptive strike is one aimed to gain control of the source of supplies, a supply line, or channels of communications. Iraq attempted to do that by grabbing Kuwaiti and Saudi oil wells and bringing western industrial nations to a standstill. Field Marshal Montgomery did so when he positioned his Eighth Army between the tanks of the Afrika Korp and their oil supply dumps in the Battle of El Alamein.

In business terms, Barrie James quotes the situation of Coca-Cola in the U.S. in 1981, when they innovated their product cost-effectively by using fructose corn sweetener instead of 50 percent of the sugar content. They ensured that their competitors could not quickly copy them, by signing such large orders with suppliers that they controlled most of the available fructose capacity.

Alliances

"Alliances are held together by fear, not by love," said former British prime minister Harold Macmillan. Perhaps the case of Apple and IBM is an example of this, since each has outmanoeuvred the other in the past, and both now find their dominance of the PC market threatened. That is how the tactics of alliances work.

Joint ventures and strategic alliances were much in the news in 1993. What seemed to escape the attention of theorists of flexible business networks, whose recommendations grew more and more grandiose, was whether they were supposed to benefit two or more weak companies, several strong ones, or a mix of strong and weak. "Enthusiasm for joint ventures is less widespread than it was," commented *Management Today*.[16] "The formula has been in general use long enough for judgements to be made about its validity—and the success rate, according to one British academic, is 'very similar to that of acquisitions.'" Commercial or personal differences almost inevitably diverge in time. Two McKinsey consultants writing in *Harvard Business Review* suggest that of a number of different types of alliances, only one has a strong chance of surviving more than the seven-year average.[17] Direct competitors with a high degree of overlap are among the worst partners. Alliances of weak partners rarely succeed. And a weak business is unlikely to benefit from joining up with a strong one. The most likely success is with an equally balanced alliance. GEC (UK) and Alsthom in France are given as an example of this.

From that, it is obvious that government-funded business alliances or networks are an anachronism, since strong business organizations hardly need government assistance to form an alliance which they consider to be in their own interest. And alliances of the weak are unlikely to benefit anyone, since they would have nothing to offer each other. If neither can succeed on its own, then each would be a liability to the other.

Alliances are a tempting solution to the dilemma of a firm seeking the home-base advantage of another nation without giving up its own. Unfortunately, alliances are rarely a solution. They can achieve selective benefits, but they always involve significant costs in terms of coordination, reconciling goals with an independent entity, creating a competitor, and giving up profits. Those costs make many alliances temporary and destined to fail.[18]

Alliances did not help Britain, France, or the Low Countries in September, 1939 when mobility and speed moved the German army across Poland and entirely eliminated an army of one million; then Guderian's Nineteenth Panzer Corp advanced through France to the English channel the following May, in the fastest race across Europe in history. Five nations collapsed from the military envelopment and 330,000 men of the British army were forced to retreat in disorder to the Dunkirk beaches and leave most of their arms and equipment behind when they were rescued by sea.

As for mergers and acquisitions, which are routinely considered as a means for entering new markets; "it should be seen in the context of a large body of evidence from the United States and elsewhere suggesting that taken as a whole, mergers add little or no value." But as far as stockholders are concerned, "The implication is that mergers do add value, that the merged concern is, on average, valued more highly than is the sum of the two merging companies. On average, the whole of that gain goes to the shareholders of the company that is acquired." But what of the acquisition? "Its average pattern is one of under performance: a portfolio of newly merged companies can be expected to do worse than the market."[19]

Of joint ventures; "General Motors, for example, responded to the demand for small cars by establishing a joint venture with Toyota at Fremont, California. But many of these joint ventures have so far mostly fallen short of their founders' expectations."

Envelopment

General MacArthur said, "The deep envelopment based on surprise which severs the enemy's supply lines, is and always has been the most decisive manoeuvre of war."

In business, it might consist of a product design and pricing strategy in which each price level commensurate with consumer demand for heavy purchases would be accommodated by a specific product designed for their particular needs. Ford has used that product strategy for many years as opposed to the mass production of the mass market "Tin Lizzie" that put them in business. A satisfied Ford purchaser in the past does not have to switch brands to buy what he or she wants: an automobile salesperson in a Ford dealership can easily sell up to a bigger model or down to a more economical one.

The same situation would apply to a first-time buyer of a major domestic appliance, for example, in the case of the General Electric brand. There would be a model to suit every household's need and budget. But it is a manoeuvre that only a very big organization can afford to use or implement to maximum effect, and it can strain their resources and present considerable risks when an economy declines. Smaller forces can cut supply lines, but it requires larger forces to outflank and encircle an enemy.

Isolation

Isolation can avoid unnecessary bloodshed by avoiding direct conflict. A business enterprise can, similarly, avoid confrontation by isolating a market niche that has been neglected by larger competitors who thought it too small or too specialized.

Darwin discovered that niches are precisely what survival is all about. He had long formulated the idea that a bloody struggle was continuously acted out in Nature, giving rise to the mechanism of natural selection as the driving force for evolution. The same thing applied to the Industrial Revolution, in which Darwin could see another force: the need for the division of labor, the filling of niches in society, the principle that an industry can succeed only if a need is there or one can be created for it. *Nature lent strength to species which fitted those niches.*[20] Those best fitted for each niche are like a key designed to turn a lock to open a door or a piece designed to fit into a jigsaw puzzle. "Any individual that could exploit a vacant niche in nature would be successful, Darwin realized, like an entrepreneur who identified a gap in the economic market place and moved into it."

A dominant design or its modified offspring is one that has become adapted to niches in the economy. That is the niche strategy, and it generally means choosing a niche that has been overlooked or purposely avoided. According to Porter, that is often because firms would need to improve and upgrade to satisfy "the most sophisticated and demanding buyers and channels; (to) seek out the buyers with the most difficult needs; (to) establish norms of exceeding the toughest regulatory hurdles or product standards; (to) source from the most advanced and international home-based suppliers; (and) establish outstanding competitors as motivators."[21]

Any of those decisions oblige a firm to improve to meet the needs of discriminating and knowledgeable customers. "They become part of a firm's R&D program," by challenging the firm to upgrade its employees, its products, processes and services, and to compete *differently* from other competitors while at least meeting their standards.

Information

Of the three great obstacles to victory referred to by von Clausewitz and van Creveld, we have examined the inflexibility of big organizations and friction arising from unforeseen hazards. The third is uncertainty.

Moltke said, "Of the three courses the enemy can take normally he selects the fourth."

Even with inside information, which is one of the five different types of intelligence gathering employed by Sun Tzu, historian Arnold Toynbee was skeptical. He wrote, "The unpredictability of the outcome of encounters between persons is a familiar datum of experience. A military expert cannot predict the outcome of a battle or a campaign from an 'inside knowledge' of the dispositions and resources of both the opposing general staffs, or a bridge expert the outcome of a game or a rubber from a similar knowledge of all the cards in every hand."[22]

Sun Tzu sought intelligence from local inhabitants as well as an enemy's own officials, turned enemy agents into double agents, spread disinformation about his intentions, falsified reports, and planted his own undercover agents. Although he appears to have been just as skeptical as Toynbee, he evidently possessed a spiral mind and subtle ways of implementing his plans, so that he achieved victory by circuitous means. In short, he was not only an innovative strategist but also an entrepreneurial general who knew precisely how to use with maximum effect the information he obtained.

Business organizations are fortunate in that they do not have to limit themselves to incomplete information. Nor do they need to be unduly cautious about possibilities of disinformation. They can choose from any number of research companies, each one specializing in different types of research corresponding with Sun Tzu's methodology. They also enjoy the advantage of information gathered by industry associations, government surveys, media or independent polls, and research that their advertising agencies may have compiled for them. And since western managers and staff habitually move from one company to another, business enterprises are even supplied with inside information about competitors without having to resort to industrial espionage.

Robots and Human Minds

While the marvels of the technological revolution are indisputable, a mistaken belief that they are a management panacea would merely reveal ignorance of what professional management is and what marketing practices can achieve. Management must recognize that however sophisticated the business technology, it is still only a tool to get things done quicker, more accurately, or more cost-effectively. When the novelty of office and workshop equipment has worn off, managers will have to return to the fundamentals of running a business in an imaginative and intelligent way; ideating, creating, making astute judgements, and leading by making appropriate decisions.

It is true that new opportunities for interactive marketing will arise from the use of electronic information systems and computer technology. New scanning technologies and smartcards can now provide customers' names and purchases almost instantly. Even whether a customer purchased a product or not after receiving a free sample, can be ascertained. "The unit of measure in the marketing future will be the lifetime value of each customer to the firm."[23]

A database of transaction histories of customers will be the primary marketing resource for many organizations. Marketing would therefore require competence in database management, statistical modelling, marketing to an installed base, and accountancy skills.

The ability to obtain direct purchasing data will make many current applications of marketing research obsolete in future, say some theorists. Some popular research techniques of surveys and observational studies to assess purchasing and frequency behavior may become meaningless compared to obtaining real data on real customer behavior through electronic information systems, if it is possible to reach a market of one customer at a time, say others.[24] Perhaps; but that does not take prospective new customers into consideration, except as another theoretical model. And as for developing existing customers, business people have been analyzing their customer records since business began.

There is a danger that companies may rely on technology instead of planning and managing suitable strategies and tactics in the workplace and in markets. Although robotics have replaced human workforces on assembly lines, in warehouses, banks, and some offices, robots cannot manage a business enterprise. Van Creveld reminds us that strategy is derived from the Greek word *stratos,* which means an army; and *tactics* comes from the Greek word for order—since it is the function of ensuring orderly slaughter in battle to achieve the best possible outcome. And although smart wartime technology seems to have eliminated the need for massive troop movements to obliterate enemies and cities, ground troops are still needed to capture territories. And they are needed in business to decimate competitors who encroach on one's own markets.

Strategic Principles

Why is there such a close affinity between business and military strategies? No doubt because both involve human behavior patterns in those who plan strategies, in those who implement them, and in those who defend their territory.

Human beings are territorial animals whose survival has always depended on defending tribal lands and on territorial expansion when they had reached their limit of supplies. Expansion of trade once went hand in hand with annexing territories or colonizing them. Now that there is some kind of general stability of national boundaries, international trade is considered to be more profitable than maintaining standing armies, competing in arms and armor, and suffering from the disadvantages of mass destruction and loss of lives. Human, financial, material, and territorial resources are now put to use with similar ingenuity to obtain economic victories instead of political or military ones.

We examined the effectiveness of the Five Cardinal Criteria for Victory, defined from Sun Tzu's *Art Of War.* Other famous military strategists have sound advice to offer us, too. A study of von Clausewitz's book *On War* leads us to consider, in particular, his chapter on the theory of war. We can extract from out of it, Eighteen Vital Principles of Combat. They are: adequate information, goal-orientation, initiative, concentration of resources, manoeuvrability, economy, co-ordinating resources, security, surprise, simple objectives, simple systems, simple instructions, avoiding complexity, technological or other innovations, internal organization, adaptability, mobility, and speed.

Every one of those principles is essential to win battles for markets and expand global market share. The speed of events taking place around us forces us to adapt to circumstances much faster than ever before if we are to survive. We must anticipate them and pre-plan for eventualities. That is where the comparison between business and warfare ceases: most businesses have lagged behind military events when it comes to speed and mobility. We too have to deter encroachment on our markets by preemptive strikes. That takes far more and more precise, and more frequent research. And the results of continuous market appraisals will oblige us to be ready to act. That is only possible if we already possess a trained and skilful management team and workforce.

Machiavelli described the disastrous consequences for those too frivolous, inept, or complacent, to heed his advice. Although he wrote the following warning to the Medici rulers in the sixteenth century, if we substitute the word *market* for state, and replace war with *strategy*, we too may find it full of relevant meaning:

> The best way to win a state is to be skilled in the art of war. The best way to lose it is to neglect the art of war.... Therefore a Prince must have no other objective or thought, nor acquire skill in anything but war, its organization and discipline. The art of war is all that is expected of a ruler...princes who thought more of pleasure than arms, lost their states.[25]

But the reality of business management as practiced by most companies today in the West more closely resembles the absence of essential information, lack of strategic planning, failure in tactical skills, purposelessness, and insufficient sense of locality or timing, as described of the civil war in England:

> Modern soldiers have noticed as one of the most curious features of the civil war how ignorant each side usually was of the doing, position, and design of its opponents. Essex stumbled upon the king, Hopton stumbled upon Waller, the king stumbled upon Sir Thomas Fairfax. The two sides drew up in front of one another, foot in the center, horse on the wings; and then they fell to and hammered one another as hard as they could, and they who hammered hardest and stood to it longest won the day.[26]

5

Satisfying Customers

The *Harvard Business Review* published a paper in 1960 entitled "Marketing Myopia" which was written by Theodore Levitt. Some considered his approach to business to be revolutionary at that time. The paper was reprinted as a chapter in a book he wrote two years later entitled *Innovation In Marketing*. He made two significant remarks in his preface: "A strictly sales-oriented approach to doing business can be suicidal"; and "The difference between selling and marketing is selling focuses on the needs of the seller, marketing on the needs of the buyer."

The first is like an echo of military strategist Frunze's statement that "those who are merely defensive are doomed to defeat." His second is an excellent definition of a marketing-oriented management discipline.

Although the connection between Levitt's remark and Frunze's statement may appear to be obtuse, they have in common the fact that making a sale is solely a one-off, short-term action to meet a sales goal. It has nothing to do with long-range profitability or survival in the long term. And defending a position is also merely a short-term objective. After both activities, another one is required to avoid failure, defeat, or suicide. In business, a proper marketing plan must be formulated and implemented, while in battle an offensive attack must be planned and put into effect—otherwise the status remains undecided.

Levitt's definition of marketing is important also because it is difficult to convince managers from disciplines other than marketing precisely what marketing is and does. At the time he wrote that article, management was still in an era of telling sales people not to make excuses for poor results, but to "get out and sell," instead of themselves providing the right product for the right market, at the right time and price. Management may even have believed that selling *is* marketing, and vice-versa—because even today, many recruitment advertisements in newspapers ask for marketing people when what they are really seeking is people to prospect for sales.

Two years after *Innovation In Marketing* was published, Charles St. Thomas was writing, "Marketing is a way of managing a business so that each critical business decision (those critical decisions made by engineering people, by manufacturing people, by financial people, and so forth) is made with a full and prior knowledge of the impact of that decision on the customer." And, "If we view marketing as *the orientation of the total business to the customer,* we find actually that business is returning to a way of operation that it has known for the past 150 years.... Consider the early entrepreneurs, with their general stores, blacksmith shops and harness-making factories. The proprietors of those businesses really knew their customers, and they were aware of their true needs and wants because they were constantly and intimately associated with them."[1]

The pebble had been dropped in the pool in 1954 when Peter Drucker wrote, "The purpose of a business is to create a customer."[2] Five years later, the ripples moved Levitt to write, "The primary business of every business is to stay in business. And to do that you have to get and keep customers. This is usually interpreted to mean that you have to sell what you have.... This just isn't so."

He wrote at a time when the post-war economy in Britain looked as if it would never recover and the best brains were emigrating. The United States wasn't doing any better. Paradoxically, South Africa was enjoying an economic boom. Meanwhile, Levitt wrote these words from America: "The reason growth is threatened, slowed, or stopped is not because the market is saturated. It is because there has been a failure of management. The failure is at the top.... The railroads did not stop growing because the need for passenger and freight transportation declined. That grew. The railroads are in trouble today not because the need was filled by others (cars, trucks, aeroplanes, even telephones) but because it was not filled by the railroads themselves. They let others take customers away from them because they assumed themselves to be in the railroad business rather than in the transportation business. The reason they defined their industry incorrectly was because they were railroad-oriented instead of transportation-oriented; they were product-oriented instead of customer-oriented."

He went on to describe a similar fate of other industries that had defined too narrowly the business they were in. Hollywood thought it was in the movie business when really it was in the entertainment business. By a wrong perception of their own business purpose, they saw TV as a threat, when they should have embraced it as an opportunity for expansion. In other words, they were not oriented toward satisfying their customers' needs.

We are well aware of advances in high-technology today. But over thirty years ago, Levitt typified high-technology as a short-sighted and product-oriented industry that was not directed primarily to satisfying customers' needs. He wrote, "Another big danger to a firm's continued growth arises when top management is wholly transfixed by the profit possibilities of technical research and development. To illustrate I shall turn first to a new industry—electronics.... Having created a successful company by making a superior product, it is not surprising that management continues to be oriented towards the product rather than the people who consume it." He went on to explain that because the high-technology industry was so complex, they had to hire an abundance of engineers and scientists who looked upon their jobs as "making things" instead of satisfying customer needs. Selling the product, to them, was something that someone else did when their job was finished. They had no conception of building the marketing into their products from the very beginning—as GE proclaimed was its policy ten years earlier.

Since engineers are oriented toward products that they make, they prefer to deal with concrete things like machines, assembly lines, and balance sheets. They are generally unaware of the realities of the marketplace and don't *want* to know about anything unpredictable like customers or sales people or competitors' marketing strategies or in-store tactics, or what advertising can and cannot do, pricing strategies, or the economic climate. They like to stick to what they know and what they can control.

Levitt pointed to the high-tech industry as being a prime example of what any efficient and sophisticated business organization should *not* do.

What horrified him in the United States in 1962 was repeated in Canada in 1980. Some eighteen years after the American electronics industry had revealed its insularity and inflexibility, British high-tech engineers arrived in Canada and opened up new business enterprises in Kanata (part of metropolitan Ottawa). Their location in the Ottawa Valley inevitably became known as Silicon Valley. And there they showed the same type of insularity and inflexibility as their American counterparts nearly a generation earlier. They seemed to have learned nothing from the American experience, or the British one in the 1970s.

Fortunately for them, the baby-boom generation was then at the right point in its life cycle to be able to afford high technology, and that was the main consumer group that had impulse-buying tendencies for novelties. Fortunately too, military markets were guaranteed by armed forces that are continually obliged to modernize their technology. And it was a boon to a civil service which always seeks to justify increased expenditures for which it has obtained annual budget approvals. Smaller high-tech firms did, however, meet more customized institutional needs in the medical profession and in research.

The perceived glamour of the industry and the anticipated affluence of its top managers encouraged builders and developers to buy residential and commercial land in Kanata, and build luxury homes for the high-tech yuppies, close to their new offices and factories. New business enterprises boasted annually that they had doubled their sales and profits—which is not at all difficult for new companies starting up from scratch. It created a similar illusion to that of the famous South Sea Bubble.

Close examination revealed that most Silicon Valley companies were very small enterprises consisting of four to six employees making components for another company's hardware. Few if any were as big as Mitel, which began in

Kanata and is now one of the leading telecommunications companies in Canada, Britain, and the U.S.

The high-tech seminar at the Chateau Laurier Hotel in Ottawa in 1981 revealed the cracks in the facade of the electronics industry. Some speakers found it difficult to hide their concern about the viability of the industry and sounded rueful about the confusion in their own companies. The moment of truth came when most had reached the limits of the capacity of their particular market niche. Dramatic claims and optimistic forecasts ceased. The high-tech bubble burst. Spec homes in Kanata were left unsold when builders closed down their sales offices and moved away.

Most or all of those companies had been started up by spirited entrepreneurs who were electronics engineers without experience of marketing or management. Their intelligence made them overconfident and their enthusiasm for their products deluded them into believing they did not need specialists from outside the industry. Those that were undercapitalized couldn't afford marketing consultants. What was needed was a government funded scheme to assist them in strategic planning, quality management, and marketing. Experienced marketing people could have told them that a product, however good, is merely a valueless mix of materials if there is insufficient demand for it.

That type of small entrepreneurial business that is not entirely oriented toward the needs of consumers, but instead in love with its products and its technology, is typical of the monumental corporate and personal bankruptcy statistics.

Customer Orientation

The following list of key marketing elements is fundamental to running a business enterprise. Its purpose is to show the difference in attitudes and approach to running a business, depending on whether a company is oriented to customer needs or to its own fixed merchandise buying policy. It exemplifies Levitt's contention that selling focuses on the needs of the seller, whereas marketing concerns itself with satisfying the needs of the customer.

The way they are used to illustrate that difference is adapted from a similar chart published in *The Canadian Retailer* in 1984. Although it was aimed at the retail trade, it offers a meaningful message to every type of industry that requires customers in order to survive.

1. *Who are the customers you target to supply?*
- Product-Oriented: "People who typically buy our kind of merchandise."
- Customer-Oriented: "When we last researched customer needs, we found a niche in the home furnishings market which was not being adequately filled; wives of busy young executives and professionals age 30 to 38 who recently achieved some kind of success and can now

afford an improved lifestyle. Although both partners want elegant modern designs they have to meet heavy mortgage payments on their new home, so we target for a medium price range."

2. Who are your competitors?
- Product-Oriented: "All other stores selling our kind of merchandise".
- Customer-Oriented: "Out of 102 furniture and furnishing companies in the city (excluding department stores because our type of customers rarely shop there) there are eleven catering for our targeted customers. But we check out their merchandise and prices regularly to ensure that we are competitive. All the other dealers cater to different age groups, tastes, or price ranges."

3. What are your strategic objectives?
- Product-Oriented: "To sell more goods than last year."
- Customer-Oriented: "Last year we achieved 7.8 percent market share in the modern and contemporary segment. This year's target is 8.5 percent share at the same average profit margin (taking price increases into consideration as well as inflation). We plan to be more aggressive in our long-term strategy to create an insulated and competitive position in the marketplace."

4. What are your Competitive advantages?
- Product-Oriented: "We'll beat all competition on all factors in all merchandise categories."
- Customer-Oriented: "We will be able to make more compelling offers of exclusive fabrics of the type our customers keep asking for but are not made locally".

5. What time frame do you plan for?
- Product-Oriented: "Next merchandising season compared to same season in the previous year."
- Customer-oriented: "We calendar to meet peak periods of customer demand with new merchandise, and promote to stimulate the quieter periods in between."

6. What is your principle planning vehicle?
- Product-oriented: "Seasonal update of annual merchandise."
- Customer-oriented: "Annual update of short-range and long-term marketing plans to meet changing needs in the marketplace."

7. What does your merchandise assortment consist of?
- Product-oriented: "Representative current styles, fabrics,colors and brands, and so forth."

- Customer-oriented: "Sufficient choice and selection to meet the needs of our market niche, and also to expand it."

8. *What is your pricing policy?*
- Product-oriented: "To maximize gross margin while seeking competitive parity."
- Customer-oriented: "To establish price points that optimize demand from our market niche and also broaden it."

9. *What is your advertising strategy?*
- Product-oriented: "To show products and prices of merchandise we have in stock, to create store traffic, and meet last year's sales in the same calendar month."
- Customer-oriented: "To communicate exciting new fabrics and furniture, also to reinforce our market position on the basis of good taste, exclusive but affordable materials, reliability and good personal service from qualified interior decorators."

10. *What is the objective for your store design and presentation?*
- Product-oriented: "To provide a stage for the merchandise."
- Customer-oriented: "To offer customers an enjoyable shopping experience in relaxing and professional surroundings, with products displayed to encourage and facilitate shopping, so that customers don't feel pressurized."

11. *What is your store manager's responsibility?*
- Product-oriented: "To maintain the store, supervise people, and sell merchandise."
- Customer-oriented: "His experience qualifies him to meet company and store objectives, and to ensure that customers are completely satisfied and likely to return with friends."

12. *What is your role in stocking merchandise?*
- Product-oriented: "We are like a selling agent for our suppliers."
- Customer-oriented: "We are really purchasing agents for our customers."

13. *What is your business orientation?*
- Product-oriented: "Oriented to merchandise coming in the back door."
- Customer-oriented: "Oriented to customers coming in the front door."

14. *What is your purchasing policy?*
- Product-oriented: "To obtain merchandise at competitive prices."
- Customer-oriented: "To create and market seductive lifestyles."

Those typical product-oriented situations indicate that retailers do not study their competitors enough, on an ongoing basis. Nor do merchandise managers address themselves sufficiently to customer needs. They either take advice from suppliers—which should be treated with caution—or feel a sense of achievement only when they are able to purchase "bargains." One of the saddest sights is a warehouse piled high with old bargains that no one will buy, and to hear the buyer or the owner say (again), "Don't worry—I'll get my price." The faulty bargain instinct arises from a buyer using his purely personal tastes instead of the customer's, or being blinded by his ego in the belief that he knows better. No one knows better than a customer what a customer wants.

Another common error is making erroneous conclusions about store offtake. The offtake of items for which there was insufficient stock in the first place will appear to show that there was little demand, when in fact the demand was high but could not be fulfilled with existing inventory. Every shopper knows the frustration of not being able to find a specific product that was excellent, because it has been discontinued. Decorators suffer the same frustration when they shop for colors and patterns in great demand by their clients, only to find out that the manufacturer has withdrawn those very ones. Those situations have worsened since computerization of inventories. It suggests that a buyer who could not interpret supply and demand situations from a simple cardex file won't know how to interpret a computer printout properly either.

There is no substitute for keeping in touch personally with customers and the marketplace on a continuing basis.

Another common problem is that management is often happy if branches meet last year's sales figures for the same calendar month, or 5 percent more if that is this year's sales target. But if the inflation rate was 5.4 percent or 15.4 percent, price increases of merchandise are likely to be at least that; resulting in an erosion of sales. Moreover, a branch manager has no way of knowing if consumer demand for his or her type of merchandise has actually increased by 24 percent or more, or less, because sales volumes for that store are unlikely to tell the manager by how much consumer demand actually increased in his or her marketplace. The only way to do that would be by continuous market research and establishing a benchmark in one year, so that gains or losses in market share could be measured against it. A manufacturer may be in a better position to analyze unit production or unit sales, but its annual sales objectives would be meaningless without knowing the size of its market and how it is growing or shrinking.

Considering the broad spectrum of erroneous attitudes arising from product orientation, or administration-orientation, or production or sales-orientation, it could be useful to be able to analyze individual reasons for business failures. We know that the most common reason for failure is generally considered to be undercapitalization, but the facts are very different: they show that only 3 percent of failures were due to financial problems. Failures due to poor management and lack of marketing skills, on the other hand, were 90 percent, according to Dun & Bradstreet.[3] Misconceptions are likely to stem from reasons given by entrepreneurs who do not possess management or marketing skills and often don't know why they failed or don't wish to admit their lack of capacity. It is so much easier to blame banks or government.

Empirical observations over time may suggest that about 60 percent of those failures could be due to both poor management and lack of marketing skills, and 40 percent to inferior management alone, but there is no accurate way to separate management from marketing. Together they may even be described as business acumen.

Customer orientation means, by definition, that management concentrates on finding out what its customers want, all the time, and provides it. But there are all kinds of customers shopping in any market, and different shoppers want to buy different things, or different types of the same thing, or different kinds of services. They therefore patronize different stores catering for different tastes or needs.

The following chart shows what single factor or bundle of factors motivate different demographic segments of a community to patronize certain types of retail business enterprises. The percentage shown for each specific group of buyers and the consumer criteria—and also the types of available stores meeting each criterion—relate to a specific market at a specific time. They would, therefore, be quite different in other places at different times. The product surveyed was domestic furniture.[4]

Income Segment:	Customer Criteria:	Shopping Venue:
Top 5%:	Exclusivity:	• Interior decorators • Exclusive fashion stores • Antique shops
Upper 25%:	Current fashions: Prestige: Enjoyable shopping experience: Style:	• Stores carrying fashionable ranges • Smarter department stores • Specialized stores
Upper-Middle 40%:	Brand names: Service: Quality: Range: Value: Reliability: Convenience:	• Better chain stores • Department stores
Lower-Middle 20%:	Price: Value:	• Family store • Price-competitive chain stores • Discount stores
Lower 7 %:	Bargains:	• Surplus warehouse stores • Price-competitive chain stores • Department store bargain basements
Bottom 3 %:	Used furniture:	• Second-hand stores

It is evident that different types of shoppers buy from different stores for a different reason or for a bundle of different reasons. For example, the top income group shown in that chart is not concerned about price when it comes to furnishing their home in style. But in other product categories, like electric appliances, they may seek out a wholesaler or discount store. There is also an assumption that they will automatically obtain good service and quality from their expensive interior decorating store. On the other hand, the upper-middle income group is concerned about value, which relates to price but is not solely price oriented. The lower-middle group is also concerned about value, but largely as it relates to price.

Those patronage motives apply to retail stores offering high-ticket items—specifically furniture and furnishings—where selling is required. The following patronage motives apply to other types of stores, mostly offering convenience and impulse items, where the pattern differs.

Patronage Motives

The following examples consist of three different types of store creating nine different types of shopping experience (figure 5.1):

- *Convenience Stores:* Stores chosen by a consumer for their accessibility rather than a need for a specific product or brand.

FIGURE 5.1
Shopping Matrix

CONVENIENCE STORES	SHOPPING STORES	SPECIALTY STORES
1 Convenience goods Impulse buying	4 Convenience goods Impulse buying	7 Convenience goods Impulse buying
2 Shopping for goods	5 Shopping for goods	8 Shopping for goods
3 Special goods or specific brand Selective shopping	6 Special goods or specific brand Selective shopping	9 Special goods or specific brand Selective shopping

- *Shopping Stores:* Those at which a consumer wishes to choose a specific product unlikely to be stocked at her local convenience store, but doesn't know which type or which brand to buy without searching for it.
- *Specialty Stores:* Stores chosen specifically when a consumer prefers to buy a special brand or specific item—even if it is not at the most accessible store.

Definitions:

1. Convenience:	When a customer prefers to go to the most accessible store and buy the most readily available brand.
2. Planned Shopping:	When a customer selects purchases from goods carried by the most accessible store with varied stocks.
3. Specialty:	When a customer selects a favorite brand from the most accessible store that stocks it.
4. Shopping Around:	When a customer is indifferent to the brand and shops various stores for better prices or better service.
5. Comparison Shopping:	When a customer makes comparisons between stores and brands before deciding what and where to buy.
6. Brand Loyalty:	When a customer is loyal to a brand but shops various stores for best prices for that brand or better service.
7. Store Preference:	When a customer prefers a specific store but is indifferent to the brand of the goods purchased.
8. Indecision:	When a customer is loyal to a store but is uncertain what to buy and examines items for the best purchase.
9. Decisive Buying:	When a customer chooses a particular store for preference and a specific brand of goods.

Shopping Malls

Women have long been considered to be the most ardent shoppers except in the case of essentially masculine items. Apart from the pleasure in acquiring new possessions, women in particular found shopping to be an entertainment in itself. Large shopping malls were intended to improve the entertainment value and facilitate shopping by enabling customers to buy everything under one roof, indeed under cover in all weather conditions, with an abundance of parking space outside or beneath the mall. They were intended to be modern or innovated "department stores." But other factors have intruded since then.

Security became a costly item that was not well enough attended to. Many teenage women shoppers are intimidated by gangs of youths who haunt some shopping malls. A tendency of independent entrepreneurs to rent space in malls and then have their stores managed by inexperienced youngsters reduces the value of shopping in places where better service is expected by discriminating customers. An increasing number of automobiles resulted in limited parking in some shopping malls and a struggle by shoppers to find space. The cost of shopping in downtown malls is generally higher; in part because of pricing to offset higher rents, and also because of parking costs in some malls. And the size and layouts of bigger malls require customers to walk long distances and take up valuable time searching for purchases.

Perhaps the most important factor mitigating against the intended convenience of shopping malls is that as more and more women enter the workforce, establish careers, or open their own business, they have less time for shopping. Shopping in malls has now become a costly annoyance for some people.

The dramatic success of Dell Computer has caused retailers to take another look at selling by mail, ironically at a time when Sears—the doyen of mail-order firms—decided to terminate the mail-order catalogue that put them in business as Sears-Roebuck. But it also took thousands of corporate bankruptcies in the recession of the 1990s to make luxurious stores, sales offices, and shopping malls appear to be obsolete. Michael Dell dispenses with such overhead costs as rents or mortgages, store managers, and floor salespeople, stock rooms, or warehouses. Dell successfully sells their computers by mail. Since they also work on small profit margins, that enables them to pass on considerable savings to customers and drum up more business.[5]

Computers themselves hastened the process of obtaining the right information to provide the right inventory at the right time in the right place, and at lower costs. Wal-Mart has exploited that formula to the detriment of traditional retailers like Sears. Appropriate information from the marketplace is accelerated directly to the manufacturers who supply Wal-Mart with what their customers want. Overhead costs are cut. And when Wal-Mart benefits from reduced costs they wisely ensure that their customers do too. Other retailers are reducing their end prices of goods or services by reducing costs in similar ways.

The consumer revolution is based squarely on factors that have always motivated shoppers—ease, speed, and affordability. Consumerism demands that retailers make their shopping more efficient, more pleasant, and more cost effective.

According to the *Nilson Report,* U.S. shoppers purchased $2 billion worth of goods *from their homes* by credit card or cheque in 1992. That showed an increase (after inflation) of 30 percent over 1988. The size of the drop in purchases from shopping centers in the same period accounted for over half of that figure. Home purchases by Visa Card doubled between 1988 and 1992 to $17.6 billion (after inflation). 3.5 million U.S. consumers used on-line computers to shop at home. Sales from catalogue stores amounted to $50 billion in 1991—up by 14 percent from 1987. 102 million U.S. customers bought at least one item from a catalogue in 1992.

All of that arose from an increase in information. Wrote *Forbes Magazine* on 24 May 1993, "The barriers to good information are crashing down. Thanks to the proliferation of buying services, catalogues and consumer product guides, shoppers need no longer leave home to gather information. It's available by mail, phone, computer or on television."

The World Wide Web is supposed to lead us into the information age via the InterNet. But, apart from a group of compulsive users, who may not be buyers, who will use it to buy goods and services by credit card? More than a billion customers by the year 2005, according to the former publisher of *Business Technology Solutions*. But at the close of 1995, a record company in Melbourne, Australia, claimed that although 8,000 people a day visited his online store, they just browsed around and he made only six sales a week. Another Australian entrepreneur described the Web as like owning a supermarket at a busy intersection, to which people drift aimlessly in and out and buy little of anything. But those were early days, and one inhibiting factor to overcome was the possibility of a customer's credit card number being picked up by anyone.

Meanwhile, nearly half of high income North Americans own PCs, but no one knows the exact number of InterNet users worldwide. We were invited to choose any number between seven million and thirty million. Whichever happens to be close to reality, the age of convenient electronic shopping has arrived.

Does that mean shopping malls will empty and become "ghost towns," main street stores will be deserted, and property developers will be registering for bankruptcy in droves? Anyone's guess will do as far as futurism is concerned. "Don't consumers like to see, touch and smell goods they're thinking of buying?" asked *Forbes Magazine*. Their answer: "Of course they do, which is why stores will never disappear entirely. But note this: The store is fast becoming a place where people kick the tires, lift the lid on a washing machine or listen to the sound of a stereo speaker—and then go home and call an (800) number to order the same item at a discount."[6]

Chain Stores versus Department Stores

From 1986 to 1987 independent household furniture stores' sales in Canada grew by 19.1 percent while domestic furniture sales in chain stores grew by only 8.7 percent. Similar sales in department stores grew by only 7.7 percent. That was partly due to the establishment image of department stores, which had turned off younger buyers ever since the 1960s. Moreover, independent stores tended to be more entrepreneurial, closer to their customers, and more flexible and adaptable to customers' needs. Bigger organizations tended to deal with suppliers instead of focusing on customer needs, but there were exceptions; in Canada there was the success of Leon's, a large chain store; also The Brick, which aimed its merchandise at young, single buyers; and Ikea, which tailored all its products to the dimensions, styles, and bank accounts of young couples, as well.

By 1996, however, it could be predicted with some possibility of accuracy that the decline of department stores might be stemmed and reversed because of the aging populations in North America and Europe. If department stores can convincingly demonstrate the advantages of shopping under one roof to older customers and the infirm or disabled, they could exploit the benefits and ensure they market appropriate assortments of products and services. After reaching a certain age, older shoppers may consider malls to be far too spread out, obliging them to walk too far from store to store and stay away from their home for longer periods than they might wish.

Psychological Types

Business managers need to understand the diversity of types of people and their different needs and approaches to buying, since the essence of marketing is defining a company's prospective customers and their particular motivations, before designing a product or service to fulfil their needs and wants.

Psychologist Carl Jung recognized the significance of the signs of the zodiac and also the symbols of the Tarot pack of cards as psychological archetypes that may influence the unconscious mind. Some business organizations use sun signs as part of their methodology to select managers, among other criteria. Sixteenth-century doctors treated their patients according to a perception of the links between four different personality characteristics, known as *humours,* and the four elements. The Phlegmatic were linked to earth; Melancholic to water; Sanguine to air; and Choleric to fire. That division of human types was derived from the ancient Greeks, who believed that the elements interacted throughout nature and through human beings, always seeking equilibrium.

A knowledge of human nature is essential to a manager who needs to be effective in selecting or motivating and monitoring people. Markinor's eight categories, listed previously, appear to be the most useful consumer segments for marketing purposes. But there are others for different purposes.

One name that comes easily to mind, among behavioral scientists, is the psychologist Abraham Maslow. His well-known theory is called the "Hierarchy of Needs." It is based on an assumption that as each need of a lower (animal or primitive) order—like hunger or thirst—becomes satisfied, then the next level of needs determines a person's behavior. His six sequential needs were categorized as follows:

1. *Physiological needs*:   • thirst, hunger, sex
2. *Safety needs*:   • shelter, health, security
3. *Belonging*:   • identification, affection, affiliation
4. *Ego needs*:   • esteem, success, prestige, self-respect
5. *Self-actualization*:   • self-fulfillment, personal growth

Maslow's name is frequently linked with Herzberg's "Dual Factor Theory," which is something quite different: it purports to show the link between certain needs and job performance. It identifies two basic job dimensions—the condition surrounding a task, and the task itself.

Another behavioral scientist is Clare Graves, who designed a seven-tier hierarchical model of needs, not greatly different otherwise from Maslow's five-tier model. It ranges in sequences from the extreme primitive person to the most highly cultured of individuals. Those categories—from the bottom or first level up—are Reactive, Tribalistic, Egocentric, Conformist, Manipulative, Sociocentric, and Existential.

At the most primitive level, people react to events by instinct, like animals. They have little or no thought of the consequences of their actions. Typical examples are spontaneous violence in prison riots, labor strikes, in sports arenas, and race riots. A more developed or mature person learns how to make choices. That type of individual has more self-control and also control of outside events. Those people know they are able to make choices from a range of different types of behavior, and they can also adapt to change. At a higher level, they become responsible, civilized human beings and consider the consequences of their actions, and other people's. Reason plays a greater and greater role at upper levels of the hierarchy where people are more mature and further and further removed from obsessions with purely animal needs. At still higher levels they form their own opinions in a rational and knowledgeable way, and are also prepared to voice them. At the highest level of personal development, their self-confidence may make them harder to deal with, if a manager is not himself a mature and cultivated person, accustomed to debating both facts and theories in a logical and reasonable manner.

Ideal Companies

Organizations have different cultural and philosophic outlooks, just like people do. The "excellent companies" is a description used for those business organizations that are so well structured and managed that they are the ones most likely to weather the ups and downs in the marketplace, and in economies, and still grow according to plan. But some of those companies once described as excellent went on to perform with less than excellent results, and some others showed extraordinarily poor judgement or poor results. It is therefore safer to refer to the high standards we expect of them by referring in future to *ideal* companies.

One such company that generations of consumers once admired for its excellence was J Lyons & Company of Britain. It was once the biggest caterer in Europe. The Lyons family began by opening tea shops throughout every major city in England. They were known for their cleanliness, the quality of their products, and the cheerful and helpful service of their waitresses, who were all dressed primly and fetchingly as parlor maids. Lyons made and cooked all its own excellent products. It was the excellence of Lyons tea shops that created public confidence in eating out, and it stimulated the opening and success of other cafés and restaurants.

So successful were their tearooms and their products that in the course of time they also opened a Lyons Corner House in each of the main cities. They were grandiose department stores specializing in the sales of their own foodstuffs, and each contained a very large restaurant which, in some cities, was open all night. The public could enjoy not only a late night meal, but also music from the palm court orchestra. They marketed over 40,000 products.

Not only did they bake their elegant cakes for sale in their Corner Houses, but they continued to provide simple and cheap fare in their tearooms, like baked beans on toast or Welsh-rarebit and a pot of Lyons tea. They also marketed packaged products like Lyons tea and coffee. And they managed the catering for the armed forces. So great was their national payroll that Lyons was among the first companies in Britain to install massive computers in their London head office. Those monsters were proudly displayed in a row of store windows along a main street in Hammersmith. They employed 30,000 people.

Lyons played an important role in the history of Britain. But it possessed one problem—nepotism. Since it wished to remain a family business for the benefit of future generations, it established, in its articles of association, that only family members could be company directors.

Many business organizations have discovered to their cost that families develop in all kinds of unexpected ways that can be harmful to a business enterprise. Some are disinterested in business, while others are temperamentally unsuited for the industry. Some are not competent in business, and some others are involved in a different vocation. Managers and directors who have no empathy for an industry or a company are unlikely to contribute stimulating ideas or manage that company well. So it was with Lyons; and good managers who were not members of the family left to join companies that offered them a career path. And other good managers did not join them. The Lyons empire suffered as a consequence. And although they attempted to make the necessary changes in the 1970s, it was too late to catch up with the rest of the world.

Eventually reorganized and opened up to new management and ideas and taken over by Allied, they became Allied-Lyons. More recently, they became the highly innovative and successful Allied-Domecq.

In 1972, Rosebeth Moss Kanter published a book called *Commitment and Community*. She described the utopian industrial societies of the companies Amana (a major domestic appliance manufacturer) and Oneida (a tableware manufacturer), and other similar types of companies that became successful. One of the significant aspects in those communities was the equality of influence and power in the workplace. They were examples of ideal companies. But as we shall see, they were merely part of a bigger trend that had been developing in Japan since the 1950s.

Perhaps the best known writer on the best and the worst types of business organizations is Douglas McGregor. His "Theory X and Theory Y" makes certain assumptions about human nature in both management and the workforce. He himself was influenced directly by Professor Argyris at Harvard University. Argyris published a book in New York in 1964 on *Integrating the Individual and the Organization*. He believed that "motivation in work will be maximal when each worker pursues individual goals and experiences psychological growth and independence."

Each writer on the management of a business, since Drucker produced *The Practice of Management* ten years earlier, has clearly acted as a catalyst for others. Drucker wrote something similar but confined it to management, while Argyris extended the theory to workers. He even went further by arguing that close supervision diminishes motivation, prevents psychological growth, and frustrates personal independence and freedom. That trend would ultimately lead in the 1980s to theories of empowerment in the workforce.

Thomas Jefferson made his own situational analysis about 150 years earlier when he declared in a letter to Henry Lee, "Men by their constitutions are naturally divided into two parties: 1. Those who fear and distrust the people, and wish to draw all powers from them into the hands of the higher classes. 2. Those who identify themselves with the people, have confidence in them, cherish and consider them as the most honest and safe, although not the most wise depository of the public interests."

Jefferson's first category is surely the prototype for what McGregor called "Theory X" companies. "X and Y" are two fundamentally different ways of managing people, according to McGregor. "Theory X assumes that people are naturally lazy and irresponsible and need constantly to be watched; sometimes threatened, blamed or punished. That attitude provokes a traditional adversarial relationship between management and labor. It is a residue from the feudal system and the divine rights of kings. It is described in law as 'the master-servant relationship." Here, such organizations are named "The Awful Companies." Those that manage according to "Theory Y" are called "Ideal Companies," and represent Jefferson's second category.

Those situations are not exaggerated to dramatize comparisons. Such problems were frequently found by consultants conducting crisis management for clients. Since they result from human failings, company size has significance only in that there are likely to be more problems where there are more personnel.

Ideal Companies	Awful Companies
1. *Staff:* Long-term commitment to staff resulting in long-term employment, continuity, and control of management and marketing functions.	• Over 50% annual staff turnover, resulting in diversion of management from effectively running the company and breakdowns in continuity resulting in increased costs and business slowdown. Quality of managers and staff declines.
2. *Planning:* Forward planning and implementation leading to attainment of goals and objectives.	• Breakdown in planning resulting from lack of continuity. Goals and objectives not met.
3. *Strategic Plan:* Equal attention to long-range and medium-range objectives, as to the short-term.	• Attention to short-term gains at the expense of long-range survival.
4. *Meetings:* Regular management meetings for free exchange of information and ideas, direction, leadership, and decisions.	• Meetings continually postponed or cancelled due to management disorganization or indifference.
5. *Management Style:* Open—with good two-way communications a priority.	• Breakdown in communications from the top down, resulting in loss of management direction.
6. *Leadership:* Good leadership from the top down.	• No leadership. Faltering direction, leading to powerlessness of managers and apathy. Disorganization and management time spent putting out fires.
7. *Work Relationships:* Harmonious relationships. Management supported at top level.	• Frustration, insecurity, anxiety and fear, resulting in inertia and lost work time with managers and staff often away sick. Impulsiveness leading to conflicts with staff and management.
8. *Accountability:* Implicit controls of finance, inventories, marketing, and sales.	• No accountability. Ineffective controls. Sloppy management.
9. *Supplier Relationships:* Good; resulting in preferential prices, merchandise, and service.	• Supplier relationships disintegrate with loss of preferential treatment resulting from adversarial attitude from merchandise director.

Ideal Companies	Awful Companies
10. *Management Performance:* Management always effective and in control of organization, accounts, customers, and market.	• Ineffective management. No control of company, debtors, customers, sales force, suppliers, or market. Management paranoia, panic decisions, nervous breakdowns. Alcohol problems.
11. *Growth or Decline:* Healthy growth and profitability. Long-term security through effective control of all marketing tools and efficient implementation of company plan.	• Regular short-term losses from loose budgeting and careless cost accounting pricing errors, apathetic managers and unmotivated staff. Gradual decline in sales.
12. *Organization:* Motivated and organized management and staff, and the gradual demise of some competitors, enable company to survive economic recessions intact and with good morale, without having to downsize.	• Incapable of fulfilling orders even in economic boom with heavy demand for their products, resulting in indifference and neglect from sales and marketing people. Even survival instincts have become numbed by the time a recession causes attrition. Sales already declined because of unreliable service and failing quality control. Company fails.
13. *Management Calibre:* Market leaders are usually "Ideal Companies." High-calibre managers apply to join them because of their outstanding reputation and pleasant work environment. Excellent workers contribute to continual growth.	• "Awful Companies" that survive a recession through massive staff cuts are generally viewed as a continuous rat race with no proper long-term planning. They provide no sense of joy or accomplishment for employees or even working owners. Good managers will not risk their reputation by joining them.

Who are typically ideal companies? Fortunately there are too many to list here. A dozen examples should suffice: Unilever, Proctor & Gamble, Colgate-Palmolive, 3M, McDonalds, Eastman Kodak, Mitsubishi, Matsushita, Eli Lilly, Hewlett-Packard, Rockwell International, and Johnson & Johnson.

All of those companies share a common factor, which is a reputation for satisfying customers. And they achieve their aim because they are marketing oriented.

Paradigms and Paradoxes

Thoughtful managers who are interested in self-improvement and the improvement of their company will invariably consider what other qualities the ideal companies have in common with each other, and also what factors contributed to their success. McKinsey & Company asked themselves the same question. R. T. Pascale and A. G. Athos were part of a McKinsey team that surveyed a number of successful business organizations to find out. They published a report in 1982 under the title of *The Art Of Japanese Management*. It included a diagram representing a model which they called the 7-S Framework. They believed that seven ingredients characterize the predominant values of the leading companies they researched. They referred to them as levers with which managers could influence their organization. They are Strategy, Structure, and Systems—which the authors consider are a dominating influence in the West—and four management-driven factors on which the Japanese place greater emphasis; namely Staff, Skills, Style, and Superordinate Goals. Peters and Waterman replaced "Superordinate Goals" with "Shared Values" when they illustrated an updated paradigm in their own book, *In Search Of Excellence*. One can see that they might have thought the expression to be uncommon and ambiguous, and that it could lead to misinterpretations. And the more one considers that criterion, one realizes that their seventh and last one would most probably have been difficult to define—because there are other significant factors open for consideration, such as "Company Mission" and *ésprit de corps*. Had they been Japanese, perhaps they would have chosen "Spirit." Certainly we know that Carl von Clausewitz considered it to be a very important factor that contributes to victory in warfare. Sun Tzu thought so too, and so did Machiavelli.

Anthropologist Ruth Benedict made it abundantly clear in her book on Japanese culture, *The Chrysanthemum And The Sword*, that whereas America depended largely on its military hardware in World War II, the Japanese possessed greater faith in "Spirit." The Japanese High Command and their civilian statesmen repeated, when they were winning as well as when they were losing, that "in such a contest material power must necessarily fail." It had been their refrain even in the 1930s: "Ships and guns were just the outward show of the undying Japanese Spirit," wrote Benedict. And in the war that followed, the Kamikazi Corps, which purposefully flew their tiny aircraft in suicidal crashes into U.S. warships, were symbolic of the superiority of spiritual values over material ones. "There are limits to material resources," the Japanese radio insisted; "it stands to reason that material things cannot last a thousand years."

Their concept and practice of self-discipline in industry, art, and in their social lives, as well as in warfare, is equally awesome to westerners. That concept is innate in their culture. Their traditions and their history are manifestations of the Japanese spirit.

Possibly those American business consultants could not find a suitable word or symbol from their own culture that would be meaningful to American readers and business organizations. But such commitment was not unknown also in France and Britain, where *ésprit de corps* is well understood and encouraged in some circles; as was *die Ehre,* or honor, among the old German military caste up until World War I. But it is true that American culture from the very beginnings of its colonial history featured the personal commitment of the frontiersman and the capitalist to their own individual purposes. It seems that after leaving Europe on the high seas, immigrants to the New World threw overboard many of the old European values. Among those discarded was the acknowledgement that the state was more important than the individual freedom of its citizens. As J. G. Frazer wrote in *The Golden Bough,* "Greek and Roman society was built on the conception of the subordination of the individual to the community, of the citizen to the state; it set the safety of the commonwealth, as the supreme aim of conduct, above the safety of the individual in this world or the world to come."

Machiavelli used the word *virtù,* not with the same meaning we attribute to virtue, but "the *virtù* of one man who knew how to grasp an opportunity provided to him by fortune." It suggests an entrepreneurial gift of innovation or leadership, or of an innovation that would give him leadership: for example, Einstein's scientific formula of how the forces of nature work, ($E=MC^2$), which won him world leadership in science. Translators of Machiavelli's works understood that it was intended to have a special meaning as well as its Latin origin meaning individual courage. Chaucer used the same word a few hundred years earlier to describe a force of nature filled with creative power.

Carl Jung described it as follows: "To put it in modern language, spirit is the dynamic principle, forming for that very reason the classical antithesis of matter—the antithesis, that is, of its stasis and inertia. Basically it is the contrast between life and death." "He (man) himself did not create the spirit, rather the spirit makes *him* creative, always spurring him on, giving him lucky ideas, staying power, 'enthusiasm' and 'inspiration.'" And, "The concentration and tension of psychic forces have something about them that always looks like magic: they develop an unexpected power of endurance which is often superior to the conscious effort of will."

The very act of considering and attempting to define such a vitally important human and organizational element creates caution. But it also offers a challenge to design a new paradigm more than a decade later, during which so many business organizations were unable to survive the economic recessions of the 1980s and the 1990s.

A paradigm is a conceptual diagram that reveals a set of assumptions about an organization or a belief. Prior to the design of the 7-S Framework, another paradigm known as Leavitt's Diamond chose for its criteria Task, Structure, People, Information, Control, and Environment. No doubt the last of those six would incorporate some element conducive to "Spirit."

A paradigm or model representing the essential features of an organization is more than a symbol of what a company stands for. It is the very essence of a company's entire ideology. It should be included in the corporate culture or philosophy document, so that new managers will understand and perpetuate the principles of the company. It is also useful to assist in diagnosing the ills of a company undergoing a crisis, by identifying which facet has become flawed. By studying the values that an organization holds dear, it is possible to speculate on which spheres are being managed suitably and which are not. It therefore follows that a dedicated manager would find it useful to think through the concept underlying the principles of each of those two paradigms, and consider which one meets the needs and challenges of today's business environment, and which does not—or whether both do, or neither does.

The following new paradigm (figure 5.2) is designed with six elements. It is named the Sextet because each criterion is intended to be like a musical instrument that management would play in harmony with the others. Each aspect has been purposely designed to emphasize the principle of people orientation, since it is clear that the main weakness of so many western organizations is the absence of it, whereas the main strength of Japanese organizations is its emphasis. That aspect has been brought home to many companies in the West in the last decade, through the use of quality circles, which has led in some instances to empowerment of workers through TQM.

Even if we agree that Strategy, Structure, and Systems are sterile unless driven by the dynamism of intellectually creative people, Japanese companies have made them the servants of management, instead of enslaving management and staff to them—as is frequently the case in more bureaucratic western organizations.

The Sextet

Organization of People

Such an organization would be based on a structure that would be oriented to people. Its organization chart would define people's positions in the company, while their individual job specification would define the responsibilities and functions of each one. *The framework would not be supported by people so much as its people would be supported by the framework.* It would be designed to avoid pressures and friction and uncertainty, and provide a safety net.

Mode

The way a thing is done. A way of planning and directing the whole operation. This would include systems oriented to people inside the organization and strategy oriented to consumers. It would be designed to avoid inflexibility, friction and uncertainty, as with the organization.

FIGURE 5.2
The Sextet

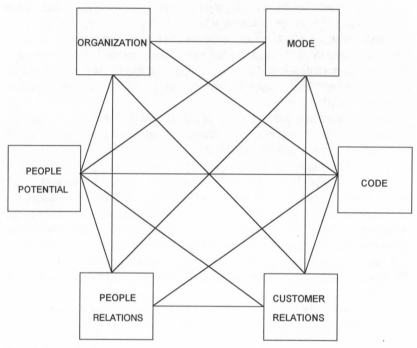

People Potential

Skills are an ability to perform a specific task well, whereas potential is an ability to be developed. People should be stretched to maximize their potential, provide pleasurable stimulation, and exploit their skills. The better the quality of their skills and the greater the fulfillment of their potential, the leaner a company can be, and the more effective.

Code

Set of laws, rules, or signals, based on established corporate principles, values, ethics, standards, attitudes, and practices in the workplace. They would be combined in a corporate philosophy and culture. It would include management style and demeanor, which is how key managers behave in achieving company goals.

The Code would involve all personnel in shared values that drive a company and create an *ésprit de corps,* or unconquerable spirit, which initiates resolution.

Today's appropriate style is shirtsleeves, hands-on management. Large companies would be required to be broken down into small, semi-autonomous splinter groups or commando units, with the flexibility and adaptability to be intuitive and entrepreneurial. Each group would be prepared to take fast actions, as if it were a small business unit run by an entrepreneur-owner.

A company's philosophy and culture is the means an organization has developed for survival in its business environment, its socioeconomic environment and its political environment. Every business organization needs a carefully considered philosophy and culture that would include management style, in order to provide and maintain a harmonious workplace directed towards customer satisfaction. It should include answers to the following types of questions:

What are the company's commitments and obligations to customers? What are its corporate obligations? What are its obligations to employees? What is its management philosophy? What is its company mission? What is its marketing philosophy? If a retailer, what is its merchandising philosophy? What is its growth philosophy? What is its chosen management style? What type of ethical conduct does it expect from its employees? What are its obligations and commitments to its shareholders? What are its duties and commitments to its community?

A manager needs to know what attitude a company takes toward his or her own department, since standards, policies, and procedures are likely to differ according to that company's culture from those of their previous employer. A financial controller needs to know what is that particular company's financial philosophy. What company policies will direct the work of a credit controller? What are the standards in this company for a quality control manager to follow? They will depend on its company culture and philosophy. A manager needs to know whether to follow without question a new employer's totems and taboos, or to make recommendations about improvements to meet changes in the marketing environment since they became company dogma to be blindly followed. A merchandise manager, a warehouse manager, or a financial controller would need to know that company's attitude toward the number of annual stockturns or returns required on every dollar invested, and so forth.

What may seem to be purely academic by a western business enterprise is recognized and practiced as a matter of course by Japanese ones. The reason why those types of obligations, duties, and commitments need to be set out with care in print and enshrined in a "Corporate Culture and Philosophy" document in the West, is because of the breakdown of social codes of behavior and the erosion of work standards in the West. As anthropologist Ruth Benedict discovered in 1945, they are a normal part of Japanese social culture, taught as a matter of custom by teachers and peer groups at school and by parents in the home. Most western children are not so fortunate, because of family break-ups and second-rate education systems. A considerable number in the U.S. are distracted, instead, by permissive sex, automobiles, drugs, and guns. One result of that is a 40 percent dropout rate; another is 160,000 American children who stay at home rather than face the violence in the schools. As a consequence, many do not learn how to interact harmoniously with other people by the time they reach maturity.

The most important of those obligations in Japan is the new employer's clear commitment to lifetime employment for its workers. In return for security new employees pledge loyalty to their company and dedicate themselves to continuous self-improvement and improvement in their work skills. The duty of their employer is to train them continuously to improve those skills and develop them for greater responsibilities. Even during the 1993 recession in Japan, industry kept its commitments to its employees. Where companies suffered from considerable loss of trade and profits, the Japanese government fulfilled its obligations to fund special training programs to change the skills of employees who would have been thrown out onto the streets in most western business organizations. Those obligations and loyalties create a network that reinforces the nation and holds communities and families together.

People Relations

In an organization that is oriented toward people there would be a corporate commitment to staff, on one hand, and a personal involvement by staff on the other hand. Quality circles would involve employees actively in improving both quality and production, and they would share in the rewards of success.

Part of a company's commitment to its employees is continuous and effective training. It creates job satisfaction and also results in continual improvements in the quality of output as well as in the volume of production.

The employer would also provide further training to provide the next generation of group leaders, department heads, divisional managers, and so forth, according to a planned career path for each individual worker or executive. It establishes a sense of identity, satisfaction in the process of self development, and loyalty toward a company that shows concern about the interests and personal ambitions of its staff.

Customer Relations

Developing ideal customer relations involves taking considerable care to know, understand, and assist every customer personally. This is of particular importance in an age of computerization using computer codes and numbers that depersonalize. If it supplies the trade, a business enterprise should take as much interest in its customer's business as its own, because it is in partnership with its customers. The same applies to its suppliers. Marks & Spencer's high level of quality in its chain stores in the UK was a result of sending its own consultants into its suppliers' workplaces to make studies and recommend improvements in total quality management. By improving their suppliers' quality, designs, productivity and unit costs, they improved relations with their own customers.

Customer Satisfaction

In order to manage the people spheres most effectively, a broad range of human relations services would require input and attention by a Human Relations Manager, and a whole range of customer services would require planning and monitoring by a Customer Relations Manager.

Key customer relations areas would include (but not be limited to) receptionists and telephonists, showroom staff, outside salespeople, product displays, trade or retail showrooms, children's areas, washrooms, the cafeteria, canteen or lounges; credit control staff who interface with customers, shipping clerks, delivery teams, and the following communications media: design, quality, packaging and handling of products; direct mail letters and flyers; media advertising; and also invoicing to customers, debt collection, and returns.

All employees who are involved in any way with customers would need to understand that the primary objective of the company is to satisfy customers by ensuring quality, dependability, and customer service

Disarray from the havoc caused by economic recessions, which may have led to company downsizing, often leaves a business enterprise unprotected, unequipped, and also demoralized. Customer service declines, quality is not as closely watched as before, and the process of innovation is disregarded in favor of cost cutting. That results from a general deterioration in management standards, and often faltering confidence by and in the CEO. The atmosphere is typically one of anxiety and impermanence.

A business enterprise that has not failed by the time an economy recovers has to address the new situation of both a weakened organization and a weak market. Disarray necessitates reorganization from a defensive posture to an offensive mode. First a company requires dynamic leadership to instil managers and staff with a determination to win. It needs intellectually creative managers to provide new ideas and marshall skills, to innovate products and services to meet new needs in the marketplace. And in order to implement an innovated strategy with new tactics it must equip itself with whatever staff are needed to satisfy customers. Then it has to woo those customers all over again and find new ones, too.

The difference between that type of trauma and the situation of ideal companies is that the ideal ones would have been attending to customer needs all along. Ongoing research would have revealed trends or cycles in sufficient time to accommodate them, and they would have ensured that they possessed the capability to do so. Their entire organization would be designed to address changes through R&D and by their possession of superior managers. Their goal is to be in control of situations, so that they are able to dominate events instead of being dominated by them.

The focus of the Sextet on people as a priority in business begs the question; "Are people more important than profits?"

Certainly they are. Nor do we need to make it a moral issue in a pragmatic society more concerned with self-interest. It is economic logic to concern ourselves primarily with full employment, if only because employees are consumers. The greater the number of consumers employed, the greater the consumption of goods and services and the greater the likelihood of social and economic stability. That is what drives an economy. It also creates a larger tax base to provide social services.

The philosopher Locke expressed a doctrine that self-interest and public interests coincide in the long run, though not necessarily over short periods. It therefore follows that people should be guided, as far as possible, by long-term interests. Long-term planning therefore demonstrates prudence, and lapses like short-termism show a failure to practice prudence. That also reveals a lack of responsibility toward shareholders, employees, the enterprise, and the community.

Japanese industry and commerce certainly appear to focus on the economic benefits to a community, over time, of full employment—rather than risking short-term gambles for higher profits. Nor do their governments squander taxpayers' money and then burden them by demanding more taxes to pay off their bad debts, as is happening in the West and preventing economies from recovering. The objective of the ideal of full employment is to lay the foundation for a happy and harmonious society, by means of personal and corporate wealth creation, as has been achieved in the leading Pacific Asian economies.

The Japanese interpret that quite differently from most western economies. Tradition dictates that people in Japan should be responsible to the community by always doing something useful. Their social contract depends on employees continually improving their skills and their workplace performance. Western aspirations, on the other hand, tend to focus on limiting work hours to a minimum and increasing leisure time. A sense of pleasure in work achievement is often lacking. Replacing workers with robots may resolve that problem, but it will create a chain of far more profound social and economic ones for us to tackle for several decades to come.

6

Planning for Survival and Growth

Management is undergoing a change of life brought about by technological innovation, deregulation leading to the metamorphosis of separate national markets into broader economic spheres like the European Union and the NAFTA, and a trend to universality of standards. Competition has intensified, and margins have shrunk while consumer choices have grown. Nonprice factors like marketing, design, and quality are even more important today, and marketing is gradually easing itself out of restrictions imposed on it by fitting it into a separate and often isolated department removed from both the workplace and the marketplace. More progressive businesses are recognizing that marketing is a function of general management and general management is a function of marketing.

Since marketing possesses internal as well as external responsibilities, it is not easy to foretell whether and how specific marketing functions can be implemented without formal departments, as has been envisaged by some practitioners. And while it has been said that marketing must be, or will be, more accountable, it already is and has been in more sophisticated corporate cultures of some multinational market leaders, like Unilever's companies for example. So although the future of marketing is presently being considered soberly and written about with enthusiasm, there can be no standard formula. Each organization will have its own individual culture and philosophy as it always had, but it is more likely to be dominated by a company's marketing objectives and mission.

There are ten major responsibilities fundamental to managing, and a company has to be marketing oriented for each sphere to be effectively managed. That means its CEO must have a clear understanding and a bias toward satisfying customers. If that is the case, so would every manager. Customer and market orientation would be reflected in the structure and systems of the organization. So would the business attitudes and style of top management teams and their staff, so that the entire organization would be customer and market driven, and all personnel would be directed to the fulfillment of customer needs and wants and satisfaction. That would permeate planning, organizing, motivating, controlling, recruiting (and training and development), com-

161

munications, developing relationships, leading, understanding organizational needs, and facilitating implementation.

Planning

Planning is the foundation of all business activities. It considers the future today. The success of a manager or an entire enterprise may depend on whether the initial planning was well done or inferior, because planning initiates a bundle of decisions. It selects and relates facts and makes assumptions about the future, then uses them in conceiving and formulating activities considered necessary to achieve desired results. It establishes in advance what is to be done and how, by whom and when. It does so by studying alternative options and ways and means to reach defined goals and objectives. Its aim is to choose the most effective option to determine every outcome to the advantage of the organization.

Each alternative plan makes an assessment of what human and financial and material resources would be required. Such a plan is likely to include a cost-benefit analysis to determine also which plan would be most cost-effective. Although that might not be the selected plan, it might justify it.

Planning is not undertaken in isolation. A departmental plan must dovetail into the corporate business plan and also into plans of other departments; since each departmental goal must be coordinated with corporate objectives, and each plan must contribute to the whole corporate plan. In that way, each supports the other and moves the company in the same direction, simultaneously, and assists in fulfilling the company's mission.

A plan commences with clearly defined terms and agreed objectives and describes how they will be achieved. It is helpful also to "glance over the shoulder," as it were, to establish how the company reached its present market position, and ascertain with hindsight whether its past strategy and tactics were the most suitable ones in terms of market activities and what was achieved. Hindsight may produce better options for the future.

Such a plan would describe how the company would reach its market share goals and marketing objectives in the short term, medium term, and long term. While it is understood that only historic numbers may be precise, assumptions for the future must be more than mere crystal-ball gazing. They must be founded on logical and rational appraisals and projections based on as precise an analysis of the past and present market situation, comprising the company and all its competitors, as possible. Each plan would consider alternative situations that could arise with each competitor's brands or product range. Part of the planning process would involve plans for research to determine changes, trends, and possible R&D innovations to meet those changes.

Management by Objectives

The strategic planning process known as MBO grew out of a statement made by Peter Drucker in 1954. It is a process whereby managers in an organization work together as a team to identify common objectives and establish activities required to lead to the achievement of those objectives. Managers are shown the overall corporate objectives, so that each can define the goals that his or her own department must achieve to assist the company in meeting its objectives; and vice-versa.

Objectives are always specific and measurable, to avoid ambiguity and inaccuracies. They ensure that a manager and his or her supervisors and staff know exactly what is to be done and why, who will undertake each particular function, how, when, and where. Methods of achieving goals and objectives are clearly stated, as are the resources required, timing, and interactions with other individuals, departments, or divisions. Each manager is held accountable and their individual performances can be measured.

Short-term objectives generally apply to one year. Five-year plans are commonplace: they require annual reviews and updates with a further year added to maintain a five-year duration. That is likely to be considered medium range. Long-term planning could cover a period from ten to twenty-five years, with similar annual reviews and updates. Updating is as important as originating plans, since all things change. Out-of-date plans are not only useless but misleading.

A miniature example of managing by objectives is the Critical Path Analysis originally developed for American industry and pioneered by Du Pont, and the P.E.R.T. chart—Program Evaluation and Review Technique—developed in the U.S. Navy to determine the critical or longest path in manufacturing submarines. Its most common commercial use is launching a new product. The design of the actual chart takes a line and follows it from inception to the completion date. It involves a series of activities, each one leading to an individual event depicted by a milestone or node. The intention of the exercise is not merely to prepare a checklist for management controls, but to determine which path is the critical one in terms of time, so that a date schedule can be established with accuracy.

Prior to the date schedule leading to the product launch, a similar date schedule would have been prepared for product research and development up to the prototype, which would undergo tests before being accepted for a trial production run. In the case of a new hair shampoo, for example, the list of events may be scheduled from: 2. plant requirements and package established; through 3. brand name established; 4. preliminary product development completed; 5. trade, consumer and advertising survey completed; 6. plan presented to board; 7. agency briefed; and stage by stage on to 19. commence trial production run; 20. commence distribution; 21. product launch. Simultaneously, a list of activities to arrive at each of those events might read as follows: 1. conduct trade, consumer and advertising survey; 2. determine brand name, legal aspects, etc; 3. estimate plant requirements and type of package; 4. prepare market plan in outline; 5. obtain board approval; and so forth, on to 14. order and await plant; 15. order and await materials; 16. install plant; 17. make trial production run; 18. manufacture launch quantity; 19. prepare advertising brief; 20. agency prepares designs; 21. prepare advertising campaign; 22. obtain approval for campaign; 23. prepare advertising for launch; 24. set launch quantities with sales manager; 25. brief sales force and distribute to trade.

Anticipated changes for updating plans can be conveniently divided between macroeconomic events and microeconomic ones. The former would be changes over which a manager has little or no control, such as an oil embargo or other sanctions, terrorism or war, economic recession, floods, tornadoes, or volcanic eruptions, which can occur suddenly; or may gradually make themselves apparent—like population increases, deforestation, soil erosion, impending free-trade agreements, changes in government, lease expiries, and the like. All such eventualities have to be taken into consideration in planning, since they could alter situations on which the plan depends.

Microeconomic situations are those that are closer to a manager's competence to deal with: product formulation that may be found to produce allergic symptoms, a new product launch by a competitor that could reduce a brand's market share by preemption, an untimely labor strike, raw material shortages, or any other such situation that could affect the implementation of the strategic plan. Management would have to act precipitately and effectively to counteract the crisis by means of an alternative plan.

The principle business of any advanced culture and the essence of marketing practices is the uniting of the microcosm with the macrocosm.

All plans should derive from the general purpose or mission of a company. That mission would be entirely consistent with the company's culture and philosophy, its policies, and previous and subsequent plans.

The main advantages of planning and plans are: they establish disciplined activities with logical purposes; they show needs for future changes; they create alternative plans as a result of continually asking "What if?"; plans provide opportunities for establishing controls; they motivate and initiate a need to achieve specific goals; they oblige a holistic understanding of necessary activities and events; they reveal needs for resources and facilities; they promote confidence; they compel initiatives; they encourage leadership.

Plans that a manager prepares also provide more personal advantages: they become useful checklists of all important activities to meet his or her goals; they direct and can support a manager's staff in the part they will play; they enable top management to feel less concern, by knowing exactly what their managers and staff are doing and how they are handling resources; they define the resources and facilities required for obtaining necessary approvals; they establish what budgets may require approval; they enable realistic forecasts to be made for production scheduling and sales targets and the like; they compel discussion, reviews, monitoring, advice, cooperation, and inputs; they provide yardsticks for measuring the performances of managers and also their staff; they provide a date schedule of proposed events for timing and coordinating salient activities which can be plotted on a network P.E.R.T. chart; they draw the attention of top management specialists to needs for controls of resources and organization functions; they emphasize what changes, improvements, and departmental or company growth will be required; they teach and compel goal orientation in managers and their staff.

Targets should always be attainable according to budgets. And although all objectives should be capable of measurement, there are some that involve creative activities such as communications objectives, design objectives, brand objectives, and graphics, which can often be measured only subjectively according to qualitative criteria instead of mathematical calculations. Those are likely to need testing in focus groups or consumer clinics, where some form of measurement can be obtained. In the case of advertisements, for example, testing would take the form of measuring degrees of awareness, comprehension, conviction, and intention to buy, and establishing benchmarks.

Managers should also set their own objectives for the improvement of their own knowledge and skills, so that they will be fully capable of undertaking their job effectively and are also prepared for career advancement when the time arrives.

Questioning

Managers will ask a multitude of questions to obtain information required for them to set objectives, targets, forecasts, goals, and determine the best means to achieve them. Effective checklists for planning therefore involve six fundamental questions; What? Where? When? How? Why? and Who?

Reviewing

Reviewing means determining all possible courses of action, then selecting that which best meets each objective with optimum effect and minimal cost in the shortest possible time frame, with least effort and fewest people. Its key principles are likely to be simplicity, flexibility, adaptability, stability, skills, and resources.

"Much of management deals with judgement, diagnosis and interpretations of events, which require a different kind of knowledge and understanding from logic and rationality. The true expert has built up his expertise from experience and an intuitive grasp of problem-solving in the real world."[1]

Marketing programs are something new in industries that were formerly government monopolies, like Ontario Hydro or Hydro-Québec, for example. Eskom went through a similar process in South Africa. It generates 97 percent of all electricity sold there. Since existing power stations were usually designed and built in periods of high economic growth, expansion results in having to market excess generation capacity. That is a new skill, particularly for managers with engineering instead of marketing backgrounds. Eskom introduced the marketing concept by building it into its corporate culture under management style.

After a false start geared to the agricultural market, their management consultants persuaded them to shift focus to the industrial market, and their program was restructured for paper and pulp, iron and steel, chemicals, food and beverages, textiles, and nonmetallic segments. The EXMAR system was used to provide a structure for their marketing planning process, because it bridged a gap identified between theory and practice.

Industrial research was undertaken in those market segments. Not only was it necessary for managers to understand new techniques but also the interrelationship between traditional and modern methods for planning. Essential differences were handling knowledge as opposed to handling data, using heuristics as compared with algorithms, undertaking inferential processes instead of repetitive ones, and using knowledge bases as compared with data bases.[2]

One result of the exercise was that the management team was able to identify the factors according to which the project should be managed, and their relative weightings: profitability—30 percent; minimum investment—12 percent; increased consumption—15 percent; growth potential—19 percent; sales value—24 percent. Inputs and tasks were identified in the EXMAR Decision Tree (figure 6.1).[3]

The contents of each strategic plan are unique for each project. Even the categories for definition or implementation, or the list of contents, will differ according to the type of plan required, different industries, individual company methodologies, and even management styles, to meet quite different sets of circumstances. The framework of a new plan or the update of an existing one is likely to follow the structure of a company's previous plans, but rigid adherence to the structure of an old approach may be a mistake. Rigidity is not a virtue in a changing marketplace with its different needs, trends, and technologies.

McDonald's description of "the true expert" is, perhaps, even more significant than he may have realized. Seventeenth-century philosopher John Locke puzzled for many years about where knowledge comes from and how we attain it. How does the mind contain all the materials of reason and knowledge? he asked. Surely they must be derived from two sources: sensation and perception? Since we can think only through ideas, and those ideas come from experience, none of our knowledge can be formed prior to that experience (as the ancients had believed).[4]

FIGURE 6.1
Decision Tree Diagram of the EXMAR Marketing Planning System

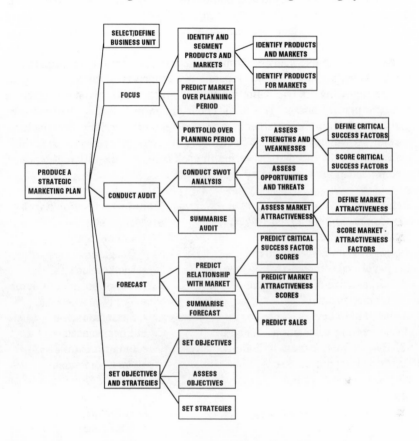

Source: M.H.B. McDonald.

Locke also, inadvertently, provides the key to the vice of short termism, by writing, "Happiness, in its full extent, is the utmost pleasure we are capable of." Russell used that declaration to unlock his theory of knowledge by amplifying that "men do not always act in the way which, on a rational calculation, is likely to secure them a maximum of pleasure. We value present pleasure more than future pleasure, and pleasure in the near future more than pleasure in the distant future." Hence the irrational leaning of most business people and politicians toward the error of short-term thinking, and their failure to plan for the long term.

But major market leaders know that it is not only reaching their future destination that depends on following long-term goals, but also meeting today's objectives. For example, Coca-Cola's 1994 annual report declared, "We understand that the best way to generate consistently strong short-term results is to keep our attention riveted on the long term. Step by step, we aggressively tackle the most important long-term priority of each day, and then move on to the next."

Note too, that like many other market leaders, it is the organization that is the marketer, and not merely a separate marketing department.

The following are two entirely different structures for two quite different strategic plans. The first is a retail chain of furniture and appliance stores seeking growth in their market area. The second is a furniture manufacturer seeking growth by exporting. The structure of each report reflected the different questions that needed answering in each case, and the different types of recommendations warranted by each situation.

Retail Chain Store

1. Company growth (last 10 years)
2. Internal problems
3. Significant consumer trends
4. 5-year sales forecast
5. Market size & segmentation by market share
6. Market forces
7. Marketing orientation
8. East & West marketing regions
9. Growth opportunities
10. Boutique-orientation
11. West end store concepts
12. Satisfying the customer
13. Options
14. Applying a corporate philosophy

Manufacturing For Export

A. Market size
   • Demography
   • Geography
   • Marketplace
B. Areas of potential volume
   • Target markets
   • Strategic factors
C. Political aspects
   • Import controls
   • Trade sanctions
D. Imports & Exports
   • Political situation
E. Distributors
   • Wholesale
   • Retail
F. Design compatibility
G. Standards & sizes
H. Pricing
I. Conclusions
   • Summary
   • Recommendations

One school of management thought advocates the separation of the planning function from operational management, and its delegation instead, to specialists, on the grounds that strategic thinking is quite different from operations orientation. Other arguments in favor of its separation are that an operational manager does not have time to perform the planning function effectively. And Professor J. G. Kotzé wrote; "Evidence also abounds that a significant number of top executives do not always fully understand the nature of the business environments in which they operate."

Not all plans are strategic marketing plans. Other types of plans are required to serve specific purposes, such as a business plan prepared for or by a new enterprise seeking venture capital. Other plans, like a SWOT Analysis, are really either a situational analysis or a proposal, a report or a paper. We therefore have to be clear about the purpose of the desired plan. It is also useful to know who has requested it. It is likely to differ in length, structure, and even style depending on the size and complexity of the business.

An entrepreneur of an SME would be likely to be closely involved with his or her plan. But, depending on the sophistication of the enterprise, developing it might be the responsibility of a vice-president of marketing. If neither possesses the specialized expertise, each might contribute to its formulation together with an independent management or marketing consultant with the appropriate skills. An ambitious or fastidious entrepreneur is likely to hire an independent consultant anyway. But a much bigger company or a multinational conglomerate is likely to use its own specialist or department; particularly if it markets a considerable product range and habitually aims at excellence.

We should also consider a theory proposed in 1969 that recommends that the entire planning process should be divided into five separate stages.[5] Each stage would have its own separate group of planners to: (a) set primary and intermediary goals; (b) search for opportunities; (c) formulate plans; (d) set targets; (e) prepare follow-up plans.

There appear to be four distinct options for a business to consider when planning: A company can either use an existing management team; it could hire a full-time planner; it can maintain a department or group of planners; or it could use the services of an independent management consultant to undertake an annual project. A larger organization would be likely to have a need and also the resources to maintain a full-time planning department. But the key question is whether or not marketing and management functions would benefit from separating the planning functions from operational management.

There are four major detrimental aspects in creating a separate planning function:

1. A planner is so far removed from operations that his plan becomes merely an academic exercise divorced from the reality of the workplace, and more akin to a thesis. As a consequence, a manager may not find it to be practical enough for implementation.

2. In the greater majority of companies there is insufficient work for a full-time planner. The result is that he is obliged to *create* work to give an appearance of being busy. All the manifestations of a bureaucracy are brought into play, including additional staff, to give an impression of overwork. That is only the beginning of "empire building," in which all types of specialist skills are recommended as essential and soon hired.

3. A planner invariably reports directly to the chief executive so that he can be informed about corporate objectives, company mission, corporate philosophy and culture, commitments to shareholders, and the desires of the chairman to whom the CEO is responsible. He therefore becomes more influenced by the attitudes of the CEO than of the marketing vice-president who would be held accountable for the implementation of the plan, and the marketing manager who would have to work the plan. The result may be a plan that will gladden the heart of the chairman or the shareholders, but has little relevance to a working plan that an operational manager can implement effectively.

4. One of the key aspects of MBO is the deep involvement and input of operational managers in their part of the business plan. That participation is intended to assist in the development of that manager and also motivate managers to achieve objectives. Separation of that function would result in their having a plan *imposed* on them, instead. It would therefore be less meaningful and unlikely to motivate them.

If we review existing situations where—in most cases—the functions are not separated, we find the following types of scenarios:

A. *Corporate Plan:*
Responsible: Chief executive
Who prepares it?   Top management team

B. *Marketing Plan:*
Responsible: Marketing vice-president
Who prepares it?   Joint effort of marketing manager, each product or brand manager, monitored and supported by marketing vice-president.

C. *Departmental Plans:*
Responsible: Relevant department head
Who prepares it?   Department head

Since a business enterprise has only two functions—marketing and innovation—it is clearly evident that the productive part of the enterprise is the marketing group. All other departments merely provide services to support the marketing function. The planning options are therefore for the marketing vice-president to choose from. But it is also clear that he has ample staff for the planning function, and it is in the interests of each of his marketing group, and himself, to be as deeply involved as possible with the planning process. The percentage of the business plan to which other department heads contribute is minimal since the main bulk of the plan is occupied with marketing. They should therefore have no problem in fulfilling their own planning functions.

When each department head completes a provisional draft of his or her section of the plan, a chief executive will have both the framework and most of the substance for the corporate plan. Through those sections, and discussions with each department head, his view will be a holistic one. And his concerns for the corporate effort—for which he is responsible to the chairman—and the chairman's concerns, would also be fully discussed before a more complete draft is undertaken. After each has given and received sufficient input, both the CEO and the business plan may well benefit from the broader and more specialized outside experience of an independent consultant.

In the case of the vast number of medium-size companies that do not have the complexity of the big organizations, the need for a full-time planner cannot be justified. There would be neither the work nor the financial resources to warrant establishing such a function. They, too, could make effective use of the input from a management consultant.

A criticism often levelled at MBO is that it is too rigid. But nobody ever said it had to be inflexible. On the contrary, an essential feature of planning is that it must take continual note of changes. It is true that a company cannot expect much, if anything, from a strategic plan based on long-range predictions—particularly a plan that is not continually adapted to changes as they occur. And changes do take place all the time, in the realms of government policy, political activity, technological innovation, economic activity, in a company's own life cycle, with each competitor, in consumer trends, and in social activity. But a strategic plan should not be founded on long-range plans, which are, after all, purely speculative.

Management by Objectives was never intended to be applied rigidly. If there is one thing that erudite managers have learned from Darwin and Wallace's theory of Natural Selection—or the survival of the fittest—it is that survival depends almost entirely on adaptability to changing circumstances and environments. Flexibility is required to meet continually changing challenges and exploit new opportunities that arise as a consequence. A business enterprise too is obliged to recognize that in the continual culling process that takes place with any species or product or company, it is only the fittest that survive.

Strategic Plans

A comparison was shown previously between the different sections of two quite different plans, in order to demonstrate how no two plans are ever identical or even closely similar to each other. Each company is likely to have quite different objectives and be experiencing different life cycles. Their budgets may vary considerably even if they have similar markets or similar products. Of the two quoted, one company owned national retail chain stores while the other manufactured solely for export, and their products were entirely different. If we examine a third strategic plan for tea, for example, we immediately see other significant differences. As a beverage, tea falls into a quite different category of fast-moving packaged consumer goods. Any experienced entrepreneur or marketing manager would therefore be suspicious of software programs that purport to be useful for every marketer. They would be as useful to a marketing vice-president as a book on how to paint by numbers would have been to Michelangelo when he prepared to paint his frescoes on the ceiling of the Sistine Chapel.

It is not only more professional to commence planning on the basis of one's own company's strengths and weaknesses, its specific markets, and the strengths and weaknesses of its own competitors, it is in fact easier. The comparison of a general making plans to win a battle are appropriate. According to Sun Tzu, the excellence of a general is shown in his planning, and he wins by making no mistakes in their execution. The plan he establishes is his recipe for victory. All he has to do is implement it.

A marketing company also has to concern itself with demographic changes. They involve trends in family formations, declines in a community's birthrate, population increases by ethnic immigration, and the inmigration of populations from rural areas into cities, from one city to another, and from east to west or south to north. In that way, continually changing demographics initiate continual changes in market needs and consumer acceptance of established products. Cultural differences influence buying decisions.

A typical marketing plan seeks measurable answers to a number of simple questions concerned with identifying and evaluating opportunities, examining strengths and weaknesses, analyzing market segments and selecting targets, matching organizational strengths to market opportunities, and planning and developing a marketing mix to meet strategic and tactical needs; such as, "What is the size of the total market? Who are the heaviest users? Where are they? Why do they buy their favorite brand? What should be our own competitive or unique selling proposition? How can we obtain a predetermined share of the total market? What is it likely to cost us? What should our objectives and goals be? When can we achieve them? What returns can we expect from our investment?"

The planner or marketing manager would continually bear in mind, while preparing the strategy, that it is intended to be a winning plan—of the type that Sun Tzu referred to when he stated that the battle is already won if the plan is right.

Business Plans

Every business enterprise begins with a plan of some kind. And each one will be quite different if it reflects the special skills of the entrepreneur and his team and its special mission.

Dr. Edward Roberts emphasizes that if you don't do it right, there is every possibility that you will never do anything beyond it. He was Professor of

Management and Technology at MIT. His own analysis of twenty business plans from high-technology companies requiring venture capital, revealed the following far-reaching mistakes:

- 30 percent did not include a rational strategic plan that seemed possible to achieve.
- 47 percent emphasized the product; 29 percent the market; 24 percent people.
- 45 percent did not cover in detail profitability or growth.
- 75 percent did not include details of competitors' plans.
- Most emphasized R&D rather than marketing.
- 75 percent gave low priority to marketing research and selling—for which those companies showed little expertise.
- 10 percent provided no financial projections; 5 percent offered no data for theirs; 10 percent only projected income up to year 3; 40 percent up to year 5; 15 percent provided an income statement and balance sheet for years 1 to 3; 10 percent for up to 5 years.

That was only a small research sample and confined to the Boston area, but it gives us some insight into the reasons for the large percentage of failures in that industry.

Dr. Joseph Mancuso offered the following suggestions for the most useful categories for a business plan.[6]

1. *The Business*:
   A. Description of business
   B. Markets
   C. Competition
   D. Location of business
   E. Management
   F. Personnel
   G. Application and expected effect of loan if needed
   H. Summary

2. *Financial Data*:
   A. Sources and applications of funds
   B. Capital equipment list
   C. Balance sheet
   D. Break-even analysis
   E. Income projections (profit and loss statements)
      - 3-year summary
      - Month by month details for 1st year
      - Quarterly details for 2nd and 3rd years
      - Notes of explanation

F. Pro-Forma cash flow
- Monthly details for 1st year
- Quarterly details for 2nd and 3rd years
- Notes of explanation

G. Deviation analysis

H. Historical financial report for existing business
- Balance sheets for past 3 years
- Income statements for past 3 years
- Tax returns

3. *Supporting Documents*:
Personal résumés, personal financial requirements and statements, cost of living budget, credit reports, letters of reference, job descriptions, letters of intent, copies of leases, contracts, legal documents, and anything else of relevance to the plan.

SWOT Analysis

A SWOT Analysis is simple enough for any level of qualified marketing practitioner to undertake for an SME, and it can also be used to develop a more detailed strategic plan for a bigger organization. Despite that, it is essentially a situational analysis. And in spite of its apparent simplicity, it can be developed into a useful strategic instrument if undertaken by a creative, as well as a practical marketing person with experience in planning strategies and marketplace tactics. It is an ideal method for a planner to establish on paper what is the current situation in a specific marketplace or segment. And it helps a planner to think through the situation methodically, as a springboard for preparing a more comprehensive plan. Its basic categories are a business and competitors' strengths and weaknesses, marketplace opportunities, and threats from competitors and the macroeconomic environment.

J. G. Kotzé published a model for what he named the Formulation of Strategic Intent.[7] He suggested that a strategic plan could be developed from a SWOT Analysis by using four management criteria: improvement, maintainer, competitive advantage of the organization, and competitive advantage of competitors.

If we are looking for a starting point in planning, it is hard to beat the old "ends, ways, and means" approach. After having determined where you want the company to go, what could be simpler than planning how best to get there and what resources will be needed?

We can see that planning is both a creative and an intellectual exercise requiring cool objectivity, but it must not possess the Procrustean symmetry of administrative bureaucrats who lose sight of the fact that strategy should be aimed at making everything easier for customers, so that they will patronize the organization and buy its goods and services. Manufacturers in particular tend, instead, to react more to factory machinery problems than to customer needs, just as service organizations—including the public service—tend to make their own job easier rather than serving the public. When workplace empowerment was practiced in Tito's Yugoslavia in the mid-1960s, there was a dearth of typewriter ribbons in stores and in government offices because they had all been exported according to centralized state planning. Government departments had an excuse to slow down, but industry, commerce, and construction projects were held up because of a lack of necessary permits and approvals. The state had also built luxury vacation resorts to initiate tourism, but they were deserted because they had not yet promoted tourism abroad. Even so, their lack of logical planning was not as damaging as state planning in the former USSR, which was imposed to suit the system instead of the marketplace.

It is one thing to produce a reasonably accurate and dependable strategic plan, but quite another to analyze and judge whether it is realistic and should be funded. Who possesses sufficient understanding of operational problems in business enterprises, and of whether the enterpriser may or may not be capable of establishing his or her services and products in the marketplace? The branch manager of a financial institution? A government employee? Who then?

"Some of the biggest white elephants in Atlantic Canada, costing taxpayers up to $100 million, were the direct result of incompetence among federal bureaucrats, a new study concludes."[8] The report examined 17 large projects which collapsed after obtaining federal grants and loan guarantees. "Federal officials routinely failed to spot trouble when entrepreneurs came calling for money, agency auditors found after examining each collapse in detail. Rosy business and marketing plans were not challenged, warnings from experts were ignored and ventures were not monitored to ensure that tax dollars were well spent." One company went into receivership in 1989, only a year after startup, and cost taxpayers $850,000. Said a document attached to the report, "A challenge of the projections would have revealed the company was actually projecting insolvency in month two." Another business plan (submitted by Presswood Pallet Partnership in New Brunswick) "ensured it would lose money."

The auditors concluded that sufficient information is generally made available to challenge the viability of projects, but most business plans were not questioned in depth. Their study said that agency officials assumed the lending bankers were monitoring the ventures, but the banks gave the projects little scrutiny, knowing that taxpayers would be forced to honor the loans in any bankruptcy.[9]

Those situations are reminiscent of similar wastage of much-needed tax funds by the socialist government in post-war Britain. They are by no means confined to North America. A pertinent question must surely be; Why should government employees or bank managers who have no hands-on operational experience in the business workplace, be chosen to make competent judgements on whether a new enterprise is likely to succeed or fail? And to judge from the admission of a senior partner in one of the Big Six auditing firms that they did not get close enough to their customers, one cannot help but wonder how else could auditors effectively assess risk management.

Considering the well-chosen criteria and the structure and implementation of the Enterprise Initiative scheme in the UK, which successfully advised chief executives of 15,650 business enterprises in a six-year period, this is surely the specialized sphere of such marketing institutes as the Chartered Institute of Marketing, which designed and managed that program. But as long as the average uninformed government employee, bank manager, or auditing firm continues to imagine that marketing is just a fancy name for selling and that marketing practitioners are some kind of creative workshop like an advertising agency, then all manner of people will continue to be co-opted to decide which business should be funded and which aspiring entrepreneur should be told not to waste their time doing something they know nothing about.

7

Right Attitude

In an ongoing struggle to do better with less, when every aspect of a business organization has been turned upside down to see how it can be improved, it was only a matter of time before organization charts would come under the close scrutiny of theorists who were itching to change its shape. But those charts can be compared to a company's nervous system or to the network of arteries, veins, and capillaries that channel blood throughout a person's body. In his contribution to a paper on "The Problem of Serial Order in Behavior," Paul Weiss wrote, "The working of the central nervous system is a hierarchical affair in which functions at the higher levels do not deal directly with the ultimate structural unit."[1]

An organizational structure is intended to ensure that activities of individuals support each other and are channeled directly or indirectly toward a common goal. It is no coincidence that the traditional hierarchical business structure was based squarely on the military prototype with its staff and line functions. And the traditional hierarchical structure is still in use because it has fulfilled its role effectively to facilitate delegation of responsibilities that enabled people to work efficiently in a group or in groups, for thousands of years.

Whenever a chart appears to go wrong—which is frequently—it is pointless to blame its hierarchical structure when it is the fault of management, not the system. Problems may arise because it was wrongly designed in the first place or because it was not adapted to meet changed needs in new and quite different times and circumstances—like the business revolution in the present decade. Or it may not have been used in conjunction with other management systems on which it must rely for its effectiveness. One such system is interlinked job specifications for each classification of management and staff. In addition, the appropriate attitude of all personnel in each company is intended to be attuned to that organization's own particular culture and philosophy. That is what develops a distinctive management attitude and style that all employees are intended to emulate.

Uninformed management, inflexible managers, or unimaginative, bureaucratic, or incompetent ones, are a threat to any business enterprise. But such failings are not caused by an organization chart. On the contrary, the structure, job descriptions, and management methodology can impose disciplines calculated to reduce risks arising from human limitations.

Some knowledge industries, like high-tech enterprises producing intellectual properties with educated and skilled executives, question whether a hierarchical structure is not a recipe for mediocrity. That would depend on the calibre of personnel chosen by Human Resources. A propensity for mediocrity is inherent in most individuals, but it can only be intrinsic to a chart that has been incorrectly designed. And the longevity of the hierarchical design is most likely due to the fact that it is a natural and widespread one all over the world, and not an artificial system invented and imposed on an organization by someone.

Koestler described such a chart as resembling an upside-down tree with its branches growing downwards and outwards, each branch delegating certain functions to a number of smaller branches growing out of it; and each of those similarly delegating to other even smaller branches at lower levels, and so on.

"All advanced forms of social organizations are again hierarchic: the individual is part of the family, which is part of the clan, which is part of the tribe, etc.... In the living organism, too, each part must assert its individuality, for otherwise the organism would lose its articulation and efficiency—but at the same time each part must remain subordinate to the demands of the whole."[2]

Delegate is defined as "entrusted to an agent." For example, a marketing vice-president may be accountable for the marketing responsibility, but she would delegate or entrust the operational function to a marketing manager. He, in turn, might delegate the operational sales function to a sales manager or the advertising function to an advertising manager. In fact, it is more than likely that all three operational functionaries would be responsible to the marketing vice-president. And each of them would, similarly, delegate other functions to other staff like a sales administrator, an after-sales service manager, product managers, or regional managers, and so forth.

The typical organization chart, illustrated in figure 7.1, is shallow because it is intended to reflect the needs of a growing small or medium-size enterprise; a GSME. The key question might be, "Is that the way to go for our firm?" The answer is "Not necessarily." But it is worth a formal study even if there appear to be sound reasons for diverting from it, like an abundance of knowledge jobs. Most importantly, it provides everyone in an organization with ample opportunity to pursue their own individual goals by concentrating on the responsibilities for which they will be held accountable, without friction or pressure from anyone else. Meanwhile, they are free to seek advice upwards and delegate downwards, or obtain inputs from downwards and provide inputs up or down. And each is free to cooperate with teams sideways, upwards and down, to assist them to meet their objectives and also develop their own skills.

FIGURE 7.1
Typical Organization Chart

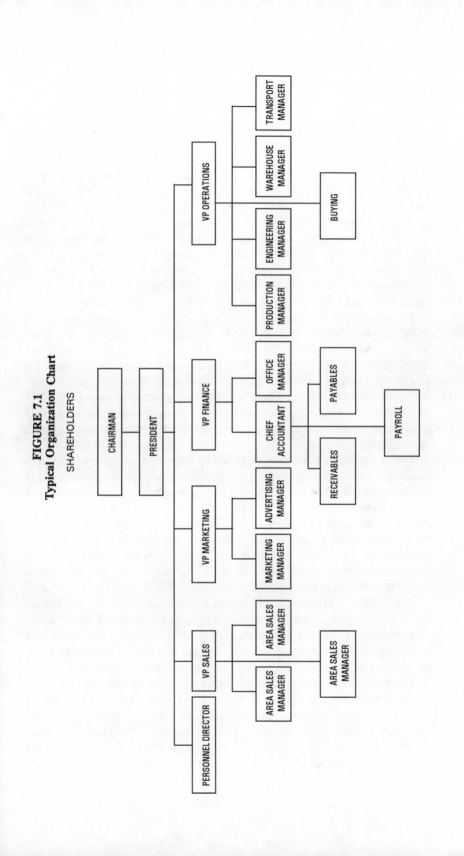

Typical Organization Chart

A chairman is accountable to the shareholders who own the company. He appoints an operational generalist who, in turn, appoints his or her own top management team. Each manager in the team specializes in a particular discipline. Each one will direct and monitor his or her own section and also advise the *generalist* on all aspects of their own specialized sphere of operation. The *generalist* may have the title of President, Chief Executive Officer, Managing Director, or Director General. In the organization chart which is featured, most managers directly responsible to the President are described as Vice-Presidents. But that won't necessarily be so.

Typically, a President and CEO requires a team consisting of a marketing specialist to recommend what customers to target for, what products and services they need, and at what volume and prices; an operations specialist to make them and be accountable for resources entering, being processed, and being shipped out to customers; a specialist accountable for sales and client services; and another specialist to control money coming in and going out. Although they don't all need to be Vice-Presidents, those responsible for Marketing, Finance, and Operations are likely to be. That is because marketing *is* the business; because Finance oils the ways and means for the marketing process to be accomplished; and workplace tools, machinery, assembly lines and workers need managing to fulfil the marketing objectives. They are all marketing forces.

The organization's structure would differ according to whether a business manufactures, wholesales or retails merchandise, or is a service industry. Other variations would occur according to differences in industry. A vice-president of marketing frequently assumes the overall responsibility also for sales, often by having a sales manager directly responsible to him or her. That may depend on the size of the enterprise or whether the company is a simple or complex one. If complex, a responsible professional marketing VP would insist on directly controlling the sales sphere in order to be in complete control of the marketing operation.

Similarly, it is more than likely that the VP Operations would have a warehouse and transport manager responsible to him. Separation of that function might depend on the size and complexity of the warehouse operation and its technological requirements to schedule and receive just-in-time inventories, and to replace customers' just-in-time inventories on instructions by satellite.

The fictitious organization chart illustrated assumes that the marketing burden and the sales burden are too onerous to be born by one top manager.

An assumption is often made that once established in their little boxes, each executive will either be totally self-directed without need of any outside direction whatsoever, or that they are puppets programmed to act out a role limited to the specifics of their job description. In fact all kinds of problems occur in the disorderly world of business, which is involved with human capacities and human desires. And although a faulty organization chart may be blamed erroneously, those problems generally arise from human limitations, such as disorganized executives, managers who lack the gift or skill of lucid communications, impulsive or undisciplined managers, autocrats, bureaucrats, managers who do not fully understand the nature of their responsibilities, paranoid managers, abrasive ones, those whose blissful ignorance leads them to work to minimum requirements, and those managers who were promoted beyond the level of their capabilities. And that is not all; there are plenty who suffer from a closed-door mentality which insulates them from their colleagues and their own personal staff, and closes their minds to changes and new ideas. They may be staff specialists who are accustomed to working on their own. Love of seclusion may appear to make them ideal for such a job, but no executive can afford to be disassociated from others; not even in a scientific or laboratory or engineering environment. Those who work in isolation reduce their value to a company, while often believing that their's is the most important role—as a consequence of not taking sufficient interest in what their colleagues actually do.

The word *bureaucracy* cannot be avoided when discussing management. It is quite simply defined as *excessive official routine*. Those three little words can riddle a business enterprise or an institution and weaken it like woodworm or dry rot. The bureaucratic manager enslaves him or herself with day-to-day office routines that are unnecessary or exaggerated and unproductive, but lead him or her to believe that they are continually busy. They *are* busy performing rituals that are intended to fill time or provide justifications for not making decisions. Bureaucracy is a state of mind that not only diverts an executive from achieving his own goals, but also inhibits a company from reaching its objectives. It wears down the resolve of other employees and can altogether slow down the dynamism of an enterprise by tying up other managers and workers with an abundance of red tape. It evinces itself in a mass of forms that are required to be completed regularly, memos relating to changes in procedures, unnecessary meetings, and indeed anything that has little or nothing to do with running a business. In the private sector, it leads to loss of any competitive edge. In government, it results in deficits.

Managers, supervisors, or other staff who suffer from those types of debilities represent unproductive investment and expenses that burden others and are stumbling blocks to a company's growth. To avoid such negative situations an organization's chart should reflect *real* needs to produce specific and measurable results; since managers must be results oriented and be held accountable for meeting budgets and rewarded for improvements. That is why the fictitious chart, which is shown, may be irrelevant to a firm's key needs. The danger of starting off with a row of empty boxes is that some kind of body can always be found to fill them, but it is the company's needs that should be addressed, not the boxes. Only when key results areas have been clearly defined should a search be made for someone to implement those needs.

The character and spirit of an enterprise will ultimately depend on the attitude of each one of the personnel shown in their little boxes. There is a right attitude and a wrong attitude: there is nothing in between. So how can we define the criteria required of those paragons who should fulfil the executive responsibilities in the ideal business organization?

Superior Managers

Old criteria that were defined to describe what distinguishes a superior manager from the others, are now out of joint with what had already happened in the business revolution by the mid-1990s. The West's economic disarray was somewhat like that moment in 1942 when Britain stood alone against overwhelming forces and skills at Tobruk, and the rest of the world waited expectantly for a miraculous victory—or defeat and a return to the Dark Ages. Britain suffered from a management crisis. Traditional management of war and battles had repeatedly failed for British High Command. But the unconventional—one could equally well say *entrepreneurial*—tactics of Heinz Guderian and Erwin Rommel had been outstandingly successful for the German army. Unfortunately, there was barely a handful of allied generals who understood technological or mechanized land warfare and could manage it operationally, like Guderian and Rommel. They included Charles de Gaulle, Benard Law Montgomery, and George S. Patton, Jr. Those five generals epitomized the personal qualities that would be required of superior managers.

They were all winners. Supremely self-confident and disciplined, independent, able to provide charismatic leadership, to train their command into a fighting frame of mind, stubbornly refusing to move until entirely ready, skilled in taking initiatives at the most suitable time and able to implement their own decisions without doubt, and ready and able to take risks and be held accountable for their own actions. Those elements require the possession of a superior intellect, and superior knowledge that can only come from practical hands-on experience.

But command of the type that is customary in the military in time of war is unacceptable in business in time of peace. Our own management crisis demands that managing managers and other employees must depend on a natural ability to work *with* managers and staff, rather than to *order* them what to do.

Discussion frequently takes place on how many managers or other staff a manager can comfortably handle well, without erosion of his or her performance. The ideal number of top managers for a president to delegate directly to is likely to be five; although he might manage six, depending on the extent of direct involvement with each one. The chart under review enables the CEO to create strong relationships with only four vice-presidents and still spend ample time on his own special expertise as well as planning, leadership, and development.

Although pressures of a bigger organization may oblige a CEO to manage eight or nine top managers, it is not advisable. But lower echelon management can cope with far more middle managers or staff. That is because of less responsibility and less complexity down the line, smaller budgets, and reduced accountability. Some organizations made their structures too shallow in attempting to cut costs after recessions, and oblige a vice-president to cope with as many as fifteen people. That strips a VP of effectiveness by reducing his or her thinking time, planning time, improving and innovating time. The quality of their performance is likely to be reduced accordingly.

On the other hand, a well-organized sales director might easily be able to handle up to forty-five or more salespeople, because they are not managers—providing they are grouped in five or six separate teams, each motivated, organized, and monitored by a sales manager or a team leader. Each team would, most likely, be responsible for a different sales region, in any case; or, as in the case of a department store, for a different department.

Much of the downsizing of the 1990s, which burdened managers with more responsibilities and less staff, is simply an attempt to restore margins. Unfortunately, it prevents value from being added and plays havoc with communications and customer service, by creating hollow companies that have been stripped of the very knowledge and marketing skills that could have created innovations, growth, and diversifications.

Key Results Areas

We gain a better idea of what a particular manager must do, when we look at the second chart (figure 7.2). We can see, for example, the folly of having a chairman assume also the role of president and CEO. A chairman's responsibility is to satisfy shareholders, for which he or she is likely to require a knowledge of finance and experience with financiers. A managing director's experience needs to be the general management of specialists, whose jobs and attitudes he or she will know from having reached the position of CEO through line management, preferably in the marketing orbit. It is the managing director who is the "conductor of the orchestra." The role of chairman might better be described as "a devil's advocate." Combining both functions generally means performing neither one nor the other—the resultant position becomes merely a personal power-base instead.

We also immediately see that whereas five top managers are directly responsible to the managing director or president, four have line responsibilities while one is a staff position advising on human resources. The concerns of those four top managers involve expanding market shares profitably. Whether the staff position will also be on the board would depend largely on

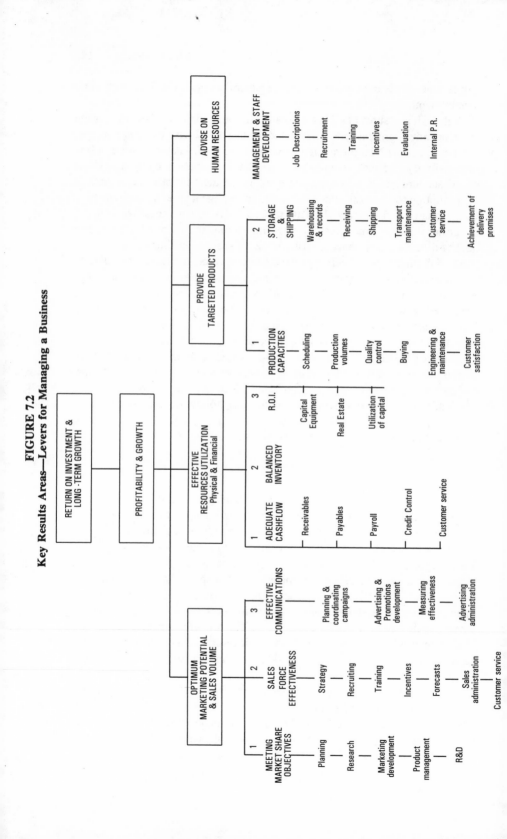

FIGURE 7.2
Key Results Areas—Levers for Managing a Business

the size of the organization and its stance according to the life cycle of the company. That position usually starts off as being a clerical one in a small enterprise in which the entrepreneur will be personally involved in hiring his or her personnel. It develops into a more responsible capacity when the clerical work has to be delegated to an assistant or secretary as the size and calibre of personnel increase.

That and the corporate culture are examined in more detail in chapter 15, since the position of personnel administrator or director of human resources is a controversial one. It is sufficient to say of the latter, that all business enterprises develop a culture and philosophy in the course of time, but unless it is planned at the outset, it is likely to develop in the wrong direction. It needs to be based on the company's unique mission, the products and services it is able to provide to a particular market niche, and the skills required to satisfy customers in that marketplace. Defining the cultural strategy in advance may prevent disproportionate growth of support areas at the cost of productive ones. Administrative empires habitually fail to support when they grow too big, because they create work for each other instead.

Autocratic managers and those who habitually procrastinate can be prevented from sprouting and creating a discouraging atmosphere, by identifying a more progressive management style at the very beginning. Autocrats often inspire fear in staff, and even in suppliers' representatives who will be discouraged from cooperating and certainly from supporting a negative customer. Discouragement on one hand and fear on the other, are likely to inhibit initiatives from other managers and staff, and prevent them from volunteering useful ideas and making the extra effort that marks the difference between a fertile and progressive enterprise and a sterile one.

While an organization chart and appropriate job descriptions may provide the framework for free communication and cross-fertilization of ideas, autocrats and bureaucrats (who are usually the procrastinators too) tend not to listen, but rather to discourage inputs and outputs. That effectively destroys opportunities for a continual learning process to develop staff by means of an open-door policy. Instead, it encourages isolation from colleagues, from the marketplace, and from customers as well as suppliers.

That is why a company's unique culture and philosophy stance needs to be thought out and set out clearly and unambiguously, so that all employees understand their obligations and commitments to each other, to their company, customers, shareholders, and the community. Starting off with a goal to maintain a lean and keen staff should gear the company toward growth of market share instead of growth of administrators who have nothing much to administer. Many of the problems of creeping overhead costs can be attributed to hiring too many of the wrong type of staff. But the people one needs with the most useful talents also possess human failings like other people. Effective leadership therefore means encouraging their strengths while reinforcing their weaknesses. Organization charts, job descriptions, and defining and maintaining a suitable culture are intended to support personnel in that endeavor.

The Round Table Concept

From an instrument to aid in scholarly learning, the desk changed to become instead an instrument of power and intimidation. One of the most important rules a manager has to learn, if he or she wishes to be productive, is to get out from under it. It prevents free two-way communications and also discourages a manager from being in contact with workplace and marketplace. The other impediment is a closed office door. Both desk and door can cause bad management habits and diminish a manager's effectiveness. A round conference table can provide a useful escape route from bureaucracy, autocracy, and procrastination.

The round table concept implies a first among equals instead of autocratic rule. We know of it from the Arthurian legend, and the positive effects of this different communications medium were described by Professor Hertha Orgler in writing of Adler's Round Table at the Café Siller in Vienna, where psychologists used to meet with him. The atmosphere, she wrote, "was that of serenity, warmth and cordiality."[3]

Using a round table for working groups is best done separately from any office, because the managing director or manager changes hats to suit the role of colleague or mentor. To ensure that everyone has done their homework and arrives fully prepared to be receptive and also provide relevant and useful information and new ideas, an advance agenda of the meeting is essential. Each particular team also needs to know that they will meet regularly each month or every six weeks, as the case may be. They also need to be made aware that such meetings are neither a chore nor a purposeless routine or ritual: they are a priority intended to inform and also to produce new ideas. To facilitate the process, a running progress list of questions carried over from previous meetings needs to be addressed at the beginning. And to introduce a fresh approach for each meeting, the role of chairperson should be rotated. Notes should be taken. Other executives or staff whose inputs may be required would be advised to be on standby, instead of taking up their time unnecessarily. A coded wall chart illustrating the section of the business plan or marketing strategy under discussion might be used to facilitate understanding and save time.

Such working groups are likely to involve separate and regular meetings with top management, a marketing work group, other vice-presidents' working groups, and Quality Circles. Whereas each VP or department head will use their own business plan as a guideline for their meeting, a Quality Circle meeting would be less formal.

It is their informal atmosphere and the mentoring process that success-fully enables each group leader to convey information through a progress report while also receiving input from staff. Since each group leader would also be involved in regular top management meetings at which different information will be bestowed from the fountainhead, as it were, each group leader is able to impart that acquired knowledge to his or her own group and also convey their own reports from the grass roots to the CEO. The network of new data and knowledge and common wisdom therefore courses throughout the arteries and capillaries, as the lifeblood of the organization. Management and current financial information may be conveyed to the marketing group in that way, while marketing information may be conveyed to the financial controller's group and the roundtable group chaired by the director of operations, and so on and so forth.

Current and future company activities may also be reviewed on an up-to-date PERT network chart, to confirm the progress of every single product or service and raise new questions or problems and address new opportunities. Every marketing executive who attends would have an opportunity to learn from the skills and problem-solving of others. That would facilitate the caretaking of different products, brands, or categories whenever a colleague might take over the responsibility for another product category or be promoted to a higher level in the hierarchy.

Using the marketing team as an example, more detailed discussion may involve research needs or the latest results from marketing research surveys already undertaken, progress on R&D activities and new needs, raw materials scheduled for a new product formulation, developments in packaging and print, production schedules, status of monthly sales forecasts, shipping dates, advertising and promotion campaigns, product strategies and market tactics, launch dates of new or innovated products, budgets, selling in to distributors, comparisons of brand barometers and changed market shares, competitors' activities, in-store shelf space and displays, category management, point of purchase materials, new research data from distributors, public relations, quality controls, and so forth.

In that way, each meeting can be made to be an enjoyable experience with learning opportunities and challenges to develop better ideas and skills.

Continual change is intrinsic to each department, and these are the ideal opportunities for conveying and discussing changes in policy or procedures or marketplace or technology changes. Just as products are always in a different position of each marketing cycle, so inventories are continually moving in, being converted to products, and moving out. The same applies to cash flow, with its payables and receivables and surpluses to meet the payroll. The objective of an efficient organization is not to store but to use and move, like the digestive system of a simple organism like a sea cucumber, where resources are required to energize it and then to be ejected to provide room to repeat the process over and over again. That process can only be initiated, maintained, and completed by skilled and dedicated managers.

Quality Circles

Meetings of Quality Circles (or Q-Circles) differ from other working groups in that all of the people involved are volunteers. None is an officer of the company. And their meetings are not structured according to the progress of items on a network chart; nor does the process correspond with an MBO plan.

What Q-Circles are supposed to do and how they do it is already well established by leading Japanese companies that have benefited from using them. Because of Japan's limited natural resources, they have become efficient at using what resources they do possess to the full. And they are well aware that it is human resources that can develop a company if those resources themselves are developed. They have been highly successful in encouraging participation by employees, and they discovered that a significantly large percentage of ideas placed in their suggestion boxes were realistic and useful in improving their company's performance. Full cooperation and loyalty from employees is one of the benefits that Japanese businesses enjoy in return for full and lifetime employment. They were quick to harness their employees' eagerness to help, to the concept of Quality Circles which initiate social interaction, harmony and self-discipline to the ongoing task of finding new ways to improve workplace processes and systems.

They found out what the Standard Register Company in the U.S. discovered in the 1950s, that users of systems and procedures often develop ways to improve them, because they are the ones who have had continual first-hand experience of observing the faults. Ben S. Graham—who was Director of the Systems and Procedures Division of the SRC in the United States—wrote, "Participation with 'know how,' built on understanding, stimulates interest, initiative, imagination, and results in enthusiastic cooperation."

Suggestions volunteered by Japanese staff also resulted in improvements to tools and assembly lines, which saved time, improved work, and reduced costs. A byproduct of Q-Circles is that staff enjoy their work more because of their participation and the recognition they receive for their contributions. Such involvement also develops their skills and opens up opportunities for gradual advancement.

The Q-Circle concept is based on a belief that standards of processes should conform to the requirements of end-users of those services or of participants in the manufacture and assembly of components and products. Quality standards can be isolated and measured and any deviations assigned a mathematical or a dollar value. Those deviations can be reduced and then prevented by improving the design or process. The technique can be applied to any activity that employees perform. And improving the system or the process often initiates re-education of workers. Improving their job can change their attitudes favorably toward it and the company they work for. But if it's not voluntary, it won't work.

The only individual who can encourage volunteers is a CEO who is known to be dedicated to the creation of an ideal working environment. He must be a passionate believer in innovation aimed at customer satisfaction, because he would have to sell the idea to employees. Each separate operational sphere might have its own Q-Circle, because improving systems and procedures and the flow of paper through an accounts department facilitates cash flow. That could be as important as facilitating the flow of products through an assembly line or a warehouse.

Continuous improvement of every facet of a business is a challenge that inferior "leave-it-alone managers" are not up to. Fortunately, every department always has a few employees who are dissatisfied with the way things are done. Their complaints may be dismissed as if they were habitual malcontents, or they may be listened to as possible sources of improvements or new ideas. Q-Circles take the positive approach. They acknowledge that employees get frustrated and demoralized from undertaking time-consuming jobs that could be simplified and laborious ones that could be made easier. But staff will be disinclined to be helpful in an authoritarian or bureaucratic regime where so-called training consists of being ordered to do just what you are told, no more and no less. It would be pointless, indeed harmful, ever to contribute constructive proposals there. Q-Circles can change attitudes favourably.

Right Attitude

All efficient organizations establish systems of one type or another to organize work and its management without friction or uncertainty. One such procedure is to be accountable to only one individual. The organization chart must clearly show that to be the case with every employee—not only in lines of authority but also by not confusing them with broken lines of communications: they should be unnecessary. People often assume that communications imply instructions, too.

Superior management and superior staff stem from possessing the right attitude as well as acquiring and practicing special skills. And yet, such are human frailties that we identify more often with symbols of helplessness like Charlie Chaplin's little man full of hopes and ideals which he hasn't the means to attain, instead of Nietzsche's superman. That is because we recognize our own limitations and are afraid to try to measure up against exceptional qualities, in case we fail.

Austrian psychologist Alfred Adler discovered what he named the *inferiority complex,* and also the compensatory mechanisms that come into play as a result of a wrong attitude toward life. In the course of his lectures he would invariably sympathize with his patients—whether neurotics, drug addicts, or criminals, by saying, "If I had his erroneous view of life, I would act exactly as he does." He considered even the worst of failures to be poor blunderers who had gone astray because of a faulty sense of direction. But with the right attitude, even very difficult tasks can often be undertaken without undue effort.

The parable of the two watchmakers is an example of this.[4]

Once there were two Swiss watchmakers whose watches were in equal demand. The name of one watchmaker was Bios: the other was Mekhos. Bios prospered while Mekhos struggled and finally failed in business. Bios hired him as a mechanic.

Each watch had about 1,000 parts. Each watchmaker assembled them differently. Mekhos assembled them bit by bit. Each time he was disturbed, he had to lay down his partly-assembled watch, which always fell to pieces: then he had to start all over again from the beginning.

Bios, on the other hand, first made sub-assemblies of about ten components each, which held together as an independent unit. Ten of them could then be fitted together into a larger system. Then ten of those systems were assembled to complete a whole watch. His method had the advantage that whenever he was interrupted and had to put down his work it did not fall into pieces.

Mathematically, a watchmaker like Mekhos, who is interrupted on average once in every 100 assembling operations with a watch of 1,000 pieces, will take 4,000 times longer to assemble a watch than Bios. Instead of a single day, it would take him eleven years.

Professor H. A. Simon, who designed computers, concluded that "complex systems will evolve from simple systems more rapidly if there are stable intermediate forms than if there are not. The resulting complex forms in the former case will be hierarchic. We have only to turn the argument around to explain the observed predominance of hierarchies among the complex systems nature presents to us." In short, "Wherever there is life, it must be hierarchically organized."

The Eightfold Path

If we switch from the cold logic of mathematical formulae to the spiritual discipline of Zen-Buddhism, which applies to morality and ethics, surprisingly we find ourselves in a similar area of self-improvement leading to exactly the same conclusions, because both depend on possessing the right attitude.

The Eightfold Path involves right views; right aims; right speech; right conduct; right livelihood; right effort; right memory; and right meditation. It emphasizes self-discipline and being discriminating about one's choices, as well as meditation. All of that is aimed at achieving harmony obtained from enlightenment, or *satori,* where even difficult tasks become seemingly effortless. That is also the aim of any superior management methodology.

An ideal business would be likely to follow such a methodology. But companies in crisis or those that have already failed are not likely to have observed one, or most likely possessed an ineffective one. And sometimes companies that once defined a useful methodology failed to take the trouble to follow it. Even in 1967 Drucker wrote, "Effective organizations are not common. They are even rarer than effective executives. There are shining examples here and there. But on the whole organization performance is still primitive." Not much of significance in the calibre of management has changed since then. But the revolutionary changes in our social and economic environment and in business demand far better management of our resources.

The right attitude from management is a focus on marketing. But that is not what the survey by the National Training Board in South Africa revealed in 1990. They sent a questionnaire to 450 companies with more than 100 employees. Similar responses might have come from Canadian or British companies:

TABLE 7.1
Management Qualities that will be Required of Future Managers

Quality	N	% of Responses	% of Respondents
Sensitivity to changing social factors	45	15.8	69.2
Leadership	41	14.4	63.1
Adaptability	37	13.0	56.9
Conflict management	26	9.2	40.0
Negotiating skills	26	9.2	40.0
Entrepreneurial ability	25	8.8	38.5
Professionalism	99	7.7	33.8
Conceptual abilities	21	7.4	32.3
Other*	20	7.0	30.8
Analytical skills	13	4.6	20.0
TOTAL:	284	—	—

*Other: management-induced change, the ability to maintain resources, knowledge of international methods, professional management, and empathy.

What neither they nor the National Training Board seemed to understand is the impossibility of separating management ability from marketing principles, practices, and skills. Dr. Nico Smith remarked at the Fourth National Marketing Educators' Conference that "it is a matter of concern that marketing skills do not feature as an essential requirement for the future manager in South Africa. In the light of developments in management training worldwide, this is an aspect that needs to be critically examined and rectified." And, "the curricula for management education are too academic; this is a finding that all educational institutions but technikons in particular, should sit up and take note of."[5]

Wrong attitudes seem to be the result of a new and less experienced generation that was never involved in superior management or outstanding marketing. That is because, apart from a few exceptional companies, business sectors and institutions appear habitually to neglect skilled people whom they took years to acquire, and possibly even train. At the same time, their key managers apparently lose abilities through neglect or carelessness. But that is only a perception of a particular time in specific western economies. Such changes are partly generational, partly due to the damaging effects of economic recessions on particular industries, partly to brain drains, and partly to declines in educational standards that are lowered even further to meet the lower reach of a broader democratic base, instead of catering for an intellectual élite. There are also national cycles in which people who have been deprived of education become voracious book readers, scholars, and self-improvers, while those in formerly successful economies have become complacent and indifferent to declining standards of competence.

One result of all that is that we find an occasional oasis of calm where management is being nurtured in some small or medium-size enterprises or some government departments. Departmental managers are younger than ever and appear to have been chosen more for their technical qualifications and computer compatibility than any management experience or marketing abilities. Their staff are mainly students not much younger than themselves, whom they mentor with care and consideration. It is pleasing to see, hear, and be aware of the relaxed atmosphere and the spirit of friendly cooperation and enthusiasm. But one cannot help wondering how they lost sight of their business objectives. Someone evidently appreciates their managers playing out the role of Mr. or Ms. Nice Guy, but managers with little knowledge or experience of the workplace have little of value to teach a group of even less experienced students, however willing they may be to learn. Meanwhile, who is running the business or the department, and with what objectives? And how long can this alleged management style last in the face of mature and knowledgeable Asian business people with whom we must compete?

Marketing Focus

Although recognition of marketing principles and the practice of marketing reached a peak in Western Europe in the decade between 1952 and 1962, a later report by the University of Warwick's School of Industrial and Business Studies in 1987 concluded that "most British companies lacked any coherent marketing strategy. They lacked ambition and commitment to market share, and reacted defensively to the Japanese penetration of their markets.... Often their products had no competitive advantages and they were left with the lower-priced down-market segments." It showed that 47 percent of British companies were not clear about their target market segments or what their needs were, compared to 40 percent of the U.S. companies and 13 percent of Japanese. Evidently they had lost their marketing focus.

A new report by Cranfield's Centre for Advanced Research in Marketing was unveiled in April, 1994 by the Chartered Institute of Marketing in the UK. "Marketing has failed to live up to expectations," wrote Professor Malcolm McDonald, in explaining the results of their research on the current state of marketing. But that was because organizations "adopted the trappings of marketing, rather than the substance, giving a veneer which fooled observers. So-called 'marketing managers' created the impression of responding to market needs, yet in reality were employed solely to sell the organization's products or services. So marketing to the uninitiated became intrinsically linked to sales promotion and sales support.... The failure of British business lies in its view of marketing as a practical, tactical function rather than a corporate philosophy. Yet for many companies, marketing is about little more than brochure writing and market research surveys to generate sales leads."[6]

As competition intensifies, margins shrink and consumers' choices grow so that they become more choosey and demand better products at lower prices. Manufacturers and suppliers of services must become as sophisticated as the more discriminating buying public. Meanwhile, many sectors have reached maturity and over-capacity. That depresses margins still further. Only the effectiveness of new business technologies and the novelty of electronic appliances keep businesses afloat. One result is a pressure for marketing to produce better results and also to be more cost-effective.

Innovative marketing must shift from old-fashioned selling from warehouse stocks, to "marketing the *capability* of manufacture to exacting customer-specific requirements." *Research by leading academics continually demonstrates that companies with a strong marketing focus outperform their competitors.* Unfortunately only a small minority of businesses appear to be able to focus on innovative marketing.

To carry best marketing practices into the future, Professor McDonald maintained that marketing must operate at three levels; a corporate culture and pervasive philosophical level; a strategic level; and a tactical level. Moreover, best marketing practices are accomplished by leadership from the CEO and board: "Until organizations have adopted a company-wide marketing ethos, the effectiveness of their marketing activities will always be limited."

Most Canadian businesses have not yet focused on marketing. They are still puzzled about what it is and therefore don't understand what it can do for them. And, as in Britain, "managers are embarrassed at admitting their ignorance."[7] Their very lack of comprehension inhibits them from seeking advice or help. South Africa was fortunate to benefit from British expatriates escaping from bureaucratic red tape and socialist discrimination against business. Its marketing skills peaked in the decade from 1960 to 1973 and then declined with the brain-drain out of Africa which was triggered by UN sanctions. A summing up was voiced in Australia, but it could just have well come from Canada, the United States, or Western Europe: "Marketing is widely misunderstood by the general public and even by those working inside the industry. Text book marketing taught at universities doesn't necessarily translate easily into real world marketing job functions as marketers' roles vary so widely from company to company. Therefore most people don't know what a marketer is, or what he/she does."[8]

Is it a matter of education? Marketing-oriented management has been openly discussed for nearly a century and leading multinational business organizations have been carefully following a marketing philosophy for almost as long. No doubt that is what helped to make them grow to be market leaders multinationally. Drucker has been writing intelligently and persuasively on management and marketing for half a century. The Japanese and other Pacific Asian economies learned it from the West and overtook them within four decades. The leading question remains: How could they master it globally when we cannot? Is it simply a matter of having the right attitude, as Adler said? And if so, what motivates people to want to possess it?

8

What Motivates People

In the course of many responsibilities a manager interfaces with colleagues, top management, staff, suppliers, and customers. To direct, satisfy, cooperate, or negotiate with them, he needs to know what motivates them and how to do so. If we study all the theories available on what motivates human beings to behave in certain ways, it becomes apparent that while there is a multitude of different theories, none of them is fully adequate.

However, theories of motivation can help a manager to understand what it is that triggers specific behavior patterns. We also need to know in what way a person can be motivated and for how long that person will persist. By understanding the psychology of motivation a manager hopes to be able to predict particular behavior patterns in people. Philosopher Hume was well aware of that when he wrote, "Nothing is more fluctuating and inconstant on many occasions than the will of man; nor is there anything but strong motives which can give us an absolute certainty in pronouncing concerning any of his future actions."[1]

Although classical philosophers concerned themselves with questioning and theorizing on what motivates people, studies in our own era originated as a consequence of the discoveries of Charles Darwin on the origin of species, and the different needs or compulsions in a particular environment that prompted quite different changes in behavior in order to survive.

Each group adapted to different circumstances in different ways. Until then, it was thought that the dynamic that triggered an arousal of behavior was physical for animals and both physical and spiritual for human beings. The earliest psychological concept for motivation was a combination of pleasure and pain. Career motivation or the motivation for fulfillment of ambition throughout most of recent history, is commonly symbolized as a carrot-and-stick approach. But in its broader sense, human beings knew that they could achieve kingdoms if they were winners, or lose their head by the axe if they failed. It is only quite recently that theorists seriously suggested that there are better ways to motivate people.

Darwin's studies on motivation of each individual member of a species are concerned with survival and reproduction in a specific environment in which it exists, and changes in characteristics of a species as some of its members manage to survive. Others become marginalized when they lack suitable survival skills in a particular environment. It has since become evident that the motive for animals and humans to adapt or change is survival. That destroyed a need, in some theorists' minds, to consider *will*, *wants*, and other *motives* when they were directed solely to survival as a reason for behavior. But other psychologists interpreted Darwin differently: "[B]ehavior, both simple and complex, animal and human, could be studied for the antecedent variables affecting and determining them," wrote Abraham Korman.[2]

That led to several different approaches and theories in the study of arousal, direction, and persistence of behavior. The main ones are: behavioristic, arousal or activation, incentive, hedonistic, achievement motivation, and frustration-aggression.

Behaviorists

Some behaviorists studied animals in zoos for many years to learn about their behavior and the behavior of human beings. Papers were written, lectures were given, theories published, and conclusions drawn—based on zoological studies. It was when zoos became modernized, animals were allowed to roam more freely in the grounds, and behaviorists went out into an animal's natural environment to study its species, that most of the theories were found to have been entirely wrong. What they had considered to be normal behavior, like the lion pacing in its cage and the chimpanzee masturbating in its cell, turned out to be abnormal behavior. What they had been studying were imprisoned and deprived animals whose behavior, as a consequence, was neurotic.

The philosopher Bertrand Russell cautioned the public as follows: "[A]ll the animals that have been carefully observed have behaved so as to confirm the philosophy in which the observer believed before his observations began. Nay, more, they have all displayed the national characteristics of the observer. Animals studied by Americans rush about frantically, with an incredible display of hustle and pep, and at last achieve the desired result by chance. Animals observed by Germans sit still and think, and at last evolve the situation out of their inner consciousness. To a plain man such as the present writer, this situation is discouraging. I observe however, that the type of problem which a man naturally sets to an animal depends on his own philosophy, and that this probably accounts for the differences in the results."

If a manager is skeptical at the very beginning, he will save himself from a great deal of confusion.

In 1913, Professor John Broadus Watson, at John Hopkins University in Baltimore, published a paper. It called for a type of psychology that would be entirely objective. "The time has come when psychology must discard all reference to consciousness," he wrote. "Its sole task is the prediction and control of behavior; and introspection can form no part of its method." By that statement Watsonian Behaviorism excluded all mental activities from science, because they cannot be observed by others. Whereas psychology was previously defined as the science of the mind, behaviorism replaced it with the conditioned-reflex chain. He favored a conditioned response model known as classical—or Pavlovian, after the Russian psychologist who first conditioned dogs to salivate at the sound of a bell. He taught that it was the basis on which to understand changes in behavior.

He showed, for example, how he could condition a boy to respond with fear to a rabbit that he had not originally feared. He then re-conditioned the boy not to fear it, as a demonstration that Watson's way of understanding the antecedents to behavioral choice and its direction was meaningful, and that he could do so without resorting to (what he believed was) the mysticism of conscious experience.

"By far the most powerful school in academic psychology," wrote Arthur Koestler, "which at the same time determined the climate in all other sciences of life, was, and still is, a pseudo-science called Behaviorism. Its doctrines have invaded psychology like a virus which first causes convulsions, then slowly paralyses the victim."

Despite Koestler's views, Watsonian Behaviorism persists today, with any number of psychologists who approach motivation with this type of model in mind. Korman points out that this psychological process is very difficult to equate with physiological processes. How, he asks, can such an approach be successful? "Can it deal with such questions as the choice of one goal as opposed to another? Can it explain the anticipation and expectancy of achieving goals and incentives? Can these really be translated into a physicalistic system?"

About fifty years later Professor Skinner of Harvard University wrote Science And Human Behavior, in which he stated firmly that mind and idea are nonexistent and invented for the sole purpose of providing spurious explanations.

Wrote Koestler, "[F]ew of the theories and concepts of modern physics would survive an ideological purge on Behaviorist principles—for the simple reason that the scientific outlook of Behaviorism is modelled on the mechanistic physics of the nineteenth century."

"The 'cynical onlooker' might now ask: if mental events are to be excluded from the study of psychology—what is there left for the psychologist to study? The short answer is: rats. For the last fifty years the main preoccupation of the Behaviorist school has been the study of certain measurable aspects of the behavior of rats, and the bulk of Behaviorist literature is devoted to that study."

Each Skinner box is equipped with a food tray, an electric bulb, and a bar that can be pushed down—like the lever of a one-armed bandit—whereupon a food pellet will drop into the tray. A rat, when placed in the box, would press the lever down with its paw, and sooner or later it would be rewarded automatically with a pellet. It soon learns how to get food by pressing the bar. Skinner called that "operant conditioning"—because the rat operates on the environment (unlike Pavlovian conditioning, where the dog does not). Pressing the bar is called a "reinforcing stimulus," or a "reinforcer." Withholding a pellet is a "negative reinforcer." The rat's rate of response depends on the number of times it presses the bar in a given period. All this was designed to arrive at a quantitative means of measurement.

Skinner's best-known books *The Behavior Of Organisms* and *Science and Human Behavior* contain data that were largely derived from conditioning experiments with rats and pigeons, "and then converted by crude analogies into confident assertions about the political, religious and ethical problems of man," wrote Koestler. "The motivational drive of the rat is measured by the number of hours it has been deprived of food before being put into the box; human behavior, according to Skinner, can be described in the same terms."

One of the consequences of Darwin's theory of evolution was a primary emphasis on the notion of *instinct*. Darwin's view was that instincts determined the likelihood of survival of both the individual and the species. Those innate behavioral tendencies respond to such stimuli as hunger, thirst, and pain. They cause behaviors intended to eliminate them. And the survival of the organism depends on them to perform or it would die.

Human behavior was considered to be a manifestation of many instincts. The invention of the instinct was useful for a time, to embrace, uncritically, almost any kind of behavior. It was frequently used in the writings of European ethologists—ethology being a study of animal behavior. McDougall, Woodsworth, and Freud all wrote of instincts. McDougall saw human beings as essentially driven by irrational instincts. He considered that the main reason for socialization was a need to control them. His concern for impulsive sources of action was incorporated into the contemporary concept of *drive*. It was Woodsworth who introduced the term *drive* into psychology, by means of the analogy of an automobile. It has mechanisms for giving motion to the wheels and for steering them, but they need an energy supply to make them go. He defined it as drive. Freud too emphasized the irrational impulse-driven aspects of human conduct, which he suggested rested on instincts. He was particularly concerned with their unconscious character.

Behavior varies in the speed with which it is triggered and in its intensity and scope, its duration, and quantity. That is its energy. It also varies in kind, and in its concentration on one goal or another. That is its direction. Some theorists are concerned with the qualitative aspects of direction—such as goals, purposes, choices, preferences, and decisions. Others consider that motivation serves to energize behavior and not to direct it.

Classical Freudian theory seemed to attribute motivation with both the functions of energizing *and* directing behavior, while emphasizing qualitative aspects. According to Freud, human beings have innate needs that must be satisfied. Each need creates tensions. The ultimate cause of all activity is the reduction of those tensions. That is why arousal occurs and takes the direction it does. He described instinctual energy as requiring discharge because it accumulates if not vented. But discharge is frequently delayed if the environment is inappropriate. A small child would therefore experience frustration in dealing with the environment. Some theorists believe that frustrations are essential to initiate the development of an ego.

The ego is a control mechanism that serves the id by reducing or preventing frustration, in allowing the libido to be discharged in such a careful or disguised way that punishment or disapproval can be avoided. But the ego also steers a person toward objects of satisfaction or gratification. In that way, the ego monitors the instinctual drive of the id. Moreover, the superego is a third internal operative that imposes a set of social and parental standards and prohibitions. It can punish the ego by inducing anxiety through threatening to diminish its self-esteem.

Freud's theory coincides with Darwin's, in that a person's survival in an environment that provides opportunities will depend on developing mechanisms that allow fulfillment of such instincts as are necessary for survival.

But drive won out over instincts as the major concept for motivation, among traditional functional psychologists. There were two main interpretations of drive. An American physiologist named Cannon described how the experience of hunger occurs from contractions of an empty stomach, and thirst from a dry mouth and throat. Sexual and other drives were considered to stem from similar local stimulation. An individual would therefore feel impelled to relieve such uncomfortable conditions, which arose from internal sources. But it was found that hunger behavior still existed in laboratory animals after they had their stomachs removed or nerves cut. Similar situations occurred with desert thirst, when people continued to drink even after wetting their mouth and throat. And sexual desire has been reported by men who have been castrated or denervated.

Another interpretation of drive described it as a central regulating state. Examples were the increase of intake of food or water by an organism after it has been deprived for greater periods of time. That was supported by studies of an American physiologist, Curt Richter, who discovered an activity rhythm in his laboratory rats during twenty-four-hour periods. Feeding was followed by low activity, which remained low for some hours, then increased to a peak as the next feeding time approached. As drive mounts, activity increases. Internal conditions leading to regulatory behavior became the major notion of the theory of drive.

Arousal or Activation Theory

The influence of the drive theory declined around 1950 when a theory of arousal (or activation) arose to prominence. Other theories also appeared to contradict the theory of drive and support the arousal theory. There was evidence from using the electroencephalogram to demonstrate brain activities arising from physical stimulation. Fluctuations were recorded in patterns that corresponded with excited or emotional states in humans and other mammals. They indicated that those emotional states resulted from high degrees of arousal. That approach suggested that both arousal and direction of behavior are due to a desire to attain a normal or balanced outcome, by rejecting too much stimulation or too little. Behavior was at the highest level of efficiency at intermediate levels of arousal.

Meanwhile, other data revealed evidence of curiosity in the behavior of laboratory animals that explored their environment, manipulated objects, oriented themselves to new stimuli, and also demonstrated preferences for unfamiliar objects or situations. None of those behavior patterns could be attributed to internal or biological drives. New drives such as curiosity and exploration now began to be considered.

Other laboratory work with paid human volunteers in conditions of sensory deprivation revealed that they found their apparently tension-free situations intolerable within a day or two, and hurriedly left to find higher levels of sensory stimulation. Many had experienced hallucinations or showed other abnormal symptoms. Other findings too did not support a tension-reduction theory. Laboratory animals like rats, for example, would work hard to obtain stimulation from electrodes implanted in their brains, even to a point of exhaustion.

There was some vagueness in the arousal theory, because the state of arousal was not related to specific antecedent circumstances, but it provided a popular acceptable theory based on motivation by external factors.

Incentives

The incentive theory rose to prominence in the 1960s, but it was already known that objects that are goals, such as food or sex, significantly influence behavior. And laboratory rats performed better when specific incentives were made available.

Evidence from experiments failed to conform to the drive theory. Some functions were found to be learned rather than innate or automatic. And in hormonally based studies on sexual behavior, it was observed that male rats showed no sexual behavior without the presence of a female in heat. Even then, considerable mutual stimulation appeared to be necessary before a stage of copulation was reached. And when an obstacle, such as an electric grid, was placed between them, an incentive had to be displayed before it was crossed and consummation was possible.

Psychologists Cofer and Appley demonstrated two mechanisms to describe the instigation of incentives. In their anticipation-invigoration mechanism, animals learn to be aroused by the presence of (or imminent occurrence of) an incentive. That is learned anticipation. In their sensitization-invigoration mechanism (which applied to behavior not previously learned) arousal appeared in the presence of an incentive and an appropriate hormonal condition. They claimed that direction of behavior is provided by the stimulus conditions of situations through innate relationships or ones that can be modified by learning. External factors such as a receptive female, were shown to be important.

The psychologist Henry Murray had already published a list of human motives or needs in 1938. They were categorized as being either innate (biological) or acquired (learned). He considered they triggered behavior by relating it to goals. Among the motives he defined that were considered most important were needs for achievement, anxiety, and aggression.

Wrote Korman, "Behavior is viewed, therefore, as a continuing series of choices designed to obtain the best outcomes possible." He described Edward Tolman's approach toward motivational phenomena, which "sees behavior as being initiated by various internal and external environmental cues and by disequilibrium situations of various kinds." The major components of Tolman's theory are intervening variables. They are demand for a specific goal, the degree to which the goal is available (or exists in an organism's specific environment) and his expectations of achieving the goal in that specific environment. They determine the direction and persistence of behavior until the goal is reached.

Tolman's work is reminiscent of McDougall's, which came into disrepute. But according to Korman, his approach and testing differed greatly. "McDougall cited the common observations that behavior is persistent, that it is variable in overcoming obstacles to reaching goals, that it terminates when a goal is achieved, and that it improves with repetition." According to McDougall, instincts include at least three parts—receptivity to certain stimuli; a disposition to behave in certain ways rather than others; and an emotional component. The problem was how those variable causes were to be defined and measured or experimentally manipulated, independently of the behavior they were designed to predict. "Tolman was very careful to meet this necessary methodological requirement," wrote Korman.

Hedonic

Pleasantness and unpleasantness produce, in hedonic terminology, behavior that is ordered on a continuum of approach and withdrawal. Approach is defined as being manifested toward goals, situations, or outcomes that are considered to be pleasant. Avoidance or withdrawal are defined as anticipation of contact with a condition that will be unpleasant.

That theory is based on a proposition that all motives are learned.

A logical assumption from that, is that human beings are motivated to achieve outcomes that involve a moderate discrepancy from levels of previous adaptation, and to avoid outcomes that involve extreme discrepancies from previous levels of adaptation.

Achievement Motivation

Henry Murray began with an assumption that people have motives and those motives should be studied as to the way they arouse and direct behavior. And what was important would be found in people's everyday lives. The laboratory therefore played only a minor role. The need for achievement was studied by Murray according to measurements, its relation to behavior, and development. Measurement was achieved by scoring stories he would have people write in response to each one of several pictures—known as his Thematic Apperception Test. Papers would be graded according to any evidence that a writer showed concern about competition against a standard of excellence—in other words, that they were achievement oriented. There was some evidence that the need-for-achievement scores reflected positive achievement factors and also elements relating to a participant's fear of failure. They included risk-taking studies, from which it was found that those who fear failure tend to choose alternatives for which success appears certain—or for which it would be unlikely that they could be blamed for failure.

Evidence demonstrated that the need for achievement is learned. There is some uncertainty as to which experience influences the development of a need to achieve, but in people with high scores, its origins were identified in emphasis on independence training at an early stage of childhood.

David McClelland added to Murray's work in the 1950s by arguing that people differ in the degree to which they consider achievement to be a satisfying experience. His concept too, enabled measurements to be made of people's achievement motivation. It also provided possibilities of defining those who will develop achievement motivation and those who will not. And it enabled predictions to be made as to who will act in an achievement-oriented mode in a specific situation, and who will not. It indicated that people with a high need for achievement are likely to be attracted to an entrepreneurial career. Since economic growth of a country depends on success in entrepreneurial roles, it follows that a nation's success would depend on the number of people attracted to that type of career. Therefore, the greater the achievement motivation in a society, the better its economic performance should be.

A general concept of reward and punishment, while having worked tolerably well in a number of cases, often has not stimulated performance. It suggests that decision to achieve could be far more complex in its motivation. For example, a psychologist named B. Zeigarnick found in her research that certain people have a compulsion to complete a task or achieve results. She wrote that "the setting of an objective does not result in its achievement unless the person or persons involved have a sufficient compulsion for closure of actions to attain the goal." And, "Accomplishments preoccupy them. In contrast, others have weak or very little compulsion to finish work assignments. Activities preoccupy them."

There are other anomalies: "Women of high self-esteem who want to go to college are more likely to engage in behaviors designed to achieve that goal than women who want to go to college who have low self-esteem" (Denmark and Guttentag, 1967)[3]. Or, "People who expect that they will have to do something unpleasant on the basis of previous experience choose to perform the unpleasant task, even when they could have chosen a more pleasant one" (Aronson, Carlsmith, and Darley, 1963)[4]. And research undertaken by Karabenick in 1972, found that females did better when competing against males than when competing against females.

In spite of what has been learned so far about achievement motivation, many questions remain unanswered and present challenges for other researchers.

Frustration-Aggression Hypothesis

Some people are believed to have considerable tolerance to frustration, whereas others have less ability to resist frustration stresses. The hypothesis that frustration leads to aggression is not always supported by observations. On one hand, different responses have been observed among frustrated people. On the other hand, aggression frequently arises from anger triggered by insults, irritations, or attacks from others. There are also displacements of aggression caused by anger, such as when a person deliberately breaks an object or hits an innocent animal. There is also catharsis, or emotional release.

Berkowitz wrote a monograph in 1962,[5] as a basis for a revised formulation of the hypothesis by Dollard et al. in 1939, which was considered to be flawed.[6] He suggested that three types of prediction follow from the original frustration-aggression hypothesis. They are—the greater the frustration, the greater the instinct to aggression; the stronger the motive being frustrated, the greater the frustration and therefore the impulse to aggression; and the greater the number of frustrations, the greater the aggressive response. Berkowitz concluded that only the first two hypotheses were supported by the research findings.

A more generally accepted theory is that aggression is simply a learned behavior for getting one's own way. It has been observed that the individuals or groups of people chosen as targets for aggressive behavior are weaker. They do not have the economic, social, psychological, or physical strength to fight back—which makes the aggression most likely to succeed.

Hierarchy of Needs

That summary of factors that are considered to motivate various behavior includes remarkably few human needs. Perhaps that is why Abraham Maslow's hierarchy of needs theory enjoys popular appeal. He considered that human beings are motivated by a whole range of different needs and that specific groups of needs function hierarchically. Physiological needs like thirst, hunger, and sex are at the first level of his hierarchical model. Only when they are satisfied would a person be motivated by needs for safety, like shelter, health, and security. Needs for belonging would not motivate sufficiently until safety needs had been fulfilled. Only then would come the turn of ego needs such as esteem, success, prestige, and self-respect, to be satisfied.

At the top of his hierarchy, Maslow proposed that a need for self-actualization was the motive, through self-fulfillment and personal growth. He held that higher needs cannot be expressed satisfactorily unless lower ones that dominate behavior are satisfied. Evidence for his theory appears to be only marginal.

Scores of professors who specialize in a particular subject, or an aspect of it under review, are quoted in specific chapters of this book. That they often contradict each other is immaterial to our discussion. What is more important is that their ideas and theories stimulate. They open our eyes and break the mold of our own learning, our customary way of thinking, and traditions. They change our viewpoint and therefore influence our attitudes. Professor von Bertalanffy humorously referred to "that slightly ridiculous figure, the professor," by defining his place in the pecking order as being below that of a manager of a five and ten cents store, a modern GP, a second-rate TV starlet, models, and boxers. After that self-deprecating introduction he carefully points out that professors (or such people who were not called that at the time) are the people "who create world views, values, problems and solutions." The creation of Renaissance Man was the work of professors, he says. "The French Revolution and the United States were inventions of Voltaire, Rousseau and the French Encyclopedists. The Soviet Union was drafted by Karl Marx in the circular reading room of the British Museum.... *The Weltanschauung,* the view of life and the world, of the man in the street...is a product of Lucretius Carus, Newton, Locke, Darwin, Adam Smith, Ricardo, Freud and Watson.... It is we who, in the last resort, *manufacture the glasses* through which people look at the world and at themselves."

Whether a business executive agrees with Professors Maslow, McGregor, Herzberg, Graves, or Argyris; or with psychographics, theories of store patronage, or paradigms and so forth, is irrelevant. What is important is that a manager knows and understands the theories. Karl Popper reminded us how scientific theories are frequently overthrown by experiments, and that *"the overthrow of theories is the vehicle for scientific progress."*[7]

Where corporate life is concerned, a consciousness of sibling rivalry can be helpful, since commonplace family behavior also shows up in business organizations. The president is sometimes seen as a father figure; particularly if he is autocratic or a benevolent dictator. And since a company is often regarded as mother—as with Ma Bell, for example—there is a potential for conflict when a manager considers that decisions of the president could damage the company. That executive may develop a classic Oedipus Complex and harbor resentment or anger against his superior. On the other hand, when a CEO is a charismatic leader who is admired, respected, or even regarded with some affection, managers frequently vie with each other for his attention and approval. Some executives make every effort to initiate a special relationship with the CEO, while others may feel rejected or defeated. Some behave irrationally through frustration. Others are so aggressively competitive that they are prepared to damage another's reputation to put him down and replace him in the chief executive's regard.

We should also take note of American philosopher William James, who directed Carl Jung's attention to *the clash of human temperaments.* By doing so, he influenced Jung's typology. According to Jung, "the chasm between introverts and extroverts...is unbridgeable." Even when they appear to share the same world, they perceive it differently; when seeming to use a common language, they attach different meanings to it. "The conflicts between the two types...are caused by prerational commitments so basic and ineluctable that attempts at compromise are fruitless."[8]

Many authors—scientists and pseudo-scientists—fell into the same trap that waited for Jung when he rejected Freudian analysis. In formulating his own doctrine of a collective unconscious, he began to label archetypal images from mythology, and attempted to provide a general rule of personality typology. But human beings are more complex than that. The point is that each is a unique individual because of a different mix of inherited and environmental factors which contribute to his or her character. It can therefore be dangerous to settle for a limited number of generalized stereotypes—even though there may be recognizable dominant characteristics that tempt us to do so.

For example, William James made a clear distinction between two basic types of people; the tough-minded and the tender-minded. According to him, the former are empiricists, lovers of facts. The latter are idealists devoted to abstract principles or ideologies. Each is antagonistic toward the other because the tough consider the tender to be sentimental soft-heads, whereas the tender look upon the toughs as callous or brutal. "Each type believes the other to be inferior to itself."

In the light of what has been learned and what is still unknown about what motivates people, the following summaries may assist in addressing seeming contradictions and reaching some kind of conclusion:

1. *McGregor's "Theory X"* assumes that people dislike work and must therefore be coerced, controlled, and directed toward organizational goals. Furthermore, most people prefer to be treated that way, so that they can avoid responsibility. "Theory Y," on the other hand, emphasizes the average person's intrinsic interest in his or her work, a desire to be self-directing and to seek

responsibilities, and the capacity to be creative in solving business problems. Professor McGregor concluded that "Theory Y" is the more desirable scenario for managers to follow.

• *But John J. Morse and Jay W. Lorsch conclude,* "For many enterprises, given the new needs of younger employees for more autonomy, and the rapid rates of social and technological change, it may well be that the more participative approach is the most appropriate. But there will still be many situations in which the more controlled and formalized organization is desirable. Such an organization need not be coercive or punitive. If it makes sense to the individuals involved, given their needs and their jobs, they will find it rewarding and motivating."

• *And Professor George R. Terry states,* "Unless a company has hired or developed managers and employees with high Zeigarnick effects, it will find that the more conventional types of management, emphasizing authoritarian practices, should be followed."

2. *Professor Maslow's theory* is that when the more basic needs of an individual are met, only then will he or she make an effort to fulfil the next level of his or her needs. And only when those are satisfied will their behavior be directed at attaining the next highest level of needs.

• *But Professor McGregor* said, "a satisfied need is not a motivator."

• *And Professor Herzberg wrote* that motivation does not lead to achievement, it is the other war round—achievement leads to motivation.

• *Terry wrote,* "the setting of an objective does not result in its achievement unless the person or persons involved have a sufficient compulsion for closure of actions to attain the goal."

3. *Frederick Herzberg identified two aspects of a task:* the conditions surrounding it, which do not themselves generate high performance but are prerequisites to job satisfaction—and the task itself. Does it provide a sense of achievement and a challenge that will result in a sense of growth? In that sense, the task itself is a motivating factor.

• *Mowrer wrote,* in his survey on motivation in the *Annual Review* for 1952, "At the level of ego-psychology there may be said to be only one master motive: anxiety."

• *Freud in 1920:* "[T]he course of mental events is invariably set in motion by an unpleasurable tension, and it takes a direction such that its final outcome coincides with a lowering of that tension."

• *Hebb in 1949:* "It is clear of course that the primitive drives of pain, hunger, and sex are often of overwhelming importance. We need an approach to motivation that neither minimizes these things nor fails to provide for the unrewarded learning that also occurs when the animal's belly is full and his sex drive is satisfied."

• *Koestler in 1964:* "In classical Gestalt theory, motivation by rewards, usually in the form of bananas, is taken for granted."
• *Drucker in 1974:* "As people get more they do not become satisfied with a little more, let alone with less. They expect much more."

In his autobiography, Darwin wrote, "with the exception of the Coral Reefs, I cannot remember a single first-formed hypothesis which had not after a time to be given up or greatly modified."

"Let us face the facts," wrote Ludwig von Bertalanffy in 1967; "a large part of modern psychology is a sterile and pompous scholasticism which, with the blunders of preconceived notions or superstitions on its nose, doesn't see the obvious; which covers the triviality of its results and ideas with a preposterous language bearing no resemblance either to normal English or normal scientific theory." And Arthur Koestler wrote in *The Act Of Creation,* "It took natural philosophy nearly a thousand years to rediscover that the earth is round; it took experimental psychology nearly fifty years to rediscover...that rats and men are pleasure-seeking creatures, that some activities are pleasurably self-rewarding, and that exploring the environment, solving a chess problem, or learning to play the guitar are among these activities."

There is a recurring theme of serious researchers as different as McDougall, Freud, Koestler, and Jung, that they perceive human beings as being driven by *irrational* instincts. We all appear to be motivated by an effort to stabilize situations by seeking some balance in our own particular circumstances. Herbert Spencer wrote, "Life is the continuous adjustment of internal relations to external relations."[9] That balancing act does not appear to be what we might call a "happy medium"; rather, it is behavior that seems to be most likely to obtain the best possible outcome for us in any circumstances.

Although motivating managers and staff is a necessary management skill, evidently it is not a clear-cut science. If a manager appeals to a *rational* desire in others to seek equilibrium, would it be likely to work if human beings are driven by *irrational instincts*? Evidently not. It seems that if an executive does all the right things in management spheres, they are likely to work. But the more that he or she must rely on inputs from others, the more problems are likely to arise. What does that tell us about delegation? And what does it say about managers and staff? Nevertheless we have to work with them and managers have to motivate them.

The Three Great Motives

Perhaps we should conclude that there may be only a very thin dividing line between what is rational behavior and what is irrational. For example, Spinoza wrote that we do not desire something because it gives us pleasure:

rather it gives us pleasure because we desire it. And we desire out of the necessity for survival. For survival determines instinct and instinct desire, which triggers thought and action.

Schopenhauer saw desire as a will to live, while Nietzsche saw it as a will for power. And Popper (writing of Marxists who try to reconcile the claims of Marx with those of Freud and Adler) proposed that they may perhaps decide that the Three Great Hidden Motives of Human Nature are hunger, love, and lust for power.[10]

All that we can be sure of in the workplace is that people have a habit of performing in different ways from what we want of them, what we expect, and what we have been led to believe. But we notice that they all possess different personalities, and—as Jung remarked—they will therefore also possess different attitudes. Because of that, industrial psychologists undertake various tests to assess the suitability of a candidate for employment in a particular job. Tests might involve numeracy or design, management skills or selling techniques, or levels of responsibility or perseverance or frustration. One conveniently divides candidates into four extreme personality characteristics and approximately eight gradations of each personality type: (1) expressive; (2) amiable; (3) driving; and (4) analyzing. They are broken down as follows:

Expressive: personable, stimulating, enthusiastic, dramatic, over-reactive, undisciplined, or creative.

Amiable: respectful, considerate, willing, supportive, friendly, cooperative, retiring, or unplanned.

Driving: critical, pushy, dominating, organized, determined, decisive, well-planned, challenging, or direct.

Analyzing: respectful, listener, exacting, stubborn, unresponsive, persistent, industrious, organized, or detailed.

Four other psychographics are ones unlikely to recommend a candidate for a corporate management position. They are: (5) dominant; (6) easygoing; (7) spontaneous; (8) self-controlled. Those are broken down into qualities that might be considered undesirable: intolerant, impatient, argues, dogmatic, loud. Or quiet, shy, submissive, passive, indecisive, humble. Or disorganized, undisciplined, impulsive, frenetic. Or cold, unfriendly, unresponsive, closed, and so on.

The originators of that test illustrate it as follows (figure 8.1)

Natural Selection

There is another, more basic way to analyze people when assessing how best to motivate them. That is by determining their primary survival skill. We often do it automatically. The drive to survive is, after all, our most basic one. It was Herbert Spencer who coined the phrase "the survival of the

FIGURE 8.1

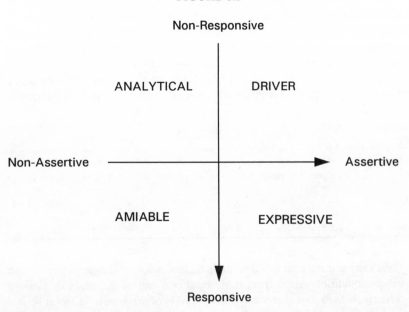

fittest." He believed that it is only those who advance under the pressures of the system who eventually survive. It is, he wrote, "the never-ceasing discipline of experience."[11]

It is that *never-ceasing discipline of experience* that developed the greatness in famous singers like Cathleen Battle, Maria Callas, and Pavorotti; great violinists like Isaac Stern and Yehudi Menuhin; extraordinary pianists like Vladimir Horowitz and Glenn Gould; superb ballet dancers like Baryshnikov, Massine, Violetta Elvin, Margot Fonteyn, and Nureyev. They dedicated themselves to a process of continuous improvement. As with Darwin's theory, that drive is nature's way of selecting the fittest of any species—*natural selection.*

In view of such a large range of different personality types with their different attitudes, it seems simplistic to believe that all of them would be motivated by exactly the same desires, like love, hunger, or power. In one retail outlet of a large textile group, a number of decorator/salespeople were employed, and each one required different motivation than each of the others. When they had been given the same sales incentives, some had been frustrated while others were filled with anxiety and could not achieve their best individual performance. Spinoza recognized an "instinct for self-preservation," but it takes a multitude of different forms, and those employees were a good example of the types of forms it can take. At opposite poles were the highest achiever who demanded a straight commission at the highest level, without any retainer, so that her earnings could be unlimited: and the placid interior decorator who felt insecure without knowing he would receive a regular modest fixed income to pay his basic household bills. He was not in the least bit motivated by earning commission. Between those two extremes was a range of varying needs for different ratios of commission and retainer, as in figure 8.2.[12]

FIGURE 8.2

Salespeople:	#1 Assertive	#2 Determined	#3 Enthusiastic	#4 Cooperative	#5 Willing	#6 Anxious	#7 Insecure	#8 Learner
Retainer:	—	20%	33%	45%	55%	67%	80%	100%
Commission:	100%	80%	67%	55%	45%	33%	20%	—

Not only did they all differ in their higher or lower Zeigarnick level, but their personalities varied from timidity at one end of the scale to extreme aggressiveness at the other. And whereas levels of drive were the most visible manifestations of a need to achieve, or the lack of it, each of them possessed different financial needs according to their individual life-styles and life cycles, and according to whether they had dependents or not, and—in one case— receiving a pension effectively lowered his need to achieve.

Another significant feature of managers and staff in the group of companies owned by that textile conglomerate, was that—skills and talents apart— many of them used different societal survival techniques. Whether they were "instincts for self-preservation" or whether they were learned, they used the most suitable techniques to get their own way. The means to do so may range from charm or sex-appeal, charismatic leadership or low cunning. To paraphrase Malthus, population multiplies faster than the creation of new jobs. That means—in today's restructuring and introduction of new technologies— that more people must compete for less jobs in order to survive. Survival skills act as a selective force, marginalizing the weak and creating a new élite from survivors who fit neatly into the job niches of the work environment. And management can find ways to appeal to an individual's overriding survival technique.

Depending on how they may be categorized, there appears to be at least eleven major ways for a person to assert their individuality to influence outcomes in their own favor, according to the limited choices at the disposal of each one. "Natural selection results in adaptation, with its several meanings and multiple manifestations. (It) involves interactions between individual organisms, their physical environment, and their biological environment— that is, other organisms."

"Thread a needle; your capacity to do so represents the cumulative effect of millions of years of selection pressures for digital dexterity and eye-hand coordination."[13]

Eleven Survival Skills

1. **Power:**	Political, military, financial, or physical strength.
2. **Cunning:**	Resourcefulness, ingenuity, skill at deception, or craftiness.
3. **Intelligence:**	Mental ability to learn and understand things.
4. **Dexterity:**	Digital dexterity and eye-hand coordination to use tools, weapons, and other technology. Ability to do something well.
5. **Adaptability:**	Ability to bend easily and change whenever advantageous in changing situations. Mimicry.
6. **Intuition:**	Knowing without reasoning or being taught. Gut-feel.
7. **Novelty-seeking or Curiosity:**	An enquiring mind with its desire for knowledge is innate in most intelligent animals; frequently resulting in discoveries likely to change goals, or the means to achieve them, to ones more likely to succeed. Nonconformity or idiosyncrasity may lead to a new way of thinking, likely to result in new discoveries.
8. **Avoidance of Harm:**	Evasion, inaction, abstention, or seeking moderation in accordance with the pleasure/pain principle.
9. **Reward Dependence:**	Working only for a price, perquisite, or bribe. ("Consider the love and devotion characteristics of the domestic dog; these are adaptations related to the procurement of food and shelter as stringently selected for as the beak of a woodpecker.")
10. **Persistence:**	The drive to continue a project in order to achieve favorable ends; or the compulsive *idée force* which can end in destruction and even self-destruction.
11. **Audacity:**	The heroic spirit and self-confidence of those for whom nothing is impossible. Absence of fear. Courage and vivacity; ardour or dash; speed and mobility; verve, daring, zeal, agility; press of business, determination, expedition and resolution.

All of those techniques are used in social intercourse, often to get the better of someone else. The first seven and the tenth "survival skills" listed above were identified in numerous workplaces and marketplaces over many years. Since they did not appear to have been scientifically researched, it was felt that there might be more of them. Now Dr. C. Robert Cloninger of Washington University's School of Medicine, has described four aspects as "basic bricks of a normal temperament." Novelty-seeking, avoidance of harm, reward dependence, and persistence are considered by psychologists to be attributable in good part to a person's genetic makeup—"the predisposition that one is dealt with at birth." Any one person may possess a mixture of varying degrees of the four temperamental dimensions, according to Dr. Cloninger.[14]

The heritability, or genetic component, of the four aspects was based on studies of identical twins who shared all their genes and fraternal twins who shared only about half their genes. In some cases, identical twins were reared apart and subject to different environments while their temperaments were being forged. It is random experience and circumstances that an individual encounters in childhood and chance exposures to reward and punishment that "may strengthen or weaken one's innate tendency toward avoidance of harm, novelty seeking and the like." But knowing a person's temperament "doesn't tell you whether the person is mature or immature. That's an issue of character development." Parental attitudes help a child to mature into a reasonable adult.

The eleventh disposition or skill is a rarity.

Transactional Analysis

The arena in which those techniques flourish is one in which practicing psychiatrist Eric Berne studied personalities and the survival skills that people use to get their own way. Since there can be no motivation without communication in the workplace, some knowledge of how Transactional Analysis works could be valuable for a manager. Berne describes social intercourse between two or more people as a *transaction*.[15] One will acknowledge the presence of the other in some way when they encounter each other. He refers to that as a *transactional stimulus*. The other person would make a *transactional response*. Interaction involves three different ego states between which anyone shifts at any moment. They are described as the Parent, the Adult, and the Child. Transactional Analysis is concerned with diagnosing which ego state initiates a transactional stimulus and which ego state responds.

Everyone who has been influenced by one or more parents carries an ego state that reproduces the parents as they were perceived in childhood. The Parent can be judgmental, critical or scolding. On the other hand, the Adult ego state is reasonable and objective and does not get emotional. Anyone can activate the appropriate Adult in themselves and be capable of responding in a mature and reasonable manner, too. But since everyone was once younger, they carry fixated relics with them from earlier years that can be activated under certain circumstances. So that everyone carries a little boy or girl around inside them, as well as the Parents and an Adult.

The objective is for an Adult ego to address another, and the response to emanate from the other Adult ego. That would be a *complementary transaction*; such as when an Adult state reacts in a mature and appropriate fashion to an Adult stimulus. For example, a secretary passes a folder of typed-up letters to her boss and he opens the folder and signs them politely. And there are other complementary transactions; such as between a Child and a Parent: when the sick child asks for some water and the mother acts appropriately and responsibly by bringing it. But a *crossed transaction* is when two adults fail to transact with each other in their Adult states. "Where the hell are my sunglasses?" asks one. A reasonable reply would be, "On the balcony." But if the respondent over-reacts like a Child, she might counter with, "How the hell should I know?" or "I didn't take them. You're always leaving them behind. Why don't you look after your things?" Berne described that as the main concern of psychotherapists, because it is the most common type of crossed transaction and one which causes most social problems.

Communication is aborted by responses like, "You're just like your mother!" or "You always blame me." or "You drink far too much!" He describes how crossed transactions can end with two speechless people glaring at each other. If the subject opened up for discussion in a reasonable adult manner was important, like gambling debts, drug addiction, or adultery—for example— the solution that requires cooperation and consideration will have been postponed, perhaps for ever.

Apart from Adult to Adult transactions and aborted crossed transactions, there are what Berne calls "Games People Play." That summary reveals just what a manager is up against when trying to communicate with colleagues and staff, let alone motivate them. But there are also ambiguities and curves; or what Berne calls *ulterior transactions* and *angular transactions*. He gives the following example of one, with which salespeople are particularly adept:

Salesman: "This one is better, but you can't afford it."
Housewife: "That's the one I'll take."

Another example of an ulterior motive is provided:

Cowboy: "Come and see the barn."
Visitor: "I've loved barns ever since I was a little girl."

That demonstrates how communications are used in different ways and that apparently simple and direct answers to what might appear to be straightforward questions may have a whole range of quite different meanings. Communications are frequently intended to conceal the truth. And, in some societies, it may be considered to be courteous to lie in order to keep a visitor happy. That evinces different cultural values, customs, and goals.

Multicultural Societies

Multiculturalism has grown in the West, and immigration, as well as tourism, brings different customs and values with it. But many societies have been multicultural for generations or even centuries. The following research survey (table 8.1) shows how psychographics can differ in the same geographical area according to different traditions and cultures.[15] Although it was undertaken in South Africa between blacks and whites, it is not skin color that produces differences. Different attitudes are prevalent between Francophones and Anglophones in Canada, between northerners and southerners in the United States, between Flemings and Walloons in Belgium, Bavarians and Hanoverians in Germany, and so forth. A slogan emerged in 1995, as most western economies were obliged to acknowledge that trade in domestic markets doesn't pay the bills: "Think global, act local." That means addressing local idiosyncrasies, customs, and cultures. For example, "Advertising, whether a brand is local, regional or global, will have to be culturally relevant in order to work," wrote Marcio Moreira.[17]

Shared motives are the glue that holds societies together and provides stability so that they can progress. And psychographics illustrate that personal attitudes can cut across demographic boundaries. For example, there are achievers or novelty seekers, socialites or hedonists, pessimists and optimists in all societies. Even the motives of extremist special interest groups, including solitaries like the unabomber, cut across national boundaries when they hold

TABLE 8.1
Multicultural Psychographics

Whites:	Needs:	Hallmark:
1. The Responsibles:	26% Security & Stability	Tradition
2. Brandeds:	27% Esteem & Belonging	Status
3. Self-Motivateds:	24% Style/Design/Harmony	Confidence
4. Innovateds:	23% Liberalism & Tolerance	Human Rights
Africans:		
1. Traditionals:	21% Black Culture	Age 50 plus
2. Responsibles:	20% Family & Community	Black causes
3. Brandeds:	19% Drugs & Alcohol	Group pressures
4. I-am-Me	22% Aggression	Toughs
5. Self-Motivateds:	17% Security & Comfort	Young & Educated

civilization to ransom. They are expected to increase in the twenty-first century, because we have not yet found an effective way to prevent their mischief.

Although their motives seem to be beyond our comprehension, Professor Edwards had no problem in conjuring them up when he described the self-indulgent or dog-in-the-manger attitude of Shakespeare's Iago. He "was born to oppose happiness. He is the sheerly satanic in man, bound by the acute malevolence that is his nature to wreck and destroy."[18] Anyone with loftier values or aspirations is an affront to him, since he cannot attain them himself. He will put them down by destroying their confidence and beliefs, stir up envy or jealousy or spite against them—particularly in those who, like himself, feel abjectly inferior to others.

They are the ones who use the negative side of the tenth survival technique, out of meanness and malice, in order to diminish society to their level. A single-minded idea takes possession of them and they cannot shake it off.

McLuhan associated today's urban bombings with a crisis of identity—linked with our new electronic culture: "The clash of the old segmented visual culture and the new integral electronic culture creates...a vacuum of the self, which generates tremendous violence—violence that is simply an identity quest, private or corporate, social or commercial.... All our alienation and atomization are reflected in the crumbling of such time-honored social values as the right of privacy and the sanctity of the individual..." We are all "scurrying around frantically in search of our former identities, and in the process unleash tremendous violence.... From Tokyo to Paris to Columbia, youth mindlessly acts out its identity quest in the theater of the streets, searching not for goals but for roles, striving for an identity that eludes them."[19]

II

Practices

*"Countries that wish to preserve their indepen-
dence must become more efficient in tapping
the energies of their populations. Elites exist in
every society and are justified if they
strengthen the community and are open to
talent and reward merit. That is far better than
the type of privilege that protects mediocrity."*

—Carl von Clausewitz

9

The Power of Words

Kant went into print in 1784 with his theory that conflict between people was nature's way to develop each individual's capabilities; that struggle creates character and initiates progress. He argued that if people were completely social beings they would stagnate. Complete harmony, contentment, and requited love would not have developed their talents. Competition is desirable for human beings to survive and grow—as it is for business enterprises. "Man wishes concord; but nature knows better what is good for its species; and she wills discord, in order that man may be impelled to a new exertion of his powers, and to the further development of his natural capacities."[1]

It was that "new exertion of his powers" that turned animallike grunts and gestures into verbal communications to direct clan members to hunt for food or work together in order to survive. People had to learn to cooperate or die from injuries caused by physical conflicts. Whether cooperation is a social mechanism or whether it is motivated by fear, it is what is required in a business organization that wants to survive and continually grow more successful.

But we have to be on our guard, because the gift of speech or literacy can also enable people to influence others to their detriment and the deterioration of the company for which they work.

Observations of social primates illustrate that they are able to order their society very well without having to use words as we understand them. But much more than that is required of business executives and technocrats in sophisticated industrial societies. Culture arose out of man's social drives, which were essential to avoid situations in which individuals were at war with everyone else. That attitude would have prevented the formation of societies, totems and taboos, matrimony, and the establishment of institutions.

"Vocal abilities appear prerequisite for language in the human sense (although, of course, man is by no means lacking in non-verbal language). To develop them, creative abilities are necessary...the basic fact in anthropogenesis is the evolution of symbolism,...Apart from satisfaction of biological needs man shares with animals, he lives in a universe not of things but of symbols.... Man lives in a symbolic world of language, thought, social entities, money, science, religion, art—and the objective world around him, from trivial surroundings to books, cars, cities and bombs, is *materialization* of symbolic activities."[2] Those symbols are freely chosen, and "the consequences of the images will be the images of the consequences."[3]

Technology may have refined the tools that a corporate executive now uses to make presentations in order to influence people, but it is the verbal skills necessary for persuasion and the charisma to inspire support that are in demand. Throw aside the technology and the skills still remain. Writing skills are required, too. It is those communication skills and the ideas they encapsulate that enable a manager to be upwardly mobile. They can persuade other managers to support her ideas and cooperate with her plans. They are also required for effective delegation. And the primary objective of words (and graphics) in advertising—whether by print, word of mouth, or electronic media—is to influence people to use a specific brand or product or service. Words can, therefore, possess the power to move people, if they are selected with care and assembled according to the appropriate formula that may be required to achieve a desired effect with a specific audience. It is no wonder that illiterate societies considered words to be imbued with magical properties: they create happenings. Two epic poems, for example, united diverse Aegean tribes into a Greek culture that would produce contemplative philosophers like Socrates and Plato, and successful generals like Pyrrhus and Alexander.[4]

Managing and marketing are group activities like hunting and gathering food. And the purpose of communications in a business organization is similar to that of hunters following a spoor that may lead them to the kill. It is to channel the individual skills of each member towards the same end, on which may depend the survival of all of them, and their families and their clan. Words can provide unambiguous direction if selected discriminately and used with simplicity and brevity.

But communications are often ambiguous and misleading. They may contain anomalies and contradictions because of errors or distortions of the truth. John Stuart Mill wrote of "the collision of truth with error." He believed that such discourse could only enhance the truth. Opening up such discourse means permitting every opinion to be expressed, since the suppression of even one dissenting opinion might deprive everyone of the *real* truth. For reality and truth are multifaceted and we need to explore every facet to understand their significance.

Mill wrote, "The beliefs that we have most warrant for have no safeguard to rest on, but a standing invitation to the whole world to prove them unfounded...if the lists are kept open, we may hope that if there be a better truth, it will be found when the human mind is capable of receiving it."[5] Hence the need for candid two-way communications in business organizations and the need for a devil's advocate; an outside consultant who can question opinions, attitudes, judgements, and decisions of a CEO or board that may have examined only one facet because it was unaware of others of equal or greater importance. Often he is likely to insist, as Voltaire did, that "if you wish to converse, first define your terms."

Gobbledygook

Communication can also be purposely distorted in order to deceive. The continued use of Latin by lawyers and doctors, when most people did not understand it, helped to conceal their incompetence or roguery from the public. And bureaucrats and technologists also use a language of their own making to numb the mind and even take control of our destinies. It has become known as *gobbledygook*. The following example was written by Hegel, who has been described as "the most influential figure in German philosophy." Karl Popper wrote of him as follows:

> In order to discourage the reader beforehand from taking Hegel's bombastic and mystifying cant too seriously, I shall quote some of the amazing details which he discovered about sound, and especially about the relations between sound and heat. I have tried hard to translate this gibberish from Hegel's *Philosophy of Nature* as faithfully as possible; he writes: "§ 302. Sound is the change in the specific condition of segregation of the material parts, and in the negation of this condition;—merely an *abstract* or an ideal *ideality*, as it were, of that specification. But this change, accordingly, is itself immediately the negation of the material specific subsistence; which is, therefore, *real ideality* of specific gravity and cohesion, i.e.—*heat*. The heating up of sounding bodies, just as of beaten or rubbed ones, is the appearance of heat, originating conceptually together with sound."
>
> There are some who still believe in Hegel's sincerity, or who still doubt whether his secret might not be profundity, fullness of thought, rather than emptiness. I should like them to read carefully the last sentence—the only intelligible one—of this quotation, because in this sentence, Hegel gives himself away. For clearly it means nothing but: "The heating up of sounding bodies...is heat...together with sound." The question arises whether Hegel deceived himself, hypnotized by his own inspiring jargon, or whether he boldly set out to deceive and bewitch others. I am satisfied that the latter was the case.[6]

That the works of some other authors contain passages that reflect either muddled thinking or carelessness, poor communications, or attempts deliberately to mislead the reader should make us skeptical whenever a writer fails to make the contents clear. The danger of gobbledygook is that it throws the responsibility on us by seducing us into thinking that a text must be profound simply because it is incomprehensible to us. Bertrand Russell wrote of Hegel's philosophy, "Like other historical theories, it required, if it was to be made plausible, some distortion of facts and considerable ignorance. Hegel, like Marx and Spengler after him, possessed both these qualifications."[7] Caird went even further when he wrote, "But the height of audacity in serving up pure nonsense, in stringing together senseless and extravagant mazes of words, such as had previously been known only in madhouses, was finally reached in Hegel."[8]

Franz Kafka described the nightmare world under totalitarian government and the misery created by its lackeys in *The Trial*. But it was surpassed by the reality of bureaucracy in the Third Reich and the USSR, and the ability of their propaganda machines to cover up and mislead the world about what was really happening. Gobbledygook is frequently described as misuse of language when, in fact, it is a purposeful deception of the public by brainwashing and reprogramming.

George Orwell wrote his treatise on the intentional misuse of language by politicians in 1946. Its intention is to make unsavory acts of the government palatable by avoiding the creation of a mental picture of what they are really doing. Their actions become legitimized by calling them something quite different. Orwell introduced the word *doublethink* into the English language to describe a process that is quite simply a confidence trick.

That trickster aspect of the English language is no more tricky than in other languages. The deception lies in what Gomperz described as "a simple and unsuspecting faith that the range of an idea and the range of the word roughly corresponding to is must in every case exactly coincide."[9] Wrote Jung, "It needed a long process of development before man recognized once and for all that the word...does not always signify a reality or bring it into being."

J. Ralston Saul emphasized the dangers of what he called blind reason. He traced the origins of its organization and administration to Loyola and his Jesuits. The objective is to implant thoughts designed to enslave us to ideology, dogma, products, or services by words and by symbols. But, as is often the case, it was part of the Greek experience too. Plato's uncle—the poet Critias—appears to have been the first to praise the use of lying propaganda in inventing religion to compel people to submit to the state. Plato shared his uncle's view that myths and rites of gods are useful lies to which people must be obliged to adhere. Any doubts must be suppressed by inquisition, punishment, or death in the interest of the state. And he anticipated Orwell's doublethink and Goebbels's lying propaganda by stating that those myths—although lies—must be true; because anything that serves the interest of the state has to be believed, and must therefore be described as the truth.[10]

Institutions sometimes delude themselves before seeking to delude us. Whereas it is clear that Hitler used the Nazis cynically and they just as cynically used the German people to fulfil their own mercenary ends, the Communist party was filled with believers whose main problem was political naivety. The only way we can prevent ourselves from being used and abused is by self-development. Without self-actualization and the armor plate of knowledge we become their innocent prey; or we become institutionalized ourselves.

Idealists and cynics alike have long asked, "What is truth?"—as did Pontius Pilate. But Napoleon did not suffer from doubt. It is, he said, "Whatever people *think* is true." That is why the media shape our thoughts. Truth in the Napoleonic age was whatever Napoleon decided to fabricate for the French to believe. Total power in his police state enabled him to use force and fear and to brainwash a nation with propaganda. His official censors controlled all media from posters to newspapers, and from books to plays in the theaters. Twentieth-century dictators took him as their role model. And as long as the leader gave status and function to the nation and provided food for their tables, they were happy to believe whatever he wanted them to believe.

Because communication is a vehicle for ideas, and words are fuelled by them, the ideas themselves can be ambiguous or purposely misleading.

The following is a small selection of euphemisms used to deceive the public by legitimizing criminal actions or to escape from personal responsibility for them through self-deception. They disguised the organized murders of millions by making them sound acceptable, appropriate, efficient, or even romantic: pacification; annexed; enemies of the people; elimination of undesirable elements; ethnic cleansing; *Kristallnacht* (Crystal Night); *Endlösung* (the final solution); friendly fire; protective reaction strike; surgical bombing; free fire zones; collateral damage; heresy; inquisition.

The CIA's special assassination unit is called the Health Alteration Committee. "Even when governments are not concerned with the discomfiture of a putative enemy they are apt at hiding realities under the euphemisms long known as gobbledygook. The Nixon administration produced the term Biosphere Overload for overpopulation. Benign Neglect (coined by the Earl of Durham in 1839 to describe England's treatment of Canada) is now used to mean, apparently, letting the underprivileged fight their own way up."[11]

Deception

Deception is the dark side of the political double agenda that is not intended to be made manifest. Instead, it is generally concealed behind a carefully contrived lie, which we would prefer to believe so that we can enjoy peace of mind.

With all that institutional language invented to conceal the truth, it is difficult to believe that it is our ability to communicate facts, ideas, and opinions that has transformed the simple, ignorant, and superstitious Neanderthal of the stone-age, pursuing a brutal life of fear and desperation, into a master of science, technology, and the arts. But of course we are not all masters of scientific, intellectual, or creative brilliance. And many executives and other employees act out a scenario of insecurity, anxiety, and desperation in order to survive in a corporate society, and support their families, as precariously as those Neanderthals. Although the times and the environment have changed, the fundamentals of human life are much the same.

One of those fundamentals is the possession of foolish thoughts. Orwell attributed them to the slovenliness of our language. But it is also our ignorance of human nature, our indifference to history or our forgetfulness of it, and our willingness to be deceived, that allow us to transform those foolish thoughts into foolish and irresponsible actions. Management jargon, for example, is as contagious in corporate society as the common cold is through social intercourse. Its prevalence and meaninglessness causes much the same bewilderment as does bureaucratic jargon. In a decade characterized by high unemployment, we heard little or nothing of employees being fired: companies *downsized* instead. That is not only socially acceptable, but forgivable, responsible, and even praiseworthy. During the recession of the 1990s, of some 200,000 people who *became redundant* in Canada, 160,000 changed their persona as easily as a chameleon changes its color to blend in with its environment, and appeared in the statistics as *consultants*.[12]

A company's future is encapsulated in its language, almost like the way that an individual's destiny is influenced by his or her DNA. And its progress could be less clearly defined, or even inhibited, by the language of its managers. *Execuspeak* is a jargon consisting mainly of euphemisms and clichés, fibs, and ambiguities. The *Financial Times* even speculated that such unclear or misleading expressions could have a deleterious effect on a company's financial performance. Inevitably it cited Orwell, who knew that bad habits are spread by imitation. The columnist listed other false words used like a masonic handshake to show that an executive belongs to a *pro-active* club together with other *win-win* management teams. Vision; challenge; wither; short-termish; I hear where you're coming from; We need to manage change; Think global, act local—those are some of the fashionable buzzwords read in books written by management *gurus* and bandied about in order to show that the executive read the latest book on management and understands what it is all about. Some expressions are more painful to hear for their transparency than their ambiguity, like; "People are our most important asset." As the columnist wrote, "They are merely camouflage. Without them, without clichés, jargon and other dead language, most businesses would work better."[13]

Poor communications is one of the most common problems among business personnel. That may be surprising when we consider the far greater number of high school graduates, BAs, B.Comms, and MBAs entering commerce and industry. Did educators lower their standards in order to be able to pass more graduates? Of course they did. So we shouldn't be surprised when so many business graduates cannot even write a reasonable letter, let alone a professional report or strategic plan. "The development of rigorous educational standards has been impeded by two fundamental tenets of the Canadian system: decentralization and universal access. At the elementary and secondary level, an emphasis on universality and the school's broader social role has tended to encourage a lowest-common-denominator orientation in which the primary goal seems to be to 'get everyone through.' Imparting basic knowledge—which should be the most important objective of the schools—has become less of a priority."[14] Much the same comment could be made of American education.

The National Commission on Excellence in Education in the United States revealed in April, 1983 that the average American graduate "is not as well educated as the average graduate of 25 or 35 years ago." Milton and Rose Friedman reproduced a chart of Student Aptitude Test Scores from 1967 to 1983 that clearly showed the continuous deterioration in verbal and mathematical scores.[15] And in 1995, Newt Gingrich described the United States as "a country where 12-year-olds have babies, 15-year-olds kill each other, 17-year-olds have AIDS and 18-year-olds get diplomas they cannot read."[16]

But it is not just the democratization of education that lowered general standards of literacy, rhetoric, debate, advertising, art, and other forms of verbal and symbolic communication. The famous cave paintings in France demonstrated to everyone's amazement that stone-age people were extraordinarily advanced in art. And "the Homeric poems, like the lays they describe, are products of an oral art, composed for, and directed to, listeners who do not read. Such an art precedes written poetry and has an enormous vogue in illiterate and semi-literate societies." Those words describe an age around 700 B.C., when "European literature starts with two long poems, the *Iliad* and the *Odyssey*."[17]

Even after World War II, masses of people read almost addictively and publishing was a respected profession because it discovered and encouraged literature of a very high standard. There was still a large market for hardcover books. And it was a commonplace sight to spot people carrying a book to work or reading it in the subways or on buses or in cafés. Numerous short-story publications continued to be read regularly, and many fine authors owed their careers to magazines that published them, like the *Saturday Evening Post, Esquire, Lilliput,* the *New Yorker, Argosy, Punch,* or *London Opinion.* Readership began to drop off when TV sets were purchased in larger numbers and more programs were made available. Many magazines and newspapers were forced to close when advertising revenues moved from print media to electronic media in the 1950s. Popular fiction on TV and cinema screens drew readers away from fiction in print, and some publishers advised their authors to switch from novels to nonfiction subjects. Coffee-table lines of books, consisting mostly of photographs and very little text, became popular. But another cultural cycle was initiated when Penguin Books won the court case brought against them in 1962 for publishing alleged pornography; namely, the unexpurgated version of *Lady Chatterley's Lover.* Censorship was discontinued in Britain as a result, and the Lord Chamberlain's office ceased to be required to license theater plays. Fiction became popular again when it could describe sexual scenes and use the very four-letter words that had annoyed D. H. Lawrence when they were used as pejorative adjectives out of context. Ironically, he had opened the door for the very thing he despised.

Some magazines followed suit with photographs of nudity and then sexually explicit scenes. Perhaps that is what brought magazines back into popularity. And it was not long before the movies, too, depicted male and female nudity and sexual play. The same very old four-letter words followed. While it may have reduced the reading of serious or well-written books, it did not save the cinema industry: perhaps only top-calibre content could do that, and it is now considered to be at its lowest level ever. Meanwhile, TV soaps and sitcoms had begun to be churned out to several well-tried formulas and standardized like any other mass market products. Electronic multimedia computers are searching for suitable niche markets of their own, and could conceivably replace traditional television. But what of the content?

Books are now synonymous with popular paperbacks which are marketed *en masse* with groceries in supermarkets and cut-price stores like Wal-Mart. The volume of book sales in those stores is now big enough to dictate what publishers will print. And the takeover of large publishing firms by entertainment businesses like Paramount has also influenced publishers to go for the mass market. Most media today has become one or other branch of show business, and much of its content is prurient or violent. That is what the media believe the mass market wants, and perhaps they are right. Since it is circulation figures, readership, and viewership statistics that influence advertisers to choose specific media in which to place their advertisement, and they pay for it, TV channels are entitled to choose whatever subject matter they believe will attract the biggest TV audiences. But the proliferation of magazines also demonstrated that there are any number of niche markets too, which TV cable companies are out to exploit. But printing and distributing books does not attract advertisements to pay for its costs, so trade publishers believe it pays to satisfy the wishes of the mass market. And violence, rape, murder, and sex with all its deviations have been subjects of entertainment since Greek drama and the Elizabethans. Audiences have always enjoyed the diversion of watching other people, either better off or worse off than themselves, as if they need role models against which to compare and judge their own successes or failures.

Content becomes obsolete very fast, whether in storytelling, research, business reports or government White Papers; just as with any other product or service. New occurrences and altered circumstances, new experiences, increased knowledge and skills and new technologies, all change attitudes. The old cliche about yesterday's news being buried under other eliminations in a garbage can has been replaced by electronic news that is out of date as soon as it is uttered. What was novel appears stereotyped, conventional and out of date, whether customs, artifacts or art—almost as quickly as news becomes old. When carnality moved from the wings to centre stage—as it were—the sameness of content became all too obvious, as did its irrelevance. Past societies found a separate and appropriate place for it, without permitting it to complicate their lives. Consequently, several leading British publishers announced in 1996 that they intended to exploit the market for erotic and pornographic literature on the grounds that it is a valid and traditional genre. The Japanese take that genre for granted. And publishers have no choice if they are to compete with blue movies on late night television, VCRs, or the Internet.

But the day-to-day affairs of business executives are not sexual ones, despite what some TV soaps would have us believe. Managers are supposed to be above all that mindless frivolity. They are considered to be an intelligent and sophisticated élite group of technocrats, whether in the West or in Pacific Asia. Even so, it must give them pause to consider the effects of predigested paperbacks and formulaic sitcoms and soaps on their customers and on the advertising media that their customers may or may not read or watch or listen to. Some effect is shown by the generally accepted duration of six minutes as the average attention span. Newscasters are obliged to feature ten-second *bites* of their predigested fare. And some surveys show that impatient Brits may use their remote control to switch over to a different channel after only four seconds; while American audiences apparently cannot wait a second longer than three.

We should consider all those deprived and unsophisticated audiences who lived two and a half thousand years ago, without benefit of electricity or electronics. They could sit in discomfort for hours, and yet be spellbound listening to epic poems from storytellers in a marketplace or a cold and damp castle, or watch lengthy plays in an uncomfortable stone amphitheater. Since they lacked the benefits of our educational system, how can we explain the ability of the masses to concentrate for many hours and enjoy epic poems about heroes like Achilles and Odysseus? Such poems might continue to be recited for weeks on end, with excited audiences hanging on every word of the narrative or of a drama.

Perhaps they could do so because the legends they listened to with such attention encapsulated their origins and migrations and their will to overcome invasions and survive. They were as impatient for the appearance of their favorite protagonists and events as Elizabethan audiences would be at Shakespeare's plays at the Globe Theatre. And, in 1584, "when Laurence Chaderton, Master of Emmanuel College, Cambridge, the town's preacher for half a century, had preached for only two hours the disappointed congregation cried out, "For God's sake, sir, go on! we beg you, go on!"[18]

According to McLuhan, "Before the invention of the phonetic alphabet, man lived in a world where all the senses were balanced and simultaneous, a closed world of tribal depth and resonance, an oral culture structured by a dominant auditory sense of life. The ear, as opposed to the cool and neutral eye, is sensitive, hyperesthetic and all-inclusive, and contributes to the seamless web of tribal kinship and interdependence in which all members of the group existed in harmony. The primary medium of communication was speech, and thus no man knew appreciably more or less than any other—which means that there was little individualism and specialization, the hallmark of 'civilized' Western man."[19]

How can we explain the decline of Western literature and its replacement by the type of paperbacks written and published for the supermarket trade—compared, for example, with de Tocqueville's descriptions of the wilds of frontier America in 1839, where "there is hardly a pioneer's hut which does not contain a few odd volumes of Shakespeare"?

One answer may be that those legends and dramas connected their audiences with their own past, whereas we have been cut off from our own roots as effectively as black slaves transported from their homelands into strange countries with alien cultures and values. In our own case, neither world history nor geography are taught well in schools. In place of our heritage, we are drawn into the unreal world of the TV sitcom and the unnatural behavior of soap opera stereotypes, or the violent underworlds depicted in movies. Both their content and their treatment have caused a disconnect to take place. Another answer might be that the more advanced our technology becomes, so that just about anyone can use a movie or TV camera, so the standards of content and treatment have declined. And whatever has no meaning is not worth thinking about.

Content and Treatment

Content and treatment are precisely what a business executive must manage: their technology is relatively unimportant. They must manage words better than the popular media, because their communications involve them in more sober spheres of influence which they are obliged to address in a more responsible fashion. They are not in the business of entertaining.

With increased competition, less support staff, and less time to devote to each responsibility, executives have to learn where their real priorities lie. Today, it is more important than ever to understand what really matters in an organization, and what activities may achieve less effect in reaching company objectives, even though they may have been the traditional ones. The same type of analysis is needed for the marketplace.

The introduction into the workplace of microcassette recorders, cellular telephones, fax machines, word processors, and computers have enabled executives to be more mobile instead of being isolated in a conventional office while all the action is taking place outside. Time-consuming rituals with secretaries and typists, receptionists, executive assistants, and middle managers have been eliminated. Business technology has contributed to shirtsleeves management and brought us back to those times when mill owners were in intimate contact with their labor and the machine floors, their transport, and their customers.

Inhibitors to writing no longer include spelling, because electronic typewriters and word processors now include dictionaries that automatically prevent spelling mistakes; electronic pocket calculators are customary at work and in examinations to prevent errors in calculations; and powerful notebook computers slip easily into a briefcase. But despite the new technological business tools, the rate of functional illiteracy is as high as 42 percent of the population in the United States: it was a prime issue in the 1992 Presidential election. So, notwithstanding the technology, it is the calibre of executive that counts. Managers must be able to express themselves clearly and adamantly on certain subjects in order to avoid any possibility of misleading or being misunderstood. Of course that means they must know their subject. Lack of concentration because of a six-minute attention span will not excuse a dispute, later on, when documents are produced in evidence during expensive litigation.

Chapter one of *The Art Of Plain Talk* commences, "This is a book on plain talk. It tells you how to speak and write so that people understand what you mean." Nothing could be plainer or clearer than that. It is an approach and style that will do very well for all of the types of business communications.[20] There are no vague generalizations in Flesch's book; he is specific. And although he does not describe *style,* as such, in his Quick Reference Chart, attention to its quantitative criteria should result in a businesslike style as clear and direct as his own. What counts more than style in business communications is *lucidity*.

Flesch identifies the types of communications that would be easily understood by different categories of readers, from fourth grade to college students. He aims somewhere in between the two at what he calls *standard*; the type of communication that is generally found in publications like *Readers' Digest* magazine. It is likely to have no more than seventeen words in an average sentence; thirty-seven affixes per 100 words; six personal references per 100 words; and would be easily understood by schoolchildren in the seventh or eighth grade in the U.S. So plain talk is based on using short sentences and plain words with few affixes, and it becomes more direct and personal when personal references like "you" or names are used. Standard English, as defined by him, would be understood by 75 percent of the population of the United States.

Only learned people were literate in the seventeenth century, and they had all the time in the world to write long and unwieldy sentences composed of very long words and exotic allusions suited to their classical scholarship. It was both a pleasure for them to study and a joy to communicate with other erudite people. But language is a living instrument and therefore subject to continual changes. Sentences have become much shorter since then, and so have vocabularies. Literacy has escaped from the realm of scholarship into a more open and democratic society that does not understand Latin, Greek, Hebrew, and other ancient languages that scholars had to know in order to translate the classics themselves. Our language has become more crisp and colloquial and uses more Anglo-Saxon words than the longer Latin ones.

Size and choice of vocabulary should not present problems, since the whole idea is to be able to communicate with anyone who possesses an average vocabulary of words. The following chart shows how quickly infants and small children develop a working vocabulary that enables them to survive very well, providing their parents talk to them from the earliest age. In the six-month period between the age of two and a half and three years the number of words learned doubled at the point when they already knew 450 words. They learned approximately 50 new words each month after that.

TABLE 9.1
Smith's Test—Average Size of Vocabularies

Age:	Number of cases reported:	Number of words:
8 months	13	0
10 months	17	1
1–0	52	3
1–3	19	19
1–6	14	22
1–9	14	118
2–0	25	272
2–6	14	446
3–0	20	896
3–6	26	1222
4–0	26	1540
4–6	32	1870
5–0	20	2072
5–6	27	2289
6–0	9	2562

Linguist Noam Chomsky believes that children possess an innate capacity for language (a view disputed by some experts). But that could be the reason for such rapid growth of vocabularies listed in Smith's test. Having reached a stage when they can survive well enough, their interests seem to move elsewhere. More mature adults lose interest in continuing to develop a bigger vocabulary unless they are scholars or technicians, who have to know the language of their trade for their careers. And popular authors comfortably aim at the standard described by Flesch.

Creating Visibility

A commonplace practice for ambitious executives is to draw favorable attention to themselves by means of unsolicited memos or reports. Each one carries the risk of doing exactly the opposite. Since anything in writing is wide open to careful scrutiny and criticism, it is best to avoid anything inessential to running the business. If written, it is advisable to put it away in a drawer for forty-eight hours and then read it again as if you are the recipient. It will often seem quite different when viewed from that perspective. Lack of clarity, ambiguity, misleading information, emotional undertones that might even seem arrogant or abrasive—all of those things and more could raise questions about an executive's competence or motives. The best course of action would be to throw it away and do not go into print unless asked. Then establish clear terms of reference beforehand, like what is its main purpose?

Presidents do not like to be bombarded with unnecessary paper when they already have to peruse so much that requires their careful attention. A better way to create visibility, if that is considered necessary, is by preparing innovative ideas and asking the CEO if he or she would like a more detailed report. Then it would have to be prepared with care and backed by sound facts and arguments.

Verbal Communications

If the danger of writing is that it may expose an executive's errors, omissions, or failings, speaking has its flashpoint too. Intended humor generally gets lost in a telephone conversation without the other person seeing the smile that was intended to accompany a joke. Then, ambiguous statements intended to encourage bonding by laughter may seem offensive instead. And in the closeness of the corporate world, even in face-to-face conversation, anything that could be interpreted as being abrasive, will be. The ways that words are communicated is almost as important as the message itself.

Unlike TV soaps which show boardroom meetings where passions run high and directors shout at each other, scream, weep, or bang the table with their fists, chief executives are more accustomed to calm meetings with passions kept well under control. Even when subjects are contentious and discussions intense, corporate managers act cooly in order to appear reasonable, and usually talk in monotones as reassuring as their executive suits or designer jeans.

Philosopher and mathematician Bertrand Russell believed that any problem could be solved by logic, reason, and moderation, and that if only people would be patient and follow reason instead of their emotions, and discuss problems with logic instead of intuition, human relations would be harmonious and wars would not be possible. His credo was one of philosophic detachment. In 1958 he wrote, "No opinion should be held with fervor. No one holds with fervor that seven times eight is fifty-six, because it can be known that this is the case. Fervor is only necessary in commending an opinion which is doubtful or demonstrably false."

In fact tensions and stress are common at board meetings because they are brought about to discuss vitally important subjects and everyone present is expected to contribute by using their own particular expertise in the best possible way. Top managers in the West know what the Japanese and Chinese have known and practiced for centuries: that if people live and work in close proximity every day under tensions, relationships will be easier to endure when they are civil to each other. Comfort level is, after all, one of the criteria used when a company selects its executives. The same applies in academia, the civil service, politics, the armed forces, and in professions like law and medicine.

It is also important to ensure that everyone is on the same wavelength, or what is said may lose its impact, its relevance, or even its meaning. That is why an experienced chairperson will commence a meeting by stating its purpose, its terms of reference, and its goals.

Communicating with top managers needs to be handled with special care. A President or a Vice-President expects support and loyalty. Communications should therefore reinforce his or her belief that the team can be depended on. Even body language should support that assumption. In today's rapid-fire business environment, with mounting bankruptcies, there are greater responsibilities and also risks at the top: one result is often paranoia. Managers who cannot be seen to be able to provide continual achievements may be seen as liabilities instead. Then, who can a manager trust, and who is after his or her job? Any member of a top management team may have someone behind him on the way up, and a CEO ahead of him who is continually looking distrustfully over his shoulder. Paranoia comes well-recommended in those types of circumstances.

Communicating with staff is somewhat different in that it requires a genuine show of interest in their careers. Managers have an obligation to train and help to develop their staff. They also need their help. But middle managers tend to have a different management style than top managers, in that they appear to be neither management nor labor. But since they work closely with labor in order to achieve their own work objectives, they often tend not to wish to be associated with management and prefer the "buddy system" instead. Predominant is a culture of the trade-off; as if helping other people is a favor that must be earned. Its hallmark is the phrase, "I owe you one." It is also a form of protection against being overloaded with work.

Advertising

Advertising used to be described as selling in print. Then, when the media decided that their objective was to entertain, advertising too became part of show business and forgot what its real purpose is. Electronic media has since taken most advertising budgets because it combines verbal and visual selling and also provides an opportunity to demonstrate a product or service in the consumer's own home. On the other hand, there are so many variable factors to weigh in the balance that it is not easy to establish and measure the actual cost per sale. With costs continually rising, an efficient advertising manager is required to determine the effectiveness of a marketer's advertising and also ensure that it is cost-effective.

Even a meticulous analysis of cost to reach each reader or viewer or listener is irrelevant if the advertisement doesn't work well enough. And it won't if the words lack the power to be persuasive. The 1920s and 1930s produced copywriters who were dedicated craftsmen. They often learned their craft in the mail-order business, because that was where the effectiveness of an advertisement could be clearly measured in terms of direct responses. Names like John Caples and Claude Bedell are part of the history of "scientific" advertising because of their outstanding skills in creating copy that sold products and services. Similarly, creative layout artists like Ashley, Abraham Games, and E. McKnight-Kauffer contributed to the visual artistry that created impact to get attention and form a favorable image. And names of admen and women like David Ogilvy, and Mrs. Havinden of Crawfords were a guarantee of professional advertising that achieved what it set out to do: sell goods and services.

The downsizing of advertising agencies when they lose major clients, and the jettisoning of creative teams; economic recessions when clients' budgets are cut to the bone; of advertising agencies bought and sold like commodities; of the dwindling creativity of advertising agencies; of creative people leaving to form their own small workshops, leaving hollow agencies behind them; of attempts to replace creativity with technology like desktop publishing—all of that has eroded the effectiveness of ad agencies, and therefore also of the general standard of advertising when marketers use freelancers or employ inhouse advertising people. The main difference between the downsizing and restructuring of advertising agencies compared with other types of industries, is that we see their tired, uninspiring, and unstructured advertisements all around us.

Any professional advertising manager who has worked with a major multinational marketer like Matsushita, Proctor & Gamble, or Colgate Palmolive can take out a one-page checklist to measure the effectiveness of hundreds of today's ads in magazines, newspapers, or on radio or TV, and reject one after another as being a waste of 80 percent to 100 percent of the advertisers' budgets.

A smart marketer hires an efficient advertising manager to eradicate waste by placing budgets behind advertising that sells; to select the best ad agency; and then to hold them to their obligations. He or she can do that only if they know at least as much as the agency, and hopefully more than they do about advertising that works. His or her function is not to provide advertising but to manage it. A manager does so by ensuring it meets its creative and its budgetary objectives. And since advertising can easily deteriorate into a subjective and often emotional area, the manager requires autonomy to achieve the best possible job. One of those jobs is to prevent the President or board from being seduced by a pretty picture that may resemble an advertisement but does not possess the components of an effective one. The essential criteria are powerful words that select prospective customers and speak directly to their needs by offering appropriate promises to provide what that customer wants. Without the power of the most suitable words, an advertisement is just a pretty face or a foolish joke which says nothing of value or may simply hold the company up to ridicule.

Typical of the decline in Britain's global competitiveness and management and marketing standards was their 1994 Government White Paper on Competitiveness that mentioned marketing only once as one of the determinants, and advertising not at all. Said Sir Michael Perry, Unilever's Chairman, to an audience of civil servants, recently; "Advertisers and their advertising agents are so preoccupied with the competitive problems of their products and services that they have totally neglected to explain the importance of the communications process in the chain of supply and demand."

Their problems are not all that dissimilar from other service industries that failed to find out what their clients wanted, but simply gave them what they had in stock—like retail stores oriented to merchandise instead of customers. Ad agencies offered creative graphics when clients wanted marketing inputs. And auditors who decided to diversify into marketing services sent round accountants or business administrators without practical marketing experience.

Despite similar management and marketing problems suffered by their clients' companies, old established multinational ad agencies like J. Walter Thompson, Ogilvy & Mather, McCann-Erickson, and Lintas, survived by retaining their professional integrity, and because of reputations they had built up by creating effective working partnerships with their clients.

Clients like Sir Michael Perry's Unilever, or Proctor & Gamble, and Colgate Palmolive, know the power of advertising to help move huge volumes of packaged goods from store shelves on a continuous basis. They know because they research each advertisement and marketing campaign, and meticulously measure their performances and establish ongoing benchmarks as a matter of normal practice. Whereas, to those who don't understand it and its support role in the marketing mix, it is still as much a mystery as the entire marketing mystique—heavily shrouded in ignorance and superstition.

One result, in unsophisticated companies, is that when their advertising doesn't wok they blame advertising *per se*. But it is unlikely to be effective if it is not based on a clearly defined communications strategy. Nor will it work if it is merely a copy of a brochure or manual. The reason for lack of response might be in their distribution, product design, pricing or product features. But to judge from so many print advertisements without a headline, where the benefit to the purchaser is probably buried in too much body copy, the fault may be in not hiring and supporting a top-notch advertising manager.

The power of advertising was expressed, inadvertently, by philosopher Hume, when he proposed *that any attendant emotion is easily converted into the predominant:*

> amidst all this bustle [of hypotheses], it is not reason which carries the prize, but eloquence; but no man needs ever despair of gaining proselytes to the most extravagant hypothesis, who has art enough to represent it in any favourable colours. The victory is not gained by the men at arms, who manage the pike and the sword, but by the trumpeters, drummers, and musicians of the army.

And in his section on the influence of the imagination on the passions, he wrote;

> Nothing is more capable of infusing any passion in the mind than eloquence, by which objects are represented in their strongest and most lively colours. We may of ourselves acknowledge, that such and object is valuable, and such another odious; but till an orator excites the imagination, and gives force to these ideas, they may have but a feeble influence either on the will or the affections.[21]

How to Influence People

It is not only advertising and public relations that are intended to influence people favorably: everyone in a business enterprise can offer something of value to customers. But they cannot stir, move, or influence customers if they are on a different wavelength. We have to connect with people at their own level of interest and understanding. And we do so by spoken or printed words, and sometimes also by body language.

The first stage of interacting with people is known by every successful sales or advertising executive who understands their job: it is to get attention. Advertisements do it by attempting to dominate the media; packages do it by dominating the shelves of a store. Salespeople and other staff who interface with customers do it by making a connection or creating a relationship. The next immediate step is to initiate interest by finding out the object of a customer's needs by asking two or three direct questions. Then a successful sales person or an effective advertisement finds a way to fulfil a consumer's emotional needs. But that is often insufficient by itself, because the human psyche requires rational justifications to support emotional impulses like making a purchase, even though those goods or services may not have been bought for rational reasons. Successful advertising agencies know and sales courses teach that what must be appealed to is a person's self-interest; to their *desires*. As Schopenhauer put it, "People think they are led on by what they see, when they are really driven by what they feel."[22]

Where salespeople and advertisements frequently fail is in achieving action, in typical judo-fashion, by using the momentum of the other person who wants to buy. That is when many salespeople and copywriters are at a loss for the most suitable word or phrase. Their loss is another supplier's gain, and the entire cost of advertising and the salesperson's costs will all have been wasted without the making of a sale. That is usually because the salesperson's real objective or the advertisement's communications objective has not been clearly defined and established beforehand.

Marcio Moreira (Vice-chairman and Chief Creative Officer of McCann-Erickson Worldwide) asks, "How many ads have you seen, lately, that seem in desperate search of a strategy? It's like meeting someone who knows how to talk, but doesn't know what to say!"[23]

He adds; "turn on the television for a few hours and you too will notice that *form* overwhelms *function* by a good measure."

In the same paper on creativity, he wrote; "I, therefore, also learned that copywriters and art directors are *hiding weak ideas* behind the *executional prowess* of film directors." And; "Too many ads today provide you with answers to questions you haven't asked."

He continues on a note reminiscent of *Kaizen*; "And yet, do we do enough? No such thing as enough. There is *no* finish line in the creative process—there will always be a better line of dialogue, a funnier ending, a better shot, a tighter cut, a clearer mix, a better performance...and it is our *obligation* to get them!"

Most personnel in business are hired to support the making of sales, even if they do not come in contact with prospective customers by phone, mail, print, or face to face. Those that do may be provided with more opportunities directly to influence sales, but the entire organization has to be customer oriented. If they are not trained, they will not know how to be. And any business that neglects to define its business goals or the objective of a particular employee will be the loser.

It has been said that transaction marketing of the 1980s has made way for relationship marketing in the 1990s, but there is a time and place for both. It should go without saying that people selling a company's products or services need to make a connection with the prospective customer, so that he or she will be receptive to influence. "Only connect!" wrote C. S. Forster of human relationships. Managers who can connect with their staff can illuminate and inspire them, imbue them with determination to succeed, and trigger positive actions that result in achievements.

But people often confuse words with actions. No sooner are they out of their mouth than they assume they have been acted on. Wishful thinking is one of our weaknesses. What is required is knowledge and effort to follow through and complete any promise made verbally or in print. The only true measure of words can be made by assessing the impact of the deeds. And the best way to achieve meaningful ones is for a company to undertake a total marketing approach to the public by the entire business enterprise. The difference between words and actions is like the chasm between theory and practice. And an understanding of theory is no guarantee that a manager will be capable of putting the right actions to the words.

Sense and Insensibility

The word held considerable powers for ancient Greeks and Jews, not only as the origin of all behavior, but also of discovery. It was the key to thinking and knowledge. Only thought could open up the world's mysteries to our understanding. Verbalized thought and mathematics became the only real truth. The sensory world that was known previously came to be regarded as illusory and was relegated to myth and legend.[24]

The decline of a literate culture with the rise of electronic media has taken us right back again to the illusions of the sensory world, because of its appeal to emotions instead of to intellect.

McLuhan described how learning became debased, stage by stage, and first of all from the prime importance of wisdom to the greater evaluation of rhetoric. Prior to Socrates, education consisted in learning how to live correctly and speak well. Socrates separated the tongue from the heart when he favored eloquence over thinking wisely. By the time the Romans influenced thought, Cicero favored applied knowledge. In his opinion, "wisom is eloquence because only by eloquence can knowledge be applied to the minds and hearts of men."[25]

Applied knowledge would also occupy the mind of Francis Bacon in England very much later on, on the basis that knowledge is growth.

That so-called knowledge was applied by isolating a particular area of learning and then hammering away with uniform repetition or mass *learning by rote.*

According to McLuhan, applied knowledge "gives new stress or ascendancy to one or another of our senses," while dulling the others: "the ratio among all our senses is altered." For example, a dentist removes tactility when he introduces continuous noise. "Hypnosis depends on the same principle of isolating one sense in order to anesthetize the others."

Anyone who heard the oratory of Hitler in the 1930s should have recognized its similarity to a cobra mesmerizing a rat or a mouse in order to grab and swallow it alive and whole while it is paralyzed as a result of the hypnosis. The common expression used to describe the phenomenon is: "He took leave of his senses."

McLuhan declared that "tribal, non-literate man, living under the intense stress on auditory organization of all experience is, as it were, entranced." The result of such hypnosis is "a kind of loss of identity."

That loss is the most profound of tragedies when we consider that the fundamental questions that thinking people ask are, "What is the purpose of my life?" and "How can I live in harmony with my true nature?"

The Chinese sage Chuang-Tzu replied with a warning of the dangers of being transformed by technology, which becomes an extension of the senses only by anaesthetizing the existing natural ones. Those who lose their senses in that way become *unsure in the strivings of their souls*. Bereft of their senses, they become schizophrenic. The old man in the philosopher's tale says he would rather be human than use technology that robs him of his senses.

Many would argue that technology is introduced in order to improve on human limitations, but Chuang-Tzu recognized that there is always a cost to replacing human methods by technological ones. In our particular case, the dilution of literacy is accelerated still further by the effects of electronic media that limit the capacity of our senses.

Part of the entrancement of television, compared with other media, is that it mesmerizes both the participants and the audiences on each side of the camera. The lens does not simply record happenings, it *creates* them. What we see, therefore, is artificial or unreal. For example, we may see and hear the most outrageous confessions or incidents from celebrants who desperately seek the spotlight for their fifteen minute fix, before returning to anonymity. The lens possesses the hypnotic power to draw out their fantasies the moment it appears in their homes or is focused on them in the studio or in the theatre of the streets. And it often creates a level of hysteria that would be unlikely to occur without it providing an audience by its presence.

Those who bare their souls to talkshow hosts or studio audiences, or riot before cameras focused on the streets, prisons, or strike lines, use the television lens as if it were the all-seeing eye of God; to seek approval for their antisocial attitudes or their extravagant behaviour.

We are justified in concluding that they have taken leave of their senses. We may even be reminded of Marlowe's *Doctor Faustus*, when he finally realizes he has gone too far with his alchemy, and desperately promises Mephistopholes, "I'll burn my books!"

There may come a time when we, too, will wish we had destroyed electronic media before it undermines our society. Meanwhile, we have to ensure that business executives possess the strength of character to prevent themselves from being mesmerized and manipulated by the technology, at the expense of achievements, or that the novelty will quickly wear off.

10

Human Limitations

If business students studying for a diploma in marketing, a B.Comm., or an MBA, were to be presented with completely irrational case histories every other day, they would probably be puzzled or peeved, because most classroom cases tend to illustrate a symmetrical pattern like an Agatha Christie mystery. Her successful fictional detective used cool logic to solve each problem, and the protagonists act out of perfectly rational motives in accordance with stereotypical characterizations. It is true that mistakes are made, just as in business organizations, but if some of the irrationalities from a multitude of workplaces were to be included in those scenarios, neither the case histories nor the murder mysteries would be believed.[1]

And yet, we have only to choose randomly from actual historical examples— like the French Revolution, the Soviet Union, or the Third Reich—to record endless lists of inconsistencies and irrational and inept behavior patterns and situations, which led ultimately to the revolutionaries being devoured by their revolution or the defeat of its principles. Regardless of the fact that they had ulterior motives, they also shared a common problem with other institutions and also with business organizations—in all of them we find the pain of human limitations. It is recognized in the famous in-basket test conducted by industrial psychologists to determine how much inconsistency and irrationality an executive can take before succumbing to similar aberrations.

It has been argued that laws would be unnecessary if people were reasonable. The fact that so many lawyers exist is evidence that a great many people are not.[2] And if we mistakenly assume that reasoning is made so much easier by education or a high intelligence quotient, then we will be unprepared. Philosopher Bertrand Russell and some other intellectuals deplored irrationality in others while demonstrating that they could be just as irrational themselves. The span of unreason in which we live is considerable. Property developers continue to pretend that the thirteenth floor of residential highrise buildings does not exist, by describing it as level fourteen, so as not to lose sales by offending the public's irrational superstition about that number. And we go along with it in a conspiracy of nonsense. Institutions have been lying since antiquity, and the public has been obliged to go along with it. That was why Roman law once insisted on signs being posted outside merchants' premises to warn buyers to beware of being duped. But that will not stop millions from buying goods and services displayed on TV screens or computer monitors. We hand our savings over to banks and investment companies whose managers and staff suffer from the same types of inadequacies as we do, without a qualm. And we elect politicians we don't even trust.

When people questioned whatever appeared to be nonsense in the dogma of the early Church, they were immediately put on the defensive by being told that they were obviously possessed by Satan—the Father of Lies—who had deliberately turned their reasoning the wrong way round. That same instrument of rebuttal is used to silence critics in all totalitarian regimes, whether they are labelled as blasphemers or enemies of the people, or of the state. But it could be argued with logic that anyone who opposes the tyranny of an all-powerful regime *is* irrational, and that irrational people *are* possessed.

That dilemma confronts management consultants when invited by business organizations to solve problems that have resulted in a crisis. They find themselves surrounded by nonsensical situations, some of which are hard to believe. But a business counsellor's code of ethics prevents him or her from making public the type of situations that may make us wonder whether "the lunatics are running the asylum."

Such workplaces would provide far better learning processes for business students to accustom themselves to real-life situations. Then they can assume a skeptical attitude and continually expect the unexpected in business, and learn how to cope with random inconsistencies that arise from inflated egos, or wishful thinking, self-delusion, and often a stubborn refusal to let a flawed idea go. Unreal situations are often the result of product orientation, where an entrepreneur has quite simply fallen in love blindly with his own product. Alternatively, it may be his workshop, the process, or the technology. Or it may be an orientation to sales instead of to real customers. Even when his flawed arguments are pointed out to him as such, he may accept the truth of the argument as well as the flawed idea—so that a company's notions can be riddled with contradictions, because he—or the entire top management team—cannot let the flawed concept go. The result is a split-minded approach to everything, and irrational behavior is bound to spring from it.

For example, whyever should Britain possess twenty times more accountants than Japan, or thirty times more than West Germany, instead of engineers or scientists as are on the board of French, German, and Italian companies? One reason is considered to be a lack of any other relevant form of professional qualification—according to Keith Allen Smith, who is head of Oxford Polytechnic's School of Business. It is assumed—quite irrationally—that bookkeeping can be equated with the possession of management and marketing skills. And academic qualifications in management, in any case, "inspire little confidence among those who appoint managers, since they merely certify academic success. They confirm nothing about the holder's ability actually to manage anything."[3]

The problem is how best to prepare business students for the follies of human nature that they will encounter day after day, after they graduate and enter the workforce. The high-tech industry, for example, is rich in foibles and folly, because it is a new and complex industry filled with essentially management and marketing hazards for which its engineering-based managers have little or no operational experience or skills. They have been trained to focus narrowly on the product instead of on customers and markets. Any other type of manufacturer would have been wise enough to understand that marketing practices grew out of continual necessity to solve their kinds of problems. But a distinctive feature of the industry is that the egos of its technocrats persuade them that they are different. Their entrepreneurial brilliance lies in the workshop or the laboratory and not in the marketplace. That compels them to launch products prematurely—sometimes when flawed, but more often when they are not sufficiently advanced in design or features. It is the excitement of technological discovery that triggers a rush to market a product to preempt a competitor who might launch a similar one. Then each of them is relaunched as the next generation. The result is that a number of market niches are saturated with products that become less desirable because consumers soon see improved models being offered at lower prices. The planned obsolescence of the 1930s and 1950s has made way for the unplanned obsolescence of the 1990s. But whereas the former took place about five years after buying an appliance, this can happen less than six months later.

Unplanned obsolescence also differs in that the old five-year cycles created employment, whereas technological advances in manufacturing are creating unemployment. It is also one of the ironies of the high-tech revolution that manufacturing products electronically is also reducing the number of consumers who might otherwise possess the disposable income to buy the goods and create new jobs, by putting them out of work.

A great many consumers are confused by a mass of prematurely distributed appliances, which, perhaps, are not even intended for them. They include VCRs that some buyers couldn't get to work properly and have abandoned, answering machines that didn't answer, computers that could produce a mass of unwanted information but not what was required, word processors that took four times longer to use than an electronic typewriter, CAD equipment that cost far more to use with skilled technicians, electronic scanners that cost four times the price of conventional typing and may result in more than ten times the errors, and so on. Once engineers create new "bells and whistles," they cannot wait to include them, even if buyers don't want them. They have still to learn sophisticated research techniques to discover what buyers really want and build the results into their R&D processes.

As John J. Tarrant wrote; "By now the computer people know this too—Isaac L. Auerbach, president of an international firm offering consulting services on computers and information systems, observes that three things went wrong in computer development. For too long it was controlled by mathematicians and engineers who were not user oriented. Manufacturers did not sell solutions; they sold hardware. And most users failed to plan their systems, methods, and procedures so that the computer could do the job it was intended to do."[4]

It may seem extraordinary that this self-styled élite of high-technology experts had no conception of how to market their products correctly, and their tunnel vision prevented them from seeking outside help. They were far more concerned to make a product than find a customer. But many builders put themselves out of business for the same reason, and auto makers similarly stumbled.

They are an object lesson for a dedicated young manager to learn how not to manage a business enterprise. In addition, they failed to learn the lessons from the follies of their industry in the United States in the 1960s, and blindly repeated them in the 1980s. The result of those marketing and management failures is that the computer industry faces the probability of an even more disorderly decade than the previous one.

At the 1991 Olivetti International Electronic Banking User Group Conference, managing director Virgilio Zaina told delegates that computer companies could forget about real growth in the 1990s. "A slowdown began emerging during 1986 and 1987—and now the industry's index is falling almost continually. During the nineties the industry will grow, but very slowly, at a rate of around five or six percent. The only thing we can be sure of during the rest of this decade is the industry's non-performance."

He based his talk on a study of the computer industry by McKinsey. Using Burroughs, Honeywell, and Control Data as examples, he said users should not judge a computer company's survival capability merely by its product excellence. *"They must realize that their people are their added value; the computer business has now become a people business."*

It has taken that industry over twenty years finally to recognize that product excellence is only one step in the marketing process, and that people are the added value of an organization. Having belatedly realized that it is people who add value and enhance the bottom line, many companies turned to eliminating them by mass firings, as a desperate resort to remedy past errors of judgment. Perhaps that was because cutting costs does not require any management expertise—providing the company does not mind emasculating itself. Freud named it the "castration complex," which arises out of self-disgust or frustration at impotence. In business, it could equally well be described as "cutting off your nose to spite your face," because it also frequently results in "corporate amnesia."

Delta Airlines and Nynex have been quoted as examples of companies in which service fell apart after downsizing. Others suffered from lack of skills, loss of direction, or reverse momentum after restructuring. Staff layoffs are rarely sensitively handled from the point of view of retaining skills, accumulated knowledge, customer or supplier relationships, but are more often based on such arbitrary reasons as an employee's age or on ledger savings from discarding high salary earners.

Less than half of the companies that downsized since 1990 reported higher operating profits in following years, according to a survey by the American Management Association. "Even fewer improved productivity." Other research, by Monitor, "found that nine out of ten firms that had outperformed their industries over a ten-year period had 'stable' structures."[5]

In effect, many that downsized "threw out the baby with the bath water." They lost expertise, commitment, loyalty, and accumulated experience that told them what works and what does not. That is the type of tacit knowledge that Japanese companies recognize and cherish.

Koestler described in *The Sleepwalkers* the lack of linear progression in the history of western civilization, by reminding us of important discoveries that were lost to us and took hundreds of years to be rediscovered. Although Plato believed that "we do not attain new knowledge; we recover what was already known," in our own case, it is other companies and other economies that recover what we have allowed to slip through our fingers.

Although activities inside many business organizations and government agencies defy description, a paragraph in a remarkable book on the group mind is appropriate.

Earlier in this chapter I referred to the tendency of overexcited organs to assert themselves to the detriment of the whole, and then went on to the pathology of cognitive structures getting out of control; the *idée fixe* of the crank, obsessions running riot, closed systems centred on some part-truth pretending to represent the whole truth. We now find similar symptoms on a higher level of the hierarchy, as pathological manifestations of the group mind. The difference between these two kinds of mental disorder is the same as that between the primary aggressiveness of the individual and the secondary aggressiveness derived from his identification with a social holon. The individual crank, enamoured of his pet theory, the patient in the mental home convinced that there is a sinister conspiracy aimed at his person, are disowned by society; their obsessions serve some unconscious private purpose. In contrast to this, the collective delusions of the crowd or group are based, not on individual *deviations* but on the individual's tendency to *conform*. I have suggested that the evils of mankind are caused, not by the primary aggressiveness of individuals, but by their self-transcending identification with groups whose common denominator is low intelligence and high emotionality.

Although it should be an intelligence industry, home building is more renown for its resourcefulness and its skills. But it is also known for its high emotionality. Part of the reason is its high-profit and high-risk factor, which can easily and swiftly swing to high losses. Builders become gamblers as a result. They gamble with numbers, time, and the economy—just like others gamble on the spin of a roulette wheel—and tensions in that industry are just as high as in a casino. The result is large-scale and widespread bankruptcies. The Florida coastline in the 1970s, with its unfinished skeletal structures taken over by lending institutions, bore testimony to it. And the Costa del Sol followed the same pattern in the 1990s. Sometimes the timing was wrong, but more often it was lack of marketing expertise that led them to cater for the wrong customer segment or spoil their designs on the offchance of making a few extra dollars. When sales slow as a consequence, debt loads increase, and the enterprise—if not already bankrupt by then—falls foul to the next economic downturn.

Any perceptive individual working daily in those types of organizations must remark on the irrationality around them. Management often does not understand the true circumstances in those situations, or what they are doing. They act out of their emotions or from reflexes, or simply follow instructions. They are generally unaware of their irrational judgements and actions. Although part of their skill is to schedule systematically, they do not plan rationally, and rarely invite marketing consultants to help them.

Why is that? A manager needs to know how people will behave in specific situations and what motivates them to behave in that way. But we have reviewed the main theories of experts and found that nobody really knows. All we know is that nature is unpredictable and nobody is perfect.

Ironically, it was machines that were feared for what they might do to human beings, ever since mechanized looms closed down cottage industries and put hand-loom weavers out of work. In Fritz Lang's early film *Metropolis,* mass production was depicted as a monster. Chaplin's *Modern Times* showed the chaos that could arise when machinery went wrong. But that fear was a projection from a much earlier era than the beginning of the Industrial Revolution. It goes back to mankind's collective unconscious memory of aberrations in human beings; as do the myths of werewolves and the legend of Count Dracula. It peaked with the creation of Dr. Frankenstein's monster, who was an aberrant human being, not a machine.

Human beings *are* aberrant. That is the central problem of human relations. It is the underlying difficulty of developing relationships in business enterprises. If relationships were easy, books would not have to be written about motivation, communications, managing people, controls, leadership, or how to organize work more effectively. *People often make stupid mistakes.*

Arthur Koestler had already written several successful books on the behavioral sciences before writing *The Ghost in the Machine* about problems of the human condition. He wrote, "When one contemplates the streak of insanity running through human history, it appears highly probable that homo sapiens is a biological freak, the result of some remarkable mistake in the evolutionary process. The ancient doctrine of original sin, variants of which occur independently in the mythologies of diverse cultures, could be a reflection of man's awareness of his own inadequacy, of the intuitive hunch that somewhere along the line of his ascent, something has gone wrong."[6]

What is it?

Koestler reminds us that the strategy of evolution is subject to trial and error, just like any other strategy, and that although our human equipment may be superior to that of other animals, we should assume, from what we know, that it may possess a serious fault in the circuits of the central nervous system.

He describes evolutionary mistakes that developed in other forms of life from microscopic mites to centipedes, insects and spiders, to ten-foot crabs. All had their ganglion built around their alimentary canal through which food travels. (Ganglion are nerve ends which are forerunners of a brain). If their primitive brains were to grow, the food tube would become more and more compressed, until nothing but liquid could pass through it into the stomach. Faced by the evolutionary prospect of intellectual development that would end in starvation, or intellectual stagnation and the impossibility of enjoying a square meal, they chose to become bloodsuckers.

According to an authority named Wood Jones, that will lead to the death of the species anyway. He provided another example of an evolutionary mistake, with the marsupials of Australia, by remarking, "They are failures. Wherever marsupial meets higher mammal, it is the marsupial that is circumvented by superior cunning and forced to retreat or to succumb. The fox, the cat, the dog, the rabbit, the rat and the mouse, are all ousting their parallels in the marsupial phylum," because a marsupial's brain is smaller and of inferior construction to that of a mammal.

Koestler therefore suggests that we should pause to consider the possibility "that man, too, might carry a constructional fault inside his skull, perhaps even more serious."

The neurologist Judson Herrick referred to this possible flaw as a likely cause of civilizations passing through cycles of growth and richness, including those of spiritual values, which have all been thrown away by wanton vandalism and destruction.[7] There have been suggestions that the growth of the human brain has gone too far and is like a "tumorous growth" in which normal control has been lost and it behaves abnormally and erratically.[8] Although it may seem plausible when we view a history of continual wars and revolutions, fallen empires and the turmoil and bloodshed of the twentieth century, he dismissed the theory as "neurological nonsense."

Koestler refers to what he calls "contemporary research," which indicates that the problem is not one of brain size, but of "insufficient coordination between archicortex and neocortex"; between the old areas of the brain, and the new areas superimposed in relative haste for a fast-developing *homo sapiens*. Our intellectual functions are carried on in the new and more highly developed part of the brain, says Professor Paul MacLean, but our effective behavior is still dominated by the earlier and more primitive system.[9] That situation provides a clue to understanding the difference between knowing and feeling, between reason and emotion, which puzzled the Ancient Greeks, too.

So, says Koestler, the older brain structures and the primitive feelings they give rise to, develop relationships with the newer structures and functions which developed in our brains later on. Wrote MacLean in a medical paper, "Man finds himself in the predicament that Nature has endowed him essentially with three brains which, despite great differences in structure, must function together and communicate with one another." The oldest brain is basically reptilian; the second was inherited from lower mammals; and the third is a more recent mammalian development, "which in its culmination in primates, has made man peculiarly man." Investigations in recent decades revealed that the lower mammalian brain plays a fundamental part in emotional behavior, since it possesses a greater capacity than the old reptilian one for "learning new approaches and solutions to problems on the basis of immediate experience." But like the reptilian brain it cannot put those feelings into words.

MacLean even went so far as to picture a psychiatrist inviting a patient to lie down on a couch, and described what is on the couch as a combination of a crocodile, a horse, and a human being. Although the crocodile can handle primitive activities based on instincts and reflexes it learned in ancestral times, it cannot face up to any newer situations. Nor can it communicate with the mammals. And although the horse can play its fundamental role in emotional behavior, it cannot put its feelings into words. Our brains retain the hierarchical organization of those three types. But the newest brain was not provided with "a clear-cut, hierarchical control over the old—thus inviting confusion and conflict." That means we all possess a propensity to be schizoid. Schizophrenia is a mental disorder in which a person is unable to act or reason rationally all of the time.

The Irrationality Factor

Kant recognized that people possess split personalities. So did Rousseau—his concern was with the dichotomy between natural and civilized people. Hegel's ideal was "the whole man who realised his full potentialities within an integrated cohesive political community."[10] And Schiller wrote of the contemporary discord between man's true nature and his actual existence. His goal was harmony between the two, and unity with a state that would safeguard the rights of individuals.

Human beings possess a recognizable and inherently schizoid attitude to the world around them. Harry Berger referred to two primal needs. On one hand we need "order, peace, and security, for protection against the terror or confusion of life." But, paradoxically, we also appear to need the exact opposite: "anxiety and uncertainty...confusion and risk...trouble, tension, jeopardy, novelty, mystery...enemies." And the reason, wrote Berger, is "human spontaneity is eaten away by sameness."[11]

Multiculturalism has become a significant factor in employment in the West. It has already led to race riots by the losers in society, who view ethnocultural immigration with fear. Paranoia drives them into an abnormal state of self-delusion in which they identify visible minorities as enemies to blame for their own shortcomings. It is the classic inferiority complex by which frustration triggers their limited resources, which are brute strength and mob power. That power often becomes exploited by extreme political or militant forces for their own purposes—particularly in totalitarian regimes.

As A. L. Rowse wrote, "Hitler knew to his fingertips what idiots the masses are: the epigraph to *Mein Kampf* read, 'Germans have no idea of the extent to which they have to be gulled in order to be led.' This piece of candor was deleted on his coming to power."[12]

And Sartre—appalled like many people at human behavior in the first half of the twentieth century—believed that Marxism was "the only philosophy of our time." His disgust was evident when he wrote, "Man is unjustifiable."

Had he lived to the end of the century he might have recognized, like others, the flaws in a nineteenth-century pseudo-philosophy that prevented most communist countries from progressing after World War I, and led to the collapse of their infrastructures and their economies.

A Pseudo-Philosophy

The English economist David Ricardo started a duel of words that would be continued by other protagonists for many years to come. He declared that the exchange value of any commodity is due to the labor of producing it. Eight years later, Hodgkin published *Labor Defended Against the Claims of Capital,* in which he argued that, in that case, all the reward should go to labor—and that landowners and capitalists must be extortionists.

James Mill responded by writing, "Their notions of property look ugly.... Rascals, I have no doubt, are at work among them."

Thus it was that socialism was born in 1817, although its name was not used for another ten years. Another letter from Mill in 1831 began the long battle that ensued in earnest between capitalism and socialism. "These opinions," he wrote, "if they were to spread, would be the subversion of civilized society; worse than the overwhelming deluge of Huns and Tartars." Through the words and actions of Marx, Engels, Lenin, and others, he was proved to have been correct—it has dominated the history of Europe, the United States, Russia, and Asia, for nearly two hundred years.

Marx's politico-economic theory was a product of the Industrial Revolution in the nineteenth century, but he inspired an attitude that was to become a significant feature of the twentieth century—that human beings are disposable. Sigmund Freud was the product of a similar period and spent his life exploring the human mind. He taught that people are essentially self-seeking and would be prepared to dominate anyone as a tool to be exploited or murder anyone who was an obstacle. Aggression and hate, he believed, are as fundamental as sexuality, and only fear of retribution prevents people from killing one another.

Events in totalitarian countries in the twentieth century demonstrated the truth of his beliefs. Indeed, if Marx had been one of Freud's patients when he became a pioneer in psychoanalysis, he could have included among his case histories a prime example of those theories, since Marx was an unscrupulous self-seeker and hater to the end of his life.

Many thought that Marx's theories derived from Engels's vivid descriptions of the long hours of soul-deadening serfdom to the mechanized machines of industrialists, the appalling conditions of child labor, and urban poverty, which was considered to be caused by the Industrial Revolution. Those descriptions of working-class life must touch the hearts of any compassionate readers. But Marx was not compassionate, and it is doubtful if he ever witnessed any employee abuse that he used to further his political ambitions.

His arguments were usually based on out-of-date statistics, falsified examples, distortions of the truth to justify the points he made, and outright lies. His propaganda was calculated to create an illusion that he was concerned with the conditions of the working classes, when in fact it was an emotional platform for an idealogy that could provide him—and did provide his adherents—with unlimited power. His philosophy provides an example of Freud's theory of *psychic determinism* as revealed by psychoanalysis and in dreams, in which there is a content made manifest solely to conceal the truth.

Marx's fiery emotions ran riot, and he used them and his dynamic energy to dominate everyone around him into submission to his ideology. Even his economic theories were out of date, because of his obsession with production and the fact that he clearly did not understand industry or capitalism.

The historian Paul Johnson listed no less than twenty-three pages of falsehoods and errors of fact and transcription in one chapter alone of Engels's book, *Conditions of the Working Class in England*. Wrote Johnson, "Marx cannot have been unaware of the weaknesses, indeed dishonesties, of Engels's book...since many of them were exposed in detail as early as 1848 by the German economist Bruno Hildebrand, in a publication with which Marx was familiar. Moreover, Marx compounds Engels's misrepresentations knowingly by omitting to tell the reader of the enormous improvements brought about by enforcement of the Factory Acts and other remedial legislation since the book was published and which affected precisely the type of conditions he had highlighted. Indeed they were often collaborators in deception, though Marx was the more audacious forger."[13]

"He (Engels) misrepresented the criminal statistics, or ignored them when they did not support his thesis. Indeed he constantly and knowingly suppresses facts that contradict his argument or explain away a particular 'iniquity' he is seeking to expose."

Marx apparently made no effort to understand how industry functioned. Either he could not understand or understanding was irrelevant to his purpose. In fact, from the beginning of the Industrial Revolution, efficient manufacturers with sufficient capital chose to improve working conditions and generally supported factory legislations because they eliminated unfair competition. So conditions continued to improve and the workers did not revolt as Marx had predicted they would.

What emerges out of the ballast of *Das Kapital* is Marx's lack of understanding of capitalism. That is not really so surprising, although an entire book was devoted to the subject. After all, he had a double agenda. He was not interested in investigating facts or even viewing objectively facts that were investigated by anyone else. When he wrote an article on the plight of the Silesian weavers in 1884, he never went to Silesia. As far as is known, he never talked to any weavers, never visited a mill or a factory, a mine, or any other industrial workplace in his entire life.[14]

The economist Sismondi—who liked to consider himself to be a disciple of Adam Smith—introduced a different view of the social classes of his time. To earlier economists like Malthus, Smith, and Ricardo, the employer—whether landlord or capitalist—was not the cause of the misfortunes of the poor. It was the fault of their own irresponsible habit of marginalizing themselves by producing too many children who had to be fed.

> The poor laws of England tend to depress the general condition of the poor in these two ways. Their first obvious tendency is to increase population without increasing the food for its support. A poor man may marry with little or no prospect of being able to support a family in independence. They may be said therefore in some measure to create the poor which they maintain, and as the provisions of the country must, in consequence of the increased population, be distributed to every man in smaller proportions, it is evident that the labor of those who are not supported by parish assistance will purchase a smaller quantity of provisions than before and consequently more of them must be driven to ask for support.
>
> Secondly, the quantity of provisions consumed in workhouses upon a part of the society that cannot in general be considered as the most valuable part diminishes the shares that would otherwise belong to more industrious and more worthy members, and thus in the same manner forces more to become dependent. If the poor in the workhouses were to live better than they now do, this new distribution of the money of the society would tend more conspicuously to depress the condition of those out of the workhouses by occasioning a rise in the price of provisions.
>
> Fortunately for England, a spirit of independence still remains among the peasantry. The poor laws are strongly calculated to eradicate this spirit.[15]

Sismondi changed that attitude. As far as he was concerned, rich and poor were in continual conflict because the rich were the enemies of the workers and of the poor.

James Mill—born in the same year as Sismondi—did not think so. His belief was that "to the individual belongs his own salvation. From the pursuit of that salvation comes the salvation of all."

"None can say this view is perfect," remarked Galbraith in 1987, "but it does come as close to perfection, he believed, as anyone can expect in an imperfect world."[16]

But it was to be Sismondi's theory, and that of David Ricardo, that would form the basis of Karl Marx's class struggle of the workers against the capitalists.

Ricardo's theory is confusing, or certainly poorly expressed.[17] He referred to "a surplus value falsely appropriated by the capitalist and the overriding case that all the proceeds from any goods produced belonged to labor." He seems not to have understood the need for a return on capital investment. Nor, apparently, did he understand the need for a reserve to be set aside from the surplus, to be invested in research and development, replacement of capital equipment, restructuring, new technology, or for periods of downturn in business or the economy, or other situations when consumption might be weak, such as market saturation. Instead, all of that capital was to be "returned to the workers." Such confused thinking or expression of thought has long lent itself to misinterpretation. In this case it provided useful ammunition for Marx's social revolution; because—like some of Marx's own *Capital*—it possessed those ingredients that influence struggling readers who find it difficult or confusing, that it must therefore be profound and true.

Marx and Engels created the Communist League and the International. Marx made sure that working-class socialists were excluded from influential positions. They sat on committees only as token workers. Although he seems to have been an intellectual snob, his main reason appears to have been that workers who had experienced factory conditions were generally against violence and preferred more modest but progressive improvements to working conditions. They tended to be skeptical of ideology that promoted revolution, whereas Marx preached that revolution was necessary and inevitable. Apparently he did not want reasonable people on his committee, particularly if they represented the working classes.

A business executive might well ask what then had Marxism to do with industry, or capital, economics, or working conditions? The answer is that they were merely used as justifications for a social revolution that could enable him to seize power. Marx was a missionary who preached an ideology so effectively that he converted millions to his creed. So emotional was marxism that they were misled by his economic theories. Perhaps that is not so surprising when we consider the arguments that have been voiced against the economic theories of John Kenneth Galbraith in our own time.

Galbraith has long been a successful author and a popular economist. In 1977 he hosted a television series produced by the Canadian Broadcasting

Corporation about the evolution of economics. At the same time, the Fraser Institute of Economic Affairs published a book on *The Conventional Wisdom of J. K. Galbraith*.[18] In it, Professor Friedman wrote, "I do not know of any serious scholars who have validated his conception."

Of Galbraith's theory of countervailing power,[19] Friedman wrote, "In any case, the whole Galbraithian argument is factually incorrect." On *The New Industrial State*,[20] the theme of which "is that the economy is dominated by giant concerns in which control is in the hands of the technical-managerial class," his "view has also been examined and attacked by many scholars. John Jewkes, in his book on *The Sources of Invention*,[21] examines Galbraith's claim that the day of the small enterpriser is past." Jewkes wrote, "Nearly all the systematic evidence has run counter to any such doctrine."

Thirty-four years later, all the statistics on small and medium-size businesses demonstrate that the present and future of new job creation rests very largely on small entrepreneurial companies.

"Ironically, after the 1971 Bolton Report came out reporting the decline of small British businesses, the number began to grow. In fact the number of new business registrations has risen in every year since 1968 except during the oil crisis of 1973–4."[22] Small businesses *had* declined in importance for most of the twentieth century. In 1968 only 19.2 percent of firms in Britain employed less than 200 people. But by 1975 it rose to 20 percent. By the end of the 1980s it had climbed to 32 percent. By 1991 it had jumped dramatically to 99.7 percent.[23] The North American trend was not so very different.

Not only are Professor Friedman and Professor Jewkes quoted extensively as to their disagreements with Professor Galbraith's economic theories, or his evidence for them—or his lack of testable evidence—but also Professors McFadzean, Allen, Demsetz, Slow, and Meade. This small volume, which contests several theories put forward by Galbraith, was first published in the UK by the Institute of Economic Affairs in January, 1977. Friedman wrote that Sir Frank McFadzean "attacked Galbraith for a lack of realism, and misunderstanding of how large enterprises are run. He attacked the realism of Galbraith's view from the inside, as it were, and demonstrated, I think rather conclusively in a lecture he gave 10 years ago, that the notion that somehow or other large enterprises were run by faceless impersonal committees with the ability to control their future was a fairy-tale rather than an accurate description." He added, "Galbraith speaks in broad general terms; he makes assertions about the world at large. But they are very seldom put in a form in which they yield testable hypotheses."

Friedman then went on to examine whether Galbraith is a scientist or a missionary. His review ended by stating, "I think we shall see that his view of the world derives from his ideological view, and not the other way round." Evidently that was the case with Marx.

We are reminded of von Bertalanffy's "slightly ridiculous professor" who creates worldviews, values, problems, and solutions; also contradictory theories. Davidson & Rees-Mogg put it another way:

> In the mid-twentieth century, the ideological power of the Newtonian "paradigm," or worldview, in social studies reached its height. Early computers increased the ease of computation, and thus made econometric modelling practical. Flush with their new tools, economists boldly announced that they could control the economy in the same mechanical way that engineers control boilers. They imagined themselves fine-tuning variables like fiscal policy to increase output, lower unemployment, and regulate inflation. It sounded like a great idea to minds conditioned to expect linear relationships. And it yielded occasional approximations of success—when the relationships between various components were stable. But when they were not, even trivial changes in inputs could produce chaotically different outcomes. Hence the dismal record of economic forecasting, government economic management, and centrally planned economics.[24]

Issues addressed by Galbraith included countervailing power and its effects, economic affluence and the quality of life in modern society, and the functioning of the industrial state. Initial response to *American Capitalism* was "overwhelmingly favourable."[25] But debate grew "increasingly hot" and more orthodox economists began to attack the book. Professor Simon N. Whitney of New York University wrote a paper that appeared in the *Journal of Business* in October, 1953, in which he listed six defects in Galbraith's argument: cannot explain consumer benefits; overlooks real reasons for the economy's success; illogical examples; defective cycle analysis; fails to explain obvious successes; and not supported by history.

Galbraith answered his critics at the American Economic Association in Washington, D.C. in May, 1954. *The Affluent Society* appeared in 1958 and became a best-seller. He gave as his reason for writing it that, "We do many things that are unnecessary, some that are unwise, and a few that are insane"—because we are guided partly by ideas more relevant to another world. He made the point that the central preoccupation of Americans is production—gross national output—and that only by an act of will can we hope to escape the preoccupation with the GNP.

He insisted that whereas the teachings of economics continue to perpetuate the myth that wants are spontaneously and independently generated by the prime urgency of production as a social goal, it is modern advertising and salesmanship that creates wants for goods that are being produced. And in view of the reduced urgency of goods, we can now address other considerations, because economic security demands new solutions. He cited an essay of Keynes' which declared that human needs fall into two classes: "those needs which are absolute in the sense that we feel them whatever the situation of our fellow human beings may be, and those which are relative only in that their satisfaction lifts us above, makes us feel superior to, our fellows." The first is capable of being satisfied, while the second class of wants might be insatiable.

The point that he was making strikes a particular chord of recognition today—that government's paramount responsibility is creating social stability by providing economic security.

In the 1970s, Leonard Silk summed up the work of fellow economists Galbraith, Paul Samuelson, Kenneth Boulding, Friedman and Wassily Leontief, by stating, "Economists have rarely been popular with the generality of people. This is strange, because economists have long insisted that their subject matter is the improvement of human welfare. Nevertheless, their critics have often called them a heartless crew, content with the calculus of more and less within the existing order, while so much of humanity suffers and dies, and the gross sins of society go unstudied and uncorrected."[26] And scientists Coveney and Highfield remarked in the 1990s, "For decades, the central dogma of economics revolved around stale equilibrium principles in a manner entirely analagous to the application of equilibrium thermodynamics in physics, chemistry, and even biology. For the same reasons as natural scientists, many economists have sought to shoehorn all economics into theories whose merits are their mathematical simplicity and elegance rather than their ability to say anything about the way real-world economies work."[27]

With all the conflicting theories of economists, it is just as well to bear in mind that the word *theory* originally meant "passionate sympathetic contemplation."[28]

It is not easy to depict the extent or types of irrational behavior to which people will resort, and which permeates so many business organizations because of the human element—because of its variations, its randomness, and the different durations of the madness. There was, for example, the panic selling off of bonds and stocks in the first quarter of 1994 when the U.S. bank rate was deliberately increased by only one quarter of one percent. The intention, which was openly announced beforehand, was to offset the possibility of a slight rise in the level of inflation, which was running at only about 2 percent. The mass impulse to unload shares in a bull market illustrated the nervousness of investors. It also shows the readiness of a mass of people to reduce the values of quoted companies and even possibly trigger a crash in the financial markets at a moment's notice by their own panic behavior.

The panic that triggered the French and the Russian revolutions threw entire populations into an irrational impulse to invite dictatorships dedicated to autocracy backed by terror. That insanity lasted for more than seventy years.

Human infrastructures are more volatile than we generally suppose, and false perceptions or wrong attitudes can very easily create self-fulfilling prophesies of doom. If enough people believe that an economy will collapse, it will. If enough people believe that their government will fall, it will. Perhaps that is what John Stuart Mill meant when he wrote of "the tyranny of the majority." Depending upon the weakness or strength of government, the majority may hold our destinies in their hands. The technology to achieve it is now available with the introduction of the Internet.

Computer technology and the superinformation highway have advanced significantly as an influential medium since McLuhan elucidated what we had begun to anticipate only dimly about thirty years ago. First there was his contention that it is not a visual medium but a tactile one: "Unlike film or photograph, television is primarily an extension of the sense of touch rather than sight, and it is the tactile sense that demands the greatest interplay of all the senses." In short, the essence of the effectiveness of TV and multimedia computer viewing is "intense participation."

> Man's relationship to the computer is not by nature very different from prehistoric man's relationship to his boat or his wheel—with the important difference that all previous technologies or extensions of man were partial and fragmentary, whereas the electric is total and inclusive. Now man is beginning to wear his brain outside his skull and his nerves outside his skin; new technology breeds new men.
>
> Already, it's technologically feasible to employ the computer to program societies in beneficial ways...the computer could programme the media to determine the given message a people would hear in terms of their over-all needs, creating a total media experience absorbed and patterned by the senses.... By such orchestrated interplay of all media, whole cultures could now be programmed in order to improve and stabilize their emotional climate, just as we are beginning to learn how to maintain equilibrium among the world's competing economies.... The content of that programming, however, depends on the nature of future societies.[29]

Investors over-reacted again, in the same quarter of 1996, when fresh statistics showed reductions in unemployment levels. Instead of reasoning positively or optimistically that more people at work would be likely to encourage spending and trigger the stagnant economy which was filled with pent-up demand, the mass mind instinctively reminded itself that more jobs could result in demands for higher wages and salaries, trigger inflation, and cause uncompetitiveness.

The herd generally reacts to any perceived danger with short-term solutions, even though atavistic instincts of "fight or flight" were based on an *animal's* need to survive the moment, with no thought at all for tomorrow. And although *homo sapiens* is empowered with an ability to consider the future and plan for it, the mass mind steals the individual's common sense with an urgent command to flee the arena immediately. Just as investors gambled on a perception of winning when they bought, so they flee from a perception of danger when they sell. The classic example of impulsive and unreasoned actions motivated by perceptions of the mass mind was illustrated soon after the end of World War I and repeated in much the same way in the years following World War II. Labor shortages propelled the living standards of British workers well above most in Europe. And those high wages destroyed Britain's competitiveness so that its industries lost overseas markets. They also resulted in a loss of 2.5 million jobs. As unemployment grew, government and employers attempted to reduce wages in order to trigger the creation of new jobs. Trade unions reacted by calling the General Strike, which put others out of work too. Despite the fact that British manufacturing costs were among the highest in the world, workers demanded still higher wages. And Britain lost more markets to Germany, Japan, America, Italy, and the Dominions.

Three million were unemployed in Britain by the time of the Great Depression. Her international trade had dwindled to such a low level that foreign nations refused to make loans to her. Unemployment benefits rose to over 125 million pounds sterling, with only 50 million available from unemployment contributions. Britain's finances were in jeopardy. And the once-proud shipyards at Jarrow became derelict, with 80 percent unemployment in the region by 1936.

In recent years, we have seen how affluence arising from economic recovery in Germany and Japan has, similarly, forced up wages and salaries and made them uncompetitive, so that trade was soon lost to the Asian Tigers, and the United States with its cheaper dollar. It was that situation that compelled the outsourcing of manufacturing to Third World economies or the movement of factories there.

The problem is how to strike a suitable balance between job creation on one hand and resultant wage demands on the other. Capitalism prefers to leave the choice to the see-saw of market forces, whereas Japan is more concerned with long term aims like social stability.

The Desire for Liberty

Irrationality also shows itself in the struggle for liberty and the desirability of free speech. Mill's vision of liberty resulted in our own rejection of authority and our belief that only each individual can define what is right, what is true, and what should be permitted in our society.

His thesis was as ambiguous and contradictory as Mill himself. In 1854 when he wrote his essay *On Liberty,* his intention was to assert "that the sole end for which mankind are warranted, individually and collectively, in interfering with the liberty of action of any of their number is self-protection." There was no place for authority, tradition or community or brotherhood. Liberty was an end in itself; it has resulted in an uncontrollable crime rate and violence, a new generation of deprived one-parent families, and worldwide terrorism.

One contradiction is that as a consequence of the declaration of liberty, bureaucracies have to be set up to protect human rights. And the more there are different groups lobbying for special right, the more a need arises for almost unlimited government to ensure that their liberty is protected. Meanwhile, the demands of each group alienate them from others. Caught between the desire for freedom and the need for bureaucratic controls, it is no wonder that so many people are schizoid in our own times.

Philosophers and intellectuals are often unworldly and frequently isolate themselves in ivory towers. Mill apparently never considered "the possibility that men would also be free to explore the depths of depravity."[30] He seems to have been unaware of the powerful forces of evil he was unleashing when he influenced political thought, since he wrote in his letters that "government exists for all purposes whatever that are for men's good: and the highest and most important of these purposes is the improvement of man himself as a moral and intelligent being." Instead, liberty has succeeded in degrading human beings by its permissiveness of crime and violence, rather than uplifting their moral standards or improving their minds.

Ambiguities, anomalies, paradoxes, and contradictions are stumbling blocks placed in the paths of people attempting honestly and courageously to seek the truth, to determine the correct approach, to define the best behavior; whether in a society, a business organization or an institution. Management consultants investigating organizations in crisis often feel like Alice in the Looking-Glass world, where everything is the wrong way round. And yet the CEO and his top management team lived with that bizarre situation for some time. Some top managers who questioned it may have been fired for revealing the reality to the chief executive. Others would have left because of nervous breakdowns, or resigned to join more healthy companies. In the end, the collision of truth with error causes the organization to come tumbling down, as did the corrupt totalitarian regimes of the twentieth century.

The paradox is that totalitarianism is a license for rulers to do whatever they want to do, but democratic freedom can mean license for *everyone* to do as they wish. Liberty is like those free radicals in our bodies. We breath them in with oxygen in the air we need to stay alive. But oxygen also rusts metal, ruins food, and destroys our internal organs in time. We cannot live without it, but too much of it can kill us.

Once again von Bertalanffy's "slightly ridiculous figure, the professor" makes his appearance with an apologetic shrug and a sardonic smile, to caution us that it is customary to find a variety of conflicting opinions on such abstract ideas as morality and ethics. The same is true of economic theories, theories about motivation and behavior patterns, management theories, political and religious philosophies, and even scientific and medical theories. It is a prerogative of specialists to align themselves to one theory as opposed to another. The public, not being specialists, choose their positions according to whim, custom, changing fashions, propaganda from special interest groups, fresh discoveries, or ingenious new concepts from elsewhere. Meanwhile, executives who possess the desirable qualities of objectivity and reasonableness would be likely to remain cautiously skeptical while they watch the latest round of musical chairs.

Arthur Koestler wrote that

"progress" can by definition never go wrong; evolution constantly does; and so does the evolution of ideas, including those of "exact science." New ideas are thrown up spontaneously like mutations; the vast majority of them are useless crank theories, the equivalent of biological freaks without survival-value. There is a constant struggle for survival between competing theories in every branch of the history of thought. The process of "natural selection," too, has its equivalent in mental evolution; among the multitude of new concepts which emerge only those survive which are well adapted to the period's intellectual milieu. A new theoretical concept will live or die according to whether it can come to terms with this environment; its survival value depends on its capacity to yield results.[31]

When George Orwell wrote for the BBC, he noted that it was impossible to take anything at face value. Every announcement made by either side required interpretation. He wrote in his wartime diary, "Nowadays, whatever is said or done, one looks instantly for hidden motives and assumes that words mean anything except what they appear to mean." Even when propaganda tells the truth, he wrote, it consists of lies.

The Bright New Life

The accepted yardstick for international competitiveness is productivity. An authoritative study of productivity released in the final quarter of 1992, and based on output per full-time worker, showed the following results.

Value of Goods and Services

United States:	$49,600	a year
Germany:	$44,200	" "
Japan:	$38,200	" "
Britain:	$37,100	" "

The study was undertaken by the McKinsey Global Institute and three top productivity experts in the United States, including Robert Solow. Researchers concluded that American leadership was due, not to good corporate management nor robotics nor bigger companies, but instead, to Washington's reluctance to protect companies from competition.

Britain appears still not to have recovered from a two-pronged policy that discouraged middle-class initiative by over-taxation, and drove some of the best business brains and executives out of the country. It also supported destructive trade union practices. By doing so, the post-war socialist regime resisted total quality management and protected the second-rate.

That Japan did not take the statistical lead is not so surprising, since they are far more concerned with maintaining full employment to drive their economy.

Why, after all, should Japan have increased its productivity at a time when there was insufficient demand for its goods? What is the point of overproduction? Merely to arrive at a situation like that of the personal computer industry, which is suffering from manufacturing three times too many PCs is surely a self-defeating undertaking?

Third World countries traditionally purchased old machinery that U.S. or European plants considered obsolete and replaced with more modern technology. But slow as the old machinery may have been, the very much reduced demand of less developed industrial countries obliged manufacturers or packers there to keep it inoperative, perhaps for as much as four days a week or three weeks each month. And if high technology equipment continues to increase production in western plants, we are likely to see those new and more modern machines similarly lying idle for much of the time. The problem is that technology is being designed and manufactured not to meet consumer needs in the marketplace, but instead to fulfil criteria relating to the factory floor. The reason for this self-defeating philosophy is an inability of industry to orient itself to the marketplace instead of the assembly lines of the last century.

Of course it could be argued that consumer demand existed but was preempted by more astute or energetic U.S. or German business organizations. But marketing in a global economy is not as simple as that. It was most likely the declining value of the U.S. dollar that made American goods cheaper, rather than any competitive marketing skills. In such circumstances a manufacturer may find itself in a Catch-22 situation. If it reduces its prices to compete—as was done in the personal computer business—it will erode its margins and risk huge losses, or even go out of business. Or it can continue to produce goods and rent additional warehouse space to store them and await an economic recovery. The risk of doing so is finding they are unsaleable later on, when they may have been replaced in the markets by better and cheaper products that made them obsolete.

Sometimes it makes more sense to switch off the machinery and close down assembly lines for several days a week, even if it converts some employees into part-time workers. It is more important for a company to survive so that it can continue to employ people, just as it is better for employees and their unions to practice similar flexibility by acknowledging a necessity to compromise over wages in order to maintain a source of employment. In fact, many employees are often happy to enjoy an extra day of leisure each week although it reduces their earnings. But diversified companies may simply move employees to other machinery that manufactures different products.

That assumes an ability to change assembly lines rapidly and economically from one product that has been overproduced or is not selling, to another for which there is increased and immediate demand. It requires flexibility. It also requires adaptable designs. But flexibility and adaptability are not characteristics of North American industry. U.S. management tends to be conservative: it prefers to stick to methods that worked in the past. It is resistant to change. And when it is finally forced to change, it generally does so with its traditional orientation to the technology of the assembly line instead of to the strengths of its people or the demands of the marketplace.

One consequence of that attitude was the recent debacle of GM, who believed they could replace human intelligence, ideas, and flexibility with robots. The result was that they made their robots in their own image—they reflected the rigidity of GM's ultra-conservative top management. After a generation or more of rigid policies and procedures from the top, instead of consumer-oriented ideas, they built robots with the same failings as themselves. And after considerable cost and extensive firings, they were confronted with robots that possessed inflexibility and a bias toward rigid mass market production methods without the human gifts of creativity or flexibility.

GM appears to have discovered—after the event—that Japanese auto makers are skilled in mixing and matching teams of trained workers with fewer robots, under the direction of dedicated team leaders. The result in Japan is a high-performance workplace where production can be switched easily and expertly from one product to another. It seems that Japan's only real problems stem from the lukewarm economies of their trading partners in the West.

The necessity for flexibility in manufacturing is also demonstrated by the trend to just-in-time inventories. Pressure on the narrow margins of retail chain stores not only obliged supermarkets to expand their share of retailer-controlled brands by achieving top quality products, but new technologies—including barcodes—propelled them into replacing inventories much faster. They are now also more selectively tuned to provide stock rotation for best-sellers and their rub-off effect on stimulating shelf offtake of other products displayed beside them. Margin management also demanded that durable goods retailers selling high ticket items do *not* take in inventories until they are actually needed, in order to avoid negative cash flows. Just-in-time inventory applies in particular to manufacturers in industries that depend on a multitude of different components. Deliveries into stock are now fine-tuned so that components and spare machinery parts arrive only at the moment they are required; thus showing savings on capital, overhead costs, and providing cash flow for other priorities.

What is surprising is Germany's position compared to the U.S. Since German currency is the strongest in the world—so strong that other European nations fear German domination—and the dollar is so weak because of the American deficit, we are left to wonder about the relative importance of productivity compared to unemployment and to a deficit. Clearly different countries have different economic goals and use different management tactics to reach them.

Before that study was released, Japanese industrial productivity had been considered to be the highest in the world and productivity in the West was thought to be declining. But those statistics in no way alter the fact that the Japanese, who are renown for their ability to imitate and improve upon original concepts, appear to have created an entirely new society that works. On one hand it is capitalist and a free market economy, and on the other it manages to combine the most attractive aspects of socialism without its traditional burden of bureaucracy. No socialist or capitalist society ever managed to achieve full employment while also remaining highly competitive. The Japanese have achieved a seemingly effortless balancing act that is the envy of the world.

That its politics are neither of the left or the right, as Europeans use that terminology, is significant. Public reaction to the 1992 elections in Britain and the U.S., and the Canadian Federal Election results, show that the majority of people in the West are now less partisan in their attitude toward traditional political parties than they used to be. Extreme political ideologies have disappeared in the West, enabling parties to move towards the center, where most votes are to be captured. Polls showed that most people are far more concerned with who can best manage the economy, create more jobs, and improve living standards, rather than with political platforms. What might be termed a new realism is not so far removed from the realistic approach to government taken by the Japanese. The majority of people seem to want a system that prevents anarchy and stimulates the economy.

Half a century ago, Peter Drucker published a book called *The New Society*. He made a case in it for a new social and economic order after the destruction of fascism. It was not his new society that was to be developed in Japan after the war, but one based essentially on Japanese culture. Even so, it is interesting to find that of his dream society, he wrote, "This would not be capitalism in the sense in which we think of it.... An industrial society is beyond Capitalism and Socialism, transcending both."

Despite instinctual flexibility—as exemplified in the fable of the oak tree and the bamboo—and their comfortable adaptability to changes, the Japanese do not abandon traditions and customs that have developed over hundreds of years and suit the Japanese psyche, which yearns continually for social and economic stability. One such tradition is its public service. Civil services in the West were considered to be, at best, an inept evil that require considerable cutting back and accountability for fiscal mismanagement. But the Japanese appear to view theirs almost with affection.

Alsushi Ueda believes that "although society has become democratic in many respects, Japan remains under bureaucratic rule," just as it has done for eight hundred years, since the establishment of the *jito* or steward system in the Kamakura period, when officials ruled the common people.[32]

When he worked as a public servant himself, Ueda found that "a government office was a revolutionary place." That could never be said of our own civil service establishments, whose function is simply to administer whatever programs are promised to the electorate by their political masters. While ours is like a mechanical toy to be wound up periodically and pointed in the right direction, quite the contrary happens in Japan. Their national assembly apparently does little more than ratify bills from policies selected by ministry councils run by bureaucrats. "Practically all the laws and policies of the Japanese nation are established by bureaucrats."

Such is their calibre that the nation is content to be ruled by them, because their main concern is the creation of social and economic harmony and stability which combats inequality. It is described as *administrative guidance*.

Their bureaucratic system dates back to "the network of guardians and stewards created by Minamoto no Yoritomo (1147–99), the first shogun of the Kamakura *bakufu*." They were called *sumurai* in the twelfth century. Their philosophy can be summed up by the words, "Allow no peasant to become extremely prosperous, nor any to be ruined." The West might describe that as *paternalism*, but they believe that "too great a gap between the rich and poor would have a disruptive influence on society." Their in-words are equality, welfare, a simple lifestyle, and regulation. Disliked, or forbidden, are such concepts as disparity, competition, luxury, and freedom.

That gives us an insight into their business and management philosophy too, because freedom begets chaos, luxury involves waste, competition encourages conflicts, and disparity results in ostentation and envy. In a society where the goal is harmony, creating discord is bad manners. Controlling those totems and taboos is the primary task of Japan's stewards and guardians.

William Ouchi studied management practices in Japan in 1973, and began to consider whether some of the essential characteristics of the social organization of Japanese companies could be transferable to America, despite the considerable differences between the two cultures. He compared their very different corporate policies:[33] lifetime employment in Japan compared to short-term employment in the United States; Japan's slow evaluation and promotion compared to America's rapid evaluation and promotion; nonspecialized career paths in Japan compared to specialized ones in the U.S.; implicit control mechanisms versus explicit ones; collective decision making as opposed to individual decision making; collective responsibility as compared with individual responsibility; and the holistic concern of Japanese organizations compared to the segmented concern of the U.S.

According to Professor Dawes, "The Japanese economic success illustrates…the beneficial effects of being problem-oriented rather than success-oriented."[34] Whereas the view of Western corporations is an economic one, Japanese companies take for granted that it is their responsibility to play a much broader role. As well as economic needs, employees also have social, psychological, and spiritual needs. It is only when all those needs are met that an individual is free for effective and productive work.

"In many ways," wrote Dawes, "the extreme work ethic, competitiveness, and ethnocentricism of Japanese culture makes it unpleasant to us."

Another way in which Japanese management differs is in their acceptance of ambiguity, uncertainty, and imperfection in organizational life. "They carry different connotations in the East than in the West," wrote Pascale and Athos. "In the United States, for example, when a situation is 'ambiguous,' the implication is that it is incomplete, unstable, and needs clearing up. In Japan, in contrast, ambiguity is seen as having both desirable and undesirable aspects. The Japanese often seek a great deal of predictable order. But in other respects, having to do with many organizational matters, they are also willing to flow with things. More ambiguity, uncertainty, and imperfection in organizations is acceptable to them than to us as an immutable fact of life.... By this they mean that such conditions just *are,* and, accordingly, the sooner we accept that they exist the better things will go. Regarding them as *enemies* gets our adrenaline pumping for a hopeless battle. Regarding them as conditions to be reduced or lived with, as appropriate to the situation, makes more sense."[35]

Ouchi became aware that the "basic mechanism" to control ambiguities and avoid misunderstandings leading to anarchy was an implicit philosophy of the organization, which defines objectives and also procedures to move toward them. They represent the values of owners, employees, and customers. That corporate culture amounts to a set of beliefs about what kind of solutions work best in that company or industry—such as who should make decisions about what type of new products they should (or should not) consider.

"Those who grasp the essence of this philosophy of values and beliefs (or ends and means) can deduce from the general statement an almost limitless number of specific rules or targets to suit changing conditions." Moreover, they will be consistent between individuals because they are communicated through the firm's common culture which is shared by all key managers, and, by extension, all employees.

But it would be misleading to generalize without pointing out exceptions, since it is by no means only Japanese organizations that establish a corporate culture combining an ethical code of conduct, in order to manage those complexities, uncertainties, and ambiguities. Some American companies have done so for years, while others learned from the Japanese or from European business organizations in the past few decades. One example of an American multinational that moved in the same direction is Johnson & Johnson of New Jersey. Its Chairman and CEO, Ralph Larsen, remarked that their management style addresses "complexity and ambiguity." (No doubt like other innovative R&D leaders who specialize in new product launches, such as 3M and Glaxo).

Johnson & Johnson's ethical code commits it to responsibilities to its 81,000 employees, its customers, its shareholders, suppliers, and also the community and the environment—as rigidly as any Japanese business enterprise. It is the biggest manufacturer of health care products, with 1994 sales of $15.7 billion, obtained approximately 50/50 from overseas and from domestic markets. Its products fall into three main categories: pharmaceuticals, consumer, and professional. Its drug business accounted for more than half of its profits in 1994. It possesses 160 businesses in 50 countries, with which it is committed to decentralization. Each of its operating companies is almost entirely autonomous. Each shares its research, engineering, and operations expertise with the others. It also forms alliances with other companies. An important key to its success is planned innovation. More than one-third of its sales come from new products launched within the previous five years. Their life cycles began to shrink to about two years in the 1990s. They have therefore evolved R&D skills to develop new products simultaneously and globally, instead of launching them one at a time in separate countries.[36]

The East discovered long ago something that western business executives and administrators found hard to tolerate: that sometimes it is better to be indefinite. Why always attempt to be explicit about everything when vagueness or ambiguity can solve a particular problem to everyone's satisfaction? The West has moved more and more in the direction of explicitness in its culture and attitudes, while the East finds it repugnant and continues to back away from it.

It was this lack of sensitivity and understanding of other peoples' values that bedeviled relationships between colonial administrators and colonies. A western manager must orient him or herself to local customs when working in other countries. Because, of course, it is not only the Japanese who possess different values and customs from the West. But even being sensitive to other customs does not mean that we can shed our lifetime traditions in an instant and emulate the Japanese (or the Koreans, Malaysians, Taiwanese, or those of mainland China). And whatever the Japanese have learned from the West, their corporate relationships—as with their social ones—are based squarely on Japanese traditions.

We would be merely attempting to simplify the problem of understanding such different cultural values if we simply acknowledge three of the pillars of Japanese culture, namely, Buddhism, Shinto, and Bushido. Adherents of Japanese traditions are also fenced in by numerous obligations, duties, and codes that must be observed. Anthropologist Ruth Benedict listed fifteen of them.[37] Those traditions have become less rigid since Benedict's study was made. And, in time, the influence of western democracy will inevitably wear away many of those codes still further, as is already happening through the younger generation.

There were times in Europe when such codes of behavior were adhered to. Similar obligations, duties, and indebtedness had to be fulfilled during the feudal system. Such moral codes and social disciplines were intended to create law, order, and purpose out of the chaos, destruction, and misery of the Dark Ages. And they did so by imposing Jewish ethics through the moral leadership of the Christian Church and the power of its military supporters. Fundamental to the code of Christendom at that time of rebirth were the totems and taboos of the Ten Commandments. They were taken up, like a banner, by evangelists. Those values have now been rejected by the West, while the East struggles to retain its own moral balance. The ten pillars of evangelical wisdom now lie buried beneath the rubble of our history, together with outworn knightly loyalties, tarnished duties to the realm, family obligations, and dedications to an ancient God. All were rejected in favor of aspirations of liberty and equality, the welfare state, and other democratic values. We have exchanged the ideal of a well-ordered and honorable society for freedoms or special interests that do not appear to satisfy anyone—since it is evident that we live in an age of dissatisfaction.

"The great behavioral experiment has failed," Professor von Bertalanffy told his students at Clark University in 1966. "The hypothesis was that, given material wellbeing, society manipulated according to scientific principles would arrive at the greatest happiness of the greatest number...permissive education; conditioning, according to the best methods of manipulative psychology, for the perfect consumer; relaxation of sexual norms to avoid formation of complexes; and so forth.... The outcome, unfortunately, contradicted expectations. Precisely in affluent society, with gratification of biological needs, reduction of tensions, education and conditioning with scientific techniques, there was an unprecedented increase in mental illness, juvenile delinquency, crime not for want but for fun, the serious problem of leisure in an automated society, and the appearance of new forms of mental disorder diagnosed as existential disease, malignant boredom, suicidal retirement neurosis and the like—in fact, all symptoms of a sick society."

We must ask ourselves seriously if we have the will, or even the desire, to adhere to business disciplines when people cannot be bothered to follow social ones. If our social will has failed, we should consider whether the West has the courage to fight for its survival through the benefits of trade and industry. Perhaps the undertow of negativism or complacency or indifference toward upgrading management and marketing practices in the West is too strong, and we are no longer powerful enough to resist being pulled under by it. The tide of history is against our old-fashioned work habits and our aging population. Historians occasionally ponder on the reasons why once-great civilizations died out. The choices they made were little different from ours. Will Durant wrote of the disappearance of the Cretan civilization, "Perhaps there too, as in most declining cultures, population control went too far, and reproduction was left to the failures."[38]

That is one of the irrationality factors. And it reminds us of the argument put by Malthus that the poor marginalise themselves by producing more children than they can handle, because statistics in our own time show that the situation has worsened. William Buckley Junior wrote in 1993, "Produce one illegitimate child and you contribute to...poverty, crime, drugs, and unemployment."[39] Illegitimate births accelerated in the United States from 1970 through 1980. Among whites it rose from 6 percent to 11 percent. Among blacks it climbed from 38 percent to 55 percent.[40] In the former case it since rose to 17 percent, and in the latter to 62 percent. The U.S. Labor department put it another way when they stated that 44 percent of white babies born to women below the poverty line are illegitimate.

China is one of the few nations to acknowledge that population increases lead to starvation, and do something positive about it rather than encourage it by continually emphasizing and applauding indiscriminate sex. Their goal is zero population growth by the year 2000. What used to work in the West was what Bernard Shaw called "middle-class morality."

But it was not only population increases that led to the breakdown of western societies. After the irrationality and destruction of the Great War, with the loss of 8.5 million men, the cost of that folly, in terms of taxes, reduced the quality of life of the middle classes. World War II inflicted similar hardships. And again, middle-class lifestyles suffered from higher taxes and a higher cost of living when peacetime came.

Four decades later, the middle classes are shrinking still further, and middle-class morality has almost disappeared with the continual erosion of that socioeconomic class. Now they are too small in numbers and disposable income to support the rest.

Compared with other animals, our uniqueness is supposed to be our free will to shape our environment in order to survive. Global overpopulation may demonstrate that our species is winning the battle against heavy odds, but—as Malthus discovered and Durant argued—our most intelligent, skilled, and moral section of the population can no longer afford to reproduce, while society's failures overproduce. They increase the Have-Not section from which conflict and terrorism have emerged to create chaos wherever it can. Karl Marx saw them in continual conflict unless the political and economic order could be changed. It was; but neither communism nor socialism could change it for the better. All they succeeded in doing was destroying middle-class society with its sense of service, morality, ethics, civility, and hard work.

Failing an ideological solution, we are left with James Mill's contention that only each individual can provide his or her own salvation; and from that pursuit will emerge the salvation of others. But Liberalism or Democracy are based on an illusion that most people are reasonable, self-disciplined, and sensible. The flaw in that argument may be the evolutionary gap which appears to be the cause of irrationality and leads to society's follies and the tragedy of western society's voluntary suicide.

Accountability

What has been lost with middle class morality is personal accountability. It is as if individuals are no longer responsible for their actions and as if today's society doesn't expect them to be. It is a society without totems or taboos. That is as true in the business sector and the public sector as it is in the larger social one.

At the tail end of the lengthy economic recession of the 1990s chief executives lost their jobs at American Express, Westinghouse, Digital Equipment Corp., and Compaq, as well as at IBM and General Motors. Their abrupt departures were triggered "by enraged institutional shareholders, who demanded that board directors act quickly to restore confidence in firms that were floundering.... Boards of directors, if themselves held properly accountable, are the best check on the power of chief executives."[41] They should be, but they cannot be held accountable for the whims or sentiments, personal excesses, or irrational impulses that cause faulty judgements of a CEO, unless they possess the authority.

A significant feature of Japanese management is that its networks of obligations, duties, and codes do not permit irrationality in the workplace. They know it can damage a business organization, and they are well aware that it is most damaging when indulged in by a CEO. Consequently decision making is collective, not individual; responsibility is collective, not individual; concern is holistic, not segmented; and there are implicit control mechanisms.

The collapse of the 123 year old Confederation Life came as a shock in 1994. It ranked fourth in the Canadian industry, with 4,425 employees, 273,000 policy holders, and assets allegedly worth $19 billion on paper. Its demise demonstrated Galbraith's description of some board directors being motivated more to make fortunes for themselves than being responsible to their shareholders, their employees, customers, and the community.[42]

"William Douglas, Confederation's sometime senior vice-president of corporate development, holds the distinction of emerging from the Confederation tragedy a millionaire, having managed, as some people see it, to stock a lifeboat with champagne and row away before the company sank."[43]

Patrick Burns was President, CEO, and Chairman by 1990. They had gambled 71 percent of their assets in the real estate boom of the 1980s; in real property and mortgage loans on residential and commercial properties including shopping malls. Bought at the peak of the boom, it was only a matter of time before the bust had to take place. Perhaps the board did not understand the inherently high risks of the property business. In any event, Burns retired in the spring of 1993.

The situation showed how a closed corporate society is as dangerous as a closed political one, in that an open society provides democratic checks and balances. The only reason that an institution may be designed to be closed is to benefit its top management. They are, demonstrably, accountable only to themselves. If shareholders of western business organizations wish to ensure the protection of their investments from irrational management judgements, they would be well advised to insist on the same types of restraining networks and safety nets as are employed by Japanese organizations. All major decisions affecting the success and future viability of their enterprise should be shared by the entire management team. The top team should be rewarded collectively and also collectively held accountable, not just the CEO or the President or the Chairman. That also identifies the inherent dangers of appointing one person for two or more of those functions: it effectively nullifies one or other acting as a devil's advocate to check impulsive judgements or irrational decisions of the others. It was the Chairman who was ousted from DEC of Maynard, Mass., and the co-founder who was jettisoned at Compaq Computer Corp.

"Confed went under because there wasn't a single director, officer, regulator, auditor, politician, or industry honcho who completely fulfilled his or her job," wrote Rod McQueen in his book *Who Killed Confederation Life?* The culprits were "greed, stupidity and sloth."

"Any government, whether that of a company or a nation, degenerates into mediocrity and malperformance if it is not clearly accountable to someone for results."[44]

Royal Trustco went into the red in 1990 and failed in 1992–93. It was one of Canada's oldest, biggest, and better-known trust companies. Its aggressive growth strategy was utterly discredited.[45] Jack Hickman (professor of strategic management at the University of Toronto) was quoted as remarking, "The failure of Royal Trustco is a board problem pure and simple." And business administration professor Thain (University of Western Ontario) said, "The function of any board is to stop management from taking survival-threatening risks." It backed an aggressive growth strategy recommended by its operational managers rather than trying to achieve a profitability goal.

The responsibility of top management is not only to manage a business, but also to create gainful employment, initiate consumption of goods and services, create wealth for shareholders and the community, and also vitalize a nation's economy. That is no small responsibility. But, as we see, it is often left to personal whims and notions, irrational judgements, chance, and foolish decisions or ulterior motives.[46] And, unfortunately, "the accursed lust for gold" frequently diverts owners and managers from achieving that holistic bundle of goals.[47]

11

Leadership and Management Styles

Psychologist Daryl Conner—a consultant with ODR Inc. of Atlanta, a research and consulting firm that concerns itself with managing large-scale change—was quoted in *The Globe and Mail* as saying, "Historically, the CEO has been required only to figure out what to do. But in today's heavy turbulence, the top executive must get the plan executed inside the organization. In other words, the pressure is on the CEO not only to make decisions, but to orchestrate the human variables to accommodate those decisions. In the past, all you had to do was be right. That's just not enough any more."

Harvey Enchin, who quoted Conner in his column, added, "They are no less skilled at figuring out what to do. They are infinitely less prepared than they were 5 or 10 years ago to implement those decisions."

A leader who looks upon a group of employees with foreknowledge of their diversity must consider how their energy and skills can be channelled in one clear direction to the benefit of the business organization. He will know that individuals are naturally dedicated to their own individual pleasures and the furtherance of their own desires. A leader's main concern should be how to harness those individual drives to meet the objectives of the business enterprise. Diversity may seem to some like a hornet's nest or a can of worms, but it is the job of a leader to use them opportunely on behalf of the shareholders who pay him for his general management skills, and expect successful leadership that will result in attractive bottom-line results.

First he must choose people with appropriate skills that relate to the company mission, then he must motivate them. When he or his human resource manager looks for people with suitable skills, they have also to choose ones with personality characteristics that can best be motivated. They need, as it were, hardy and fast-growing plants that will flourish in their rich and fertile soil and be abundantly fruitful.

Fortunately we are confronted with only a very small percentage of pessimists and strugglers in the psychographic model we have chosen, and a very large number of achievers and aspirers. They are obviously going to be easier to motivate, because the momentum of their own ambitions has only to be directed to achieving company aspirations. Their own personal drives will motivate them with the minimum of outside encouragement.

Personnel requirements in any organization are not limited only to achievers. Routine jobs need to be filled by people who are content to undertake them daily, without feeling frustrated at never reaching a final conclusion. They are likely to be employees with low Zeigarnick effects who are motivated more by means than ends; the contenteds.

Knowledge industries require introspective thinkers and intellectuals who can harness original thinking to meet the needs of an enterprise. Some who might be considered to be pessimists are frequently idealists with considerable drive who strive for the highest standards and are generally gloomy only because of repeated disappointments. As for the socialites and hedonists in that psychographic framework, they are often valuable in public relations, advertising, or sales. Those personality characteristics alone include 85 percent of candidates in our model, who could contribute towards the success of a business organization, providing they are employable. They also provide evidence that diversity is precisely what most enterprises need.

It is unfortunately also true that not so many managers or chief executives possess the character, intellect, or experience to handle themselves well in the company of diverse types of people. Some feel comfortable only among their own kind, who share their values and talk their kind of language. Others are biased against certain types of people. Still others simply do not understand people outside of their own personal experience with whom they cannot identify. In any of those situations there is a need for a strong individual to be in charge of the human resources function. But it is also essential for the CEO and his or her top management team to be dedicated to a company culture that takes into account the need for diversity, because the result of it being severely limited in any culture is sterility or inertia through lack of intellectual interaction or stimulus.

While there has been a tendency to believe that money is the main or even the sole stimulus in business, it is only the means to achieve social acceptance or respect among one's peers. Ongoing research of over six thousand white- and blue-collar workers in the U.S. reinforced that impression and also added two more needs that stimulate activity: a desire for autonomy, and the wish to do something original.[1]

Those may be their ideals, but do they understand their role as manager or leader? Management institutions have often been uncertain in defining the role of a manager. Such uncertainty is understandable because the management role continually changes according to different challenges at different times. And different styles become fashionable in different circumstances. As well, Professor Koontz's paper on "the management theory jungle" demonstrated that there is more than one approach to management, and there are bound to be different opinions about each of them. Since wars generally force the pace of development of new management skills, technologies, strategies, and tactics—because survival is at stake—we took a quick look at what qualities contributed to the turning points in World War II, and whose they were. What we found was that spirit of imagination that draws on latent ideas and applies them to defining solutions to daunting situations; that hyperactive energy and self-confident single-mindedness that plans and establishes clear objectives and goals to be achieved—then implements the winning plan decisively.

What else distinguishes superior managers from others? Superior management analyses the effectiveness of its activities and the value of its goals in order continually to improve ways and means to achieve a superior performance. It must also possess an ability to predict well in order to be able to seek out and aim at those goals.

Superior management periodically sets new standards and continually measures its results in order to do so.

Superior management aims at superior content in its communications, rather than simply dressing up empty gestures to deceive or entertain.

Superior management is disciplined management that, nevertheless, also possesses the flexibility to bend in order to achieve predetermined objectives in disorderly and uncertain circumstances.

Superior management must anticipate and use change skillfully in its own favor, as a black belt judo expert uses the momentum of an opponent to achieve victory—instead of defensively attempting to keep change at bay or merely reacting to it at the last moment, when forced to, and when it is already too late.

Superior management creates such management controls as policies, procedures and systems, to increase efficiency. But it also recognizes that the standardized and ready-made answers they provide may prevent employees from rethinking and recreating something more suited to changed conditions.

Superior management recognizes that responsibilities often cannot be undertaken without authority, and that having authority also obliges a manager to be willing to be held accountable for his or her own actions.

Instead of providing top management with analyses of information and leaving it to someone else to draw suitable conclusions as to what should be done, superior managers take initiatives to make and implement their own decisions. To do so, they require knowledge accumulated from the results of their own practical experience. In short, executives have to be more entrepreneurial and be responsible for their own work.

Since outsourcing will grow and more work will be undertaken outside the company or by subcontractors within it, outsourcing and subcontracting skills will be required. Joint venturing, too, may grow, despite its inherent dangers. Being able to work advantageously with other companies, while maximizing the benefits accruing to one's own firm, may be a useful skill to be able to offer.

Sorting quickly and discriminatingly through overloads of all types of information also requires knowledge born from practical shirtsleeves experience that has matured into instincts based on a buildup of latent ideas. It requires an ability to recognize the small but vital percentage of data that could prove to be useful, while automatically rejecting the 80 percent or more that will be irrelevant, misleading, self-serving, or otherwise distracting and time wasting.

Superior managers now need an ability, continuously or periodically, to analyze, destroy, and recreate every aspect of a business, its processes, its systems, products, services, and plans—including the manager's own contributions—and to improve them.

A 1959 article by the American Management Association was entitled *What Is Management?* It referred to three possible ways that a manager could fail to be effective: either he or she may lack capacity, fail in devotion to duty, or put their own ends ahead of those of the enterprise. But in assessing the calibre of a CEO, as opposed to any other operational manager, we have to acknowledge that any and all the ills of a company can validly be laid at his door, because he is accountable for the leadership and effective management of the entire business enterprise. On the other hand, he or she might have been appointed with a crisis management function, to clear up the mess left by a predecessor.

The most common ways a chief executive might lack capacity are by not leading; through poor communications (generally from isolation); an erroneous belief that administration is the main function of managing a company; by self-aggrandizement or arrogance; by dabbling in the marketing function without a proper knowledge of what it is, and thereby preventing an experienced marketing vice-president from performing effectively; through greed; or by making irrational judgements and decisions. There are many others of lesser frequency.

If we are looking for the ideal attributes for chief executives, von Clausewitz considered leadership in battle for most of his life, and made copious notes as he studied generals in the field. Since he lived during the Napoleonic wars, he had ample opportunity to observe winners and losers and the reasons for both victory and defeat. "Four elements make up the climate of war," he wrote; "danger, exertion, uncertainty, and chance."[2]

Business managers are fortunate that their lives are unlikely to be endangered, but their companies can be, and so can their careers. They do not have to endure the exertions of war, but business stress and an overdeveloped sense of responsibility can take their toll. Although uncertainty can be reduced by research, the unexpected can always happen. And a great deal may depend on chance, with its accompanying risks. Leadership in business therefore requires closely similar personal characteristics as ones that von Clausewitz considered essential for a commander in battle. If we compress the very essence of his chapter on leadership into a few dozen key words, we are able to construct a profile of the ideal leader.

Commanding Attributes

The following list encapsulates the characteristics von Clausewitz considered essential for leadership: spirit; courage; responsibility; training; discriminating judgement; powers of intellect; determination (*courage d'ésprit*); presence of mind; strength of will; strength of character; rapid and accurate decision (*coup d'oeil*); and a sense of locality.

The type of determination he intended as that seventh characteristic is one that, by its very single-minded purposefulness, *dispels doubt* from the minds of followers. Of the ninth characteristic—strength of will—he added the words *staunchness* and *endurance*. What he intended to convey about rapid and accurate decision making in the heat of the moment was an ability to make correct and rational judgements, *in the flash of an eye*. The last of those special criteria was intended as much more than a knowledge of the topography or the disposition of his and his competitors' forces, or the status of battle at any given moment. In terms of a large diversified manufacturing organization, for example, or a national chain of department stores or hotels, it would be such a thorough knowledge of every single aspect of the enterprise which could be conjured up in an instant, that exploitable opportunities or potential problems could be immediately addressed.

Those twelve ideal attributes, over which he pondered probably for many years, are certainly highly desirable in a CEO of a large organization, or a top manager with a broad scope of responsibilities.

The functions of a CEO are general management ones in their broad scope, and each one should be marketing oriented. They would therefore benefit from someone with an abundance of practical experience of the daily hazards in the career of a general manager. But circumstances leading to such appointments differ according to a company's life cycle, the type of industry, and whether the country in which the enterprise operates has a developed economy or is a developing one or an undeveloped Third World nation. A company that had barely managed to survive a recent crisis would probably have jettisoned its CEO. In that case it would be difficult to move someone out of a secure position to take on a sensitive one in a company with a tarnished history. A search for a suitable candidate might locate a potential president who was unemployed for reasons other than his or her own mismanagement. But in a situation in which shareholders cannot find a suitable candidate because of bad publicity, they would probably decide to settle for continuity instead. And they would identify the most suitable of their existing top managers, who could at least control its assets for a while, even though he or she could only play a defensive role to protect their investments in the short term.

It would mean settling for second best; choosing an accountant or controller for the sake of expediency, not to attempt to put the company back on its feet. The newly promoted accountant would be in a similar position to a subaltern promoted at the front in wartime because more senior officers have been killed or incapacitated. He is often promoted beyond his competence. And if he is still alive when the crisis is over, he is generally demoted. He is therefore likely to exploit the opportunity to the full. Sometimes the challenge of new responsibilities discovers in him an ability to lead.

In a developing country where supplies are limited and opportunities abound, a head office might appoint a CEO with a strong sales background. If the industry is capital intensive and necessitates setting up factories to manufacture industrial or electronic equipment, the background of an ideal candidate may be production or engineering. In the sphere of packaged consumer goods, it could possibly be someone who rose in the ranks through marketing. The management style of each alternative CEO would therefore be influenced by their own individual background. And each would believe that his or her own particular approach to management is the best one, because of their training and experience in that particular discipline.

The Ivory Tower

There is a type of leader who is insensitive to the impression he creates on his staff and their reactions to him. His management style is one of aloofness, and his management team might well say that "he lives in an ivory tower."

Before reviewing traditional categories of leadership and management styles, we should reflect on the Ivory Tower syndrome, because it is more prevalent than might be supposed. What most of the former leaders of failed companies, mentioned previously, had in common, as well as those that survived after suffering heavy losses, was a false view of the world outside and of their own self-importance within. Arrogance misleads a CEO and his top management sycophants into believing they know better than their customers what their customers want; that they know better than long-term employees what is wrong with processes, systems, design, production, assembly, and quality of their products or services; that they know better than their distributors what to offer the public, and how to sell it.

Arrogance frequently conceals ignorance of opportunities in the marketplace and of real problems that need solving in a workplace or in customer service. Often after discovering why and how their business organizations lost millions or billions of dollars, top executives will deny that their own people in sales, marketing, or on production lines, knew what was wrong beforehand and repeatedly warned them what would happen. Those executives had isolated themselves from reality in their ivory towers and did not practice Management by Walking Around.

Arrogance that stems from ignorance often leads to complacency and sometimes to pomposity. They are the four deadly sins of commerce and industry, because they result in blindness and deafness, and inhibit two-way communications. Meanwhile, executive offices and the board room become arid arenas of pointless daily performances. Essentials are brushed aside to make way for self-congratulatory presentations of spreadsheets promising paper profits, and flattery of the CEO. It is left to more dedicated and entrepreneurial employees with spirit to leave and start up their own small business enterprises with the very ideas that top management lacked the ability to evaluate. Alternatively, they were deliberately ignored as being subsidiary to their own personal career interests. The Ivory Tower syndrome results in hundreds of small, aggressive companies eroding the market shares of bigger organizations. It aborts in-house discoveries and ideas, which are exploited, instead, by overseas business organizations with more vision, initiative, and drive.

Often it is specialization and departmentalization that isolate them from key results areas that make the business work, and their unproductive type of administration style turns minds inward instead of outward. Often, too, they possess little or no solid operational line management experience relating to customers, markets, or production lines: they are more accustomed to staff positions.

CEOs who have not risen through the ranks are generally afraid to reveal their ignorance of manufacturing processes or marketing strategies, and find safety in being remote. They are often happy to build up a bureaucracy to protect them from the operational realities of the business. Those administrative or staff layers are self-serving, and multiply, so that they are in a position to filter out information that might go to the CEO and be detrimental to their career advancement or even their survival. Not only do they represent unnecessary costs but they also discourage productive employees and keep them off-balance. That leads to slowdowns in responding to customer needs, and a company's competitive edge is blunted.

Management Styles

There are two opposite poles in a range of management styles. There is the autocracy of a Napoleon, who believed that people could not be trusted and had to be firmly controlled, ordered what to do, and punished ruthlessly if they did not obey. There is Rousseau's belief that the only source of law is the will of the people; or worker empowerment.[3] And there are gradations in between them.

Autocratic Leadership

It was the autocratic leader who was the subject of Jefferson's letter to Henry Lee, which compared that dictatorial style unfavorably with "those who have confidence in the people." The latter lead by means of a consultative style. Professor McGregor referred to those opposites as Theory X and Theory Y.

An autocrat *drives* personnel, whereas the consultative style inspires resolve and a will to win. The autocrat *uses* managers and staff to achieve purely immediate and short-term results, whereas a consultative leader develops managers, who, in turn, develop their staff. Autocracy rules by threat and fear, while the consultative style *involves* managers, who involve their staff. Autocrats tend to procrastinate on commitments to staff and customers, because their actions are primarily centered on self—whereas a consultative manager is concerned to fulfill internal and external obligations. Whereas the autocrat is continually driven to extinguish crises that divert him or her from meeting company objectives and goals, the consultative leader achieves goals. While autocratic leaders are adept at placing blame on others, the consultative approach enables managers to solve crises as soon as they appear, because they are prepared.

Those differences indicate that while autocrats are continually involved in trying to push through short-term solutions to problems as they arise, a consultative leader plans ahead of time by defining clear objectives and manages by meeting goals aimed at reaching those objectives. The former style could be described as purely administrative, while the latter is a marketing approach.

Managers dedicated to a marketing approach are often disappointed when they see the autocratic one seeming to work. But whenever it does it is generally only short term. And when it may seem to be working long term, it generally ends in a monumental disaster.

Successful autocrats are rarely liked but often respected when they appear to get things done, while unsuccessful ones are generally despised or pitied. They succeed for a time because of their tremendous drive and their enjoyment of tensions, but only when the market is in their favor or fortune shines on their endeavors. But they can rarely withstand setbacks, because their style seldom attracts dedicated high-calibre employees, and their high rate of staff turnover does not provide a firm foundation for long-term success.

Benevolent Dictatorship

Whenever the relative flaws in totalitarianism or democracy are discussed, there will often be someone to raise the question as to whether a benevolent dictatorship is not the best compromise. Although they have no experience of one, they are likely to say, it might avoid the rule of fear on one hand, and a permissive and anarchic society on the other. But the terminology confuses by its seeming contradiction—benevolence is kind whereas dictatorship is cruel. So is the caring but scolding father or mother to a beloved child.

They do exist in business, and many of those enterprises are independent family ones. One such company was a successful market leader in the retail furniture trade; another was a successful carpet wholesaler. Industry statistics showed them to be competitively managed in terms of comparable sales per square foot, return on investment, and other quantitative measurements. The owners, who were also the chief executives, were both well-respected in their own industries and in their communities, because of their knowledge and success.

In each case, their management style could best be described as paternalistic. They knew exactly what they wanted and their entire staffs knew they had to get their own way. When they did not, their explosive personalities inspired fear and insecurity. The explosions took place whenever either of them believed that they were being frustrated in their pursuit of perfection. Their demeanor was not like the iciness of the autocrat, which continues for some time after each confrontation. A paternal or maternal entrepreneur may swell in anger as an instinctive means of immediately getting their own way. And when their staff are running in all directions, in a state of shock, their temper subsides as quickly as it arose, and all is forgotten.

Staff take great pride in their company's excellent image, because it also enhances their own perceived value in the eyes of suppliers, the industry, and customers. Consequently they respect and like, and even feel affection for the owner, and therefore allow his or her dictatorial style. Managers or staff who might leave the company, invariably regret having done so. Some return, and the owners show no ill feeling. On the contrary, they are flattered. But paternalism, with its edge of fear, seems to work only if the owner is a brilliant and dedicated perfectionist in his own sphere. That sphere is generally discrimination in selecting superior merchandise and negotiating favorably for it.

Socrates preferred a leader who is aware of what he does *not* know. He considered such an admission to be a measure of the spirit of scientific enquiry, intellectual curiosity, and honesty. He was skeptical of academic smugness, and felt that those who did not know how little they knew, knew nothing of consequence. Paternal or maternal entrepreneurs tend to fit into that category because they generally possess enquiring minds and a desire to improve their performance. But they will only trouble to listen to those they respect.

Bureaucracy

The sign of a bureaucratic organization is that it pays more attention to the form than the substance. The wrong format or cover of a report takes precedence over its content. Rules and regulations are imposed to create power, and a sign of bureaucracy is that its proponents are in love with the power structure. Each cog believes it controls all the others. But while they are attending to the structure, no one is running the business.

Although we are not primarily concerned with institutions, which are usually, or usually become, self-serving, in government cities like Washington or

Ottawa, bureaucratic complexity, confusion, and sterility tends to seep into the private sector from the movement of public service personnel. It slows down business, increases costs, and lends it false values to inflate its self-importance. Output drops as overheads increase. Losses cannot be recovered by increasing the marketing effort, because the bureaucratic style of administration effectively obstructs or even suffocates ideas and their implementation in a welter of doggerel.

It is questionable whether a bureaucracy possesses any leadership at all, outside of a government deputy minister and the direction of the minister. Based on the definition previously quoted, it is purely ritualistic and self-serving, like some archaic priesthood.

Consultative Leading

Typical patterns of consultative leadership have been shown by comparison with autocratic management. Consultative leaders of over fifteen large business organizations were studied in depth, and all practiced a distinctive style of management that reflected their personalities and was demonstrated by their demeanor. Most had been accustomed to a working methodology akin to MBO. That naturally applied to their top management teams, who applied it to the management of their staff. All were sophisticated companies in a variety of different industries, including: fast-moving packaged consumer goods, consumer durables, multinational advertising agencies, tobacco and confectionery distribution, chemicals, agricultural and veterinary products, confectionery manufacturing, publishing, sewing machines, textile distribution, and manufacture of domestic appliances.[4]

Marketing directors in most or all of those companies undertook sophisticated marketing studies and R&D, and presented the results at board meetings with such clarity that their strategic marketing plans followed naturally, so that decisions could be easily made. The same meticulous but easy style of management was practiced by their advertising managers, their sales managers, promotional and brand managers, and others on their staffs. Their companies and their meetings were run with fluidity and efficiency. Personal relationships were excellent because of respect for each others' skills, and because of the close involvement in decision making through consultation between managers and staff. And in all cases, the benevolent personality, courtesy, and consideration of an intelligent CEO played a crucial role. Those qualities were equally in evidence in head offices in London, New York, Johannesburg, and Durban. The same thing applied to the multinational advertising agencies used by those companies.

Management and board meetings were a model of what such meetings should be. They were facilitated by the distribution of formal agendas long enough beforehand for everyone to arrive fully prepared. Senior managers would invite the opinion of everyone present. Even when the CEO was already well-informed of the current status—which they all took care to be—they would listen with care and patience to every word without unnecessary interruptions, other than to ask relevant questions at appropriate times. Department heads would apprise the CEO of their particular situation, using commonly understood principles. Everything said was directly to the point, and it was carefully weighed before finalizing each decision, which was always reached unanimously, so that everyone left meetings feeling they had contributed to those decisions. That was partly because of the care taken by the CEO, or whoever chaired those meetings, that friction, uncertainty, and inflexibility had been avoided.

It was significant that in all of those companies practicing consultative leadership and management, the chief executive inspired not only respect but friendship, and even affection. Managers were developed with a gentle and considerate touch so that they were hardly aware of being directed at all.

Obligations and commitments to shareholders were met by the high standard of management and a dedication to the first-rate; obligations to customers were met by providing excellent and dependable products at affordable prices; commitments were made to their communities by providing employment; and to their management by establishing clearly defined career paths.

The smooth running of each company was undertaken apparently without undue effort and in a calm and pleasant atmosphere, despite the fact that most were complex and sophisticated companies. Several were multinational market leaders. Professionalism was the key, and most of their top management were cultivated and erudite individuals. Beneath their urbanity they were all street-smart. And their association was one of equals communicating with equals.

Consultative leadership could be described as charismatic authority, since it relies more on personal devotion between leaders and followers rather than on the authority of status.

Participative Leadership

Because consultative leadership invites participation, there is only a thin dividing line between it and participative leadership, but it is a borderline that can separate hero from eunuch.

While *participate* means to have a share or take part in something, *consultative* is defined as "advisory"—seek information or advice from; or "of or for consultation." Terminology often persuades a consultative manager or CEO that their style is participative when it is not.

The chief executive officer is called upon to play a decisive role as leader of a company, for which he has to direct a top management team in a sufficiently firm and assertive manner, so as to initiate response leading to actions. If he were to be merely participative, he would be just another member of the team. But in a consultative capacity he can take leadership initiatives with the certainty that his top management team will support his actions and cooperate with them; or his charisma will persuade them that he is the first among equals; or—depending on the calibre of the team—he may sometimes have to cajole them into activity. Whichever way he chooses to lead, he can trigger appropriate action. And his or her consultative style will invite employees to participate whenever they have useful opinions, suggestions or advice, or interact if they have questions or doubts.

All line managers play a tutorial role in their consultative capacity with their staff, in order to improve their performance, and, sometimes, gradually to prepare them for promotion. Staff managers, too, offer suggestions or advice, but more often when they are *asked* to provide their expertise. That being the case, something different is apparently expected from participative leadership. However, in the final analysis, people need direction, even in knowledge industries where there is more independence. And they usually become confused when leadership is transformed into a more passive state. Often, after a meeting in which staff members have been asked to participate and the person chairing it has stepped back to play a less assertive role in order to invite participation from others, the meeting ends inconclusively. Those who know they are supposed to act on the conclusions that were arrived at don't know what they were or what is expected of them. In such cases, they seldom approach the participative chairperson, because he or she left a nebulous impression. They will ask a more decisive manager what the meeting was all about and what precisely they should do.[5]

It could be claimed that a participative management style is a more *democratic* one inviting consensus, but it may do so in such a nebulous way that those supporting consensus may not understand what it is they are supporting. But despite the fact that the terminology may be an oxymoron meaning no leadership at all, it does border on ambiguity, and ambiguity can be used purposely, often to enable decisions to be approved without causing confrontations. It can also work to advantage when a CEO wants to ease out of the leadership role into some other capacity—perhaps to become chairman, or to head up a separate autonomous division or company—and wishes to pass initiatives to other managers. One general manager of a leading multinational advertising agency, practiced an open-door policy that stimulated participation by inviting anyone to step in at any time, when he would stop whatever he was doing to give them his undivided attention. He was also adept at Managing by Walking Around. Like several of the other successful CEOs who had strong ideas of their own, he would not push them forward, but rather get things done through the other's momentum, by talking *around* the subject, to clear the way until it was *they* who thought they had initiated the idea in the first place, not him. He used his benevolent, almost self-effacing manner to inspire trust and invite ideas from others, because he knew that a knowledge environment of that type can be very competitive and ambitious people can easily feel threatened. He would never summon staff to his office, but wander around the corridors and drop in on their's for an informal chat. That way he knew they would be more relaxed and candid and more ready to accept oblique suggestions. His strategy usually started by asking an apparently innocent question as he plumped himself down in their visitors' chair. Since he had aroused their curiosity with the question, they would have to think about it, and once they answered, they had taken the bait, and he would gradually pull them in. Unlike many advertising people who feel threatened by other people's brilliance, he had the quiet self-confidence to think out loud, and sometimes even frankly admit to errors of judgement. His very openness invited participation and he himself acted as if he were just another member of that person's team.

Although his self-effacing leadership style worked for him, it did so only because his was a knowledge industry. With other types of workers, there can be resentment at being pressed to make decisions, because it is the manager who is paid for being accountable, not them. They prefer to perform their own functions to the best of their ability and feel pride whenever they achieve a performance out of the ordinary, but unloading management responsibilities onto them is often met with resistance.

If consultative leadership works through charismatic authority, participative management can deprive a leader of his charisma, like the fabled emperor who was deprived of his clothes without realizing it until a small child announced that he was naked. More often than not, a manager changing from a consultative style to a participative one does so gradually as he loses interest in the job and the company and can no longer be bothered to take the lead. Consequently he is happy to pass responsibilities and decisions to others. That could hardly be described as leadership.

Democratic Leadership

Democracy is what leaders give us the illusion of but not the substance— because they know how quickly chaos can occur, either from the "tyranny of the majority" or from manipulation by special interest groups or individuals who justify mischief-making by claiming their so-called "democratic rights."

In Athens, where it originated, it did not represent what we like to delude ourselves it did. The only empowered citizens were men from aristocratic families who had settled the territory. Women were not entitled to vote, nor were slaves or freemen. The only reason that it was described as "democratic" was because it was not ruled by a tyrant.

In the mid-1990s, the closest management fad to "democracy" was dubbed "bottom-up management." That is an oxymoron, since tails do not wag dogs. Workplace empowerment failed in socialist and communist countries. Committees were elected, ostensibly to represent the people. But, as with democratic political systems, it is rarely the best who get elected. It is naive to believe that there is not an art to forming committees to gain individual power: Marx and Lenin were but two who exploited it to their own advantage.

Democratic management promises much because of its ambiguity—it means different things to different people, and is as seductive a theory as Marxism once was. It is known generally for its ability to protect mediocrity or to impose it. In Tito's Yugoslavia, workplace empowerment had to be stopped: "[T]he working class simply voted itself pay rises when it was given a choice about what to do with excess funds."[6] That surplus should have been used to replace worn machine tools, provide new technologies, be invested in R&D, or otherwise ensure the industry's future. But how could iron-curtain workers be expected to understand capitalist fundamentals or economics?

If a manager is hired to provide bottom-up management, he or she can be sure that—despite democratic consensus to share responsibility—he or she will be the person who is fired when the enterprise fails. How, after all, can a manager advance a company's interests if he or she has to obtain consensus on every issue? The collapse of soviet industries provides the answer.

Just as no one can do your living, loving, or dying for you, it is unwise to delegate leadership if it is your responsibility. Those who do so are generally disappointed, and it can be a costly experiment. Leadership and direction are essential. Despite that, some entrepreneurs like to court popularity simply by seeking occasional consensus on easy issues.

Laissez-Faire Management

The theory of *laissez-faire,* or individualism, implied that "individuals acting independently for their own advantage will produce the greater aggregate of wealth." According to Keynes it was based on several unreal assumptions and gained ground in the nineteenth century because it gave full scope to captains of industry who were the heroes of the age, but were now becoming "tarnished idols."[7]

While *laissez-faire* management in the hands of unscrupulous twentieth-century entrepreneurs could be dangerous, it is something altogether different in the hands of managers who are less than brilliant. The late Barings merchant bank, Confederation Life and Royal Trustco, all suffered from its consequences, because today it simply means no management controls at all, or no management responsibility or accountability, rather than unlimited management power. The latter may be best exemplified, in more recent times, by Onassis, on one hand, and Robert Maxwell, on the other. The former should rather be described as "Leave-it-Alone Management."

Leave-it-Alone Management

No company can survive for long today without continually taking initiatives to innovate in order to improve every aspect of a business. Leaving things alone on the grounds that "if it ain't broke why fix it?" is—as Barings demonstrated—today's *laissez-faire*: an absence of management controls that would otherwise reveal fault lines that can break a company apart.

Top management teams and other executives easily become complacent in a leave-it-alone environment in which they are unaccustomed to any form of leadership. Complacency relaxes any sense of urgency, and with it any desire for change or challenge. New concepts are viewed as a nuisance that might disturb the comfortable *status quo*.

When a crisis manager is brought in to solve such problems that cause inertia, or the CEO has been replaced because of it, management that has become accustomed to a complacent style—whether democratic, participative, permissive, or bottom-up—generally fail to understand any need for urgent repairs. Nor do they show much concern for a company's deficit—since government practices suggest that deficit spending is a perfectly normal way to conduct one's affairs. We all live on credit nowadays. In fact the very terminology is double-think. And, in that case, a consultative management style rarely works, although the new CEO would be justified in thinking it should. But the longer that *leave-it-alone* management is practiced, the more difficult it is to convert top management into a more dynamic or innovative team. And autocratic leadership fails too, because, when warned of the precariousness of their jobs, managers freeze or run around in useless circles instead of being motivated to smarten up. Years of being left on their own destroys initiative and drive, so that they can no longer function effectively as top managers. They possess neither the self-discipline nor the dedication, nor any necessary resolve to do so. Without having experienced direction or authority from a leader for years, they lose all sense of purpose.

Free Rein

When riding a well-trained and intelligent horse that knows exactly where it is going, it is not unusual to loosen the reins. If there is mutual confidence the horse will react well to the loosened reins and both will enjoy the run. The same is true of dedicated and creative executives who understand their goals and enjoy improving and demonstrating their skills. Free rein is a valid leadership style in knowledge industries, and perhaps also in some other service sector industries, in similar circumstances.

Ego States

Regardless of those different categories, a good leader is flexible and changes style on occasion to meet the unique needs of different situations, different companies, different industries, and different personnel.

But we should never forget the role that emotions can play in even the best managed company, because of the enlarged ego of any manager. If we bear in mind the method of Transactional Analysis, we find that each management style corresponds to a different ego state:

Parent:
- Autocratic
- Benevolent Dictator

Adult:
- Consultative
- Participative
- Free-Rein

Child:
- Democratic
- Laissez-faire
- Bottom-Up

The approach of the Parent is to choose how to lead and control. The Adult seeks to understand and motivate. The Child prefers to leave the burden of responsibility to someone else.[8] So that when we talk loosely of a manager's ego we really mean his or her domineering Parent state. And when we say a manager lacks leadership qualities, it is often because he or she possesses a low capacity for responsibility.

Sycophants inevitably flourish in the reign of an autocratic leader. His or her scolding or contemptuous attitude necessitates a means to obtain feedback from managers who may be afraid to express their own opinions in the face of such a forceful and powerful personality. Autocrats know that and are never sure that their employees are telling them the truth. Although they despise yes-men, the paradox is that they may deliberately have to employ one to find out what their managers really think. They may even be afraid that their authority could be undermined and their career go awry. In that case they might appoint a personal assistant, or P.A., as old-fashioned, family owned department stores once hired a floorwalker.

That is one aspect of the emotional arena that easily prevails without strong or positive leadership.

Traditional Authority

Charismatic authority, which is required for consultative leadership, has been depicted throughout history. But in order for it to succeed, everyone has to know their position and function, whether in a corporate culture or the larger society, as if each one scrupulously followed a clearly defined job description. Only then, it seems, can individuals feel free to fulfil their responsibilities with singleminded resolve, dedication, and industry.

There appears to be no western tradition still intact that might serve as a foundation for a new management style in an ideal industrial society, compared with the residue of the Japanese feudal system or Confucian philosophy in which everyone knows their place and what is expected of them.

What we find in the West is two management styles that appear to work well enough for us—a consultative style in a properly structured business organization and a benevolent dictatorship in smaller or family business enterprises. And a free-rein style may be used in each, in special circumstances. Certain values and codes are essential for both of those management cultures to work effectively. And those values and codes have endured, or reappeared after some time—just as the codes of *Shinto, Bushido, Zen,* and Confucianism have in Japan. And Confucianism appears to be returning to China, in order to reestablish status and function in a changing society. *Bushido* incorporated such characteristics as self-discipline, correct demeanor, simple living, thrift, and loyalty, from Confucius, as well as emphasizing bravery.

Most of the shards left over from formal western traditions have to be excavated in order to identify them and their origins. Then we find, to our surprise, that some date back to the ideals of perfect knighthood from long before the Arthurian legend. Some were transplanted to the New World, where they grew into the fabled heroism of Wild West frontiersmen and gunfighters as mythologized in romantic American movies like *Shane.* Indeed, President Reagan's popularity was due, in part, to his "lone gunfighter" image.

Instead of *Zen* disciplines or self-denial, there is only the remains of gentlemanly virtues from Edwardian England; of quiet courage, self-restraint, modesty, and sometimes even self-effacement ("Never complain and never explain"). It became converted in the United States, by Ernest Hemingway, into a philosophy of "grace under pressure."

Since the specific position and function of each social class in Japan was clearly defined according to the imported Confucian philosophy and code that developed into something characteristically Japanese, and the formal German caste system continued even up to the 1950s, both Germany and Japan were enabled to rebuild their societies after the devastation of World War II. They already possessed role models, whereas Britain and other western nations chose to reject the old models to pursue the goal of a classless society.[9]

It should not be forgotten, however, that post-war Japanese workers fought hard against autocratic management in giant corporations like Mitsui, in order to achieve the Bright New Life. The violence of strikes like that of the coal miners left great bitterness in its wake. But it also acted as a warning to powerful companies that they could no longer misuse their authority against workers as if they still possessed a feudal right to do so.

Pragmatism

Thomas Cromwell interrupted the scholar Pole's discussion on how to serve a prince with honor, at Cardinal Wolsey's house, to say that he would do better to exchange theoretical classroom learning for practical experience as could be found in Machiavelli's new book. The theme of *The Prince* could be summed up in his phrase, "A ruler will perish if he is always good; he must be cunning as a fox and as fierce as a lion."[10]

Niccolò Machiavelli considered that while a ruler should appear to possess such virtues as conscience, morality, and religion, he would be wise not to practice them, because he dared not risk such weaknesses when he was responsible for the security of the state. In order to be feared, he should seek a reputation for cruelty. Consequently, the word *machiavellian* is erroneously used to illustrate evil or despotic rule. But Machiavelli's aim was simply to instruct the Medici ruler how to protect his principality and stay alive at a time of blood feuds, insurrections, and assassinations by powerful families who sought to steal territories with the aid of mercenaries. A prince's life could easily be shortened if he were not continually on guard.

In fact, Machiavelli's *Discourses* led Bertrand Russell to conclude that he was a disappointed romantic.[11] The person more suited to bear the designation "machiavellian" was Louis XIth of France, who built a political system in Europe through remarkable deceit, cunning, deception, cynicism, and lies. Today we would probably describe it as diplomacy.

His leadership style was despotic. Its significance is that Louis turned his back on established codes of honor and chivalry, which had been inherent in knightly virtues—even though they were not often practiced—and replaced them with the services of ruthless mercenary soldiers of the Scottish Life Guards, and the Swiss who were even more brutal. In diplomacy, he was without scruples: while other parties to his negotiations still felt bound by religion, honor, or morality, he did not. And if they appeared to hold an advantage over him, he would smile to conceal his duplicity and use his engaging wit to disarm them, until such time as he could hold them in absolute power in his dungeon prisons and torture them at his pleasure, or leave them there to rot.[12]

That dying system of knighthood and its chivalric principles that revered consideration for others are the characteristics that form the foundation of charismatic business leadership. Louis considered them to be romantic notions in a violent world inhabited by scheming and callous opponents. But those principles would reemerge in England as part of the courtly demeanor during the reign of Queen Elizabeth the First.

Chivalry represented a code of ethics and behavior of a knight. It was an ideal of moral nobility, as opposed to nobility of birth. The poet Geoffrey Chaucer summarized the knightly virtues between 1380 and 1383 as truth, integrity, loyalty, honor, courage of convictions, liberality, and courtesy. And courtesy implied tact, humility, gentleness, and mercy. A person who practiced such virtues in those times could justifiably be described as "civilized." But actions define the individual, and the Crusades and other sustained overseas military engagements created a need for conscription and the hiring of professional soldiers instead of knights. Even so, we see some similarity between those knightly values that crept surreptitiously into Edwardian customs, and a recent remark by a leading Japanese politician who tried vainly to avoid the media spotlight at a world summit conference; "Leadership should be modest, not bold."

That remark reveals an attitude toward politics that was once held by the English, too. But the turn of the century marks a return of the very changes that took place in Louis XI's time—from well-intentioned amateurism to brutally effective professionalism; from values of chivalry in a well-ordered society to cynical ones in an era of intense competition in which there will be only winners and losers.

We see winners and losers come and go in the business world and in the world of high finance. Sometimes it seems that only an element of luck weighed down the scales on one side rather than the other; that the dividing line between the two is almost invisible. But when we take a deeper look, we find that qualities that were inherent in the winner were lacking in the loser.

If we use a historical parallel again, in order to benefit from vivid descriptions by chroniclers of Frankish and Norman successes in the Mediterranean regions (like Malaterra, Vitalis, William of Apulia, and Amatus of Monte Cassino) we find that they did not attribute success to the advantage of overwhelming numbers or to new weapons technology, but to "character." The winners enjoyed a special mix of drives, of which the most important was "sheer energy." It enabled them to press an enemy harder and for longer than was accustomed. And in business negotiations or marketplace tactics, we see major corporations led by brilliant entrepreneurs who possess the same type of drive, persistence, and audacity. "Their goals were wealth and domination," wrote Amatus. And Geoffrey Malaterra wrote that they were autocrats "greedy for booty and power." Tough, vigorous, and hard working, they thrived on adversity and were driven by *inner ambition*. At the turn of the twelfth century, Anna Comnena wrote, "Whenever battle and war occur, there is a baying in their hearts and they cannot be held back."[13]

Those colorful descriptions fit most of the winners in business battles for fame and fortune—or greed and booty, whichever way one perceives it. And many people view a business career with repugnance because it seems to them to consist of taking money from other people to put into one's own pocket, as it did seven or eight hundred years ago by those types of adventurers or *conquistadors*.

Even if that description were true, there is a valid argument that losers are less skilled, poorly managed and led, and uncompetitive companies that do not therefore contribute to social stability by creating new jobs and circulating money to improve the economy. Those that lose business to their competitors, as a consequence, should therefore be pressed to improve through competition, or be toppled into bankruptcy as an ineffective and useless species.

In fact, that vision of business is flawed. Progressive enterprises fulfill new needs by creating new or innovated services or products. The invention of the silicon chip is a good example of this. So was the steam engine. So were the automobile, the jet engine, penicillin, and pasteurization, the discovery of DNA, and biotechnology. Each of them created new industries and new jobs, as well as providing numerous benefits to society.

That greed occupies the minds of some entrepreneurs, business leaders, and bank presidents is indisputable. But it does not guarantee success and is more likely to contribute to failure. We have no difficulty in comparing certain business people of our acquaintance with the greedy dog in Aesop's fable. It was also stupid, ignorant, or naive. It was happy trotting along with a juicy bone in its mouth, until it saw its own reflection in a river. What it thought it saw was another dog with, surely, an even bigger bone. When it opened its jaws to steal it, the real bone dropped out of its mouth and was lost in the river. Its moral was that a business manager should not throw away something tangible for the sake of an illusion. But it happens all the time, and greed is at the bottom of it.

When we consider the moral ideal in conducting business and in our workplace practices, we are, perhaps, fortunate in having Spinoza's advice, because his ethics manage to reconcile opposites by identifying our goal simply as happiness. He predicated that we have three alternatives to choose from. The first is a belief that all individuals are equally precious and therefore unlimited democracy should prevail. The second recognizes the inequality of individuals and prefers autocratic rule, because power is a virtue in such circumstances. The third one—which he chose—considers neither one to be applicable in the real world. That belief was held also by Socrates, Plato, and Aristotle—that only educated and mature people can judge when it is wise to rule benevolently or through power. The key is to use intelligence, which would surely counsel a mix of both democracy and autocracy. From that, it would seem they all believed in what we have called "benevolent dictatorship."

Parameters

The case of the highly successful pictorial magazine, *Picture Post,* became a *cause célèbre* in its own industry in Britain in 1950. It is an example of borderline management.

Here was an outstanding publication of which the industry was rightfully proud. And to judge from its sales of 1,380,000 it was also highly regarded by its readers. Much of the credit for its high standards of photo journalism must go to its editor, Tom Hopkinson, who was knighted in 1977. And yet he had been fired by the publisher in 1950.

Since magazines like *Picture Post, World Review, Time,* and *Life* help to mold public opinion by their revelations and comments on world events, the demise of *Picture Post* seven years after Hopkinson was fired, turned him into a hero. It also involved the publisher and his wife in considerable criticism.

Long after the event, many of its old readers assumed that it was the advent of TV, with major advertisers switching their huge budgets from print to TV commercials, which destroyed *Picture Post,* as it did so many other publications. The publisher took that approach when interviewed on TV in 1977. But since most publications that were ruined by lack of advertising failed much later, and others—like *Reader's Digest*—survived, one must look for other reasons for the drop in circulation to 1,225,000 by June, 1951 and to only 935,000 twelve months later. The really significant effects of TV advertising in Britain only began to be felt by print media between 1954 and 1957. The crux of the matter was that the editor had refused to be emasculated by the publisher.

After taking over as editor from Stefan Lorant, who invented *Picture Post,* Hopkinson became "Mr. Picture Post." Even though by his own admission, with hindsight, he would have modified his management style and concerned himself more with the social side of his job, the fact remains that the magazine's considerable success was due very largely to him. It was his enthusiasm, talent, and the hours he devoted to the magazine that not only motivated an excellent staff of creative individualists, but also carried the publisher along with it, until the social and political aspirations of Mr. and Mrs. Hulton began to interfere with their business sense.

Evidently the Hultons had no clear idea of the objectives of *Picture Post* or of their business enterprise. They had already wound up *World Review* earlier in the same year, because (according to Hopkinson) "Edward Hulton had run *World Review* as a vehicle for his own comments on the state of the world, and for the contributions of his friends and people he admired."[14] And its editor (Schimanski) had devoted its June issue to George Orwell, a leftist writer of renown, who had died several months previously—while Hulton's own political views and friends were of the right. The final clash between publisher and editor arose from pictures of the Korean war, which showed the allies in a bad light, and could have involved the publishers in criticism from their friends that their magazine was pro-communist.

It appears that Hopkinson never established a formal business plan with clear objectives and a mission, for which he might earlier have obtained approval from his employers. Had he done so, there would have been a clear commitment as to what he could and should not do. And the publishers would have had an opportunity to think through the situation in a more businesslike and less personal way. Without it, we are left with an impression that the magazine was merely a rich man's hobby, and that his editor was dismissed for turning it into a professional publication of considerable merit. Finally, by firing an editor who refused to be turned into a eunuch, he was free to appoint a number of subsequent editors, to whom he was able to dictate both content and style. He therefore had no one validly to blame for the failure of *Picture Post* but himself.

Hopkinson subsequently edited a successful look-alike magazine for black readers in South Africa, called *Drum,* and emerged from the situation as a hero.

That situation reveals how management parameters need to be clearly defined in an executive's own job description or in a formal agreement or written contract. It should also be framed in an organization's own culture and philosophy document, or in a manifesto. Without a clear definition of a manager's thresholds, an individual with initiative and drive who is dedicated to the success of an enterprise, can easily overstep the threshold of the job without being aware of it, until he is axed for his outstanding contribution.

That was not only the situation in which Hopkinson found himself. There was also the case of General MacArthur, who was dismissed by President Truman around the same time, during the war in Korea. MacArthur's biographer quoted no less an expert than General de Gaulle, who wrote, "The man of character...in relation to his superiors...finds himself in a difficult position. Sure of his own judgement, and conscious of his strength, he makes no concession to the desire to please.... More than that: those who do great things must often ignore the conventions of a false discipline. Thus in 1914 Lyautey kept Morocco despite orders from above; and after the battle of Jutland, Lord Fisher bitterly commented on Jellicoe's dispatches: 'He has all Nelson's qualities, except one: he has not learned to disobey.'"[15]

12

Responding to Challenges

Every age has its turning point. And, with hindsight and distance we can generally see how some key incident was instrumental in triggering a revolution almost overnight; like a terrorist bombing in a city center that challenges attitudes to change direction, or the assassination at Sarajevo. But new thinking, leading to suitable actions, takes longer to develop and apply. In the case of current technological and geopolitical or economic changes, different types of organizations will meet those challenges in somewhat different ways—whether big business, growing medium-size enterprises, small ones, or government.

As far as big business is concerned, perhaps Sir Michael Perry, chairman of Unilever, is an appropriate person to sum up the challenges for marketers as the century turns. Unilever's UK group includes Birds Eye, Walls, Van den Bergh, Brooke Bond Foods, Lever Brothers, Elida Gibbs, Rimmel International, Unipath, Elizabeth Arden, and Calvin Klein Cosmetics; with annual revenues of around 28 billion pounds sterling in Britain alone.

There had been considerable soul-searching by marketers, the media, researchers, and advertising agencies, and some talk of "transforming the theory and practice of marketing." But observing the almost unbroken success of the fine marketing of Unilever companies, the impression conveyed is not that marketing is changing—or even needs to change—but markets and marketers.

Despite the size of the American market, the rest of the world is now more profitable, and growing even more so. By the end of 1994, for example, India was the target for America's fifth largest foreign investments, tying with China. Tops were Britain, France, Canada, Mexico, and Germany, in that order. And Latin American countries like Brazil, Chile, and Argentina were attracting investments from other nations. "Unilever's acquisitions in the first few months of 1994 included a Malaysian flavors and fragrance business, two margarine firms in Kazakhstan, three ice cream businesses in Venezuela, France and Canada; a Russian personal products firm, and an olive oil business in Italy."[1] When Perry was prodded about global umbrella brands, retail brands, and a need for innovation in 1994, he retorted, "All that's been going on for donkey's years."

For the past five years or so, the traditional organization of marketing on national lines has been consigned to the dustbin. Instead, regional and global marketing and innovation centers with speedy electronic flows of information have been erected. Said Perry, "What competitors are doing the other side of the world could change the shape of the world you are operating in within six months." And spotting new developments and reacting to them at the speed of light is what "sorts the men from the boys these days."

More emphasis is being placed on trade customers, without moving the brand manager's focus from consumers. Reliability and quality are no longer enough, since a manufacturer must offer the same price as own-label brands. It is innovation and new concepts that revolutionize consumption patterns and enable a company to *own* a new "category." That means a move to "category managers." In the past, innovation started with a marketing brief, which went to R&D, which changed the product, which was rushed to the agency, and only when the campaign was ready was Sales asked, "Can you sell it?" "Essentially it was linear."

"Where we have changed our thinking *vis-à-vis* the past is that in the past we had a personnel function, a marketing function, a sales function, a production function and each one operated within its tight walls. Increasingly, we think in terms of the main business processes, supply chain management, innovation, and those processes are multifunctional." The entire innovation process is now "iterative and constant. You've got to have all the components in place all the time." And, "at any one time in the structure you have got to handle total centralization and total decentralisation."

"Thinking in terms of 'marketing functions' and 'marketing departments' is '*old* thinking,'" Perry declared firmly. Putting the consumer at the heart of the business is general management's responsibility as well. Although Britain is viewed highly by the Japanese for the quality of their industrial products, they consider Britain's marketing to be poor. Quality does not guarantee a successful product. It is the "willingness to modify designs, to adapt, (and) this focus on consumer needs is what it is all about—not how good the advertising is, or how strong the brand is…. How focused is it on the precise solution of customer problems?"

The other side of innovation is that "brands die when they deserve to die; when they cease to be meaningful to the consumer." The objective is to clear the shelves so that innovated brands can have room and resources to grow. That is what marketers do. In short, the marketing philosophy is as sound as it has always been—it is only a matter of how a company practices it.

Proctor & Gamble, too, reacted to changes in its domestic markets while examining overseas opportunities. They had continually failed to take leadership away from Lever Brothers in the UK market. Persil, Surf, and other Unilever brands are household words despite P&G outspending Lever by three times their promotional budget. And its hallmark in the U.S., too, is its massive advertising and promotions spend to buy and maintain its market share. That acts as a strong deterrent to many other companies seeking to enter any market dominated by P&G, or to increase their existing share. For example, Colgate-Palmolive diversified into markets where they did not compete head-on and were therefore not so vulnerable to P&G's huge budgets and marketing activities.

The stand-off situation in Europe and the U.S. must have become intolerable when supermarket chains eroded their market shares with own-label brands and also obliged them to reduce their margins. Profitable growth in developed economies became too expensive. In July, 1993 they announced that they would close thirty plants and eliminate 13,000 jobs worldwide over three to four years. Cuts represent 12 percent of staff, and 4,000 administrative jobs will be in the United States. The reason Edwin Artzt—chairman and CEO—gave is a necessity to slim down to stay competitive; "We are simply going to have to run faster to stay ahead, and we intend to do that."[2] Their net earnings for the fiscal year 1991/2 were $1.9 billion; up 6 percent from the previous year.

One means that business organizations are using to reduce costs in order to remain competitive, is manufacture their products abroad in countries with large pools of labor and high unemployment rates. And Proctor & Gamble had commissioned a new study of the South African market in 1991—according to news leaked through the supermarket chains. In fact, they had conducted a pilot test many years before by having SmithKline Beecham manufacture some of their products there under license, but the experiment was abandoned; probably because of established brand loyalty for Lever Brothers and Colgate, which might have cost them too much to erode in their own favor. But a new black middle class has emerged since then and is expected to grow very fast. The size of the black population alone is greater than the entire population of either Australia or Canada. And South Africa's economy is four times bigger than all its nine African neighbours together."[3] And yet, a recent survey "by Ernst & Young...suggested that few Japanese, American and European companies are even considering investing in Southern Africa."[4] That omission should provide a bonanza for home-grown conglomerates like SA Breweries, Rembrandt/Richemont, Anglo-American/De Beers, Sanlam, SA Mutual, Liberty Life, and Anglovaal, who, together, control around 86 percent of the Johannesburg Stock Exchange.[5]

The expected entry of Proctor & Gamble into southern Africa was confirmed in 1993. It was in February of that year that *The Economist* stated, "Africa will have the largest population growth of any region in the next century, doubling its share of the world total from today's 11.9 percent to 23.9 percent by 2100, according to the World Bank." It also brought up to date the comparison between the population growth on the continent of Africa and other continents.

"Europe's share will dwindle from 15 percent today to 8.1 percent by 2100, while Asia's will stay much the same." But only one year later, western businesses were recognizing that China showed by far the biggest growth of any economy. The Taiwanese and business people in Hong Kong and Korea and Japan had been acutely aware of that fact long before. They got in first as a result.

"Africa's population in the early 1990s has been growing at 2.9 percent a year, nearly six times as fast as in Europe (including the former Soviet Union)." In fact, the growth rate of the black population in South Africa has been growing at that rate for over a decade, and their total disposable incomes caught up with those of the white market segment several years ago.

"The World Bank reckons that global population will stop growing in the late 22nd century, when it reaches 12.2 billion (more than twice today's 5.4 billion). Nearly 90 percent of those people will live in today's poor countries. Africa's population is expected to level off at 3 billion, up from 627m today."[6]

Growing Medium-Size Enterprises (GSMEs)

Canadian economist John Kenneth Galbraith published *The Sources of Invention* in 1959 and has been censured for it ever since, because he claimed that "the days of the small enterpriser are past."[7] In fact, all historic evidence in the twentieth century up until that time showed it to be the case. Then, almost immediately after the 1971 Bolton Report on the decline of small businesses in Britain was published, the number of small businesses began to grow. New business registrations rose every year after 1968, except during the oil crisis of 1973–74. In 1968 only 19.2 percent of firms in the UK employed less than 200 people, but by 1975 the proportion of small to big had risen by 20 percent. By the end of the 1980s it had climbed to 32 percent. And by 1991 it had leapt to 99.7 percent.[8]

More studies of small businesses have been made in the UK than in most other economies, and more effort and funding has been made by government and qualified marketing practitioners to help them grow to provide more new jobs in the British Isles. By 1993, 90.1 percent employed less than 10 people; 9.7 percent employed more than 10 but less than 500; and only 2 percent employed 500 or more people. Only 2 percent produced between one million and ten million pounds of annual revenues; 19 percent created revenues of more than 100,000 pounds; and 78 percent earned less than 100,000 pounds.[9]

Professor David Storey attributes the growth of SMEs (small and medium-size enterprises) in the UK "more to the impact of technology and the worsening performance of very large firms rather than solely to a flowering of entrepreneurship." He was quoted as saying that "during downswings, a lot of people start their own business because they don't have any option. The sector acts as a sink which absorbs the fall-out from larger firms."[10] Although there was considerable fallout during recessions, births have exceeded deaths. The problem, he says, is that new businesses tend to be ever smaller.

Startups in the 1980s encouraged people to believe that it was relatively easy, but they saw or felt the downside in recessions which followed. However easy it might be to start up a new business, the major problem is to survive and persist in the face of microeconomic and macroeconomic factors that conspire against their very existence.

What are the factors that contribute to a firm's survival and growth? If we knew that we might be able to accelerate the growth of SMEs to provide more new jobs, increase exports, and improve our economies. Some researchers have defined what they call a *growth corridor* into which 20 percent of SMEs enter with five to fifty employees, but out of which only 2 percent survive to grow. They are known as GSMEs, which are now considered to be the "engines of economic growth," with turnovers of 5 million to 10 million pounds.

"The key characteristics of these companies is that they can grow far more rapidly than a large group like ICI can. Big companies have achieved critical mass where growing more than GNP is virtually impossible. They may grow 3 percent, 4 percent or 5 percent maximum. The kind of business we look at can grow from 40 percent to 50 percent up to 100 percent. *So they deliver growth, innovation and exports. Even more to the point, they deliver the jobs.*"[11]

SMEs make up nearly 50 percent of the economy in Germany and the United States, and 60 percent in Japan. "In the twelve years from 1979-1991, employment in large firms with over 500 people fell by 1.9 million. It rose in the small and middle-sized sector by 2.2 million." Between 1985 and 1989, small businesses created one and a half million jobs in Britain—13 times more than larger companies did.[12]

Investment capital group 3i (along with Cranfield European Enterprise Center) pinpointed the powerful contribution made by SMEs in the UK. They identified 3,500 middle-sized private companies whose growth they studied over a two-year period at the end of the 1980s. All together they employed over 244,000 people, and they generated 62,000 more jobs in that period alone. That was an increase of 30 percent. Total turnover doubled to about 18.4 million pounds in the same period.

Twenty-six percent of those particular GSMEs were manufacturers, compared to a national average of only 10 percent. Twenty-nine percent were distributors; 16 percent transport services; and 18 percent construction. Eighty-eight percent of the total grew by increasing sales of their own products and services (not by business acquisitions). *By far the majority focused not on reducing costs but on creating sales to niche markets.* And although it is generally supposed that small businesses concentrate on a few big customers, that was not the case. Sixty percent of the GSMEs sold less than 4 percent to their three biggest customers. Only 15 percent appeared to be dominated by their major accounts—with over 60 percent of their sales going to their three biggest customers.

Perhaps it is significant that the typical entrepreneur of those particularly successful GSMEs was aged between forty-five and fifty, with long experience of his or her own business sector, and not the young whiz kid who attracts media hype.

Growth Factors for GSMEs

Statistics Canada recently released its research findings on what factors make business enterprises grow.[13] Top management in selected GSMEs were asked to assess the relative importance of factors which they considered led to their success. They rated them as follows: (1) Management skills; (2) Marketing ability; (3) Skilled labor; (4) Access to markets; (5) Access to capital; (6) Cost of capital; (7) Ability to adopt technology; (8) R&D-Innovation capability; (9) Government assistance.

Management skills were given far the highest score. And although marketing ability came second, skilled labor was a close third. And here we have to be very clear about two aspects: One is that management skills depend on the effectiveness of marketing concepts, marketing objectives, marketing skills, and a holistic marketing orientation of the entire company; otherwise management merely *administers* what is handed to it by someone else. The other is that Canadian entrepreneurs who provided the basis for measurements as well as their own scores, would be unlikely to be able to separate management from marketing functions.

StatsCan noted that the scores on the ability to adopt technology ranked "well ahead of R&D-innovation capabilities," but GSMEs in Canada are far smaller than those in western Europe and generally less sophisticated than Germany's *Mittelstand* or Japan's workshop artisans who supply the big organizations. R&D appears to be neglected by most Canadian GSMEs because of a lack of marketing orientation. But no matter that measurements might be accurate of their opinions or even in fact, what matters more is the order of priority.

There was little difference in the sequence or scores between the manufacturing sector, construction, wholesale, retail, and service companies.

Those businesses were also asked to evaluate their position in relation to their main competitors for ten attributes. The order of priority in which they placed them was: (1) Customer service; (2) Flexibility in responding to customers' needs; (3) Quality of products; (4) Employee skills; (5) Range of products; (6) Frequency of introduction of new products; (7) Price of products; (8) Cost of producing; (9) Labor climate; and (10) Spending on R&D.

The first three criteria enjoyed almost equal importance. "Growing firms feel very much superior to their main competitors," in those areas. Scores for R&D were very low again: "Some 50 percent of firms filling in one of the other responses felt R&D activity was not applicable; that is, they did not perform R&D." Only 12 percent felt that their R&D gave them a competitive edge. Short-termism dominates business thinking in Canada too.

Although it is interesting to see that those entrepreneurs considered management and marketing to be of the utmost importance, there is a clear perception that businesses in Canada do not know what marketing is and believe the terminology applies to either selling or advertising.

Government

National and provincial debts have forced governments to borrow tactics from the private sector. They are downsizing like some large corporations, merging some departments, and getting out of providing some services. Where they feel obliged to replace some staff, they are choosing to outsource services and also bring in people with other skills who are not public servants. They are also using students. Although the main objective is to reduce costs one way or another, contracted staff from outside are also changing the management style. In Britain's Department of Trade and Industry, employing youth and multicultural staff changed the work environment to one of challenge and innovation instead of custom and routine. Some young employees possessed overseas work experience in the private sector, while retired business people were employed to manage regional branches of the Business Links program.

The Decline of Manufacturing

Whereas a quarter of America's labor force worked in the manufacturing sector in 1960, that number dwindled to only 15.4 percent by 1992. A similar trend took place in western Europe. And the proportion in Canada dropped from 22.3 percent two decades ago to only 15.9 percent by the end of 1993.[14] That erosion was not as steep in Germany and Japan, which are at 30 percent, and the UK at 20 percent. That decline has affected the West's capability to export, since it is simply producing fewer and fewer products. Britain, at its peak, once enjoyed half of the total world market; it now possesses only five percent. And three-quarters of Canadian merchandise exports are undertaken by only one hundred companies. Of that merchandise, the amount which is simply trucked or piped across the U.S. border has grown to 82 percent.

Because most of Canada's products are not manufactured but are merely either chopped down, dug up, harvested, or netted, Canadians continue, in the main, to be "hewers of wood and carriers of water." Most of their exports are natural resources like lumber, wood pulp, primary energy, unprocessed aluminum, nickel, wheat, fish, and crustaceans. Only a very small amount involves machinery and equipment. One result is that marketing has never been a priority and is therefore not clearly understood in Canada. And without marketing, Canada's management style has remained very much in its original sterile form of administering the *status quo*.

Some economists argue that the trend in the West from manufacturing to service industries is a healthy sign for developed nations that enjoy high standards of living. But those standards are clearly declining. They say we should leave manufacturing to Third World countries with lower labor costs, lower environmental standards, and lower expectations. But during and immediately after economic recessions, when economies cease to be consumer driven and corporate and personal bankruptcies grow, so does unemployment in the service sector. People with less disposable income have no choice but to eat out less, curtail visits to taverns or bars, travel and vacation less, indulge in fewer hairdos and manicures, stop attending health clubs and theaters, make their existing automobile and even their shoes last longer, and buy fewer luxury items. That effectively reduces employment in trade, catering, accommodation, transport, finance, real estate, and other personal services. And in situations where there are fewer available buyers, advertisers always cut their budgets; so that advertising agencies are obliged to reduce their staff, and their suppliers—like printers—suffer, too.

If we search for reasons for this state of affairs, we can choose from short termism on the part of some manufacturers who failed to modernize their thinking or their plants and remained uncompetitive when others did; political agendas or business ineptitude by governments that imposed payroll and other forms of taxes that discouraged hiring and expansion; trade union practices that may have led to high labor costs, low productivity, or plant closures; cheaper production in Third World countries; improved marketing and management in Pacific Asian economies; a declining work ethic in the West; and so on. But regardless of past failings, we are confronted with a situation in which our global markets have been eroded for two decades by Japan, the Asian tigers, and other, smarter, enterprises in Pacific Asia. Meanwhile, response by Britain to such challenges has been to fall back on its North Sea oil and tourism for its revenues. From Canada it has been simply to increase its trade with the United States. We have to ask ourselves whether that is responding to challenges or merely copping out.

Working people today, who once would not have thought that economics was their concern, hopefully examine leading indicators almost daily, to reassure themselves that their economies are still alive, while lacking sufficient confidence in their security to buy goods or services. Confidence arises from perceptions. And there is an uneasy perception that there are not enough manufacturing jobs to provide and maintain a stable economy. There may be merit in that view, because if we look at the proportion of manufacturing jobs of G-7 and other nations, we find those with the highest percentage appear to enjoy the strongest economies. For example, at two extreme poles are Germany and Japan with 30.8 percent and 28.9 percent of their GDP respectively in manufacturing, and Canada with only 17.8 percent.[15]

It is significant that when Canada's manufacturing sector does occasionally run at close to full capacity, it provides new jobs. But there are not enough to create the necessary impact to trigger its domestic economy. And nobody knows what is the minimum percentage of manufacturers or employment in that sector needed to provide a safety net for social stability in any economy. Japan's manufacturing sector is the only one among developed nations that is expanding. And although its unemployment rate crept up gradually from 2.8 percent to 3.2 percent in the mid-1990s, it still enjoyed by far the lowest rate of any G-7 economy. Since it continues to demonstrate economic success and social stability, despite its particular problems, it could be argued that economic power and social harmony require a solid manufacturing foundation. The ideal formula appears to be the utilization of approximately one third of a country's labor force in manufacturing jobs.

The Rise of the Service Sector

Establishment institutions in the West justify their inaction to save and upgrade the manufacturing sector by reassuring business, the media, and the public with friendly statistics. At first glance, they appear to reassure us that service industries are preferable to manufacturing jobs, simply because they seem to illustrate stability and even growth. For seven straight years from 1983 to 1989, 73.1 percent of Canada's labor force worked in service jobs. Those jobs rose annually thereafter to 77.1 percent in 1993.[16] It may therefore seem comforting to allow the manufacturing sector to run down so that labor can be freed for more congenial service jobs. But, by and large, we happen to be remarking on two different labor forces.

In fact, as more laid-off executives and bankrupt entrepreneurs were pushed into selling real estate and into other commissionable sales areas like telemarketing and consultancies, and university graduates joined them, they would most likely be earning less than blue-collar workers did in manufacturing industries. Those workers rose socioeconomically for three straight decades and joined the middle classes. Now the middle classes are shrinking, because instead of manufacturing jobs we have an abundance of graduates waiting at tables and serving at bars for tips.

Manufacturing provided full-time employment, whereas much of service sector employment is part-time, irregular, and poorly paid. Behind those stable statistics there is considerable movement from one job to another, and unpaid downtime in between jobs when unemployment insurance benefits must come into play. In larger and larger segments of the community there is a continual struggle to rise above the poverty line. Waiters and waitresses whose tips are pooled by an employer often never receive them because their employer goes under; and the rate of restaurant bankruptcies is particularly high. Employees who are fortunate enough to hold down regular service jobs often do so for minimum wages. They have become *declassé*.

Even sedentary jobs like travel agents are poorly paid and often only part time. Workers whose wage levels and hours were once regulated and protected by the Teamsters' Union or the Automobile Workers' Union are unlikely to fill those types of jobs. With the advent of fast-food outlets, a great many of those jobs merely involve turning hamburger patties on a griddle; so that service jobs in general have become known as *McJobs.*

Had the service sector not burgeoned as it did, government and the business sector would have been forced to address a challenge to improve the manufacturing sector to provide jobs, instead. As it is, entrepreneurs might well ponder on why the number of service jobs increased. One reason was that—small though the proportion of manufacturing jobs might be in the West, they include a base of constantly innovating high-tech companies. Telecommunications companies like Nortel, Newbridge, and Mitel; printing and photocopying equipment makers like Kodak and Zerox; computer manufacturers like IBM, Compaq, Apple, and Dell—all produce complex multipurpose machines that frequently require servicing. Consequently many service jobs simply accompany the manufacture of complex machinery. When that hardware is exported, so is a percentage of the service jobs that travel with it. Sixty-two percent of Canada's service exports naturally go to the United States.

While those better-paid service jobs in factories or in customers' workplaces are élite ones in the huge and multifaceted service tertiary sector, we should never forget that they are likely to dwindle with each generation of improved models. Once upon a time, there was a service sector that repaired radios, TVs, washing machines, Roneos, gramophones, kettles, and electric toasters. The ghost of the unwanted Maytag repairman hovers over this service segment. As more and more manufacturers firmly embrace the principles of total quality management, radios and TVs no longer require continual servicing as they once did. Superior designs, quality planning and controls, innovative construction, ingenious new materials, and more accurate robotic assembly lines are just as likely to reduce servicing needs for laser printers, computers, CAD/CAM and telecom equipment, and even automobiles.

Obsolescence takes its toll on everything we rely on. It should force us to reevaluate everything we take for granted, such as the possible depletion of natural resources or those that become too expensive to mine profitably. And yet, no sooner does a new or innovated sector hold out promise for potential revenues than we habitually abandon a whole range of less profitable ones instead of improving them by innovations. Change stares us down and challenges us to manage it before it replaces us, and frequently we do not accept the challenge and, instead, it leads us by the nose. We are being led, struggling, in any number of different directions against our will. And new customs and technology prevent us from going back. With labor costs rising in Japan, for example, it has already increased investments in manufacturing plants in China and South-east Asia where labor rates are lower.

One cannot help but admire the spirit of entrepreneurship that may burgeon in time into successful companies like Honda, Corel, Rembrandt, Bell, IBM, Microsoft, or Virgin Airlines—or, alternatively go belly-up like O&Y, Campeau Corporation, Royal Trustco, or Maxwell. What is there to provide an incentive other than their "innate urge to activity which makes the wheels go round?"

So varied are their industries that if we search for a common factor for their success we are likely to end up with the time-worn cliché that they saw a need that required filling. That could be true of any product or service, but entrepreneurs also have to possess suitable skills, drive, ambition, and an ability to assemble all the necessary components of a successful enterprise, including an ability to meet the payroll every month. Even when they achieve all that, they only become heroes on the basis that they can create new jobs. Anything else could be considered to be self-indulgence.

Whether their skills are in engineering, chemistry, physics, medicine, optics, biotechnology, or bookbinding, they are inventors or innovators. Often they bring with them a particular knowledge or technique they learnt in a service company. And sometimes they succeed not because they are perceptive enough to recognize a need or an opportunity, but because of a change in momentum in their particular market or industry which moves in their favor at a particular moment in time. But even when such an opportunity may seem to fall into their lap, they have to know how to exploit it to the full in their own favor.

One such example was the change in a trend from more or less stable interest rates to a continually fluctuating bank rate, which created much heavier demand on financial institutions and investment management companies. Another was the self-indulgence of the permissive society in the late 1960s, which was to grow into a splurge of even more acquired wealth in the materialistic 1980s, by those same baby boomers who had matured to raise families. They indulged themselves and their families still further. That generation initiated and led a trend that others aspired to or followed, in customarily eating and drinking out and vacationing more often. It kept wealth circulating and created new jobs. That it also created a high rate of inflation was a boon to them, because they had equity and capital to invest, even if it became a curse to some others.

Now that the inflation rate is down, and so are bank rates, a fluctuation of as little as half a percent either way has investors and debtors alike on the edge of their seats, ready to acquire or sell mortgages or mutual funds in a moment. Many investors have put their savings at risk in a desperate attempt to increase their small incomes or pensions, because of the low rate of more conservative returns.

Those and other pressures placed on our lives, as well as workplace stresses, now oblige us to take vacations out of necessity instead of as the luxury they once were. So that, despite the inconvenience of travelling en masse and the disappearance of individual charm and character of holiday resorts that become overdeveloped, and the mass-market nature of tour operators and their look-alike hotels, tourism, finance, transport, catering, and accommodation businesses succeed in spite of themselves, because of our necessity to use their services. Where some outstanding companies succeed in marketing their services innovatively—like Virgin Airlines or Sun City in Bophuthatswana—it is to increase their own market share by taking some business away from the others.

But the main reason that the service sector burgeoned is simply that the vast numbers who became unemployed from downsizing programs do not possess enough capital to set up as manufacturers, or do not have the necessary abilities, and turn, instead, to various forms of personal and business counselling which merely involves selling their advice; and the lowest overhead costs apply. Marx predicted that trend long ago when he visualized small business people downgraded to join the proletariat through lack of capital. Government therefore finds itself in a dilemma when it comes to funding, in which obviously the biggest share of federal or regional budgets will be allocated to bigger companies that possess the know-how and are already proven winners. Big business has always needed government and government has always needed big business, while smaller businesses must develop skills to compete.

In addition to such regulated service industries as hospitality, finance, teaching, health care, law, the retail trade, and transport, the service sector includes a multitude of home-based businesses where a great many "offices" are situated between an entrepreneur's ears, or in her handbag, her briefcase, or a laptop computer. This sector involves "virtual corporations" and also flexible business networks that may provide new contacts or related services. Consequently, the service sector is divided into two categories, with the successful established careers at the top—like medicine, law, finance, accountancy, and academia—and a new proletariat at the lower level. In fact, many lower-level service occupations evolved when the middle classes and landed gentry could no longer afford the upkeep of their large homes or estates and the employment of their domestic servants. Domestic servants almost disappeared as an important and established class, and the service sector now employs individuals who would once have earned their living as a housekeeper, a cook general, scullery maid, parlormaid, nanny, valet, butler, chauffeur, gardener, tutor, comptroller, estate agent, and the like. They did not develop themselves further, as some of the artisan class were forced to do or disappear.

Apprenticeship

The artisan class was more independent and entrepreneurial. Those who did not recognize a need to change to meet different needs naturally did not survive. In Japan, they are described as *machi-koba,* or subcontracting workshops that "function as safety-valves for the survival of the large industrial corporations in times of recession."[17] Like the *Mittelstand* in Germany, they are considered to be the hidden strength of the Japanese economy. This is where apprentices train to become skilled workers. Many of Japan's SMEs consist of less than ten employees and may not even be supplying big industrialists direct, but rather firms that supply those industries; or even companies who supply the firms.

Their value to industry is not only their low prices or the quality of their work, but that they provide greater flexibility for larger manufacturers. Often, most parts on assembly lines of mass production companies are outsourced to *machi-koba.* They are the direct descendants of artisans in crafts and trades centers, like Osaka in the eighteenth century, where specialization was the key to the very high quality of knives, swords, building materials, agricultural equipment, locks, decorative metal parts, clothing, and other merchandise. Human skills are still valued and perpetuated in Japan through those types of family firms, whereas former manufacturing nations in the West, like Britain and Canada, allowed such skills to be lost.

Their importance to the West can be seen from the way that the comparatively new industry of high technology relied for many of its components on smaller firms that specialized in particular skills. They were started up by entrepreneurs who left bigger companies where their skills had been developed, and where they had managed to accumulate seed capital. That was the customary way that manufacturers grew in the past. Their success often turns them into GSMEs, by which time they can provide historic figures to obtain bank loans for further development.

In fact, despite frustrations and hardship suffered by unemployed people in the West, there is considerable demand for machinists, engineers and systems analysts, moldmakers, and computer graphics software designers. But a large number do not want to work with their hands and consider working in science and technology to be boring. Perhaps that is because lawyers, physicians, surgeons, and even accountants have been glamorized for so long by the media. The chief economist of the BC Credit Union was quoted as saying that "somewhere between 144,000 and 432,000 Canadians, currently without jobs, would be productively employed if they had the skills the labor market needs." The availability of unskilled jobs has declined to 35 percent of all jobs, and by the end of the twentieth century is expected to drop to only 15 percent.

President and CEO William Waite of Siemens Electric Ltd. was involved in a crusade, for several years, to develop apprenticeship schemes in Canada like those in Germany, where 65 percent of engineers commence as apprentices and become much better engineers as a result of hands-on training. Siemens is a multinational corporation based in Germany. Its global revenues in 1992 were $60.5 billion. They make high energy transformers, medical equipment, and other electrical devices, but suffer from a shortage of trained and skilled tradespeople in Canada, which inhibits their growth. Despite an unemployment rate of 11 percent at the close of 1993, Waite finally resigned from a task force of business and government interests, labor and community colleges, because of an adversarial standoff between business and labor unions.[18]

According to Waite, 1.8 million Germans enrolled in apprenticeship programs in 1991 (approximately 4.5 percent of the workforce). Enrollment in Canada was only 0.8 percent of the workforce, and the dropout rate was 40 percent. The main reason for that failure was that Canadians are late starters: they meander from one job to another before they mature. The average age of their start as apprentices was, therefore, twenty-six, compared to seventeen in Germany. Consequently, they needed to earn far more than such a scheme could provide for adults—often with families to support—living away from parental homes. Waite and other business community members on the task force wanted to create job security for apprentices, but the unions adhered rigidly to rules of seniority that "often forced employers to lay off apprentices first in the event of a downturn." The labor co-chairman of the task force and the representative of the Canadian Auto Workers' Union maintained that older workers with homes and families on the line would not support the program. And the CAW was adamant that tying in apprentices for four to five years could create a situation in which management could enjoy the benefit of a perpetual workforce of low-paid employees.

Imagination and Innovation

In this case, the reality of the situation is precisely the opposite of what Marx preached and Engels wrote—business has to use intelligence and imagination continually to innovate in the struggle to survive and create employment. On the other hand, government and labor unions have continually increased the burden of costs and prevented employees from using their skills, to the ultimate detriment of the labor force, which is forced out of work whenever it is uncompetitive.

A four-day work week might end all that, and by reducing labor costs, enable more people to find employment and keep their jobs. Options studied in the Report of the Advisory Group on Working Time and the Distribution of Work were; shorter working day, shorter week, longer vacations, sabbaticals, earlier retirement, flexitime, less overtime, more part time. Analysis was based on 10 percent reductions and 5 percent increase in productivity. The study showed that "a reduction of working time by those currently employed can lower unemployment while allowing more leisure time for those reducing their hours." They found little change in output.[19]

Instead of looking nostalgically over one's shoulder into the past, business and labor should be prepared to design a more modern vehicle to support their aspirations. It requires courage and ingenuity to replace the obsolete one by means of innovation. Volkswagen are an inspiring example. From the relatively happy days of their three-shift system employing 29,000 workers in one Wolfsburg plant after World War II, Volkswagen AG's six plants began working a four-day, twenty-nine-hour week in January, 1994. The alternative would have been to cut 30,000 of its 100,000 jobs.

The Japanese, similarly, view each situation as a unique opportunity, and are adept at addressing it holistically as one demanding a special solution, instead of an inflexible, unimaginative, or bureaucratic one. Nissan, for example, announced a hundred million pound expansion program and one thousand new jobs in the UK in 1992. "Nissan is producing 124,000 cars a year, Honda has gone into partnership with Rover, and Toyota is about to produce in Britain. The numbers of cars produced by Japanese-owned companies in Britain is expected to reach 400,000 in the next four years and one million by the year 2000."[20] One reason why Japanese-owned plants in the UK are so successful is that they deliberately sought new labor in new locations. Instead of sourcing labor where there was a lifetime of experience in the industry—in cities like Cowley, Coventry, or Birmingham—Nissan chose Sunderland. Sunderland assured them that they would not be provided with workers geared to traditional British auto workplace experience, customs, and skills. In an area of high unemployment they could carefully choose one worker out of every twenty who wanted to work for them. Toyota, similarly, chose Derbyshire. It is easier and quicker to train new workers in their own methods than having continually to correct or eradicate bad work habits from the post-war era.

Part of the training was involving workers in the improvement of quality standards. That alone saved heavy costs of repairs and replacements under warranties in the first year of purchases. And reliability of their products won customers. "Another innovation has been flexible working. Nissan's workers in Sunderland are willing to take on virtually any task and are trained to do so." Japanese auto makers also brought with them their expertise in outsourcing components, over which they maintain detailed controls of quality and cost. And they are securing long-term relationships with specially selected suppliers who are efficient and possess high quality standards.

The alternative to innovative solutions was exemplified in the new year of 1995 by long line-ups of more than 15,000 job-hungry applicants waiting in the snow, day and night, in the hope of reaching the door of General Motors in Oshawa, Ontario, before the 200 advertised jobs might be filled. Newspaper cartoonists and others could not help but compare it to the queues of dispirited unemployed outside U.S. soup kitchens in the Great Depression of 1929. The possibility of earning $22 an hour drew not only unemployed auto workers, but also service personnel from retail stores who earned very much less than that.

Economists have always been pessimists expecting future declines. Europe's swing to a four-day week epitomizes what happens when manufacturers overproduce, not to meet market needs but technological ones instead.

Marx prophesized that "each capitalist lays many of his fellows low"; that when businesses fail their entrepreneurs may be reduced to the position of wage earners. That trend may increase wealth but concentrates it in fewer and fewer hands. "The small tradespeople, shopkeepers, and retired tradesmen generally, the handicraftsman and the peasants, all these sink gradually into the proletariat; partly because their small capital, insufficient as it is for the scale on which modern industry is conducted, is overwhelmed in the competition with the bigger capitalists; partly because their specialized skill is rendered worthless by new means of production." That is a fair summary of the Great Depression of the 1990s.[21]

Government-Funded Programs

The job crisis topped agendas at G-7 and OECD meetings in Europe in June, 1994, when unemployment levels in the twenty-five industrialized countries had reached 35 million. Unemployment rates ranged from 8.1 percent in Holland up to 24.6 percent in Spain compared with 6 percent in the U.S. and 2.9 percent in Japan.[22] Like Lord Young—some years earlier in Britain—Spain had decided that tourism was more important than developing industries, and suffered from a shrinking service sector because there was not enough disposable income to feed it. The European Union's six-point program listed three major priorities: cutting bureaucratic red tape which inhibited small businesses; providing easier start-up capital for new small businesses; and improving management and marketing skills.

Those objectives had already been defined six years previously by Britain's Department of Trade and Industry and they had done something about it: they had launched their Enterprise Initiative program, funded by the DTI and managed by the Chartered Institute of Marketing. Michael Heseltine, President of Britain's Board of Trade, was now implementing a follow-up program to provide 200 permanent one-stop business centers across the British Isles, named Business Links. They would provide the same counselling service for small and medium-size businesses but it would no longer be funded by government. This was made possible by the success of the Enterprise Initiative, described by the DTI as the best business program ever to be funded by the British government.[23] Only one experience of that program had been enough to instil confidence in marketing; in qualified and experienced business counsellors provided by the CIM; in government (the DTI); and in the Chartered Institute of Marketing.

The Institute was contracted to Britain's Department of Trade and Industry to investigate the weaknesses of small and medium-size enterprises and provide them with suitable management and marketing skills. The Enterprise Initiative Scheme received applications from 140,000 business enterprises. Some 95,200 were approved for government funding and 65,000 of those were serviced by June, 1994. Budgets were provided for another 10,000 such businesses to be enhanced before the commencement of the new Business Links program. The DTI funded only established companies by up to one-third of the cost; or two-thirds in some areas of high unemployment.

Sixteen percent of their projects involved business planning; 36 percent centered on quality; 10 percent on financial and information systems; 7 percent on design; 5 percent on manufacturing; and 26 percent on functions commonly considered to *be* marketing, such as advertising, promotions, print, and sales management. Research undertaken afterwards showed that 92 percent of clients considered the counselling to be value for money; 80 percent fully intended to implement recommended strategies; 91 percent rated the project designed for them as good, very good, or even better. Most significant was that 56 percent are likely to follow the marketing philosophy, with its strategies and tactics, and to develop and use marketing skills in future.

Business Links in the UK closely resembles SBDCs in the United States. They are 900 Small Business Development Centers established across the U.S. One benefit is that "every dollar spent on counselling established companies generates $1.55 in subsequent tax revenues. Results from counselling startups are even better: every dollar spent yields $5.82 return." One of their main advantages is that "They encourage people who don't have any business being in business to get out of the market faster."[24]

That emphasizes the problem that several federal and provincial task forces were attempting to solve in Canada. Their objectives, like other G-7 nations, was either to cut bureaucratic red tape or provide sources of start-up capital for new small business enterprises. But statistics had already clearly revealed that the main reasons for failures were not problems in obtaining financing but lack of management and marketing skills.[25] In that case, the very high rate of bankruptcies should rather deter governments from assisting others into the bankruptcy courts by making startups easier. Instead, they should rather slow down the process for careful consideration. Then, if a proposed new enterprise were unable to produce a convincing business plan that stood up under scrutiny, candidates should be encouraged to acquire necessary skills or be dissuaded from starting up in business.[26]

A major flaw in Business Links, SBDCs, and other types of small business centers is that owners and managers of SMEs and GSMEs have neither the time nor the single-mindedness to use them. If they possessed the time and the inclination, they would surely have taken every advantage to study some of the excellent books which have been available for nearly half a century, or they would have attended advanced management seminars or become members of a marketing institute. Now the advent of InterNet and the World Wide Web have initiated schemes like Industry Canada's Management Information Network, which on-line business managers can access for information, sources, referrals, and other data. Whether they will use this source of data or whether the type of knowledge they need can be provided or used in that way remains to be seen.

What is known and demonstrated by statistics is that the weight and challenges of running a new business distract entrepreneurs and business managers from the constancy of purpose required of a scholar. Instead of being dedicated to book learning, their dedication is to their workplace. That was the considerable advantage of the UK's Enterprise Initiative scheme whereby clients were counselled individually in their place of work; at the first stage by "business people" with a wealth of acquired business knowledge, then by qualified and specialized Enterprise Counsellors. Failing that, SME entrepreneurs seem to have only time or funds to try out the latest quick fix. Most fail to understand that there is no such thing and that their particular situation requires knowledgeable inputs tailored specifically to their own company, their special skills, their industry, and their market niche.

The extraordinary success of the Enterprise Initiative scheme was due, quite simply, to the fact that it was custom-made to achieve specified objectives, and was implemented and managed by the right organization that designed it. Therefore, we are left to assume that the sole reason for its discontinuation was the crippling national debt. Business Links is not a substitute for it; it is an entirely different program that appears to have been more politically motivated than business oriented.[27] When the Enterprise Initiative scheme was recommended to the federal government in Canada by the Canadian Institute of Marketing, because Canadian businesses obviously desperately needed marketing and management help, it was rejected, as the industry minister's mandate was to cut $2.3 billion from government funded programs over three years.

Both situations could be viewed as typical ones in which the correct prescription for the malady was tossed aside in favour of a surrogate. Cheaper in the short term though it may be to use a sugar pill, long-term results of avoiding taking the most appropriate measures could be economic pain.

The problem is compounded by statistics that show SMEs have created more than 80 percent of new jobs in some economies, like North America. In Canada, they account for 52 percent of total employment and provide nearly 40 percent of Canada's GDP. Governments also know that Germany's *Mittelstand*—which are mostly family-run GSMEs, although some are large and also sophisticated—have long been described as the hidden champions of the economy. They represent nearly half of Germany's industrial output and retail sales, and account for even bigger shares in other service sectors. According to the Institute for *Mittelstand* Research, however, many are in industries badly affected by economic recession and some are losing the ability to innovate. Many focused on premium-priced quality goods, whereas customers have become price conscious. Japanese competitors were quick to exploit that opportunity by providing cheaper products. And a great many

Mittelstand are still run by an older generation which started up businesses in West Germany's postwar industrial revival. They are the ones considered most likely to grow at a slower rate than enterprises run by professional managers from outside the family. This too points to the need to upgrade management and marketing skills and practices.

But governments generally admit that they don't know of practical or cost-effective ways to prevent SMEs from failing so fast and in such numbers, or even how to develop GSMEs. Consequently, small business feels that "government small business programs don't work and aren't wanted by entrepreneurs."[28] Eighty-seven percent of respondents in a national survey conducted in Canada in 1994 said that government isn't representing the interests of entrepreneurs. Despite that, Industry Canada studied a program of Flexible Business Networks designed for Denmark by the Danish Technological Institute.

The Institute had directed a three-year program to its 7,500 manufacturing companies in 1989. Denmark's problem was that it possessed a great number of SMEs that did not cooperate with each other or export. Their concern was that they could be outclassed by the combined skills and size of European Union nations. They formed 500 business networks consisting of 3,000 manufacturers.

About 50 percent of the budget for the program amounting to over $20 million (US) was funded by the government. They claimed that considerable product innovation was achieved; new competitiveness skills acquired; new business developed; the size of exports became significant; new jobs were created; and new capital investment followed as a result. Most companies continued to network after the budget was spent, and business networks in Denmark became industry led and industry funded. But did all that result from the program? Denmark overcame its twenty-five-year deficit; within the three-year period, it achieved the highest per capita positive trade balance of any OECD country; and the 1993 World Competitiveness Report showed that it rose to third place, behind Japan and the U.S.

Italy and some other members of the EU—the United States, Japan, Australia, New Zealand, and India—have all developed some type and size of business networks to increase their international competitiveness. But alliances of one kind or another are not new. High-tech companies formed alliances from the beginning and many still do. Many smaller ones supplied components and consultants to bigger firms. More and more companies are finding benefits from outsourcing. One problem is that if a bigger company fails, the ensuing domino effect could put others out of business too. And often networks strengthen competitors who may cause damage later on. But generally each Silicon Valley has developed into a specialized and incestuous community in which employees move from company to company and most know each other and exchange ideas. The difference between those informal alliances, the more formal corporate alliances of big businesses, and the Danish program, is that Danish networks were structured to meet specific objectives, and their's employed full-time *facilitators* who coordinated activities of companies within a particular network. Despite the "sensitive egos" of competing firms, as opposed to complementary ones, the success of Danish networks of SMEs—which should probably more appropriately be described as GSMEs—resulted in corp groups of GSMEs. They claim to be energized by entrepreneurial values, flexible and versatile, to possess simple organizational structures, to innovate, to develop niche markets, to deploy new technologies, to share knowledge, and to build skills. They also handle group purchasing like a cooperative, share resources, and establish consistently high quality standards.

But their success depends on existing high levels of management and marketing sophistication that are up to international standards to begin with—otherwise they might have nothing worthwhile to learn from each other, and could easily learn processes and skills which might be flawed. As well, the cost would be likely to be much higher than the UK's Enterprise Initiative, while its effectiveness would be likely to be lower.

In general, companies that have something to offer each other already form alliances on their own, without government funding. Otherwise it would be far simpler for independent management consultants to act as advisers, facilitators, or coordinators to make purchases in common, on behalf of a particular group of companies with similar goals, so as to reduce material costs; organize joint training to enhance staff skills; organize shared research, development and design; arrange group financing; apply advanced technologies; improve quality standards; organize the process to manufacture selected items in common or in a complimentary mode; initiate joint productivity improvements; develop innovated and new products and services; organize joint marketing, export development and commercialization. Management and marketing consultants have done it before, as well as cooperatives—to gain access to markets from which those companies might be excluded individually because of their particular limitations in being unable to provide a full service or a full range of products.

But the biggest weakness of most SMEs and many GSMEs is a failure on the part of the owner to establish firm foundations for future growth and survival of the enterprise. It is simply not enough to produce a good product today. Ongoing research and development must be in the pipeline in order to compete in the future. And sound marketing practices need to be initiated as the vehicle to project what might easily be a purely short-term success into the future—as so many bigger market leaders do.

13

Picking Winners

Professional product management involves both the consumer and a company's marketing management at the very beginning, at the conceptual stage of a new product. Otherwise a business enterprise cannot know if there is sufficient need for such a product. Nor can the marketer include all the essential marketing elements in its design. The same applies to the service sector.

A product manager should be the type of individual who possesses an innate drive to perfection. Perhaps it can best be characterized in the 1990s, by Loblaws's creation of The Decadent Chocolate Chip Cookie. It is a retailer-controlled brand, a private label competing successfully with national brands.

The challenge to provide a better product arose from a pressing need by consumers with less disposable income to find lower-priced goods that did not sacrifice quality. In response to that demand, Loblaws International Merchants took considerable care to improve the quality of their private label products in order to switch customer loyalty, in their own supermarkets, from previously preferred national brands. Loblaws's campaign enabled them to overtake a similar product manufactured by Nabisco, by substituting butter instead of shortening, introducing 50 percent more chocolate chips, and offering a lower price. Their product therefore provided three distinctive, even unique, consumer benefits. And since it is available only at Loblaws's stores— which is a unique selling proposition for the store—its supermarkets automatically offer the other three consumer benefits to their own advantage, too.

To market their product they used their sixteen-page *Insider Report* as a loose insert distributed by newspapers throughout Canada, or in the localities of their supermarkets, approximately every quarter. It advertises a whole range of President's Choice Products and generates sales in the region of $30 million to $50 million (Canadian). President Dave Nichol appeared frequently on TV and radio commercials to sell those products. By doing so, he became an effective salesman for his company's private label brands, and therefore the supermarkets that offer those exclusive products.[1]

If it seems ironic that the prime example of excellence in product development should be a fast-moving packaged consumer good, in an age of high-technology products, it should be born in mind that the FMPCG industry has

311

been involved in R&D and marketing for very much longer than the electronics industry, and is therefore more sophisticated in its top-to-bottom marketing orientation.

Back in the immediate post-World-War-II era, there had been little problem for business enterprises to increase their sales, because populations had been starved of so many commodities that there was a ready pent-up demand to be met. While they responded to that demand, most manufacturers imagined that the market would continue to grow for ever, in accordance with growing populations. The baby boom did at first provide that growth in developed countries in the West, but heavy buyers declined as a consumer niche after the peak of what became known as the baby bust. Population growth and the need for basic commodities became identified more with underdeveloped countries of the Third World, while populations aged in the West; more women entered the workforce, married at a later age, if at all, and produced fewer, if any, children. The divorce process was made easier, and single-parent families became more numerous and moved closer to the poverty line.

When markets shrink and become saturated with products, competition intensifies and companies are compelled to consider other tactics to dispose of surplus inventories in order to survive. Overseas dumping became a symptom of the post-war industrial expansion of both Germany and Japan, until their overseas markets grew and became more organized.

In those circumstances, a company that wants to grow can make a choice from ten basic options: (1) increase national sales of existing products; (2) export; (3) innovate existing products for other market segments; (4) research and develop new products; (5) manufacture an overseas company's products under license; (6) merge with another, smaller company with different product ranges that are synergistic with their own; (7) manufacture overseas; (8) diversify; (9) source and make acquisitions; (10) form alliances.

Although it may be simpler and more advantageous to continue manufacturing the same products and exporting the surplus, that is only a short-term strategy.

From the other side of the border, the United States market looks greener to Canadian businesses, because it is ten times the size of their own; while from the perspective of the U.S., Canada looks ripe for exploitation. The United States is already Canada's main trading partner: Canadian exports there were worth $94.5 billion in 1988, while imports were worth $79.1 billion. When the economic recession of 1980 began to reduce European markets for consumer durable good, Italian companies like Zanussi, and its German and Japanese counterparts, looked speculatively at South Africa as a low-risk and high-profit market opportunity for their goods, and discussions on joint ventures took place. Prospects there looked attractive despite the continuation of economic sanctions by the United Nations. But any such ideas were hurriedly abandoned when the recession spread to South Africa in 1981.

Meanwhile, burgeoning unemployment in Britain made the concept of a European Free Market begin to look attractive to British manufacturers who were not already having their products manufactured in Taiwan, Malaysia, or elsewhere. Continental Europeans were themselves busy looking elsewhere for markets to buy their surplus production capacities. The French made overtures to Francophone former colonies in Africa, while German and Italian companies explored the potential in the Canadian market. Fragile governments and economies also triggered interest in foreign investment.

By 1991 a new recession had taken hold and the American economy showed no signs of recovery, while the Canadian economy was in even worse shape with unemployment at 11 percent compared to over 7 percent in the United States. The Australian economy was even worse. And national accumulated deficits of all three countries were increasing through faulty government judgements and poor fiscal management by their bureaucracies. A dispassionate observer, at that time, might well have wondered whether South Africa's economy was in such bad shape after all, by comparison with the West's. Competition in the American automobile market had intensified too, with the installation of robotics, to a point where U.S. and Japanese auto makers had squeezed out most foreign competitors, finally including Peugeot. But Japan's market share continued to increase at the expense of America's, and General Motors was in trouble.

Some Japanese companies had already established themselves in British Columbia, close to the U.S. border, in readiness for the North American Free Trade Agreement (NAFTA) between Canada, the United States, and Mexico. Vancouver had been penetrated by Hong Kong business interests, and its orientation as the capital of a Pacific Rim country was gradually transforming it into another Hong Kong; but without their dynamic economy.

If all the market activity that took place in the past forty years did nothing else, it stimulated markets and improved products and technology by obliging manufacturers to spend more and more money on R&D, advertising, and promotions. But viewed from a perspective closer to the turn of a new century, it all seems like nothing more than a huge and disorganized game of musical chairs, played by the giant multinational corporations against everyone else. Most well-managed companies are winners when there is adequate consumption. But in a recession with declining consumer demand for goods and services, smaller undercapitalized businesses are squeezed out of the game at a rate of over a thousand a month; depending on which economy is under scrutiny. They are small enough to disappear without a trace, like obsolete biological species. Successful big organizations that have planned for this maintain their skills even though they may restructure to withstand the storms of the economy. In many cases they emerge from out of the storms with lower operating costs which improve their profit margins. But, meanwhile, everyone scrambles for whatever business remains, and a natural culling process takes place because there is never enough business available in a recession. Marketing-oriented companies that have established their infrastructures, their products, and their markets in good times are better prepared than those that have aimed at purely short-term goals. The weaker, the less skilful, and disabled business organizations fall in their tracks or are eaten up by more virile and smarter ones that continue to take an aggressive stance; or by more efficient or powerful ones. But smaller companies with unique new products or services designed for specific market niches often gain ground.

Opportunities of one kind or another are always there for innovative businesses, which search for them and possess the flexibility to adapt to them. The collapse of infrastructures opened up opportunities in all former communist countries that still had enough money to buy goods. On the other hand, markets in Latin America and black Africa, which once seemed to show promise, had to be written off as high-risk and low-profit areas. They left western banks drained as a consequence of unrealistic judgements. About five years afterwards, as a result of debt write-offs, western companies began to benefit from Latin American economies which had been stimulated into extraordinarily rapid growth by 1993–94. The NAFTA was implemented in January, 1994, and Argentina, Chile, and Brazil's markets grew, as well as Mexico's. But the rapid fall in the Mexican peso, which dropped by 40 percent in value at the end of 1994, revealed to startled investors that they had been caught again; this time by the "perfumed boys" in their Armani suits. *Los perfumados* with their PhDs in economics from Harvard, Yale, and Stanford, were so self-assured and convincing after the stereotypical Latin-American image of rough military *juntas* that the West was ready and willing to be taken in.[2] The fallout from the United States and Canada buying pesos to shore up the Mexican economy was a drop in value of the North American dollar.

Exporting overseas is not the only way to penetrate foreign markets, as Proctor & Gamble and Heinz's interest in South Africa showed. There are abundant precedents for American companies, as well as others, to manufacture overseas. An article written in 1964 recommending the establishment of overseas manufacturing bases, is of as much interest in today's economic climate. Comparisons of reasons why U.S. firms began producing abroad then, as compared with market conditions today, show that little has changed: (1) lower production costs; (2) lower plant construction costs; (3) lower wages; (4) lower fringe benefits; (5) superior quality control in some cases; (6) concessions from foreign governments which may include tax advantages and capital cost allowances for R&D; (7) increased efficiency and competitiveness of new and automated plant facilities; (8) availability of special raw material and labor skills (such as in the paper industry, petroleum products, and petro-chemicals); (9) availability of specialized skills.[3]

When exported products become successful, local manufacturers frequently exploit opportunities for making me-too products and even imitating branded goods that can easily be sold at much lower prices. And domestic manufacturers may press governments for protective tariffs to be imposed on imports. That is why the successful exportation of goods requires brand protection by manufacturing them overseas or entering into licensing agreements.

That is what took place in Mexico, as well as Pacific Asia. And South Africa is now being recognized as a suitably stable economy. As with the Mexican peso, there is considerable leverage for companies possessing dollars, with the favorable exchange rate with the South African rand. Not all the skilled managers have left South Africa, and many more are being trained; as can be seen by the considerably increased membership of their Institute of Marketing Management and the enrolment of 10,004 students who wrote their marketing exams in 1995, as well as activities of universities and business schools. Their IMM is the second biggest marketing institute in the world after Britain's and is spreading its membership across southern Africa and north up the continent. Their aggressive activities reflect concern at the 1991 United Nations report, which showed that a $128 billion five-year program for forty-five black African countries has not only *not* improved anything at all, but Africa is actually in a worse state now than it was five years earlier. Per capita incomes are down. Levels of illiteracy, mortality, and malnutrition are up. Food aid requirements in the program increased by 45 percent. Thirty million more people are unemployed. Another 90 million are severely underemployed. Wages declined up to 75 percent to 80 percent in some countries. Mortality rates at birth rose to 600 per hundred thousand, compared with 75 per hundred thousand in developed regions. Ninety-four percent of rural women cannot read, and work twelve to thirteen hours more per week, on average, than men.

The lesson that the West is only now beginning to learn is that such aid provides a barrier to protect bad governments from their own incompetence. It also encourages them to spend money on grandiose public building projects instead of attempting to elevate the living standards of their populations.

Why do international organizations and financial institutions continue to give away money on bad risks? The United States, Germany, Britain, Italy, Japan, and Canada courted Latin-American countries as well as African ones in the late 1960s. Most ended up by not being able to pay interest on the loans. The false optimism of those developed economies reveals how desperate they must have been for markets and also shows their naivety in wanting to believe that future economic growth would be guaranteed because "various international organizations help contribute to economic development."

Robert Heller remarked:

> Nor are most financial men especially knowing about business and business management, in their own trade, or in other people's. Financial institutions are better at burying their million pound mistakes in multi-million aggregates than at displaying commercial drive, managerial acumen and marketing enterprise. The ex-

316 Management Crisis and Business Revolution

pertise needed on Wall Street or in the City of London is not that of the industrial executive suite—and the financier's judgement of directors is therefore fallible. That is why banks lend gigantic sums to managements of bewildering incompetence and on propositions of worse than dubious worth—like the dud U.S. loans to real-estate investment trusts, less developed countries, and (very probably) over-leveraged buyouts.

Salient economic features of such undeveloped countries are: (1) low per capita capital values; (2) absolute over-population in agriculture; (3) practically no savings for most people; (4) high fertility and mortality rates; (5) low per capita volume of trade; and (6) absence of employment opportunities outside of agriculture.[4]

Those factors also apply to Mexico. And had it not been for the problems arising from mass illegal Mexican immigration into the United States, it is arguable whether the NAFTA would have been endorsed. In theory, increased new jobs and disposable income of Mexicans would provide a growing market for American and Canadian goods and services as well as improving Mexican living standards. In fact, the introduction of new technologies reduced the number of new jobs and increased unemployment. The fall of the Mexican peso eroded confidence in targeting aggressively for the Mexican mass market, although some Canadian and American businesses had already moved south. But the north-south dichotomy has always existed in Canada, because of huge distances from east to west and less costly weather conditions down south. Another reason in 1991 was that labor costs in Canada rose higher and faster than in the U.S., and leading indicators showed that Canada's consumer price index and producer index were both higher than in the United States. Canadian competitiveness was shown to have fallen still further, in global terms, from fifth to eleventh ranking. And the continual threat of Québec separation caused political and economic instability because of uncertainty. That also affected the domestic economy and caused nervousness in the value of the Canadian dollar.

The Global Market

United Nations research showed that there are more than 35,000 multinational business organizations with over 170,000 foreign affiliated companies, as well as banking and financial institutions. The top hundred are likely to represent over 40 percent of cross-border assets. *The Economist* estimates that they probably possess only approximately 16 percent share of global productive assets. The cross-border business has been driven by three major factors: (1) falling regulatory barriers to overseas investments; (2) tumbling telecommunications and transport costs; and (3) freer domestic and international capital markets in which companies can be bought, and currency and other risks can be controlled. "All these have made it easier for companies to

TABLE 13.1

Multinationals (non-financial)			Total Assets ($ billions)	Foreign Sales
1. Royal Dutch/Shell:	Oil	Britain/Holland	106.3	49%
2. Ford Motors:	Cars & Trucks	U.S.	173.7	48%
3. General Motors:	Cars & Trucks	U.S.	180.2	31%
4. Exxon:	Oil	U.S.	87.7	86%
5. IBM:	Computers	U.S.	87.6	61%
6. British Petroleum:	Oil	Britain	59.3	79%
7. Nestlé:	Food	Switzerland	27.9	98%
8. Unilever:	Food	Britain/Holland	24.8	42%
9. Asea Brown Boveri:	Electrical	Switzerland/Sweden	30.2	85%
10. Philips:	Electronics	Holland	30.6	93%

invest where they choose to, to do so more cheaply and with less risk. Yet such factors favor small firms as well as big ones, new boys as well as old."[5]

The top ten nonfinancial multinationals—as ranked by foreign assets by the UN—show an average of over half their sales are made overseas.

Of the 35,000 companies surveyed by the United Nations, less than half are from the U.S., Japan, Germany, and Switzerland. Britain is seventh in line. Now there are also increasing amounts of businesses from Third World economies and from Taiwan and South Korea, although still small.

If we select the next ten multinationals in order to form a different mix of countries and also avoid duplicating those particular industries, we find that the average percentage of foreign sales differs very little: eleventh is Alcotel Alsthom (Telecommunications) in France; fifteenth is Hanson (Diversified) in Britain; eighteenth, Mitsubishi (Trading) Japan; nineteenth, General Electric (Diversified) U.S.; twentieth, Mitsui (Trading) Japan; twenty-first, Matsushita Electric Industrial (Electronics) Japan; twenty-second, News Corp. (Publishing) Australia; twenty-third, Ferruzzi/Montedison (Diversified) Italy; twenty-fourth, Bayer (Chemicals) Germany; and twenty-fifth, Roche Holdings (Drugs) Switzerland.

The main advantage of being a multinational company is that business risks are spread across a number of different types of economies, many of which are passing through different life cycles, in much the same way as a wise investor chooses a balanced portfolio for its financial investments. But there are also disadvantages, such as: government restrictions on investments; restrictions on imports, taxes, and subsidies; uncertainty of supplies; volatile exchange rates; uncertain consumer evaluation of unfamiliar products; negotiating costs; advantages enjoyed by established companies; infringements of brands or patents; uncertainty about competitors' reactions; and unexpected risks through insufficient information. Perhaps that is why American companies usually prefer to trade on the American continent, European companies trade mostly in Western Europe, and Japan trades predominantly in Pacific Asia.

Export Dynamics

Despite a natural propensity for preferring to trade with immediate neighbours, a 1991 study made the point that, "one sign of truly competitive industry is sustained exports to many countries because this signals more robust competitive advantages."[6] However, Canada relies almost entirely on the competitive advantage of lower, overland, transport costs by simply shipping greater and greater loads of commodities over the U.S. border. And the trend of shares of global exports of most G7 economies since 1950 can be described as one of slow decline.

We can compare Canada's burgeoning exports to the United States of 75 percent in 1989, with Switzerland's more prudent exports to European Union nations of 56 percent—the EU being roughly the size of the U.S.A. And despite the dangers of placing the greater majority of one's eggs in one basket, Canada's exports to the U.S. increased to 82 percent and continue to grow, rather than seeking other global markets. Apart from losing opportunities in overseas markets, which are steadily declining, the danger of such a practice is America's historic leanings toward protectionism.

If we consider the main determinants for success in supplying overseas export markets (apart from usages of technology, marketing and innovation skills, company organization, effective communications, and the calibre of management), high labor costs and low productivity are at the very core of a company's and a nations' failure to compete. That is particularly so when labor costs rise faster than the rate of productivity; as they did in the 1980s in Italy, France, Canada, and Britain.

The study pointed out that "the severity of the 1990–91 recession is itself a sign of underlying structural problems—including poor cost performance and inflexible labor markets." Compared with 5.5 percent productivity growth in Japan, Canada's growth was only 1.8 percent, Germany's 2 percent, Italy's 4 percent, and Britain's 4.8 percent.[7] That is the sector that most influences success or failure in international trade.

> Since productivity is the critical determinant of real income growth over the long term, it is not surprising that Canada has experienced very weak growth in real incomes and wages in recent years. In contrast to previous decades, the average Canadian family experienced essentially no gain in real, after-tax income in the 1980s.

That study of the Canadian economy, which was commissioned by the department of Supply and Services Canada, also explored slow development and adoption of new technologies, weaknesses in education systems, and training practices, all of which may contribute to or inhibit export capabilities. Meanwhile, Canada's labor costs grew more than twice as fast as comparable U.S. costs.

Since as much as 45 percent of Canada's exports consist of natural resources, it hardly stretches the mind to recognize that Canada would have been obliged to give priority to manufacturing if it had not inherited, by chance, an abundance of resources. But, at the same time, we also see that its high labor costs prevented that from happening. Similarly, had Britain not discovered North Sea oil, it would have been forced to rebuild its declining manufacturing sector instead. Then again, high labor costs in the U.K. were the root cause of loss of international markets which resulted in the disintegration of its manufacturing sector.

In the same way, oil-rich Arab World nations would have had to develop sound economies instead of living on "unearned income" (as it has been called), and poorer socialist Arab countries might have been motivated to develop workable economies had they not relied, initially, on reserve funds inherited from previous governments.

We can only conclude that the economies of nations rest on a razor's edge and are caught between uncompetitive labor costs, declining manufacturing competitiveness, and a remarkable inability to learn, develop and sustain sophisticated management and marketing skills which could solve their problems.

A picture of the global market gradually emerges as we examine more and more of these kinds of statistics.

U.S. exports rose in 1992 and displaced Germany as the leading global exporter, largely as a result of a cheaper dollar. At the same time, Germany's internal political and economic problems arising from unification of East and West (and perhaps also the aging of the *Mittelstand*) eroded their previous lead and put them in second place after the United States. The most dramatic performance of all economies was the persistence of the giant leap forward of

TABLE 13.2
1992 Global Share of Exports

	U.S.:	12.3%
	Germany:	11.6%
* Hong Kong,	* Asian Tigers:	9.5%
Singapore,	Japan:	9.3%
S. Korea,	France:	6.3%
Taiwan,	Britain:	5.2%
	Italy:	4.8%
	Others:	41.0%

Source: IMF

the Asian Tigers since 1976. They challenged not only western exporters but also exceeded Japan's performance for the first time.

More recent statistics released by the General Agreement on Tariffs and Trade, soon after the first quarter of 1994, reveal how Hong Kong alone leaped past the Netherlands and Belgium-Luxembourg in 1993. It became the eighth largest global exporter of goods. In doing so, it challenged Canada. Back in 1983, Canada was in seventh place with 4.2 percent share of the global market, compared to Hong Kong in seventeenth place with only 1.3 percent. Canada has since dropped to 3.9 percent with Hong Kong tripling its own share to 3.7 percent.

Hong Kong is the major shipping port for Chinese-made goods. It is expected to leap ahead of Canada in 1994. China's own position as exporter advanced in the same decade, from eighteenth place to eleventh.

The rate of growth of western economies is weak in exports, compared to the more virile Pacific Asian economies scrambling energetically uphill. Malaysia became the nineteenth largest exporter of goods between 1992 and 1993—displacing Australia, Austria and Saudi Arabia. Singapore vaulted two places to fourteenth, displacing Spain and Switzerland.

While Canada is complacent about its shrinking potential as a manufacturer on the dubious grounds that it is more healthy to switch to service industries, it is now in fifteenth place as a global exporter trading in services; well behind Hong Kong, which is thirteenth.

Market Segmentation

After World War II most companies tended to think in terms of a mass market as a single group of customers who would purchase any product designed for it. In more recent years manufacturers realized that different segments of the market wanted different products. The concept of market segmentation began to be considered seriously in the mid-1960s and became a popular theme by the 1980s. As companies differentiated their products to meet different needs in different market segments, they came in time to find even smaller niches among each segment, which wanted modified or innovated products.

What seems like a glut of special magazines in the West today, shows evidence in the advertisements of a proliferation of different life styles, life cycles, and psychographic groups of consumers. Each magazine has identified itself with a particular market niche.

But the major factor in the ascendancy of American manufacturing and marketing since Henry Ford invented the assembly line, was the minimization of unit costs resulting from mass production. That philosophy pervaded American manufacturing right up to and through the 1970s. But, gradually, market segmentation showed itself to be an irresistible market force which

TABLE 13.3
1993 Global Shares

Exporters: ($U.S. billion)			Importers: ($U.S. billion)		
1. United States:	$465	12.6 %	United States:	$603	15.9 %
2. Germany:	362	9.8	Germany:	327	8.6
3. Japan:	361	9.8	Japan:	241	6.3
4. France:	209	5.7	Britain:	210	5.5
5. Britain:	183	5.0	France:	201	5.3
6. Italy:	168	4.6	Italy:	147	3.9
7. Canada:	145	3.9	Hong Kong:	143	3.8
8. Hong Kong:	135	3.7	Canada:	139	3.7
9. Netherlands:	134	3.6	Netherlands:	126	3.3
10. Belgium/ Luxembourg:	116	3.1	Belgium/ Luxembourg:	118	3.1
Others:	1,409	38.2	Others:	1,541	40.6
Total:	3,687	100 %	Total:	3,796	100 %

Source: GATT

TABLE 13.4
Products in Global Trading

Machinery & Transportation Equipment:	37.3 percent
Automotive Products:	9.9 percent
Office Machines & Telecom Equipment:	9.6 percent
Food:	9.6 percent
Fuel:	9.1 percent
Chemicals:	9.0 percent
Clothing:	3.6 percent
Textiles:	3.2 percent
Iron & Steel:	2.8 percent
Other:	5.9 percent

Source: GATT 1992

could no longer be ignored. Advertising and promotions today tend to direct their claims to selected consumer segments who are discriminating in their choices, as opposed to meeting the primary buying motives of the 1930s and 1950s. Distinctively different features appeal to differentiated consumer groups.

If we consider an electric stove as an example, we find that some people prefer an eye-level oven and a separate unit containing the hob. But most people do not have a big enough kitchen to accommodate both components separately within the tight design of their cabinets. There was once a demand from one section of the community for an eye-level grill. But since the popularity of microwave ovens and electric toasters, eye-level grills have lost favor.

There are also two different opinions as to where the operating knobs should be positioned on a conventional stove. Parents of small children do not want knobs placed at the front in case their children turn them on and burn their hands on the hot plates. But adults—apparently without children—don't like the knobs positioned at the rear, in case they scald their hands with steam or cooking fat from pots and pans on the hob, as they reach over them to adjust the knobs. Some customers will not buy a stove without the traditional deep drawer at the base, if there is insufficient storage space for pots and pans in a small kitchen. And some consumers insist on a heating element in the drawer, to keep their dinner plates hot before serving a meal—whereas some manufacturers reduce the price by excluding the element. Many stoves no longer offer a drawer at all. Those that do, rarely include the heating element. But that, like other factors, can differ according to customs in different countries. As far as the cooking hob is concerned, some people prefer heating coils, while others prefer heating plates because they are easier to clean. And for those who use a microwave oven and prefer a separate cooking hob, a manufacturer must consider several other choices. Should the hob be easy to clean, but potentially breakable black glass with concealed elements, or a surface of stainless steel, or baked enamel, with heating plates? And if we home in on the conventional oven—whether eye-level or beneath a counter-top—a manufacturer is obliged to make other decisions: should convected hot air be introduced? And if so, what about a fan to distribute the air evenly for baking cakes?

Supplying all or some of those variables is product differentiation. It leads to market fragmentation. While most manufacturers would prefer to concentrate only on the heavy users of any product variation and ignore the other variable factors, a company can lose market share by ignoring consumers' needs. But when sales people return to their offices with lost orders because included among them were a few units with product differentiations their companies don't supply, the marketing vice-president may find himself between a rock and a hard place. How much business is he prepared to lose? On the other hand, is it practical to create confusion in assembly lines, slow down production because of short product runs, increase costs because of machine changes, complicate warehousing and administration, and confuse specifications in brochures and manuals? Surely it must all add to the end cost? Yes it does. But there are other types of costs involved from loss of sales.

As long ago as 1962, Kenneth Schwartz wrote an article on "Fragmentation of the Mass Market" in Dun's *Review*. He referred to a sociologist named David Reisman, who suggested "that marketers may need to categorize consumers along more subtle lines than income or occupation—perhaps in terms of psychological and sociological profiles of what goods they need to fit their style of life."

He also referred to sociologist Paul Lazarsfeld, founder of Columbia University's Bureau of Applied Social Research, who "thinks that marketers must isolate the opinion leader in each social class. One of Lazarsfeld's earliest studies found that the 'large family' wife sets the tastes for coffee and cereal, whereas 'unmarried girls' influenced purchases of some clothes and cosmetics. Lazarsfeld believes that business executives also must pay more attention to the role of 'word-of-mouth' advertising in selling new products to a segmented market. In a study for the Chas. Pfizer Co., the Bureau analyzed the pattern of adoption of a drug by physicians. Buying influence, the study showed, spread through four different groups of doctors: first the 'innovators,' who took the lead, but whose action did not result in a rush to follow their example; next the 'influentials'; shortly thereafter, the 'followers,' (the largest group): finally, after a long interval, the remaining small group of 'die-hards.'"

"In packaged goods such as soap and foods, manufacturers have added to segmentation by bringing out differently priced versions of the same goods, thus competing not only with each other but with themselves as well."

Wherever possible, however, the tendency among mass marketers is to achieve a perception of product differentiation by means of advertising claims or image building and promotions, followed up by different packaging or labels, while continuing to standardize the formulation of the product—so as to permit mass production at the manufacturing stage, with all its economies of scale. An example that comes readily to mind is aerosol shaving cream. The same foam is made, but differentiated by means of a variety of additives: standard foam, extra foam, formula for sensitive skins, formula for tough beards, fresh lime, or lemon. Potato or corn chips or other snacks follow a similar pattern, like a choice of ice cream flavors.

On the other hand, many factories are accustomed to producing both standard products and also differentiated products made to order (MTO). The former option reduces the number of changes required to machines and assembly lines and reduces unit costs by increasing production capacities. The other option demands many changes and comparatively short production runs, with accumulated downtime in between, to set up production for different customer specifications. The production styles differ. Some manufacturers with several plants separate the manufacturing and assembly functions by establishing a mass production plant in one factory and an MTO plant in another. Each factory can then develop its own individual production culture to optimize volume on one hand and particular variations on the other.

Product Innovation

Product innovation is a strategy used often to resuscitate ailing brands. One example is sherry—that product of the grape that was marketed in Jerez for many generations and imitated by other wine-growing countries. Dry Sack had suffered from declining sales for several years. Its image was male oriented, but not in a way acceptable to the giant U.S. market. It was an aperitif for connoisseurs who, in North American culture, are not considered macho.

American importers held discussions with an advertising agency (Chirurg & Cairns Inc.) to analyze the causes of their sales problem. They decided that their sherry should be identified among on-the-rocks drinks, which are an American preference, instead of recommending it be served in an elegant sherry glass at room temperature. Bourbon and rye whisky on the rocks have a macho image that Americans liked and Dry Sack needed. The new image achieved the desired result—so much so that other brands of sherry followed the same style of advertising as Dry Sack.

Another of Chirurg & Cairns's clients was the International Silk Association (U.S.). Silk had been one of the most prominent fashionable fabrics before DuPont patented nylon in 1937. Silk sales declined thereafter. The agency designed advertisements equating silk with quality and exclusivity, and placed them in authoritative publications with high aesthetic standards. Despite having almost disappeared from view for an entire generation, silk became a trend-setter in American fashion, not only in women's apparel, but also for men's wear and home furnishings. Wallace L. Shepardson, president of the agency, wrote: "Silk has once again regained its position of leadership in the fashion field as the 'queen of fibres'; and, despite the fact that it is at an all-time price high, demand for silk is greater than it has ever been since nylon appeared on the scene."

Shepardson described another product innovation, which was developed by Dow Corning Corp. They had worked with silicones for airplane tubing to withstand wide ranges of temperatures during World War II. At the end of the war, Dow Corning were left with available plant capacity but no business. They developed new uses by creating the "Barrier Finish" with silicone emulsion on textile fabrics. Advertising was concentrated in the trade press, emphasizing mills that were starting to use the Barrier Finish, and promotions were aimed at driving buyers into retail stores to seek garments made with Dow Corning silicones. With the idea of the trade name "Syl-mer," Dow Corning established itself in a strong position when competing finishes came onto the market later on.

New Product Marketing

There is insufficient information to determine the percentage of new products that fail. A rule of thumb is nine out of ten. Another guesstimate is 33 percent to 90 percent.

No doubt the broad range of speculation accommodates different suppositions from different types of industries. One thing for sure is that developing new products is a time-consuming and expensive business. But there is no choice for those companies that have geared themselves up for continual new product development and have been successful at it. Many other manufacturers simply wait for a new product launch that is successful, and then imitate the product.

Development of a new product might be assigned to a special new products division or development group, as was the case with General Electric. Or it might be monitored by a new products committee that does not involve itself in operations at all—like American Standards. Otherwise it might be supervised by a group brand manager whose brand the new product would belong to. And there are variations on those themes. S. C. Johnson & Son established a new product department as early as 1955.

3M estimated that approximately half their profits came from products that did not exist ten years previously. But then, 3M are well-known for their drive for new product development. They owe their origins to it. Their policy has long been that growth should come from internal ideas and operations. And it is the *environment* that is the key to new product development. It requires a climate of imagination and enthusiasm, inspiration, determination, and direction. It also has to have both the research and the manufacturing facilities, and a readiness to provide big up-front investment. But the most important ingredient for success in the development of new products is people who can select good ideas and make them work by their own enthusiasm, energy, and resolve.

Dr. C. W. Walton (who was then vice-president of research and product development for 3M) gave the following as the most important criteria to measure the potential success of a new product:

- Is it the first of its kind in the market?
- Is it useful, and of a quality which will command a profitable price?
- Is it novel enough to be patentable?

3M produce a new product every day of the year, on average. Nearly one-third of their $15 billion sales consist of new or innovated products launched within the previous four years. They are, perhaps, the ideal example of a company that wedded innovative marketing to TQM. *Fortune* magazine recently ranked them as the eleventh most admired company in the United States.

It is interesting to follow the critical path that led to the product launch and unusual success of Proctor & Gamble's classic Crest Toothpaste. Teamwork by several P&G laboratories, their process development department, and product research department, combined with Indiana University School of Dentistry, resulted in the patented Crest stannus fluoride formula by the early 1950s. Clinical tests between 1952 and 1954, and test marketing in 1955, culminated in the national introduction of Crest in 1956. It was not until 1960 that the American Dental Association printed its recognition of Crest's effectiveness. By 1961, Crest had become the top-selling toothpaste in the United States.

A company that depends on developing its own new products never rests. There is, understandably, an exciting entrepreneurial atmosphere of risk and gamble in many of those companies.

Samuel C. Johnson (of S. C. Johnson & Son) once revealed what he said was the secret of successfully marketing new products with an extraordinarily low percentage of failures. That was combining three operational elements:

1. The screening technique of picking winners;
   - taking a quick look at the total market for the product,
   - making an estimate of the growth possibilities of the total market,
   - estimating the share of market attainable,
   - making a rough calculation of potential gross profit margin.

2. The "sponsor group" concept of broad participation in new products; consisting most probably of the conceiver of the new idea, a laboratory technician, a marketing man, financial man, a production man, and a member of the new products department.

3. A demonstrable "product plus," to earn consumer acceptance.

Borden Co. introduced 179 new products in 1963. Something over 22 percent of its total sales in that year, of $1.119 billion, came from products that had been added to the company lines within the previous ten years. James V. Bassett, who was president of Borden Foods Co. at that time, was quoted as follows:

We have several criteria in addition to quality, for judging the marketability of a product;
- Will it upgrade our profit margins?
- Will it benefit from our knowhow, experience and reputation?
- Does it have prospects of becoming an established item in our product line?
- Will it retain the status of a "specialty"?
- Does it fill out a product line, or have prospects of being developed into a product line?
- Does its volume potential warrant the management attention that will be necessary?

Managing The Brand

The essential difference between a product and a brand is that a product only offers functional benefits, whereas an established brand creates confidence, offers psychological or emotional benefits, and may provide worldwide availability, as well. For example, so many refrigerated beverages perform a similar function of quenching thirst or tasting good and cooling down the drinker that, without both tangible and intangible benefits, it would be difficult to explain the success of a simple product like Coca-Cola, other than to state that it is one of the world's best managed brands.

A product manager would therefore be described as a brand manager in companies that market branded goods or services. And responsibilities would most likely be more sophisticated because of the intangible as well as the functional benefits. The brand manager would be held accountable for brand integrity, brand awareness, brand consumer preference, and consumer loyalty to the brand; in other words, for total brand sanctity.

Instead of being assigned more products according to category, they would be chosen because they form a group of synergistic products marketed under the same brand name. The Lux brand range once included Lux Beauty Soap, Lux Soap Flakes, and Lux Dishwashing Liquid, whose common factor was that they all came in contact with a woman's skin. Gentleness and even skin improvement were the main consideration in their formulation and therefore their advertised promise. Advertising and awareness of brand image were intended not only to expedite shelf offtake in retail stores, but also to bond consumers to the brand. That can happen only if the quality of the product itself creates consumer preference.

We see why managing a brand takes precedence over managing the product, if we watch a TV commercial for Lipton Chinese Tea in Hong Kong. It features an old man; since we all know that most tea experts are senior citizens. He is skeptical but studiously polite when told about the new tea blend, even when the package is opened to reveal whole tea leaves instead of the usual chopped up pieces. Finally, after having tasted it (although secretly convinced that it is quite as good as his customary blend), he restrains himself from admitting it, in order to save face. Like most successful advertisements, it illustrates a simple concept told with credibility. It helped Lipton gain 13 percent market share in the first year of the product launch. But, of course, the Lipton brand already enjoyed considerable *momentum of image*, which acted like a springboard, because the brand had been nurtured with care all over the world from the beginning.

Category Management

The idea of branding a product or a range of products in the same category was intended to create consumer demand through brand advertising and promotions. The concept worked well enough for a long time because, if consumer loyalty to the brand became strong enough, dealers were obliged to stock those brands or risk losing business to competing dealers. But intense competition that threatened to marginalize some supermarket chains, and new technologies that shifted the power from national brand manufacturers to more progressive and combative supermarkets, changed the old supplier-dealer relationships. Whereas the objective of those brand marketers was to outwit other brands in order to increase their own sales, now it is to help their distributors to increase their total retail sales to consumers.

Or is it? The difference in aims is significant, because if a national brand marketer chooses not to focus on the retailer's goal, its products might be cut out of those chain stores. The leverage that has placed marketers in that dilemma is electronic evidence of the fickleness of consumers caught in a tighter economy in which the patronage motives of some of them switch away from such factors as brand preference.

Superstores became tough negotiators out of necessity, and when their growth flattened out they squeezed their suppliers still harder. Since brand manufacturers have been forced to reduce their margins, and so have supermarkets, both are aware of a new reality in the marketplace and a need for a new type of supplier relationship. On one hand they need each other to solve their mutual problems, and on the other hand to exploit new opportunities revealed from analyses of electronic data obtained at points of purchase, points of shelf offtake, and from repeat orders to warehouses. Both parties began to realize that they could benefit from pooling customer information.

The catalyst for the new partnership is category management. And the objective is to maximize returns on a category of products on a dealer's shelves rather than increase sales of a single product or brand. Whereas suppliers have always tried to replace competing brands with their own, that does not benefit the dealer. A dealer's bottom line is derived from increasing the entire shelf's offtake. The essence of category management is marketing tactics. And winning tactics are based on propositions arising from out of cooperative customer research and electronic data, such as what it is that a particular consumer segment generally purchases *altogether* in one shopping expedition. Obviously it is better to sell more of the entire category than spend money just to compete one brand against another on the same shelf. The prize goes to the category manager who can define the category in such a way as to increase total customer spending in that store.

Some pundits argue that the days of young business graduates starting careers as brand managers will soon be over. Responsibilities of category managers, who may replace them, are more complex, subtle, profound, and demand different skills. Not only do they include an ability to design and manage large databases but also the special and broader responsibility of relationship marketing. But pundits frequently forget that such activities are likely to apply only to that three percent of big businesses locked in the battle of the giants for limited territories and their resources. Most other businesses are likely to carry on using product or brand managers, whatever they wish to call them. And it may well be that fast-moving packaged consumer goods manufacturers of size will find they need brand managers as well as more senior category managers.

Some brand manufacturers may simply brush off the trend as just a passing fad for new buzzwords when they have practiced the concept for years within their existing framework. They may always have coordinated their advertising, promotions and merchandising with selected chain stores. And they would always have innovated particular products to increase sales and margins. The responsibility for doing so might have been that of a Product Group Manager. And, as with all alliances, some will not wish to share their innovative ideas and their marketing expertise in case they build up a partner into a powerful competitor, as frequently happens with alliances. Many brand marketers will be reluctant to abandon a strategy that put them in business or built them into a power that distributors were forced to do business with— that of creating mass consumer demand for their branded products over the heads of the dealers. They are more likely to finesse their consumer research, their brand advertising, their packaging, merchandising and promotions, in order to establish more powerful motives for consumers to buy their products and remain loyal to their brands. That is how they met the challenges of market saturation before.

By 1995, they were obliged to reposition themselves. Now they have to interact with consumers who may be loyal to their brand, to interface with their retail distributors, and also to concern themselves with electronic data about shoppers who may be loyal to their retail distributors. From a cost-benefit point of view, they may think they would be better to concentrate their time, human resources and budgets on the first two factors and leave the third one to the dealer, as they probably did in the past. But there is another powerful factor that the dealer may wish to negotiate with—that is the dealer's own brand. Its value to the dealer may depend on the size of its sales or margin, while its value to the brand manufacturer may be one of economies of scale if it can be added on to other production runs. But both of those factors may now be of lesser importance than creating more impulse buying of other complementary instore products when a customer patronizes the store with the intention of purchasing only one or two items.

Relationship marketing, which involves counselling retail distributors on more effective store tactics, and on which products they should buy, has, in turn, spawned *personal marketing*. More appropriately named one-on-one marketing, it uses data from EPOS technology (or electronic point of sales) that is analyzed and evaluated, then transformed into a useful illustration of each important shopper's purchasing behavior. Then relationship partners can predetermine their future needs from past habits, and influence their buying patterns. One-on-one marketing is the link between supplier-dealer relationships and dealer-shopper relationships. How the latter will develop may depend on electronic multimedia, sophisticated direct mail, or even telemarketing. Family grocers used to phone their regular customers when fresh produce or their favorite brands arrived in stock, and customers used to phone in their orders for delivery, before those local street-corner grocery stores were marginalized by supermarkets. Now that instant data of typical customers' individual orders is available electronically, some chains may prepare a customer's order in advance and have her goods parcelled ready for pick-up. That could take some of the hassle out of weekly household shopping or provide more time to browse around and buy more goods. And it might create customer loyalty to that retailer.

Research and Development

Who would be involved in research and development of new products would depend on the size and type of company and how well-structured they might be. Although it is a marketing responsibility, it is a multidisciplinary process like quality management. Bigger companies therefore tend to separate responsibilities under the operations of an R&D department, as opposed to a marketing one. Therein lies the essence of a problem: "Collaboration among people from different functions is difficult, uncertain, and suffers because of too little mutual understanding."[8]

A study of 123 companies and 252 new product histories was undertaken to analyze their management of new product systems. Each firm was shown the following list of thirteen activities as a basic structure for the R&D process. Results showed that many of those stages were omitted from a company's disciplines. Only 1.9 percent of all projects in that study utilized all thirteen activities prior to marketing their new products. They were: idea generation; initial screening; preliminary market assessment; detailed market study/market research; business/financial analysis; product development; in-house product testing; customer test of product; test market/ trial sell; trial production; precommercialization business analysis; production start-up; and market launch.[9]

The primary product marketing objective is to obtain a sufficiently high consumer trial rate; the advertising objective is to create measurable brand awareness and awareness of consumer benefits to initiate shelf offtake; the objective of point of purchase material is to identify the product and induce impulse buying. It is up to the quality and features of the product to achieve repeat purchases, the advertising being a constant reminder. Its formulation must therefore be preferable to other similar products. If the formulation is only comparable, then its container must be preferable, or its price lower, or the quantity or weight greater for the same price, or its advertising or its promotional budget may be greater, or its communications may be more effective.

After initial store offtake at the launch of a new product, and immediate replacement of store inventories, the advertising should create new customers and also repeat purchasing. Repeat purchases would provide evidence to merchandise managers that the new product has created consumer demand. The objective of creating brand loyalty should have been achieved several years before maturity and should contribute to a momentum of image. Prior to the stage when purchasing momentum is expected to level off, the marketing team may choose between considering the product as a cash-cow to be milked thereafter, or a *star* for reinvestment or innovation to extend its life cycle. If new market and consumer research show hard evidence that an innovated product could meet changed consumer needs and fill a gap in the market, a pilot test might be arranged. A small preliminary production run of the innovated product in its new package may be made to test demand, possibly by limited distribution into selected outlets or into an isolated test market.

The reason for failure is often that unfounded assumptions were made when they should have been tested.

Ample time should be given to testing the fundamental proposition that some sector of the market will be eager to buy the product or pay for the service, and can afford to do so. Often the concept does not match *real* marketplace needs or even the actual demographics of the market. And an overseas branch of an international marketer may be pressed to launch a product that was successful in another economy when it is irrelevant to local needs. Consumer benefits and communications goals should be tested, as well as local availability of raw materials. On the other hand, a new product may seem to be excellent when viewed in isolation from the emotional and practical needs of the market segment to which it may be aimed. Obviously it would be the wrong investment vehicle for a company's resources if it is not marketable, but that may not be so obvious to an entrepreneur who has thought up the process or invented the product. That is why top calibre measurable research is essential. It is a tool of the devil's advocate to uncover the truth.

Research is the means for removing uncertainty; of the concept, the product, its design and packaging, the marketplace and the intended consumer. Then all communications require thorough research; so do the media and distribution channels. By first testing the proposition with consumers who match the profile of the intended market segment, a great deal of waste may be prevented. And even after a launch, it is the consumer who should be surveyed again, because shelf offtake may turn out to be only a measurement of the effectiveness of advertising and promotions: *the public may never buy the product again.*

Meanwhile, the company will have made preliminary calculations in order to arrive at an estimated return on investment with the aids of rules-of-thumb, inhouse records and historic costing formulae.

Research can cover a far broader range of types and techniques than is realized by the public or the trade: product research and development, technical and engineering research, laboratory and formulation research, overseas research of similar products and services, package research and testing, design research, surveys of consumer trends, desk research, store audits, pantry checks, dustbin audits, taste tests, market research, distribution analysis, consumer research surveys, motivational research, advertising copy research, pre-post advertisement research, display-material, and pilot test-market research, among others.

Consumer research techniques, alone, include on-street or at-home personal surveys and polls, focused interviews in consumer clinics, telephone and panel and direct mail surveys. Questionnaires may be prepared by a Yes/No/Don't-know formula, or by multiple-choice answers, or as responses to open-ended questions. The number of consumers would vary according to quotas, random samples, or multistage, depending on what needs to be found out. There are also likely to be pilot surveys to correct any possibilities of misunderstandings beforehand, and to improve questionnaires.

Desk research is secondary research gathered from published material or material gathered by others. In its micro form, it would include such data from company records as sales figures, inventory purchases and store offtakes, prices and gross and net profits, R&D costs, and so forth. In its macro form, it would consist of outside statistics obtained by industrial and trade organizations, government census statistics, regional government surveys, or demographics, geographic or trade information from the media. Original research involves obtaining unknown facts.

Obtaining facts through research is a plodding affair that should never be hurried or undercut, because it is like seeking clues and other evidence for a murder trial, in that a picture slowly takes shape. And information invariably emerges at some point, which is unexpected and may cause a marketer to change direction. Companies that attempt to cut research costs by reducing the numbers in a survey or using an unsophisticated research company, can very easily miss the crucial information they should be looking out for, and waste a great deal of money in an abortive launch instead.

The above list is by no means exhaustive, since different research specialists discover and develop better ways to obtain meaningful information which may assist marketing companies to make vital decisions.

As with most sciences or practices, there is a qualitative and a quantitative approach to research. It is not only how many and how much, but also what, how, where and why? Consumer research can be either quantitative or qualitative. Qualitative consumer research has come to be known generally as motivational research.

Motivational Research

If we wish to establish a date when marketing companies first began to show interest in motivational research as a marketing tool, it would probably be the summer of 1947, when a paper was presented on "Psychology In Market Research" by Dr. Ernest R. Dichter, president of the Institute for Motivational Research, Inc. There was confusion in some circles, for some years afterwards. There were misunderstandings and differences of opinion among researchers. And from manufacturers there was mostly neglect. Now that the dust has long since settled, the friction and bitterness between the two main schools of research is generally forgotten, except for two articles published in 1955 and still on file. One was a report on the "Battle of Embittered Ph.D.'s" on 19 September in *Advertising Age*. The other was entitled "Research Rivals Trade Blows" in *Business Week* the following month.

Today, most sophisticated marketing-oriented companies use both types of research because they know that there is a special need for each.

A basic distinction is that whereas market research can ask such questions as "What? When? How? Where?" and "How much?" and expect to receive suitable answers, it is most unlikely to receive true answers by asking "Why?" Most of the time, people who are asked "Why?" do not know the answer—but they will usually say something. In those cases it is more dangerous to undertake poll research than not to. In some cases an answer may be distorted according to an individual's emotional reactions or his or her character traits. In other cases, social mores may inhibit people from selling the truth about why they buy some products or brands and do not buy others; or why they shop at one supermarket and not at another one; or why they shop with or without a prepared list; or why they will pay certain prices for particular goods. But the biggest problem which creates misleading answers is a misunderstanding of the questions.

The claim of motivational researchers is that their techniques are able to uncover the *real* reasons why.

When the dust was still flying from feuding researchers in 1956, *The Journal of Marketing* (of the American Marketing Association) published an article by Percy Black, in which he wrote,

Motivation research claims that to get at the "Why?" of consumer buying, one must unearth hidden or unconscious motives; one must discover the basic needs, desires, and tendencies of consumers *as people*. And the only way to do this, it says, is through the use of procedures such as free-association interviews, projective tests, and nondirective questionnaires which bring these motives to light. For it is evident that people often don't know why they prefer one brand to another, or why they buy one thing and not another. The reasons they give for their brand attractions—if they give any at all—are surface explanations, that is, what appears rational to them. Moreover, we do not always voice what we feel, if indeed we know what we feel. Our social mores prevent it. Unless we can therefore get at our basic motivations indirectly and round about, by methods which do not embarrass or shock us with direct confrontal of our desires and intentions and which do not take it for granted that we ourselves know what they are—unless we can do this, we will never understand the fundamental dynamics of attraction between consumer and brand.

Motivational research claims to be able to see beneath the rational layers of buying, beneath the expected, customary responses to inquiry into buying behavior, and to understand the basic motives, the personality needs, the *emotional* impulsions which attract people to one product and not to another. Market research, it says, never reaches this unconscious level in human activity because it uses techniques like direct questions and the tabulating of "yes" and "no," which only reveal reasons. Such techniques lend themselves easily to statistical manipulation and therefore result in nice, tidy, systematic answers to marketing problems. But they so limit the scope of enquiry that the researcher is closed off before he begins from what lies deepest in the individual and subtly but forcefully determines his buying trends.

The Meaning of "Why?"

Black goes on; "Why? is an ambiguous word. Sometimes it means the underlying needs which shape desire. Why does the woman *want* a new dress? Because she wants love and admiration. That is her deepest need relevant to the situation. When motivation research asks "why?" it asks, "what motivates the consumer?" and its answer explains the consumer in terms of psychosocial desires, drives, motives, and needs. Motivation research reveals to industry the motives for the urge to buy. Knowing these, industry knows the most effective stream through which to channel its persuasion.

But "why?" also means the causal conditions which determine buying. Why does the woman *buy* a new dress? One reason is that she can afford it. Another is that the kind of dress she wants is available. When market research asks "why?" it asks, "what conditions the consumer—that is, what conditions are operating to enable the purchase to take place, and without which the purchase would not take place?"— and its answer explains the consumer in terms of prevailing market factors which help to satisfy consumer needs or which inhibit them from being carried out. Market research gives industry facts about the changing market spectacle in which the motivated buying act takes place. Knowing these facts allows industry to direct its promotional media and monies to areas which most can profit by them.

Disagreements among researchers about procedure, sample size, usefulness or meaningfulness or applicability of results—even disagreements about what men are and what as consumers makes them tick—spring from the failure to realize the dual function of "why?" and the legitimacy of its answers in both regions of investigation.

Test Marketing

The objective of test marketing a new product is—as with any other type of market research—to minimize risks before incurring further and larger costs. As with other market research, its method is to find a small "world" which resembles the big one outside, in which a company plans to launch its product, in a number of significant ways.

This is how the consumer profile and market profile of "The Iowa Test Triangle" compared to the national profile of the U.S. market some years back:

TABLE 13.5
Iowa Test Market

Major Similarities	Triangle	U.S.
1. Rate of growth (1950–1960):	18.5%	18.5%
2. Urban population:	68.9%	69.9%
3. Rural population:	31.1%	30.1%
4. Incomes 4 to 5 thousand:	11.6%	11.1%
5. Incomes 9 to 10 thousand:	5.0%	4.9%
6. Professional-technical population:	10.4%	10.3%
7. Sales-clerical population:	13.1%	13.8%
8. Retail sales by food stores:	22.0%	24.6%
9. Retail sales—gen. meds. stores:	16.5%	17.2%
10. Retail sales by auto stores:	15.5%	15.9%

Instead of inviting in small consumer groups for interviews—comprising some twenty people at any one time and maybe ten separate groups with the same demographics as the selected target market for the product—which the marketer probably did for a consumer probe at an early conceptual stage or after making a limited number of prototypes for testing; or taking a questionnaire to 2,000 randomly sampled consumers' homes for an attitudinal test, a manufacturer will confidently use a far bigger market area at a much later stage.

"The Iowa Test Triangle is an eight-county market in Eastern Iowa with a population of 477,983 people in 44 towns and cities, including three standard metropolitan areas," advised Frank N. Magid Associates of Cedar Rapids, a research firm located in the test area which had 200 trained research workers living in the community.

The faithfulness of the consumer profile (and possibly the market profile, too) is one of two essential factors for an acceptable test market. The other is that it should be controllable in terms of its advertising media, and preferably sealed off from the invasion of outside media. States the advertisement for the area; "The Iowa Test Triangle is ideal for testing *media mix*, inasmuch as the market is served by 3 TV stations, 4 newspapers, 11 AM radio stations, and 3 commercial FM stations—with negligible penetration from outside media."

Another ideal location for test marketing, advertised by *Peoria Journal Star* newspaper, was Peoria, which claimed the following advantages:

1. *Isolation*: A self-contained distribution and retail trading area, with negligible penetration by outside media. Chicago is 160 miles to the northeast; St. Louis is 175 miles to the southwest.

2. *Population*: Peoria ranks as the second biggest metro area in Illinois, with a correctly diversified farm/industrial labor force...no dominant nationality ...balanced population composition.

3. *Saturation*: With one newspaper. The *Peoria Journal Star* is Peoria's *only* daily newspaper. Run-of-paper color is available seven days a week with 1,000-line minimum. Split run testing is offered on every-other-copy basis. Complete merchandising service includes trade calls, point-of-purchase placement, mailings, checks on distribution and product movement.

4. *Distribution*: Peoria is a distribution and transportation hub served by fifteen railroads, wholesalers in all lines, sixteen major general merchandise stores, 100 "chain" food outlets and eighty drug and cosmetic outlets.

5. *Research*: Continuing Consumer Audit sponsored by the *Peoria Journal Star,* this exhaustive and continuing survey reports to you accurately on Peoria brand preferences and user characteristics...adding important data to test results.

Does Test Marketing Work?

"New product testing is like checking to see if there's any water in the swimming pool before jumping off from the top diving board," said some anonymous person. That seems to be the only comment on which everyone agrees. Its main function is to find out what is wrong, so that a marketer can correct certain erroneous assumptions before they result in a disastrous product launch.

But it does not work according to precise principles of laboratory conditions, because there are too many variable factors involved. It is simplistic to believe that the only significant ones are consumer and market profiles and isolated media.

One researcher referred to test marketing as "retrieving large and expensive chestnuts from the fire." It could therefore validly be argued that test marketing does serve a useful purpose if it tells manufacturers the bad new *before* further budgets are wasted by throwing good money after bad. The real problem is that marketers expect more from test marketing than that. They would like to analyze and quantify the results and project them in such a way that they will know with certainty what production volumes, inventories, and sales levels are possible for state and national distribution. Sometimes the projections are close, sometimes not. They also want to evaluate their marketing strategies and prove that a product can be marketed profitably, by projecting test-marketing results to prove that specific profits can be anticipated.

But the big argument *against* test marketing is security. Manufacturers try to preserve secrecy to give them sufficient lead time in the marketplace to make a reasonable profit to recover their research, development, and initial production costs, before competitors market me-too products. Many companies tremble with anxiety from the moment a concept for a new product has been approved, in case it will leak out to a competitor. And there is also, with some sensitive products, industrial espionage.

Conversely, a reputable company that has gradually built up an established position as a market leader in the industry does not wish to make a fool of itself in public and risk damaging its reputation by destroying confidence in its other products because of a dramatic failure.

The bottom line is that management makes judgements and takes risks all the time. That is what it is paid for. And nobody is perfect. But a manager needs the constitution also to be able to withstand failures and still have the courage of his or her convictions to take initiatives in the future.

Demographics

One important lesson that manufacturers find hard to learn is that the rules change all the time. That is because the players are always changing. And it is not only the competitors and products that change but, more importantly, the customers.

For example, a manager would be well-advised—if he or she is considering test marketing in the Iowa Test Triangle—to compare the most recent demographics in that area. The same would apply to all the factors quoted meticulously for Peoria. It is very doubtful if any of them are true today; except that Peoria is still 160 miles from Chicago and 175 miles from St. Louis.

A fundamental truth about markets is that local industries move or die, young people leave to find employment, others leave to create their own families elsewhere, older people leave the frost belt areas to go down south or move to the West. For example, Calgary in Alberta, enjoyed an oil boom in the late 1970s that attracted very large populations of young couples from all over Canada. It became the fastest-growing Canadian city. But when oil prices dropped, some oil wells became uncompetitive. The boom turned suddenly to bust. With large-scale unemployment, many couples abandoned their homes and their downpayments, left the deserted factories and offices, and returned home.

Demographics change as birth rates rise in underdeveloped countries and fall in developed ones. Household incomes change as more wives go out to work, and change again as the divorce rate increases. One moment there is a teenage market, then one consisting largely of mature adults, then an aging population of senior citizens. In Vancouver, British Columbia, more and more Hong Kong capital is invested in commerce, industry, and real estate. Not only has the skyline altered with more narrow high-rise buildings—as in

Hong Kong, and for similar reasons of availability of space—but the ethnicity has changed with the influx of Chinese populations. A similar situation occurred in the UK when rising oil prices in the Middle East enabled a large Arab population to buy summer properties, and then blocks of flats, hotels, department stores, and banks. In the United States, the ethnic balance changed from legal and illegal immigration of Mexicans, Cubans, and Haitians, particularly in cities like Miami. Large-scale movement of families from East Germany to West Germany changed the balance of labor to one of intense competition in the West and skilled labor shortages in the east. Oil embargoes against South Africa obliged that country to develop its own successful oil-from-coal technology, which resulted in the growth of Sasolburg. Sanctions, on the other hand, created a brain drain to overseas countries from the white population sector, and massive unemployment for the black population, resulting in population movement to the cities for food, and the erection of squatters' shanty towns. France suffered a similar movement from Algeria when that country won its independence. The north-south problem still troubles Italy. And into Israel comes a mass exodus from Russia.

It is said that 45 million Americans can trace their ancestry back to Ireland, although only some 2 million Irish emigrated and settled in the United States by 1870.

No marketer can ignore demographics today. Population instability is a fact of life, just as it was in the ninth century and other eras when empires fell and were replaced by new ones. Meanwhile, western governments will be pressured to stop the flow of multicultural immigrants. Economic recessions create dire problems in integrating ethnocultural workers into the labor force and entrepreneurs into the business community, because local populations are afraid of being marginalized. There is also the problem of Have-Not societies in Third World countries and underclass societies in the West, where teenagers follow criminal and terrorist lifestyles. That too leads to demographic flux.

Trends in overcrowded cities in California reveal population introductions of approximately a million a year from 1989. "Los Angeles has more Mexicans than any other city but Mexico City, more Koreans than any other city outside Seoul, more Filipinos than any other city outside the Philippines and, some experts claim, more Druze than any other place but Lebanon."[10] And, "Whatever happens now in California, or to California, will be happening to America before long, and to the entire world a little while after that."

In fact it has already happened by now. Similar changes, but on a smaller scale and with different ethnic mixes, took place across the border in Canada when capital poured in from Hong Kong and Japan; and also in the conservative capital city of Ottawa, closer to the Eastern Seaboard. Out of a total of 45,505 immigrants in the decade from 1981 to 1991, the majority were Lebanese.[11] Nationally in Canada 54 percent of its 4.5 million immigrants came from Europe and 46 percent from Asia. More than half settled in Toronto, Montreal, and Vancouver. Forty percent of the population of Richmond (Metropolitan Vancouver) were immigrants from Hong Kong, by 1994.

Movements of populations have always taken place—that's how the founding fathers reached America. Immigration, emigration, and inmigration are major forces in the dynamics of change, and change is the marketing challenge. America's foreign-born population now stands at twenty million. And 300,000 illegal immigrants entered the United States in 1993. All present market niches for goods and services, whatever their job, their business, or their income. Entrepreneurial businesses would have researched markets beforehand and also on an ongoing basis to determine at what point the changed circumstances would provide new opportunities.

14

Oiling the Works

When Drucker declared that "so much of what we call management consists in making it difficult for people to work," he was most probably describing a bureaucratic style of management—because it generally ends up by
causing the very three failings that von Clausewitz and van Creveld identified as bedeviling the whole process. They are inflexibility, friction, and uncertainty. They dislocate business organizations as well as military expeditions,
because both involve people choosing ways and means to achieve goals, and
there are bound to be hurdles to overcome all the way along the route.

Someone is needed to facilitate activities of every project a company undertakes, to ensure that it is completed as planned. That manager must massage situations to their advantage where inflexibility prevents activities from
occurring at their required destinations on time. He or she must oil the "machinery" of processes, to avoid abrasiveness causing friction and jamming up
the works; and must be able to provide relevant knowledge to reduce uncertainties and minimize risks.

The following chart lists fifty-two key results areas in which business managers of an average GSME become involved. There are many more in a big
national or multinational market leader and less in a typical SME. Sometimes a manager controls situations directly by actuating. At other times, he
or she may delegate but still be held accountable. In most cases, a manager
facilitates by making malleable what was inflexible, by oiling the works, and
by applying appropriate knowledge, ideas, and wisdom to making things easier
for people to get things done.

A manager will facilitate whatever has to be done in any of those key
results areas that are his or her responsibility, or in all of them if he or she is
chief executive officer. It will be facilitated by discussion, analysis, problem
solving, judgement, decision making, or by implementation. A manager also
reserves the right to do nothing if alternative options appear to involve unnecessary risk. In some cases he will postpone if he feels intuitively that a
course of action under consideration may be inappropriate. He will deal with
facts. He will offer considered opinions. He will also consider other people's
opinions. He will rely on his experience of similar situations, but also seek

the experience of a departmental manager, or a user of a particular skill, or a knowledge worker, or the topmost executive. Sometimes he will request more hard facts and other people's opinions. He may convene a meeting to obtain inputs from other managers or employees. And so, of course, will she.

She will do so in a particular way, but is likely to be more successful if she uses a consultative style. The following example illustrates how that management style tends to facilitate, whereas an autocratic one can be abrasive and cause friction:

Options: An autocratic manager is likely to *tell* an employee what to do, whereas a consultative one asks the employee what she thinks needs to be done. The former approach is likely to cause resistance to the idea, whereas the latter invites useful suggestions through participation. The autocratic manager may not bother to tell his staff the purpose of the project. And if the employee asks what the objective is, he might even respond irritably by saying, "Just do it!" The other manager invites his staff to consider if there are other options that may be better. If not, he may suggest some for her to pass judgement on. Then, after discussing several alternatives, the ends and means are agreed on by both parties and trust is implicit.

The employee in the first example may undertake the work grudgingly. And, although she may know a better way to undertake the job, she is likely to decide that it would not be advisable to point out the problems in the manager's approach that might prevent the project from being completed on time or to the best possible advantage. In the other situation, personal involvement in the ways and means are likely to inject a feeling of pride in producing the best results.

When the autocratic manager checks back to make sure his employee is working, he is already prepared to find fault because of the tension created and a feeling that the employee may deliberately obstruct the process. Resistance to her employer may cause her to choose simply to take her time and keep him waiting, to show him how indispensable she is. The other manager, who is equally responsible for the project, must monitor it. He will check back to satisfy himself that the method they both agreed on actually works in practice. And the employer will offer his help if it is required to facilitate completion of the job.

If the autocrat shows impatience on returning to see how the project is going, the employee might even slow down further, to impress on him the fact that it is she who possesses the specialized skills, not he. The satisfied and involved employee would probably have completed the job efficiently by that time and asked for her employer's opinion. No doubt he will show his satisfaction that the job was done well and in good time, so that mutual confidence and trust is generated. The autocrat would have probably not bothered to conceal his displeasure and might even have showed his annoyance or contempt for his staff, by a gesture or a rebuke. For his discourtesy and lack of consideration, he is kept waiting each time he is obliged to return to attempt to accelerate the work—until it is finally finished in the worker's own good time.

That commonplace situation illustrates how an insensitive manager can make work disagreeable for others and harder for himself. The right to human dignity should never be questioned or abused. And a natural show of it by treating an employee as a person who knows something about her own job and whose opinion is worthy of consideration, is evidence of respect and trust. Employees are not rats in Skinner boxes, or components in some academic theory like Vroom's Valence-Expectancy model or Porter's Diamond. Since people are human they behave in ways that are characteristically human according to typical strengths and weaknesses, skills, and failings that need to be taken into consideration. The last word has not been said on what motivates them or how best to attempt to do so. Meanwhile, a manager has to assume that most people are brought up to react well to courtesy and consideration, while also being skeptical in the knowledge that many people are antisocial and even enjoy provoking trouble by creating mischief.

Union Members

Edwin Stringer, Q.C., who specializes in management and labor problems, also takes that straightforward approach. He is a partner in the legal firm of Stringer, Brisbin, Humphrey, of Toronto, and he counsels companies on employee relations and problems with trade unions. He assumes, just as we would, that employees chosen to work for a company are the type of people who would naturally react well if they are treated as decent, reasonable human beings who are seeking security and job fulfillment. In his 1985 address at the annual convention of the Retail Council of Canada, he told them, "Managers can't afford to think of themselves as a class apart, insulated by rank, perks and bonuses. Show me a two-class company and I'll show you a union in the making. You don't automatically get respect with the job title. You must earn it." And "The workplace can frequently appear to be a hostile, frightening, closed community to a new employee. His first few days in a new workplace may determine his attitude for a long time to come. If a company takes the time and trouble to make a new employee feel comfortable and welcome from the first day on, then that employee is more likely to develop a positive, co-operative attitude towards his employer."

On unions, he said, "Once a union member doesn't mean always a union member. If he or she finds no need for a union, there is no reason to suppose that he or she will attempt to form one. Unions are most frequently simply tools for change; a response to management failure. In fact, employers of well-managed businesses have often found employees who may have belonged to a union at a former workplace are the most vocal opponents of a union because they have experienced the realities, frustrations and disadvantages of working in a union shop."

Perhaps the most vociferous complainers and troublemakers are to be found in the two most tedious and frustrating areas of a business enterprise; the administration or accounts department and the factory or warehouse floor. The routine and monotony of the work creates an environment conducive to complaint instead of challenge. That is because employees never seem to reach any goal or conclusion after all their repetitive striving. And although administrative offices are generally more comfortable to work in than workshops or assembly lines, they can also be a breeding ground for gossip, rumors, bickering, and backbiting, where employees are apt to take sides in disputes about nothing tangible. But, like some administration departments, a factory floor can suffer from instructions and counter-instructions where there is indecisive management. Employees can easily react with irritation at different sets of directions or misdirections emanating from too many bosses.

Boredom, dissatisfaction, and frustration all cause discontent with the job, the workplace, and the boss. And some employees are quick to complain, even if what they complain about is not what is upsetting them. All that is needed is an insensitive manager to come along and ignite the fuse. And when an emotional explosion takes place, he is left wondering what he could possibly have said that caused all the fuss. In fact he just created an opportunity for pent-up frustrations that needed an outlet. He provided it by being at that particular place at the wrong time.

Ways to relieve boredom have always been known—it is simply a matter of relieving the monotony by creating personal involvement. For example, when a property developer constructs a high rise apartment building from a design that results in long unbroken corridors, he can choose from a number of alternative ways to relieve the perception of endlessness and tedium. He may decide to instal carpeting with very large and colorful patterns, or divide the walls with panels of wallpaper, or use decorative wall brackets for the lighting instead of concealing it. Sections of the corridor might be lit differently, or wall mirrors or artificial windows might be used; or he may make a feature of each doorway. Management, too, is required to relieve the monotony of work that involves considerable routine.

Apart from occasional improvements of the workplace—which have been shown to improve the quality and output of work, whatever they involve—the monotony of repeat work can be broken up in all kinds of ways. By setting intermittent goals, peaks and intervals can be introduced as something for employees to look forward to. In that way, work will seem to have a beginning, a climax, and an intermission. And work in between those anticipated moments can be divided up into individual projects.

In the case of salespeople, for example, despite a delusion by many sales managers that salesmen and women just work for commission, they too tire and get bored and their sales decline. Introducing sales competitions each season, between teams, stimulates interest and injects a spirit of pride, on one hand, and competitiveness on the other. If awards are geared to achievement, the best and the worst will achieve more sales and become accustomed to higher targets.

In some factories where specific runs of products are made to individual orders according to different customers' own specifications, each project is naturally separated from each other by product type, color, gender, material, or pattern. Employees should be made aware of the separation of one production run from another by dramatizing it. In the case of much longer production runs of the same or similar products, an imaginative way is needed to identify differences, even if only between orders for one customer as compared to another one.

Since some complaints that stir up sufficient trouble to result in unionization stem from boredom, they are often simply appeals for change, and boredom welcomes any change to overcome the monotony of daily repeat work.

Facilitators

Quality Circles are likely to be the best catalysts for positive change, because they introduce employees to new and different challenges all the time. As well as the considerable advantages of improved processes, systems, tools, or technologies, which can improve production and lower costs, Q-Circles can also solve less tangible emotional problems of restlessness, insecurity, depression, or the perception of drudgery. They stimulate imagination in the very types of people who possess a low tolerance for monotonous work, by involving them personally. Their voluntary and informal structure and procedures provide an opportunity for issues to be raised not as complaints but as suggestions, ideas, and proposals. And the feeling of having made a worthwhile contribution creates pride in work and self and a feeling of community with fellow workers and the business organization.

Employees often feel low in spirit because they feel they have no control over their lives. Q-Circles can be uplifting and energizing. And when employees are provided with opportunities to overcome work problems, they feel less manipulated by management and by the workplace. They are facilitators that management has only to initiate and then wait for suggestions and show sufficient interest to benefit from employees' contributions.

New business and plant technologies that are designed to improve work or increase productivity or quality or exactitude can also be facilitators. But new machines can divert employees from work, like new toys. It is difficult enough to get managers and staff to establish the right objectives and continue to follow them, but it is very easy for them to be diverted from their objectives by technology. For love of technology, many executive presentations at workshops and seminars are spoilt by diverting the audience's attention away from the substance of the talk and the speaker, to the technology instead. Often, overhead projectors or slides with elaborate charts are not needed and only end up by creating confusion in the minds of the audience. Computer nerds love to play with the latest model, and executives love to play with laptop computers even when the connection with their real work is marginal. And so-called communications technology like answering machines and voice-boxes actually isolate customers from the business and executives from the marketplace.

Other facilitators are outside service industries that managers may need from time to time, like market research or motivational research companies, industrial psychologists, recruitment consultants, public relations specialists, sales trainers, executive seminars, advertising agencies, printers and sign painters, freelance commercial artists, finance companies, truck hire companies, corporate lawyers, and so forth. As outsourcing of services, as well as hardware components, becomes an even greater trend, more such facilitators will be sought to provide specialized services and reduce fixed overhead costs. But the manager will still be the supreme facilitator, because all of those outside companies to whom work is subcontracted require sourcing, negotiations, monitoring, and measuring for performance standards. That is part of a manager's responsibility.

Within the workplace itself, a manager will continuously place himself or herself in positions where they can be available to assist in making things happen, by enabling employees to work more effectively. Sometimes it may mean offering useful advice, at other times it may be by discussion with a department head who may be short of staff during an unexpected peak period. Or it may mean picking up a phone at a crucial moment to obtain quicker deliveries of components, spare parts or raw materials to facilitate activities required to meet a goal or a date-schedule. At any time or place where there is a work stoppage, for whatever reason, a manager must show his or her leadership by taking much-needed initiatives to get workflow back on target. He can smooth out misunderstandings between departments, patch up conflicts between the company and its suppliers or its customers, or obtain the support of the chief executive in a crisis. In short, a useful manager is like an oiling can that keeps the cogs turning smoothly in an important machine.

Another way that a manager can keep other managers and staff moving in the right direction is to know the goals or objectives of each one of the key results areas of a company. Most personnel are remarkably lacking in knowledge, or simply forgetful, about what their objectives are, or the objectives of their own department, or the company's primary objectives. They can waste everyone's time and other resources simply by veering off the rails that lead to those objectives. One inhibitor to meeting goals is to employ too many people. It may be that several phases of massive company downsizing in the past decade has taught management how dangerous all those layers of fat can be, but it is doubtful; because statistics over many years reveal the propensity of business organizations and institutions to hire more clerks, accountants, administrators, assistants, middle managers, and other executives as soon as an economy begins to recover. What is surprising is how companies often penny pinch when it comes to hiring productive people who can create customers and provide growth for a company, while administration departments grow exponentially. When that happens, lines of communications lengthen, more layers of command have to be penetrated, and more friction overcome by a manager seeking to facilitate or delegate to effect. They became known as "MUSH" jobs during the past two recessions and were weeded out. The result was, generally, quicker action and more productivity at lower cost.

Eight spheres are illustrated in figure 14.1, in which managers can facilitate activities leading to separate goals and requiring objectives of their own. They are market share objectives, sales objectives, communications objectives, resource objectives, productivity objectives, customer service objectives, human resource objectives, and corporate objectives.

All fifty-two key results areas must have clearly defined goals of their own in order to establish realistic budgets and forecasts for those eight measurable objectives. In that way, each key results area may be managed as if it were a "lever" with which those objectives might be capable of achievement. And a general manager or CEO who is accountable for profit or loss of the enterprise should possess that faculty or skill described by von Clausewitz as *a sense of location*. That is to say, his or her familiarity and thoroughgoing knowledge of each function in all key areas should enable him or her, at a moment's notice, to visualize the importance of each one in a grand strategy.

Like a general considering the terrain and disposition of forces on a field of battle, the CEO would know immediately where a weakness might require reinforcements to avoid the possibility of disaster, or where a strength might be used successfully to exploit any opportunity that might present itself.

If a function of each departmental manager is to facilitate the achievement of those objectives of the sphere for which he or she is accountable, in any one or several of those fifty-two key results areas, either directly or by delegation, then he or she must first be able to facilitate his or her own personal objectives. But a manager is unlikely to be able to achieve a free-flowing, calm, and self-confident style and continually achieve, unless that manager is well organized for facilitating. What often makes a manager ineffective in facilitating the work of others is an intermittent concern that he may have mislaid some document or other, failed to confirm an important order or directive, may be unprepared for a meeting, or forgotten particular information that may be required. In short, a manager must be able to manage himself without effort if he wishes to manage others without overloading himself.

External Factors

In addition to those fifty-two—or more, or less—internal factors that a manager must control, he or she will also be involved in somewhat different ways with external factors.

One of the objectives of Keynes's *The General Theory* was to escape from the false division of economics between the *Theory of Value and Distribution* and the *Theory of Money*. He proposed that the correct distinction was between the Theory of the Individual Firm or Industry, and the Theory of Output and Employment as a whole. That dichotomy is now recognized in the difference between microeconomics and macroeconomics.

Organizational needs are likely to change in accordance with macroeconomic factors, over which a company may have little or no control. Either one or a combination of several of the following external factors could and should influence a company's direction. They would include but not be limited to; government restrictions, the national economy, political situations, security aspects, trade unions, sanctions or embargoes, the global economy, acts of God, inflation, bank rates, balance of payments, foreign exchange rates, patents or copyright violations, import duty, availability of raw material supplies and their price, advertising infringements, consumer groups, human rights, technological innovations, ethics, market saturation, unemployment rates, consumers' disposable income, legal considerations, and so forth. Each person motivated to exercise power must judge which of those factors could be controlled in some way, or manipulated or exploited to provide an outcome favorable to the company, and which cannot.

Internal Factors

Organizational needs are also influenced by factors centered within key results areas of a company. Management is required as a matter of course, to understand the needs of each of those fifty-two or more key spheres of operation, as well as decisions arising from external factors.

But managers can easily lose themselves in a maze of business functions and soon become so administration-oriented that they may lose sight of what the business enterprise is there for—to get and keep a customer. Whenever an executive forgets that, they become distracted from a company's real objectives and may propel it and their job onto the slippery downhill slope to oblivion. Most businesses in the UK and the U.S. demonstrated generally poor performances in the recent past. Their statistics reveal the type of mismanagement that unseated numerous CEOs in the 1990s, because it was no longer considered acceptable by owners. "The top 50 U.S. companies made a feeble showing from 1973 to 1983: in 4 cases, earnings per share fell over the decade; in 7 further cases, they rose by less than 2% compounded annually; 10 others grew

FIGURE 14.1
Key Results Areas

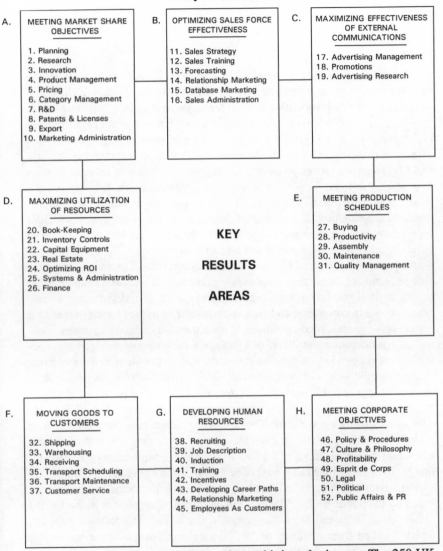

A. MEETING MARKET SHARE
    OBJECTIVES

    1. Planning
    2. Research
    3. Innovation
    4. Product Management
    5. Pricing
    6. Category Management
    7. R&D
    8. Patents & Licenses
    9. Export
    10. Marketing Administration

B. OPTIMIZING SALES FORCE
    EFFECTIVENESS

    11. Sales Strategy
    12. Sales Training
    13. Forecasting
    14. Relationship Marketing
    15. Database Marketing
    16. Sales Administration

C. MAXIMIZING EFFECTIVENESS
    OF EXTERNAL
    COMMUNICATIONS

    17. Advertising Management
    18. Promotions
    19. Advertising Research

D. MAXIMIZING UTILIZATION
    OF RESOURCES

    20. Book-Keeping
    21. Inventory Controls
    22. Capital Equipment
    23. Real Estate
    24. Optimizing ROI
    25. Systems & Administration
    26. Finance

KEY

RESULTS

AREAS

E. MEETING PRODUCTION
    SCHEDULES

    27. Buying
    28. Productivity
    29. Assembly
    30. Maintenance
    31. Quality Management

F. MOVING GOODS TO
    CUSTOMERS

    32. Shipping
    33. Warehousing
    34. Receiving
    35. Transport Scheduling
    36. Transport Maintenance
    37. Customer Service

G. DEVELOPING HUMAN
    RESOURCES

    38. Recruiting
    39. Job Description
    40. Induction
    41. Training
    42. Incentives
    43. Developing Career Paths
    44. Relationship Marketing
    45. Employees As Customers

H. MEETING CORPORATE
    OBJECTIVES

    46. Policy & Procedures
    47. Culture & Philosophy
    48. Profitability
    49. Esprit de Corps
    50. Legal
    51. Political
    52. Public Affairs & PR

by less than 10%; the magic 15% mark was hit in only 4 cases. The 250 UK largest were no more inspiring. After allowing for inflation, 206 showed declines; another 34 grew by less than 7%; and only 46 managed 15%."

"The recession of the seventies can't be blamed, either. In 1983, a marvel for growth in sales, there were 20 U.S. firms in the top 50 whose earnings per share were worse than in the previous year: for the next 50 companies, the delinquents were 17 in number. As for return for investors, in which the stock

price is dominant, 17 of the 500 biggest companies produced a negative figure; stockholders had not obtained a 7% annual return on investment in 62
more cases."[1]

Consensus

Econometrics are gauges required by managers in order to know where to
oil the works of an enterprise and where to facilitate by massaging situations
or seeking suitable information needed for judgement calls. Where consensus
may be necessary before making an important decision that could involve the
entire company, it is essential for the chairman of the meeting to ensure that
all parties to the decision are on the same wavelength. It is frequently the case
that a manager may make an emotional judgement because of subjective opinions when a rational judgement is required. Or an administrator may make a
purely pragmatic assessment when a creative approach would be more appropriate to the situation. It is therefore necessary to understand how different
individuals in a meeting are likely to think through a particular situation in
quite different ways, because of the human factor.

As we have discovered by now, the human condition can make for unreliable judgements, because it combines weaknesses as well as strengths. That
is why institutions and business organizations spread the risks between a number of people in committee and seek consensus. The human factor in this case
may involve genetic predispositions of each member, personality traits, ideological considerations, attitudes of a particular professional discipline, corporate political agendas, or personality feuds, and so on—*and neither element
that is brought into play to contribute to the final decision may have anything whatsoever to do with the real decision required of the meeting.*

That is why many aggressive entrepreneurs have little or no patience with
decisions made by a committee. They know that democratic consensus may be
entirely self-defeating and that the real prime mover may be prevented from
advancing the real interests of the business, through compromise or a misdirection brought about by a consensus of largely irrelevant personal opinions.

Consensus is common in Canada where the private sector has been infil-
trated by the public sector. The opposite is true of management in the United
States which is geared more to aggressive marketing. The following report,
which resulted from a survey of 15,000 managers from all over the world,
could also apply to Australia's management style.

American managers are by far the strongest individualists in our national samples.
This means that they regard the individual as the basic unit and building block of
the enterprise and the origin of all its success. They are also more inner-directed,
i.e., they locate the source of the organization's purpose and direction in the inner
conviction of its employees. No culture is as dedicated to making each individual's
dream come true. Americans believe you should "make up your own mind" and

"do your own thing" rather than allow yourself to be influenced too much by other people and the external flow of events. Taken together, these are the prime attributes of entrepreneurship: the self-determined individual tenaciously pursuing a personal dream.[2]

The short-term approach of the West excludes so many possibilities from consideration, by limiting the choices from which we prioritize, that our judgements are often flawed. We make hasty, uninformed decisions out of a narrow view of circumstances. And as if that were not limiting enough, irrational thoughts impinge on our decision-making process. Or—if we head up an enterprise or department that we like to perceive as being democratic, and make consensus our goal—we may divert the entire organization from its objectives by attempting to strike a compromise out of all the clutter of uninformed and unscreened inputs from a team of people who have not considered the full implications of their contributions.

Surely we cannot favorably compare our style of muddling through to the broader and deeper vision consistently under scrutiny by Japanese business leaders, which provides a richer choice of possibilities in readiness for the creative thinking process?

Of course, the human factor, with all its flaws, often plays a disruptive role, as well as a creative one, there as well as here. But whenever they realize that a false attitude is leading them in the wrong direction, they are adept at performing an immediate about-face.

Intelligent and rational executives would like to believe that a reasonable thinking process characterizes the management of all business organizations, but that isn't so. The creative or intuitive process, which some call "gut-feel," appears to possess two sides—good and bad—like a coin that rotates. When we are illuminated by an idea, sometimes we light up one side, and sometimes the other: you win some, you lose some.

The Thinking Process

Professor George Terry draws our attention to five different types of thinking, which he categorized as creative, causative, inductive, deductive, and problem solving[3]:

Creative thinking "deals with deeply impressing a problem upon one's mind, clearly visualizing it, contemplating it, all towards the formulation of an idea or concept along new and different lines." *Causative thinking* "emphasizes the shaping of future events and achievements instead of waiting for destiny to decide them." *Inductive thinking* "is reasoning based on building up to a general principle or conclusion from various particulars." *Deductive thinking* involves breaking down the whole into separate elements and analyzing them. *Problem-solving thinking* "is a judicial type of thinking... concerned with securing facts about a situation, ascertaining the problem, analyzing and evaluating the facts logically to determine meaningful relationships among them, and finally evolving the solution to the problem."

Despite the very real value of intuitive thinking, it is often that and emotional arguments that present management with problems of misunderstanding or conflict. Terry describes the creative process by explaining how "the generation of ideas normally follows a process which is made up of closely related, yet distinct, steps": (1) develop favorable attitudes toward ideation; (2) exhibit problem sensitivity; (3) prepare for creativity by acquiring needed raw material; (4) apply idea fluency; (5) allow incubation of unconscious brain action to take place; (6) permit illumination of new idea.

He makes the process sound much simpler than it is: those six steps toward illumination involve actuating something abstract, although each may appear, with analysis, to be a logical step up the ladder of creativity. He defines step 4: "Idea fluency means an ability to pile up a quantity of ideas about a given problem. The value of this is that the more ideas available, the greater the chance of disclosing a usable one."

But where do ideas come from? According to Koestler, "All reasoning, even of a trivial order, is steeped in unconscious process.... When a situation is blocked, straight thinking must be superseded by 'thinking aside'—the search for a new, auxiliary matrix which will unblock it, without having ever before been called to perform such a task." In his *Act of Creation* Koestler quotes at length from a lecture by Henri Poincaré at the *Société de Psychologie* in Paris, on one of his best-known mathematical discoveries; the theory of the "Fuchsian functions."

Poincaré described how he had tried for fifteen days to prove the uniqueness of what he would later call Fuchsian functions. He would sit at his work table trying out numerous mathematical combinations for hours without any results. Only when he could not sleep one night after having drunk too much coffee, did ideas rise in crowds. Some collided until pairs interlocked and made stable combinations. By morning he had established the existence of a class of Fuchsian functions: all he had to do was write out the results.

An excursion out of town made him forget his mathematical work. But on entering a bus, in the course of conversation with a friend, he was suddenly illuminated to realize that the way he had defined the Fuchsian functions was identical with non-Euclidean geometry: he was therefore presented with a formula to advance his work. Nevertheless he carried on his conversation as if nothing significant had occurred. When, on his return, he began to study other equations, he was unsuccessful and felt disgusted with his failure.

He became involved with other things on a trip to the seaside for a few days. But he was suddenly illuminated again one morning, with brevity and certainty so that when he returned home to meditate on the results, he was able to deduce the consequences; that there were other Fuchsian groups. He applied the theory he had deduced to his calculations, and all but one of them worked. That one was crucial, because if it failed, so would all the others. But his conscious work on it was to no avail.

Again he left home, this time to be fully occupied with military service. Then, walking down the street one day, he was suddenly stopped by the solution to his mathematical difficulty: it "suddenly appeared" to him. Only after his military service was he free to resume his mathematical work. He found that he now possessed all the elements and had only to sit down and write out his final demonstration paper at a single stroke and without difficulty. He described his illumination as "a manifest sign of long, unconscious prior work."

Koestler also quoted another example, of André Marie Ampère, whose memoir demonstrated, among other things, that habitual gamblers are, in the long run, bound to lose. It gained him a professorship at the Lycée in Lyon.[4] Again it was a matter of sudden illumination after having abandoned a mathematical problem seven years previously because he could not solve it *directly*. Instead, it came to him by chance and he knew instantly that it was correct.

Poincaré described the process: "Among chosen combinations the most fertile will often be those formed of elements drawn from domains which are far apart.... Most combinations so formed would be entirely sterile; but certain among them, very rare, are the most fruitful of all."

What he described was an unconscious or intuitive process that marketing managers or creative advertising people call gut-feel. But they are usually well-read, with broad interests, compulsive absorbers of a variety of facts and theories, out of which they can unconsciously *think aside* to discover innovative approaches to exploit opportunities and solve problems. They are knowledge workers and ideas people, and often not managers.

This intuitive approach, gut-feel, or process of thinking aside is clearly quite different from the sequential thinking of, for example, an accountant. Instead of an accountant's logical step-by-step auditing approach that continues in one reasonable line, it resembles more a vacuum cleaner sucking in data and ideas from many sources, then making meaningful and appropriate patterns from what was apparently unconnected information, to discover a pattern that will solve the problems under discussion. Bureaucratic thinking is different again, because of the restrictive and often illogical codes which control its activities. It tends to move in spirals around a problem, like an inquisitive dog circling a screwed up ball of newspaper in the street, half afraid of what it might find inside if it is unravelled. The thinking process of a sales person differs too. Although it appears to be linear, as with an auditor, unlike him it is flexible and targeted to the ultimate sale ahead of time. A creative sales person uses that flexibility continually to think aside, as Koestler described it, whereas an accountant cannot progress further than her next calculation, to which she must respond before she is free to progress to the next one, trapped in the logic of numbers. "For the artist with his organic, vivisectional (or living section) point of view of man and society, the natural enemy is the bureaucrat, the man with the tidy desk, the big file, the orderly mind devoid of simultaneous modes of awareness or observation."[5]

Just as confrontational is the unimaginative and old-fashioned accountant with a mind equally insensitive to creative thinking or simultaneous concepts and time channels, whose sole skill in any circumstances is to sharpen his pencil. New research by the Institute of Practitioners in Advertising describes what seems to be a continual struggle between marketing practitioners and financial directors to win each other's confidence and the favourable attention of the board. The survey, conducted with KPMG consultants, reveals that marketing and advertising come a poor second or third to other disciplines, in the eyes of financial directors. Although 58 percent believe that marketing and advertising is a long term investment, they consider training, IT, human resources and R& D to be somewhat more important (70 percent). A quarter said that marketing should be the first budget to be cut if the need arises, compared to less than 10 percent who would give the same treatment to R&D or IT. [6]

Either marketing and advertising practitioners failed to communicate their disciplines or accountants were not listening. The separation of "marketing" from R&D, training, human resources, and other marketing spheres of influence, is suspect—just as the linkage of marketing with advertising seems suspiciously like old-fashioned thinking. The old-fashioned accountant seems to picture himself as benefiting rather by jockeying for power in the top management stakes and keeping well away from marketing, which he does not fully understand. Fortunately, there are others that do.

But, regardless of integrity or power politics, remarks by marketing consultants working in the same auditing firms as accountants emphasize the very real problems of quite different mindsets in those suited to each individual discipline. There are forward-looking creators who are customer oriented, and there are the counters and budget-cutters who choose to imprison themselves in historic numbers on computerized spreadsheets.

It is the diversity of types of thinking and attitudes, and the different values which attach to them, of each manager in a team, which obliges leadership to be a complex and subtle skill. Obtaining two-way communications between manager and CEO and manager to manager, requires an empathetic personality dedicated to ferreting out the best ideas and the best solutions. It requires a consultative approach, and also an understanding that diversity is highly desirable to provide a rich assortment of elements for the creative process to be fed with an abundance of opportunities.

But because of the quite different thinking process and attitude of each manager, each is naturally suspicious of the other's foreign way of thinking. That uneasiness can create a level of intolerance between managers and also between their departments. Each manager must therefore be able to handle the intolerance of the other. A perceptive CEO would recognize the impatience of a sales person to the rigid production orientation of a factory manager; an assembly-line manager may smile at what he thinks of as the impulsiveness or the untidy mind of a sales manager; a marketing manager may frequently have to control any impatience at the plodding systems orientation of an administrative manager. But to be judgmental according to one's own particular attitude is to miss the whole point, which is that those differences of temperament are not wrongful but essential for the different types of responsibilities involved. That is why a business enterprise must be constantly alerted to placing the interests and needs of a customer first. Only then is it possible for each type of thinking process and attitude to converge at the same point, which is customer satisfaction.

Another type of response to challenges is an emotional one. It has been called *thinking through the blood*, but it is not thinking at all: the excessive pumping of the blood when anger or other emotions well up inhibits thinking. It is impulsive and irrational behavior brought about by people bringing subjective attitudes, biased opinions, personal prejudices, superstitions, or other immature judgements to bear on subjects requiring calm and reasonable objectivity. It is a symptom of the child ego that is centered entirely on self and stubbornly wants its own way to prevail.

Koestler described how emotions trigger chemical and biological actions on the whole body, unlike the process of thinking, which is confined to the roof of the brain. "The chemical and visceral states induced by the action of the sympathico-adrenal system tend to persist; once this massive apparatus is set in motion it cannot be called off or 'change its direction' at a moment's notice. Common observation provides daily, painful confirmation of this. We are literally 'poisoned' by our adrenal humours; reason has little power over irritability or anxiety; it takes time to talk a person out of a mood, however valid the argument; passion is blind to better judgement; anger and fear show physical after-effects long after their causes have been removed. If we could change our moods as quickly as we jump from one thought to another we would be acrobats of emotion."

An example of this is the self-defeating strike, or threat of one. Most such threats in the West, nowadays, are a last desperate attempt to put back the clock when the past has already gone for good. A company's demise is generally accelerated by the refusal of employees or their trade unions to come to terms with change. Meanwhile, we marvel at their determination to put themselves out of work to spite their employers rather than try to keep their jobs. Frequently the public's perception is that those strikers have long been overpaid, particularly when they are public servants paid out of taxes. If that is so, it seems to determine their irrational refusal to let go of all the benefits they enjoyed when times were prosperous instead of being willing to reduce future expectations when times are hard. Mature and reasonable people know that hard times require sacrifices, that business enterprises or institutions have to be lean and cost-effective to survive. But human beings prefer to believe what they want and see only what they wish to see. The spoiled child within us all clutches desperately at fallacies, fancies, and notions, rather than giving way to change or compromising with it. It is not in the nature of a child to practice grace under pressure.

Therein lies the stumbling block to progress, which is the human factor. And executives are always being drawn into an emotional arena. That is one of the reasons why a CEO often invites an independent management consultant to find a reasonable and objective but creative solution to special company problems, rather than being misled by a *false reality*.

15

Hiring the Best Brains

The Swinging Sixties were a time of considerable change that took the unchanged establishment by surprise. McLuhan saw through all the hype and predicted what would follow: "The medium, or process, of our time—electric technology—is reshaping and restructuring patterns of social interdependence and every aspect of our personal life. It is forcing us to reconsider and re-evaluate practically every thought, every action, and every institution formerly taken for granted. Everything is changing—you, your family, your neighborhood, your education, your job, your government, your relation to 'the others.' And they're changing dramatically."

A generation has passed since then and we are now confronted with the awesome reality that "The major advances in civilization are processes that all but wreck the societies in which they occur." A. N. Whitehead wrote that. McLuhan was well aware of it, because he quoted Whitehead.[1]

Despite the ring of truth that astute critics heard when they read those words over thirty years ago, and the evidence of change staring at us from every side, the hiring of managers and staff proceeds in much the same way as before. Three examples of haphazard recruitment and their results should suffice, from the first half of the 1990s. The first and last items are from the first quarter of 1993.

Item 1: "The man the Ottawa Congress Centre plans to hire as general manager was fired by the Winnipeg Convention Centre two weeks ago amid allegations he persuaded employees to falsify expense accounts," ran the front page of the *Ottawa Citizen* on 30 January. The vice-chairman of the Congress Centre was quoted as saying, "Our executive search team assured us that he has the highest qualifications. He stood head and shoulders above the other candidates." He also said that the board was unconcerned about the Winnipeg event. The newspaper reported that the top candidate chosen from 154 applications for the $100,000-plus job, "quit as general manager of the Centre in the Square—a performing arts centre in Kitchener, Ont.—several months after news broke that he took unauthorized loans of about $3,000 for private purposes. These included two personal vacations, a golf trip to Myrtle Beach, S.C., and a family Christmas visit to Regina."

"Earlier, he had angered staff with such cost-cutting measures as turning down the heat, removing light fixtures and reducing the number of flushes in washroom urinals."

On 7 February it was reported that the board of directors for the Ottawa Congress Centre decided after all, not to hire the general manager they had appointed on 11 January. It was said that the provincially owned Congress Centre had previously agreed to pay a "golden handshake" of $237,000 to the *previous* general manager, who had agreed to step down on 31 March in exchange for two years of his base salary of $116,000 a year. As a consequence, the Crown Corporation could wind up paying three managers at once. Besides the incumbent and his eventual replacement, the Centre may have to pay to sever the three-year contract of the general manager they decided not to hire.

By 3 April, the NDP head of the Congress Centre's twelve-member board had been fired by the NDP party. He was replaced by a sixty-nine-year-old woman—a well-esteemed Conservative who possessed all the experience required in the first place, as former head of the National Capital Commission.

Meanwhile, the Centre is expected to lose $500,000 in 1993 and is a prime example of the muddle and waste of money resulting from haphazard management selection.

Item 2: The prison psychologist couldn't be fired from the Edmonton Institution, although his work had to be investigated after two inmates he had recommended for early release committed killings in Edmonton. The report by two Calgary psychologists who were hired by the Correctional Service of Canada to assess his work concluded he lacked even the most basic skills and did not follow ethical standards. The government established that he was incompetent and the Warden recommended that he be dismissed. But the chairman of the Appeal Board with the Public Service Commission of Canada ruled that he can't be fired because he was not warned his incompetence might cost him his job (source: *The Edmonton Journal*).

Item 3: President Bill Clinton was responsible for selecting the best top management team for his new cabinet. When he came to the important position of Attorney General—who must be seen to be beyond reproach—he was caught up in a similar muddle through haphazard recruitment. He decided to limit his choice to a woman. And his first choice was a woman who was obliged to withdraw her nomination because the glare of media spotlights revealed that she had been harboring two illegal immigrants. Furthermore, she had illegally hired them for less than the minimum wage for a chauffeur and a nanny.

What caused the public outcry that resulted in her withdrawal was that both she and the president's advisers appeared to think it was okay for an Attorney General to break laws that other U.S. citizens are obliged to obey.

Former President Bush lost the election to Clinton because he did not hear the voice of the American people. Clinton heard it but did not listen carefully enough to what the polls said—that government was out of touch with the wishes of the electorate.

Democrats breathed sighs of relief when Clinton got lucky with his third choice. Meanwhile, a government invasion of the Davidian cult's base in Waco, Texas, got out of hand before the new Attorney General could rein in the government agencies and avoid the ensuing slaughter. The public was left with a perception of politicians muddling through. And whenever another foul-up occurred, the media drew attention to the youth and inexperience of the White House staff.

Body Shops

Just as it is the right people who provide imagination, spirited energy, and activities that create profitable growth for a business enterprise, it is the wrong people who demoralize and destroy it from within.

The entire area in which management of subordinates is centered is fraught with numberless problems, because of its links with recruiting. That is the sphere of human resources. It is a territory in which the blind lead the blind.

Personnel are sourced either by a company's personnel administrator or by one of the operational managers, or through the services of an outside company that specializes in recruitment. The latter range from what are commonly known as *body shops,* to management recruitment consultants—who like to describe themselves as management consultants. Their ranks include companies that specialize in finding engineers, accountants, or sales and marketing people; but most of them are generalists. They work on commission. That is their main weakness from which others stem.

The first decision that a company must make in sourcing new or replacement staff is who will do it—not who is best suited to perform that function most effectively. Like so many activities in a business enterprise, it is often a question of who has the time to perform what is an onerous function that no one else wants to do. That attitude frequently pervades the entire process of recruitment, induction, supervision, training, and motivation in so many organizations and institutions. But not all the blame for mediocrity in management can be attributed to pressures of work or lack of time. The public service rarely suffers from overwork and generally has ample time, yet it too suffers from appointing too many wrong people, and from failure to train or motivate them effectively.

Those who are in the best position to perform those tasks in the private sector are busy managing the business. Although they know perfectly well that successful business enterprises are created and managed by people, they feel they cannot suspend management of their own operations while a search is undertaken for a number of prospective candidates who then have to be interviewed, some several times, before the best judgement can be made.

Moreover, most managers do not relish making that final judgement in case they are proved to have been wrong. Their judgements may become suspect thereafter as a consequence. In order to avoid that, they sometimes interview jointly and share the risks. In that case, a final decision gets made by two inexperienced executives instead of one.

If mediocre or inferior staff are hired, the company too will soon become mediocre or inferior. The best companies are those that have taken great care in the realm of human resources. They know the damage that second-rate executives can do, and they know that the result of a brain drain can be failure. They therefore do everything they can to attract and keep the best personnel. But then, successful companies enjoy an incomparable advantage over others in that—by their very reputation—they will attract the best candidates.

In post-war Britain there was little incentive to improve the quality of management or the quality of work because—among other disincentives—of supertax and the shrinking quality of life of the middle classes. The resultant brain drain from Britain was an asset to the United States economy. At the same time, gifted British entrepreneurs departed for tax havens overseas. Each economic recession in the UK drove skilled workers, top managers, and ambitious professionals to the U.S., Canada, Australia, and South Africa. That was one reason why the South African economy boomed in the 1960s.

In Canada the trend has always been for many of the best brains to move down south into the United States. When Canadian commerce and industry was initiated by the merchant adventurers of the Hudson Bay Company about three hundred years ago, they were supported by the British government and aided by the North-West Mounted Police—later to became the Royal Canadian Mounties—who established law and order and created stability. There was little room for other adventurers between them. Many left for America where there was plenty of scope for initiative, innovation, courage, and hard work. A great many Canadians with those qualities have been going down south ever since.

Japan, on the other hand, did not benefit from floods of immigrants. Its policy has always been to take care of its own people. With its innate ability to adapt to change and make irresistible leaps forward, it developed its own excellent companies, trained its own workers in skills, and its own executives in management, and nurtured them. The Japanese do not waste their resources like so many other countries which are concerned solely with short-term benefits. They have a long-term vision that is also holistic in its scope. And they know precisely how to obtain the utmost value out of all their resources, but in particular their human ones whose skills they continually hone.

There can be little doubt that one of the ways they manage to develop their personnel is by providing lifetime employment. In return they benefit from the loyalty and hard work of their staff. Instead of the workplace being an adversarial arena or somewhere from which to escape at the end of each day— as in most western countries—Japanese companies are an integral part of the life of their managers and workers, and of their families, too. That results from their company cultures. Few European or North American business organizations have purposely set out to plan an ideal working environment and company culture into which to induct the best available personnel, and with which to motivate them, like the Japanese have done.

A comparison was clearly evident in 1992. Britain was undergoing one of its worst economic recessions ever, with widespread unemployment. The United States and Canada suffered a similar trauma with personal and corporate bankruptcies running into over 7,000 in some months. Canada's personal bankruptcies mounted to over 62,000 and its corporate failures to over 14,000 in that year alone. U.S. unemployment amounted to 7.4 percent of the workforce while Canada's was 11.4 percent. The continent of Europe was suffering from a cataclysm resulting from the collapse of the unrealistic economic ideology of Marxist Socialism. Its totalitarian regimes had protected management mediocrity and industrial and commercial incompetence for generations. The only country functioning economically on the continent of Africa was the Republic of South Africa, and it too was in recession. Japan, on the other hand, enjoyed a situation that had always been considered to be impossible—that of full employment. They were the wonder of the world.

Notwithstanding the post-war miracles of Japanese industry, the continuation of the global economic recession and the continuation of United Nations sanctions against South Africa eventually eroded Japanese export markets. The domino principle ultimately worked to the detriment of Japan too. Even so, Japan showed a record trade surplus of $107.06 billion in 1992, while Canada, Britain and the U.S. each showed huge national deficits.

Recruiting

Wrote Drucker of personnel management, "Some wit said maliciously that it puts together all those things that do not deal with the work of people and that are not managed."

To judge from what else he wrote about it, that wit was probably Drucker himself. In 1955 he described it as "partly a file clerk's job, partly a housekeeping job, partly a social worker's job and partly fire-fighting to head off union trouble or to settle it. The things the personnel administrator is typically responsible for—safety and pension plans, the suggestion systems, the employment office and union grievances—are necessary chores. I doubt, though, that they should be put together in one department; for they are a hodgepodge, as one look at the organization chart of the typical personnel department, or at the table of contents of the typical text-book on personnel management will show."

This is a much neglected sphere that management needs to take a cold hard look at. Meanwhile, in each and every case where a member of the staff has to be replaced, or whenever a new position is created, management has to decide who will do what to recruit and induct a new individual. Whether a separate personnel manager is employed to perform the fundamental tasks appears to depend on the number of employees in the company, the type of industry, annual percentage of staff turnover, and the life cycle of the company. It might be undergoing growth or have peaked, or be in decline, or in a state of crisis. It will also depend on whether the company is an ideal or an awful one, and the primary objective of its personnel department. Is it to hire the highest calibre of staff, the cheapest people, or merely to administer layoffs?

Many personnel managers have difficulty in defining their functions or describing how they fill their time. That may partly explain why the responsibility is frequently given to the most junior member of the staff who has the least experience in dealing with personnel. One management trainee in a large company in England explained that the function was part of his training: management trainees *took a turn at it* for one year before moving on to another department. A student performed that function in a retail store chain in Canada, and was replaced by another student when she returned to the university. A similar functionary in a Top Ten Company in South Africa juggled continually with a variety of printed forms, files, reports, and dockets. Some dealt with the complexity of such problems as the make of company car that each executive was entitled to, or the hotels where they were allowed to stay on vacations—providing a more senior manager was not staying there. "Well, someone has to do it!" he said, defensively.

The extent of staff turnover in some companies is remarkable—quite apart from those industries where high turnover is typical, like advertising agencies, direct sales companies, real estate, movies, and the theater. Massive staff downsizings were a commonplace of the recessions of the 1980s and 1990s, but considerable replacement of personnel was customary in badly managed companies even before then. Reasons ranged from inept hiring, failure to provide proper job descriptions, a gap in the process of induction and training, poor communications, lack of understanding of the job and its objectives by management, inferior management style, failure in leadership, disorganization, absence of a clear company mission or vision. Then there are mergers, takeovers, and business failures. And in each case, someone is required just to complete the paperwork involved in hiring and firing.

It should go without saying that the cost of continual bad management far outweighs the cost of doing the job of hiring in the right way in the first place. But however good its operational managers may be, a major policy change at head office can initiate a series of traumas that may result in the loss of hundreds, or even thousands, of jobs. In such an event the personnel manager has to be retained just to clear up the mess of paperwork, then restructure whatever remains of the company with more suitable people.

But having disposed of MUSH jobs, and others that are considered to be no longer required, how do they define who is "more suitable"?

Whichever of several ways of hiring is finally undertaken, an operational manager has to be involved, because it is she or he who will have to work with the new recruit, and not the personnel manager or administrative clerk. Since, in most cases, there is no separate personnel manager, the operational manager is likely to be the one to hire her own staff. The advantages are that she will know the functions and aims of the job best, and the type of individual best able to fulfil them. The disadvantages are that she would be unlikely to choose someone good enough to be perceived as a possible threat to her own job. But, from a company's point of view, that would be the ideal replacement if she should fall sick or leave. Another disadvantage is that she may not have the time to do justice to the recruiting process because of the pressure of her own work.

On the other hand, a personnel manager would be likely to be more objective and also have ample time to undertake a thorough job of selecting the right candidate. But a personnel manager is unlikely to know and understand fully the implications of the whole range of responsibilities and functions in a medium-size or bigger company. Consequently, she would be obliged to work closely with the operational manager anyway. In so doing, she might lose the advantage of objectivity.

Since outsourcing of services as well as components began to be the norm in the latter half of the 1990s, more staff selection may go to outside recruiters who are known colloquially as "body shops." They recruit fast because they work on commission and depend on fast turnover. Their advertising costs are generally low, through using classified columns. Sometimes they provide a six months guarantee to replace without additional charge if the employer is unsatisfied. But their staff is often young and inexperienced, and would be likely to require close monitoring by a personnel manager who would insist on perseverance and the best quality of employee available at the time.

Established management recruitment consultants are likely to possess more experience and have a more mature or sophisticated approach to selecting top managers. Some are adept at psychological testing of a short list of candidates. They are therefore more likely to match the candidate to the job profile. But consultants work on commission and therefore may not persevere long enough to locate the most suitable person, since their time must be made cost-effective.

The "head hunter" generally works differently. He makes a point of knowing which managers are the most successful in their particular industry category. He makes direct contact with individuals whom he often knows personally, who are employed by a competitor. His objective is to seduce a successful executive on his client's behalf. To do so, there must be sufficient inducement to leave a good job for the risk of landing in one which might not be quite as good. That may mean a higher salary, more perks, or—more likely—stock participation. Sometimes the head hunter may recommend someone who is held back from his career aspirations but is ready to move up. The head hunter may also offer his client a guarantee that he will never steal his client's staff, providing he has exclusivity to search for all his client's new personnel.

Author John Tarrant described Drucker in a typical situation with a client in 1976: "Smith goes on to talk about a job he is trying to fill.... 'The way we have worked out the job description, it doesn't seem to be too demanding. But the last guy we had in there fell apart completely after six months...How can I find the person I need?'

"Drucker says, 'if you go on looking for someone to fit a job, it may take you forever.... In interviewing a lot of people you are giving yourself a wonderful opportunity to look for strengths. But you are wasting the opportunity by blinding yourself to the strengths of the applicants and simply running a comparison test, seeing if any of them fit into the outlines of the job. Don't think of yourself as 'having a job to fill.' You need some strengths in the organization. Look for strength.'"[2]

A personnel administrator would be unlikely even to consider offering such useful advice—particularly if he or she were too young and inexperienced to have earned the respect of the CEO. The title of Human Resources Manager would change nothing. That would apply also to a young eager beaver from a body shop, struggling to earn commission through fast turnover.

An older and more experienced recruitment consultant would think very carefully before recommending someone against a client's desired profile. He too works on commission and owes loyalty to his employer for sourcing someone who matches that profile, as quickly as possible, so that his company can bill the client and he can get on with his next assignment. In terms of ethics, he would be fulfilling his client's request.

A head hunter works somewhat differently, since his or her function is to seduce an employee from an existing job and into a client's company. Fast turnover is the key to head hunting, too. But success in the game depends on initiative and resourcefulness in motivating both employer and employee. It is he who is more likely to say, "I've got the person you need, although she's not what you asked for. She's better. When can I arrange to send her over?"

The bigger the responsibility of the position that has to be filled, the greater the pressure to find someone suitable who would be likely to remain. An operational manager would feel obliged to become deeply involved for a bigger managerial position. And he would want a high level of performance from someone he might have to rely on in future. In that case he would be wise to minimize the risks by sharing the responsibility with the managing director.

Perhaps the most illogical bias of all irrational hiring customs in the West, where the population is aging, is discrimination against age.

The main reason for this cultural trap in which the West has caught itself is that western European countries and their former colonies were once young and virile. Despite statistical information that shows they are aging—and so is their culture and their industries—they still picture themselves as they were when young. Reality is now beginning to confront them with the replacement of western populations by Eastern immigrants and those from south of the Mediterranean basin. The main reason for this is the higher birth rate in Third World economies, while the West's declines. Meanwhile, older employees are being shown the door because of their age, to be replaced largely by ethnocultural immigrants or inexperienced juniors. Experience is always preferable.

Some American employers have addressed the problem of the aging population and evidence that improved health care is slowing down the aging process. When McDonald's Restaurants started hiring older people they discovered that they work harder because they grew up in an era when work ethic was still admired. And they more easily empathize with aging customers and very small children. Sir Simon Marks discovered that older people are generally more responsible and dedicated to their employers and to customer service, when he began hiring them as part-time employees in Marks & Spencer in Britain.

A Canadian client who employed thirty-four sales people in his retail chain stores found that the older ones were more productive. His best were over the age of sixty-five. As some retired, he tried out younger salespeople, but found them to be less effective and did not therefore inspire customer confidence.

Despite the reality, South African recruiters rarely specify anyone over the age of forty in their advertisements, and when they use the word "mature" they usually mean around thirty. Often it is merely a justification for not paying enough for the job. But many retired people with energy, drive, and dedication would work for less to rejoin the workforce. Indeed, the reality of present-day economies is that many are driven to carry on working in order to maintain their standard of living. But another problem is that managers prefer not to hire anyone with more experience than themselves, who may show them up as being less than mediocre. The result is the management vortex, as elsewhere.

But it is competition from colleagues as well as from other companies that keeps managers alert and forces self-improvement on them. Managers who cannot be honest enough to hire better people because they are riddled with misgivings about their own capabilities should not be allowed to recruit. It should be given to someone more senior. Then inferior managers would be obliged to improve or be jettisoned.

In Japan, where they diligently make the best use of all resources—whether material, financial, or human—it seems that top managers only begin to mature at age sixty-five. They are often accorded special advisory roles after seventy, unless they are too busy running a company at the age of eighty-four. According to Drucker, selecting, hiring, and developing managers in Japan was the job of the *Chief Banto,* who would spend a great deal of time getting to know every manager in order to develop him. Although a top *honcho,* in Japanese terms his title was *chief clerk.* A company invested time, training, and resources in its managers. Some would be graded as *top manager* at age forty-five. The best could remain until their eighties, if they wished. The best do not leave to join other companies. The worst are not upgraded and they retire at age fifty-five. Pay is tied to length of service. Training is continuous throughout the length of employment. It is holistic in that it covers all responsibilities and functions in a company, although there is a dividing line between management responsibilities as opposed to worker responsibilities.

The outstanding success of the Japanese in industry and commerce should be evidence enough that they are doing something right and the West is doing it wrong in the sphere of human resources. What is remarkable about Japanese companies is not only their maximization of resource usage and their adaptability to changes, but the fact that they do not even consider settling for second best; nor should the West. Whether or not they have the excuse of the brain drain, high labor costs, over-taxation, or a bias against the work ethic or élitism, nobody cares in the final analysis. In the struggle to survive, history makes it abundantly clear that those countries which do not set high enough standards and maintain the discipline and resolution to sustain them, disappear from its pages.

It should be clear by now that management cannot recruit, train, or develop subordinates without having hired the right top managers in the first place. Sourcing and hiring the right people is even more important than sourcing and purchasing components for a company's products or spare parts for its capital equipment. As Drucker wrote, "To depend on the personnel department to do management development is basically a misunderstanding. A marriage counsellor can help with a marriage, but it's your job." The same is true of recruitment.

Tarrant wrote, "More and more an upper-echelon executive holds himself aloof from what is going on beneath him. He figures that his responsibility lies in hiring somebody to do a job, telling him the 'bottom line' results that are expected, and then rewarding the subordinate if he delivers or firing him if he does not deliver."

But a recruitment process is far more complicated than that; and should be because the responsibility is far greater than that. And the cost in terms of people's time is formidable but rarely measured. That is why a company suffering from a high staff turnover can be likened to an old house suffering from woodworm and dry rot. The damage is gradual and goes unnoticed until the floorboards break through and reveal the extent of the damage to the structure, and one is confronted with the cost. Even after the recruit is hired there is a whole process of induction to go through and the filling in of employment and tax forms, and information on company procedures and benefits. Then there is groundwork to be laid in starting the new employee off on the right relationships with his or her colleagues and other staff. Most companies rush through the entire process as quickly as possible to "get it out of the way" so that the new staff member can get on with the job. In reality, it is so that the manager and everyone else can get on with their's. The manager never seems to find sufficient free time to undertake on-the-job training and will probably have neglected to prepare a training program. Before he can allocate enough time to do so, the personnel administrator is handing him more forms and requesting a performance review of the new member of the staff.

This gives him pause. It is at this stage that he wonders whether he made a mistaken judgement in the first place. But it's too late to withdraw without a lot of harm being done; including harm to his own reputation. The result is that another employee is thrown into the deep end to sink or swim—and even if they swim, there is every likelihood that another misfit has been added to the payroll.

In a company with the intelligence to practice Management by Objectives, such risks are minimized in direct proportion to the degree of efficiency with which it is undertaken, monitored, and managed. MBO involves meeting two of its own objectives; one to do with the preparation of a business or marketing plan, and the other involving the development of those people who use the plan and whose performance can be measured according to the ways in which the plan is being achieved.

A company's plan must include a strategy to be at all effective. And it would provide tactics to meet established objectives for which a new executive would be accountable. Each employee will have and know their own key results areas and the levels of targets or improvements that are expected. And if they are results oriented, they will achieve their work targets.

Meanwhile, their departmental manager would monitor them on a regular basis and help them to achieve their goals. The manager would also be required formally to review their performance in writing. If they and their work progress satisfactorily and they show potential for further development, they would be assisted toward that objective; so that when suitable openings occur which they might be able to fill, a career path would begin to open up for them within the organization.

A sophisticated business organization that wishes to grow by improving the calibre of its staff will set specific standards for improvement so that an employee's performance can more easily be measured. It would also provide in-house training programs or ones offered by outside seminars. They may include lectures, talks with participation, job training, discussions with free exchanges between employees and lecturers, practice enactments of roles on the job, case studies, projects with opportunities to show initiative and innovation, and the infamous in-tray test. That timed test, under the pressure of an industrial psychologist's stopwatch, simulates the chaos of managing a department or a factory with simultaneous problems that require an executive to prioritize and solve them before further damage can occur. In business games, teams are assigned roles and given information about a specific company, products, and markets. The objective is to lead and take decisions for a working group. Group dynamics are also practiced with a qualified supervisor, who can criticize behavior and provide inputs to improve it.

No doubt all ideal companies offer in-house training as part of their MBO or some other methodology. Many use outside facilities provided by industry associations and even suppliers. Medium-size enterprises also need those types of facilities but are often unaware that they do if they are not sophisticated marketing-oriented companies.

The 1947 Urwick Report on management education noted the serious lack of men and women in Great Britain who were competent to train managers. Lack of proper training caused major problems in implementing business strategies. The top six problems were: took more time than expected; inadequate coordination in implementing activities; unexpected major problem surfaced; management attention distracted; inadequate capabilities of personnel; and inadequate training of lower-level employees.[3]

Another report in 1987 showed that more than one-third of British managers had no management training since starting work.[4] A study by Professor Alan Mumford at the International Management centre found that "most directors...have learned through a mixture of relatively accidental and unstructured experience." It also concluded that formal management development processes did not provide the continuous education necessary for senior level jobs. And Bryan Nicholson (chairman of the Manpower Services Commission) considered that Britain's boardrooms were "blighted by amateurs because no one had prepared them for it."

It seems that no sooner had the better and larger companies begun to learn the error of their ways than competition from overseas obliged them to do something about it. The demand for management courses was so great by 1987 that INSEAD (the business school in France) took more MBA students from Britain than from any other country. INSEAD received 2,000 applications for only 300 places. Perhaps that was because its electives include Analytic Marketing, Strategic Implementation, Buyer/Consumer Behavior, and Market and Competitive Analysis, that many other European business schools do not offer. Copenhagen, too, differs from most in offering Market Modelling, Business-to-Business Marketing, and International Marketing Consulting. Most probably their reputations rest on an orientation to marketing principles rather than to old-fashioned business administration.

Perhaps the strangest phenomenon is those candidates straight out of business school and with no experience of the workplace, who believe that after graduating they possess the capabilities to manage GM, GE, P&G, or Sears, when, in fact, all they possess is a "Starter Kit." Perhaps they should consider what happened when former British ambassador Lord Franks headed a commission to Washington to compare the somewhat jaded management in the UK with energetic American business management. He could not help but notice an abundance of business schools at a time when Britain possessed none. The solution seemed obvious: if Britain were to open up institutions like Harvard's School of Business, British management must inevitably improve. It seems he failed to notice that burgeoning economies like Japan and Germany had no such schools, either. What they had instead was a combative culture with role models still intact from their feudal systems; with duties, obligations, and commitments to family, employers, and country.[5]

The Learning Process

Where does learning begin and what form does it take? The type of learning we need to know about starts in the home by emulation. Then we learn "all about" a specific subject, like management, in a classroom. We learn "how to do it" in the workplace.

There is a continually changing perception of what being an educated person means. It is undergoing reassessment at the present time because our society finds itself embarking on an unsettled and insecure road into a new century, by way of a knowledge revolution. New technologies are not only the vehicles for the journey into the future, but they require specialized knowledge to drive them there.

It has long been debated whether education is simply a matter of absorbing a body of specialized knowledge essential to earning one's livelihood, or whether it should be something more than attending a polytechnic. What education is, what it should achieve, and who is capable of providing it are questions that travel round and round the universities, community colleges, and business and technical schools with regularity. The modern purpose of education became clear during the Enlightenment in France—it was to overcome ignorance by acquiring rational and scientific knowledge to sweep aside the cobwebs of "superstition, prejudice, intuition, habit and custom."[6] As John Stuart Mill wrote, "The despotism of custom is everywhere the standing hindrance to human advancement." Why? Because it is antagonistic to anything better. Bertrand Russell even asserted that if people are properly educated—as long as they live in a democratic society—they will understand that their true interests are peace, freedom, justice, and cooperation. He considered that people are beset by evils of a physical nature, of character, and of power. In his opinion, the main methods to combat those evils are science, education, and the political and economic reform of society—by which he meant, by socialism.

Russell often tended to view life from the straightjacket of his political ideology, instead of defining his political views in accordance with real life.

As a scholar, he should have known that the expulsion of ignorance by knowledge is not enough to deal with a lack of moral or ethical scruples, irresponsibility, or mischief making. He would have read Cicero, who knew that "knowledge and virtue are not identical."

What then is education? Is it really "nothing more than a kind of forensic laboratory where the embalmed corpses of geniuses are slid out of their drawers for periodic examination by students"?[7]

Education should certainly not be confused with knowledge if it is classroom education as opposed to on-the-job training. An accumulation of knowledge can be achieved only by and through actual experience. And if the aim is to acquire wisdom, then it can only emerge from knowledge, as opposed to data. In this electronic information age it is necessary to repeat that data do not necessarily equal knowledge. Data, like statistics, often tend to be passed off as information while still requiring someone with experience and knowledge to convert them into useful and relevant information. That may be done by opening them up to discussion or argument with others who possess experience and knowledge of the subject, and comparing outcomes with their personal opinions. Even though their opinions may be subjective or based on false or unproven theories rather than actual experience, results can be examined critically from the point of view of personal experience and valuable knowledge acquired from that experience. But since knowledge and knower are not something static that we search for, but are constantly changing or accumulating, we must continually pursue it. Marx called the process "dialectical," as if it were an endless argument.

Psychologist William James was an empiricist who believed that "pure experience" is "the only one primal stuff or material" of which everything in the world is composed. Depending on its context, a given and undivided portion of experience can be both a knower and something known. He maintained that pure experience "is the immediate flux of life which furnishes the material to our later reflection."

The type of education that the privileged once enjoyed was a grounding in history and the classics, which also embraced the arts. But the development of science and industry that arose out of the Industrial Revolution was to change all that. When the two protagonists thought to embody education or culture confronted each other, it was the technocrats who won the battle, and classical scholars became an endangered species.

But the goal of post-secondary education in-between the two world wars was not necessarily graduation or even intellectual stimulation, but rather to effect socially desirable friendships between sons of old monied families and those of the new rich. Then the advance of socialism introduced working-class scholars into the academic fold. As for scholarship, after World War II—as Drucker wrote of the North American scene—the quickest way to earn a middle class income was to work for a manufacturer rather than attend college.[8] As in Britain, it was advisable to conceal an academic qualification if one wished to make a success of a business career. Neither trade not industry would consider an academic to be of any use in the workplace.

What we have, on one hand, is classroom theorists without real business experience. On the other hand, we have specialized business administrators who do not possess an all-round liberal arts education, as used to be taught to the privileged. Consequently, many managers are still only semi-literate. According to Peter Emberley at Ottawa's Carleton University, it is the humanities that teach students how to think for themselves and continue to educate themselves.[9] He claims that he is trying to save the joy of learning history, philosophy, literature and the arts, as a solid foundation for an all-round education. Certainly, workplace evidence demonstrates that is precisely what is missing as an impetus to personal maturity, holistic awareness of problems and opportunities, making wise decisions, and being able to manage work and lead people.

However, the state does not take the view that it is their responsibility to enrich people's lives or improve the ability of business managers to achieve. So it seems that an all-round education to develop character and individuality is still a luxury for the privileged. Unfortunately, where the education gap is at its widest is in the spheres of business and public service management, whose insularity, naivety and ineptitude almost destroyed our economies in the past two decades. Now it seems that both government and business wish to have streams of graduates produced on assemblyline principles like identical clothes pegs from out of a factory.

We should bear in mind that mass produced products have a very short life-span nowadays. That is the more pragmatic reason for not penny-pinching when it comes to educating the next generation. Setting a pattern for a joyless and empty life style in which technical education simply fits young people for routine jobs that may quickly become obsolete, is the type of bureaucratic thinking which was typical of totalitarian regimes in the 1930s.

For more literate, erudite, or cultivated individuals, the joy of learning is in possessing the self-confidence of *knowing*. That is to say (to paraphrase Walter Allen), *understanding the organic relationship between one person and another, between employee and workplace, management and society, industrial society and its past, and the impersonal past of our own and our competitors' cultural history—and in excelling by using the acquired knowledge with meaningful and joyful panache*

Before the days of organized education for the mass of the population, the privileged classes could afford private tutors, and the guilds taught apprentices their specialized skills and maintained the monopoly of certain trades through secrecy. The church maintained their monopoly of classical education for scholars by possessing a working knowledge of Greek, Latin, and Hebrew. Our business schools hoped to obtain a similar monopoly of top management and management consultancy careers through the acquisition of a much-coveted MBA degree. Perhaps if the big multinational manufacturers had continued to displace small family businesses, as they once looked like doing—and as large department stores and chain stores succeeded in doing in the retail trade—the MBA might have achieved that objective. But the trend reversed itself instead. Now, entrepreneurs who manage small businesses view MBAs in a very different light. Whereas inexperienced or inept executives could once conceal themselves among a growing number of bodies in administration, a business enterprise consisting of less than fifty employees leaves them exposed to scrutiny. Then they are evaluated daily according to their workplace achievements.

That is of no concern to graduates of business administration, since they aspire to bigger companies and higher salaries, which is precisely what a Harvard MBA apparently achieves.[10]

We have come full circle after two generations—theory is not enough. Practical knowledge gained by experience, which produces superior performance, and continual improvement, are required. Perhaps it is time for executives to serve apprenticeships on the factory floor, once again.

Rightly or wrongly, there is still a tendency to view universities as places of scholarship intended for academic careers and the professions, while community colleges and polytechnics limit themselves to teaching students what will be expected of them in the workplace. But—like political parties of the left and the right, which moved to the center to attract more votes from the electorate—learning institutions made similar compromises to meet the needs of their customers.

Ever since business schools were established in Britain there has been some concern that they may be inadequate to meet workplace needs. The Harvard MBA program achieved considerable prestige, but it appears that 71 percent of its graduates did not enter manufacturing industries, and that more than 80 percent are not in line functions and therefore do not manage. They entered staff positions, became management consultants or went into banking or property development.[11]

Business schools were created in the West to improve business management and therefore marketing skills, but there is no evidence that they have done so. They were intended to lead to real growth and to improve western economies, but aggressive competition by Japan and the Asian Tigers, which won them global market shares at the expense of western economies, demonstrates that they did not do so.

One service sector category of business to hire MBA graduates to advise their clients how to run their business organizations was the multinational accounting firms. They created problems for themselves that still torment them. According to the senior partner of KPMG, the biggest of the Big Six in the UK, problems of clients' lack of confidence in their services arose because they "did not get close enough to their clients."[12] That would mean they were not sufficiently conversant with their clients' workplaces. Since the core concept of marketing is that business must be oriented primarily to the needs of customers, clients, consumers, or the public, it would seem that they were simply not marketing oriented.

John Butcher—who was junior Industry Minister in Britain in the 1980s—said that British businesses were, with few exceptions, not as good at marketing as their main international competitors. Although he was describing the manufacturing sector, the point he made is of equal relevance to the service sector, if we substitute *knowledge* for *production*. He said that "too many companies limit their perception of marketing to the task of getting current production out of the warehouse. That is not marketing. Marketing is being in a position to provide the customer with what he wants, not just persuading him into taking what you've got."

In *Voltaire's Bastards,* John Ralston Saul wrote that the London Business School "claims that the central concept of its Masters Program 'is that management can be taught as a unified body of essential knowledge which can be applied to an organization.'" That, he says, is a misrepresentation of the word *knowledge,* because "there is no such thing as knowledge which is universally applicable to all organizations.... What they mean by knowledge is method. And the casual throwing in of the adjective *essential* is positive charlatanism."

Of Harvard's case method, Saul wrote, "There is nothing empirical about the process because it begins with a solution and a predetermined argument into which the problem must fit in order to arrive at that solution."

"*Imagination, creativity, moral balance, knowledge, common sense, a social view—all these things wither.*" That sentence, which I have italicized, lists some of the fundamental problems of old thinking about administration as opposed to creative management inspired by the marketing philosophy instead. But for reasons that will become clear, those elements are unteachable in a classroom prior to graduation. They can develop only from workplace experience and self-actualization.

It is quite obvious that no business school can teach a student everything that a business manager needs to know. Kant argued that knowledge is not a collection of gifts received by our senses and stored in the mind as if it were a museum, but that it is very largely the result of our own mental activity; that we must most actively engage ourselves in searching, comparing, unifying, generalizing, if we wish to attain knowledge.[13] The reason for the gaps in knowledge and skills is not only a failure to pursue continuous education, but also the failure of employers to lead, to direct, and continually to educate themselves, their managers, and workers, and to encourage and support them in continuous self improvement.

Wrote *Marketing Business* magazine in 1996, "If you are one of the thousands of young professionals who have recently forked out around fifteen thousand pounds, quit your job, and taken a year out for intensive study, all in the name of an MBA, you will be bitterly disappointed to learn it may not be worth it. The gilt edged qualification you thought was your passport to career success (to say nothing of the megabucks) is losing some of its shine."[14] But is it? Kotter wrote an entire book, published in 1995, about the extraordinary earnings of 115 Harvard MBAs from the class of 1974, whose career activities he analyzed during the next two decades.[15] And there is no doubt that winning an MBA designation serves a special purpose in that it replaces much of the qualifying of job candidates previously undertaken by executive placement companies. The main reason that business students enter management degree courses nowadays is to find employment in better-paid jobs—even though few are in management. Most are in staff positions.

Analysis of twenty-seven Canadian universities offering an MBA program shows that the greatest number obtain jobs in finance. Although the second largest number became consultants, the likelihood is that many of those too are in finance or with accounting firms. Other job categories they fill are real estate and project management, followed by telecommunications and health care. But a handful do end up in marketing and manufacturing. While it is true that a few CEOs of big business organizations boast of having achieved an MBA, that is unlikely to be what propelled them to the top. More than likely they took an opportunity to sign up for a part-time course at their company's expense when they were already top managers.

Success in obtaining employment fast appears to be guaranteed for MBA graduates, if we can believe the claims made by one university after another; 80 percent working in three months, or 85 percent to 98 percent of graduates finding work in six months, and so forth.[16] Since the number of years of previous work experience ranges from three to seventeen years—most likely averaging out at around eight years—the MBA might just be the icing on top of the cake. But that is what it is meant to be.

However, management changed dramatically after the class of 1974 graduated. It is precisely during those two decades afterwards that workplaces, technology, and economic and social changes accelerated and grew into a business and social revolution. What was being taught in classrooms then may well have been little different from James Burnham's description of management as it existed in 1941. He referred to management as the "functions of guiding, administering, managing, organizing the process of production." In that management category he included production managers, operating executives, superintendents, administrative engineers, supervisory technicians." To him, as to many before and soon after World War II, production was still of primary importance. That meant manufacturing, converting, fabricating, assembling, and the administration and organization required to produce "things."[17]

By 1952, it was beginning to dawn on top management in larger companies that growth, expansion, or diversification required ensuring that a company was making the *right* things—meaning those that consumers or other businesses wanted. That initiated properly structured marketing research, product R&D, and the best means to plan strategies and tactics to market their products.

The next huge change was a trend toward outsourcing manufacturing processes to countries that could do it cheaper. Then the service sector of western economies accelerated its growth. If those trends could be called evolutionary ones, the introduction of new technologies and the shedding of jobs at just about every level began a business revolution intended to increase profit margins by cutting overhead costs. That revolution continued through such management processes as category management, database marketing, internal and external relationship marketing, and the merging of management with marketing so that it has become impossible to separate the two in a well-run business organization.

What may well have started the process was the introduction of Management by Objectives, or MBO. The main reason for its success is that it holds each manager accountable and provides a yardstick for measuring a manager's results. It removed the chaos out of managing and became an effective substitute for seat-of-the-pants management. It also took management out of the self-defeating realm of bureaucratic rituals. Once installed, it enables a manager to measure, monitor, and regulate his or her performance as if they were independent entrepreneurs requiring little direction from the top. Being entrepreneurial means innovating; and innovation is part of the marketing process.

From the theories of a classroom, an executive is obliged to move swiftly to the realities of a workplace and the practical demands of the marketplace. Sir Austin Robinson probably spoke the last words on that subject shortly before his death in 1992. He was a leading Cambridge economist who was greatly respected. He was closely associated at one time with John Maynard Keynes. Although he spoke of economists, his remark could also justifiably be used to illustrate the realities of management and marketing, research or advertising, R&D or production: "No economist is more dangerous than the pure theorists without practical experience and instinctive understanding in the real world...seeking precision in a world of imprecision."

Marketing and Management Institutes

Up until 1995, the mission of the Chartered Institute of Marketing in the UK was "to be an internationally recognized catalyst for the improvement of marketing skills to the benefit of our members, their companies, and others in the marketing profession." They achieved that through governments, learning institutions, and the business sector, and by being a role model for other such management and marketing institutes in Canada, Australia, New Zealand, Ireland, Hong Kong, Singapore, Malaysia, South Africa, and other countries.

One way was to create a marketing diploma program which, by 1994, would be in use in 91 countries, when 37,142 students were registered for the CIM diploma in marketing. In view of the upsurge in management and marketing skills in Pacific Asian countries, it is interesting to note that 3,598 candidates for the diploma were in Singapore, 3,536 in Malaysia, 2,299 in Sri Lanka, and 1,038 in Hong Kong.

The program includes two streams at the first two levels, namely sales or marketing: the first-level sales or marketing certificate, then an advanced certificate in either sales management or marketing management; with both leading to the common third level diploma which covers international marketing strategy, marketing communications strategy and strategic marketing management.

The CIM diploma in marketing has been accepted for some years as a qualification for entry to MBA and teacher training programs in leading UK universities and by their Department of Education and Science. It has also become a recognized marketing qualification within the member states of the European Union. After the introduction of a revised and updated program which was published in September 1995, the CIM internationally recognized and preferred diploma was awarded seventy credits in the Accumulation and Transfer Scheme (CATS) and exempts holders from certain marketing elements of masters courses. Since masters courses are equal to 120 CATS points, a holder of the CIM Diploma In Marketing now needs only to accrue fifty points to achieve masters level—including an MBA.

Playing Safe

Recruitment is so much easier when a company knows what it wants. A candidate's list of academic qualifications may help or hinder judgement on how he or she might fill a need or meet a company's objectives. But very often the real objectives of a job are not clearly defined first. A corporate manager may be trapped by established procedures that compel him or her to ask, "What procedures must I follow so that the company will see that I have done what I should?" Long-established procedures may need to be questioned and modified to ensure they can achieve the objective of the exercise, as well as reducing the number and extent of uncertainties.

The most effective way to reduce uncertainties after making a judgement to employ an executive is to schedule half a day or even an entire day of analytical tests under the supervision of a professional industrial psychologist. The cost is more than compensated for by the savings an organization makes in avoiding problems and hidden costs in hiring the wrong person.

Another way to recruit a manager is borrowed from the old Chinese civil servant exam. After a short list of candidates has been made, each one would be invited alone into an office. There they would find pens, paper, and a typewriter. Each candidate would be asked to write an essay on any subject of their own choosing, in any style and of any length they wish. They could take an hour or an entire day if any of them wished. Not only would the employer have an essay to examine on its own individual merits, but it could also be compared for its merits against the others. Each essay would be likely to tell far more about a candidate's attitudes, values, priorities, intellect, interests, and motivations. It would also judge his or her communications skills far better than an application form or a contrived interview.

What would not matter would be a candidate's gender, color, religion, size, age, whether they are physically attractive or not, or whether they need crutches or a wheelchair to get around. As common Chinese wisdom has it, "It doesn't matter if a cat is black or white so long as it catches mice." Having assessed their character, the bottom-line question would then be simply, "Do I believe that they could undertake the job effectively, and could I and other managers and staff get along with them well enough for them to contribute and succeed?" People with strong characters also frequently possess strong failings too, but a manager's job is to manage people.

Unfortunately, the most common request made to a recruiter is, "Find someone like us." Conservative cultures often oblige a manager to do the safe thing instead of the best thing. Not only does it show a lack of imagination but also an absence of common sense; because it is the very diversities of character and skills that create a life-giving, dynamic force that energizes an organization by imbuing it with original ideas. Doing the traditional thing is an admission that a manager does not possess enough character to manage people who do.

Unfortunately too, most managers automatically reject candidates who appear to be too good. They feel threatened if they believe that they themselves may not be able to live up to his or her high standards.

The Management Vortex

It is clearly evident that those successful national and multinational market leaders that survived the long haul with good annual results possess two ingredients in common, which those that failed did not; a constantly practiced top-down marketing philosophy and superior managers with marketing skills. Now that business has grown in complexity in order to meet and beat global challenges, it is equally clear that this is the formula for others to be competitive and survive. But in the overwhelming mass of small businesses and in less structured bigger ones, experienced managers have gradually been replaced by less effective ones who may be cheaper in order to cut costs, but who do not fully understand the parameters of their jobs. They are casually abandoned to those jobs by top management, which may know even less about the uses of marketing and the abuses of management than they do. If they accept the isolation of their employer's style, it is because they have not known any other way to manage. And if they protest it, they risk becoming unpopular.

An eager young graduate who may think she knows, and expresses, what must be done to improve a company's market position by innovation, may be viewed as arrogant by top management with longer tenure; since recommended changes imply criticism of their own management capabilities in the past. On the other hand, "a business school graduate with his head stuffed full of nostrums about situations he has yet to encounter is likely to spend much of his working life trying to cram these ideas into the heads of recalcitrant subordinates. He will talk more than he listens and 'see' mostly those phenomena for which he already has constructs."[18]

Something has to be done about the management vortex in the West, in the realms of education, apprenticeship, recruitment, induction, training, monitoring, supervising, mentoring, and creating career paths for those who can contribute to a company's success. The responsibility is far too great to be delegated to a personnel administrator-cum-clerk. What is required is a more mature and experienced senior manager who can be a confidant of the CEO. A smaller business that cannot afford this full-time role might use the help of a management consultant to undertake the following responsibilities, instead.

1. The analysis of each job requirement, and preparation of individual job descriptions and specifications;
2. The development of a personnel and recruitment philosophy that suits that particular organization, together with a strategic plan for human resources;
3. Sourcing and recruiting appropriate personnel whenever necessary;
4. Reducing the average annual volume of staff changes by improving workplace conditions and incentives;
5. Induction of new personnel according to a properly planned program;
6. Training and development of all employees and definitions of their career paths;
7. Establishing and updating appropriate incentives including fringe benefits; health, safety, and security; wages, bonuses, and salaries;
8. Administration of employee evaluations by department heads;
9. Examination of job fulfillment at each of the key results areas, in conjunction with Quality Circles, to define any necessary improvements;
10. Establishing and maintaining harmony in the workplace through good employee and labor relations;
11. Internal public relations including communications and the betterment of working conditions;
12. Development of a practical working knowledge of what is involved in the fifty-two key results areas (or more or less, depending on the size and type of business enterprise) in terms of responsibilities and functions of each department head, supervisor, inspector, skilled worker, knowledge worker, clerk, assembly line staff, systems operators, laborers, and all other employees;

13. Establishing working relationships with all managers and the chief executive and gaining their confidence and respect as a knowledgeable and experienced senior manager; obtaining ongoing information on all changes made or planned that might require additional staff or modifications of functions or skills, or training and development of existing staff;

14. Practicing an open-door policy for all employees to feel free to communicate urgent problems; otherwise being freely available at specified days and times for interfacing with staff regarding their development or suggestions or problems.

Those fourteen responsibilities with all they entail would create an impossible workload for an inexperienced or immature manager. And such a person would be unlikely to know how to "create" such a job, depending on the size and type of company, and its previous history of management style and staff turnover. Creating a dynamic job with a quite different perspective on people and the workplace is what is required. It is clear that this manager of human resources must fully understand not only those fifty-two key results areas, but also how they interrelate with each other and what is expected to materialize from that interaction, and its implications to the business enterprise.

The relationship of each key results area and that of managers and staff must be harmonious. What is therefore required is a charismatic personality which attracts people and causes them to confide.

The title presently in use—Director of Human Resources—sounds exploitative because it is oriented to a company's administration instead of to its people. The real job is concerned with *human relationships,* because each employee is a "customer" of the others.

A fresh look may persuade management that what is needed is a Human Relations Director. And what is essentially required is a practical and sensitive means to tackle three primary objectives:

A. To ensure recruitment of more suitable personnel and to induct, train, and develop them so that they become prime assets to the company;

B. To establish job parameters and expectations at the outset;

C. To minimize staff losses by means of appropriate incentives and work enrichment and personal fulfillment, so that personnel would prefer to stay with the company.

It should go without saying that every single job category in a company requires a formalized description, which would be prepared by the Human Relations Director after discussion with the appropriate department head, and sometimes with the CEO. This top-calibre manager must be prepared not to compromise herself by hiring second-rate employees, and she must have the strength of character to prevent managers from preferring inferior subordinates. The right person would soon recover the cost of employment by improving standards throughout the company and reducing the level of staff turnover, with all its hidden costs that not only erode a company's margins but also lower work performance by destroying self-respect.

One way that some companies use to select personnel is hard to take seriously but needs to be addressed in case it becomes popular. It is when a CEO decides that a new employee should be chosen by a group of co-workers. Quite apart from the pressure of their own jobs and their lack of competence to perform such a responsible function, there are implicit dangers. Human nature being what it is, it is almost certain that anyone of a high calibre would be rejected as a threat to their own peace of mind. Having established their own pace and style of work, they would be most unlikely to choose or approve of a newcomer who was quicker, smarter, or more accomplished than them. And yet, from a company's point of view, it is precisely the challenge of a superior manager that is required to uplift the standards of all of them.

That situation was underscored by the furor over continual firings at Michael Cowpland's Corel Corp. Corel produces the world's best-selling PC graphics program of software called Corel Draw. "People are terrified they could be let go any time," said a previous employee who was fired. Cowpland said the firings were justified. He made a name for himself as co-founder of Mitel Corp., from which he had long since resigned. Interviewed by the *Ottawa Citizen,* he said, "One of the problems is when you go from a company that's got close to 300 and is beating out the whole world—and we're talking about Silicon Valley and Boston and all those Harvard MBAs—you're not going to do it with an average team. To expect that is to expect miracles.... If you don't raise the level of the team, the team won't do well."[19]

After being told of the firings, but not which company was involved, the president of the Canadian Advanced Technology Association added, "That's the role model we have to send to all Canadians, because we're under-performing in all areas.... I like the idea of a model that insists a little more on excellence and over-achieving.... We need that for the Canadian economy, period."

That Cowpland's attitude was the right one was shown by the fact that whereas Corel Corporation employed 270 people at that time, it was able to employ 440 two years later. Revenues increased from $130 million to $200 million by 1994. Corel exports 95 percent of its software products; about half to the United States.

If we are looking for an ideal role model, perhaps it should be based on criteria that were defined for the selection of officers to manage the U.S. Navy. Their selection form provides space for comments on each candidate to be made against each of the following criteria, in columns headed Outstanding, Excellent, Average, and Unsatisfactory.

1. Intelligence:	• Comprehension and mental acuteness.
2. Judgement:	• Discriminating perception.
3. Initiative:	• Constructive thinking and resourcefulness.
4. Force:	• Moral power.
5. Leadership:	• Directing, controlling, and influencing others.
6. Moral Courage:	• To carry out dictates of conscience and convictions, fearlessly.
7. Cooperation:	• Working harmoniously with others to accomplish common duties.
8. Loyalty:	• Faithfulness, allegiance, constancy.
9. Perseverance:	• Maintaining purpose despite obstacles or discouragement.
10. Reaction in Emergencies	• Instinctively logical actions in difficult and unforeseen circumstances.
11. Endurance:	• Ability to carry on under any and all conditions.
12. Industry:	• Energetic performance of duties.
13. Military Bearing and Neatness of Person and Dress	• Dignity of demeanor, correctness, and smart appearance.

The idea that corporate managers should possess the same characteristics as U.S. Navy officers may seem to be absurd, but it is no coincidence that the first planned management concepts and principles that were put into practice in the United States were applied to the armed forces at the beginning of the twentieth century.[20]

But a profit-oriented company has also to match its personnel to its life cycle; as Cowpland remarked, a company that grows requires different attributes of its executives to one that is still small. That means staff should anticipate growth and continually develop themselves to grow with the company. Indeed, they are the ones who should be in a better position to lead it into the future. If they cannot do that they should look elsewhere for their career when the company has overtaken them, *before* they are fired. It seems that they were too young and inexperienced to understand the extraordinary challenges caused by success, which require extraordinary responses. That can come only from self-development.

The calibre of suitable managers is not a new problem but a recurring one. Every civilization has had to address it when a new management class was required. When the feudal system was broken in China, and the clan basis of the old aristocracy destroyed, the Han Emperor opened up the imperial civil service to outside talent instead of patronage, which is commonplace in North America. Provincial public authorities were directed to select candidates on a test of merit, for recommendation to the government. That merit was defined as proficiency in writing in the style of Confucian classical literature and in interpreting Confucian philosophy to the satisfaction of experts. A new civil service was created in that way out of traditional Chinese culture. Confucianism inspired a common bond of corporate professional ethics that lasted for nearly two thousand years, until 1911.

By comparison, when the Roman imperial civil service similarly required improvement and expansion, it took some three hundred years after the Emperor Augustus before entry was open to Roman citizens, on merit and without class distinction. But it too was created out of their own social and cultural heritage.[21] And when the British East India Company was obliged to convert itself from a purely commercial enterprise of merchant adventurers into a body of public servants at the breakup of the Mughal Raj, it changed from a predatory band of freebooters into a public service whose incentive was not personal financial gain, but "the honour to wield enormous political power without abusing it." The training of those public servants was "superior even to that in force for Britain's own civil service at the time," according to Toynbee.

Perhaps democracy's greatest flaw is its tendency to place mediocrities in power. They, in turn, hire other mediocrities to do their bidding. And the public pay dearly for their ill-judgement and irrational decisions. In the case of government elections, referendums, or job competitions, choices are made by consensus—which means counting the noses of committee members or majorities—instead of limiting such offices to trained and experienced people with demonstrated achievements. Or they are patronage appointments.[22]

It is that type of challenge that faces western economies today. If the West does not respond to it by creating a new management culture, then its industries and its economies must decline in the face of more dynamic, better disciplined, and highly-motivated competitors trained in management skills.

That challenge has long been addressed by the Japanese, whose priority in business is a commitment to their employees' careers. That is the type of democratic right that should be practiced in western economies too.

On the other hand, Western history shows that whenever labor is required to be competitive, it always demands higher rates than are compatible with competing prices. That leads inevitably to loss of markets and large-scale unemployment. Close alliances between banks, government, management, and labor in advanced economies like Germany and Japan were considered to be progressive and successful. But those alliances did not prevent their labor costs from rising beyond competitive boundaries. And even in Japan, it led to manufacturing in Third World countries.

Despite that, Japan's unemployment rate is still only 2.9 percent in 1995. And it should not be forgotten that their dedication to full and lifetime employment was the foundation for their remarkable post-war recovery. They should be our model. But the Americanization of Japan may result in social changes that could create similar social decline as is taking place in the West.

For example, the U.S. suffered from its worst ever spate of bankruptcies in the four-month period from January to the end of April 1996, despite fear of inflation from a "buoyant" economy. Total bankruptcy filings rose by 27 percent to 318,893. 1.1 million Americans were expected to file for bankruptcy in 1996. Personal bankruptcies accounted for 90 percent to 95 percent of total bankruptcies over the past six years.[23] Rising bankruptcies are a "danger sign for the economy that may well reflect the growing disparity between the haves and the have-nots in society."[24] Causes are listed as job losses, divorces, unexpected medical bills, or auto accident costs.

Professor Lipset posed a question in 1950 as to why there had never been any socialism in the United States. The answers led him to examine America's social class system in 1959. By that time he had become acutely aware that America was exceptional in most ways. "Some worry that our best years as a nation are behind us," he writes. "Americans distrust their leaders and institutions." His new book on *American Exceptionalism* was released in 1996. In it, he asks, "Is the country in decline economically and morally? Is Japan about to replace it as the leading economic power?"[25]

16

Dynamics of Change

"For you to succeed in the future you will have to abandon every single thing you've learnt in the past." So says Jack Welch, CEO of General Electric Corporation.

Other ominous predictions are being made as we pass into the twenty-first century. But this is not the first time we have been confronted by social and economic change. "Seeing that everything swayed and shifted aimlessly, I felt giddy and desperate," wrote Plato about 2,500 years ago in his Seventh Letter. It was the era when Heraclitus realized, with a similar culture shock, that "Everything is in flux"—therefore the existing social order could not remain for ever. Plato thought otherwise and spent the rest of his life trying to protect the state from all change by totalitarian government that would create a closed society. Theories that arose out of that discovery have been described as "an expression of a feeling of drift; a feeling which seems to be a typical reaction to the dissolution of the ancient tribal forms of social life."[1]

One of our idiosyncrasies is wishful thinking; and we are pleased to imagine that our customs, laws, and institutions should remain exactly the same forever. Heraclitus discovered the contrary to be the case as long ago as 500 B.C. The theory of social dynamics sprang from that moment. And yet nowhere do we see the management of discontinuous change as being an important criterion for managers or leaders to learn and apply. An ability to "create the new" is one thing, but equally important is the skill to abandon to history all those useless practices and senile institutions that proved themselves to be counterproductive and culturally damaging: the *laissez-faire* management of absolutely nothing.

Whatever happened to that entrepreneurial spirit that produced such useful and meaningful original ideas, like the ingenuity of James Watt or those magnificent British ironmasters, and the entrepreneurship of pioneers like Josiah Wedgewood? It was exemplified in America by the intellectual abilities and skills of inventors like Benjamin Franklin, Thomas Edison, Alexander Graham Bell, and George Eastman, who achieved success also by managing change to their own, and our, advantage. It was innovation that triggered the Industrial Revolution in eighteenth-century Europe. But in the nineteenth century, Britain created a centralized civil service structure to administer India and its other colonies. It was composed of bureaucrats who simply did what they were told by Whitehall. Intellect, creativity, or initiative were frowned on and brilliance was suspect. Managers were hired merely to carry out instructions, and the entrepreneurial spirit lost ground to administrators. The reason for the alarming growth of bureaucracies all over the world is that they create work for each other.

An accumulation of unnecessary problems caused by management without reasonable or relevant objectives acts as a stumbling block to a nation's economic recovery, similar to the way it creates inertia in a business organization. Few countries in the mid-1990s, if any, could genuinely claim to possess governments or business sectors that were in complete control of a healthy, well-ordered, and progressive industrial society. It would have been difficult to identify which was "the sick man of Europe," between Italy, Spain, the former Yugoslavia, and the former Soviet Union. Each suffered from past and present mismanagement. Each had attempted to impose a closed society by force of arms. But the roots of their problems existed beforehand: a police state was their reaction to the collapse of tribal systems. But it was a vain attempt to impose order by procrustean means—to cut up its people so that they could fit into preconceived patterns designed by fascist or communist bureaucracies. We were fortunate to escape their trauma, if only by a narrow margin, but we did not entirely escape their dedication to bureaucratic mismanagement. In our own case it left us with huge national and provincial debts which are holding our society back.

But back from what? The world is no longer an area of vast territories and dense forests awaiting our exploration. Nor is it being shaped any longer by a variety of tribal migrations or wanderings. The geographical borders are mostly fixed. Our adventurous spirit with its technological advances has enabled us to examine practically every square inch of our global village, and yet we are continually surprised at the arrival of the unexpected.

There came a lull in activity in the mid-1990s, as if world economies had reached a similar stage as at the end of World War I, when the depleted and demoralized armies of France, Britain, and Germany came to a standstill from sheer exhaustion, loss of direction, apathy, and hopelessness. Today it is our economies that have come to a standstill through lack of direction, but there is a similar feeling of despair as we reexamine our values and wonder where our society is going. What makes the similarity ominous is that post-World War I military regimes were enabled to grow because of widespread unemployment in Germany, Italy, Spain, and Russia. Creating employment for them in the armed forces was viewed as a sensible solution. Today's high technology is creating similar stresses by causing large-scale unemployment.

Peacetime technologies are being initiated by workshop problems instead of marketplace ones or social needs or requirements for a stable economy.

And our democratic free market economy is not faring as well as we had hoped. A naive vision of Third World countries in which employment would be created so that they could develop into markets for our goods, belied the reality that new technologies take jobs away. Mexican novelist Homero Aridjis recently remarked that the image of a prosperous Mexico "has fallen like a deck of cards under the brutal reality that was hidden all along: unemployment, poverty, corruption, violence, armed uprisings and kidnappings all over the nation." The situation of anarchy from which they, India, Palestine, South Africa, the former Yugoslavia, and other countries like Russia, are trying to escape, may be the destiny of the West. On one hand, chaos can be brought about by the tyranny of totalitarian governments or military *juntas,* and on the other hand by the tyranny of the majority who demand too much liberalism and unleash aggressive special interest groups who can do as they wish. That includes breaking down old values.

Once again we find ourselves at the crossroads, but whichever way we turn we are confronted by mankind's baser characteristics. Perhaps that is why we are placing our faith in technology instead. But it can only lead us into another dead-end, because it does not arise from social needs for stability. Instead, it is being imposed by a capitalist system that is directionless and supported by a government that follows purely political agendas. While it is true that technological innovations have won wars, when all other considerations but survival were thrown aside, peacetime demands more enduring values.

History reveals how societies all over the world created similar traps for themselves and became discouraged, and sunk in torpor as a consequence. Some disappeared and left little trace of their culture or even their existence. Others remained inert for centuries and barely managed to survive. Some others were displaced by more virile societies when they ceased to possess the power or the will to resist competition, or were overwhelmed by superior skills. But others did manage to extricate themselves from their inertia, in time, by organizing a new culture and an élite which enabled them to contain their competitors and propelled them out of obscurity and into economic or military dominance. Some of them even developed into great civilizations. The question frequently asked is how did they manage it?

A Historical Perspective

When Toynbee decided to write an unconventional history of civilization, he searched for a positive factor that could have been responsible for shaking a part of the human race out of its habitual torpor and directing it into change, differentiation, and growth.[2] He posed several crucial questions: If mankind had been held back by inertia for about half a million years at a pre-civilized level, because it was so entrenched in custom, how was it that some members of the human race managed to overcome that inertia in only the past five thousand years, to propel themselves into dynamic activity? Why did it happen only in some societies? If custom, or tradition, is a retarding factor, then the momentum would have had to be even greater to catapult those societies into the future. What could that positive factor be to initiate such dynamism?

He considered how Hegel thought of history as a spiral development from one form of unity to another, through a phase of disunity; as in Chinese history, for example. He observed how Saint-Simon viewed the history of civilizations as a series of alternating organic and critical periods. He reviewed the way that Empedocles had attributed the changes of the universe to "the alternate ebb and flow of two forces which are complimentary to one another and at the same time antithetical"—an integrating force, which he called love, and a disintegrating force, which he called hate. (The *Sinic* world called them *Yin and Yang*: water and fire, rival and partner). "Without contraries there is no progression," wrote William Blake.

It seemed possible that the positive force (or *Yang*) that drives resolution may be found in either a special quality in human beings or in a special feature in those environments where transition took place. Toynbee considered that they might even be in "some prowess of the race when confronted with some challenge from the environment." But his original theories broke down because when each appeared to be fruitful in one case, they were shown to be sterile in another. Then he realized that his method had been at fault, because he had applied a scientific approach used for inanimate objects to the study of human beings. Whereas he had looked for cause and effect, initiatives taken by people are not causes but challenges. Their consequences are not effects but responses. And he realized, too, that human response to challenge cannot be predicted, because it is not uniform in all cases. He decided to view the problems through new eyes.

He decided that challenge is produced by an adversary (or an adversarial situation). It is "an impulse or motive which comes from outside." It might be "a critic to set the mind thinking again by suggesting doubts; or an adversary to set the heart feeling again by instilling distress or discontent or fear or antipathy.... This is the role of the Serpent in the Book of Genesis, of Satan in the Book of Job, of Mephistopheles in Goethe's *Faust,* of Loki in the Scandinavian mythology...of the environment in the Darwinian theory of evolution."

"To jolt the individual...and also...to break up the collective frameworks in which he is imprisoned, it is indispensable that he should be shaken and prodded from outside. What would we do without our enemies?"[3]

The state out of which mankind needs to be shaken, Toynbee called "the integration of custom." The activity that drives resolution, he named "the differentiation of civilisation." The western world learned of *Yin* and *Yang* from the analogy of the sleeping princess who is finally awakened by a kiss of life from a handsome prince. At the time of that myth, principalities that suffered from inertia knew that as well as the arrival of a dynamic force from outside, they also needed genetic diversity in the royal bloodline, in order to restore its greatness. Other legends describe how a hero, with his dynamism and differentiation, would be welcome.

Western economies are not entirely lifeless, only inert, and awaiting that breath of life to resuscitate them. Henri Bergson named it the *élan vital*. He wrote, "It is useless to maintain that (social progress) takes place by itself, bit by bit, in virtue of the spiritual condition of the society at a certain period of its history. It is really a leap forward which is only taken when the society has made up its mind to try an experiment; this means that the society must have allowed itself to be convinced, or at any rate allowed itself to be shaken; and the shake is always given by *somebody*."

That was the stimulus that compelled human beings to emerge from their pre-human ancestry; that initiated the crafting of the first tools; that caused the invention of agriculture; and led to the first dawnings of civilizations in city states. And the somebody who is responsible for giving the shake or the *élan* is an *outsider*. For "creation is the outcome of encounter." Devil or hero, rival or partner, the creative role is the property of the adversary.

> Companies seldom change spontaneously; the environment jars or *forces* them to change. A company must expose itself to external pressures and stimuli that motivate and guide the need to act.... The difficulty of innovation means that it is often 'outsiders' to the firm, the industry, the established social structure, or based in other nations, that are the catalysts for innovation. Outsiders can perceive changes that go unnoticed or contradict conventional wisdom. Outsiders are neither wedded to past strategies nor worried about upsetting industry or social norms.[4]

Meanwhile, the West is creating its own technological trap by firing employees, losing skills, and replacing them with high technology. While there is no doubt that new technologies reduce unit costs in the short term, it is purely a production-oriented philosophy that takes us all the way back to Taylor, Fayol, and Henry Ford. It has little to do with markets or customers. Indeed, it is the antithesis of marketing. Nor is it the glorified knowledge revolution it is made out to be by media hype. The fiber optic tail is trying to wag the dog in the case of the proposed five-hundred-channel TV Super Information Highway, because TV production houses have long demonstrated that there is not enough quality content to provide consistently high-calibre programs even for as few as five channels. Fibre optic cables can be compared to electronic assembly lines that simply create overproduction in manufacturing plants. The products are likely to be unwanted.

The West is taking high technology like an analgesic to deaden the pain of social and economic failure, while the real problems persist and the ailment intensifies. New technologies may seem like a quick fix, but they cannot create customers, and that is what keeps economies going. There is a profound need for social innovation with employees at the center instead of being marginalized.

The real drama today is not being enacted on TV screens, or on the monitors of the latest multimedia computers, or the assembly lines of the automobile industry. In the real global amphitheater, the East is playing the role of the adversary to the West. Rival or partner, it is shaking western economies out of their complacency, while it reshapes the economy of the East. Japan and the Asian Tigers made their great leap forward toward the global economic summit, in the last two decades, without benefit of any resources other than their own culture, their work ethic, their alertness to opportunities and challenges, and their ability to manage change—as can be seen by their share of world exports in figure 16.1.

Between 1972 and 1992, France, Britain, and Italy, shown lying along the base of the chart, barely managed to maintain their shares of the global market and ended that period with smaller shares. (The same was true of Canada, which would be shown beneath Italy, if it were included.) Similarly, Germany and the United States, at the top, ended that period in much the same positions as they began. Real growth was achieved by Japan, which leapt from around 7.5 percent global share to about 9.5 percent, and the Asian Tigers, who jumped from around 2.5 percent to 9.5 percent approximately. The question is whether the West can react positively and aggressively or whether it is in irreversible decline.

Toynbee directed our attention to "the stimulus of hard countries," where great civilizations once developed in response to great challenges. But history also reveals that yesterday's dynamic forces, which once fired the imagination and created great resolve to struggle against enormous difficulties, become, in time, today's prison bars of stale custom, out of which we prisoners beg to be freed. The presidential election of Bill Clinton in the United States and the overwhelming rejection of the Conservative government in Canada's Federal Election were examples of this; as was the divestment of totalitarianism in former communist countries. The public had lost faith in partisan politics and in government, but have not yet found a satisfactory way to replace it.

Japan, too, found itself in such a trap in the nineteenth century. It sought out its own adversary through *mimesis.*

Mimesis is a Greek word meaning social imitation. Toynbee defined it as "the acquisition, through imitation, of social 'assets'—aptitudes or emotions or ideas—which the acquisitors have not originated for themselves, and which they might never have come to possess if they had not encountered and imitated other people in whose possession these assets were already to be found."

It was for the sake of regeneration through mimesis that in 1858 the Japanese opened their country to the influence of the outside world. Times were desperate: Japan was bankrupt and the grip of poverty was at everyone's throat.

FIGURE 16.1
Share of World Exports

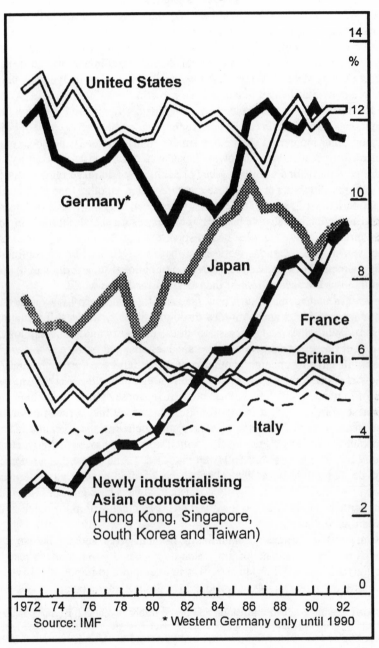

14
%
United States
12
10
Germany*
Japan
8
France
6
Britain
Italy
4
Newly industrialising
Asian economies
(Hong Kong, Singapore,
South Korea and Taiwan)
2
0
1972 74   76   78   80   82   84   86   88   90   92
Source: IMF   * Western Germany only until 1990

Despite that, they managed to exert considerable control over outside influ-ences. Their aim was to use the best western methods while remaining Japa-nese. When mimesis is directed toward the past, custom rules, and that society remains static. But societies in the process of civilization direct mimesis to-ward creative personalities who command a following because they are pio-neers on the road toward a common goal of endeavor. In such forward-directed societies, the "cake of custom" is broken and society is set in dynamic motion along a course dedicated to change and growth.

Japanese culture was molded by geography, climate, and geology. Only about one-sixth of Japan can be used for cultivation between a chain of volca-nic and other mountains situated on small islands. Before its post-war emer-gence as a great industrial power, Japan was described as "a country that hides poverty behind a smiling face."[5] Lacking the natural resources of west-ern nations and living at such close quarters with each other, one of the prime characteristics of the Japanese has always been frugality. And disciplined social behavior has always been essential to ensure social harmony in such tight circumstances. They learned to solve their problems through organiza-tion, self-discipline, and a work ethic that involved *kaizen,* or continuous improvement. Their dedication to a vision of national superiority was to posi-tion them as the second-largest industrial power in the world.

Western management must now face similar challenges by acquiring the best Japanese ideas and aptitudes through mimesis, while still remaining western. While the West possesses both the ingenuity and the technology, it no longer possesses the work ethic: its values changed in the postwar world. They will have to undergo another change, or fall even further behind Pa-cific-Asian economies. One problem mitigating against the West is its rejec-tion of hierarchy, which is the backbone of Japanese culture and beliefs. The Japanese consider that it is top-to-bottom hierarchy that creates mutual re-spect leading to social harmony. The same applies to the workplace. Ruth Benedict called it a "meticulously explicit map of behaviour" that "guaran-teed security as long as one followed the rules."[6] And in the eighteenth cen-tury, de Toqueville wrote that although he admired egalitarian America, it lacked true dignity. "True dignity consists in always taking one's proper sta-tion, neither too high nor too low. And this is as much within the reach of the peasant as of the prince."

Class differences are not humiliating in themselves. Indeed, the constant goal of the Japanese is honor, for which it is necessary to command respect. The mistake made by the Japanese was in attempting to impose their type of hierarchy onto the rest of the world, which did not appreciate it.

Japan, having attained unification and peace in her homeland, having put down banditry and built up roads and electric power and steel industries, having, ac-cording to her official figures, educated 99.5% of her rising generation in her public schools, should, according to Japanese premises of hierarchy, raise her backward younger brother China, being of the same race as Greater East Asia. She should eliminate the United States, and after her Britain and Russia, from that part of the world and "take her proper place." All nations were to be one world, fixed in an international hierarchy.

This would be achieved through the Japanese spirit. In the Japanese context, *spirit* appears to mean what Machiavelli called *virtù*. "What then is this *virtù*? It is force and ability, daring and prudence, efficiency, energy, *dynamis*, the combination of force and talent (Burckhardt), capacity, ability or power. Ercole gives a larger and more complicated definition: It is the concrete exercise of liberty typical of a man of energetic and conscious will-power not to stop or control, but to mould the course of action in which he lives in order to stamp it with his own imprint, for the purpose not only of setting a goal but of translating action into reality."[7]

Ercole's definition also synthesizes the qualities that form the essential difference between the traditional administrator of yesterday's vintage and a superior manager designated to be successful in the twenty-first century.

Japan's entry into the sophisticated marketing arena stamped the age with a Japanese imprint. They set their goals and translated them into reality—as the calendar of inventions, developments, innovations, and patents shows very clearly. The marketing orientation of management that took place in Japan differed from its progress in Western Europe and the United States in that it was a steady and determined one that advanced in a very much shorter period of time than occurred in the West. In 1953, Japan was still in a commercial sciences mode, with emphasis on basic needs and production. Then they progressed to random sampling and marketing research; gained in technology; improved the image of Japanese products; and concentrated on the necessities of life. TV became a catalyst. Their calendar of events has been summarized as follows—beginning at a time when the quality of marketing and advertising appears to have peaked in western economies.

1953–1964: First marketing research agency; Japan Productivity Centre (1955); Japan Marketing Association (1957); rapid economic growth; first consumption revolution; liberalization of trade; product planning emphasis; translation of marketing articles and books; first periodicals on marketing; first marketing course; marketing study team visits.

1965–1969: Spreading influence; mass consumption; supermarket growth; Association of Voluntary Chains (1966); Tokyo distribution center (1967); advertising and TV; product diversification; electronic technology and new products; acceptance of Japanese products; rationalization of distribution; marketing approaches adapted; status products; Japanese approaches to marketing; Japanese Institute of Marketing Science; research institutes.

1970–1973: Oil boycott; environmental and pollution issues; social issues and responsibilities; productivity and efficiency emphasis; consumerism movement; Japan becomes a major market; quality of life improves;

high consumption; liberalization of foreign exchange and trade; expansion of exports.

1974–Present: Global markets; mature and saturated markets; importance of autos and steel; oil shock; increase in efficiency; international focus; expansion of exports; trade surpluses; reduction of barriers; increased competitiveness; orderly market agreements; increasing market share; knowledge industries; high-tech industries.[8]

The Way Ahead

Ruminating on wasted opportunities, Malcolm Muggeridge observed that "history, like wood, has a grain in it which determines how it splits; and those in authority, besides trying to shape and direct events, sometimes find it more convenient to let them happen."[9]

Henry Adam had a similar notion. But, for him, the grain split about fifteen or eighteen years after each century turned. According to his assessment, the sixteenth century was dominated by the Italians (1515–1615); the seventeenth century by the French; the eighteenth century by the English; and the nineteenth century by the Germans. To bring him up to date, the twentieth century belonged to the Americans. And all leading indicators, at present, point to the twenty-first century being appropriated by Asia-Pacific nations.[10]

The goal of western business organizations and governments could therefore be defined as ensuring that we shape our enterprises and our managers to direct our activities toward our own best outcome at the beginning of the twenty-first century. If we do not mold and control our destiny, the grain at the centenary may well split of its own accord in favor of the East—from the sheer size of the Chinese market, the marketing skills of the Asian Tigers, and Japan's constancy of purpose.

At 6 percent annual growth rate, Asia-Pacific economies represent the world's fastest-growing markets. They now contain 50 percent of the World's total production, 40 percent of world trade, and two-thirds of the world's population.

Some thought should be given to Hegel's theory that all change and progress is produced by the conflict of great forces. A challenge (or thesis) is thrown by an outstanding world-class individual, nation, or event. It is opposed by an antithesis. And the conflict is ultimately resolved by a synthesis of the two adversaries—when, in effect, they become partners. Certainly that is the way that events are shaping at the end of the twentieth century, according to a new model that is gaining popularity, called the Triad.

The Postmodern World

Western economies and Pacific-Asian ones are on a see-saw and we are at the declining end of it. "Most advanced countries are becoming politically unstable," declared Professor Jagdish Sheth at the Seventh World Marketing Conference in Melbourne, Australia, in 1995. They are suffering from lack of growth and social disruption. At the same time, most emerging markets are gaining political stability. Instability and civil strife discourage investment and widespread unemployment results. The power base is shifting significantly and emerging economies will dominate in the twenty-first century, including China, India, Indonesia, and others—and geo-economic alliances will take place, instead of political ones, because politics are now driven by economic pragmatism.

A new model gaining in popularity is the Triad, consisting of European Union states and other Western European nations with 475 million people; North and South America with 750 million; and the Asia-Pacific region with a population of 1.5 billion (excluding India).

China is expected to surpass Japan by the turn of the century, and is likely to be the largest single economy in the world by 2030. India will most probably be the fourth largest economy by the year 2000; the U.S. will remain number two, and Japan will drop into fourth or fifth place.

Contrary to the traditional theory of population expansion and control, this model shows that nations with greater populations will be better off.

Each regional trade bloc will be led by one or two stronger economies—the Asia-Pacific bloc by the Chinese and the Japanese; Europe by the French and the Germans. Britain is most likely to align itself with the North and South American bloc because of cultural differences with continental Europe. Brazil will become the major agricultural producer for the Americas. The African continent—led by South Africa—is likely gradually to align itself with the European Union bloc by 2010. There will be closer integration between the Eastern European economy, including Russia and the Northern Baltic states, and the EU. The Middle East is already aligned with the American and British bloc, and India will be informally aligned with it too.

Countries driven by ideologies instead of fundamental economic considerations will be left out as religious, political, and social ideologies continue to decline in the Triad Blocs. One consequence will be a change of focus from east-west trading partners to north-south ones. U.S. manufacturing will go to Mexico and South America. Italy is expected to become the second largest economy in the EU.

Professor Sheth predicted that there will be regional "Fortresses" within which members will be given advantages in trade wars between regional blocs, and "Enterprise Nations" will emerge. Privatization of public sector enterprises will continue, and so will outsourcing, in the continued downsizing of government.

Conflicts will continue to increase, but they will be between generations within the rich and the poor classes. The key issue, particularly in traditional Asian cultures, will be managing intergenerational conflicts to stabilize situations. Social and culture shocks will take place in China, India, and Eastern

Europe. Politics are unlikely to run smoothly in those situations, and party political coalitions will be necessary to ease gridlock in order to govern.[11]

The Betrayal of Democracy

Behind that geopolitical vision of the twenty-first century are western disillusion with party politics and government. And, instead of the "tyranny of the masses," which grew out of a desire for liberty, equality, and brotherhood in the French Revolution, there is another kind of tyranny that holds the public to ransom. It is the justification by individuals, who also form part of special self-interest groups, for violent and ruthless actions in the name of so-called "democratic rights."

Christopher Lasch wrote how, among European intellectuals and artists one hundred years ago, there was a revolt against self-denial and self-control; against civic authority, family, and religious obligations, class conventions, bourgeois solemnity, stupidity, and ugliness. Political and social agitators were hailed by intellectuals as absolutely necessary for the advancement of civilization. Anarchists, Troskyists, Marxists, Bolsheviks, and Fascists plotted to free the working classes from the opiate of religion and the chains of industrial labor. And the women's movement promised to emancipate women from the bondage of domesticity by agitating for the vote. Capitalism and bourgeois culture were under continual attack. But the postmodern world in which we live "is defined on the one hand by a disillusionment with grand historical theories, and on the other with an ideal of personal freedom." "Postmodernism is rooted in the modernist idea of individuals emancipated from conventions, constructing identities for themselves as they choose," and leading their own lives as if they were playing a role in a TV soap opera.

Lasch recognized the danger (as did Schiller) that our disenchantment with the world would lead to emotional and spiritual impoverishment, because we are deprived of the necessary illusion that our activities have any real significance. "A man for whom nothing exists beyond his immediate situation is not fully human."[12]

"Does democracy have a future?" asked Lasch, shortly before he died. "The decline of manufacturing and the consequent loss of jobs; the shrinkage of the middle classes; the growing number of the poor; the rising crime rate; the flourishing traffic in drugs; the decay of the cities—the bad news goes on and on."[13]

Meanwhile, the erosion of the manufacturing sector and disillusionment with ideologies have both helped to change the working environment. Drucker has been proved to have been quite right when he predicted in *The New Society*, two generations ago, that the new industrial society would be neither socialist nor capitalist. There is a bland absence of workplace politics or party politics in the workplace. Today's workplaces are very different from the factories and workshops of the 1930s. They are more likely to be exemplified by the comfortable open-plan offices of financial institutions, hospitality industries catering to tourists, retail chain stores, Silicon Valley, resource industries, health-care organizations, or auditing firms.

Competitiveness Rating

Not many years before Malcolm Muggeridge's death, as if he were admitting his sins in the confessional, he wrote, "What hurts most is the preference I have so often shown for what is inferior, tenth-rate, when the first-rate was there for the having."

His regret at wasted years and lost opportunities no doubt stemmed from having been taught from childhood that, where competition is concerned, the goal is to be first—or, at the very least, in the first three places.

The World Competitiveness Report is compiled by the Economic Forum and the International Institute of Management Development in Switzerland. It is based partly on statistics and also on a survey of the views of 18,000 business managers. The report released in June, 1993 covered thirty-eight countries, of which twenty-three were classified as developed, while the others were categorized as newly industrializing economies.

Competitive ratings not only reflect the ability to balance national budgets, create new jobs, and maintain social stability, they also relate to such other changes taking place as management standards, government effectiveness, internationalization, and the attitudes of the people in each country. The ability to compete as a trading nation is changing very fast. Whereas Japan was our model in 1993, because it had been ranked first for nine consecutive years, the United States regained top ranking in 1994.

In 1995, the U.S. and Singapore increased their lead in competitiveness and the gap widened between the U.S.—in the lead—and Japan in fourth place and continuing to slide down. The U.S. ranked first in Domestic Economic Strength, Internationalization, and Management. Their aggressiveness was particularly evident in new technologies like computers, software, telecommunications, and the like. It also ranked first in science and technology. Weaker points are sixth place for government and ninth for people. Singapore ranked first in government, finance, and people—and thus becomes a new model.

	1995	1994	1993
1st:	United States	United States	Japan
2nd:	Singapore	Singapore	United States
3rd:	Hong Kong	Japan	Denmark
4th:	Japan	Hong Kong	Switzerland
5th:	Switzerland	Germany	Germany
6th:	Germany	Switzerland	Netherlands
7th:	Netherlands	Denmark	Austria
8th:	New Zealand	Netherlands	New Zealand

9th:	Denmark	New Zealand	Sweden
10th:	Norway	Sweden	Belgium/Luxembourg

Most Asian economies showed strong domestic growth combined with internationalization.

Japan had still not solved its political or economic problems, which are exemplified by its ranking twenty-seventh for government—whereas is was ranked second in 1991. Paradoxically, this land of social innovation has its present problems described as social ones. Confidence in Japan's economy fell to twenty-third place in the Executive Opinion Survey.

Instead of Europe's economies converging, as intended in the Maastricht Treaty, European countries are even more dispersed than before. German management was ranked only fourteenth, whereas Switzerland was third. Although both France and the UK performed well in internationalization, France is ranked as low as thirty-fifth for government. The UK was ranked fourteenth. There is little difference in their management ranking—at twenty-first and twentieth, respectively. Their people factor is fifteenth and twenty-fourth.

Canada slipped from fifth place in 1991, all the way down to eleventh place in 1993, then to sixteenth place in 1994. Reasons cited were rising personal income taxes and mismanagement of government expenditures that resulted in the highest per capita debt of the U.S., Britain, and Canada. Canada moved up to twelfth place in 1995. The UK was sixteenth in 1993, fourteenth in 1994, and eighteenth in 1995.

Singapore and Hong Kong had been rated at the top of the second league in 1992, as newly industrializing economies. By the following year they had both burst into the "developed" classification. In 1995 they were the leading stars in Asia.

But the tendency in 1995 to 1996 to write off Japan may be due in large part to the media's preference for headlining depressing news and the political fashion of denigrating competitors to avoid providing solutions. Despite the prevailing pessimism of the times, sales figures of Top Industrial and Service Companies in 1994 revealed that the four most successful ones were Japanese, as were nine out of the top fifteen:

1st:	Mitsubishi	9th:	Nissho Iwai
2nd:	Mitsui	10th:	Royal Dutch/Shell (Holland & Britain)
3rd:	Itochu	11th:	Toyota
4th:	Sumitomo	12th:	Wal-Mart Stores (U.S.)
5th:	GM (U.S.)	13th:	Hitachi
6th:	Murubeni	14th:	Nippon Life Insurance
7th:	Ford (U.S.)	15th:	AT&T (U.S.)
8th:	Exxon (U.S.)		

Source: Fortune, 1995. (Fiscal year ends differ in some cases.)

In fact, Japan can do nothing about the weak purchasing power of its trading nations, and its stagnant domestic market differs little from Europe's or Canada's. As well, while the better unemployment figures there had risen to around 10 percent, Japan's had grown to only 3.2 percent by 1996. And while it is true that 21.4 percent of jobs in Japan were only part-time ones by 1994, 23.8 percent was typical of the UK, France, and Canada, and around 25 percent in the United States.[14]

While the opinion of western media was that Japan must change its entire attitude and cut up to half of its expensive labor force to be competitive internationally, their *jito* and their politicians know full well that following a short-term, ruthless, and narrow-focused western management style could result in western-type social problems and an even worse economy. It is not in the Japanese tradition to throw employees out onto the streets—particularly as the marketing philosophy at the end of the twentieth century was to regard employees as customers.

A reason frequently given for the uncompetitiveness of some western economies is that we have to compete with prices of Third World countries with low labor costs. That is both a simplification and an exaggeration. "While the United States does some trade with low-wage, Third World nations, the great bulk of its trade is with countries that are more or less as advanced as it is, and that pay wages close to or even exceeding its own."[15] Canada is a good example of this, and European nations trade mainly in Europe. The cost of competing labor is virtually equalized because it is customary to trade mostly with close neighbors.

Metamorphosis

The self-inflicted agonies of IBM must have come as a surprise to the authors who lovingly baptized it as an "excellent company" when it was actually falling further and further from grace. Others had observed symptoms of its decline for some time. Of the proliferation of clones that were nibbling at IBM's market share at that time, *Computer Weekly* wrote (in 1982), "Dinosaurs, like IBM, once dominated the earth. Then they vanished overnight, leaving the planet to the ants, who remain the most prolific form of life on earth. The ants nipping at IBM's heels are the micros, which will soon, like the ubiquitous formica, be resident in every home."

Of the myopia of Peters and Waterman, DeLamarter wrote:

The authors' search quickly led them to IBM—a firm they claim to be expertly managed. Their opinion is based in part on IBM's stellar financial performance, which is explained by, among other things, the fact that IBM is action-oriented and close to its customers; it encourages entrepreneurship, values its people, and sticks to its main business. According to the authors, IBM has benefited from a strong central philosophy that was originally laid down by its charismatic leaders, the Watsons. They present a simple, appealing model for IBM's success—excellence in management. But this view is dead wrong. IBM's success comes from the power of its monopoly.... The two authors failed to realize that what they had understood as IBM's caring for its people, was in fact a mindless regimentation, as psychologically brutal as the physical regimentation in an army.[16]

Business Age's editor and publisher, Tom Rubython, wrote, "When *In Search of Excellence* was published in the 1980s it became the guidebook for many managers. Its authors were lauded. Unfortunately, the book was fatally flawed—and not only as a result of the problems which have emerged at one of its role models, IBM. The whole book is based on misnomers that really don't work in the long term, or the short term for that matter."

At a London Business School seminar in the 1990s, Professor John Kay stated that "there are no generic strategies, no recipes, for corporate success."

Another professor who taught at the same business school wrote, "You can know everything there is to know about business and still be a lousy manager."[17] So perhaps there is some truth in Harold Laski's claim that education is the art of teaching people to be deceived by the printed word.

By mid-1994, in IBM UK at least, the agonizing seemed to be over and the patient lived. Perhaps because Sir Anthony Cleaver commenced his career at IBM straight from Oxford, as a trainee instructor, in 1962, his thinking process is more marketing oriented than former top managers in his company. Or perhaps it is because he also serves as a vice president of The Chartered Institute of Marketing. In an interview for *Marketing Business*—the CIM's magazine—in May, 1994, he asked a rhetorical question: "Did we get too remote and stand too far back? Undoubtedly. But given that we were growing at 25–30 per cent a year, it was quite hard to resist. *It was a question of people taking orders rather than creating new opportunities.*"

Like most other businesses, IBM had been satisfied for decades to blindly follow all the conventional short-term and historic measurements that seemed to demonstrate success; such as last month's sales figures, last month's production capacities, and last year's bottom line. Meanwhile, marketers like Unilever practiced ongoing and disciplined analysis of their and their competitors' monthly market shares for each brand and continually built on a long-established foundation for future growth. From that, it would seem that management that practices old thinking looks over its shoulder at the past, whereas marketing management continually builds in preparation for future challenges. But— like so many high-tech manufacturers—IBM was product-oriented and sales-led, instead of being wholly oriented to customer needs. Chairman Cleaver appeared to be rotating one hundred and eighty degrees from old-fashioned business practices to a marketing methodology. In order to facilitate marketing practices, he is also presiding over IBM's fragmentation into a federation of separate businesses, each with its own profit and cost center.

Cleaver insisted that "the real bite is the determination to go beyond corporate speak (i.e., "We are a marketing-led, customer-focused organization and our people are its greatest asset") to actually demonstrating how such statements can be put into practice. *If you can't measure it, you can't manage it.*" Such indices "would be better predictors than pure financial numbers, because the bottom line, the profit, is essentially a historic statement."

How can we turn old thinking into more purposeful new thinking? How can the calibre and attitude of managers be improved so that they will seek out and embrace challenges and resolve problems? What does an intelligent executive with career aspirations have to do to obtain recognition? And what does an alert business enterprise have to do if it wishes to be profitable in the short term and also establish itself securely in the marketplace for the long haul? They have first to develop a capacity continually to innovate. To do so, they might consider adopting an improvement program based on the following fifteen dynamics for progressive change:

1. The CEO and board must understand and commit themselves to marketing principles and also possess the leadership skills to ensure the company continually puts them into practice;

2. A total quality management program should be initiated and maintained in every department as part of that commitment;

3. Long-term planning should be undertaken to achieve the company's mission, as well as establishing short-term and medium-range objectives;

4. Think holistically to determine the purpose before defining objectives;

5. Continually improve ways and means—of processes, plans, design, R&D, equipment, and management and work, with the aim of optimizing performance and quality;

6. Practice constancy of purpose in preparing and aiming at goals and in continually improving on them;

7. Build in marketing, quality, and dependability, right at the beginning of planning and designing products and services;

8. Make use of apprenticeship training, training for export and global competition, and continuous management education, linked to actual achievements and to planned career paths;

9. Practice hands-on, shirt-sleeves, out-of-the-office management;

10. Fragment bigger organizations into smaller, more flexible and entrepreneurial units, with autonomy to promote initiatives; adapt systems and processes to mobility and speed; and separate each unit with its own cost and profit objectives;

11. Minimize layers of management and eliminate bureaucracies;

12. Employ only dynamic and original people, with the diversity of a well-balanced portfolio;

13. Ensure that all managers are constantly alert to prevent any sidetracking away from a company's primary objective, which is to satisfy customers;

14. Dedicate the company to preparing and managing an employee program that is both caring and also in the interests of the company both in the short and long term;

15. Maintain open and democratic two-way communications, internally and externally. Management should be advised to listen more and talk less.

While there is nothing there to surprise leading management philosophers with a lifetime of experience of markets and in workplaces, those fifteen points represent a drastic change for most businesses. And human nature fears and therefore resists change. But economic survival demands changes that improve the ways and means we use to tackle global challenges.

We have to recognize that we are confronted by a predatory world that has forced its way into our living rooms and our workplaces. It impinges on us whether we want it to or not. And it is not a mechanistic world, as it may have seemed at the beginning of the Industrial Revolution: it is a world largely inhabited by people. While it is true that philosophers began by considering the mind looking inwards, we are not concerned with the self-absorption of a Descartes or a Marcel Proust. We are obliged to look outwards at the dynamics of a global marketplace, and to consider its effects on our own lifestyles and on the life of our business enterprise, in order to choose how we should react to them. *And our responses should always be different.*

Bergson wrote that the future can never be the same as the past, because new accumulations of impressions build up with every step forward. We have to change and mature in order to exist: therefore reality is changing and becoming, becoming and changing. And memory carries each step into the future, to act as a catalyst, by presenting alternative responses to each new situation in which it finds itself. The mind tests each option with the aid of memory and free will, before making its choice. That is why each thinking man or woman is a center of creative solutions. And each can improve their skills because of the continual accumulations of memories and free associations.

"The primary function of memory is to evoke all those past perceptions which are analogous to the present perception, to recall to us what preceded and what followed them, and so to suggest that decision which is the most useful."[18] Instead of the depressing theories of mechanisms involving struggle and degeneration, illustrated by Malthus, Darwin, and Spencer, we see that memories accumulate with time as each of us acquires a knowledge base. And—providing that the impressions on which they are based are of a quality to generate a fund of useful information for the creative process to take place— we are presented with "the continual elaboration of the absolutely new."

Social Dynamics

When Heraclitus realized that the existing social order could not remain for ever because everything continually changes, he expressed the view that we must not act like children with a narrow outlook that was handed down to us: we can communicate with each other, control, and check one another. We do not have to act like sleepwalkers or dreamers in their private worlds. If we are awake, we can reason.

What he faced then confronts society today. But we have seen how reasonableness appears to be a rare quality, and that much of life is ordered by instincts, by myth and misunderstanding, by prejudice and superstition, and by emotional outbursts that solve nothing except to enable some individuals to have their own way. Progress can be achieved only by design and an effort of will against those who exist from day to day largely by the automatism of instinct. What may work very well for ants does not work for human beings. Civilizations progress by the risk-taking creativity of intelligence and free will, and a human yearning, in some, for betterment.

"In every country a tiny minority sets the pace, determines the course of events. In the countries that have developed most rapidly and successfully, a minority of enterprising and risk-taking individuals have forged ahead, created opportunities for imitators to follow, have enabled the majority to increase their productivity."[19]

But, as Machiavelli discovered, "the reformer has enemies in all who profit by the old order."[20] One example of this was the experience of Semmelweis in Vienna in 1840.

Puerperal, or childbed fever, was a major cause of death in the nineteenth century. It was caused by doctors and midwives who carried the organism *Streptococcus A* bacteria. But since bacteria is invisible to the naked eye, surgeons were unaware that they existed. And they habitually infected patients on whom they were operating, through unwashed hands, unsterilized instruments, and blood or puss encrusted on their street clothing they wore when operating. The death toll perpetrated by medical practitioners appalled Semmelweis, who realized what the cause must be; but he had no way to prove it.

Medical scientists like Lister and Pasteur would prove him right later on. But the medical profession refused to endorse his theories that they were spreading death to their patients. Instead, they were scandalized by what they took to be accusations of murder. Fearful of the spread of such rumors that could threaten their livelihood, they drove Semmelweis into exile and continued to kill their patients.

Closed minds, like closed societies and closed doors, prevent progress by blocking encounters with new ideas. We have seen how family businesses often fail by following a policy of promoting only from within the family, but promoting solely from within a company is a risk practiced often by big corporations, too. By doing so, they effectively close the door to the outside world for the sake of slavishly following outworn policies or customs. And executive placement firms that are afraid to recommend disabled people, dyslexics, thalidomide cases, epileptics, and the like, may also be slamming their client's door in the face of candidates who may possess the character, drive, resolve, energy, or imagination and originality that they need.

Whereas Pacific Asian countries respect age when it represents a storage of unique experience and wisdom, the West chooses to waste such valuable resources. Older employees can provide suitable counsel for young people to test out new ideas. It is the lack of conformity in the young that inspires novelty and innovation, but someone is needed to encourage it, counterbalance impulsiveness by providing organization and experience, or provide a means to develop new ideas, or contribute added value. The patience of an older manager may help to turn a crude idea into an intellectual property.

Tests by Meredith Belbin at the UK's Henley Management College showed that everyone who produces an idea needs someone to receive and recognize its value, someone to champion the idea and develop it, someone to evaluate and improve its, someone to find the necessary resources, someone to undertake the detail work and ensure its completion, and someone to maintain the morale of the group in the meantime.

Francis Bacon wrote: "Young men are fitter to invent than to judge, fitter for execution than for counsel, and fitter for new projects than for settled business; for the experience of age in things that fall within the compass of it, directeth them.... Certainly it is good to compel employment of both...because the virtues of either may correct the defects of both."

That is precisely how progressive Japanese companies view the generational gap—not as a problem but as an opportunity to be nurtured and exploited. The older member of such a team is the *sempai* and the younger the *kohai*. That is one way the Japanese ensure continuity of skills and the accumulation of valuable corporate memories.[21]

Western companies that indulge in mass firings as short-term solutions to high overhead costs indiscriminately throw out well-tested ideas, invaluable knowledge, and processes that took many years to develop. So that instead of a corporate renaissance evolving and burgeoning when an economy recovers, there is discontinuity from the loss of useful memories. That psychosis has become known as *corporate amnesia*. And those discontinuous companies are obliged to begin reinventing in all kinds of areas and in different ways, all over again, with newly acquired staff who cannot replace the value that was thrown away.

Deficit Spending

Debts caused by mismanagement by previous governments are an example of public servants taking value away from the public. It may turn out to be the biggest single factor to prevent the growth of western economies, if the accumulated deficits cannot be reduced before interest rates on foreign borrowing become unmanageable. Meanwhile, the public is taxed to cover losses and monetary values are eroded. The situation destroyed public confidence, and now federal and regional governments are downsizing the public service. But it won't end there. When Adam Smith wrote *The Wealth of Nations,* he stated that government has only three duties: (1) to protect society from violence and invasion from other societies; (2) to protect every member of society from injustice, oppression, or otherwise establish and maintain the administration of justice; and (3) to erect and maintain public works and institutions that require large-scale funding. The problem lies in the third duty.

According to economists Milton and Rose Friedman, he intended the third duty to be limited because it could be—and has since been—"used to justify a wide range of government activity."

Jefferson drafted the American Declaration of Independence in the same year, aimed at disposing of British bureaucracy and taxes. It is ironic that the American War of Independence, which was fought over tax disputes, became the role model for the French Revolution. Due to the bankruptcy of the French monarchy and government, and a considerable national deficit, the middle and lower classes were handed a heavy tax bill. They decided that if the colonists in America could reject the demands of the British government, they could do the same with their's; and the revolution got underway.[22] At the G-7 summit in 1993, all government heads who attended were out of favor in their own countries, except for Yeltsin. Anger at the U.S. deficit was manifested when President Bush lost the election. Canadians showed their contempt for their government, not only by voting them out of office but also by making the Progressive Conservative party entirely ineffective with only two seats left in parliament. Britain's Labor party, which was expected to be voted into office, was rejected instead, because of its history of excessive taxes and deficit spending.

Milton Friedman pointed out that inflation in the government sector is more than three times what it is the private sector. He said, "In the United States it has grown from about ten per cent of the national income in 1929 to something over 40 per cent today. In the United Kingdom it has grown from ten per cent of the national income at the time of the Diamond Jubilee of Queen Victoria to something like 60 per cent today."[23] The Ross Perot phenomenon in the U.S. demonstrated how a large section of the public was prepared to show more faith in a successful businessman than in a politician. And Plato, long ago, expressed amazement that the public would consider that anyone should possess the skills to run a country when all he had demonstrated was an ability to win an election.

Friedman quoted the four-point policy of both President Reagan and Prime Minister Thatcher: "Reduce regulations, reduce government spending, reduce tax rates and have a steady and stable monetary growth."

The Auditor-General's report frequently points out that government departments have misspent or squandered taxpayers' funds and are not held properly accountable for shortfalls, ineptitude or waste. So they are naturally disinclined to reduce taxes when they may need funds to cover their lack of any reserve. (The exception is political promises in an election year). But whenever successful business people or professionals are properly motivated to spend large sums on capital equipment, research and development, advertising and promotions, or invest in hiring new staff by expanding their enterprises, wealth does trickle down to suppliers and shopkeepers and those who provide services.

And yet, theories with glib or ambiguous names like "Supply-side Economics" or "Trickle-down Economics" are abused when taken out of the closet again. That is either because they were so politicized that people take sides, or because they weren't understood. They are based on the elementary maths of the 80/20 formula in which the *vital few* create ideas, initiatives, wealth and jobs for those less-skilled or less ambitious or less motivated, as well as for themselves. We can either encourage that twenty percent who possess eighty percent of the wealth, to create and distribute *more* wealth and *more* new jobs to stimulate our economy; or we can show our envy, mean spirit and malice, by penalizing them for their ingenuity and effort, through imposing high taxes. In the latter case, we punish ourselves by retarding the economy and placing our own life-style at risk.

Public office has long been considered to be a sphere demanding vigilant scrutiny. Adam Smith remarked, "There is no art which one government sooner learns of another than that of draining money from the pockets of the people." The Roman Empire was rife with bribery and high office was one of the best means to acquire enormous wealth. Public opinion polls revealed reasons why politicians are held in such low regard today. One was that leaders of governments are entirely out of touch with what is going outside of their homes and their political caucuses. Another is patronage appointments. They create privilege and wealth at the expense of taxpayers, and are rarely seen to have been earned by merit.

More than 650 people were appointed to patronage posts in the final year in office of former Prime Minister Mulroney, and a similar number were made by Trudeau before him. One of them was a seven-year appointment as head of the Standards Council of Canada. The *Ottawa Citizen* wrote of it, "The truly disrespectful say that McSweeney rounds out Mulroney's tacky triumvirate of patronage—The Hairdresser, The Innkeeper and The Babysitter. (Rinaldo, Mila's hairdresser, was appointed to the Federal Business Development Bank. Fernand Roberge, manager of the Ritz-Carlton Hotel, the Mulroneys' home-away-from-home in Montreal while living in Ottawa, is now a Senator)."

Patronage, McSweeney said, "is part of our democratic system."

The Act of Creation

While there often seems to be a contradiction between the practical aspects of running a business and the process of invention or innovation, those who possessed the entrepreneurial gift in abundance, like Franklin, Edison, Marconi, Wedgewood, or Ford, had no problem whatsoever in reconciling the two. But many companies do have problems in providing an environment suitable for encouraging originality and discoveries. Those types of enterprises or departments might be laboratories, advertising agencies, R&D departments, think-tanks, marketers, commercial art studios, or electronics companies. One thing that is known with certainty about the act of creation is that conformity inhibits it or puts a stop to it. And entire and reasonable concentration on a creative project can frighten the solution away. That is where peripheral thinking and serendipity come into their own.

Keynes believed that creativity requires a dual nature—a combination of opposites like reason and intuition, consciousness and unconsciousness, harmony between thought and feeling, reason and imagination, of male and female characteristics. It is instructive to observe the workings of an intellect like his, because of a natural ability to reach complex conclusions through a blend of reason and intuition. Sometimes his intuition betrayed him, and what saved him was the objections and arguments of a network of brilliant mentors, colleagues, and students. It is sometimes questioned as to whether his economic theories derived rather from the interchanges between members of his team and himself than from his own genius. Sometimes he was leader, sometimes led—an ideal example of a consultative management style in which he depended on the loyalty and affection he had carefully built up over time.

He is also an excellent example of how a creative individual recognizes that opposites play a significant role in linking matrices of thought that may lead to the truth. The formulation of oppositions and antitheses plays a crucial role in the development of scientific creations and advances (Gerald Haton). And "The creative process progresses from the formulation and specification of polarities, dichotomies, and extremes towards moderation...the creator is willing to deal with the risks of contradiction and conflict. He modifies and shapes the conflicting extremes in forming a creation" (Dr. Rothenberg).[24]

"Thinking is a constant oscillation between conscious and unconscious processes," according to physician and philosopher E. Platner. Goethe likened them to the warp and the weft. The problem in a business enterprise is the unreliability of the unconscious process. Notwithstanding Freud, the unconscious mind was not a discovery of the nineteenth century. Plotinus knew that "feelings can be present without awareness of them," and, "the absence of a conscious perception is not proof of the absence of mental activity."

It would appear that the only time when intuition can be trusted is when individuals who *know by instinct* are recognized as being possessors of considerable practical experience of that subject or a broad range of knowledge in that particular sphere. As a result of the accumulations of their own experience and of the experience of others, a data bank will have been stored in the unconscious over a number of years, which can be drawn on, at the appropriate time, to create moments of illumination. This is by no means a linear process: unusual combinations of otherwise disparate ideas and facts join and part company, and rejoin with other elements or combinations of elements, like Poincaré's mathematical combinations which produced, for him, the discovery of Fuchsian functions.

Whether the discoveries prove to be of value would be likely to depend on the quality of inputs over time; whether the original impressions are true or false; and on how discriminating are the unconscious speculations in ultimately recognizing which combinations will provide the key to all the problems, by means of a new discovery, a new way of doing things, an invention, or new uses for an existing discovery.

Conversely, the danger of *hunches* is that often they are merely wish-fulfillment, like daydreams or dreams at night time that seem to provide momentous conclusions but do not stand up to sober scrutiny when we awake. Jung remarked, "The anima might then have easily seduced me into believing that I was a misunderstood artist, and that my so-called artistic nature gave me the right to neglect reality. If I had followed her voice, she would in all probability have said to me one day, "Do you imagine the nonsense you're engaged in is really art? Not a bit." Thus the insinuations of the anima, the mouthpiece of the unconscious, can utterly destroy a man."[25] Gut-feel is therefore at its most dangerous to a business organization when acted on by a CEO, not only because he may possess a wrong conviction based on false facts or premises, but because he may also possess the authority to override all advice to the contrary. That is why every chief executive requires the checks and balances of a top management team who are not sycophants, and sometimes also an independent management consultant who can test his proposition by argument.

When it comes to deliberately creating something new, all the time, we are in a somewhat different realm, because ways need to be found to initiate or encourage ideation. The dream factories of Hollywood had their ways, in the past, of combining fresh ideas, or innovations of old ones, with technology and commercialization. Comparison with far lower standards coming from the movie and TV industries today, shows how technological improvements allow a much lower calibre of film-maker to produce entertainment that generally demonstrates how technology has become a substitute for real talent. The same thing is happening in other types of business enterprises in which time is consumed in creating elegant models to demonstrate that computer technology is a substitute for real-life situations. "[O]ne must understand clearly how real-life situations are different from computer situations, exactly because they do not have the precise solutions that chess or engineering calculations do."[26] Nevertheless, we cannot ignore the movie industry or the sausage-machine factories that devise continual sitcoms and soap operas for TV networks. Despite the evidence that quality has given ground to quantity and the limited amount of available talent is spread too thin, their dynamic influence on society and the economy is such that they can initiate social innovations and also provide much-needed employment.

The dreams of scientists also create social and industrial innovations and provide employment, but for different types of workers. They have a more sober and profound influence in that their weapons technology can destroy on a large scale and their medical technology can heal. Their consumer technology can not only provide new products but also the means to manufacture them. Science cannot use the same means as show-business does, because entertainment is generally contrived or derivative, frequently imitative and repetitive, and also transient. It is rare to find originality in entertainment, but it is original ideas that are required of science.

Whatever their similarities and differences, both depend upon a continual production of ideas. Perhaps original ideas have never been so important, because Japan has now caught up with the scientific discoveries of the West, and Korea is not so very far behind. In order to take another leap forward they must depend, instead, on their own creativity. Meanwhile, the West must struggle not to be overtaken. And shrinking product lead times place considerable pressures on their creativity.

Scientific discovery takes inventors and innovators on a journey without maps. All is mystery, and often discoveries are made only after considerable periods of speculative work. That work and time has to be funded without possessing realistic schedules, and may lead nowhere. In that way, exploratory journeys of the mind can be compared to the discoveries of unmapped continents by the great navigators and explorers of the past. Fortunately, more often than not, applying educated curiosity to one thing ultimately leads to a discovery, even if it is of something quite different.

"The original writer is not the writer who thinks up a new story—there aren't any new stories, really—but the writer who tells one of the world's great stories in a new way."[27] Both art and artifice assert themselves by innovations.

"Most geniuses responsible for the major mutations in the history of thought seem to have certain features in common; on the one hand skepticism, often carried to the point of iconoclasm, in their attitude towards traditional ideas, axioms, and dogmas, towards everything that is taken for granted; on the other hand, an open-mindedness that verges on naive credulity towards new concepts which seem to hold out some promise to their instructive gropings. Out of this combination results that crucial capacity of perceiving a familiar object, situation, problem, or collection of data, in a sudden new light or new context."[28]

Staff are generally self-motivated in intelligence industries where they are chosen specifically for their unusual skills or intellectual curiosity and creativity. Talented people enjoy change and challenge, and obtain self-fulfillment in mental voyages of discovery. They are accustomed to working alone for long hours or for months at a time without direction from above, and often without supervision from project managers. The traditional hierarchical organizational chart might not exist in their case. New products marketers are likely to give them free reign, and may be lucky to receive regular progress reports. But it could not happen if they were not exceptional people. What is most important in such organizations is that they should feel as free as a composer, and be single-minded in pursuit of a goal which might otherwise slip through their fingers as they try to grasp it.

In a more conventional organization, however, imaginative and creative individuals with character and originality tend to make other employees uncomfortable. So do resolute managers who know exactly what they are doing and have the courage of their convictions, which are born from knowing where the business enterprise should be heading. Consequently, there is a tendency to disqualify such candidates or let such executives go, because they do not appear to fit in. A broader-minded CEO with marketing experience and a creative Human Relations Manager would understand that it is the insular mediocrities who are the misfits: they hold back what should otherwise be a progressive business organization. They are typical of many of yesterday's managers who failed to grow with their company or should not have been hired in the first place. Losers are bound to resent hardworking and talented people who enjoy challenges and respond with enthusiasm to solving problems instead of complaining about them. Standards can only be upgraded by employing winners as role models for others to emulate.

The Hand of God

Legends we read as children, of the allegorical kiss of life that a handsome prince of so many tales bestowed on a sleeping princess, probably arose out of the dynamic trading cultures that a prince like Lorenzo de Medici helped to develop in a city-state like Florence. They could be likened to the added value that a modern manager contributes to an inert corporate body to revive it.

But there is also the matter of "the hand of God."

It is ironic that Japan's record-breaking trade surplus in 1992 should have been viewed by the OECD as a weakness in Japan's economy. They diagnosed that it was not a conspiracy to keep out western goods and services, but an inability of Japanese customers to be able to afford imported goods. Their GDP fell in both the second and third quarters of 1992. Industrial production tumbled 8.2 percent. Retail sales fell 5.7 percent. "Fortunately for Japan," wrote *The Economist*, "it can reduce the swelling by actions it should take anyway; to stimulate its domestic economy through more government spending and/or tax cuts. Inflation is hardly cause for concern; at 0.7 percent, Japan's inflation rate is the lowest of any OECD country."

Why be concerned when all they have to do is apply a few traditional economic levers? Classical economists thought it was the hand of God that pushed or pulled them to restore balance and harmony out of economic chaos. But in the case of Japan it is their own constancy of purpose. And it is poor economic performance in the West which failed to provide markets for Japanese goods, because it prevented western consumers from being able to afford to buy much, whether of domestic manufacture or imported.

While anticipating a crash in the Nikkei 225 at the close of 1993, *The Economist* made the following analogy: "Like a geisha who cakes her face with make-up, Japan's leaders are adept at masking economic blemishes. Big companies are restructured discreetly by their bankers, not allowed to go bust. Unwanted workers are found new jobs, not pushed out onto the street. A weak stock market is supported, not left to crash. As a geisha does with a fretful customer, Japan tries to charm and soothe recessions until they eventually go away." But it is more than mere charm and it is more than merely cosmetic. It is a national social contract with industry, commerce, and Japanese employees.

Meanwhile, the West appeared to be entering a new economic cycle with recovery expected to be slow, because North America and Europe are out of joint with Pacific Asian economies. Their's are consumer driven, whereas western governments squandered their surplus and are desperately trying to appropriate any residual savings of the public that they can get their hands on to pay their bills.

"It is increasingly difficult to hang onto capital in America, and it pays to remind ourselves that 25 percent of those who are classified as rich fall from affluence every year.... The dollar earned, if it is a dividend, is first taxed to the corporation, reducing it to about 60 cents. Then it is taxed to the individual, reducing it to about 42 cents. It then reduces in value every year by the amount of that year's inflation, on average about 5 percent, reducing it to 39 cents. Then, when you die, state and federal taxes will move in to the extent of about 65 percent, reducing it to 25 cents, less the cumulative inflation."[29]

Classical economists (as designated by Marx) searched for agricultural cycles to explain the disaster of lean years following fat ones. Apparently the hand of God was at work before the Industrial Revolution spawned Marx. But since John Maynard Keynes's economic theories in the 1930s, we tend to view equilibrium as being a result of the contributions of millions of different factors arising from the behaviour of millions of people. Each one appears to offset others by some law of compensation that neutralizes the whole. But whenever everyone behaves alike, they weigh down one side of the boat and tip it over. It is reminiscent of Koestler's argument that "the collective delusions of the crowd are based, not on individual *deviations* but on the individual's tendency to conform." Whenever a large enough number of people in a society *conform* by showing loss of confidence in government and the economy, consumers stop buying inessential goods and services. What is uncertain is whether a fall in public confidence is the cause or the effect of economic recession.

If Keynes were still with us, he would very likely advise lowering taxes to increase consumption and thereby trigger economic recovery. Now that we no longer order our lives by agricultural cycles but by industrial ones, we realize that most of our problems are man-made and there is no point in waiting for the hand of God to pull the appropriate levers, any more than believing in a mythical Golden Age when Cronos ruled the world during one cycle, which was followed by an age ruled by Zeus. Voltaire remarked that man's intellectual history is simply the replacement of one myth by another. The industrial era provided new myths for Marx, who tried to find solutions to imaginary problems. No doubt he was influenced by Plato, who covered a broader canvas by describing political cycles of a typical state, and not just industrial capitalist economies.

Plato defined his position by explaining that "men are acquisitive, ambitious, competitive, and jealous; they soon tire of what they have, and pine for what they have not; and they seldom desire anything unless it belongs to others. The result is the encroachment of one group upon the territory of another, the rivalry of groups for the resources of the soil, and then war."[30]

"Any city is in fact two cities, one the city of the poor, the other the city of the rich, each at war with the other."

In nineteenth-century Britain, Prime Minister Disraeli would call them the Two Nations. Today we refer to them as the Haves and the Have-Nots, and the army of Have-Nots is growing through bankruptcies, the shrinkage of the middle classes, and unemployment.[31]

To paraphrase Plato's theory of typical social dynamics: Aristocracy collapses by limiting the circle of power too narrowly and creating a closed society; a growing merchant class seeks social positions through wealth and conspicuous consumption. The change in distribution of wealth produces political change; the oligarchy of capitalists and politicians is wrecked by their greedy scramble to acquire wealth; then democracy comes and gives the people an equal share of freedom and power; but democracy ruins itself by excess (of democracy) because its basic principle is the equal right of all to hold office and determine public policy.

That is disastrous because people are not properly equipped to select the best rulers and the wisest courses of action; democracy is simply the tyranny of mob rule. Then, because the masses love flattery and are "hungry for honey," they support the wiliest and most unscrupulous flatterer who calls himself the protector of the people (or the state) and he quickly becomes a dictator.

Plato questioned how to devise a method for barring incompetence and knavery from high office and find a better way to choose more suitable people to govern wisely and efficiently for the common good. We have still not come up with a solution. And now that Marxism has finally lost credibility and capitalism was mismanaged, society is left with a vacuum waiting to be filled by a new ideology or religion, or a new form of government to bestow the kiss of life on a society that has lost its purpose.

The Kiss of Life

The reason why classical scholars have for so long admired ancient Greek civilization is that when we observe their attempts to shape their society in accordance with reason, we recognize the same issues that confront us today. And it comes as a shock to find that Schiller was writing hopefully about solving the same types of problems over two thousand years later on. He referred to specific fragmentations in human beings—between people as they are and ideal beings, between the individual and the community, between one person and another, and between reason and feelings. "Man is inwardly at one with himself" only when he manages to transcend those dichotomies by attaining a higher harmony. But if he fails to do so, he is "at odds with himself." Schiller claimed that if the split within human beings were to be healed, then the conflict between people, and between individuals and society, also would be healed. To Hegel it was a matter of ethical conduct in a rational society—a society in which actualization of certain rights would be guaranteed.

When a father asked a follower of Pythagoras what was the best way to educate his son in ethical conduct, he was told, "Make him a citizen of a state with good laws." In a similar way, an ethical manager should ensure that he or she is part of an industrial society, or a business organization, with a philosophy and culture that is both rational and ethical. "In an ethical community it is easy to say what man must do, what are the duties he has to fulfil in order to be virtuous."

What Hegel was stating was that an individual has a right to belong to an ethical order with which he or she can identify—"a station in life" with identifiable rights and duties, in which he or she can achieve self-respect. The ethical philosophy in such a society is Right Attitude (*Rechtschaffenheit*) and *ésprit de corps*.

It comes as no surprise that Hegel's words faithfully describe Japanese culture and traditions, as briefly summarized in earlier chapters. But those societal elements are precisely the ones that are missing in the sad state of a declining ethical and moral environment in the West. We are caught up in a tyranny of democracy which—like the "despotism of freedom" that followed the French Revolution and led to the guillotine—attaches itself to the values of a mass or pop culture (*Massenpsychologie*). In our nostalgia for the democratic culture we admired in ancient Greece, we forget that the majority of its population were either slaves, free men, or women, without citizenship rights. It was not the masses who set the standards but the higher values of a small élite, like Aristotle, who were descended from the aristocratic families who originally settled the territory.[32]

"We are concerned," wrote Koestler, "with a cure for the paranoid streak in what we call 'normal' people, which is revealed when they become victims of group mentality. We are a mentally sick race, and as such deaf to persuasion. It has been tried from the age of the Prophets to Albert Schweitzer."

Each time we take a step forward we are pushed two steps back. How can we stop regressing? Only, apparently, by means of that vital force, like Bergson's breath of life, or *élan vital,* or Machiavelli's *virtù.* Nobel prizewinner Albert Szent-Györgyi re-named it *syntropy.* And he defined it as an "innate drive in living matter to perfect itself."

If we pause to consider the existence of such a drive, we are obliged to acknowledge its rarity in human beings. Syntropy seems rather to describe Lamark's theory about animals striving to adapt to their environments, while Rousseau considered that "everything degenerates under the hand of man." And Jung drew our attention to "the phenomenon of that widespread regression to paganism which has made itself increasingly felt ever since the Renaissance." Perhaps we are therefore being romantic even to consider that syntropy—which can be scientifically observed in very low organic forms—could also be present in human beings. Their innate drive to perfect themselves must surely be unconscious, whereas the collective human unconscious, according to Jung, "holds the earlier low intellectual and moral level before the eyes of the more highly developed individual.... Seldom does man understand with his head alone, least of all when he is a primitive. Something in man is profoundly disinclined to give up his beginnings."

Industrial societies and corporate cultures differ little from the much larger society in which they form a particular part, in that they too are composed of people. And the specific problem of people is their often faulty discernment between reality and illusion. Between those two states falls a shadow which blurs their edges.

The *shadow* is a negative archetypal figure of the collective unconscious, according to Jung, who studied it in his own psychiatric patients, in Otto Gross's studies of psychopaths, and also in mass psychology. "The mass is swayed by *participation mystique*[33]...The regressive identification with lower and more primitive states of unconsciousness is invariably accompanied by a heightened sense of life; hence the quickening effect of regressive identification with half-animal ancestors in the stone age.... That is why masses are always breeding grounds of psychic epidemics, the events in Germany being a classic example of this." So too was the recent religious cult in Waco, Texas, which chose to destroy itself and all its children in a fit of paranoia, by fire, in 1993, and the Oklahoma City disaster in 1995.

"Why is it that we still remain barbarians?" asked Schiller.

Jung answered the question by gazing back into history, where we see "personality disappearing beneath the wrappings of collectivity. And if we go right back to primitive psychology, we find absolutely no trace of the concept of an individual. Instead of individuality we find only collective relationships...the earlier all-powerful collective attitude prevented almost completely an objective psychological evaluation of individual differences."

"It is that primitive collective mentality" that seeks to suppress self-actualization and civilized values. "It is a relic of that archaic time when there was no individual whatsoever."

But the drive to perfection—rare though it may be in human beings—does exist in mature personalities seeking self-actualization. It also exists in compassionate societies. What Hegel, Schiller, and Rousseau described was a social schizophrenia that causes paranoia in less developed individuals and societies. And it compels them, out of frustration, to debase standards they themselves cannot attain. They denigrate or degrade minorities who do not have the power to protect themselves, in order to create an illusion that they are "superior." They demonstrate Adler's "law of compensation" carried to neurosis. Thus, the innate drive to perfection, which Szent-Györgyi named "syntropy," is destroyed again and again because of ignorance, a bias toward inferiority, delusions, or fanaticism in a sick society.

As for the *idée fixe* of the individual; in one of two major personality types—the *introvert* as defined by Jung and studied in psychopaths by Gross[34]— we see that the after-effect of an initial idea persists for a prolonged period: "The idea has a lasting influence, the impression goes deep." But "the associations are limited to a narrow range...at the same time the complex (of ideas) is shut off from everything extraneous and finds itself in isolation." "In pathological cases it turns into an obsessive or paranoid idea, absolutely unshakable, that rules the individual's entire life. His whole mentality is subverted, becoming 'deranged.'" That is not to say that all introverts are deranged: what is described are those who develop an *idée force* detrimental to themselves and others.

Both of those abnormal drives and the ideal one of syntropy are important for managers to understand in an age of growing multiculturalism, because with it comes prejudice and racism. While ethnicity is one of the prime sources of diversity for the West, racism is the last resort of failures who cannot adjust to it.

It is not easy to be a whole person poised between reason and emotion. People tend to be either reasonable and unemotional or emotional and unreasonable; mostly the latter. "As passion without reason is blind, so reason without passion is dead" (Spinoza). On one hand there is the dead hand of the bureaucrat or the dry academic, but a greater danger is *primitive* thinking and feeling, as Jung described it. Most of human history, with its paranoid focus on mystical atrocities—which were nothing more than the degradation and crude butchery of other human beings—makes that abundantly clear. The door to the unconscious may lead to creativity, but it is also dangerously like opening the lid of Pandora's box.

Tomorrow's managers should be able—like Renaissance man—to control the dumb savagery of "the crocodile in the soul" and turn instinctively, instead, to his or her drive to perfection. But to do so requires self-improvement. Renaissance man was soldier and poet, adventurer and philosopher, artist and craftsman, inventor and merchant, politician and monk, hoodlum and hero, alchemist and scholar, astrologer and astronomer, all in one.

Continuous personal growth is demanded of today's business executives, despite the continual battle against a maelstrom of mediocrity and worse. Most executives are unaware of a continual need for regular analysis of activities and events, in order to discover better ways to perform every function and achieve each goal. That is how improvements are made, instead of merely repeating bad habits. Most managers choose to be enslaved by habits, in the erroneous belief that routine is good. They do not realize that even habits that are not bad in themselves prevent improvement by change, differentiation and growth.

Evolution has been compared to a maze with a number of blind alleys into which some animal species, including earlier humans, came to a dead end. Yesterday's executives who were slaves to bureaucratic habits thought and behaved as if management consists of repetitions of stale customs and routines. They too have reached a dead end, through failure to improve themselves and to strive continually to improve on previous performances.

High technology has propelled us into the twenty-first century ahead of time. We can no longer escape economic realities in illusions like "deficit spending," which seek to justify management incompetence. And it is self-defeating to hope for miracles and rely passively on the hand of God. Yesterday's managers winged it, by investing the minimum of time and effort required merely to keep old routines going for the time being. But increasing competition between Pacific-Asian countries seeking to overtake North America; a European Economic Community; and the struggle by overpopulated Third-World countries to improve their living standards, will no longer allow mediocrity in management. Managers will be expected to provide intellectual skills and creative solutions, and innovate continuously in order to compete. They will be required to be more holistic in their approach, and dedicated to nurturing their business organization.

By now we have taken a number of steps backwards in order to view the management situation from the broadest possible perspective. What we have seen are executives incapable of rising above mediocrity in the West—who do not possess that *élan vital* to breathe life into a business enterprise—as allegories described the process of syntropy. But real princes like Lorenzo de Medici often developed or revived dormant societies like Florence. And there were talented women as different as Queen Elizabeth the First and Joan of Arc, for example, who transformed "ugly frogs" or "beasts" into self-respecting princes (or societies) by virtue of their kiss of life.

We have also witnessed the extraordinary achievements of the Japanese Spirit founded on Confucian principles and working with constancy of purpose to achieve perfection. While the West has been talking, Japan has opened up markets for its goods right across Pacific-Asia.

The West has a choice. It can refuse to stir out of its present torpor, and yesterday's managers can ensure, as before, that newcomers toe the line of mediocrity and become part and parcel of the sterility of second-rate establishments. And the 1990s will be described by historians as the decade when the West finally became too apathetic to survive and gave up all the social and economic benefits we have worked for since Magna Carta. Or we can work instead to restore our self-respect and our fortunes, through syntropy.

But the second law of thermodynamics states that entropy always increases. Some things rust or wear out, others burn out, cool down, or melt. Everything disintegrates, collapses or dies. We cannot afford to be indifferent in the face of such relentless destruction. Nor is there any point in taking purely defensive measures. General Patton—who knew a thing or two about battling to win and not just to survive—said, "Soldiers in defensive positions are just waiting to die." That is what the West has been doing for more than two decades.

A Golden Age

The business and technological revolutions in the 1990s revealed a management crisis in the West, which had been partly concealed for several decades. The key question is whether business leaders will wake up in time to realize either that their companies are hollow and sterile without skilled senior marketing management, or that their present calibre of less experienced managers—who were probably originally intended to be stop gaps—is far too insubstantial to provide real growth.

But to view trade and commerce in isolation from society is a meaningless endeavor. What, after all, are we striving for unless it is to improve our quality of life? We can do so only through economic and social progress—as took place, for example, over 2,500 years ago in Athens, and also in the fourteenth and fifteenth-century Italian *Renaissance*. Of course, those changes for the better were far broader and more profound than just technological advances. They were scientific and economic as well as cultural in Greece; and the social and cultural advances in Italy were made possible only through the riches obtained by financial innovations, trade, and aggressive marketing. The blossoming of Greek culture

> bequeathed itself in an incomparable legacy to the nations of Europe and the Near East.... Our handicrafts, the technique of mining, the essentials of engineering, the processes of finance and trade, the organization of labor, the governmental regulation of commerce and industry—all these have come down to us on the stream of history from Rome, and through Rome from Greece.... Our schools and universities, our gymnasiums and stadiums, our athletics and Olympic games, trace their lineage to Greece.... Our literature could hardly have existed without the Greek tradition. Our alphabet came from Greece through Cumae and Rome; our language is littered with Greek words; our grammar and rhetoric, even the punctuation and paragraphing of this page, are Greek inventions. Our literary

genres are Greek—the lyric, the ode, the idyll, the novel, the essay, the oration, the biography, the history, and above all the drama—tragedy, comedy, and pantomime—are Greek; and though Elizabethan tragedy is unique, the comic drama has come down almost unchanged from Menander and Philemon through Plautus and Terence, Ben Jonson and Molière. The Greek dramas themselves are among the richest portions of our inheritance.... The liberation of science from theology, and the independent development of scientific research, were parts of the heady adventure of the Greek mind.

Greek mathematicians laid the foundations of trigonometry and calculus.... Democritus illuminated the whole area of physics and chemistry with his atomic theory. In a mere aside and holiday from abstract studies Archimedes produced enough new mechanisms to place his name with the highest in the records of invention. Aristarchus anticipated and perhaps inspired Copernicus; and Hipparchus, through Claudius Ptolemy, constructed a system of astronomy which is one of the landmarks of cultural history. Eratosthenes measured the earth and mapped it. Anaxagoras and Empedocles drew the outlines of a theory of evolution. Aristotle and Theophrastus classified the animal and plant kingdoms, and almost created the sciences of meteorology, zoology, embryology, and botany. Hippocrates freed medicine from mysticism and philosophical theory, and ennobled it with an ethical code; Herophilus and Erasistratus raised anatomy and physiology to a point which, except in Galen, Europe would not reach again until the Renaissance.[35]

The rebirth of Italy was initiated by cultivated banking families like the Medici. The kiss of life was given first to the City of Florence because its culture was endowed by a grand conception of an intelligent, educated and dynamic leader named Cosimo d' Medici. Perhaps he was the archetypal *Renaissance Man* gifted with an abundance of interests and skills and a passion for perfection in all of them.

Through the organization of her industry, the extension of her commerce, and the operations of her financiers, Fiorenza—the City of Flowers—was in the fourteenth century the richest town in the peninsula, excepting Venice. But while the Venetians in that age gave their energies almost entirely to the pursuit of pleasure and wealth, the Florentines, possibly by the stimulus of a turbulent semi-democracy, developed a keenness of mind and wit, and a skill in every art, that made their city by common consent the cultural capital of Italy...rival families contended in the patronage of art as well as in the pursuit of power.[36]

The fortunes of the Medici family were founded "by bold commerce and judicious finance." Their emblem of six red balls on a field of gold became reduced, in later years, to the familiar sign of three golden balls outside of every pawnbroker. But Cosimo loaned his money to foreign kings and to popes.

It should be born in mind that earlier even than the turn of the fourteenth century, the European world was relatively densely settled, productive and culturally innovative. In Flanders tens of thousands of looms were producing textiles for export; in northern Italy sophisticated international banking empires were elaborating credit, insurance and investment; in northern France intellectual life of the highest sophistication and political power of exceptional effectiveness had developed side by side. Everywhere in Europe in the twelfth and thirteenth centuries trees were being felled, roots laboriously grubbed out, ditches delved to drain waterlogged land. Recruiting agents travelled in the overpopulated parts of Europe collecting emigrants; wagons full of anxious new settlers creaked their way across the continent; busy ports sent off ships full of colonists to alien and distant destinations; bands of knights hacked out new lordships.[37]

The Elizabethan Renaissance in England was no less spectacular for its intellectual vitality, individuality, hustle and bustle, and its talents. "[I]t may well be that early seventeenth-century England was at all levels the most literate society the world had ever known": It was the age of Shakespeare, Marlowe, Ben Jonson, Beaumont and Fletcher—whose entertainments have been described as "the most intellectually demanding" ever put before a large audience in the history of England.[38]

What is so striking about this period is not the appearance of individual men of genius, who may bloom in the most unpromising soil, but rather the widespread public participation in significant intellectual debate on every front. It is no accident that the monarchs, Elizabeth, James I, Charles I and even Charles II, were more interested in things of the mind than any before or since; that James was even flattered to be called 'King of the Academicians'.[39]

"If it is accepted that over half the male population of London was literate, that a high proportion of the one third of adult males who could sign their names in the home counties could read, and that 2½% of the annual male seventeen-year-old age-group was going on to higher education, then the English in 1640 were infinitely better educated than they had been before."
What brought about that age of bustle, planning, projects, and progress? To find the answer we must go back, link by link, in a chain of circumstances that lead to challenges to which some individual or society responded effectively enough to be established by name in the history of western civilization. Either they exploited opportunities to their own advantage or improved on situations by using their survival skills—intelligence like Charlemagne; power like the Church; cunning like Louis XIth of France; intuition like Joan of Arc; adaptability and pragmatism like Queen Elizabeth the First of England; technical knowledge acquired by Peter the Great; political skills like the Empress Catherine of Russia; innovations like Frederick the Great of Prussia; and other remarkable individuals of their time. Each one generally emerged opportunely when civilization stood on the brink of a chasm and had no choice but to wait hopefully for someone to erect a bridge across it.
The catalyst for change at the new dawn after the Dark Ages in Europe was the institution of the Church of Rome. It had survived the collapse of the Roman Empire and was then nearly eight hundred years old. And it pos-

sessed the monopoly of education. Its thesis was that it could survive all the schisms and heresies of Christianity and the onslaught of Islam only if it possessed a military force to establish a new Holy Roman Empire. The other protagonist—or antithesis: the *somebody* alluded to by Bergson as an *outsider* who could provide the breath of life to that dormant period in western civilisation—was to become known as Charlemagne. He inherited the Frankish Empire in the ninth century, held back the marauding Vikings from the north, and repelled the Moors from invading France from the south. The Church lent him legitimacy by crowning him Emperor, and he gave it legitimacy by providing an army to spread its creed. Wherever he carved out the Holy Roman Empire, the Church founded a network of bishoprics, a church, a succession of clerics, its own saint, often even a relic, and an endowment. Its hierarchical system established it to the present day, in one form or another.

New technologies played a significant role then and there, just as at other times and in other places. By the year 1100, knights and castles, crossbows, and siege machines had been instrumental in shaping new societies. New technology and tactics resulted in victory when the Normans invaded Britain and when Germans sought to conquer new territories in Eastern Europe. Dynamic forces competed for estates, cattle, slaves, and other resources owned by indigenous peoples and their rulers. The more virile or adaptable of them reacted in the end as most survivors must do: by *mimesis*. "By the mid-thirteenth century the rulers of, for instance, Wales and Pomerania had become virtually indistinguishable from their foes in armament and methods of waging war (as in much else)."[40]

That century and the following one were times when urbanization spread to most parts of Europe and urban networks developed through family connections and trading contacts, as well as legal ties, and extended outwards from central Western Europe. Trade and commerce, which developed in the eleventh century, burgeoned across Europe in the twelfth and thirteenth centuries and was born across the Mediterranean in the fourteenth by Italian merchants in particular, and also German ones. Trade, plunder, and piracy quickened in Genoa, Venice, Constantinople, North Africa, and the Middle East. Venetian merchants gained a virtual monopoly of trade in the Crusader States.

The city walls of Florence surrounded more than 1,500 acres by 1284. And the Golden Age of Renaissance Italy would become the pinnacle of a western civilisation that had developed out of the challenges of overland and overseas trade.

But there are also societies that imprison themselves in their past, and they exploit the collective delusions of the mobs to hold back the future. Christian nations were retarded by a worldview that was, by this time, hundreds of years out of date and frozen in time. That frigid perception began to be thawed out from the twelfth century onwards by a gradual warming process emerging from Asia Minor and Alexandria, where the wreckage of Greek science and philosophy was discovered. Classics "or fragments of works of Archimedes and Hero of Alexandria, of Euclid, Aristotle, and Ptolemy, came floating into Christendom like pieces of phosphorescent flotsam."[41]

Just as "the ruins of Rome were pillaged by the builders of the Renaissance and worked into the temples and palaces of a new civilization," so the shards of Greek philosophy, mathematics, map making, astronomy, navigation, and culture, were reunited to provide a solid foundation for a new Golden Age in the walled city state of Florence.[42] So the stirrings of the modern mind in the thirteenth century were initiated by the rediscovery of Greek philosophers who demonstrated the superiority of scientific and measured observations and intelligent reasoning, compared to myths and superstitions. "[T]he stirrings of a patient who emerges from a long, comatose state," resembled the legendary sleeping princess being awakened from her torpor by the kiss of life.

Despite the closed society of Christendom, which had managed to control thought, attitudes, and custom, and hold back the future for over a thousand years, better-educated, more knowledgeable, and experienced people in more developed cultures react in a more positive way to changes they can manage through their innate drive to perfection. The catalyst in the Florentine Renaissance was Cosimo d' Medici. He contributed enormous sums of his own money to public works and private charities. He was an educated man of good taste, who "cared as much for literature, scholarship, philosophy, and art, as for wealth and power." He spent a fortune on searching for ancient manuscripts which had been lost, and buying them. He had them shipped from Greece and Alexandria, and hired copyists to transcribe those that could not be bought. He ensured that classical philosophy and culture were revived. But he was not the first or only one to revive the *Golden Age*: Petrarch and Boccaccio were among the best known of the scholars and writers who did so. But, "if we embrace in our judgement not only Cosimo…but his descendants Lorenzo the Magnificent, Leo X, and Clement VII, we may admit that in the patronage of learning and art the Medici have never been equalled by any other family in the known history of mankind."[43] It was Cosimo who presided over the awakening of the modern mind.

When a printing press was installed in Florence, his son Lorenzo saw the revolutionary possibilities of the new technology of movable type. It was the ideal means of propagating the works of Homer, Euripides, Lucian, Horace, Virgil, Pliny, and Dante, which were included among over a thousand volumes that were to become known as the Laurentian Library.

Our own high-tech revolution cannot compare with the revolution of ideas and the dedication and energy to realize them in pursuit of perfection. Our technological advances—extraordinary though they may be—simply create better or faster machinery without regard for its devastating effects on our society. Only the Japanese, it seems, take the human aspect into consideration, because their more holistic vision embraces society in its entirety and the future as well as the present. But they are under intense pressure by the United States to change their views to short-term ones and their values to purely materialistic ones. Doing so would not be a kiss of life for them, but possibly the destruction of their well ordered society, which should rather be a model for the West.

The Pursuit of Happiness

The pursuit of perfection is the philosophy that underlies all great religions and is the objective of classical philosophers. Not many of us can achieve it: perfection is an ideal that seldom, if ever, is achieved, because those who seek it most strenuously are the ones least satisfied with their achievements. The more their minds know and the more their skills grow, the higher the standard they set to achieve perfection. Continuous improvement may lead to excellence, rarely to perfection. But striving for it exercises the wits and advances standards of proficiency. Japan and China, which were influenced by Lao Tzu and Confucius, were more aware than most cultures of a need to strive for perfection rather than consider life to be pointless and abandon the struggle by giving only enough of oneself to satisfy conventions, or compromise with the tenth-rate. The results were the ideals and disciplines of *Zen* and *Bushido*; to fix the objective and provide the means to achieve it.

Every amateur or professional in sport, and every musician, composer, author, artist, ballet dancer, or opera singer who is dedicated to their career, strives for perfection. How can we think otherwise of Beethoven, Bach, Wagner, Sibelius, Mahler; Horowitz, Menuhin, or Lortie; Kirsten Flagstad or Teresa Stratas; the great painters or great conductors and their famous orchestras; Markova, Fonteyn, Ashton, Nijinsky; Chaucer, Shakespeare, Milton, Joyce, or T. S. Eliot? They all understood and practiced a philosophy of continuous study and practice, discipline, reappraisal, and still more practice, in a continual attempt to achieve perfection. Should business managers—with all their responsibilities and obligations—be any different? Perfectionists are always aware that what is second-rate is simply not good enough. They know how easy it is to backslide the moment they might allow themselves to settle for second-best. Their performance is constantly submitted to their own disciplined judgement and improved through analysis, comparison and discussion—sometimes through argument. But first we have to know what we are and what we ought to be.

The sheer volume of outstanding talent in sports and the arts in North America and Europe, in particular, is extraordinary. Whether we are thrilled at watching the dedication and disciplined training of fourteen year olds performing gymnastics and acrobatics at the Olympic Games or thirteen year olds excel on the violin or cello at Carnegie Hall, we cannot help but be impressed by their perseverence to reach such heights of accomplishment.

If we consider the enormous gap between the entire sphere of competitive sports, music and the arts at the Lincoln Centre, the Kennedy Centre, Glyndebourne, or the Albert Hall and Festival Hall, compared with the entire sector of business management, we are left admiring the skills of one and disappointed at the mediocrity of the other. And whatever their international acclaim or their financial rewards, we are forever in the debt of those sports men and women, conductors of famous orchestras, opera singers and musicians, for the joy they give us, and for the constant reminder that there is so much more to life than materialism. Material things do not endure in the way that our love and enchantment of real talent uplifts and inspires us throughout our lives. So much so that, more than ever before, we continually see audiences rise spontaneously to give standing ovations in appreciation at theatres, stadiums, concert halls and opera houses.

The ancient Greeks used the word *aretē* to denote functional excellence of any person, animal, or thing. For example, "the *aretē* of a shoemaker is that quality which makes him produce good shoes; in a race horse, it is the quality which will make the horse run to victory; and the *aretē* of a musical instrument will make it respond well and correctly to the manipulations of the player...This means that the overtone of divine sanction of human morality, which is the cornerstone of any Judaeo-Christian system of ethics, is absent from the Greek. The value of *aretē* is that it is an end in itself..."[44]

Aretē in the economic arena of business, too, requires dedication, disciplined training, and skill in the use of management and marketing principles. Those who took business seriously, like the Venetians, the Florentines, the Dutch, and the British, were able to develop great cultures based on trade. It was trade that laid the foundations of democratic civilizations. On it depends the employment and the quality of life of millions, the stability of nations, the maintenance of law and order, sovereignty, and the creation of a suitably powerful and self-confident environment for a nation's culture to spring forth and flourish.

The awakening of the modern mind requires continual inputs by innovators and technologists. But we should not enslave ourselves to the marvels of electronics, fiber optics, silicon chips, robotics, or computers. First and last should come the miracle of awareness and of the human spirit, with its ability to transcend, its drive to learn and compare, to analyze and to surpass its previous performances and the performances of others.

To continue to transcend the merely materialistic pursuit of production and unit costs requires resolution and dedication. But as the twenty-first century dawns on the West, a state of demoralization seems to have set in, instead of optimism or hope. Perhaps it is because we are standing on the brink of a chasm once again, and all we can see is the gap before us. We are waiting hopefully for someone to erect a bridge across it, but there is no help coming from any direction. The established institutions have demonstrated their powerlessness, and we have thrown our traditions and customs away.

The myth of care and comradeship in our tribal or familial origins may be exaggerated or mere illusion, but we miss them none the less. And we are ready to believe in them as a reaction to feeling trapped by the manipulations of bureaucrats on one side and technocrats on the other.

At the same time we are continually confronted by the media with social and economic problems. We are bombarded with everyone else's personal problems when we are desperately struggling to solve our own. Today's complexities seem to be overwhelming us because of the repetitive communications that overlap and overload, so that we are in danger of losing control of our lives. Fate waits patiently, it seems, to snare us in its web. The more we struggle, the less likely does escape seem possible. Indeed, there is nowhere to escape to. We could surely be forgiven for sometimes succumbing to despair? But pessimism is a certain way to failure. We should rather recall Adler's understanding of our vulnerable condition, and his remark that, "If I had his erroneous view of life, I would act exactly as he does."

The Golden Ages of reform and rebirth came into being and were developed by extraordinary individuals; not as a result of the popular will or established institutions. They need not, therefore, be confined to the distant past. The key is *individualism*. Lord Clark wrote, " I believe that almost everything of value which has happened to this world has been due to individuals...They are usually men of genius waiting for these moments of expansion, like ships waiting for high tide..."[45]

We should not allow self-serving lobby groups to marginalize them or us. Nor should we be drawn to the illusory tribal fireside with its participation mystique that leads to alienation and violence between and within societies. Bertrand Russell expressed the view that people's passions and instincts render them incapable of enjoying the benefits of any scientific civilization. It seems we can return to reason only by self-actualization.

George Orwell's view of emerging modern societies, as he saw them in the 1930s, was that they were not very promising. He was one of the first left-wing writers to see through Soviet tyranny. He detested the tribal Nazi dictatorship; and there was the materialistic United States.

These societies seemed to have made a disastrous mistake. Each claimed that it sought the welfare of its people but in each of them the quality of life was being debased. Nineteenth century America and Edwardian England were unjust societies, yet Orwell knew from literature in the one case and personal experience in the other that people in those days lived under much less strain than they do today, when so much is supposedly being done to make conditions easier.[46]

He faced the same question that confronts us today: "Modern capitalism is bad and must be replaced by a juster society; but how can we ensure that the best qualities of the old society will be retained while destroying the worst?" He had been impressed by the simple decency of people in comparatively backward societies.

Decency was not a virtue solely of gentlemen or of the middle classes, although it is considered to be just as old-fashioned today. His guide was his love of pre-war England with its decent values, and the English society he loved was at the point of disappearance. "And for a time he was rather like a man who doesn't know in which direction to take the next step." In that way he was remarkably like us at the turn of the century.

By now, the tides of democracy have almost entirely drowned gentlemanly codes and middle-class morality. Whatever remains of those traditional values is on the point of being washed away as technology and money take precedence over human decency in the business revolution. And yet, it is not too late to reconsider what is necessary to govern a nation well. In Renaissance Italy, the Duke of Urbino had no doubt: it was simply "*essere umano*—to be human."

That is what Orwell asserted in all his writings. "Our problem," he wrote, is "how to salvage civilization."

It is our problem too.

Appendix

Management Ranking in the World Competitiveness Report

The extent to which enterprises are managed in an innovative, profitable, and responsible manner

	1995	1994	1993
1st:	U.S.	Japan	Japan
2nd:	Sweden	Sweden	Denmark
3rd:	Switzerland	Switzerland	Sweden
4th:	Japan	Hong Kong	Switzerland
5th:	Singapore	U.S.	U.S.
6th:	New Zealand	Denmark	Belgium/Luxembourg
7th:	Denmark	Singapore	Netherlands
8th:	Hong Kong	New Zealand	New Zealand
9th:	Chile	Finland	Germany
10th:	Finland	Netherlands	Austria
11th:	Netherlands	Austria	France
12th:	Austria	Germany	Ireland
13th:	Norway	UK	Norway
14th:	Germany	Malaysia	Canada
15th:	Taiwan	Norway	Finland
16th:	Canada	Chile	UK
17th:	Belgium/Luxembourg	Belgium/Luxembourg	Australia
18th:	Israel	Australia	Italy
19th:	Australia	Canada	Turkey
20th:	UK	France	Spain
21st:	France	Taiwan	Greece

Categories used for rankings: Use of Information Technology; Implementation of Strategies; Willingness to Delegate; Long-Term Orientation; International Experience; Employee Relationships; Managerial Constraints;

Source: IMD & World Economic Forum, Switzerland.

Notes

Foreword

1. William Zikmund and Michael d'Amico, *Marketing* (John Wiley & Sons, New York, 4th edition, 1993).
2. George W. Terry, *Principles of Management* (R. D. Irwin, Homewood, Ill., 1982).
3. Multinational management consultants McKinsey & Company.
4. PA Consulting, London, England.
5. Robert Heller, *The Naked Manager* (Hodder, London, 1974).
6. *Harvard Business Review* (Boston, 1960).
7. James Burnham, *The Managerial Revolution—What is Happening in the World* (The John Dale Company, Inc., New York, 1941).
8. John P. Kotter, *The New Rules* (The Free Press, New York, 1995).
9. *The Pocket MBA*, Book Division of *The Economist*, UK (1995) and the AMBA (The Association of MBAs).
10. Peter F. Drucker, *Post-Capitalist Society* (Harper Collins, New York, 1993).
11. *The Economist* (17 April 1993).

Introduction—The Management Jungle

1. *Sources:* The OECD, the Japanese embassy, *The Financial Post* (Toronto, Canada, January 1993), The Canadian Department of Finance, and the UK Treasury Department.
2. Harold Koontz, Cyril O'Donnell, and Heintz Weihrich, *Essentials of Management* (McGraw-Hill, New York, 1986). Harold Koontz, "The Management Theory Jungle," in *Journal of Academy of Management* 4, 3(December 1961): 174–88. Also "Making Sense of Management Theory," *Harvard Business Review* 40, 4(July–August 1962): 24ff.; and "The Management Theory Jungle Revisited," *Academy of Management Review* 5, 2(April 1980): 175–87.
3. James Champy, *Reengineering Management* (Harper Business, New York, 1995).
4. Meredith Belbin, *Management Teams* (Heinemann, London, 1981).
5. Paul Klugman, *Peddling Prosperity* (W.W. Norton, New York, 1994).
6. *Source: The Economist* (London, England, 5 August 1995).
7. Peter F. Drucker, *The Practice of Management* (Heinemann, London, 1954).
8. *Source: Business Age* magazine, UK (March 1993).
9. Jacob Bronowski, *The Ascent of Man* (Little, Brown and Company, Boston/Toronto 1973).
10. Henry Mintzberg, *Mintzberg on Management* (The Free Press, New York, 1989).
11. Joseph A. Schumpeter, *The Theory of Economic Development* (Transaction Publishers, New Brunswick, N.J., 1983).
12. John Maynard Keynes, *The General Theory of Employment, Interest and Money* (Macmillan, Cambridge University Press, 1973).
13. Details of rankings in the final chapter and in the Appendix.

Chapter 1—The Marketing Evolution

1. Statistics are quoted in chapter 12.
2. Edwin Stringer, Q.C. of Stringer, Brisbin, Humphrey of Toronto.
3. *Source:* Dr. Michael Gershon, professor of anatomy and cell biology at Columbia-Presbyterian Medical Center, New York.
4. Walter Allen, *The English Novel* (Penguin Books, London 1954).
5. Vilfredo Pareto discovered an economic law in the nineteenth century. It showed that, for example, 20 percent of customers account for 80 percent of revenues; 20 percent of components account for 80 percent of costs, and so on. A detailed analysis of customer accounts revealed the same ratio in this case. It became known as the 80/20 formula.
6. Michael E. Porter, *The Competitive Advantage of Nations* (The Free Press, New York, 1990), 580–81.
7. W. Edwards Deming, *Out of the Crisis* (Massachusetts Institute of Technology, 1986).
8. Koji Miyake, *Small Factories: The Underpinnings of Industry.* An essay published in *The Electric Geisha,* translated from the Japanese by Miriam Eguchi (Kodansha International, Tokyo, 1994).
9. *Source: New York Times* reported on two papers—one by Dr. Richard Ebstein and his colleagues at Herzog Memorial Hospital in Jerusalem and Ben-Gurion University in Beersheva; the other from Dr. Jonathan Benjamin and Dr. Dean Hamer and colleagues at the National Institute of Health in Bethesda, Md. The dopamine system has long been proposed as a factor in impulsive, extravagant behavior, but this is the first clear evidence of a connection between the neurotransmitter and the personality type, and the first known report of a link between a specific gene and a specific normal personality trait, according to Dr. Ebstein. Research on animals and studies of human twins indicate that about half of novelty-seeking behavior can be attributed to genes and half to environmental circumstances so far ill-defined. (Genetic origin theory as yet unproven.)
10. Markinor (South Africa).
11. *Modern Marketing Thought* (Macmillan, UK, 1964). Edited by Charles St Thomas.

Chapter 2—Innovation, The Key to the Future

1. John Ralston Saul, *Voltaire's Bastards* (Viking/Penguin Books, New York, 1992).
2. Joseph A. Schumpeter, *The Theory of Economic Development* (Transaction Publishers, New Brunswick, N.J., 1983).
3. *Source:* Dr. Andrew Sentance's report, *Innovation and Design in a Changing World Economy* (1996).
4. Research company: New Solutions, UK, 1996.
5. John Kenneth Galbraith, *The Affluent Society* (Houghton Mifflin, Boston, 1971), quoting from Thorstein Veblen, *The Theory of Business Enterprise* (Scribner, N.Y., 1932).
6. *Source: The Financial Post* (Toronto, Canada, 16 July 1993).
7. James M. Utterback, "Dominant Designs and the Survival of Firms," chapter 2 of *Mastering the Dynamics of Innovation* (Harvard Business School Press, Boston, Mass., 1994).
8. Ludwig von Bertalanffy, *Robots, Men and Minds* (George Braziller, N.Y., 1967).

Chapter 3—The Killing Fields

1. John Gribbin, *In The Beginning* (Little, Brown, New York, 1993).
2. *Source: Chicago Tribune* (June 1995). Gerstner replaced John Akers after IBM lost markets to Microsoft and began showing annual losses, which reached $8 billion in 1993 alone. Promotion had previously come from within, and this outsider quickly showed that he was not prepared to be gentlemanly about managing change (as IBM's founders had been regarded). In mid-1995 he made IBM's first ever hostile takeover of Lotus, the third biggest manufacturer of personal computer software in the world (after Microsoft and Novell Inc.). IBM is likely to expand Lotus's market share because it already possesses customers in 140 countries, and Lotus is dominant in Groupware, which is catching on in corporate America. In announcing the Lotus takeover, Gerstner also established a new policy to acquire more companies and overwhelm the competition by buying market shares.
3. "At every step the expansion of Rome was aided by the mistakes of her enemies." Will Durant; *The Life of Greece* (Simon & Schuster, New York 1939).
4. As in eroding market share.
5. In business terms, pin them down so that they cannot obtain essential supplies of raw materials.
6. John Kenneth Galbraith, *The Great Crash, 1929* (Houghton, Mifflin, Boston, 1961).
7. Charles H. Hession, *John Maynard Keynes* (Macmillan, New York, 1984).
8. According to a 1988 translation edited by James Clavell (Delta, New York).
9. John Hemming, *The Conquest of the Incas* (Macmillan. UK, 1970).
10. Unilever claimed 20 percent share of the global fabric detergent market, while Proctor & Gamble claimed 24 percent. Unilever claimed 23 percent share of the European market to P&G's 32 percent. *Source: The Economist* (London, England, 11 June 1994).
11. The aim of a market leader is to seek control of the market or a particular segment or niche. That business can sensibly be considered as if it were a martial art is demonstrated by the fact that the great military strategist Carl von Clausewitz had long considered writing a book comparing business strategies and tactics to military ones. But since he never even had time enough to complete his famous book *On War,* he never got around to it.
12. A tactic favored by Napoleon and some other renowned generals.

Chapter 4—Disposition of Forces

1. Barrie G. James, *Business Wargames* (Penguin Books, London 1984).
2. "We do not want things because we have found a reason for it, we find reasons for it because we want it."—*Schopenhauer.*
3. *Source:* The survey undertaken for the New York-based *Financial World* (published 11 April 1995) was prepared by Robert Meschi & Partner using a complex value formula in which they showed that IBM's brand value fell from third place in 1992 ranking to 290th in 1993. In 1994 its name was valued at only $3.7 billion; one-third of its software sales. Microsoft's brand value had risen to $10.3 billion.
4. W. Edwards Deming, *Out of the Crisis* (Massachusetts Institute of Technology, 1986).
5. Richard Tanner Pascale and Anthony G. Athos, *The Art of Japanese Management* (Simon & Schuster, New York, 1981).

6. "Packaging adds value to a product." P. Kotler, *Marketing Management-Analysis, Planning and Controls* (Prentice-Hall, N.J., 1991)."Protection, Containment, Storage, Advertising, Information, Identification, Facilitating Usage." E. J. McCarthy and W. D. Perrault, Jr., *Basic Marketing* (Irwin, New York, 1993).
7. Martin van Creveld, *The Transformation of War* (The Free Press, New York, 1991).
8. Nancy Mitford, *Frederick* (Hamish Hamilton, London, 1970).
9. *Source: The Economist* (London, 17 September 1994).
10. *Management Today* magazine, UK (March 1995).
11. Frederick the Great of Prussia.
12. Friction that resulted in a British force being wiped out by Zulu warriors arose when the bureaucratic quartermaster kept the ammunition locked so that he could ration it out personally, piecemeal, upon request.
13. Zhukov (like the Duke of Marlborough and the Duke of Wellington) never lost a battle.
14. Haim Laskov, the Introduction to *The Fighting Man* by Brigadier Peter Young (Routledge, London, 1981).
15. In 1994, IBM claimed to have turned away from rigidity to flexibility; from autocracy to encouraging initiatives by self-motivated groups; organizational structures became shallower; they made best use of information technology and cellular phones for instant decision making and implementation; they dispensed wherever possible with assistants, middle managers and secretaries; and some former middle managers became part of empowered teams—in Canada, at least.
16. *Management Today* (UK, March 1995).
17. Joel Bleeke and David Ernst, *Harvard Business Review* (January/February 1995).
18. Michael E. Porter, *The Competitive Advantage of Nations* (The Free Press, New York, 1990).
19. John Kay, *Why Firms Succeed* (Oxford University Press, New York and Oxford, 1995) pp. 148/9.
20. *Source:* Michael White and John Gribbin, *Darwin—A Life in Science* (Dutton, New York, 1995).
21. *Source:* Michael E. Porter, *The Competitive Advantage of Nations* (The Free Press, New York, 1990).
22. Arnold Toynbee, *A Study of History* (Oxford University Press and Thames and Hudson, London, 1972).
23. R. Blattberg and J. Deighton, *Interactive Marketing: Exploiting the Age of Addressability* (Sloan Management Review, Fall 1991).
24. D. Pepper and M. Rodgers, *The One-To-One Future* (Century Doubleday, N.Y., 1993).
25. Niccollo Machiavelli, *The Prince* (Penguin Books, UK, 1961).
26. John Morley, *Oliver Cromwell* (Macmillan, UK, 1994).

Chapter 5—Satisfying Customers

1. Charles St. Thomas's editorial, *Modern Marketing Thought* (Macmillan, London, 1946).
2. Peter F. Drucker, *The Practice of Management* (Heinemann, London, 1954).
3. John Case, *Looking for Jobs in All the Wrong Places* (*INC* magazine, March 1994), pp. 27 and 28. Other categories were External Economic Factors: 3 percent, Overexpansion, Market Failure or Fraud: 4 percent.
4. Time: mid-1980s. Market: Ottawa, Ontario, and the Outaouais, Québec, Canada.
5. Dell's profit margin strategy in 1992 was to aim at 5 percent.

6. Interactive home-based shopping is expected to amount to up to $300 billion in the United States by 2004. That represents 15 percent of today's retail sales of $2.1 trillion. *Source: Forbes* magazine (May 1993).

Chapter 6—Planning for Survival and Growth

1. M. H. B. McDonald, *Technique Interrelationships and the Pursuit of Relevance in Marketing Theory* (Quarterly Review of Marketing, 1990).
2. M. H. B. McDonald, *Marketing Planning and Expert Systems: An Epistemology of Practice* (Marketing Intelligence and Planning, 1989).
3. *Source:* Professor H. E. C. de Bruyn, Department of Business Management, Rand Afrikaans University. (Paper presented at the Fourth Marketing Educators' Conference in Durban, Natal, September 1993).
4. John Locke, *An Essay Concerning Human Understanding* (Oxford University Press, UK, 1990). "His influence on the philosophy of politics was so great and so lasting," wrote Bertrand Russell, "that he must be treated as the founder of philosophical liberalism as much as of empiricism in theory of knowledge." *History of Western Philosophy* (Allen & Unwin, UK, 1946).
5. Haynes and Massie, *Management: Analysis, Concepts and Cases* (Prentice-Hall, N.J., 1969).
6. Joseph Mancuso, *How To Write a Winning Business Plan* (Prentice Hall, N.J., 1985).
7. J. G. Kotzé, *Boardroom* magazine (South Africa, 1991). Kotzé was Professor of the Post Graduate School of Business Management at Potchefstroom University of Christian Higher Education.
8. The *Globe and Mail* (Toronto, 5 September 1995).
9. *Source:* The *Globe and Mail* (Toronto, 5 September 1995).

Chapter 7—Right Attitude

1. Arthur Koestler, *The Act of Creation* (Macmillan/Pan Books, UK, 1966).
2. Arthur Koestler, *ibid.*
3. Hertha Orgler, *Alfred Adler: The Man and his Work* (Sidgwick & Jackson, UK, 1973).
4. Arthur Koestler, *Janus: A Summing Up* (Hutchinson, London, 1978).
5. Dr. Nico Smith—formerly Professor in Marketing, now Executive Director of Technikon South Africa, included these results in the paper he delivered at the University of Natal in 1993.
6. Professor Malcolm McDonald, Co-director of CARM at Cranfield School of Management in England.
7. Sir John Hoskyns, Director General of the Institute of Directors in the UK.
8. Russell Scrimshaw, Marketing Director of Optus *Australian Professional Marketing* magazine (April 1995).

Chapter 8—What Motivates People

1. David Hume *A Treatise of Human Nature* (Dent, London; Dutton, New York, 1972). Volume Two, p. 37.
2. Abraham Korman, *The Psychology of Motivation* (Prentice-Hall, N.J., 1974).
3. F. Denmark and M. Guttening, "Dissonance in the self-concepts and educational

concepts of college and noncollege oriented women." *Journal of Counselling Psychology,* 1967.

4. E. Aronson and J. M. Carlsmith, "Performance expectancy as a determinant of actual performance." *Journal of Abnormal and Social Psychology,* 1962. E. Aronson and J. M. Darley, "The effects of expectancy on volunteering for an unpleasant experience." *Journal of Abnormal and Social Psychology,* 1963.

5. L. Berkowitz, *Aggression: A Social Psychological Analysis* (McGraw-Hill, New York, 1962).

6. J. Dollard, L. W. Doob, N. E. Miller, O. H. Mowrer, and R. R. Sears, *Frustration and Aggression* (Yale University Press, New Haven, 1939).

7. Karl Popper, *The Open Society and its Enemies* (Princeton University Press, N.J., 1962).

8. *Source:* Paul J. Stern, *C.G. Jung The Haunted Prophet* (George Braziller, New York 1976). pp. 157/8.

"From time immemorial, amateur and professional psychologists have relished drawing up more or less elaborate typologies promising cheap insights into—and power over—their fellows. There is no end to this sort of invention. Schemes of character have been innumerable—from Galen's four temperaments (sanguine, phlegmatic, choleric, and melancholic) which dominated western characterology for centuries, to fairly recent attempts, like those of Sheldon, to establish empirical correlations between character and body build. When the basic types are sketched with a quasi-artistic intuition—as, for instance, with Ernst Kretschmer's "pyknics" and asthenics"—such schemes have the power to fascinate the reader...The fact that typologies are manufactured in endless succession is a sure sign that they promise much more than they deliver...What the German physicist Georg Lichtenberg said about physiognomics over two hundred years ago holds true for typology today: "I have always found that people of mediocre knowledge of the world expected most from systematic physiognomics. Men who know the world are the best physiognomists and expect least from general rules"." (Paul J. Stern pp. 159/160).

9. Herbert Spencer, *Principles of Biology* (New York, 1910).

10. According to Alfred Adler, lust for power is simply the urge to compensate for feelings of inferiority by demonstrating one's superiority.

11. Herbert Spencer, *Social Statics* (1878).

12. Cyril Darlow (Pty) Ltd, Durban, Natal, South Africa.

13. Helena Curtis and N. Sue Barnes, *Biology* (Worth Publishers, New York, 1989).

14. *Source: New York Times Service* (January 1996).

15. Eric Berne, *Games People Play* (Penguin Books, UK, 1970).

16. *Source:* Market Research Africa (Pty) Ltd. (Johannesburg 1986).

17. Marcio M. Moreira, *Global Marketing 1994* magazine (Sterling Publications Limited, London, England).

18. Philip Edwards, "William Shakespeare." In *The Oxford Illustrated History of Literature,* Pat Rogers, ed. (Oxford University Press, New York, 1987).

19. Marshall McLuhan (interview by *Playboy* magazine). *Source: Essential McLuhan,* Eric McLuhan and Frank Zingrone, eds. (House of Anansi Press Limited, Concord, Ontario, 1995).

Chapter 9—The Power of Words

1. Immanuel Kant, *The Natural Principle of the Political Order considered in Connection with the Idea of a Universal Cosmopolitical History* (1784).

2. Ludwig von Bertalanffy, *Robots Men and Minds* (George Braziller, New York, 1967).
3. Heinrich Hertz.
4. Homer's *The Iliad* and *The Odyssey* (Penguin Books, UK).
5. John Stuart Mill, *On Liberty* (1859).
6. Karl Popper, *The Open Society and its Enemies* (Princeton University Press, N.J., 1962).
7. Bertrand Russell, *History of Western Philosophy* (Allen & Unwin, London, 1946).
8. Edward Caird, *Hégel* (AMS Press, New York).
9. Theodor Gomperz, *Greek Thinkers* (Murray, London, 1901–12).
10. Karl Popper, *The Open Society and its Enemies* (Princeton University Press, N.J., 1962).
11. Anthony Burgess, *But Do Blondes Prefer Gentlemen?* (McGraw-Hill, New York, 1986); and Judith S. Neaman and Carole G. Silver, *A Dictionary of Euphemisms*.
12. *Source:* Canadian Manufacturers' Association, Toronto, Canada.
13. Simon Gibson, *The Financial Times* (3 June 1994). He quoted George Orwell's advice as follows: (1) Never use a metaphor, simile, or other figure of speech which you are used to seeing in print; (2) Never use a long word when a short one will do; (3) If it is possible to cut a word out, always cut it out; (4) Never use the passive where you can use the active; (5) Never use a foreign phrase, a scientific word or a jargon word if you can think of an everyday English equivalent; (6) Break any of these rules rather than say anything that is outright barbarous.
14. Michael E. Porter and The Monitor Company, *Canada At The Crossroads* (Business Council on National Issues and the Ministry of Supply and Services Canada, 1991).
15. Milton and Rose Friedman, *Tyranny of the Status Quo* (Harcourt Brace Jovanovich, New York, 1983), pp. 148.
16. Newt Gingrich quoted in *Time* magazine (17 April 1995).
17. Sir Maurice Bowra, *Homer* (Duckworth, London, 1972).
18. Daniel J. Boorstin, *The Creators* (Random House, New York, 1992).
19. Marshall McLuhan (interview by *Playboy* magazine). *Essential McLuhan*, Eric McLuhan and Frank Zingrone, eds. (House of Anansi Press, Limited, Concord, Ontario, 1995).

    "The term 'literature,' presupposing the use of letters, assumes that verbal works of imagination are transmitted by means of writing and reading. The expression 'oral literature' is obviously a contradiction in terms. Yet we live at a time when literacy itself has become so diluted that it can scarcely be invoked as an esthetic criterion. The Word as spoken or sung, together with a visual image of the speaker or singer, has meanwhile been regaining its hold through electric engineering" [Albert B. Lord, *The Singer of Tales* (Harvard University Press, Cambridge, Mass., 1960)].

    McLuhan remarked, "That such a study of the divergent nature of oral and written social organization has not been carried out by historians long ago is rather hard to explain. Perhaps the reason for the omission is simply that the job could only be done when the two conflicting forms of written and oral experience were once again co-existent as they are today." Considering a whole range of implications arising from the effects of electronic media, he added that electronics takes us back to our primitive tribal existence, because television and multimedia are not intellectual, literary, or oral in tradition, but "they reorganize the sensorium, appealing as they do to feelings rather than thought" [Marshall

McLuhan, *The Gutenberg Galaxy* (University of Toronto Press, Canada, 1962)].
20. Rudolf Flesch, *The Art of Plain Talk* (Collier, London, 1962).
21. David Hume, *A Treatise on Human Nature* (Dent, London; and Dutton, New York, 1972). Volume One. Introduction, p. 4, and Volume Two, p. 137.
22. *Source:* Will Durant, *The Story of Philosophy* (Simon & Schuster, New York, 1926).
23. *Source:* A paper by Marcio M. Moreira entitled *Creativity is a Risky Business,* in *The Marketing Challenge* (the official magazine of The Canadian Institute of Marketing. August/September 1996).
24. *Source:* J. C. Carothers, "Culture, Psychiatry and the Written Word" (*Psychiatry,* 1959).
25. Marshall McLuhan, *The Guttenberg Galaxy* (Toronto University Press, Canada, 1960).

Chapter 10—Human Limitations

1. "Business schools' cases, which are generally based on interviews with company management, provide both qualitative and quantitative information about company activities, especially for U.S. corporations. They vary considerably in quality. Few contain much analysis, which the instructor or student is expected to provide, and they often reproduce, in an uncritical fashion, the opinions and perceptions of the managers involved."
   John Kay, *Why Firms Succeed* (Oxford University Press, New York and Oxford, 1995). p. 14. (John Kay is Professor of economics at the London Business School).
2. The United States has 312 lawyers for every 100,000 of its population. That is one lawyer per 320 people—more lawyers per capita than any other nation. It has an incarceration rate four times that of Canada and five times that of Britain. Source: Seymour Martin Lipset, *American Exceptionalism* (Norton, New York, 1996).
3. "Where the boards of French, German and Italian companies are studded with engineers and scientists, ours [Britain's] are dotted with accountants instead." (Britain 170,000; France 20,000; Japan 7,000; Germany 4,000)
   Source: Charles Handy, *Beyond Certainty* (Harvard Business School Press, Boston, Mass., 1996).
4. John J. Tarrant, *Drucker* (Cahner's, New York, 1976).
5. *The Economist* (20 April 1996).
6. Arthur Koestler, *The Ghost in the Machine* (Pan Books, UK, 1970)
7. Judson Herrick, *The Evolution of Human Nature.*
8. Morley Roberts. Source: Koestler, *The Ghost in the Machine.*
9. He initiated the Papez-McLean theory of emotions.
10. Bernard Cullen, *Hegel's Social and Political Thought* (Gill & Macmillan, UK, 1979).
11. Harry Berger, *An Essay on Historical Structuralism.*
12. A. L. Rowse, *The Poet Auden* (Methuen, London, 1987).
13. Paul Johnson, *Intellectuals* (Weidenfeld & Nicolson, London, 1988).
14. Source: Johnson, ibid.
15. Thomas Malthus, *An Essay on the Principle of Population* (1798).
16. John Kenneth Galbraith, *Economics In Perspective* (Houghton Mifflin, 1987).
17. Austrian economist Joseph Schumpeter identified what he called "the Ricardian vice"—"the habit of theorizing at such a stratospheric level of refinement that 'nothing lacks save sense.'" *Source:* Robert Heilbroner, *Teachings from the Wordly Philosophy* (Norton, New York, 1996).

18. Milton Friedman, *Friedman on Galbraith* in *The Conventional Wisdom of J. K. Galbraith* (The Fraser Institute of Economic Affairs, Canada, April 1977).
19. John Kenneth Galbraith, *American Capitalism: Concept of Countervailing Power* (Hamish Hamilton, London, 1952).
20. John Kenneth Galbraith, *The New Industrial State* (Pelican Books, UK, 1969).
21. John Kenneth Galbraith, David Sawers, and Richard Stillerman, *The Sources of Invention* (Macmillan, London, 1959).
22. David Clutterbuck and Stuart Crainer, *The Decline and Rise of British Industry* (W.H. Allen, London, 1988).
23. *Source:* Professor David Storey, Director of the Centre for Small and Medium-sized Enterprises at the University of Warwick, England.
24. James Dale Davidson and Lord William Rees-Mogg, *The Great Reckoning* (Simon & Schuster, New York, 1993).
25. Charles H. Hession, *John Kenneth Galbraith and His Critics* (New American Library, 1972); and John Kenneth Galbraith, *American Capitalism* (Hamish Hamilton, London, 1952).
26. Leonard Silk, *The Economists* (Avon Books, New York, 1976).
27. Peter Coveney and Roger Highfield, *Frontiers of Complexity* (Fawcett Columbine, New York, 1995).
28. Bertrand Russell, *History of Western Philosophy* (Allen & Unwin, London, 1946).
29. Marshall McLuhan (interview by *Playboy* magazine). Source: *Essential McLuhan*, Eric McLuhan and Frank Zingrone, eds. (House of Anansi Press, Limited, Concord, Ontario, 1995).
30. Gertrude Himmelfarb, *On Liberty and Liberalism* (Knopf, New York, 1974).
31. Arthur Koestler, *The Sleepwalkers* (Hutchinson, London, 1959).
32. Alsushi Ueda, *How Bureaucrats Manage Society*. From *The Electric Geisha* (Kodansha International, Tokyo, 1995).
33. William Ouchi, *Theory Z* (Addison-Wesley, New York, 1981).
34. Robyn M. Dawes, *House of Cards* (The Free Press, New York, 1994).
35. Richard Tanner Pascale and Anthony G. Athos, *The Art of Japanese Management* (Simon & Schuster, New York, 1981).
36. *Source:* The *Economist* (London, 29 April 1995).
37. Ruth Benedict, *The Chrysanthemum and the Sword* (Routledge & Kegan Paul, London, 1967):

> *Obligations*: Each *On* is an automatic debt which must be paid; to the Emperor, to parents, to one's lord, to one's teacher, and to any individual who lays an obligation on us by performing even the smallest of good turns gratuitously. Such good turns lay a heavy burden of indebtedness on the recipient, which may lead to resentment since it was not called for.
>
> *Indebtedness* (which is continually repaid but never fully paid off): Duty to the Emperor, the nation and the law; duty to parents, ancestors and descendants; duty to one's work. These debts are known as *Gimu* and one never pays one ten-thousandth of this type of *On*.
>
> *Debts* (which can be repaid in return for a favour and in accordance with its true value, and required within time limits): Duties to liege lord; Duties to relations; Duties to persons not related but due to a gift or favour or work performed; Duties to persons not closely related but due to favours from common ancestors. (Known as *Giri*-to-the-world).
>
> *Codes of Honour* (*Giri* to one's name): Obligations to clear one's name of insults or of scorn for failure; to even the score by a feud or vendetta. Obligations not to admit to ignorance or failure. Obligations to fulfil Japan's priori-

ties, including respect for behaviour, not living above one's station in life, and, curbing any emotional displays at inappropriate times.

38. Will Durant, *The Life of Greece* (Simon & Schuster, New York, 1939).

39. William F. Buckley, Jr., *Happy Days Were Here Again* (Random House, New York, 1993).

40. *Source: Newsweek* magazine (July 1985).

41. *Source: The Economist* (London, 6 February 1993).

42. John Kenneth Galbraith: "[I]n half of these firms, the stockholders had ceased to have any significant role. Power, for all practical purposes, had passed, and irretrievably, to the management, which was responsible, if at all, to a board of directors of its own selection.... There now existed power without property. The corporate bureaucrat, not the greatly celebrated entrepreneur. Bureaucracy, not entrepreneurship. All this being true, would the managers maximize revenues for themselves? Or, perhaps, would they have other and conflicting goals; would they encourage the size of the enterprise, the objective that most enhanced their own prestige and power, not profits for the unknown stockholders?" (Comments on a study by A. A. Berle, Jr. and G. C. Means, *The Modern Corporation and Private Property* (Macmillan, London, 1932)—from *Economics in Perspective* by John Kenneth Galbraith (Houghton Mifflin, Boston, 1987).

43. *Source:* The *Globe and Mail* (Toronto, 22 December 1994).

44. Peter F. Drucker, *Post Capitalist Society* (Harper Business, New York, 1993).

45. *Source:* The *Globe and Mail* (Toronto, 19 July 1993).

46. Salient points of the UK's Cadbury Code: (1) Chairman and Chief Executive should be separate roles; (2) Executive Directors' contracts should not run for more than three years; (3) Their pay, pension and stock options should be monitored by a remuneration committee mainly composed of Non-Executive Directors (NXDs); (4) NXDs should be independent and appointed for limited terms and selected by a formal process by the whole board; (5) Boards, including three NXDs, must meet regularly and provide effective leadership and control of a business; (6) The board should be monitored by an audit committee of at least three NXDs, and give a clear, balanced assessment of the company's position; establishing that it is a going concern and confirming the effectiveness of internal controls. *Source: Management Today* (UK, April 1995).

47. Charles H. Hession, *John Maynard Keynes* (Macmillan, New York, 1984). "The love of money as a possession—as distinguished from the love of money as a means to the enjoyment and realities of life—will be recognised for what it is, a somewhat disgusting morbidity, one of those semi-criminal, semi-pathological propensities which one hands over with a shudder to the specialists in mental disease." John Maynard Keynes's 1928 speech on the "Economic Possibilities for our Grandchildren."

Chapter 11—Leadership and Management Styles

1. Srully Blotnick, *Ambitious Men* (Viking, New York, 1987).

2. Carl von Clausewitz, *On War* (Princeton University Press, 1976). Edited and translated by Michael Howard and Peter Paret.

3. Jean-Jacques Rousseau, *The Social Contract* (Hafner Press, New York, 1947).

4. Chapelat Confectionery, Easy Washing Machine Co., Hoover SA., J. Walter Thompson, Reader's Digest, T.W. Beckett, Singer Sewing Machine Company, SA Cyanamid, SANA Petersen, L. Suzman & Co., Pitco/Lipton Ltd., Feltex Ltd., Shoecorp Ltd., several Unilever companies, Defiant Industries & General Electric Corporation, SB Lintas SA—all in South Africa. And in the UK, the London

Press Exchange (LPE), Lipton Ltd., Unilever Group of companies, Lintas, Marks & Spencer, Great Universal Stores, and others.

5. Most brilliant conductors of famous orchestras are either autocrats like Toscanini or benevolent dictators like Sir Thomas Beecham. They had to get the very best from extraordinarily talented musicians. They succeeded by understanding the music and those musicians and creating respect by virtue of their own special talents. And it is self-evident that an orchestra leader must be decisive. Audiences who have witnessed discord in an orchestra commencing a symphony on their own instead of in unison, because they missed the signal from an indecisive conductor, know what division is caused by failure to lead decisively.

6. Mischa Glenny, *The Rebirth of History* (Penguin Books, UK, 1980)

7. John Maynard Keynes on currency management, in his campaign against the restoration of the gold standard; *The Return To Gold*, in the *Nation*, 1924. *Source:* Charles H. Hession; *John Maynard Keynes* (Macmillan, New York, 1984).

8. Dr. Eric Berne, in *Games People Play* (Penguin Books, London, 1970) described the three basic ego states as follows: "'That is your Parent' means you are now in the same state of mind as one of your parents (or a parental substitute) used to be, and you are responding as he would, with the same posture, gestures, vocabulary, feelings, etc. 'That is your Adult' means you have just made an autonomous, objective appraisal of the situation and are stating those thought processes, or the problems you perceive, or the conclusions you have come to, in a non-prejudicial manner. 'That is your Child' means the manner and intent of your reaction is the same as it would have been when you were a very little boy or girl."

9. Japan's population was divided into four classes under the nobility: samurai, farmers, artisans, and merchants at the lower level. Outcasts who undertook jobs which defiled (like slaughtering) or were involved with death or the removal of excrement, were excluded from society. Each class was "differentiated from each other by strict regulations of dress, location and type of residence, form of transportation, and many other aspects of daily life." *Source:* Miriam Eguchi's introduction to *The Electric Geisha* (Kodansha International, Tokyo, 1994).Some formalities of the German caste system continued even as recently as in the 1950s, when well-bred young men bowed stiffly at the waist and clicked their heels together to show respect. Young woman curtsied automatically to their elders and social superiors. And the pastor's wife would instinctively take her appropriate place next to the wife of another professional person or academic, at even informal gatherings, according to a well-established pecking order. Everyone was comfortable with such rituals providing everyone else addressed each other appropriately and did what was expected of them (*Source:* author).

10. A. L. Rowse, *The Elizabethan Renaissance* (Scribners, New York, 1971).

11. Bertrand Russell, *History of Philosophy* (Allen & Unwin, London, 1946).

12. *Source:* Sir Walter Scott's 1831 Introduction to his historical novel, *Quentin Durward* (Macmillan London, 1831).

13. Anna Comnena, *The Alexiad* (Penguin Books, UK, 1969).

14. Sir Tom Hopkinson's autobiography. (Out of print).

15. William Manchester, *American Caesar: Douglas McArthur* (Little, Brown, New York, 1978).

Chapter 12—Responding to Challenges

1. *Source: Marketing Business* magazine (UK, September 1994), from an interview by Alan Mitchell.

2. *Source:* The *Financial Post* (Toronto, 16 July 1993).
3. *Source:* World Bank, 1991.
4. *Source:* The *Economist*, London (August 12, 1995).
5. *Source:* McGregors Information Online (disputed by some of those companies).
6. *Source:* The *Economist* (London, 12 August 1995).
7. John Kenneth Galbraith, David Sawers, and Richard Stillerman, *The Sources of Invention* (Macmillan, London, 1959).
8. *Source:* Professor Storey, Director of the Centre for Small and Medium-sized Enterprises at the University of Warwick, UK.
9. *Source:* Federation of Small Businesses, UK.
10. *Source: Marketing Business* magazine UK, May 1994 edition. From a feature article by Laura Mazur.
11. Christopher Woodward, marketing director for 3i, UK (a leading financial investment service firm).
12. *Source: Marketing Business* magazine UK, 1995.
13. John Baldwin, *Strategies For Success* (Statistics Canada, 1994). A research paper by Garnett Picot and Richard Dupuy was published by Statistics Canada in 1996, entitled "Job creation by company size class: Concentration and persistence of job gains and losses in Canadian companies," no. 93. It aimed at a more accurate assessment of relative advantages of small versus big companies in creating new jobs. Examples show that it depends how *big* and *small* are defined, on what industries are being scrutinized and why, on how many firms are new ones, and on whether job creation numbers are offset by job destruction statistics to arrive at net figures. The fact that most new companies by far are small ones appears to be overwhelming in stating that more new jobs are provided by small businesses than by big ones. Another factor emerging from the study is the rate of growth of new companies: "A few firms grew rapidly, while others either grew slowly or lost employment." A mere 5 percent of the small companies reviewed generated as many as 43 percent of the new jobs created by small businesses. That alone indicates thinking about *average* employment growth among small firms can be misleading. In addition, some large and mid-size companies were also major job creators. Even so, when net new jobs were measured as the difference between total jobs created and those destroyed, small businesses created more of them.

The study's base year was 1978 when SMEs added 156,000 new jobs in Canada, while larger companies with 500 or more employees shed 37,000. But in the growth period of 1984–88, the growth rate for small businesses mushroomed to 48 percent.
14. *Source:* Statistics Canada.
15. Percentage of GDP by manufacturing: Germany 30.8 percent (1990); Japan 28.9 percent (1990); South Africa 22.5 percent (1992); Canada 17.83 percent (1993); *Sources:* OECD National Accounts (1992), Statistics Canada 1994, and the official 1993 South African Year Book.
16. Source: Statistics Canada's Labor Division.
17. Koji Miyake, *Small Factories: The Underpinnings of Industry*—an essay in *The Electric Geisha* (Kodansha International, Tokyo, 1995).
18. *Source: Report On Business* magazine, Toronto. Published by the *Globe and Mail* (December 1993).
19. *Source:* Human Resources Development Canada, December 1994.
20. Walter Ellis in the *Evening Standard,* UK (25 March 1992).
21. From Karl Marx's theory of the Trade Cycle and Surplus Populations.
22. Other unemployment rates in June 1994: West Germany 8.4 percent; UK 9.4 percent; Australia 10.1 percent; Canada 10.7 percent; Italy 11.5 percent; France

12.3 percent; Denmark 12.6 percent; Belgium 13.1 percent.

23. As described to the author at the UK's Department of Trade and Industry in June, 1994.

24. *Source:* A study by James Chrisman, University of Calgary in Alberta; published in *Inc.* magazine, U.S. (October, 1994). His analysis was made from 29,088 pre-venture clients, of whom 14,696 launched start-ups, and 14,220 established businesses.

25. *Source:* Dun & Bradstreet: 90 percent of SME failures were due to lack of management and marketing skills; 4 percent to overexpansion, market failure or fraud; 3 percent to difficulties in financing; 3 percent to external economic factors.

26. *Source:* Dun & Bradstreet: 40 percent of SMEs failed in the first year, and another 40 percent of those still operating in year four.

27. Project Manager Ron Alexander of the CIM's Consultancy Services, said; "The Business Links have been given a difficult task because they have been asked to set up a local business advice provision from scratch but also to do it on the basis that they will be commercially viable at some short-time scale point in the future. The Business Links have, therefore, to think commercial; they have to think service provider; they have to develop their skills at the same time; and they are all working unilaterally. I suggest this is a difficult task, and when one looks back at the Enterprise Initiative system with an established track record of helping SMEs, one does wonder why we did not build on the past rather than walk away from it and start again."

28. *Source:* A national survey commissioned in Canada by the *Financial Post* of Toronto, and undertaken in 1994 by Arthur Andersen Enterprise Group. Twenty percent of businesses surveyed revealed sales of less than $2 million; 35 percent showed sales of $3 to $5 million; 19 percent sales of $6–$10 million; 14 percent of $11–$20 million; 8 percent of $21–$50 million; and 4 percent achieved sales of more than $50 million.

Chapter 13—Picking Winners

1. Dave Nichol left Loblaw's in 1994 to join Cott.

2. *Source:* The *Globe and Mail* (Toronto, 10 January 1995): "66-year-old Rafael Conde, Director of a Mexican shock-absorber plant, growled, 'The *perfumados* are little boys with PhDs who have never set foot in a factory like mine.'"

3. *Source:* Morris L. Sweet (a planner with the Housing and Redevelopment Board of New York City) and Dr. S. George Walters (a development projects manager of Socony Mobil Oil Co.).

4. *Source:* C. James Reilly, Member of the faculty of the Department of Economics at Lehigh University.

5. *Source: The Economist* (London, 27 March 1993).

6. Michael E. Porter and The Monitor Company, *Canada At The Crossroads* (Business Council On National Issues and Minister of Supply and Services Canada, 1991).

7. *Source:* U.S. Bureau of Labour Statistics.

8. *Source:* Department of Business Management, Rand Afrikaans University, South Africa.

9. R. G. Cooper and E. J. Kleinschmidt, "An Investigation into the New Product Process: Steps, Deficiencies and Impact" in *The Journal of Product Innovation Management,* 1986. Used to illustrate a paper presented by Ms. Riana Kruger and Mr. Reinholdt Just at the Fourth Annual Marketing Educators' Conference in 1993, Durban, South Africa.

10. 3,000 British, 1,000 Germans, 800 Polish, 1,000 Romanian, 5,000 Russian, 10,000 Chinese, 10,000 Koreans, 5,000 Taiwanese, 16,000 Vietnamese, 24,000 Filipinos, 5,000 Laotians, 5,000 Indians, 900 Irish, 10,000 Iranians, 1,000 Canadians, 33,000 Mexicans, 2,000 Guatamalans, 7,000 El Salvadorans, 1,000 Peruvians, 40,000 from other countries, 656,000 from other states, and 100,000 illegals. *Source: Time* magazine (November 1991).
11. 11.4 percent Lebanese, 6.7 percent British, 5.6 percent Polish, 5.5 percent Vietnamese, 4.9 percent Chinese, 4.5 percent Somali, 3.5 percent Indian, 3.3 percent Hong Kong, 3.3 percent American, 3.2 percent Iranian, *Source:* Statistics Canada.

Chapter 14—Oiling the Works

1. Robert Heller, *The New Naked Manager* (Hodder, London, 1984).
2. Source: Charles Hampden-Turner and Alfons Trompenaars, *The Seven Cultures of Capitalism* (Doubleday, New York, 1993).
3. George W. Terry, *Principles of Management* (R.D. Irwin, Ill., 1982).
4. André Marie Ampère, *Considerations of the Mathematical Theory of Games of Chance*.
5. Marshall McLuhan, *The Gutenberg Galaxy* (Toronto University Press, Canada, 1960).
6. *Source*: *Marketing Business* magazine (July/August 1996).

Chapter 15—Hiring the Best Brains

1. Marshall McLuhan and Quentin Fiore, *The Medium Is The Massage* (Random House, New York, 1967).
2. John J. Tarrant, *Drucker* (Cahner's, New York, 1976).
3. *Source:* David Hussey, Managing Director of Harbridge Consulting Group.
4. Charles Handy, *The Making Of Managers* (NEDO Books, UK, 1987).
5. The London Business School estimates that most participants in their MBA courses possessed an average of five years business experience. The Association of Masters in Business Administration in the UK claimed that applicants had spent an average of eight years in business before achieving their MBA.
6. John Burnham, *Suicide of the West* (Gateway Editions, Chicago, 1985).
7. Jaroslav Pelikan, *The Idea of the University* (Yale University Press, New Haven, 1992).
8. Peter F. Drucker, *Post-Capitalist Society* (Harper Business, New York, 1993).
9. Peter C. Emberley, *Zero Tolerance: Hot Button Politics in Canada's Universities* (Penguin, New York 1996)
10. John P. Kotter, *The New Rules* (The Free Press, New York, 1995).
11. John Ralston Saul, *Voltaire's Bastards* (Viking, New York, 1992).
12. KPMGs Colin Sharman advertising in *Management Today* magazine, UK (March 1995 edition).
13. *Source:* Karl Popper, *The Open Society and its Enemies* (Princeton University Press, N.J., 1962).
14. Nicky Wnek, *Marketing Business* magazine, UK (February 1996 edition).
15. John P. Kotter, *The New Rules* (Free Press, New York, 1995).
16. *Source: Canadian Business* magazine (April 1995 edition).
17. John Burnham, *The Managerial Revolution* (The John Day Company, Inc., 1941).
18. Charles Hampden-Turner and Alfons Trompenaaars, *The Seven Cultures of Capitalism* (Doubleday, New York, 1993).

19. *Source: The Ottawa Citizen,* Canada. Reporter Dominique Lacasse.
20. Definitions of the criteria are more fully described on the actual forms. These are abbreviations.
21. Arnold Toynbee, *A Study Of History* (Oxford University Press & Thames and Hudson, UK, 1972)."They were perhaps two of the finest secular institutions that the world had yet seen."
22. "The fickle disposition of the multitude almost reduces those who have experience of it to despair; for it is governed solely by emotions, and not by reason" (Spinoza).
23. *Source: The Wall Street Journal* (7 May 1996).
24. Elliott Platt, chief economist for Donaldson Lufkin & Jenrette, Inc.
25. Seymour Martin Lipset, *American Exceptionalism—A Double-Edged Sword* (W.W. Norton & Co., New York, 1996).

Chapter 16—Dynamics of Change

1. Karl Popper, ibid.
2. Arnold Toynbee, ibid.
3. Pierre Teilhard de Chardin, *The Phenomenon of Man* (Collins, London, 1959).
4. Michael E. Porter, *The Competitive Advantage of Nations* (Free Press, New York, 1990), 581.
5. G. B. Sansom, *A History of Japan* (Stanford University Press, California, 1958–63).
6. Ruth Benedict, *The Chrysanthemum and the Sword* (Routledge and Kegan Paul, London, 1967).
7. Giuseppe Prezzolini, *Machiavelli* (Macmillan, UK, 1967).
8. Stephen, Helms, and Tillotson, *Marketing Intelligence and Planning* (MCB University Press, Bradford, Yorkshire, 1994).
9. Malcolm Muggeridge, *Chronicles of Wasted Time* (Collins, London, 1973).
10. Henry Adam, *A History of the United States of America* (1890).
11. Jagdish H. Sheth, *Bringing Innovation To Market: How To Break Corporate and Customer Barriers* (Wiley, New York 1987).
12. From an essay by Mannheim in 1932.
13. Christopher Lasch, *The Revolt of The Elites And the Betrayal of Democracy* (W.W. Norton, New York, 1995).
14. *Source: OECD's Employment Outlook,* 1995.
15. Paul Krugman, *Peddling Prosperity* (W.W. Norton, New York, 1994).
16. Richard DeLamarter, *Big Blue: IBM's Use and Abuse of Power* (Dodd, Mead, New York, 1986).
17. "An MBA is no longer a license to name your own salary but is increasingly a starter kit." Charles Handy, *Beyond Certainty* (Harvard Business School Press, Boston, Mass., 1996).
18. Henri Bergson, *Creative Evolution* (Greenwood Press, London). Translated by A. Mitchell; *Matter and Memory* (Zone Books, 1988). Translated by N. M. Paul and W. S. Palmer.
19. Milton and Rose Friedman, *Free To Choose* (Harcourt Brace Jovanovich, New York, 1980).
20. Niccolo Machiavelli, *The Prince* (Penguin Books, UK, 1961).
21. *Source: The Economist* (20 April 1996).
22. Neither the French aristocracy nor the Church was obliged to pay taxes, in case the monarch's life would be in danger in the former case, and his soul in the latter.

23. Milton Friedman, "[W]hereas the average inflation rate is about 12 per cent, it is 6 per cent in the private sector and 20 per cent in the government sector." From an interview on BCTV-Vancouver by Jack Webster (25 March 1982) and a lecture delivered at the end of 1976 and published in the UK by the Institute of Economic Affairs in January, 1977 and by the Fraser Institute in Canada in April, 1977.

24. Charles Hession, *John Maynard Keynes* (Macmillan, New York, 1984).

25. Carl G. Jung, *Memories, Dreams, Reflections* (Pantheon Books, New York, 1963).

26. *Source:* Jacob Bronowski, *The Ascent of Man* (Little, Brown and Company, Boston, 1973), 433. "Chess is not a game. Chess is a well-defined form of computation. You may not be able to work out the answers, but in theory there must be a solution, a right procedure in any position. Now real games...are not like that at all. Real life is not like that. Real life consists of bluffing, of little tactics of deception, of asking yourself what is the other man going to think I mean to do." John von Neumann and Oskar Morgenstern, *Theory of Games and Economic Behaviour* (Princeton University Press, N.J., 1943).

27. Northrop Frye, *On Shakespeare* (Fitzhenry & Whiteside, Markham, Ontario, 1986). Winner of the Governor General's Award. Editor: Robert Sandler, 29.

28. Arthur Koestler, *The Sleepwalkers* (Hutchinson, London, 1959).

29. William F. Buckley, Jr., *Happy Days Were Here again* (Random House, New York, 1993).

30. Will Durant, *The Story of Philosophy* (Simon & Schuster, New York, 1926).

31. In the mid-1990s the composition of homeless poor street people in the United States changed from largely single men to 43 percent families and 30 percent small children.

32. *Source: The Story of Philosophy,* by Will Durant, ibid. "Of the 400,000 inhabitants of Athens 250,000 were slaves, without political rights of any kind."

33. Lévy-Bruhl, *How Natives Think* (Ayer, New Hampshire, 1980). "Participation Mystique" is what Marshall McLuhan was talking about with his claim that electronic media like TV (and now multimedia computers) are tactile, not visual, and therefore become a technological extension of our biological sensorium. In doing so it numbs the other senses. "Virtual Reality," which was developed later, demonstrates this trancelike state.

34. Otto Gross, *Über Psychopathische Minderwertigheiten* (Germany).
    Jung's reference to the word *introvert* gives it a different meaning. It took him nearly ten years to develop a theory of typology that satisfied him. And, "In Jung's era psychoanalysis, and western civilization in general, favoured the extrovert at the expense of the introvert, tending to view the former as "healthy" and the latter as "neurotic". (Paul J. Stern, ibid)

35. Will Durant, *The Life of Greece* (Simon & Schuster, New York, 1939).

36. Will Durant, *The Renaissance* (Simon & Schuster, New York, 1953).

37. Robert Bartlett, *The Making of Europe* (Princeton University Press, N.J., 1993).

38. Emrys Jones, *The Origins of Shakespeare* (Oxford University Press, Oxford 1977) p. 7.

39. Lawrence Stone, *The Educational Revolution in England, 1560–1640 (Past and Present,* vol 28, 1964. pp. 68 & 80).

40. *The Making of Europe*; ibid. So indistinguishable that Normans were no longer Norsemen from Scandinavia but French; Britain was largely Saxon or Danish instead of being inhabited solely by Britons (i.e., Celts); history interchanges Franks with Normans; and all territories settled by the Roman Empire became Romanized.

41. *The Sleepwalkers,* ibid.

42. *Source:* Holbrook Jackson's introduction to *The Anatomy Of Melancholy* (J. M. Dent, England, 1932).
43. *The Renaissance,* ibid.
44. *Source:* Martin Ostwald's glossary to his translation of Aristotle's *Nichomachean Ethics* (The Bobbs-Merrill Company, Inc., Indianapolis 1962).
45. Kenneth Clark, *Civilisation* (Harper & Row, New York and Evanston, 1969)
46. John Atkins, *George Orwell* (Frederick Ungar, New York, 1954).

Index

447

MANAGEMENT CRISIS AND BUSINESS REVOLUTION
John Harte

Management Crisis and Business Revolution describes the enormous gap between business theories on the one hand, and the realities of the workplace and uncertainties of the marketplace on the other. In place of reasoned management and disciplined organization John Harte depicts daily disorder, vagueness, and confusion instead of the logical processes of classroom case histories with rational solutions. He provides tales of an abundance of irrational judgments, personal foibles, and business follies. Once a top operational manager with multinational organizations, Harte applies his hands-on knowledge of the business world to a realistic examination of workplace conditions. He describes methodically how to handle human limitations in the average business enterprise, as well as how to develop management strengths.

The author observed superior and inferior management firsthand, and therefore witnessed the painful demise of many companies—some of which, in his opinion, could have been saved. With thirty years' experience to draw on, he analyzes why so many businesses and products fail, while others succeed. He examines the amazing progress of Japan and other Pacific Asian countries; explains the decline of German, Canadian, British, and French management practices; and provides strategies for the marketplace.

The business sectors described in this all-encompassing book include: high-technology, fast-moving packaged consumer goods like detergents; manufacturing and retailing consumer durables like furniture and appliances; soft goods; fashion products; service sector industries; manufacturing, wholesaling, and retail trade; and a whole range of new service industries. Harte stresses that

Marcelene Transiori

Dynamic
Mental
Laws

NORVELL's

for
Successful
Living

NORVELL's

Dynamic Mental Laws

for Successful Living

Anthony Norvell

WEST NYACK
N. Y

PARKER
PUBLISHING
COMPANY, INC.

LIBRARY OF CONGRESS
CATALOG CARD NUMBER: 65-25251

PRINTED IN THE UNITED STATES OF AMERICA
62378—B&P

How This Book Will Give
You Secrets for Achieving
Everything You Want in Life

How This Book Will Give You Secrets for Achieving Everything You Want in Life

Throughout the ages there have been illumined souls who possessed extraordinary powers of the mind and spirit. These great teachers possessed universal wisdom which they carefully guarded, revealing it only to the few neophytes who were ready for these great mystical and spiritual revelations.

These great souls had discovered the secrets of the universe through contemplation and meditation on the deeper mysteries of life. They advised kings and princes; they safeguarded the arts, music, literature and scientific knowledge all through the dark ages. They gave inspiration and guidance to the few who were ready for their revelations.

Civilization advances and man rises to greatness under the impetus of the wisdom and knowledge that he gathers throughout the centuries. Formerly this wisdom was denied to the masses, because they lacked the institutions of learning. Now, in our modern twentieth century, this accumulated wisdom can be revealed in all its radiant splendor.

In this study we shall walk together, teacher and student, down the golden path of history, gleaning the priceless secrets of the ages and applying them to your own daily life for achieving the health, wealth, and happiness which is every person's secret dream.

Norvell's Dynamic Mental Laws will reveal the secrets of ancient lands and cultures, India, China and Tibet, all explained in modern language which can be easily understood and applied

9

to your own life. We shall explore the glories of the Golden Age
of Greece and learn of the wonders revealed by such great minds
as Socrates, Plato, Aristotle, and Epicurus. Many of the profound
truths uttered by these mystics and sages apply to modern living,
and your life will be greatly enhanced and enriched by gleaning
these pearls of wisdom from these great minds.

Carved in stone, penned on parchment and papyrus, blocks of
wood and marble, these great teachers of the past left their forbidden secrets of the ages to guide the initiates in the Temple of
Wisdom. Now we shall study these universal and mental Laws
of the past and present and learn how you may apply them to
your own everyday life to achieve the fulfillment of all your
dreams.

In my twenty-five years of lecturing and teaching in world-
famous Carnegie Hall in New York City, literally thousands of
students have studied these great spiritual and mental truths with
me, and now, for the first time, they are being given to the world
so that you may study them in the privacy of your own home.
You need not be a cloistered mystic in some sacred shrine in
India or Tibet to be able to use these forbidden secrets of the
ages. You can begin instantly to avail yourself of the benefits of
this cosmic and universal knowledge.

What benefits may you expect?

As a student of Universal Wisdom, you may naturally ask,
"What benefits may I expect in my personal life from this book?"

The benefits are many. First, you will grow and expand mentally, so that your mind will release its own dynamic and mysterious powers in every department of your life.

You will then learn how to live under the Cosmic and Universal
Laws which determine your measure of success, health, and happiness in this life. You will also learn how to channel the great
power of universal magnetism in every area of your life, so as to
attract to yourself the work you should do, the people who will
help you, and the destiny which you secretly desire.

This course of study will help you unlock the tremendous reserves of power that reside within your own soul. Then you may
accurately know yourself and your higher intuitive mind will

reveal to you the pattern of your future, so you may more intelligently shape the events of your present and future life.

You will be shown how to tap the Cosmic Mind and release the creative power that God used to create the universe and all therein, and with this new dimension of mind and spirit, you will be able to achieve fame, fortune, honor, riches, and wordly recognition, if that is your wish.

These secrets of Universal Wisdom will also give you peace of mind and peace of soul. You will be able to motivate the forces of life and shape in the invisible interstices of the universe, the world of beauty, peace and joy in which you wish to live.

You'll enter the world of effortless ease

Instead of laboriously wrestling with physical and material problems, as you may have in the past, and being worn out with fears, worries, anxieties and perplexities which kill people off prematurely and make them sick, you will learn how to enter that secret sanctuary of the soul, where the true mystic power resides. There you will find the world of effortless ease, the Pathway to Heaven which Lao-tse tells about in his mystical philosophy. There you can command the secret power that liberates man from slavery and drudgery and you will rise on wings of song and hope into the unlimited celestial realm of infinite intelligence, infinite beauty, infinite good, and infinite peace and love.

Life will be yours to command

Life is yours to command when you once have the wisdom and power that sure knowledge gives. People will admire and respect you, because you will possess a serene and poised personality in which they sense some secret inner power. When you speak, others will listen, for your voice will have the unmistakable ring of authority and truth which commands attention in high places and low.

You will become a presence, not just another person, when you release these ancient truths in your mind, and thought-atmosphere. You will possess the mystical power of the ancients, which gives you instantaneous awareness of every situation that may arise in life. You will know that the center of this power resides within your own mind and soul, and your personality will reflect to the outer world a majestic dignity and aristocratic bearing that make you the center of all eyes. You will seem to be literally surrounded by a golden magic circle which protects you from danger and which, at the same time, attracts into your orbit of experience only those persons and situations which benefit you and add to your future enjoyment.

You'll know yourself and what to do with your hidden talents

Know thyself! This is the basis of all philosophy and wisdom. This study will give you an excellent understanding of the forces that make up your mind, your emotions, your soul, and the unlimited powers of your psyche and your higher mind. Any study of esoteric or occult teachings must begin with a sure knowledge of your own powers, your motivations, your desires, your emotions and your surging hopes and expectations. In this course of study we shall analyze all the great truths of the ancient teachers, as well as the modern school of psychology, philosophy and psychosomatic thought that pertains to life and its many problems. You will be given hundreds of illustrations, examples, and exercises, which will sharpen your powers of perception and unfold your own unlimited powers.

You'll learn how infinite riches can be yours

The universe is filled to overflowing with treasures in the visible and invisible world. Infinite riches can be yours when you once understand the great spiritual laws which show you how to tap these treasure troves of the infinite. Gifts of the mind, the emotions, the soul, are revealed in these mystic studies, that can begin to enrich your mind and life immediately. You will learn how to translate these dynamic spiritual truths into the pure gold of mind and spirit and instantly have peace of mind, inner tranquility, and joy. If you wish to use this knowledge to enrich yourself materially, you will learn of the ancient Alchemists secrets of how they tried to turn base metal into shimmering gold. They did not succeed, but they left behind a priceless formula which can cause man in the twentieth century to turn his creative energies into ideas and inventions for bridges and skyscrapers, paintings and sculpture, novels and plays, industry and science. You will learn how to mint the purest of gold from your mind, and release ideas that will transform your own life and enrich the entire world.

You'll achieve the miracles of creative mind

See the miracles of creative mind all about you which brought fame and fortune to the illumined souls who conceived them. From the wagon wheel to modern jet planes that travel at twenty-five hundred miles an hour; what a span of time! And yet, man's creative spirit can bridge the centuries and devise new miracles in the future that cause our modern world to pale into insignificance. No potentate of the Far East with all his fabled wealth could turn on a magical box and have music and pictures, such as the miracle of modern radio and television give us. And yet this power was in the universe throughout the ages waiting for man's glorious discovery. Think what magic it was considered when Marconi first sent his messages through space without wires; and how startled the world was when Alexander Graham Bell talked into the first telephone and his voice came through the receiver at the other end. Think how man has tapped the invisible reservoir of creative power in his modern electronic microscope, which reveals an invisible world so vast it baffles the imagination. And our two-hundred-inch telescope at Palomar brings the planets in outer space so close to the earth that scientists now know many of the secrets which will make space travel easier in a few short years.

The miracles of creative mind are all about you, when you once have the unlimited vision to see and know the world of the invisible. The mystery of a robin's egg, with its miracle of life, is so great that it baffles the greatest of scientific minds. And yet somewhere, somehow, this creative miracle of all life must be known and is explainable in terms that may be understood and a technique which may be harnessed to perform still greater miracles.

You can now begin a journey into the unknown

In this mystical study together, let us take a journey into the unknown. Let us discover the outer dimensions of the mind and soul and learn how to explore the secret, hidden realms of universal power, so we may channel this Cosmic Intelligence for our everyday purposes. You will have signposts to guide you along the way, on this mystic journey into the unknown, for other voyagers have trodden this cosmic path of truth in search of the light of wisdom.

I shall be your Mentor and Guide, pointing out the highlights for you to observe, showing you the pitfalls which can spare you agony of mind and body, and revealing the fundamental principles that can cause you to rise above the limitations of the material and physical universe into the stratosphere of spirit where you will expand your vision to encompass the grandeur of an unlimited universe replete with all the splendor and beauty of the Infinite.

Dynamic
Mental
Laws

NORVELL's

for
Successful
Living

Contents

Law One

Visualizing the Master Plan Back of Your Life

There is a Master Plan back of the entire universe. We see it reflected in the order and harmony that exist in the rotation of the planets in their orbits without confusion, collisions or interference from outside sources. In fact, this Cosmic Plan in the stars is so perfect and punctual that man sets his clocks on earth by the stars in the heavens.

We see a great Master Plan also in the rotation of the seasons: spring, for preparing the soil and planting the seed; summer, for growth and maturity; fall, for harvesting the crops; and winter for the earth to rest and restore itself.

The same Master Plan exists in relation to your own life. There is a springtime of youth, in which the seeds of education, morality and conduct are implanted in the young mind through education. A time of summer when we grow and mature, when we love and marry and rear our families. Then the falltime of life when we reap the rich rewards of our labors and prepare the mind for intellectual growth and culture, leisure and enjoyment. Then there is the wintertime of life, a period for soul-search and spiritual growth, in which man finds the true purpose back of life and prepares for his mystic journey into the vast unknown.

The mystic pattern back of life

From star to snowflake, from the macrocosm to the microcosm, man, there is a mystic pattern back of all life. This invisible design is set into motion through the cosmic law of vibration and externalizes in all forms of creation.

25

A scientist in France studied snowflakes for a period of forty years and never found any two designs alike. So vast, so complicated, so profound is the Master Plan back of the created universe that no two blades of grass or grains of sand are ever exactly alike.

The mystic pattern back of life decrees that all things shall respond to an invisible law of vibration, which Pythagoras called "the music of the spheres." Scientists say that if a giant violin could be built upon which the vibratory note that governs the Brooklyn Bridge were played, the vibration would shatter the bridge to bits.

In fact, the great opera singer Enrico Caruso used to amuse guests at dinner parties by proving this theory. He would rub the rim of a crystal drinking glass and obtain the hum of its vibratory pattern, then he would sing that note into the glass and shatter it to pieces. This was startling proof that man can create or destroy material and physical objects by learning the secret vibratory power that is back of all creation.

The cosmic plan

There is a Cosmic Plan that includes all creation. The word Cosmos comes from the Greek *Kosmos* and literally means universal order, harmony, and oneness. It is a totality of all creation. You belong to this Cosmic Order, and you can do a great deal to build your own personal Master Plan so that it is in harmony with the universal Cosmic Plan that God has back of His creation.

What are the principles of this Cosmic Plan? They include:

1. Order
2. Harmony
3. Balance
4. Intelligence
5. Growth or evolvement
6. Attraction (The law of capillary attraction)
7. Fulfillment
8. Disintegration

All creation reflects these eight elements of the Cosmos.

Let us see how they work universally and then apply them to

your own personal Master Plan and see how you can vibrate in harmony to the Cosmic Plan and achieve the fulfillment of your destiny.

ORDER. Everywhere we look in nature we see order. The tides ebb and flow under this law of universal order. The earth rotates around the sun, and the moon around the earth with perfect order and rhythm. In nature all things evolve and mature under this law of order. Only when man interferes with nature's law does this sense of order disappear and chaos result.

When man depletes the soil we have crop failures and soil erosion and famine. When man disrupts nature's order and becomes greedy and selfish, we have war and mass starvation and death.

HARMONY. The universe, according to Pythagoras, operates under a mathematical system that is as harmonious and scientifically fixed as the laws governing music. When anything disrupts this harmony on a universal scale there is confusion, disorientation and chaos. When man's moral nature is out of tune or harmony with the universal laws of justice and balance, he suffers the disquieting experiences of lack and limitation, periodic wars and disasters.

Kant, the noted philosopher, said there is a moral law within that is as fixed and definite as the laws which govern the stars in the heavens.

Confucius also spoke of the imperative need in man's conduct to observe the laws of order, harmony, and balance. When an ancient king asked the great teacher how he could preserve order and harmony in his war-torn kingdom, Confucius answered, "First there must be order and harmony within your own mind. Then this order will spread to your family, then to the community and finally to your entire kingdom. Only then can you have peace and harmony."

BALANCE. One of the great precepts of Oriental philosophy is the law of equilibrium or balance. Mind must balance the body; the inner must balance the outer. Work must balance play, also sleep and rest must balance work. Nature works unerringly to preserve balance between all her parts. If man upsets this delicate balance in nature he suffers the dire consequences of his acts.

INTELLIGENCE. In every atom and cell of the visible and invisible universe, science has found that a vast intelligence exists. This intelligence seems to be a reflection of a Master Mind which rules the universe. In religion this Intelligence is called God or Spirit. In ancient times it was believed that everything reflected this infinite intelligence of the God-mind. This form of religion was known as Pantheism . . . a belief that God was in His universe.

In modern days philosophers and religious leaders have come to the conclusion that God, being Infinite, cannot be in Matter, which is finite. Therefore it is assumed that God's intelligence, or creative spirit is an invisible force that animates all creation and gives it life and cohesion. This reflection of the infinite mind of God in His creation is much like the sun which, by reflection, gives life and growth to all things on earth without actually being in the earth.

GROWTH OR EVOLVEMENT. This universal law of Growth is a part of all creation. Put a seed into the ground and the forces of intelligence, order, balance and harmony within the soil cause it to grow. So too, man plants seeds or ideas in his own consciousness and they evolve into miraculous things like autos, jet planes, television, and space ships. Or creative ideas in the same mind may evolve and grow into systems of philosophy, science, art, literature, invention, and industry.

The Bible speaks of this law of growth: "As ye sow, so shall ye reap."

It is essential that we continue growing and evolving mentally, physically and emotionally all our lives, or we stagnate and grow prematurely old. Any form of creation that loses its ability to grow and falls into disuse is soon removed by nature. A dead tree cannot resist the powerful force of the wind and is soon uprooted and destroyed.

ATTRACTION. Between all the elements and atoms making up the visible and invisible universe, is the silent law of attraction. All things attract the elements they require for their growth and survival. The plant and tree, even though lacking mobility, have the power to attract the elements they need for their growth and fulfillment, through the universal law of capillary attraction.

Man has this same ability, and further in our study of these principles of life we shall learn how to use this law of magnetic and capillary attraction to attract all the things we require for our future growth, survival, and fulfillment.

FULFILLMENT AND DISINTEGRATION. When a thing has fulfilled its cycle of usefulness in nature and is no longer of value, it begins the process known as disintegration. Science has now found, in the study of aged and aging through the science of Geriatrics, that even people who have no further purpose in living, and literally retire from life, begin to disintegrate mentally and physically. Statistics show that most men who retire from their jobs at the age of sixty-five die within three to five years.

It is vitally important that you learn how to live under these universal laws and that your Master Plan for your life in the future include all the elements that make for growth, evolvement, and fulfillment.

Your personal master plan

Your own personal master plan must include the following elements, if you wish to be complete and fulfilled.

1. The physical side of your life.
2. Your mental and intellectual side.
3. Your emotional nature.
4. Your social side.
5. Your moral and ethical side.
6. Your Cosmic or Spiritual relationship to God.

These six basic elements must be present in your life if you wish to have order, balance, harmony and growth or fulfillment in your future life.

The physical side of your life

Be aware of the fact that you are physical as well as mental. The body has its needs and must be fed and clothed. There must be balance in your life physically. The law of moderation should prevail in everything you do. The cross of balance should prevail. Work balanced by play; love balanced by spiritual worship and belief in God. This psychological cross of balance will take care of all your needs, if these four elements are present in your life each day.

Your body requires the right food and nutrition, and time should be spent in studying the latest scientific facts regarding food, vitamins, minerals and other elements the body requires for good health. Later in this course of lessons, we shall study some of these latest scientific revelations for maintaining the balance of good bodily health, youth and vitality.

Your body also requires rest, exercise, fresh air and at least eight hours of sleep nightly. If your body does not get these essentials it is apt to suffer from lowered resistance and germs more easily infect the bloodstream.

Your mental and intellectual needs

Your mind has needs that are as specific and definite as your body needs. Your thinking processes shape your body and affect its workings; they also shape your destiny.

Goethe spoke of this inter-relation between mind and destiny in these words:

> Sow a thought, reap a habit.
> Sow a habit, reap a character.
> Sow a character, reap a destiny.

Your thoughts should be shaped in the direction of health, happiness, prosperity, optimism and good. Thoreau, the philosopher and naturalist, once said that we must hold mental pictures of what we want to do and what we want to be. He suggested that we hold these visual pictures in our minds as often as possible during the day, and to mentally see the experiences, persons, and situations that we desire. This helps focus the powers of the mind upon the desirable things we wish to attract.

What mental adornment do you wear?

What adornment do you wear mentally? Is your mental world clothed with beauty or ugliness? Do you search each day for beautiful experiences? Do you look for the good in people? Are you aware of the beauty in all of nature? You can mentally choose the environment you wish to live in. You may have only a small furnished room but it can be kept clean and it can be furnished tastefully and beautifully.

Beauty is in the eye of the beholder.

The world can take on a mantle of loveliness or ugliness, depending on your own state of consciousness. Money can help beautify and change your environment, but it isn't always necessary. You can begin now, wherever you are, to have order, harmony, balance, and beauty in your environment. You can wear your best clothes, adorn your face in a bright expression with a happy, radiant smile, and soon you will find your entire life beginning to change for the better because of your changed mental attitude.

When the Muzhiks or peasants of Russia freed themselves from the Czars, they took over their palaces. Being untrained in cultural and intellectual values, the peasants fed their horses out of the rosewood pianos, and tore the beautiful tapestries off the walls and made blankets which they threw over their horses to keep them warm. They built fires in the middle of the rooms and broke up the priceless antique furniture to feed the fire.

Obviously these unfortunate people had never had the opportunity to become educated. They were ignorant and insensitive to the higher values of life. No amount of money could wipe away that ignorance overnight. It takes generations of study and work to evolve the mind intellectually. This is done by absorbing the wisdom and knowledge of the great philosophers, seers, mystics, and teachers of the past. In this course of study we shall have an opportunity to study all these great thoughts that have added to the world's sum total of knowledge and culture. These great thoughts will help mold your mind and shape your intellect in the paths of wisdom and greatness which will in turn inspire you to achieve a greater destiny.

Destiny is a matter of choice

Bryan said, "Destiny is not a matter of chance; It is a matter of choice. It is not something to be waited for; but, rather, something to be achieved."

Your Destiny is definitely a matter of choice. If you have the necessary mental and intellectual knowledge, you will choose the persons and events of your life in a pattern that reflects good, truth, beauty, peace, harmony and love. These intrinsic values will be inextricably woven into the warp and woof of your tapesty of destiny and will reflect in every aspect of your life.

Using the tools of mind

Your mind has certain valuable tools which will be considered in this course step by step. Some of these tools are: Imagination, Vision, Memory, Reason, and Logic. The way you use these mental tools determines to a great extent how your future life will be shaped.

When you grow wings of the imagination you may soar upwards and scale the very heights of achievement. Man's flight into space and the miracles of the jet age undoubtedly began when some primitive man unlocked the power of his imagination as he saw a bird in flight and visualized man growing wings and flying like a bird.

In fact, the first man to carry this imaginative picture a step further towards reality was the great Italian artist Leonardo da Vinci. He designed an airplane without a motor, built it, and a house servant actually flew with it off the roof of the house. The Church ordered the flying machine destroyed as a tool of the devil.

Today the original sketch of that first airplane may be seen in the Louvre in Paris with these words in da Vinci's handwriting: "Man shall grow wings."

It is in wings of imagination that man possesses his greatest creative power. Apply this rule to your own life today; begin in your imagination to see ways in which you can improve yourself, your mind, your environment, your job, your life. Start to run through your imagination all the problems that beset you and visualize ways in which you can solve them.

Imagine ways in which you might increase your income, and soon you will be guided by your higher mind to doing the things that actually bring you more money.

Build your ideals in your imagination, and see yourself living in an environment of beauty, order, and harmony. As you aim higher and higher in life, you will somehow find the means to achieve your dreams. There is a saying in philosophy,

> What man can conceive,
> He may achieve.

Your emotional nature

You are more than mind and body working harmoniously together; you are emotional in nature, and the emotions must be considered and fed, just as the body and the mind are fed.

What are man's emotional needs? Man needs to love and to be loved. He has a sexual need for fulfillment with the opposite sex. His love nature extends to more than just his physical and sensual satisfaction, however; there is love of family, love of friends, love of country, love of people and love of the world. Added to these emotional needs there is also the love of God.

If any of these emotional elements are missing in man's life experience he is unfulfilled, and cannot know completion. There are men and women who serve God in religious orders who deprive themselves of the sensual appetites, but because they transmute physical love to spiritual love, they are able to serve God and humanity and this brings them a peace and satisfaction that fulfills their basic human need for love.

Your soul's need for beauty and love

Man's soul requires the adornments of beauty and love. Without these no human life is complete. The beautiful words of Shakespeare exemplify this in Juliet's speech when she tells of her love for Romeo.

> Give me my Romeo, and when he shall die,
> Take him, and cut him out in little stars,
> And he will make the face of heaven so fine,
> And all the world will be in love with night,
> And pay no worship to the garish sun.

When your life blossoms with the divine emotion of love for your fellow men and the love of God more than love of life itself, you will pay no worship to the garish sun of materialism and physical values only, but you will see the spiritual radiance of God's loving countenance in each and every person you meet.

Your social side

It is when you have established the divine emotion of love that the true social values will fall into their right place in your life. You live for people and for social reciprocity. No millionaire ever makes his millions for himself alone, unless he is a miser, and then he is miserable even though rich. We live and work and attain worldly goals of fame, money, power, or their equivalents, so we may share them with others.

There is a deep need in every human being for ego-recognition. No composer ever composed his music for himself alone. It is this desire to please others and win their recognition and approbation that leads the creative geniuses to create their great works in art, literature, music, science, and industry. They have a desire to create for the good of the world and to share the products of their creative minds with other people.

Florence Nightingale had this humanitarian impulse which caused her to be the first woman nurse to go out onto the actual battlefields and minister to the wounded.

Jane Addams, of Hull House in Chicago, founded her home for underprivileged children because of her desire to serve the world and God. The doctors gave her only six months to live because she was so sick and frail. She said, "If I have only six more months to live I shall spend that time in serving humanity." She turned her home into a social welfare center and took in all the underprivileged children of that city and forgot herself so completely in serving God and man, that she was completely healed of her sickness. In her autobiography she tells how she lived to bury four of the doctors who pronounced her doom!

The Bible says, "Man shall not live by bread alone, but by every word that proceedeth out of the mouth of God." When you learn to live your life for the good of the world, you will have added health, inspiration and power . . . and, incidentally, you will live longer.

Mme. Curie and her husband toiled for twenty years to isolate a gram of radium to help heal humanity. Their lives were richly blessed for this struggle to better the world.

Helen Keller and her teacher, Miss Sullivan, did magnificent work for the deaf, dumb, and blind, through their patience and hard work to educate the handicapped of the world.

Gandhi of India died a martyr, but his name will long be remembered by millions for his humanitarian work to free India.

Father Damon gave his life in service to the Lepers of Molokai, and advanced the cause of these poor unfortunates and led to modern therapy and methods of arresting the disease.

Pasteur's name will live long in the memory of mankind because of his unceasing efforts to discover germs, the cause of disease, and to eradicate sickness from the face of the earth. Today, in Paris, there are two statues, both to men named Louis. One, Louis XIV, people pass by without even looking up at it; the other, that of Louis Pasteur, tourists seek out and stand before it almost reverently, paying homage to one of the great servant's and beneficiaries of humanity.

Try giving yourself away

If you want to enrich your life, to inspire your mind, to stimulate your physical and mental energies, try giving yourself away. By that I mean, give something personal of yourself to the world; a smile, a kind word, encouragement to one who is depressed. Help a blind person, work for the handicapped veterans who gave so much for all of us, give your services a few hours a week to an orphanage or a foundling's hospital, and soon you will see a remarkable change in your life. It will bring you great happiness and health and inner peace. The law of the harvest is to reap more than you sow, and you will get back ten times to a hundred-fold more than you give to the world.

Your moral and ethical side

Many people become sick because they live under a pall of mental guilt. Psychosomatic medicine now finds that most sickness is due to man's feelings and emotions. When the moral and ethical code of life is violated, then conscience pangs begin and dis-ease of mind becomes disease of the body.

Example: A man struck down another man in anger and the person died. The man who had committed the act of violence became insane and was committed to an insane asylum. While working in a machine shop this man suddenly plunged his arm into a buzz saw and amputated it to the elbow. He became sane immediately and was later released.

How may we account for this man's strange act? Psychologists say that his guilt at having killed a man drove him crazy. By assuaging that guilt through self-mutilation, by cutting off the offending arm, he became restored to mental health. The Bible speaks of this moral law in these symbolic words: "If thine eye offend thee pluck it out."

This does not mean literally to pluck out your eye if it offends you, but rather to remove the offending thought or act from the realm of consciousness.

The moral and ethical laws are given in the Ten Commandments, the Sermon on the Mount, and in the Golden Rule of Christianity. These values are concerned with justice, integrity and honesty, goodness, truth, forgivenes, compassion, charity, and love. When these laws are violated there is suffering and punishment.

Your cosmic or spiritual relationship to God

The sixth and last need that man has for a perfect Master Plan in his life is a Spiritual one; the need to know God. The shining star of God's love for His creation is the most radiant one in His firmament. In civilization's darkest night of war, hatred and barbarism, that star, coupled with the stars of Faith, Hope and Charity, causes man to rise to the loftiest pinnacles of achievement.

Man's need of soul-nourishment is beautifully expressed in this poem:

> If of thy mortal goods thou art bereft,
> And of thy slender store alone,
> Two loaves to thee are left;
> Sell one, and with the dole,
> Buy hyacinths to feed thy soul.

When your mind is attuned to the divine concord and harmony of the music of the spheres, your life will blossom with good. Your relationships with others will be pure and noble and you will strive to live only under the highest and most idealistic principles. It is within the inner Cathedral of your soul that you will find the radiant presence known as God. When you find Him, you will never again dwell in the dark and dismal dungeons of sin, sickness, and despair. The sun of His illimitable presence will drive away the shadows of life and you will discover the secret of immortality within your own soul.

Apply the following dynamic Principles for creating your own Master Plan for a successful and happy future.

FIRST PRINCIPLE: *Set a high goal for yourself in life.*

Do not worry about not achieving it. You can only aim high if you think high, and you will achieve a goal that is in keeping with you mental concept. Browning said, "A man's reach should exceed his grasp, else what's heaven for?"

Until you achieve the high goal you set for yourself, do not minimize or deprecate your present work or situation in life. No one is ever low, and no work is ever dishonorable. The only dishonorable thing is to refuse to strive to reach a high goal.

Confucius said, "Do not worry about becoming great, but, rather, strive to be worthy of greatness."

Some of the so-called lowly men of life have produced some of the greatest works for humanity. Socrates was the son of a midwife and yet became one of our greatest philosophers. Voltaire was the son of an attorney. Shakespeare was the son of a butcher. Mohammed was the son of a goat herder. Christ was the son of a carpenter.

SECOND PRINCIPLE: *Cultivate the habit of knowing exactly what you want from life.*

A master plan can only work for you if you have definiteness regarding what you want in life. Before the builders can create a house, there must first be a blueprint of that house. The details must be set forth clearly or there will be confusion among the workers who try to build the house.

Put order in your thinking

There must be order and harmony in your thinking. Nature never gives anyone anything without exacting a price. Be willing to give time, energy, and perseverance to achieving your life goal. You can only know what you want if you have sufficient knowledge to guide you. You must decide if you want fame and fortune, or if you will be satisfied with a position where you are happy in a small way, doing the things you love. You can probably have anything you want in life, if you are willing to pay the price. Someone has said, "Better to rule on a pumpkin alone, than to rule on a crowded throne." Sometimes one pays dearly for the White House.

Calvin Coolidge and his wife always lamented the fact they were so busy being President and First Lady in the White House that they neglected their young son and his health. He died of blood poisoning from a simple infection in his foot. If they had not been so busy they would have detected this injury and had medical care for it. It was too late when they found out about it.

THIRD PRINCIPLE: *Constantly expand your consciousness so you will continue to grow mentally as you grow older.*

Too many people are robbed of the intellectual and cultural joys that come in middle age and the latter years of life, because they are so busy making money and being a material success. Take time out to enjoy the beauty of nature, the stimulation of good books, art, and music. Be aware of the lives of the great composers, scientists, inventors, and authors. The intellect should never stop growing and expanding, for as we get older we need the stimulation that comes from a well-stocked mind.

FOURTH PRINCIPLE: *Believe in the power of your mind to shape your destiny.*

William James, the noted psychologist and philosopher of Harvard University, said that if a person cares enough for a result there is no reason why he cannot achieve it. He warned that one must concentrate exclusively on the things one wants to achieve and not do it spasmodically. He claims that if a person wants to become wealthy he can will himself to be rich. If he wishes to be good or to become intellectual, he can do so, only he must not keep thinking at the same time a hundred other incompatible things that negate the positive power of the mind.

FIFTH PRINCIPLE: *Transform your life when it is ugly or unbearable through the power of your imagination.*

Sometimes the environment in which you live or work, may not be to your liking. To change may be impossible. It is at such times that you must invoke the power of your imagination and rise above the limited circumstances of your life. What you cannot change you must endure, until such time as you can successfully change it to your liking.

SIXTH PRINCIPLE: *Utilize the law of the harvest and sow in your garden of destiny the seeds of the crop you wish to reap.*

If you use this universal law of the harvest in your personal Master Plan for your future, you will see to it that you put into your mind only thoughts of good, kindness, love, generosity, unselfishness, truth, honesty, beauty, peace and forgiveness. The thoughts you put into your mind are causes and will produce effects that are in keeping with the original causes.

SEVENTH PRINCIPLE: *Build the power of your mind through absorbing knowledge from the greatest minds of the ages.*

Knowledge is power. You will have the ability to direct your life if your mind is fortified by the great thoughts of the ages. Study the lives of the great philosophers, scientists, authors, artists, composers, technicians, industrialists and political leaders of all ages, and emulate the pattern of thinking that has made them great. Then apply their thoughts to your own everyday life.

EIGHTH PRINCIPLE: *Control your thoughts and emotions.*

When you fritter away mental and emotional energy through worry, fear, hatred, or other negative emotions, your mind and body will be enervated and lack the magnetism and power that a controlled mind will give. Later in our study together we shall learn more about this important subject of mental control.

Summary of law one

The Master Plan regulating the universe applies to the mind as well as to matter. This Master Plan gives order, harmony, balance, and growth to everything you think and do. With the tools of the mind you may shape any world you choose. These tools are: Imagination, Vision, Memory, Reason, and Logic. Man's cosmic or spiritual relationship to God is established through love and creative effort. Eight dynamic principles help you create your own Master Plan for a happy and successful future.

Law Two

Using the Scientific Method for Starting a New Life

Let us now explore the scientific method by which you may actually begin a new life. It is essential that you pour out all the old habit patterns you have built in your mind in the past and then build new habit patterns of health, happiness, riches and success.

The Master Jesus gave the formula for doing this in Matt. 10:17: Neither do men put new wine into old bottles: else the bottles break, and the wine runneth out, and the bottles perish: but they put new wine into new bottles, and both are preserved.

This same analogy exists with your mind. Up until now your mind may have been filled with all kinds of negative and discouraging ideas. You may have thought in habit patterns of fear, worry, hate, sickness, accident, failure and unhappiness. This is true of most people brought up in our modern age. It is difficult to change your life philosophy overnight and build new mental habits that are positive.

The land of beginning again

To change your entire life, you must first change your mental attitude about yourself and about your life. No longer think of yourself as being limited, inferior, or inadequate. Fortify yourself with the knowledge that you are created in the image and likeness of God, and that this Divine Image within you is perfect and has all potentialities for health, happiness, and success. An acorn bears no resemblance to the giant oak which it later becomes,

41

but latent within it is the image of its future perfection and giant strength.

There is a poem which is called "The Land of Beginning Again," and it starts with this wonderful sentence:

> I wish that there were some wonderful place,
> Called the land of beginning again.

There is such a wonderful place, and it is in the realm of your own mind. Here it is that you may quietly appraise yourself, your talents, your potentials, and your desires and hopes. Here it is that you may implant the ideas which we shall explore together and watch them flower and grow until they become the sturdy oaks of your future destiny.

Your beginning this course of study is the first step which you are taking to organize a new life and which will lead you to the heights of achievement. Your full potential can only be explored and plumbed by this process of self-analysis and inner search.

Voltaire said, "The first step, my son, which one makes in the world, is the one on which depends the rest of our days."

The first step is mental

The first step which you must take towards shaping a new life and a glorious future destiny is a mental one.

You must decide that you want a new life. You must look about you and see the conditions of lack and limitation, frustration and impotence which may exist in your present job, your home environment, your circumstances of life. Then you must firmly decide that you want to change your life and have the glorious experiences which you have dreamed could someday be yours.

What is the difference between a man or woman who makes twenty-five thousand dollars a year and one who only makes four or five thousand?

It is *the difference in mental values!* The person who is educated to believe he can make more, usually will not settle for *less.* This is one reason why those who obtain a college education succeed sixty-five percent of the time, whereas those who never go beyond high school seldom achieve great success. It is *not* that college gives one knowledge that could not be obtained in other ways, but that it trains the mind of the college student to *believe that he is important* and will succeed because of his college degree. His mental values are shaped in the direction of importance, ego-recognition, dignity, superiority, and social acceptance by people who are worthwhile and important.

If one has not been fortunate enough to obtain a college education, it is still not too late to shape the intellect in the direction of success and achievement. All the great teachers and philosophers of the past have stressed the importance of continuing to grow and expand mentally, even after we finish our formal education. You can start now to infuse your mind with that form of universal wisdom which has illuminated the minds of all our great geniuses of the past. Most of these great men lacked a formal education, and did not go to college, but minds like Socrates, Galileo, Newton and Shakespeare built their own systems of philosophy and reflected in their works the wisdom of the ages.

An ancient Hindu Proverb says,

> Men are four;
> He who knows not and knows not he knows not,
> He is a fool—shun him;
> He who knows not and knows he knows not,
> He is simple—teach him.
> He who knows and knows not he knows,
> He is asleep—wake him.
> He who knows and knows he knows,
> He is wise—follow him!

Every person comes under one of these four categories. You and you alone can determine which fits you.

The slumbering mental giant of genius may be within your own mind at this moment, awaiting the gentle nudge of Desire to awaken to its full power and potential.

Or you may be one of those who does not know of the unlimited dimensions of mind and spirit which have inspired men to dream great dreams and achieve great things. You must then have a desire for wisdom and knowledge, and strive to put these lessons to work in your everyday life, so you may become mentally enriched.

Build your sense of value of yourself by first building the power of your own mind and intellect. You must work to find your hidden talents, and then by study and patience bring them forth to enrich yourself and the world. You must polish your personality and refine your manners, so you will attract people on the higher levels of life who will want to help you unfold your hidden talents.

Shatter the mold of past failures

You must begin at once to shatter the mold of past failures, disappointments, and frustrations. Do not feel your life has been spent in useless pursuits. Everything that has happened to you, even your failures and disappointments, your heartaches and sufferings, have been for a purpose. Nothing in the Cosmic scheme is ever without purpose. You may have needed these negative experiences to give you compassion and understanding of other people and their weaknesses. However, if you wish to build a new life, you cannot do it on the mental foundations of continued negative thinking. You must shatter the mold of past failures and disasters. Reverse these failures in your mind; do not rehearse them by going over them one by one and bemoaning the fact that you cannot change your destiny. The following quotation from a poem is a good illustration of how we must look at the past with its mistakes and sufferings:

> Look not mournfully into the past;
> It comes not back again.
> Wisely improve the present.
> It is thine.
> Go forth to meet the shadowy future
> Without fear and with a manly heart.

You can only do this by busying yourself here and now to improve yourself. You can do this through a system of daily study and growth. Set aside one hour a day in which you study this course of lessons. Let nothing interfere with this schedule. It may be in the morning before you busy yourself with the day's work, or before you are caught up in the activities of others, or it may be at night, just before retiring, when your mind is still and quiescent. Make it a point to study one lesson a day until all the lessons are completed, and then go over the lessons in the years to come, absorbing the teachings little by little and applying them to your everyday life.

Do not give away your book or even lend it to others. You magnetize an object that is yours, and put into it your own personal thought atmosphere. When others share it with you they destroy this mental image which is strictly your own. You will begin to change so profoundly that those close to you will realize something momentous is happening to you. Tell them of this book, show it to them, if you wish, but refuse to lend it to anyone. This is vitally important in your future growth and evolvement.

Then each day for the next week or two, mentally review the mistakes you have made, the lacks and limitations you may possess, not because you want to emphasize them in your consciousness, *but because you want to eradicate them once and for all!* To shatter the mold of past failures and negative conditions you must *know* what they have been, and strive diligently to avoid making the same mistakes in the future.

How the remolding process begins

In the moment that you review your past mistakes and limitations, you begin the remolding process which establishes the new mental habit patterns of success, health, happiness, social acceptance, love fulfillment, and all the rich rewards that go to those who build mental awareness and true inner power.

What shall you put into the new mold which you are mentally shaping for your future?

Principles to incorporate in your new life

FIRST PRINCIPLE: *Build basic integrity and strength of character.* No great destiny was ever built except on a solid foundation of integrity and strength of character. "He that climbs a ladder must begin at the first round" (*Scott*).

The first round on the ladder of success and achievement is basic honesty. If you build on this foundation you will have integrity and strength of character. Shakespeare said it in these words:

> . . . to thine own self be true,
> And it must follow as the night the day,
> Thou canst not then be false to any man.

When you give your word, mean it, and live up to it. Nothing will profit you as much as being known among your friends and business associates as being a person who keeps his word.

Be punctual and show up early for an appointment. This is a basic trait of character which you should build into your character at an early age. Time is valuable and when you develop dishonesty in stealing other people's time, it weakens and undermines the entire basic structure of mind. I know one young man who applied for a position at a salary of twelve thousand dollars a year, and he was fifteen minutes late. He had every other qualification for the job, he had appearance, grooming and intelligence but he *stole his prospective employer's time,* and the man could never forgive him for that. It shows basic dishonesty if a person is habitually late. One might argue that sometimes a storm makes it difficult to get a cab or bus, or that one awakened late, but all such excuses are evasions. One should always prepare for such eventualities by starting for an appointment at least half an hour early.

SECOND PRINCIPLE: *Organize your mind and your environment.*

What does "organize" mean? It means to bring into a systematic relationship all the parts of a whole. This means your mind should be organized in its thinking first, then your environment will reflect order and harmony, and soon your habits will reflect order, punctuality, neatness and harmony.

How do you scientifically organize your mind? By first controlling the thoughts that come into your mind. This is easier said than done. Thoughts have a way of just popping into one's mind in an incoherent and disorderly fashion. The oriental system of philosophy teaches one to sit in meditation and concentrate on ones thoughts for an hour or more a day. At first the thoughts will jump around in confusion, like monkeys in a treetop. The Oriental teacher says that one must mentally pluck each thought (or monkey) from the branch of the tree, and unceremoniously stuff him into a bag. He will scream and struggle, but if you keep doing this for a few days, you will soon have removed all the unruly, uncontrolled thoughts that harass your mind and take your energy and inspiration.

When you have once controlled the thoughts you shall think,

then it is time to feed your mind systematically only those thoughts which conform to the pattern you wish to shape your life by. What shall these thoughts be?

Weaving the Glowing Pattern of Greatness:

Your thoughts shape your destiny. Into the fabric of your thoughts, then, weave a glowing pattern of greatness. How? By thinking the great thoughts that have motivated and inspired the lives of great men and women throughout history. These are thoughts of love and kindness, generosity and mercy, beauty and idealism, happiness and peace, faith and charity, goodness and forgivenes.

"What is beautiful is good," someone has said, "and who is good will soon be beautiful."

There is something contagious about thoughts. When you once fill your mind with these glowing patterns of thought, they will reflect in your personality, your voice, the expression of your eyes and face, and will be as visible as the garments you wear. Emerson said, "What you are speaks so loudly that I cannot hear what you say."

Yes, people judge us by our thoughts, not by the things we say or do. Our thoughts speak eloquently and actually determine our conduct in the outer world.

Make it a point to think and talk success. Do not dwell on failure and defeat. Talk happiness; people run from one who weeps and talks about his problems. Talk and think of beautiful things, tell of your happy and wonderful experiences, rather than your operations and sicknesses. Some people measure time in their lives by referring to a thing having happened before or after an operation or a broken leg or arm. They wear a mask of misfortune that marks them for experiences of doom and disaster.

THIRD PRINCIPLE: *Expand your mental horizons to include experiences you want to have in the future.*

Too often people are limited to a dull pattern of routine existence because they have no mental vision. The Bible says, "Without vision the people perish." Your life will expand miraculously if you expand your mental horizons and include experiences that you want to have in your future.

Visualize yourself going on a trip to Europe or Hawaii. Obtain travel literature and look at all the glamorous places there are in the world and have a mental plan to visit some of these places in the future. Study books like the *National Geographic* magazine so you may acquaint yourself with the wonderful world in which you live. Then mentally exercise your mind by visualizing yourself on boats, planes and trains, taking trips to these thrilling lands. This will help expand the horizons of your thinking and make more tolerable the present monotonous routine and give you hope of a change in the future.

You can also expand your thinking by visualizing yourself doing the work you would like to do. If you gather as much information about it as possible, you will soon see ways and means to achieving the new position. You can go to evening school and take courses now in so many things that help prepare you for a new position that it is no longer necessary to remain imprisoned by a job you do not like.

Consider being an interior decorator, a commercial artist, a TV or electronics technician, a beauty parlor operator, a dress or hat designer, a stenographer, or bookkeeper. Anything you want to do *you can do*, if you will expand your thinking to include the experience you wish to have.

FOURTH PRINCIPLE: *Build your sense of values so you will actually be worth more in your job or to the world.*

Some people feel inferior because *they actually are!* You can only rise above mediocrity and inferiority by building your sense of values so you will actually be worth more in your job or to the world.

A story is told of Catherine, Empress of Russia, who one day commanded Caterina Gabriella, famous opera star of Italy, to sing at the Royal Court in Moscow. The singer sent word to the Empress that her fee would be five thousand gold ducats, payable in advance.

Indignantly, the Empress sent word that her Field Marshal did not receive that much salary in a year. The Diva answered, "then get your Field Marshal to sing at the Royal Court."

Needless to say the opera singer got her big fee and she was a tremendous success at the Royal Court. She knew her value. She had spent years in perfecting her great art and she was not selling herself short.

Know Your Worth And Ask Your Price: Know your true worth in life and do not be afraid to ask your price for your services and talents. But be sure *you have built your values to a point where they are high!*

Demand respect from people and they will give it to you, if you are worthy of that respect. Do not demean your mind and personality by indulging in coarse stories and jokes, and obscene remarks. Such people may have a temporary popularity but it is not built on solid value. It is better to be remembered for quality than for some smutty story which embarrasses people of culture and good taste.

FIFTH PRINCIPLE: *Idealize your mind and your life.*

The philosophy of Idealism is one of beauty and perfection. You may never achieve the ideal, but you can strive constantly to raise your mental and physical standards and eventually you will achieve a fair approximation of them in your life.

> Two men looked out from prison bars.
> One saw mud; the other stars.

Which are you seeing in your life, the mud or the stars? There's plenty of mud, for those who search for it. Alleys and cans of trash may exist, but if you are searching for the fragile morning-glories that bedeck the sagging wooden fence, you will not see the trash.

> How wondrous are thy works, O Lord!
> From rotting logs thou makest banks of violets grow!

Hoot owls do not sing like nightingales and frogs do not pour forth melodious sounds and sonorous music or words. If you do not cultivate your mind and perfect your talents, and organize your life according to the highest standards of which you are capable, then you cannot expect the rich rewards that others receive when they have spent years in organizing their lives to a high peak of perfection. Many coarse, crude and unevolved people try to depreciate and tear down the high standards of art, music, and literature, and we see periodic flurries of distorted images in these fields of culture, but the classical standards which have endured for the centuries are the ones we should study and absorb into the fabric of our minds and souls. Beautiful music, great art, fine poetry and literature, these are the idealistic forms of beauty to put into your mind.

Throughout this course of study we shall explore the highest and best in philosophy, art, poetry, literature and religion, so you will have only the greatest standards by which to build your new life.

Technique for reorganizing and starting your new life

1. Write down on a piece of paper the following facts:
   A. What is your basic purpose in living for the future?
   B. What do you want of life?
   C. Is your goal money or personal achievement? (It can be both, but should not be only money.)
   D. Analyze your past mistakes and ask yourself these questions:
      What mistakes did I make?
      What should I avoid in the future?
      Do I have sufficient desire to achieve greatness?
      Do I let myself be influenced neagtively by others?

2. Have a course of study which includes basic reading of some of the great classics of history. This should include poetry, drama, novels, and biographies and autobiographies of great people. Check your library for lists of books stressing cultural and intellectual values.

3. Sit each day for at least fifteen minutes and review the day's activities. What would you do differently? What would you have avoided? What could you have done to improve yourself or your situation in life this day?

4. Analyze your surroundings and ask yourself: Do I have order in my environment? Is there harmony between myself and members of my family? What can I do to improve my personal surroundings?
   Do I try to create beauty and harmony in my home?

Strive diligently each day to improve yourself and your surroundings. If there is bickering, chaos, and confusion between you and your family, your friends and co-workers, start now to improve your relationship with the world. Try to find out what is bothering you and then correct it. If it is the other person's fault, try to be more understanding, tolerant and forgiving. Realize that no one is perfect and that we must all tolerate certain imperfections in others, as they must ours.

5. Realize that you are on a mystical quest in your life and that you search for ultimate perfection, happiness and fulfillment. Great men of the past changed the course of history through their quests and crusades. Ponce de Leon searched for the fountain of youth, Admiral Byrd sought the South Pole, Lindbergh overcame time and space in flying the Atlantic, Columbus discovered new lands, and Marco Polo expanded the horizons of the world of his time with his travels. Man constantly quests for that which will add new dimensions of mind and spirit. In this mystical quest of your life be adventurous and daring, and explore new horizons of wisdom and knowledge. Constantly discover something new about life and people, and fully understand yourself and the motives that keep your eyes on the stars in this mystical voyage of life.

Summary of law two

Man may discover the mystical land of beginning again, where he may build his dreams and ideals in the image and likeness of God. The mental image you choose determines the kind of world you externalize. Build positive values to overcome past failures. Organize your mind, expand your mental horizons to include new experiences. You are on a mystical quest for ultimate perfection and fulfillment. You can achieve this goal by applying the dynamic laws and principles we shall explore further in our study together.

How to Think Your Way to Fame and Fortune

All creative effort begins in the Mind. You do nothing that the mind does not first conceive of and then approve, either consciously or subconsciously. Later in our studies together we shall have much to learn about the subconscious and the superconscious minds, but in this lesson let us be concerned with the power of your conscious, volitional mind.

It is your mind that is the selector of the events of your present and future life, just as it has chosen the past events. No matter how hard you may try, you can never erase those past thoughts or the actions that resulted from them. By analyzing the past with its mistakes and regrets, you can carefully avoid making similar mistakes in the future. You can begin this moment to harness the positive power of your mind, so that you can *think* your way to fame and fortune.

Heaven or hell in your thoughts

Milton wrote in *Paradise Lost:*

> Mind is its own place, and in itself
> Can make a heaven of hell, a hell of heaven.

This is very true. We can create a paradise in whatever environment we choose if our thoughts are positive, happy and creative. But no matter how much money we may have or how famous we may be, if our minds are not attuned to the right thoughts and creative patterns, we can be lonely, unhappy and isolated. See how many millionaires kill themselves. Even though

us and rich, their minds cannot stand the pressure
they have no sustaining philosophy to back them

itiful youthful star like Marilyn Monroe could not
fortune because she lacked mental stability.

Develop a strong, resilient mind

It is important, then, that you build your mind first, so it is
strong and resilient, and can rise above the negative circumstances of your life. Then you will not only be able to meet the
challenges of life but you will be able to withstand good fortune
and wealth.

If you can once learn to use the power of your mind constructively and creatively, you can literally *think your way to fame
and fortune.*

If you investigate the lives of great men and women throughout history, people who have achieved enduring fame, you will
see that behind every great fortune, every invention, every song,
every story, every business, there is, first, a great creative idea.
Creative ideas can be deliberately courted and cultivated by
anyone, no matter how limited his education.

You can think your way to health. You can think your way to
riches. You can attract friends and social popularity through the
power of your mind. You can find fulfillment in love and marriage
by building mental power. It is only necessary that you think each
thing into existence, persistently and over a period of many
months and years. The cumulative effect of thought is very much
like water that is stored behind a dam. The trickle that passes
over the dam and turns the dynamos, creating electric power, is
only a small part of the total mass. The real force and power is
the reserve water back of the dam.

Reserves of power within your mind

Your mind also has this reserve force which may be tapped
when you want to achieve greatness. What is the true key to
greatness? How can you unlock these reserves of power which
can cause you to scale the heights and achieve fame and fortune?

FIRST KEY: *A desire to advance yourself or your family.*

Many of the great things which have been attained in life were inspired by the desire to advance one's interests. This is *not* a selfish desire, but a natural one, which is inherent in all people under the instinct of self-preservation.

This desire often expresses itself in creative action of the mind and evolves ideas that bring success. McCormick invented the reaper when he was only twenty-four years of age, because he wanted to improve his station in life and help his family. This was one of the great inventions of all time and brought the young man millions of dollars. If he had not been inspired by a desire to help his family and himself, he would no doubt have remained poor the rest of his life.

Henry Ford had a desire to perfect a car that would be reasonable and furnish mass tranportation for people. He undoubtedly also wanted to make money and improve his own position in life. When he died he left a fortune of five hundred million dollars. The motivation which inspired him was this desire to advance his own interests and those of the world.

SECOND KEY: *A desire to create something for the good of the world.*

When Dr. Salk worked quietly for years to perfect his polio vaccine, it was obviously not for himself alone. He was motivated by a desire to create something good for the entire world and to spare millions of children and adults the agony of polio with its resultant paralysis. The proof of this unselfish motivation is the fact that he gave all profit from the sale of the vaccine which bears his name to charity.

When you are motivated by this unselfish desire you will have greater inspiration to achieve a high goal than if you merely have a desire to have a large fortune. People who made big fortunes or became famous and successful were generally infused with this creative spirit of unselfishness.

THIRD KEY: *Stimulate your imagination by imagining the life you desire.*

The imagination is one of your most powerful aids to achieving fame and fortune. Einstein said, "Imagination is more important than knowledge." It was in his imagination that Einstein envisioned the great Theory of Relativity that set the stage scientifically for our modern atomic age.

Napoleon said, "The human race is governed by its imagination." Although he was ultimately defeated in the Battle of Waterloo, Napoleon, through the power of his imagination, achieved a position as Emperor and nearly conquered the world. He would have been nothing if he had not imaged the picture of what he was to do and be.

It is said that in order to help himself imagine being an Emperor more forcibly, Napoleon called in Talma, the greatest tragedian of his day, and had him teach him to think, look, and talk like an Emperor. In a few weeks the short, uncultured, and unprepossessing Napoleon acquired the bearing and dignity of an Emperor and for twenty years the crowned heads of the world were to bow before him—a task that would have been utterly impossible if he had not used the power of his imagination.

Exercises for developing the power of your imagination

1. Stand before your mirror and read a dramatic passage from a book. It can be a poem, a political speech, Shakespeare, or some other drama. As you read look up and watch your expression in the mirror. Then mentally imagine that you are delivering this reading before an audience on a stage. Become alert to the sound of your voice, study the expression on your face in the mirror carefully. Convey all the intensity and meaning that is inherent in the words.

2. Also before your mirror, without the aid of a book, imagine that you are standing before the Congress of the United States. You have been called upon to deliver a speech. Make up in your own words what you would say on any subject you choose. At first this idea will appall you, but gradually, as your imagination becomes more and more fired, you will find yourself delivering quite a good speech. But most important of all, this exercise will do wonders for your mind; your personality will become more magnetic and forceful, your voice will ring with a new note of

authority, and your entire attitude will change to one of power and importance. Practice this speech-making as often as possible, for it is one of the best ways to project the power of your imagination to your personality and your environment.

3. Use this same power of your imagination to change your mental picture of your job, your financial conditions, or any other situation that you desire. Practice saying aloud what you would tell your boss if you were to ask him for a raise in salary. Point out your unique services for the company, why you are worth more, and why you believe he will give you the raise.

Mentally imagine yourself going to the bank and depositing large sums of money; or withdrawing money and going on a mental shopping spree, buying all the things you desire. Actually, it is only a short step between imagination and reality. When your mind grows strong enough in mental imagery to make these things a reality, you will have bridged the gap between dreams and reality and actually find yourself doing the things you formerly only imagined.

It was in imagination that primitive man first saw a stone rolling down a hill, and imagined it attached to a cart. This led to the invention of the wheel, which scientists call the greatest invention of all time. For with the creation of the wheel man set the stage for automobiles and our modern jet planes. All our machinery depends on this fundamental principle of the wheel.

FOURTH KEY: *Practice thinking about Money and Fame as often as you can.*

Change your former ideas about money: that it's wrong to have it, that it's difficult to get, that only the rich have a chance to succeed in life. Your entire mental attitude toward fame and fortune will change if you begin to think of money as a commodity which can be used to obtain things of value.

Many people think it's wrong to be rich. They remember the Bible injunction that it's more difficult for a rich man to get into heaven than for a camel to go through the eye of a needle. Actually the needle referred to was the gate in Jerusalem, before which a camel had to kneel to pass through. Also the Bible says

"Love of money is the root of all evil" and *not* "Money is the root of all evil" as many suppose.

Begin to think that you wish to achieve fame and fortune and be rich and successful because it is God's wish that you have all the good things of life. Even the Bible promises you this. It says, "Know ye not that ye are heirs to a Kingdom?" Also, "It is the Father's good pleasure to give you the Kingdom." Act as though you are a spiritual heir to all the good things of life, and you will begin to attract them.

Also in the Bible we are told this about money, "Wine maketh merry: but money answereth all things" (Ecc. 10:19.)

Bacon said of money: "Money is a good servant but a bad master."

And Aristodemus, one of the wise Greek teachers, said of money: "Money makes the man."

You will achieve the degree of fame and fortune that you *believe you can achieve*, and your desires must be whetted by the thought of the good you can do for others.

Summary of law three

Creative mind paves the way to fame and fortune. Vast reserves of creative power exist within your mind. This power may be released through a desire to advance yourself or to help others in life. Imagination is the key that unlocks the invisible doors to the storehouse of universal riches. Money in itself is not evil; only the love of money. Act as though you are an heir to a kingdom and ask for what you want of life.

Law Four

Using the Master Mind Power That Can Build Your Future

In building your future you may feel that you need external help, that someone or something must happen which can elevate you to the place you dream of in the future. This persistent thought may actually keep you from ever achieving the heights of which you dream.

You must realize that external forces can help you but *only* when you have tapped the full power that is available to your mind. This is the power of the Master Mind which rules the entire universe and which can guide you unerringly to your right destiny.

The master mind in nature

This Master Mind exists in all nature. It is the working of a vast force or intelligence which shapes the visible and invisible world in which we live. Call this power Nature or God, or Cosmic Intelligence, whatever you wish, but certain it is that something external to man is at work in the universe which is constantly busy refining, changing, evolving and perfecting.

When I was a youngster on the farm I went to Sunday School one morning and heard the minister tell of miracles. My ten-year-old mind could not comprehend what he meant by the word. When we got home, my father took me by the hand and led me to an incubator where some chicks were about to hatch. As the first tiny beak broke through the egg, my father said, "That my boy, is what the preacher meant this morning when he spoke of a miracle."

I watched in amazement as the tiny chick pecked its way out

59

of the egg shell, and then said, "The miracle to me is how he got in there in the first place."

This profound fact—which came first, the chicken or the egg—has baffled scholars, theologians, and philosophers throughout the ages. We know that some First Cause exists in the universe which created all forms of life, but which came first—the Creative Idea or the Thing? Obviously, if we want to be logical about it, we must state that the Creative Idea had to be first. There can only be a chicken if there is a Cause—the egg, or the parent hen that laid that egg.

So too, in the natural universe all things have a predetermining Cause, which leads to all effects. If you want to use this great creative principle of the Master Mind in your life for achieving fulfillment of your destiny, you can plan the Causes you want to issue from your mind, and you may be sure that all the effects will be of the same kind and character, quality and degree.

How the master mind works its miracles

The Master Mind of the universe works its miracles through the universal law of Cause and Effect. It determines the kind of universe it wishes to create, what kind of creatures shall inhabit it, and then sets to work from this predetermined Effect to create the Causes which can produce it.

Examples: A camel is a strange creature, with a great ability to store water and to live for days on the desert. His feet especially fit desert travel. No other animal quite so perfectly fits a traveller's needs on the desert as the camel. How could this strange, ungainly beast be created to so specifically fit its intended task? Some intelligence in nature shaped that animal to do its intended work in its predestined place.

A certain breed of fish is extremely rare in the ocean, and the chance of running into another of its species with which to mate is improbable. What does the Master Mind do? It creates a male fish that attaches itself to the body of a female shortly after it is born, and becomes fused with her body. At all times in the future this mate is attached to the female's body, making breeding simple, to perpetuate that species. This is a miracle of some creative

Master Mind which is endlessly experimenting with all forms of creation.

This Master Mind possesses amazing intelligence in nature. It is able to adapt specially constructed creatures to the environment it chooses. Squirrels are adapted by nature to climb trees and store nuts and grains for its winter food. The bee instinctively builds a six-sided honey comb because it will store more honey than a five-sided comb. How does the bee have this knowledge? It is a part of its race instinct, implanted by a Master Mind that was in existence for centuries before the bee was created.

Did life start in the water?

Scientists believe that this Master Mind began its work of creating and adapting all forms of life to the earth by operating in the sea first. There is much proof of this fact. One species of fish in Africa is called the lungfish, and it has lungs which permit it to remain out of water for indefinite periods of time. If a drought comes along, the lungfish will bury itself in mud and survive until the rains come again.

A sea anemone cannot move from its rooted spot, but the Master Mind has provided it with a perfect way to get its food. It has long, cord-like tentacles which have little bombs of poison attached to them. When a fish goes by, the sea anemone darts out its tentacles, penetrates the body of the fish, and the bombs of poison explode, paralyzing the fish. The anemone then devours it and is able to live and reproduce.

How this master mind works within you

The same Master Mind force that takes care of all creation, also exists within you, as a higher form of intelligence than your conscious or subconscious minds. It is the race instinct that exists within your cells. It is the power that causes you to be different from animals. You can shape and direct this Master Mind Intelligence in any way you wish, to adapt it to your environment, your talents, your needs. This Master Mind works automatically for you, but it can be directed by your desires and aspirations. It can give you ideas for future work, for building a fortune, for inventing something that will make you a million, for creating new ideas that can help change the face of the earth.

How to use this master mind power

Your own mental power can be built and made stronger, just like the muscles of your body, through use. The Master Mind works better when you form mental habits that are positive and constructive. It is always prejudiced in favor of health, life, energy, youth, success, happiness, and good. As it is God's agency for creating a better and more perfect world, it will work best for you when you desire a better life than you now have. You set this higher mind to work with the following basic forces:

1. A desire to refine your personality.
2. A desire to improve your mind and your body.
3. A desire to accumulate wisdom and knowledge.
4. A desire to help your family.
5. A desire to succeed in business.
6. A desire to make money for constructive good.
7. A desire to increase your gifts and talents.
8. A desire to elevate your standards in life.

Choose your destiny

Remember, this Master Mind will adapt you to any environment you consciously choose. Choose your Destiny, then, and depend on this higher Mind to fit you to that Destiny. Form the mental habit of thinking you are worthy of the best, of knowing you will achieve your inner dreams, and these habit patterns of thought will attract to you the things you habitually dwell on.

William James, the noted psychologist and philosopher, said of habit, "Habit simplifies our movements, makes them accurate and diminishes fatigue."

The Duke of Wellington wrote of habit, "Habit, a second nature? Habit is ten times nature."

You must persistently build habits mentally that are persevering, positive, and optimistic. The Master Mind of the universe will show you how to achieve the things you desire if you build the power of your own mind. Choose the people you want to associate with, the work you want to do, the environment in which you wish to live, the amount of money you want to spend, the trips you want to take.

Then, do not question *whether you can or cannot do these things. Know* that you can, and persistently hold to that thought, until the habit pattern is one of success and fulfillment rather than failure and frustration.

I once appeared in a one-hour television show in Honolulu, on a station owned by Henry J. Kaiser, the ship builder and industrialist. One of the other guests was Lloyd Bridges, who was preparing some television shows in Hawaii. Bridges told me he had been to Kaiser's home, and the noted builder showed him a dictionary in which the word "impossible" had been carefully cut out!

This was the secret of Kaiser's phenomenal success. When the government asked for steel ships with which to win the war in the Pacific, and wanted them within a matter of weeks, every other ship builder said it was impossible to build them that fast. Kaiser said he would build them. He established an assembly line method and produced his first liberty ship in a matter of weeks; others followed in rapid succession, and they are credited with having helped bring the war to a quicker end.

How to build positive habit patterns

You can build positive habit patterns by refusing to think that anything that you want to be or do is impossible. Then each day make it a point to think of something unusual you want to do, and then *go out and do it*

If you are a salesman, and want to increase your sales, *believe that you can do it*. You may get an idea to write a certain type of letter to prospective customers. Or the Master Mind may intuitively guide you to join a certain country club where you play golf with leading citizens, thus making contacts for future sales you could never make in any other way.

> God works in a mysterious way,
> His wonders to perform.
> He sets His footsteps on the sea,
> And rides upon the storm.

You never know how the Master Mind will express itself in your life, when you once begin to help this power set the mental stage for action, and believe that all things are possible, and somehow, somewhere, this Master Mind will catch you up and sweep you on to fame and fortune. If you build habit patterns that cause you to think of failure, fear, frustration, misery, sickness, and lonelines, you will be shaping this Master Mind power into forms that are negative and unwholesome.

God helps those who help themselves

You've heard the saying, "God helps those who help themselves?" This is a truism. The Master Mind works in and through nature, carrying out God's universal laws of action, capillary attraction, gravity and growth, but the Master Mind must be gently nudged in the direction you wish to take.

A simple story illustrates this point. A minister was visiting a farmer nearby one lovely fall day, and the farmer showed him over his farm. The Minister pointed to a waving field of wheat and said, "My, but that's a fine field of wheat the Lord has produced."

The farmer thought of the back-breaking hours of labor he had put in tilling the soil and planting the seed, but his only reply was, "Yes, it sure is."

Next they came to an apple orchard, where the trees were heavily loaded with fruit and the Minister said, "My but that's a wonderful orchard of fruit the Good Lord sent you."

When they came to a field of waving corn, the minister again said, "That's sure a great crop of corn the Good Lord gave you."

By this time, the farmer was getting a little impatient with the minister's remarks, and next they passed a field of weeds, that had been completely uncultivated, and the farmer waved his hand in the direction of the wheat, apples and corn, and said, "The Lord and I did all that together, but, Reverend, the Lord had this weed patch all to Himself."

You and God a majority

Nothing more graphically points up the truth that the Master Mind, God's Infinite Intelligence, can work miracles for *you* also, if you work with the power. If left to itself a garden will go back to jungle, but with cultivation and labor, it remains a beautiful, productive garden. So too with your mind power; it grows and evolves with usage, and stagnates and falls into desuetude with disuse. You and God are a majority, but if you try to work without the aid of this higher Master Mind, the job will be all uphill work and will never be as perfect or complete as if you enlist the aid of a higher power within your own mind.

Regimen for channeling power of the master mind

1. *Have an intense desire to improve yourself and to help your family.* Let this desire include the possession of money and material objects for your comfort and security. Do something about this desire; take the first step by improving your mind (as you are doing in this course of study), by reading good books, and by cultivating your natural powers of perception, absorption, and reasoning. The Chinese say, "A journey of a thousand miles begins with but a single step."

Take that first mental step in the direction of building power of the mind through forming mental habits that are orderly, precise, constructive, persevering, patient, and creative. You can apply these six elements of thought to your everyday life, until they become solid mental habits which operate constantly without your conscious thought.

2. *Have faith in yourself and in the power of the Master Mind of God.* Faith must exist within your mind that this Power will perform the same miracles for you that it performs in nature. Remind yourself a dozen times a day that God is a living reality, not just a name, and that His Master Mind is an Infinite Intelligence which can work wonders in your life.

3. *Use positive affirmations or suggestions which implement the natural power of your own conscious and subconscious minds.* Learn the value of giving yourself mental suggestions to implement your own mental powers. The higher mind works better when it is shaped and channeled in definite directions. You should say these affirmations each morning upon awakening, and also as often during the day as you can. They help give you mental

strength, and they also form the positive habits of thinking which create your destiny.

AFFIRMATION FOR HEALTH: I am healthy and strong, vital and young. I now breathe deeply of the life force which gives me strength and energy. I imprint upon my conscious and subconscious minds the creative ideas of health, energy and vitality which I wish my body cells and organs to express. I live with a dynamic purpose to achieve success, and to make a fortune. I am perfect.

AFFIRMATION FOR SUCCESS: I now affirm that I am successful. Everything I do is marked with the imprint of success. I have faith in myself and my talents. I will give of value to the world and the world will give in turn recognition, money and other rewards. I now express my creative ideas in dynamic action that will lead me to the fulfillment of my destiny.

AFFIRMATION FOR DYNAMIC PERSONALITY: I now project the mental image of the perfect personality I wish to possess. I desire qualities of honesty, kindness, goodness, and forgiveness in my personality. I express Divine Love to every person I meet. I am tolerant, understanding, compassionate, and merciful towards others. I know we are all children of a loving God and that we are all under His divine protection and guidance.

AFFIRMATION FOR HAPPINESS AND PEACE OF MIND: I express radiance and happiness in my mind and personality. I see the good in the world, and I enjoy all of life's good and wholesome experiences. I strive to be happy and to share that happiness with others I meet. I practice honesty and righteousness and I forgive everyone who has ever hurt me or tried to hurt me. I now release myself from all feelings of guilt by having only moral and ethical conduct that is on the highest level of consciousness. I am peaceful, serene, and calm in the midst of life's storms.

4. *When you retire at night review the day's happenings, and correct all the mistakes in thought or action that you have indulged that day.* Remove all negative thoughts and supplant them with positive thoughts. This will give you refreshing sleep and keep you from tossing and turning at night because of pressure on your mind of regret, guilt, or other emotional inadequacies.

5. *Remove hate and resentment from your consciousness by trying to reason out why you hate someone or some situation.* Hate is a vitiating emotion and the Master Mind Power operates only under the impetus of Love. Hate releases a deadly chemical from the glands which poisons the mind and body and destroys it.

6. *Have a definite course of action in your mind for each day, and try to stick with it.* This schedule should include ideas for your work, your social life, for bettering and improving your mind, for learning new words, better expressions in your conversation, improved diction and English. The Master Mind works better when you channel it in a definite way.

7. *Keep your mind young and resilient by keeping it active.* Action is nature's first law. Apply it to your mental activity. Have mental plans for your spare time, and have a program of self-improvement and study that goes on all through your life. An active mind also helps keep the body cells and organs youthful and science now says that a mind that is active actually causes the body to live longer.

Summary of law four

There is a Master Mind Power in the universe that creates all things. This power is in nature, it is within your own mind. It can be harnessed by man to create anything he desires. The Law of Cause and Effect can be used to perform miracles. Mind power grows with usage. You and God are a majority. Man may use positive affirmations to release more of this Master Mind Power in his own life for performing great deeds.

Law Five

Dynamic Steps to
Achieving Your Life's Goals

Do you really know what it is you want in life? Some people want large sums of money, others want social position, fame and recognition; still others want love-fulfillment and happiness in love and marriage. There are as many different kinds of goals as there are people and you may include one or all of the above desires in your future life goal.

It is important to realize that everyone is *not* striving for the same goal in life. Some people want to be famous and rich; others are satisfied with a small salary, and to remain in obscure positions. To be a big fish in a big pond is difficult and exacts a penalty which many people are not willing to meet. Many people choose to be big fish in small ponds, and they are the people who remain in their home towns, where they build a reputation among the citizens they have known all their lives. These people are just as happy in their way as those who achieve higher goals and build vast fortunes.

What is your goal in life?

You must determine what your goal in life is and then carefully shape all the events of your life towards that goal. No matter whether you want to be world-famous and rich or are merely satisfied with simple pleasures and ordinary achievements, your Destiny is important to *you*. What, then, are the seven Basic Elements you will need in your life, and how shall you go about achieving them?

Man's seven basic requirements

There are seven basic requirements which every person should have in his life, no matter what degree of success he may wish to achieve. These are:

1. Your right work
2. Financial rewards or other rewards
3. Friends and social life
4. Love and marriage happiness
5. Expression of creative talents other than your work
6. Mental and intellectual growth and evolvement
7. Spiritual needs: faith in God and daily prayer

STEP NO. 1: Prepare your mind by absorbing necessary knowledge to fit you for the achievement of the goal you set. This preparation should include specialized knowledge that fits you for specific tasks. Professional workers, such as doctors, lawyers, architects, dentists, and others, have to prepare by going to college for several years. If you are in a field that does not require higher education, you will go further in life by taking a course of study in some evening high school or college for adult education. Any study you do along these lines will be helpful in achieving your goal.

In fact, you should study the rest of your life, even when your work is set, for a mind that has many facets developed will be more interesting and will attract more friends than one who remains unschooled in the finer things of life.

Education helps shape the mind so that we appreciate the better things of life and understand the laws which govern the universe. Pope said of education:

> 'Tis education forms the common mind;
> Just as the twig is bent the tree's inclined.

You should not only absorb as much knowledge as possible from books or courses in high school and college, but you should daily train your mind by reading magazines of current events such as *Time, Newsweek, Life, Reader's Digest, Saturday Review, Look, Harper's,* and any others that give you a view of the contemporary world in which you live.

STEP NO. 2: *Use the Law of Expectation.*

To expect something means to look forward to achieving it. This is a positive approach to achieving your goal. It is obvious that if you do *not* expect your good, you will almost certainly miss it. If you expect to succeed, you will shape your thoughts and actions in the direction of success.

Disraeli said, "Everything comes if a man will only wait." If you wait patiently and keep expecting to achieve your goal in life, you will not be disappointed. Most people color their entire life experience with fear of failure and violate this dynamic Law of Expectation.

Live with the thought of success

Most people think of success spasmodically. They seldom persist in holding the thought that they are going to succeed or that they will have money, or fulfillment in love and happiness in the future. To succeed, one must live with the thought of success constantly. Every day indulge this Law of Expectation and remind yourself a hundred times a day of the reasons for your hard work, for studying and improving yourself, of the rich rewards that will soon come to you because you have persevered.

Not only will this Law of Expectation help sharpen your mind but it will add enormously to your joy of life, for instead of going through life with an empty and uninteresting mind, you will have exciting and stimulating thoughts to constantly accompany you.

"The happiest person," said Timothy Dwight, "is the person who thinks the most interesting thoughts."

STEP NO. 3: *Expand the horizons of your mind to prepare you for the big rewards of life.*

Most people come into an unsatisfactory destiny because they have constantly thought in patterns of limitation and lack. The horizons of your mind can only be expanded if you make real effort every day of your life. Begin this moment to realize that the world is filled with infinite treasures. You need not be limited in your quest for success or riches by the limitations of your present job or environment.

Hilton, the hotel man, once told me at a party that even as a fairly young man, when he had his first small hotel, he had visions of one day owning a world-wide empire of dozens of big, first-class hotels. His dream came true because he learned early in life how to expand the horizons of his mind.

One day at the old R.K.O. studios in Hollywood, I was being photographed with a beautiful redhead who was working on a picture. She seemed rather sad, so I asked her what was wrong.

She replied, "I am being fired today and I haven't even begun to make a name for myself yet."

I replied, "Oh, I'm sorry to hear that."

She flashed a big smile that banished her expression of sadness and said brightly, "Oh, don't worry. I'm not finished yet! Someday I'll come back here and buy this studio!"

We both laughed, for it was obviously a joke. Fifteen years later, Lucille Ball, for that's who it was, came back to R.K.O. and bought the studios for fifteen million dollars! She may have been joking when she said it, but this woman had something of vision when she made that remark. Her subconscious mind went to work from that day on, and made her more determined than ever that she would succeed.

STEP NO. 4: *Recognize the essentials for which you are struggling in working toward your goal.*

Is it just money that you are working to make? This is one of life's seven essentials, as we have seen in the first part of our lesson, but is it *all*? You must have a higher goal than working merely to make a fortune. Is it just to become famous and well-known? This is not enough either. Witness the fact that famous people in the public eye are not always happy people. Is it for others that you are living? To share your joys and sorrows with friends and loved ones is probably one of life's more satisfactory rewards. If you keep this in mind you will begin to shape your life in the direction of people, and every move will be motivated by what is good for others as well as yourself.

When General Booth, the founder of the Salvation Army, wished to send a Christmas message to the world-wide branches of that organization by cable and telegram, he chose one which not only expressed his sentiments, but was brief and to the point. He wrote the one word, *Others.*

Limit desire, increase happiness

You are striving for friends, money, recognition, love-happiness, possessions, satisfaction in your work, and many, many other things. However, in our study of philosophy we must never lose sight of the fact that the more unfulfilled desires we have the more miserable we are. Learn to limit your desires to life's essentials first, and you will increase your happiness immediately.

Franklin said, "It is easier to suppress the first desire than to satisfy all that follow it."

This does not mean you should deprive yourself of anything in life that gives you enjoyment, but merely to limit your desires to your present level of accomplishment. As you are able to prove your ability to demonstrate more and more of the possessions or desirable conditions you are working to achieve, then you can add to your desires without fear of being unhappy. However, it must be remembered that when we get our first million we always want the second. I remember a man in Los Angeles who made a million on property he owned during the real estate boom of the forties. I said to him, "Now you and your wife can surely retire and take that trip around the world you have dreamed of."

His answer surprised me. He said, "Not at all. I'd feel terribly insecure with only a million. Why, I could lose it in one or two investments. Now I need two more million to back up that first million."

In one year that man was dead and his dream of true success and happiness had never been fulfilled.

"Our desires always increase with our possessions," Samuel Johnson said. "The knowledge that something remains yet unenjoyed impairs our enjoyment of the good before us."

STEP NO. 5: *Study the lives and thoughts of great men of history to use as examples and ideals by which to build your own life.*

Nothing tells such a graphic story as history. It reveals to man his past mistakes and shows him how to remove those mistakes and build on a more solid foundation. So too, the lives of great men in history leave for us examples and inspiration which can help us build better lives. In the words of Longfellow:

> Lives of great men all remind us
> We can make our lives sublime,
> And, departing, leave behind us
> Footprints on the sands of time.

Study the biographies and autobiographies of great men and women who have helped shape the world in which you live, and take notes of the things that are pertinent to you and which will help inspire you to higher levels of thinking and achievement.

For example, the lives of the great men of the world show us the value of various positive qualities.

Lincoln: integrity, dedication, and high purpose.

Burbank: Curiosity to know nature's profound secrets; patience and perseverance to achieve the goal we set.

Edison: Ingenuity, desire to help humanity, and the determination to succeed. When an assistant said to Mr. Edison, "You've tried ten thousand experiments to make an electric light that will burn. Why don't you give up?" The great inventor replied, "Indeed not! We now know ten thousand things that won't work!" His next test proved successful. What if he'd given up and been discouraged with those ten thousand failures? The world would have been deprived of the blessings of electric light for many years.

Columbus: Vision, courage, imagination, and fearlessness.

Pasteur: Imagination, courage, curiosity, desire to help humanity. When he discovered germs the whole scientific world laughed at him and called him crazy. It was only when he persisted with his theories and finally proved them that the world acclaimed him as one of our greatest benefactors and geniuses.

Shakespeare: Beauty of expression, vast knowledge, persistence, and ability to rise above a lowly birth.

Walk with kings and princes

Leonardo da Vinci: This great artist who painted the Mona Lisa, the Last Supper, and many other superb paintings, was also

the first man to draw a picture of the flying machine and actually
build a glider which flew a few feet. When he was only twelve
he knew poverty, and the world's cruelty. He was an illegitimate
child, and everyone told him that he was doomed to a life of
failure and misery.

He made up his mind at twelve that he would become a great
artist. He felt in that way he could win the rewards and recognition of the world which his soul desired. He said at that age,
"I shall one day walk with kings and princes, and the great of the
world will honor me."

Less than twenty years later the crowned heads of Europe
acclaimed the talent of this genius and he truly walked and lived
with kings and princes, and the great men of his age paid him
homage.

STEP NO. 6: *Be definite in what you want from life.* A blueprint
for a house must definitely show where the windows, doors and
stairs are, before the workers can build the house.

So too, the Master Architect of the universe can only create for
you the great destiny you desire when you know definitely what
you want. This means that you should know your over-all goal,
but you should also know the individual events, persons, and
situations that you desire from day to day.

Set a definite life-sum goal of the money you wish to achieve
and write it down on a sheet of paper, with your other desires
and aspirations. For instance, would you be willing to settle right
now for $200,000. cash? Or do you think you need more to bring
you fulfillment in old age?

You may think that you can never have such a sum of money.
I can prove that you will have it, whether you are conscious of
it or not. If you live to be sixty years of age and spend only a
minimum of three thousand dollars a year (which is extremely
low), you will have spent the large sum of one hundred and eighty
thousand dollars! You are probably already rich without realizing it!

How to stretch your thinking

It is only a matter of stretching your thinking a little to make
that figure higher. If you live in thoughts of limitation and lack,

you will never be aware that you are already rich in health, sanity, your five senses (think what your eyes mean to you! You would not sell your sight for any amount of money!), the enjoyment of your friends, and the love of your family is worth more than money. If you think in this positive way you will begin to enjoy life more and you will stretch your thinking to encompass ever bigger and richer goals in your future.

STEP NO. 7: *Seek the aid of important people to help you achieve your goal.*

You cannot achieve your goal in life alone. You need the help of others. Whom shall you seek? Those who are poverty-stricken? Those who are failures and has-beens?

No. You must deliberately seek the friendship and aid of important people to help you. Make it a regular campaign to seek out men and women who have accomplished important things. Join clubs, work with civic groups, seek out the friendship of men and women who are leaders in their fields and socialize with them. These people are hard to meet at first, but when you once get in with them, you will find that important people are easier to know than people with petty minds and accomplishments.

Make known your needs to people who can help you. Do not be timid or frightened. They have had to struggle to achieve their present goals, and they will usually be most sympathetic with your problems. Very often such people in high places will give you a letter of introduction to someone who can be of help in seeking a better job or some other favor.

STEP NO. 8: *Avoid waste of time, for time is golden.* Time is money, and time is the only substance with which you can work to create the future you desire. Make the most of your wasted hours. Do you spend hours a day before the TV set? It may be amusing, but is it really helping you achieve your goal? Wouldn't you be better off enrolling in an evening course in high school or college studying writing, accounting, public speaking, dramatic acting, interior decorating, or bookkeeping?

Twenty-four golden hours to spend

You have only twenty-four hours a day to spend. Eight of these are spent in working; eight in sleeping, and you have eight precious, golden hours to spend recklessly. Two hours a day should be spent in self-improvement and preparing yourself for the higher goal towards which you aspire. Two hours can be given over to social activity, TV programs, movies, bowling, or other sports. You still have two hours left with which to improve yourself in some way. Read good books, listen to inspiring music, go to art galleries and museums, spend some of this daily time in spiritual meditation and prayer, for your soul needs daily nourishment as well as your mind and body.

It is said that when Queen Elizabeth the First of England was on her death bed, her last words were, "Time! Time! Give me one more moment of time! I would give my kingdom and all I possess for one more moment of time!" But time had run out on her and there were many things left undone and unsaid which she regretted not having done and said.

The poet has put it in these words:

> Catch then, O catch, the transient hour;
> Improve each moment as it flies;
> Life's a short summer . . . man a flower,
> He dies, alas! how soon he dies.

STEP NO. 9: *Remove the clouds of discouragement which gather daily in your mind.*

This mental clearing of the clouds of discouragement should be a daily exercise, before they grow so dense that they obscure your future life goal.

How can you avoid feeling discouraged? By being so busy that you never have time to sit down and commiserate with yourself! This is a good formula, for a busy mind seldom has time to think discouraging thoughts.

You can also work each day by setting small goals you are trying to achieve, and as each one is attained, your mind will feel a glow of satisfaction. This will keep you from thinking that you are not getting anywhere.

Also, by studying the lives of the great men of the past, you will realize that without exception they all had discouraging experiences, defeats, disappointments and disasters which, instead of making them quit and admit they were failures, only spurred them on to greater effort.

"Times of great calamity and confusion have ever been productive of the greatest minds," Colton said. "The purest ore is produced from the hottest furnace and the brightest thunderbolt is elicited from the darkest storm."

STEP NO. 10: *Believe in your abilities and do not let others minimize your gifts and talents.*

Sometimes failure comes early in life because we listen to the disparaging remarks of our family and friends regarding our talents and gifts.

Every great man of history had this type of negative condition to meet when he set out to do something unusual. Remember, "A prophet is without honor in his own country." No one who knows you well can ever visualize you any different from the person you are at present. Don't try to impress people who know you too well, but seek to expand your mind, to enlarge your contacts with people who have done big things, until it becomes second nature for you to think and be successful.

Faith is a miracle-worker, not only in healing the body but in preserving the mind and keeping it intact against the eroding forces of adversity and discouragement. Believe that you were born to be someone important. Believe that you can have more money and make a bigger salary. This faith in your destiny and in yourself releases mental and physical energy which can help carry you on to your high goal.

Tolstoy said, "Faith is the force of life."

STEP NO. 11: *Search within yourself for your greatest gifts and talents. Follow your own intuition as to what you can do best or should become in the future.*

How to find answers within yourself

Too many people search in the outer world for a clue as to what they want to be and the things they want to do. It is all right to study the lives of the great and learn how they accomplished their great deeds, but you should not make your decision as to what you want to be by their lives alone. You must seek within your own mind and heart to find out what you want to do more than anything else in the world.

The Bible asks, "What hast thou in thine house?" This means

literally to look within your own mind and find out what gift or talent you already possess as a natural, God-given talent. Everyone has something that is specifically his and which no other person possesses. You may be a better cook than someone else, and have no other talent. One woman I know who had three children to support lost her husband in an accident. She had no unusual talent, no formal education, no friends or relatives to help her. But she did have one gift: everyone raved about her good cooking, her home-baked pies and cakes and desserts. She searched within and found the thing she could do best—cook appetizing food.

She took the last of the insurance money she got, opened a little restaurant featuring home-style cooking and soon she was making five hundred dollars a week! She educated her three children and lives in a beautiful big home and has servants to wait on her. What if she had wanted to be an actress or an executive in business, for which she was unfit? She might have eaten her heart out with discouragement and frustration and never have achieved her goal of financial security.

How a has-been became a will-be

However, many times a deliberate slap in the face by Fate will help one achieve his goal in life faster than if he encounters a path of roses. A shabby, tired old actress walked in the rain on Broadway one night, lamenting the fact she was finished in show business. A friend saw her and gave her a pass to a Broadway theater. As this once-famous actress sat watching the stage show, she heard the woman behind her whisper her name and say to her friend, "You know who she is? That's that old has-been, Marie Dressler."

Tears of impotent rage stung the old actress' eyes as she got up and stumbled out into the rain-soaked night. Her feet were wet from the water which seeped through the holes in her shoes, and tears ran down her cheeks, mingling with the falling rain. Suddenly the cruel words "old has-been" enraged her and she muttered to herself, "I'll show them! I won't be a has-been. I will be a success!"

Armed with this determination, Marie Dressler went to Hollywood at an age when most people would have thought they were finished with a career, and in her late fifties and sixties made millions of dollars as one of our greatest character actresses.

It is never too late for you to succeed. "What hast thou in thine house?" God has given you some special gift which can be your passport to fame and fortune, if you will but search within your heart and mind for it.

STEP NO. 12: *Do not regret past mistakes, but go on to other experiences.*

Many people spend half their lives regretting past mistakes and wishing they had done differently from what they did. You hear them lament, "If I had only bought that piece of property, I'd be rich today " Or, "If I only hadn't put all my money in the stock market!" It's always the same story; the wrong investment, the wrong decision; mistakes and misfortune because one did or didn't do something.

Lincoln was one of the most colossal failures on earth in his early career in Springfield, where he was a young lawyer. He couldn't even win the lowly office of dog-catcher. He failed nine times. It is said of Lincoln that he was too big for the little things of life. His one outstanding success has had effects that have reverberated throughout the ages.

Profit by your mistakes and realize that everyone errs at some time or other in his life.

To err is human; to forgive, divine.

It is only unfortunate if you keep making the same mistakes over and over again. Life experiences should teach us what to avoid and how to improve our actions in the future. From your mistakes you can learn valuable lessons.

"The man who makes no mistakes does not usually make anything," said Edward J. Phelps in a speech at Mansion House. Cicero said of making mistakes, "To stumble twice against the same stone is a proverbial disgrace."

STEP NO. 13: *Check your present environment carefully to see if you are overlooking possibilities for goal achievement where you now work or live.*

A farmer was annoyed when he saw scum gather each day on the pool of water that his cattle drank from. He sold the farm and the new owner had the curiosity to sniff at the scum which formed daily on the water. It was oil, and soon the new owner was rich from the oilwells that gushed on his farm.

Perhaps in your own environment there are opportunities for making more money, becoming more famous, or being happier than you have been in the past. Sometimes it's a question of being aware of these hidden opportunities.

You must be constantly aware of your hidden opportunities, to be prepared to take them. Perhaps some person you know is the key to a better job or a higher income. Have you probed all your present contacts, your present work, your present environment? Before you go looking frantically on the outer periphery of your own experience for your golden opportunity, make sure that you have exhaustively checked every avenue of your present circumstances for your greater good.

Two other quotations about opportunity are:

"Do not suppose opportunity will knock twice at your door" (*Chamfort*).

"There is an hour in each man's life appointed to make his happiness, if then he seize it" (*Beaumont and Fletcher*).

STEP NO. 14: *Cultivate patience and perseverance.* We have mentioned these qualities of character before in our study together, and we shall mention them again. Every great person has had to cultivate patience and perseverance in achieving a high goal. A Dutch proverb states, "A handful of patience is worth more than a bushel of brains."

And Emerson said of patience: "Adopt the pace of nature: her secret is patience."

The trouble with most people in striving to achieve a high goal in life is that they expect life's biggest and richest rewards immediately, and without making too much effort. But life refuses to yield its rich rewards to those who do not make great effort and have great patience. Plant the seed within your mind for future riches, success, health and happiness, and then patiently wait for the crop of destiny to mature. It will surely bring you your goal eventually.

STEP NO. 15: *Build mental patterns of efficiency and quality.*

A slipshod mind will produce a slipshod destiny. Your mental patterns should reflect efficiency and quality, if you wish a satisfying life experience. Psychiatrists say that a person's mental health depends on whether or not he is an efficient person. What are the marks of efficiency?

Regulate your thinking and control your thoughts.
Be positive in your thinking.
Be definite in making your decisions.
Avoid vacillation and changing your mind too often.
Stick with your decisions, even if sometimes they prove wrong.
Any decision is better than indecision.
Be punctual and live up to your word.
Rise quickly in the morning and have a daily routine to which
    you faithfully adhere.

A German proverb states: "The best carpenters make the fewest chips."

STEP NO. 16: *Set high goals for your future, but do not make them so high that they are unattainable.*

It is good to aim high and set goals that are lofty for your mind to aim at, but do not make them too high, for if you do not achieve them, you are apt to feel that your entire life was a failure. Actually, failure may only be delayed success in your case, and the best may still be ahead of you.

Have high ideals and high goals, for they will surely cause you to aim higher than if you are satisfied with mediocre experiences and goals.

"Ideals are like stars," Carl Schurz said, "you will not succeed in touching them with your hands. But like the seafaring man on the desert of waters, you choose them as your guides, and following them you will reach your destiny."

In having your over-all high goal, however, be sure that you also have smaller goals which are like steppingstones to help you reach the high place you have chosen for yourself.

General suggestions on goal achievement

Remember, you will never rise any higher than the vision you have of your future life goal.

You will be great in proportion to your ability to think great thoughts.

Do not lower your dignity or self-esteem in the presence of others who are famous or great.

Master your mind, your emotions, your actions, if you wish to master life.

A man is judged by the friends he keeps. Do your friends and acquaintances measure up to the high goal you have set for yourself?

The higher the goal you have chosen, the longer it takes to achieve. It takes God only two months to make a pumpkin, but one hundred years to create a giant oak. Yours will be a pumpkin or oak destiny, depending on which you choose. Have the patience to wait for your fulfillment.

Summary of law five

Choose your goal in life, high or low, and keep it in mind constantly. Realize that there are seven basic needs in life: right work, rewards, friends, love and marriage, expression of talents, mental growth, and spiritual fulfillment. Seek the aid of important people in trying for goal-achievement. Discover your hidden talents. Never admit you are a has-been. Look for riches in your own back yard.

Law Six

How to Attract the Things You Want in Life Through Universal Magnetism

There is a vast sea of etheric intelligence in the universe which man may tap and use. He must first know the laws governing this life force—universal magnetism.

Magnetism is the cohesive power that exists between all the cells of the universe, binding them together under the centrifugal and centripetal force which governs all matter. "Centrifugal" means the force in gravity that causes an atom or other object to rotate away from the center of rotation. "Centripetal" means a force that causes an atom or a body to move toward the center of rotation.

The dictionary definition for magnetism is: "The property, quality, or condition of being magnetic. The force to which this is due. Personal charm."

The dictionary defines the term "magnetic" as: "Having the properties of a magnet. Producing or causing magnetism. The earth's magnetism. That which can be magnetized. Powerfully attractive."

How you can become a human magnet

What are the properties of a magnet? Any piece of iron, steel, or loadstone that has the property of attracting iron or steel. Also, a magnet is *anything that attracts*. This means that the human magnet is as real as that made of iron or steel. In iron or steel the atoms are driven in magnetic lines of force which have the power to attract any metal which has the same property. In the human magnet the mind has the same power of attracting anything that

85

it has put into its atomic structure or cells. The body also has this property of magnetism. Note the magnetic attraction to each other of a boy and girl who are in love. They are impelled towards each other almost as if pushed by invisible hands.

In a sense, it is almost like giant invisible hands which hold up our earth as it spins in space, in a field of solar, lunar, and stellar magnetic attraction which keeps the earth spinning at one thousand miles an hour around the sun without any visible support. The centrifugal and centripetal force of gravity, the push and pull power which attracts and at the same time repels all objects in space, is responsible for the earth and moon, sun and stars staying in their orbits in the heavens.

Newton discovered the power of gravity, but it was Dr. Felix Erenhaft who proved the existence of magnetism as the power behind all creation. This discovery was so great that in nineteen forty-five, when Erenhaft made his experiments at Columbia university, *The New York Times* carried front-page stories for five days in a row reporting the great event.

What magnetism means to you

You can use the great universal power of magnetism in your own life. It can be directed, built, channeled, so that it will exert its influence in your affairs. You can make your mind a powerful magnet which has the power to attract to you that which you consistently put into your mind.

You can magnetize your body so that it is healthy, youthful, and energetic, and you will seldom ever tire. You can learn how to magnetize or attract objects, such as money, cars, houses, land, persons you want in your life, by using this dynamic universal law of magnetism.

Your body has magnetism

Your body already has magnetism within its cells and atoms. It is the life force. Electricity and magnetism constitute an indivisible unit, which gives man life and health. The power of your mind is electric, and the nerves of the body operate through electricity. When God created your body He knew that the only way in which your mind could operate in your body was by making the blood a saline solution, as salt is a perfect conducting medium for electricity.

The brain, which sends out its electrical messages to your body through your mind, stores up quantities of this magnetic substance in the cells of the brain and body. When this store of magnetism and electricity is depleted, you suffer fatigue and sickness. The magnetism that builds your brain and body energy is in the very air about you; the breath you breathe helps renew this powerful magnetic substance. Also, the thoughts you think, the foods you eat, all help in keeping your fund of magnetism high.

Magnetism is of three kinds

There are three kinds of magnetism:

1. *Mental Magnetism*
2. *Physical Magnetism*
3. *Spiritual Magnetism*

Regimen for building mental magnetism

1. Keep your thoughts positive, happy, and optimistic. Have you ever noticed how you are attracted instantly to a person who has a bright, happy smile? By the same token, people avoid those who are worry-birds and who wear expressions of sadness and gloom. A smile is magnetic, a frown is unmagnetic. One attracts people to you; the other repels. The two poles of magnetism or gravity are attractive and repellant. You can increase your polarity to popularity, friendship, success, and love fulfillment if you keep your mind magnetically attuned to friendship, love, beauty, good, and truth. The mind that is magnetized by these positive qualities is automatically more attractive and radiates in the personality the things that are magnetic and charming.

2. As magnetism is action, the mind that is active and filled with interesting thoughts is more magnetic than a mind that is bored with life and has little or no interest in anything.

Keep your mind and body active as long as possible. Young people, who have magnetism naturally, are usually very active and restless. Their minds are usually curious, enthusiastic, and searching constantly for new experiences. If you can keep this magnetic quality of the young when you grow older you will not only feel younger but you will look younger and be able to do more in life.

This means that you should never stop studying something all through your life. Study French or Spanish or some other foreign language. Take a course in music, singing, dancing, or painting and drawing. Anything you like, which keeps your brain cells active and magnetic, will help give you more of this life-giving substance of magnetism.

Churchill an example of magnetism

The late Winston Churchill was an example of this principle of magnetic action for remaining young, dynamic and active until the very time of his death. He wrote great historical books, painted, had many hobbies, was a great statesman and leader, and kept abreast of the times through extensive reading. His brain cells were alive and magnetic throughout his entire life.

General Eisenhower is another excellent example of how mental and physical action gives one great magnetism and keeps one alive to a ripe old age. Despite a severe heart attack, during his years in the Presidency, Eisenhower has kept active, writing his memoirs, playing golf, and taking an active interest in political affairs. Action and magnetism might almost be said to be synonymous.

Scientists now say that we actually can live as long as we wish —that is, within reason—and that people should live to be one hundred to one hundred and fifty years of age at this stage of evolution. It is all controlled by the magnetism of the brain and body, and having activity that is useful, and a desire to live, to create, and to achieve something worthwhile. Science tells us that the organs of the body are affected by the various brain centers, and that as these centers lose their magnetism and life force, the corresponding organs begin to weaken and die. Mental inactivity lessens the body's magnetism and causes sickness and premature death.

3. Mental Magnetism is built when you hold high ideals in your mind and high standards of conduct. To idealize means to try to perfect something. When you make the effort to perfect

your mind, to expand your interests, to perfect your gifts and talents, your personality and your conduct, the magnetism built thereby becomes a powerful stimulus to the body and creates more energy and more health.

What are some of the highest ideals you can achieve? A desire to be good and do good. To be truthful and honest. There is nothing more magnetic than honesty and truth. People sense it when one responds to this high ideal with conduct that is based on integrity.

Charity or the impulse to help others is also a magnetic urge, and shows in a person's outer personality. Faith is a magnetic emotion and attracts people and circumstances that one believes in.

Love is one of the most magnetic of all emotions, and perhaps that is the reason why the Bible defines God as love, and also as Good. Jesus also said, "A new commandment I bring unto you; that ye love one another." This emotion of love, coupled with forgiveness, gives the human a magnetic quality that is almost divine in its beauty and inspiration.

Hope or optimism is also a magnetic quality of the mind and emotions. If you constantly think that things are going to be better, you will be magnetized to a point where you will actually attract the better things.

Again the Bible speaks of three of the above qualities in these words, "faith, hope, and charity," as being three of the most desirable of all virtues.

Magnetism through the imagination

4. Mental Magnetism is also built and stimulated through the channel of your imagination. If you imagine yourself in certain interesting situations, even though it is only a mental exercise, it tends to create dynamic energy in the mind and body and stimulates the glands to greater activity. This is one of the reasons why people with very active imaginations tend to achieve the things that they imagine. They set up magnetic forces within the mind and body which tend to attract the experiences that shape the destiny they have imagined.

When Admiral Byrd was only twelve years of age, he read of

the exploits of Admiral Peary. He wrote in his diary, "I shall be the first man to discover the South Pole." That fact, although only imagined as a youthful dream, became somehow caught up in the magnetic attraction of Byrd's subconscious mind, and years later he actually did make that important discovery.

Stimulate your imagination daily by trying to imagine improvements in your work, your home, your environment. See yourself mentally doing things that you want to do. Soon you will build mental action that becomes magnetic, and which leads you to doing the things you have already imagined.

Building physical magnetism

You can build Physical Magnetism through a regimen of thinking and acting. The power that you will use issues from your mind and communicates itself to your body and causes the body to respond and be stimulated by your thinking.

Mental action leads to physical action, for by reflex action everything you think has an effect on your body. You can build Physical Magnetism through a regimen of simple exercises. This can include dancing, walking, swimming, playing golf, tennis, bowling, or any other games that require muscular and mental co-ordination.

Obtaining magnetism in the air you breathe

As magnetism is in the air you breathe, anything that causes you to breathe more deeply increases the fund of magnetism that you take into your lungs. This oxygen, which is laden with magnetism, is dispersed throughout your body through your blood stream. The more deeply you breathe, the more quickly is your body replenished with fresh magnetism.

Your daily regimen should include magnetic tensing and deep breathing upon arising in the morning, before you have your breakfast. It is a wonderfully stimulating way to start your day. Magnetic tensing means simply tightening all the muscles of your body and then alternately relaxing them. You can begin with the head and neck muscles, then tense the shoulders and arms, then on down to the trunk of the body and finally the legs. The tensing

should be done at the same time as you breathe ⌐
to the count of four, then as you relax your body
you should also count four.

The purpose of magnetic tensing is to flush th⌐
from the tissues of the body and replace them with new,
magnetism and oxygen. Science says it is the fatigue acids
cause old age and tissue degeneration. By daily practicing mag
netic tensing, you avoid the accumulation of these toxic poisons
in the body and keep the body youthful, energetic, and magnetic.

Facial rejuvenation through magnetic tensing

Of particular interest to the ladies is the fact that actual facial
rejuvenation is possible through magnetic tensing. Here is how
to tense the face and neck muscles for firm, youthful contours and
the removal of wrinkles.

Lift the face as though you were smiling, but *more so*. Tighten
all the facial muscles in an upward direction, including the neck
muscles. This will be a grimace, and if you look in the mirror it
will seem to be a terribly tense and exaggerated smile . . . but
don't worry how it looks; hold that upward, tight expression for
a count of four, and as you do, breathe deeply, so you will get
more magnetism and oxygen into your lungs and blood stream.

Then relax your face and neck muscles and let out the indrawn
breath. Do this ten or fifteen times, watching in your mirror, and
be sure that all the muscles of the face are pulled up tightly in
an extreme smiling position when you tense.

Caution: Do not think you have to go around with a perpetual
tense grin on your face, for this exercise is only that—an *exercise*
of the muscles and tissues of the face, and you resume your normal pleasant expression after you have finished the exercise.
However, the youthful contour of the face always requires a
slight amount of facial tensing; that is, the lips should have a
slight upward pull of the facial muscles, and the cheeks should
have a firm roundness. The flesh will stay firmer and age will be
deferred indefinitely, so far as your appearance goes, if you practice this magnetic facial tensing every morning upon arising and
every night upon going to bed.

Eating the magnetic diet

Certain foods have a tendency to give more magnetism and life to the body than others. The magnetic foods are those that have live cells, such as fruits and vegetables, leafy and underground: nuts, eggs, meats, fish, fowl, and wheat and wheat products. (However, denaturalized wheat products, such as white flour, are *not* as healthful nor as magnetic as the natural whole wheat, or the natural brown rice.)

Each day you should start your morning with the juice from a whole lemon in a glass of water. A half hour or so later you may take your regular breakfast. Be sure you take fresh fruits or vegetables in your daily diet, and, if possible, a glass or two of fresh vegetable or fruit juices between meals. The fruit juices tend to alkalize the body and keep it healthy.

Scientists have determined that the American diet of meat, potatoes, white bread, coffee, and pie or cake, is one of the contributing factors to early death. Such a combination of foods is unmagnetic and unhealthy. It is better to avoid mixing starchy foods and protein foods at the same meal. If you desire starch foods, such as spaghetti or rice, eat a whole meal of the starchy food alone, and do *not* mix it with the meat, fruit, and vegetables.

Avoiding unmagnetic foods

There are certain foods which are unmagnetic and which should be avoided. Salt, the type known as sodium chloride, is a poison, and scientists suspect it as a cause of cancer. You can get artificial salt in some groceries and in all health food stores.

White sugar, the type that is refined, is considered highly acid, and one should use either the raw sugar, or honey for a sweetener.

Too much coffee and tea are stimulating and cause the body to become highly acid and destroy magnetism. They may pep one up for a time, but the body's reaction is one of fatigue and lowered energy. Restrict the drinking of coffee to one or two cups daily.

All alcoholic drinks are unmagnetic and lower the body's natural energies and should be avoided. Cigarette or pipe and cigar smoking are in the same category and should be eliminated if you wish your body and mind to function at a peak of perfection.

Pork, fat foods, pies and desserts are also considered unmagnetic and should be taken in small quantities, if taken at all. It is best to eat fresh fruits, dates, figs, nuts, and even cheeses for dessert than to eat pie and cake and ice cream.

How to build spiritual magnetism

Spiritual Magnetism is the power of inspiration when it is elevated to the divine plane of consciousness. The spiritual definition of God in the Bible is, "God is good." Also, "God is love." Therefore, anyone who is good, and who loves his fellow men and God, automatically has Spiritual Magnetism.

However, there is more to Spiritual Magnetism than just being good and loving God and man. The following regimen tends to increase your Spiritual Magnetism and give you soul-power and beauty.

1. Build faith in God and His power to sustain you in life. You will be more magnetic and have greater power in every way if you hold your thoughts on God as the source of all life, power, and intelligence.

Faith in God stirs the body cells into action also and makes them normal and healthy. To gain more Spiritual Magnetism study the Bible daily, and try to live under its tenets.

2. Spiritual Magnetism is built by living under the spiritual laws that rule the universe. These laws are: the law of Truth; the law of Good; the law of Love; the law of Charity; the law of Forgiveness; the law of Morality.

The Ten Commandments have the spiritual laws which all society is built on. When you live according to these Ten Commandments your Spiritual Magnetism will be extremely high. The Golden Rule, "Do unto others as you would have others do unto you," is also a spiritual law.

3. Memorize and use as daily affirmations, which you repeat at times when you feel you need extra power or mental and physical energy, such powerful injunctions from the Bible as the Twenty-third Psalm, the Ninety-first Psalm, and many of the quotations from the Sermon on the Mount.

A very powerful statement which you can write down on a

filing card and carry with you in your purse at all times, and which you consult several times a day, is from Col. 3:12:

> Put on, therefore, as the elect of God, holy and beloved, mercy, kindness, humbleness of mind, meekness, long suffering, forbearing one another and forgiving one another, if any man have a quarrel against any; even as Christ forgave you, so also do ye. And above all these things put on charity, which is the bond of perfectness. And let the peace of God rule in your hearts, to the which also ye are called in one body; and be ye thankful.

If you will examine the above spiritual statement closely you will note that it contains all the mental and spiritual qualities which are the most magnetic and lofty: mercy, kindness, humility, forgiveness, charity, and peace. If you follow this spiritual formula carefully, applying these mental qualities to your own daily life, you will see an amazing change in your personality. You will become more magnetic mentally and physically, and people will find you attractive and will try to help you.

The magnetism of divine love

Follow this spiritual formula for achieving more Spiritual Magnetism, and then add that creative spark of Divine Love to your life. Learn to get up in the morning with a prayer on your lips, and think of God every time you see something of good or beauty around you. Then end your day with a prayer each night.

Realize that suffering in this world is the shadow cast by the soul when it is out of love with God, in the Divine Romance which is back of all creation. When you are out of tune with God and His Divine Love, the soul becomes lonely and sick.

You are searching for one thing ultimately, on this mystical journey of life; you are searching for God and His Divine Love, the Love that inspired your creation. This spiritual purposefulness motivates every single element of your being, from the moment you were born until the end of this earthly experience.

Love is God's magnetism, issuing from the throne of His illimitable mercy and streaming earthward in a constant outpouring of celestial fire and Divine inspiration. God is more than your Creator; He is your life and your life force. He is your friend, your intelligence, your life power. In the moment you accept the mantle of His divinity, then you will experience that gentility of spirit, that beauty of soul, and that wonder of a human heart kindled with a spark of goodness, that will cause your soul to shine forth in the darkness of civilization like a golden light. Then the world will see the results of your Spiritual Magnetism in your personality, in your creative works and in your high ethical and moral conduct. This has always been the mark of great and good men throughout history. This has been the signature of the soul that the great creative geniuses have always borne, which distinguishes their works from the mediocre ones of the earth-bound and material-minded.

Exercises to build magnetism daily

On Monday practice Mental Magnetism; all day practice being positive, happy, and optimistic. Smile as often as possible and feel that every person you meet this day will be a friend.

On Tuesday make your key word for the day *Goodness*. Think only good thoughts, do only good, kind acts. All day today say as often as possible, "God is Good. I am good. Therefore, I am Godly."

On Wednesday let your key word be the magnetic thought of Beauty. Look for beauty in every person you meet; some quality of personality which shines, and is beautiful. Say this little poem several times today to remind yourself of the value of beauty:

> Who walks with beauty has no need of fear,
> The sun and moon and stars keep pace with him;
> Invisible hands restore the ruined year;
> And time itself grows beautifully dim.

On Thursday practice building magnetism through your imagination. Sit for half an hour or more and picture in your mind's eye something that you especially want to happen to you, such as taking a trip, moving to a new home, having a raise in salary, or going to some special event that you dream of attending. Go through the actual emotions that such an event would inspire, and see as many details of the event as you can imagine.

On Friday magnetize the thought of Money all day. Think that

will come to you from unexpected sources. Every time
end a dollar or money passes through your hands silently
.......m to yourself, "This money will multiply and grow under the
law of the harvest and will return to me tenfold."

On Saturday let your key word be Love, and send loving
thoughts to everyone you meet. Then expand your thoughts of
love to embrace the whole world. Keep the warm, happy glow of
love all day long, and forgive everyone who has ever tried to hurt
you, and send them loving thoughts.

On Sunday practice Spiritual Magnetism all day. Awaken with
the thought of God in your mind; and go to some place of worship where you can join others in paying homage to God.

Summary of law six

You may tap a vast sea of universal magnetism and channel
it in any department of your life. You can magnetize people, jobs,
money, anything you desire, through this universal law. An active
mind is a magnetic mind. The body can be kept healthy and one
can live longer through building Physical Magnetism. Spiritual
Magnetism can be built through faith and prayer and living under
the spiritual laws. Love is one of the greatest emotions for building magnetism.

Law Seven

How to Release Your Creative Power with Mental Projection

There is a creative principle back of all things in life. We see this invisible creative power shaping and forming all things. This same creative power exists within your own mind and it can also be used to shape and form the events of your life into patterns of success, health, happiness and peace.

Back of all created things there is a form of invisible atomic action. This atomic action is started by some invisible higher intelligence which man calls Nature, and which, in religion, we call God. Actually it is *not* God, for God cannot be confined to matter; it is only His Infinite Intelligence which we see expressing itself throughout nature, as intelligence and creative imagination.

We know enough about the atom in this scientific age to realize that every form of creation can be changed in its molecular structure if we once get the key to its composition. In fact, science is now creating completely new forms of substance such as nylon and plastics by utilizing this principle of manipulating the invisible atoms. For the first time since Einstein gave us his Theory of Relativity science is able to change matter and to create new combinations of atoms and even create new substances and chemicals to serve mankind.

Your mind is a creator

Man's mind has the same ability to create and to shape the invisible atoms of the universe as the Infinite Intelligence which works under the Law of Cause and Effect. Your Mind is a cause, from which issue all the effects of your future life. If you wish to project certain effects in your life—like greater prosperity, more money, a better job, a happy marriage—all you need do is know how to form these creative ideas in your own mind. Then, through the law of Mental Projection which we shall study in this lesson, you can send those creative ideas to the invisible spiritual protoplasm that fills time and space, and shape the events and the destiny that you desire.

These various conditions, events, and persons or things that you wish to attract represent a fixed pattern in your mind first, before they are projected to the outer world and become a reality.

The subjective world of mind

There is an inner realm which we call the Subjective world. Here it is that ideas and creative energy exist in a state of flux. They can be general ideas such as, "I'd like a million dollars. I wish I had a better job. I'd like a home of my own. I'd like to know interesting, intelligent people. I wish I could attract a sweetheart who has all the qualities I want in my mate." All these general ideas are Subjective only. That is, they have form and tangency and reality *only in your mind.*

Until these creative ideas are projected by your mind to the outer world they never become reality. The outer world of form and reality is known as the Objective world. Until and unless the creative ideas held in the pattern of your mind are projected to this outer, objective world, they will never become a complete reality.

Difference between daydreams and reality

This is the principal difference between daydreams and reality. A daydream remains a daydream indefinitely until it is projected to the outer, objective world.

Example: When man needed tools with which to shape his world of reality, he had only examples from nature to go on. When he saw animals' claws, he undoubtedly got the idea for inventing the rake and the hoe, which changed his world and caused him to become agricultural and control his own food sources. The desire for a steady food supply, the dream for security was always there: a subjective mental pattern or idea. *Only* when some ingenious man first attempted to project this mental idea and actually create a rake or hoe did man begin to benefit from his creative intelligence.

Some observing man saw the woodpecker drilling holes in a tree, and had the subjective idea of inventing a gimlet, with which he could also bore holes in wood or metal. Only when he attempted to project that mental concept to the outer objective world of reality was he actually able to perfect the gimlet.

Similarly, some man saw a rolling log or stone, and got the subjective idea for the first wheel. Primitive man had no way of controlling or using fire until someone projected the mental dream or desire to the objective world of reality by striking a spark from two stones, and later from a piece of metal, and still later, through conducting the rays of the sun through a magnifying glass to a combustible material.

All creation is within your mind

All the forces of Creation actually exist within the subjective pictures of your mind. Man has had the dream of flying like a bird ever since he first wanted to emulate these feathered creatures. Man's mind has within it all the power he needs to create everything that he requires in this world for his advancement and preservation. He also possesses the tools within this subjective mind for destruction. Atomic power may be used to release man from backbreaking labor, or as a destructive force in the atom bomb, capable of killing millions in a few seconds. Electricity may be harnessed in refrigerators, vacuum cleaners, and air-conditioners, or it may be channeled through an electric chair to kill a man.

You can form the pictures mentally of the things you desire in your life, but they will not become real until you learn how to project them from the inner subjective realm of mind to the outer objective world of reality.

Three elements of creation

There are three elements behind all creation:

1. *Structure*
2. *Form*
3. *Design*

Let us study these three elements carefully and see how you may use them to project your subjective ideas to the outer world of reality.

STRUCTURE. This means something that is built or constructed, such as a building or a car. It also means the arrangement of all the parts of a whole.

Your Mental Images of the things you want to create in the outer world must have this element of structure even before you project the idea to the outer world.

Someone has said, "An idea is as real as a bridge or a skyscraper." In other words, an idea already possesses the element of structure, even in the subjective realm of mind. All the parts of the whole must be present in your mind before you try to project them to the blueprint of reality so they may be built into a solid, three-dimensional structure in your life.

Do you know what you really want? There can be no reality to the things you want until they have structure within your mind first.

Exercise to build the element of structure. Review your mental desires. What are the things you really desire? You want a home of your own, let us say. Do you know the type of home? You should know the style of architecture and the floor plan, the number of rooms, the location you wish to live in. Only then will your home have the element of structure in your mind.

How will you project this dream home to the outer objective world? Spend at least a few minutes a day looking at some home magazine, which pictures types and styles of homes. Go out and actually look at homes in the neighborhood in which you wish to live. Investigate financing of homes, check your status as a veteran (if you are a veteran). Plan your life in that dream home. Visualize yourself entertaining your friends, see the garden you plan to plant. Try to visualize all the things in that home that you want to furnish it with, and then actually obtain a big scrapbook, call it your Scrapbook of Destiny, and paste in it all the pictures of the home you want, the rooms of furniture, the patio, the garden, and all the things you want in your home.

Be definite in everything you desire. Make it a point to be definite in everything you desire from life. This includes the work you want to do, the friends you want in your life, the trips you want to take in the future, the money you want to earn, the car you want to have. *Only* if you are definite in your desires will your life begin to take on the element of structure, form, and design, which is behind all creation.

FORM: *How to develop a fixed pattern of life:* Form literally means a mold or shape in which things are formed. Your mental ideas should also have form before they can be projected into the objective world of reality. This means that you must create the mold in your mind which you hold as a fixed pattern through which nature can work in creating the things you desire.

Most people do not have a fixed pattern in their minds or lives. They change the structure and form of their lives every moment. They get an idea in one moment, and then, before it can become fixed in its form, they change their minds and go on to something else. It is pretty much like planting an acorn and then digging it up every few moments to see if it has begun to grow into an oak tree. The tree is inherent in the acorn, for it has structure, form and design in its molecular composition, and it will eventually obey the law of nature, which is the Law of Capillary Attraction, and grow into a giant oak. But if it is dug up every day or two to see if it is growing, it can never mature into an oak tree, no matter how perfect the original form of the acorn is.

Be; do not seem to be: Emerson said, "Be, do not seem to be. Remove your bloated nothingness from the paths of the Divine Circuit." In your thought-patterns be big and important. Plant the seedling of reality of your future greatness, your success, your health and happiness. Then act with supreme confidence that the things you have formed in your mind are already a reality. This pattern of positive conviction which you form mentally should permeate your entire personality and every word you speak, every act you perform. The saying "nothing succeeds like success" is a reality. There is a contagion about success, and it begins first in the form that takes place in your own mind.

DESIGN: *How to design a perfect destiny.* To design a perfect destiny do these things:

1. In your mind plan the daily events of your life. Even write them down, so they will have form and structure. Put down such things as: "I want a raise in salary. I want to meet a certain person. I want a better job. I want to make a certain number of sales.

I want to attract a certain sum of money." Write down the things in detail. They may not all come true on that one day, but if your mind has a definite plan to follow, it will begin to bring these things into reality in the outer, objective world.

2. Stick with your original ideas; do not change them every day or two, but persist in your desires until you see the things you desire coming to pass.

3. Mentally prroject your creative pattern or idea into the outer world by taking some constructive step toward the achieving of your objective.

Example: You may want to learn touch typing, and this is a subjective idea, but until you actually get a typewriter and learn how to touch type, you will only have a subjective idea.

Let us go even further and say that you have a desire to write a play or a great novel. This is a subjective idea, and will only be projected to the outer world of reality when you take a step to make this dream a reality.

What are some of the steps you might take? You can join a playwriting group in your local night high school, or by correspondence. You can go to the library and obtain books by experts in the field of the theater. You can read books of plays which have been performed on Broadway and learn the technique of playwrighting.

Then you can sit down at the typewriter and *begin to write!* This is your first actual step toward projecting the mental plan you have for being a playwright. The next step, after the play is once written, is to get a good agent, someone who has faith in your work and who will sell it to some producer. This is a difficult thing to do, but you cannot let yourself be deterred by the difficulties in your way. If everyone who ever achieved anything considered it impossible there would be no inventions, no books, plays, or other creative forms ever produced by man.

Have a big dream within your mind: If you want to achieve a big destiny, a big fortune, or anything that is outstanding, have a big dream within your mind first. This is the creative pattern from which all other factors will stem. The creative idea is the seed or germ principle which is behind everything produced in life by man or nature. Nothing ever is created without the big dream; that dream can be anything you choose, no one can limit you. Imagine how men have scoffed at every great idea that anyone ever had in the past!

When Harvey announced his discovery that the blood circulated throughout the body people called him mad and threatened to lock him up in the insane asylum!

When Fulton announced the first test of his steamboat going upstream on the Hudson, thousands gathered on the shores and shouted as one man, "It won't start! It won't start!" When the paddlewheels began to turn and the steamboat moved irresistibly against the currents, the bleating of the sheep-like spectators did not stop, only now their chant changed to, "It won't stop! It won't stop!"

When Galileo announced that the earth revolved around the sun, not the sun around the earth, he was threatened with excommunication from the Church unless he recanted his heresy.

Creative thinking: The beginning of riches: Behind every great achievement, every fortune, there is creative thinking. Some of the greatest fortunes were built by a single creative idea. A poor boy watched his mother struggle against overpowering poverty when they were left to shift for themselves. She had only one bag of flour left but her mind was inspired with a creative idea. She baked batches of hot biscuits and took them to men who were working on the railroad nearby for their lunches. The money she got she invested in more flour and finally she was doing a thriving business.

The creative idea that was implanted in this young boy's mind flourished and grew as he reached manhood. This man later became the president of the National Biscuit Company and made a fortune. The inspiration? The creative ideas his mother implanted in his youthful mind.

Big thoughts create big things: On a recent program over radio station WOR, four presidents of big companies whose salaries are from $250,000 to $500,000 a year told their secrets of success. All four started life without much education, they were all poor when young, and began their careers witth absolutely nothing. Each had an overpowering ambition to achieve something big in life, to be successful, to win recognition. They never gave up the big dream, the high goal with which they started. They forged success from the elements they possessed within their minds!

The big secret behind success: The big secret behind success is first to be able to conceive of the goal you wish to achieve. Never underestimate the tremendous creative power of the higher mind within you. There is an omniscience about this higher mind which causes it unerringly to bring you what you desire in life. You must work with the invisible laws of the universe and be sure that you have a big dream within your mind. Then you must have faith in that dream and never waver from your goal.

When you once release the creative power of your higher mind, you will be able to shape all the events of your life in the direction of success. Even misfortune or personal handicaps will not deter you from achieving your high goal.

An example of this from life is a very inspiring one. Harold Bell Wright had an accident in the early days of his career, and lay at death's door for weeks, unable to move a muscle. However, his brain was not injured and his creative mind began weaving together stories of his various experiences, which kept him from being conscious of the pain and boredom he felt. While convalescing he began to amuse himself by writing down his ideas, and gradually a story began to form. He called his book, when finished, *When a Man's a Man,* and it made him over a million dollars in his lifetime and started him onto a profitable and brilliant career as an author.

No matter what obstacles stand in your way, no matter how discouraged you may be, or how limited your circumstances in life, let nothing dim the bright dream within your soul. Project the power of your creative mind and achieve a brilliant destiny!

Summary of law seven

There is a creative principle behind all nature. Man's mind also possesses this creative ability. Mind is a Cause which can create Effects in the visible and invisible universe through structure, form, and design—the three invisible elements of all creation. Plant the seedlings of reality for greatness in the big dream that creates the big destiny, for creative power flows from creative thinking.

Law Eight

How to Unveil the Power of Your Subconscious Mind

There is a tremendous power within your mind which science is only now beginning to realize can be tapped for achieving miraculous things in your life. This is the power of your subconscious mind. It was Freud who first discovered this other mind, which he called the unconscious. It is one of the most potent forces which you may use to heal your body, if you should be sick; or, if you are healthy, to maintain health and vitality.

The subconscious mind may also be given instructions to bring you financial success, to reveal new ideas for business, to improve your personality, and to give you a better memory. In fact, no act of your life is free of the influence of your subconscious mind.

How to summon this power at will

You may summon this subconscious power at will. You can change your entire life by applying the scientific principles which we shall study in this lesson. You can set up new habit patterns within your subconscious mind, which will affect everything you do in the future.

Do you want to gain or lose weight?
Do you want to increase your income?
Do you want to have a more magnetic personality?
Do you want new gifts and talents?
Do you want to prevent colds?
Do you want happiness in love and marriage?

The above list of questions presupposes that your subconscious is literally a miracle-worker. It actually is. It can do all of the above things for you and many, many more.

The automatic functions of your subconscious

Following is a list of the automatic functions of your subconscious mind. Just look over this list and realize that all the things included here are actually miracles, which require no help on the part of your conscious mind.

1. The subconscious of the mother builds the baby within her womb in nine months' time.
2. It repairs the body and maintains its working organs in good condition.
3. The subconscious controls your body's metabolism and digests the food, and distributes the various elements throughout the body.
4. It circulates your blood.
5. It regulates your heartbeat and blood pressure.
6. It operates your lungs and breathing, even while you sleep, without your conscious control.
7. It rules your imagination, your memory and the faculties of reason and judgment.
8. It controls your sympathetic nervous system, and the reflex action of the nerves and muscles of your body.
9. It controls the hearing, seeing, and feeling centers in your brain.
10. It controls the entire glandular system of your body and regulates the amount of secretion which each gland releases into your blood stream.

Control your subconscious to control your destiny

We might even go so far as to say: he who can control his subconscious mind can actually control his destiny. That is how important this automatic brain is.

The wonderful thing about your subconscious mind is that, despite its superior power to your conscious mind, it *likes to take orders from your conscious mind!*

Yes, you can give this superior mind suggestions and orders

and it will blindly accept them and carry them out automatically, creating the conditions within your body that you desire. It also causes you to carry out the actions you decide on through the reflex action of your nerves and muscles, under control of the sympathetic nervous system . . . which is ruled by your subconscious mind.

Dynamic principles for reaching your subconscious

PRINCIPLE 1: *The Law of Predominant Mental Impression*

The word "predominant" means having influence or authority over others; superior, most frequent, prevailing. Your subconscious mind is most affected by the thoughts and words you most frequently indulge in. The things you say, the things you do, what you write, read, and think most frequently are imprinted on that subconscious mind most forcibly.

Knowing this Law you can do many things to influence your subconscious mind. You can consciously suggest anything you desire to that subconscious and if it is done frequently, persistently, and with deep emotion, it will eventually come to pass.

Example: A woman went to a gypsy fortune-teller with her six-year-old son. The fortune-teller told this woman that when her son reached twenty-two years of age he would shoot himself to death over a love affair. The woman forgot this prediction, but her son's subconscious mind did *not*. When the boy was twenty-two he fell in love with a girl who rejected him, and he shot himself. Only then did his mother remember the fortune-teller's dire prediction.

The reason why this suggestion lodged in the six-year-old boy's mind is that it was of such a shocking nature that it had an emotional effect on the boy, without his mother's realizing it.

Using the law of predominant mental impression

You can work with this Law of Predominant Mental Impression by registering on your mind *only* those things that you want to register in your subconscious mind.

Remember the Law: that which you see, hear, think, or say— and even what you write, if it has a deep emotional effect on your mind—will affect your subconscious mind.

does this work in your everyday life? When you
[read]ing in a newspaper or a book, read it without emo-
[ti]on, especially if what you are reading is of a negative
[or dangerou]s nature. This means you should avoid reacting to
[what y]ou read in the daily press of killings, rapes, thefts,
[an]d accidents.

If you read of these things just once, it will undoubtedly have
little effect on your subconscious mind, for your reaction might
be mild. But over a period of years think of how many such events
you have registered in your subconscious mind. How many thousands of times have you reacted, probably saying, "Oh, isn't that
terrible!" "Poor thing. I feel terrible that such a thing happened
to her!" "Wouldn't it be awful if that happened to me?"

Emotional charge in your thoughts and words

There is an emotional charge in your thoughts and words. If
you make something you hear or read personal and apply it to
yourself, it has such an emotional charge on your subconscious
mind that it becomes caught up in the sympathetic nervous system and is communicated to the reflex action of your nerves and
muscles, incorporating its negative action in your own body.

Example: A thirteen-year-old boy had observed a hanging on
television in a western movie. He had no doubt reacted emotionally to many such killings on TV. His reflex action caused him to
put a rope around his neck, simulating a hanging. The chair he
was standing on turned over, and he hung by his neck and died.
Imagine how shocked his parents were when they found his body!
They would certainly never connect the TV program with this
tragedy, and yet there is no doubt but what it was the guilty
culprit, as it is in so many cases of juvenile crime, murders, thefts
and other acts of violence.

Children are especially susceptible to this form of subconscious
suggestion and should be shielded from movies and television
programs and books that feature violence, sex crimes, and other
acts of viciousness.

Another example of how this negative force can work in the
subconscious is that of a fourteen-year-old boy who killed his
grandmother with a butcher knife. When he was asked why, he

said that every time he went into the kitchen and saw a butcher knife, he wondered what it would be like if he killed his grandmother with it. This frightful thought, repeated over and over, had a mental and emotional charge that finally led to the reflex action of killing his grandmother. The boy was repentant afterwards, but it was too late. How many crimes occur because of this subconscious conditioning on the negative side!

Sickness caused by negative thoughts

It has been found by scientists in a study called psychosomatic medicine that many types of illness are caused by a person's negative thoughts. For instance, it was found in industrial accidents that ninety percent of all accidents occurred to only ten percent of the workers, and these accidents kept occurring over and over. Also, colds and sickness resulting in absenteeism in industry were traced to the same percentage of the workers. This proved to science that some emotional or negative mental conditioning was furnishing the reflex action in these cases which led to accidents and sickness.

Example: A man developed ulcers, and they were so bad that doctors considered operating on him. A psychiatrist gave him a word association test to try to determine what was troubling the man subconsciously. The man was given barium meal, and his stomach was observed under a fluoroscope during the testing.

Innocent words like sky, baby, house, dog, etc., were given to the man and there were normal reactions. However, when the psychiatrist said the word "mother-in-law," the patient's stomach was observed to jump, as if it had experienced a shock, and it locked on the barium meal, retaining it for twenty-four hours.

The man confessed that he hated his mother-in-law, that she lived with him and his wife and interfered in his marriage. When the mother-in-law was moved out of the house, the man's ulcers disappeared and he had a complete healing!

Is arthritis psychosomatic?

Some psychosomatic doctors now believe that such diseases as arthritis, rheumatism, some forms of heart trouble, high blood pressure, asthma, respiratory infections, hay fever, and ulcers are

aused by emotional disturbances that have their basis
onscious mind of the patient.

one of these doctor's records concerned a woman who
m arthritis for a period of twenty years. Under ques-
admitted she had hated her sister for that period of
time because the sister stole her boy friend and married him. She
had not spoken to this sister in all those years. When she forgave
her sister and understood the cause of her condition, this woman
had an amazing healing within six months.

How the law works positively

If the Law of Predominant Mental Impression works negatively
with such disastrous and dramatic results, it also works positively
if you use it correctly.

The regimen for positive action:

A. Try to think positive thoughts all the time.
B. Do *not* react emotionally to things that happen or things
   you read about. Apply reason and logic and never let the
   effect get to your heart or emotions.
C. Say only positive things that you want to have happen to
   you, not negative statements that might get caught up in
   your sympathetic nervous system.
D. Avoid hating or resenting people, but use the law of love
   and forgiveness to free you from emotional negative charges.
E. Read books that inspire and uplift you, rather than books
   dealing with crimes of violence and negative things that
   leave a negative emotional charge.

SECOND PRINCIPLE: *Reach your subconscious mind through autosuggestion*

It was Emile Coué who first used autosuggestion successfully
to heal the sick. He found that when he gave these suggestions
to other people warts and tumors disappeared in a short time, and
open sores and wounds healed faster.

Autosuggestion actually means talking to your own subconscious mind. The following autosuggestions can be memorized
and used whenever you need them.

FOR HEALTH: *I am healthy, strong, and vital. My subco[nscious] mind now takes over the workings of my vital organs an[d gives] me perfect health. My heart operates under this subco[nscious] control. It is now beating perfectly, and maintaining my body in perfect health.*

To be most effective you should use autosuggestion at least ten times for each one you say. The best time to treat your subconscious mind is at night, upon retiring, just before you go to sleep. You can whisper the autosuggestions to yourself, or say them aloud, whichever best suits your convenience.

You can make up your own, using the ones given here as a pattern. You may have some specific condition that you wish to treat subconsciously, which we do not cover here. Speak to your subconscious simply, just as you would to another person.

FOR INCREASING YOUR INCOME: *I desire a better income. I now instruct my subconscious mind to find ways and means by which I can increase my income through a raise in salary or through unexpected sources. I want ideas for creating a bigger income. I need more money to ———— (State the things that you want money for).*

You may also ask the subconscious mind for a specific sum of money for some specific purpose. The subconscious knows more ways for obtaining money than you do consciously, and it may send the ideas to you through your conscious mind.

SUGGESTION FOR SPECIFIC SUM OF MONEY: *I need the sum of $1,000 to help me pay my bills and get me out of debt. I have faith that my subconscious mind will give me ways by which I may obtain this sum of money. I ask for ideas that will lead me to getting this money from some unexpected sources.*

SUGGESTION FOR HAPPINESS: *I now ask my subconscious mind to bring me events that make me happy. I wish to overcome the negative conditions and problems that keep me from being happy and having peace of mind. Show me how to think, how to live, and what to do to be happy and complete.*

Mastering general autosuggestion

If you do not have time to give yourself a long autosuggestion when you go to bed, you may memorize some short one which you make up to fit your general needs or say the following one:

"I am successful. I am happy. I will attract the right conditions in my life to give me completion. I now ask my subconscious mind to guide me each day to the experiences that will bring me happiness, success, peace of mind, and perfect health."

When you make a positive statement such as "I am happy, I am successful," you are invoking the law of reflex action and the conditions you state as being real will actually become caught up in your sympathetic nervous system and be a part of the automatic habit patterns of your brain. Soon you will build such a positive conscious and subconscious mind that every act of your life will become colored by the thoughts imprinted there. These subconscious thoughts will externalize themselves in everything you say and do, and produce the conditions you desire in your life.

PRINCIPLE NO. THREE: *Subconscious may be impressed through the art of personification*

To personify means to think of or to represent a thing as a person. Also, to be a perfect example of something which you hold in your mind. If you want your subconscious mind to make you a success in your business, how will you use the art of personification?

You will begin to think and *act* like a successful peron. You will wear the best clothes you can afford. You will speak as though you already are successful. You will build a nature that is confident, poised, and forceful. You will watch your voice and the expression on your face, being sure that they reflect only successful attitudes. In other words, even before big success has come to you, you will begin to *act as though* you are already successful. Can you see how this will impress, not only your subconscious mind, but those who might be in a position to help you?

Example: A young lady who came to our classes and lectures in Carnegie Hall learned this secret. She got a job as secretary in an office of a cosmetic firm. She was just another stenographer, so far as outer appearances were concerned. However, within this girl's mind there was at work that mysterious force of her subconscious mind; she was using the art of personification and giving herself suggestions that she would be noticed and given advancement in a short time.

Within six months time she was chosen by the woman who was the head of her department as her own private secretary, at a substantial raise in salary. Other girls who had been with the firm for years complained bitterly because this comparative new-comer had been given this choice job. What was the secret of this girl's success? She *thought and acted*—and consequently *looked*—like the successful type who would be in the position of confidential secretary.

This girl wore neat, plain clothing. She used make-up sparingly. She had studied diction and speech and her voice was softly modulated, but clear and precise. Her tones were gentle and easy to listen to. She smiled pleasantly on her job, and when she contacted the boss of her department she was courteous, without being forward, friendly without fawning on her, and she communicated to her boss this dominant thought: "You will like me and give me advancement in my job. I shall prove worthy and deserving and give of my best to my job."

As you involve so you evolve

There is a law in psychology: the Law of Involution. As you involve, states this law, so you evolve. What you put into your consciousness, including your subconscious mind, is the material which will work its magical transformation within your mind and evolve in the facets of your personality, in your speech, and ultimately your actions creating your destiny.

Therefore use this rule of the subconscious and involve in your consciousness the thoughts that you are already rich and successful, beautiful and poised, gracious and charming, dynamic and magnetic. Begin to act this moment as though you possess the world and all therein. Soon you will have involved this positive thought so deeply in the fabric of your conscious and subconscious minds that you will begin to attract good luck, better jobs, important friends, and fulfillment of your destiny.

...ilt Hollywood's greatest stars

...et of the subconscious is what I used over a period ...ing and helping train some of Hollywood's great- ...photographs with such stars as William Holden, Barbara Stanwyck, Claudette Colbert, Gary ...ooper, Jimmy Stewart, Robert Taylor, Jeanette MacDonald, Gloria Swanson, Tyrone Power, and Susan Hayward, as well as hundreds of others whose fame is legendary. In each instance, when I gave these players (who were generally unknown in the days I gave them this principle) the secret of stardom, it was with the injunction that they begin to *act immediately as if they were already stars*. Not in some future day, but here and *now!* Then I gave them a regimen which I called The Magic Circle, in which I showed them how to become important and radiate in their personalities the qualities of value, which I told them encompassed them like a golden circle of light. Everywhere they went they were instructed to be aware of this magic circle, which made them magnetic and unusual.

In building this consciousness of value in their minds, these actors and actresses began to radiate a confidence and poise they had not known before. Soon they became great stars.

One of the latest instances of how this success secret worked is that of Vincent Edwards, who is Dr. Ben Casey in television. It was only a few years ago that this talented star began to absorb these principles and use them in his life. From the time he started to study these principles to his big success was only a matter of a little over a year. This secret works miraculously for those who have faith in it and use it faithfully all their lives.

Other pointers on the subconscious mind

1. The subconscious may also be reached by writing down the things you want to imprint upon it. Keeping a diary is a good exercise, for it emphasizes the things that you wish to do, and presents your hidden dreams and aspirations to the subconscious daily.

2. Your subconscious mind can also be strongly influenced by your imagination. Elsewhere we will deal with the methods for strengthening your imagination and using it to reach the

subconscious. Anything you picture happening in your mind, which you believe will happen and which you emotionalize, *as if it has already happened,* has a good chance of coming to you through the power of your imagination and your subconscious mind.

3. Your subconscious mind is affected by your emotions. This is true if the emotions are negative or positive. To have *only* good things happen to you, try to indulge only the emotions that are positive, such as faith, hope, good, love, charity, and courage. Avoid the emotions of fear, hate, envy, jealousy, worry, and resentment.

4. Repetition of a thought, where you repeat it over and over each day for a period of months or years, also imprints your subconscious mind.

Example: A child of twelve was badly burned, and the muscles of both legs were practically destroyed. The doctors said he would probably not live, and if he did live, he would never be able to walk or run like normal children. This child kept saying over and over to himself in the following weeks, "I shall walk and run and play with other children. I shall walk. I shall run!"

Ten years later that child, who was Glenn Cunningham, ran the fastest mile that any human being had ever run at Madison Square Garden in New York City and became one of our leading athletes!

What was the magic power used by Cunningham? Without even knowing he was doing it, he was calling upon the amazing reserves of the subconscious mind which built new muscles and nerves in his legs and completely healed him because of his faith and because of the emotional intensity of his *desire to walk and run.*

5. You can overcome bad habits such as smoking, drinking, laziness, and procrastination, through suggestions to your subconscious mind. You must *want to overcome* the bad habit first. Then you must work every day giving auto-suggestions to your subconscious that it will overcome the unwanted habit. Then you must take conscious steps to help yourself break the habit.

6. Remember, your subconscious is affected by the things you

:, think, read, and feel. Choose the events you wish
in your life, choose and control your thoughts; read
onstructive books and magazines, and feel or emotion-
only those experiences you wish to imprint upon your
onscious.*

osuggestion for the following purposes:
1. For attaining happiness and peace of mind.
2. For building your social life and making friends.
3. For making more money and increasing your financial security.
4. For overcoming bad habits and building new positive ones.
5. For healing the body, or keeping it healthy.
6. To build energy, vitality, and a youth-consciousness.
7. For strengthening the power of your imagination.
8. For building a magnetic and forceful personality.
9. For strengthening your will power.
10. For improving your memory.
11. To give you increased intellectual power.

Make up your own autosuggestions to fit any of the above
needs. Remember to keep your suggestions simple and to the
point, and to repeat them each time at least ten times to be most
effective. It takes from one month to three months to involve
some of the suggestions into the sympathetic nervous system, so
do not be impatient if there are no immediate results. For instance, to set into motion the mechanism that distributes the fat
and keeps you slender cannot be an overnight thing, but takes
time to become involved in the sympathetic nervous system.

Summary of law eight
The subconscious mind can be tapped at will to achieve health
and increase the life force. The subconscious mind is literally a
miracle-worker. Use the law of predominant mental impression
to reach the subconscious. Psychosomatic factors in sickness.
Positive autosuggestions used by Coué. The art of personification
for reaching the subconscious mind. The Magic Circle used by
the Hollywood stars. Autosuggestions for building will power
and overcoming bad habits.

Law Nine

How to Receive Divine Guidance for a Richer, Fuller Life

There is an inner voice which speaks to man in the silence of his own soul. This voice of the spirit reveals many secrets when man learns how to put himself in tune with the highest spiritual forces in the universe. There is a creative spirit or principle in the universe which unfolds all things from within. The creative spirit of the rose tells it in spring to unfold its petals and reveal its beauty, color, and perfume to the world.

The creative spirit within your mind and soul possesses all knowledge and all power. You can learn how to unfold your own precious gifts and talents by listening to this voice of divine guidance. If you listen to the babble and confusion of the outer world you will suffer from disorientation and chaos.

How the universal mind guides all life

There are three manifestations of mind in the universe:

1. The subjective, inner mind of man, made up of the conscious, subconscious, and superconscious minds. These we have studied elsewhere in this course.
2. The objective mind, which is aware of the physical and material world of reality.
3. The Universal Mind which permeates all creation and works in animals, birds, insects, and growing plant life, as well as in man. This is the Intuitive Mind which is above right and wrong, and which can guide you to doing the right thing at the right time.

Why the objective mind makes mistakes

You cannot always depend on your objective mind: that part of your brain which talks, sees, hears, and counts. You know how often you will make a mistake when adding up a row of figures. If something intrudes in your mind and distracts you you can make terrible mistakes.

The Universal Mind, which gives man divine guidance, never makes mistakes, for it is the intelligence which rules all natural law in the universe. This creative intelligence can be relied on to give you guidance in all your affairs of life.

To show you how erroneous the objective mind of man can be, look at history; see how at one time witches were burned and persecuted, in Salem in this country as well as all over the world. See how men were imprisoned for believing the world was round, that the earth revolved around the sun, that there were germs, that the blood circulated throughout the body. How long was the human race kept earth-bound because men believed the flying machine was a tool of the devil. When the telephone was first invented it was condemned as a thing of evil.

In 1842 it was illegal to take a bath in Cincinnati and Philadelphia. Boston also had laws against bathing, unless one had a doctor's order! In Hartford, Providence, Wilmington, and many other cities in the U.S., heavy water taxes were put on to force people to not bathe. In Virginia there was a tub tax of $30 a year on every bathtub. By 1922 there were only 889,000 bathtubs in the U.S.

How can we trust such a mortal mind?

How can we trust such a mortal mind as would wage war and kill millions of people on the field of battle? How can we depend on an objective mind that allows sixty thousand a year to be killed on the highways, and another million maimed and crippled? It is obvious that such a mind cannot be fully trusted with anything so precious as your future destiny.

There is a mind which you *can* trust. This is the higher mind, the voice of the spirit, which gives you divine guidance and which speaks to you through four strong instincts.

These four instincts are:

1. The instinct to live
2. The instinct to love
3. The instinct to fight for survival
4. The instinct to have spiritual identity

Divine guidance works under laws

Divine guidance works under definite universal laws. It will work for you under certain conditions. We know that it works to make all things in nature obey their natural, instinctive impulses, such as the caterpillar spinning its cocoon and becoming a butterfly. It makes the ant build its nest, herd its cattle, and store food for the winter. It causes the maple sap to flow into the roots in the fall and emerge again in the spring in the trunk and branches. It causes the swallows at Capistrano, in California, to return on the same day every year. It makes the salmon swim upstream to spawn before it completes its life cycle. A certain eel in the Saragosa sea swims three thousand miles back to the exact tributary where it was born, to spawn before it dies. What unerring instinct guides it on such a long and perilous journey? It is the voice of the spirit which gives divine guidance to all God's creatures.

How divine guidance works best

The voice of the spirit gives divine guidance and works best under the following conditions:

1. If you have an unselfish purpose in living
2. If you are motivated by the emotion of love
3. If you have a high goal or dream in life
4. If you have a deep faith in God and His power
5. If you live in peaceful surroundings
6. If your mind is orderly and calm
7. If you live in surroundings that reflect beauty
8. If you have control of your emotions
9. If your soul vibrates to the higher impulses of the human mind, such as goodness, truth, charity, and forgiveness
10. If you pray and meditate daily, keeping yourself attuned to the Infinite Mind of God

Divine guidance through your instincts

Let us now study the method by which you can receive divine guidance through your four instincts.

1. THE INSTINCT TO LIVE: This instinct rules such matters as your physical health, the functioning of your body's organs, your length of life, and the maintenance of youth and vitality and energy.

Should you or shouldn't you take vitamins?

What should you eat? What should you avoid?

Should you be a vegetarian or a meat eater?

Should you smoke, drink alcohol, take medicine?

What kind of exercise should you take, if any?

Every one of the above questions can be answered in several ways. There are experts who can point out the right and wrong diets, and government figures to support almost anything you wish to prove or disprove. You know the saying, "The devil can quote scriptures to suit himself." So too there are experts in every field of science and medicine who can give you statistics to prove anything. I have statistics on people who lived to be ninety-five years of age or more, and it shows that most of these people did not smoke or drink during their lives, but, on the other hand, some of these oldsters drank as much as a pint or more of liquor every day for years, and smoked cigarettes for a lifetime and it seemingly did them no harm.

The rule seems to be: *Do what your instinct tells you is good for you.* What if a cow were to question its instinct to eat grass by saying, "But how can green grass make white milk?" Obviously no such thought can issue from a cow's mind because it knows only one absolute power: the higher mind within governed by an instinct that is always correct.

Some people have been vegetarians, like George Bernard Shaw, and lived into their nineties. Others have been meat eaters and have lived just as long. Then on the other hand there are those who have died young, no matter what they did or did not eat.

The instinct to live is strong within you. It is prejudiced in favor of life, not death. You can implement this instinct by sitting in meditation and listening to the Divine Voice speak to you through intuition.

Ask this higher mind where you can get an apartment, how to get a better job, where to obtain the money you need. Take your personal problems to this Divine source for guidance as to the solutions to them. Then sit quietly and wait for the strong urge within your mind which will tell you of a definite course of action to take. Or, sometimes, if you will just go about your regular business, the answer as to what you should or should not do will just pop into your mind unexpectedly, but this is also the Divine Voice speaking to you.

2. THE INSTINCT TO LOVE: The Divine Voice tells every human being to fall in love and procreate. Some, however, do not follow this divine injunction and they choose to live lives of celibacy or to go through life frustrated emotionally, never fulfilling their natural instinct to marry, have children, and complete their life cycle like all of nature's living creatures. In many cases of people who become mentally unbalanced it is found that lack of fulfillment in love and sex is often the cause of their misfortune.

Sometimes early parental disapproval of the normal impulse to love will cause a child to become suppressed and to fear sex, or to have guilt feelings about the normal functions of the body. This leads to serious problems in adult life which often require the aid of a psychologist or psychiatrist.

A good rule is to follow the instinct of love; to fall in love early and marry and have a family as early as is consistent with educational requirements, and social form. This is generally around the age of twenty-one or -two. It is natural to want children, for it completes the life cycle to rear a family. If for any reason one cannot have children, one should consider adopting one or more children. This is a matter of personal preference.

The instinct to love can also express itself in other ways. The emotion of love may be expressed for one's family, friends, humanity, and love of God. It is important that each facet of love be explored and utilized. We have studied elsewhere in this course the importance of love in relationship to man's fulfillment.

3. THE INSTINCT TO FIGHT FOR SURVIVAL: To meet the challenges

of life and overcome them requires a superabundance of energy and determination. The glandular system is set up in such a way in the human body that sources of inexhaustible energy may be summoned up at will. One of the instincts is to survive, and when anything threatens survival the human being will fight such a threat with all the power at his command. The adrenal glands secrete vital chemicals which give you the power to fight the negative forces of life.

There is a will to live, a will to die; a will to succeed, a will to fail; a will to be happy or a will to be miserable. Man stands in a neutral zone in life between two opposing forces: one a negative polarity, the other a positive one. Success will come to you in the degree to which you wish to succeed. The instinct to survive has within it also an element of ego-recognition, which can spur you on to greater achievement. The will to survive can cause you to do those things which develop caution, and to protect yourself from danger and accidents. Such a person will not drink excessively, for it would cause him to endanger his health and life. He would be moderate in his eating habits, because science believes over-eating and obesity are causes of heart trouble and high blood pressure.

When you implement the will to live, you will train your mind to be alert and aware. Your higher instinct will show you how to survive in a hostile atmosphere. Your inner spirit is anxious for you to live, to express health and happiness, to fulfill your divine destiny. You will be guided by your higher mind to achievement and fulfillment, if you are aware of this fight for survival as a positive instinct within your mind.

4. THE INSTINCT TO HAVE SPIRITUAL IDENTITY: The instinct to know and love God and to serve Him is deep in the human soul. The Divine Voice speaks to man in language of the soul many times. In prayer man speaks to God, but God speaks to man in myriad voices. Sometimes divine guidance comes as an irresistible impulse to do something or to write a letter to a person who will be a channel for your future good.

Many times the Divine Voice actually comes as a whisper or an actual voice within the ear, sometimes as words that spring to your lips in a situation where you need divine aid. More often the Divine Voice speaks as a subconscious force, impelling you to take action in some way that later turns out to be right for that particular situation. Many times the answer to a problem will come through a dream, as Edison said many of his inventions came to him.

When you search within your own immortal soul to find the spiritual light of God, it can change your entire destiny.

It is said of the noted Russian writer Leo Tolstoy that when he was young he was rich and profligate, and professed to be an atheist. One day, while strolling through the fields, Tolstoy saw a worker in the field, who seemed to be happy and who was singing joyously. Tolstoy, who had been so miserable that he had wanted to commit suicide, asked the peasant the reason for his joy.

The man replied, "I am happy because I have found God." Tolstoy walked through the forests pondering this mystery. Then he tells in his autobiography of how suddenly, as he saw the golden sunlight shining through the tree tops and heard the birds sing, he felt a surge of faith spring within his heart, and in that moment he believed in God. He said of that experience, "In that instant I realized that to know God is to live; not to know him is to die." He went on to become a good man for the rest of his life because of this sudden spiritual awakening.

The uplifting power of God

When man believes in God and worships him daily, he becomes in tune with the highest spiritual forces in the universe. He then goes into the silence every day for half an hour or more and says to himself this statement from the Bible: Peace, be still, and know that I am God.

Then as he sits there in the stillness he can feel and know God's presence within his own immortal soul.

God's Divine Intelligence communicates the following qualities and states of being to man's mind: God's mind inspires, energizes, rejuvenates, heals, unites, beautifies, consecrates, elevates, ennobles, dignifies, enriches, completes, and immortalizes man's mind and body and soul.

Being in tune with divine mind

1. To be more in tune with divine mind so you may better hear the voice of the spirit that gives you divine guidance, try to discard all negative thoughts and emotions from your mind.
2. Overcome animalism and greed and selfishness, the three things that cloud the mind's intuitive power and prevent man from communicating with the Divine source of all life and intelligence.
3. Build the positive emotions of beauty, faith, love, good, and charity, for God speaks in the language of the most inspired and uplifting of all emotions.
4. Build the soul's true prototype in your personality. Your soul grows spiritually through beautiful music, poetry, classical literature, and a pattern of man's noblest achievements.
5. Avoid defiling the divinity within by coarse, crude conduct. Elevate your speech and thoughts and avoid acts that degrade the temple of the living God, which is your body.
6. Still your conscious mind so God's mind may speak to you at least half an hour a day in meditation.
7. Pray daily, for this communication with God makes known your needs and shows your faith in God as a living reality.

Summary of law nine

Man may receive divine guidance for his every act in life. There is subjective, objective, and universal mind in the universe. Man may operate on a threefold level of intelligence. There are five instincts to guide man to intelligent living: the will to live, to love, to survive, to create, and to have spiritual identity with God. Man may attune his mind to the divine mind in the universe and achieve universal harmony and fulfillment.

Law Ten

Utilizing the Law of Demonstration

You have the power within your mind to demonstrate anything that you want in life. To demonstrate means to bring something from the invisible to the visible realm.

God has given a mysterious power to all His creation to achieve completion and fulfillment of destiny. This is as true of the plant and animal kingdoms as it is of the human kingdom. However, demonstration works under definite universal laws. This is a world of law and order. Everything from the constellations in the heavens to the tiniest, invisible atom, operates under this universal law.

Gravity . . . the power behind the throne

Gravity, or the law of attraction, is the true power behind the material and physical throne of life. Just as gravity holds the planets in empty space and causes them to revolve around each other without collisions, so too there is a gravity pull exerted between people and objects. When you learn how to use this law of gravity, you can attract into your orbit of experience the persons, jobs, material objects, money, and things that you desire.

However, as the universe operates under law and order, so too you must obey the invisible laws that are back of time and space. If you violate these laws or unbalance them, you suffer the consequences in poverty, sickness, failure, and defeat.

What are the laws of demonstration?

There are many laws of demonstration, but in this lesson we are concerned with only seven of the most important ones. Elsewhere in this course we have covered other mental, physical, and spiritual laws. The following seven laws concern the method by which you can demonstrate or bring into existence in your life the money, land, cars, jewelry, furs, friends, love-happiness, and other things that you consider of value and which you desire.

The seven laws of demonstration

1. THE LAW OF ATTRACTION
2. THE LAW OF THE HARVEST
3. THE LAW OF USAGE
4. THE LAW OF RECIPROCITY
5. THE LAW OF TRANSMUTATION
6. THE LAW OF INVOLUTION
7. THE LAW OF EVOLUTION

Let us take up each of these laws in turn and study them thoroughly.

1. THE LAW OF ATTRACTION: The law of attraction is defined in physics as the mutual action by which bodies tend to cohere. It also means the power of attracting. Cohere relates to the cohesive action that exists among all of nature's elements, made up of atoms and molecules. Everything you see is a mass of vibrating atoms, constantly in motion. Things are held together by this law of attraction or cohesion. The thing that makes them cohere, or stick together and appear as a solid mass, is the power of gravity or magnetism.

Your body has this power of attraction within itself, and exercises it constantly in its attraction to certain people. Lovers know this power well, and find that they are irresistibly drawn to each other physically, in an ardent embrace. Your body feels the magnetic pull of sexual attraction physically, and this leads to marriage and the perpetuation of the human race.

There is the same law of attraction within your mind. Being electrical and magnetic in its proper sense, your mind has the power to reach out in time and space and motivate other people and attract matter or objects to yourself.

See how the miser uses this law of attraction. He concentrates so much on money that he magnetizes his brain to attract nothing but money. He often dies of starvation, it is true, because he is unbalanced in his love and worship of money. But, despite his negative use of this law, he does attract money!

If you wish to use the magnet of your mind to magnetize money, you may do so, but try to use the law of balance also, otherwise you will become warped and your money will do you no good.

Back of every great fortune is someone's mind working this law of attraction. This is true of the Rockefellers, the Fords, the Morgans, the Carnegies, the Gettys, the Astors, the Vanderbilts, Onassis, or any other multimillionaire who has ever built a fortune.

How to concentrate on success: It is not necessary that you concentrate the magnetic power of your mind on money, as such. You can concentrate on success with such emotional intensity that you will inevitably be led to the making of a big fortune. However, do not want money just for yourself, but for the good you can do with it. Carnegie gave away over five hundred million dollars in his lifetime. He established twelve hundred public libraries. When he died he still had many millions left in the Carnegie Foundation, and Carnegie Hall was established from his funds.

Carnegie said, "Someday it will be considered a sin for any man to die rich." He believed that big fortunes should be used for the good of the world and returned to the people. This follows our Law of Reciprocity, the fourth law we shall deal with in this section of our study.

How to magnetize money: You can magnetize money by desiring it for some useful purpose. Each day sit down for a few moments and concentrate all the power of your mind and attention on how you can increase your income. Do this consciously. Review in your mind the steps you might take to make more money. Visualize yourself receiving large sums of money from unexpected sources. You may not see the connection between concentrating on money and actually attracting it to you, but there is some mysterious power of the mind which has the ability to reach out in time and space and trigger action which brings money to you.

This money may come to you through a relative, who would put you in his will. It may come through something you have done in the past, which suddenly becomes valuable (like a piece of land where a new development suddenly takes place and makes the land worth many times what you paid for it). Or it may come to you through an idea that you get for inventing some object or developing some new business method that makes you rich.

How the mind magnetizes money: Back in the depression years a painter got the idea of repainting old cars for a reasonable sum, something like twenty-nine dollars and fifty cents. Business zoomed, and in a few years' time this man had made a fortune. His income from this business on a national scale is now something like fifteen million dollars a year. Recently his company was put on the New York Stock Exchange. One idea can magnetize riches for you!

"No army can withstand the strength of an idea whose time has come," William James said. "An idea, to be suggestive, must come to the individual with the force of a revelation." You must desire money, and that idea must so permeate the structure of your brain that it forms a magnetic attraction between you and success.

How one woman magnetized $250,000: One young woman who came to my Carnegie Hall course of lessons on Demonstrating Money and Supply had real need for more money. She had a growing daughter who needed an education, and her husband had deserted them for another woman. After taking the course this lady told me there was seemingly no way by which she could ever magnetize a fortune. I asked her if she had any living relatives.

She said she had a father and a brother. She had not seen her father for nearly fifteen years, as he had highly disapproved of her marriage, and they were estranged. He had been ill of late, she told me. I urged her to write a letter to her father showing concern for his well-being, and to forgive him for what he had done in the past. This letter led to her father taking a visit to New York to visit his daughter. She treated him with love and care, as he was an invalid, recovering from a recent illness.

A year later her father died, and he had changed his will leaving her two hundred and fifty thousand dollars cash! In a former will he was leaving it all to his son, but her kindly act had so touched the dying man's heart that he made provision for his daughter.

There is magnetism to love and kindness and forgiveness. Sometimes it can be counted in actual dollars and cents!

A negative instance of this same sort was that of a young man who had an uncle in Texas worth many millions. This young man was too busy to ever write a letter or visit this rich uncle. When the man died he left the nephew only $500 cash, and left the bulk of his fortune to relatives who had been kind to him in his later years, and to charity.

Remember, there are two poles to gravity—the negative and the positive. If you constantly exercise only the negative polarity of fear, hatred, envy, jealousy, worry, and selfishness, you will *keep good fortune from you!*

Why fear and hatred work disaster: Fear and hatred can work disaster for a person, for just as the positive emotions have power to attract good things to one, so negative thoughts and emotions can bring disaster. The Bible tells of how fear attracts that which we fear. Job laments, "For that which I greatly feared is come upon me, and that which I was afraid of is come unto me."

Fear and hatred can magnetize on the negative side, just as love and happiness, confidence and faith can magnetize on the positive side.

Example: A young man and his wife were living in Hollywood, California. They expected a baby in a few months. They feared the heavy street traffic in the city might endanger their coming child when he was old enough to be out. They moved to a high hill overlooking the city, built a house with a high steel fence around it, and when the child was born they felt safe and secure. When the child was at the crawling stage, the husband went out one morning to get his car out of the garage, and the child crawled onto the driveway. The father ran over his own child, killing him instantly. The thing which they feared sought them out, even on a hilltop where there seemed to be perfect security!

2. THE LAW OF THE HARVEST: *The law of the harvest is also given in the Bible: "As ye sow, so shall ye reap."*

The seed you plant mentally will yield the same type of crop. You never get cabbages from rose seed, nor oak trees from corn. The law of the harvest states that everything produces according to its kind. God created the universe under universal laws, which work mathematically. There are cycles in nature which determine that tides which come in must also go out, that summer will follow spring, and that fall, with its harvest, shall precede the barrenness of winter.

So too there are cycles and tides in the affairs of men which work unerringly to bring back that which goes out from the mind. Shakespeare told of these tides in these words,

> There is a tide in the affairs of men,
> Which, taken at the flood, leads on to fortune;
> Omitted, all the voyage of their life
> Is bound in shallows and in miseries.

What seed have you planted? What kind of seed have you planted in your garden of Destiny?

Plant seed of kindness and reap friendship.
Plant seed of generosity and reap abundance.
Plant seed of good and reap success.
Plant seed of love and reap peace and happiness.
Plant seed of forgiveness and reap love.

The *ideas* that you put into your mind are the mental seed that take root and sprout and grow in your life. Emerson said, "Ideas must work through the brains and the arms of good and brave men, or they are no better than dreams." Your ideas can be high and noble, or lowly and ignoble. The results in your life will follow suit, and be of a like kind.

If you imitate the examples of good and generous men, you will eventually begin to attract a similar destiny to the ones they have had. Study the lives of great men of history and strive to emulate their highest and best thoughts. Soon your actions will be patterned after them, and you cannot help but achieve the greatest and best in your destiny. "It is impossible to imitate Voltaire without being Voltaire," someone has truthfully said.

3. THE LAW OF USAGE: An arm or leg that is not used soon atrophies and loses the functional purpose for which it was created. If your brain cells are not exercised and used daily, they soon atrophy and are incapable of being used constructively. Then

the brain resembles a garden where there are some flowers but also many weed patches. The weed patches make the garden unsightly and untidy.

Are you using your brain to full capacity? Scientists say that even a great genius like Einstein used only about ten percent of his full brain potential! Imagine if you used your full brain potential what great things you could accomplish! Even if you add only ten percent more mental action to your total mental power after completing this course, you should be able to soar to the loftiest heights of your full potential in the future.

> Let each man think himself an act of God.
> His mind a thought, his life a breath of God.
> *Bailey*

Your creative mind is God-like: When you rise to your full spiritual stature, your creative mind can actually be God-like! In fact, in the Bible in the first chapter of Genesis, verses 26-28, it says:

> And God said, Let us make man in our image, after our like-ness: and let them have dominion over the fish of the sea, and over the fowl of the air, and over the cattle, and over all the earth, and over every creeping thing that creepeth upon the earth.
>
> So God created man in his own image, in the image of God created he him; male and female created he them.
>
> And God blessed them, and God said unto them, Be fruit-ful, and multiply, and replenish the earth, and subdue it: and have dominion over the fish of the sea, and over the fowl of the air, and over every living thing that moveth upon the earth.

You are a spiritual idea: This means that you are literally a spiritual idea, with the same creative power that God Himself possesses. You can create in your own image and likeness, phys-ically, and mentally you can certainly build the world you choose. Jonathan Edwards goes so far as to say, "The material universe exists only in the mind."

What kind of world are you creating in your mind? As you use the creative power of your higher mind, you will form the world of your choice and this will externalize in your actions, words, and deeds.

Buddha, Confucius, Mohammed, and the great Christian mystic Jesus all taught the same idea: that man could *shape the world he desired in his mind.* "As a man thinketh in his heart, so is he" is a spiritual truth. Use your higher mind, then, to form the world of beauty that you wish to live in. Use your higher creative mind to imprint health upon your body cells. Call upon this higher mind of God to bring you riches and success in your work. In your imagination see yourself living a life of peace, health, happiness, beauty, and goodness.

The Bible speaks of making man in God's image. The only place where you can hold an image is in the *imagination.* We have studied elsewhere in this course about this powerful image-builder. You can shape the world you choose and it will externalize under the laws of action and reaction.

Pascal said, "Imagination disposes of everything; it creates beauty, justice, and happiness, which is everything in this world."

Use the powers of your mind every day. Exercise the memory, the imagination, the ability to concentrate and visualize, the creative power of the mind, the attributes of the subconscious and the intuitive functions of the superconscious mind. All these various attributes of mind are given throughout this entire course, and sometimes repeated under various subject headings for greater emphasis.

4. THE LAW OF RECIPROCITY: This law is at work constantly in nature, equalizing and balancing all forces. It is the give and take in the soil, which takes the seed but gives back a crop, generally ten or a hundredfold more than the original seed. Plant a kernel of wheat and you reap a pint; plant a pint, and you reap a bushel. Always the law works to give you back more than you give.

This same law of reciprocity works in your mind and in your relationship to the world. If you give service or labor, the world gives you money or something else of value. If you give a smile, people trust and befriend you. If you open your heart generously and give of whatever gifts you have, nature rewards you with recognition, fame, fortune, peace, health, and happiness.

"You give but little when you give of your possessions," Gibran said in *The Prophet*. "It is when you give of yourself that you truly give."

And the Bible speaks of this law of reciprocity in these words: "It is more blessed to give than to receive." (Acts 20:35.)

What are you giving to life? Reciprocity means literally a mutual exchange of goods, thoughts, actions, or other things of value. What are you giving to Life? If you give joy and beauty, goodness and truth, love and happiness, service and labor, you can almost certainly expect to receive, under the Law of the Harvest which we have just studied, something of commensurate value.

You may complain, "But I've given all these things to people and I get nothing back but ingratitude and disrespect and enmity." This does not mean that the law of reciprocity has failed to work; it means merely that you did not get your good back from the source you expected.

But how many wonderful things have come to you from other sources in life? How has God blessed your life? You may have been looking for your good from limited human channels, but stop for a moment and think how lucky you are. You have eyes that can see the beauty of God's world. You have good hearing so you may listen to birdsong, the laughter of children, the music of great artists on radio and television and recordings. You have a sane mind that can enjoy the wonder of books and the art treasures of all ages. You possess an immortal soul that may know and love God, and foresee the immortality promised God's loving children.

Indeed, when you stop to count your blessings, do they not far outnumber the misfortunes of life? So maybe the good you have done for your children, your relatives, your friends, which does not seem to be repaid by them, is coming back to you through a hundred other channels which you were not aware of until now.

5. THE LAW OF TRANSMUTATION: Transmutation means the act of changing something from one form to another. Nature is a past master in the art of transmutation. She changes black soil, sunshine, and air and water, into the pink flesh of a watermelon, and

black seed, and green rind. She creates a masterpiece of a yellow rose from the same elements. In addition, she gives it a sweet scent that delights the senses.

The same law of transmutation works in your own mind. You have it within your power to wave the magic wand of faith and create the miracles you desire in your own life. Perhaps one of the greatest wonders of childhood is this amazing power of belief in magic and miracles; in a universal Santa Claus which can bring it the greatest treasures of earth. Perhaps this is why the Master Jesus said, "Except ye have the faith of a little child ye shall in no wise enter the kingdom of heaven."

The Magic Scepter of Belief: Each person possesses the magic scepter of belief within his mind. Here it is that he can literally command the forces of life to obey his dictates and bring him the things he desires. "What things soever ye desire, when ye pray believe that ye receive them, and ye shall have them."

The law of transmutation uses this divine act of faith to work its miracles. Have faith in God, and faith in yourself, as a child of God, to be able to work the miracles of transformation and you can literally work miracles.

Again, Jesus said of belief: "If thou canst believe, all things are possible to him that believeth."

Amazing Miracle Through Faith: One of the most amazing miracles of modern times occurred through the simple act of faith and prayer. Captain Eddie Rickenbacker and his crew came down in the Pacific on one of their bombing missions. They floated in a rubber life raft for three or four days, without food or water. They all prayed to be saved. On the third day a storm broke and they were saved by the rainwater. On the fourth day when the pangs of hunger were getting unbearable, they prayed for food. Suddenly, a thousand miles from land, a seagull mysteriously appeared and landed on Rickenbacker's head! He caught it and they ate it. For eleven days these men drifted, each day bringing them enough sustenance to keep them alive until they were sighted and saved. Rickenbacker called it a miracle. He never lost faith throughout that ordeal that they would be saved.

Do You Have Faith Enough? Do you have faith enough in your talents? In your ability to make more money? In your power to attract the best life has to offer? If you do not, implement this faith and begin to use the law of transmutation to change the negative conditions in your life into positive ones.

Instead of seeing your present job as a prison which you hate, transmute it with your power of mind and see it as a stepping-stone to something better. Your present job will be more tolerable if you begin to see ways in which you can improve your services and enjoy the work, as much as possible, until you can get some other job.

Instead of seeing your marriage as one of failure and disappointment, transmute it through the power of your mind, into one of love and patience, kindness and consideration. Let it be a discipline in which you will gain a valuable lesson in human relationships that will make it more bearable and happy.

How Thoughts Can Work Magic: Instead of looking at your present room, apartment, or house, as a bleak, drab, or ugly environment, see what you can do to transform it. A can of paint, curtains at the windows, clean floors and windows can work magic in a place. As you prove yourself capable of keeping your present home bright and clean, you will find yourself gradually being led into the more spacious, luxurious type of home you dream of.

Instead of accepting the limitations of your present income or financial situation in life, transmute it, and see yourself earning more money; study and work evenings, if need be, to prepare yourself for the bigger income. Hold the picture in your mind that you will come into a bigger fortune in the future. You will externalize that which you hold most frequently in your mind.

6. THE LAW OF INVOLUTION: The word "involution" means literally to involve or take into itself. The process by which nature evolves all forms of creation is through this act of involving into itself first the seed or germ of its future growth.

We see the law of involution at work in the creation of an egg. The sperm or seed is first planted within the chicken, and then, after a period of gestation, the egg is formed with the growing life of the future chick involved within it. Science never has been able to explain which came first, the chicken or the egg. That is God's mystery.

However, we do know that whatever is involved—that is, put

into the mind—will eventually have to externalize or evolve itself in some form or other.

What Are You Involving in Mind? Are you involving in your mind thoughts of health and happiness? Or do you dwell on thoughts of sickness, accident, age, and misery?

Do you involve in your mind thoughts of peace and order, or are you suffering from confusion, disorder, and chaos?

Do you involve thoughts of beauty, goodness, truth, and love in your mind? If you do, these qualities must externalize in your environment.

If you spend time putting thoughts of success and money into your mind, they must eventually externalize in your getting rich.

Example: A great pianist like Van Cliburn, who has won some of the world's greatest honors in his concert appearances, spent eight to ten hours a day for at least ten or more years, practicing and perfecting his art of playing the piano. During those years he was using the law of involution. He involved into his consciousness the idea of perfection, harmony, beauty, rhythm, knowledge, excellence, idealism, high standards, and value. With such a mental involvement, and with natural talent, he couldn't possibly evolve anything else but a great career.

Edison said of genius, "It is one-tenth inspiration, and nine-tenths perspiration." Hard work, useful knowledge, concentrated effort, a desire to evolve and perfect a talent, these are the great qualities that most geniuses involve in their consciousness before they produce magnificent masterpieces.

Perfection Is No Trifle: A friend visited the great sculptor Michelangelo in his studio where he was working on the magnificent statue of David. Three weeks later the friend visited the studio once again and saw that Michelangelo was still polishing the same section of the statue he had been working on before. He said, "But Michelangelo, you were working on that same place three weeks ago. Why do you waste time on such trifles?"

The great master replied, "Trifles make perfection, and perfection is no trifle."

7. THE LAW OF EVOLUTION: Evolution means an unfolding process of development or growth. When you involve something in your mind, it must evolve or externalize itself and develop ac-

cording to the initial seed or germ which has been planted.
is the law of evolution. We see this law at work everywhere
universe.

This law of evolution also works in your mind. That is why it
is so vitally important not to allow all kinds of negative thoughts
to be planted carelessly in your mind.

The Effect of Negative Thoughts: What is the effect of negative thinking?

Each time you think a thought, good or bad, it makes an inroad
in the gray matter of your brain. It involves itself electrically in
your brain. Your consciousness, which is the sum total of these
individual thoughts you think, becomes predominantly negative
or positive, depending on the nature of your thoughts.

If you think constantly such thoughts as the following—"I am
sick; I am old; I am a failure; I am miserable; I hate everyone and
everyone hates me; life isn't worth living; I am afraid I'll lose my
job; I'll be poor all my life; I am ugly and unloved; I cannot make
a fortune"—you will be involving such negative forces that they
can never evolve in dynamic, positive action.

How to Involve Positive Thoughts: If you want positive things
to happen to you, you must involve only positive thoughts in
your mind. They will then evolve in situations and conditions that
are good. When you arise in the morning, and prepare for your
day's activities, run a series of positive thoughts through your
mind.

Example: "Today will be a wonderful day. I shall meet people
I like and who will like me. I shall see many new opportunities to
advance my interests. Money will come to me from unexpected
sources. I am healthy and happy. I now put my thoughts in order
and refuse to be disturbed by external conditions. My work will
be easier and more pleasant because I am evolving through my
job to something better. I see only that which is beautiful and
good. I refuse to be involved in quarreling, confusion, and discord. I refuse to gossip and demean myself by uttering negative
words or using obscene language. I control my temper and my
tongue. I now accept the fact that I am created in the image
and likeness of God and I will act in a dignified, gracious, and
loving manner all day today."

If you do this every day of your life, you will be involving *only* the best thoughts and you cannot help but evolve the type of destiny which reflects prosperity, friendship, love, abundance, health, and happiness.

Summary of law ten

The law of demonstration for bringing that which is invisible into the realm of the visible. The seven laws which may be used for demonstrating what you want in life. The magnetic idea back of most big fortunes. The golden law of the harvest for increasing supply. The laws of reciprocity and transmutation for increasing good and changing conditions you do not want in life. The regimen for establishing positive thoughts.

Law Eleven

How to Energize Your Drive Towards Wealth

People who have attracted large fortunes have usually done so by energizing their mental drive to wealth. When all the power of your mind is concentrated on growing rich, it becomes an irresistible force which energizes your mind and body and causes you to do the things that make you wealthy.

Let us study the channels that this mental and physical energy expresses itself through in our desire to become rich.

Why money is an idea

Money is actually the expression of an idea. Therefore the mind is the first channel which must be energized in order to attract a large fortune. How is this done? By the following regime:

1. *Have something definite that you wish to accomplish in life for which you wish money in large sums.* The great men of history, who also became rich men, were those who had an overwhelming desire to do something for others. Edison's fortune was built by his desire to help humanity. Carnegie wanted to give the products created by his ideas to the world so people could live better. His steel mills and coal mines and other industrial holdings were all consecrated to this ideal.

In *Gospel of Wealth,* Carnegie said, "Surplus wealth is a sacred trust which its possessor is bound to administer in his lifetime for the good of the community."

In his lifetime Carnegie gave away five hundred million dollars in cash! He contributed twelve hundred public libraries to various communities. He built Carnegie Hall for cultural pursuits, and it has given joy to millions through the years.

139

Henry Ford, Sr. knew this secret about wealth. He was worth over five hundred million dollars when he died, but it was not money he worshiped. He loved the creative power which his money released. He labored long years in poverty and with discouragement as his constant companion before he perfected his first horseless carriage. His mental and physical energies were built by his desire to improve the lot of mankind.

Cecil Rhodes was told by his doctors he was dying of tuberculosis. He went to Africa to die. While there he became stimulated by an idea: to give education to people who were too poor to afford a college education. This desire so energized his body that he was healed physically. Then his intuition guided him to the discovery of a diamond mine, and Rhodes established the Rhodes Scholarship, and lived a long and useful life, using money as a tool with which to do good.

Horace said of money, "Riches either serve or govern the possessor."

It is true that misers energize money too, but in the wrong way. They achieve their goal and build a fortune through scrimping and saving, and generally it serves to destroy them. They do not know the secret of using money as a channel with which they may give good to the world. Money becomes an evil force which destroys them.

The Bible does *not* say money is evil. It says, "The love of money is the root of all evil."

A woman was discovered on the streets of New York in a condition of starvation. She was taken to the hospital where she died of malnutrition. In the cheap, cold-water flat where she lived the authorities found a trunk with five hundred thousand dollars in it! This unfortunate miser energized her mental and physical energies in the direction of wealth, but it was a negative manifestation and her money did her no good.

2. *Set a financial goal for yourself which you strive to reach. Example:* If you are in your twenties, say to yourself, "By the time I am thirty I want at least ten thousand dollars in cash or property." This setting of a goal is most important, for it helps activate the energies of the mind and body and somehow causes you to make greater effort to fulfill the goal you have set for yourself.

If you are older and already have some money saved, set another goal: that you will be financially independent in a period of ten years or less.

If you wish to use this system of mentally energizing your mind and body towards owning your own home, say to yourself, "I wish to own my own home in a period of two years." Set whatever time schedule you feel is reasonable and intelligent. You may not see how you will ever have sufficient money in that period of time for the down payment on your home, but somehow it will come to you.

I once knew a man and his wife who were in their late twenties, and they had a desire to own their own home. The husband energized his drive to make more money by preparing himself with special studies in the evenings so he could earn extra money in electronics. He repaired TV and radio sets on Saturdays and in his spare evening time. Instead of going bowling as much as he used to with his friends, he spent his extra time in working and studying.

He used to enjoy drinking beer as he watched TV, and he smoked an average of two packs of cigarettes a day. When he began to energize his mind in the direction of owning his home, he gave up smoking and drinking, and saved that extra money.

He and his wife used to entertain their friends at their little apartment where they played harmless games of cards for money. As small as the stakes were he usually wound up losing from five to ten dollars on those evenings. The bill for the drinks, smokes, and food was another ten or fifteen dollars. He soon found that his mental drive to own his own home was greater than the desire to indulge in social activities which were depleting of both his money and his time and energy.

He and his wife sought out other, simpler pleasures: going to the beach, visiting art galleries and museums, taking in a free lecture or concert given by organizations in his town. This, coupled with his work at home, filled his time so completely that he did not have the time or energy to waste with people who contributed nothing but took everything.

In two years' time, with all his scrimping and saving, he only had saved two thousand dollars. But his desire was so great for his own home, and a baby was on the way, that he decided he would start to search for that dream home.

He hounded real estate offices on Sundays and searched the papers. Finally one day he saw an ad that said: "Widow wishes to sell her beautiful home and furnishings. Sacrifice." He rushed to the address with his wife, and they met the widow, a charming, elderly lady who had recently lost her husband. She showed them the house and they loved it, but when she told them she wanted five thousand dollars as a down payment they saw their dream go up in smoke.

The man told her he only had two thousand dollars and he and his wife thanked the widow and were about to leave when she stopped them and said, "I don't know why I'm doing this, but if the price is right otherwise, I shall take the two thousand dollars you have offered for a down payment. I want to travel and I don't want the burden of a home any longer."

They concluded the deal, moved into their dream house, and it was exactly the way they had pictured it.

What strange almost mystical force is back of such an event as I have just described? Dreams do have a way of coming true. They possess in their intensity and inspiration a drive that causes one to seek out and create his own opportunities. The dream of flying brought man the jet age. The dream of beauty created our artistic masterpieces. The dream of love in the human heart energizes man to seek out shelter, security, companionship, and happiness.

3. *Concentrate at least ten or fifteen minutes a day on The Value of Money.* Think of money in terms of ideas, labor, time, supply, spiritual energy, anything that will help you crystallize a better image of what money is. As the electrons and atoms of your brain become energized with a big concept of money, they will tend to drive you in the direction where you can do the things that build wealth.

4. *Remove from your mind the unhealthy idea that money is sinful or evil.* Think of all the good things money can buy. It furnishes food and shelter, it helps the sick in hospitals, it gives transportation to millions, it creates art, music, literature that enrich the mind and soul. Money has a multitude of benefits that it

showers upon humanity. See this positive picture instead of believing that you were born to be poor, and that God wants others to have the good things of life but is denying them to you. The Bible says, "It is the Father's good pleasure to give you the kingdom."

5. *Write down on a piece of paper all the things that you want to obtain, and which you will require money to get.* Then keep this paper where you can see it a dozen times a day. In this way you will be involving the idea of building a fortune in the sympathetic nervous system, until it becomes a reflex action of your brain and body.

6. *Whenever you spend any money, such as a dollar, mentally affirm: "I now bless this money and under the law of the harvest it will return to me multiplied tenfold."*

7. *Use the Seed Money principle in your life.* Just as a seed put into the ground grows and yields a crop, so too you can plant sums of money and they will multiply and grow. For instance, money you give to your church, to charity, to some needy family, these sums of money should be thought of as seed money. Make the mental law that all such sums of money given out will yield a hundredfold. This law of tithing is also given in the Bible. Whatever money you give to anyone for a good purpose comes under this higher spiritual law.

8. *Remind yourself many times a day "time is money"* and make it a point not to waste time, any more than you would waste money. With the time that you waste you could study some course that would prepare you to make more money, or you could think of some idea that might make you rich. Ask yourself these questions whenever you plan on doing something that takes your valuable time: "Is this act helping me towards my goal of attaining wealth? Am I using my time constructively to achieve my goal?"

9. *Are you getting your money's worth out of every dollar you spend?* When you go into a store to make a purchase, be sure that it is the best value you can get for your dollar. Check on the object you want to purchase in one of the consumer's research publications to see how it is classified in relation to its price and quality.

10. *Look for special bargains on objects you wish to purchase.* Anything that saves you money increases your future wealth. It

may sound silly to walk a block to save a few cents on some object, but it isn't. It is not the money that counts but the principle back of the action. Such thrifty habits condition your mind to respect wealth and to hold it. I know a lady who is worth ten million dollars. She drives her own car most of the time, and when she goes to park she looks for a place on the street even if it is two or three blocks from the place where she is going. She refuses to throw away half a dollar or seventy-five cents unnecessarily. Many of her friends think this is ridiculous for a woman of her wealth. She gives thousands of dollars away to charity every year. She has a fortune because she is thrifty and she will probably never lose her wealth.

11. *Study the financial pages of the newspapers each day for a few moments.* This helps orient you to thinking about money and investments. Such knowledge, when used with growing capital, may be the means for making a fortune in the stock market. Buy such magazines as *Forbes, Fortune,* and others that reveal the secrets used by men who have made millions, and which keep you up to date on the happenings in the financial world. Such knowledge will help energize and stimulate your mind in the direction of building a fortune.

12. *Study the lives of some of the great financiers of the past and present.* Try to apply their techniques to your own life. Learn from their mistakes, profit from their advice. Some of the world's richest men were: Vanderbilt, Astor, Gould, Carnegie, Rockefeller, Getty, Hearst, Ford, Morgenthau, Baruch, Schwab, Whitney, Insull, Doheny, and Edison. There are books which relate their exploits and you may learn much from such a study. Some in this list lost their fortunes, or were disgraced because of illegal manipulations, but learn how they accumulated their fortunes, then find out what mistakes jeopardized those fortunes and brought them disgrace. For instance, Charles Schwab, who was a worker with Andrew Carnegie and became enormously rich, lost all his money during his lifetime and died broke. Carnegie died rich. What mistakes did Schwab make? Find out by studying his life. Even this negative approach will help you understand the secrets of making and losing fortunes.

13. *Study the following quotations from the sayings or writings*

of famous men regarding wealth and see what you can learn from them:

Benjamin Franklin: "If you would be wealthy, think of saving as well as getting."

Sam Johnson: "Life is short. The sooner that a man begins to enjoy his wealth the better."

Thoreau: "That man is the richest whose pleasures are cheapest."

Henry George: "The ideal social state is not that in which each gets an equal amount of wealth, but in which each gets in proportion to his contribution to the general stock."

Ask yourself these questions

1. Do I waste time now that I could convert into useful knowledge that might win me a better job with more money?
2. Do I read worthwhile books that contain helpful information for self-improvement and which might help me make a fortune?
3. Do I study the lives of the great men of industry and finance and apply their techniques for obtaining wealth to my own life?
4. Am I spending at least one hour a day in visualizing and imagining myself with more money and doing the things I want to do?
5. Am I using my present job as a steppingstone to a higher goal?
6. Do I seek out contacts with important people who might help me achieve my money goals in life, or do I waste time with people who discourage me and negate my big ideas?
7. Am I conscious of the value of every dollar I spend? When the late John D. Rockefeller, Sr. gave a ten-cent tip someone once asked him why he gave such a small sum. The multi-millionaire replied, "A small sum indeed! Why ten cents is ten percent interest on a dollar for one full year!"

   I might add, when you spend ten or twenty dollars, stop and figure out how many hundreds of dollars would have to work for you at the current rate of interest in a savings bank to make that money back. When you are lavish in tipping, buying harmful cigarettes or liquor, candy, and excess food you do not need, stop and realize that this is probably why you have not built a working capital which you can use to make a fortune. One man wrote a book on how he converted a thousand dollars into a million in real estate. But he had to save that one thousand dollars first!

9. Am I building hobbies and avocations that might later be useful to make money? (Perhaps you already have some such talent. A woodworker began cutting toys out of wood in his workshop at home in his spare time. They were little figures like chickens, ducks on wheels, and other wooden toys. A neighbor saw these toys and wanted some for her children. Soon this man was selling his toys to a big toy manufacturer and making as much money in his spare time as he had on his job.)

10. Am I using the money I now have to good advantage?

11. Do I take advantage of all the free services that the U.S. Government gives its citizens? (You can send for a book from the Government Printing Office in Washington, D.C., telling of these numerous free benefits which will save you money.)

12. Do I know all my health and pension benefits which I am entitled to?

13. Am I wasteful of nature's goods and my own resources? (Remember the saying, "Waste not, want not.")

Summary of law eleven

Using the irresistible force of mind for attracting wealth. Money as an idea. Secret power used by the great men of history for attracting fortune and fame. The importance of creative daydreams for bringing things into existence. Man's dreams created the marvels of the space age. The seed money principle for increasing your abundance. Time is money. Let the world's richest men guide you to the building of a fortune.

Law Twelve

How to Control Your Destiny Through Mind Power

Man has it within his power to control his destiny to a great extent. He may shape and select the events of his life in about ninety percent of the cases and predetermine what his future shall be. The instrument through which he does this is the power of his mind. There are actually five mental agents which you may use to control your destiny. But first, before we study these thoroughly, let us define what we mean by the word Destiny. The dictionary defines destiny as: "The inevitable succession of events. One's fortune, or fate."

You may not be able to choose your parents, or the shape and size of your body, the color of your hair or eyes, but these are *not* destiny. No matter with what limitations you were born, you can do something with your mind to determine the inevitable succession of events, and thus shape your fortune or fate.

What a startling change man went through from the stone age to the atomic age! In the stone age he used brute force; his mind was unevolved, and there was only one law: the law of the jungle. Man was subjected to all the destructive forces of nature, including the ferocity of wild animals, and it was all he could do to survive and avoid extinction. This phase of man's evolvement is scientifically proved by science, and it represents man at the lowest point in his long evolutionary climb from the primordial ooze to the glorious space age which he now enjoys.

Ingenuity simply means cleverness or originality. When man started to develop his mind, he began to form weapons from stone and metal, and with these he was able to till the soil, hunt for food, and protect himself.

147

With the coming of the metal age man was able to leave his lowly caves and build homes in trees and on land, to make bows and arrows, to harness fire, to discover the wheel, and to utilize nature's forces to help him in his struggle for survival. This was the beginning of his amazing mental evolution. Then came the machine age, in which man learned how to use his higher mind. He was able to harness electricity, to make machines that did his work for him, and he had more leisure in which to develop the arts and sciences, to write books, to evolve systems of philosophy, and to explore the universe in which he lived.

With the dawning of the atomic age man learned how to truly harness the secret power back of all creation, and he dared grow wings of the imagination and explore outer space and aim at the very stars in the heavens! Truly, this is man's most audacious achievement.

With the awakening of his true higher, spiritual self, man is on the way to conquering his animalism entirely, and overcoming war and starvation in the world. For the first time he possesses the mental and spiritual power to achieve the world-wide goal of peace and prosperity for all humanity.

How your mind determines how far you will go

You are a product of this, the most illumined age in history. Man's mind has achieved everything you see in the world of miracles about you. Your own mind determines how far you will personally go in the achievement of your own destiny. There is no doubt but what you can soar as high as you dare envision. You and you alone can set limits on the type of destiny you shall achieve. The sky's the limit, so far as the power of your mind is concerned.

Emerson said of this mental power: "The key to every man is his thought. Sturdy and defying though he look, he has a helm which he obeys, which is the idea after which all his facts are classified. He can only be reformed by showing him a new idea which commands his own."

Your mind is the helm which steers your ship of Destiny either into the harbor of self-realization and fulfillment or onto the hidden shoals of life. You have it within your power to choose the persons, the events, the work, the income, the friends, the mate you shall marry, and the type of home you shall live in. All these things may be predetermined by you if you have the wisdom to act in a positive and constructive manner.

"It is the mind that maketh good or ill," Spenser said; "that maketh wretch or happy, rich or poor."

Understanding the five realms of control

Now we shall study the five realms of control, which can help you choose and determine the type of destiny you shall have.

1. THE POWER OF YOUR MIND: It is your mind that is the final arbiter in all things. You may consciously choose anything within reason as your goal in life, and this conscious choice immediately sets into motion events that trigger you into instant action. You may not see the connection between mental and physical action, but it is there, in the reflexes of your nerves and muscles. You cannot make any decision, nor feel any emotion, good or bad, without experiencing an anatomical change, or without being impelled in the direction of your choice.

Examples: A man decides he is going to become rich. He does not know how. Something in his mind impels him to go to a real estate school evenings to learn about buying and selling property. In a few weeks or months, armed with this knowledge, he obtains a job in a real estate office. Inspired by his desire to become wealthy and successful, he works harder than most of the other salesman. In two or three years he obtains his own real estate broker's license. Soon he has an opportunity to open an office of his own, and in two more years he is such a success that he employs fourteen salesmen and is on the way to making his first million!

Sounds fantastic and impossible, doesn't it? This is a true case history of a man inspired by these teachings on the West Coast, who is now one of the biggest real estate operators in California.

There is a definite connecting link between mind and matter. The saying "mind over matter" is a true one. Your mind has the power to rise above obstacles and negative situations and carve for itself any career you choose.

A veteran came back from the war with both arms shot off. He sat for miserable hours in a veteran's hospital trying to while away the time. Suddenly he got the urge to paint pictures. At this stage most people would have told him, as many did, "Forget it! Be grateful to just be alive and have others wait on you."

This young man did not take such negative advice. He had someone buy him a paint set, some pieces of canvas board, and then he began to laboriously train himself to hold the paint brush in his teeth and paint!

He was soon turning out saleable paintings, and came to the attention of an art dealer, who gave him an exhibit in his gallery. The newspapers heard of his work and covered the story. Crowds gathered to see his work. They were so impressed, not with pity but with genuine interest in the quality of his work, that they bought his paintings. Now this armless genius sells more paintings than he can paint!

Grandma Moses and Her Gift: A frail old lady of seventy-six got tired of being put on the shelf of life because she had reared her family and was seemingly finished with her life work. Indeed, she seemed so frail that it was thought she would die at any moment.

Some mental impulse caused her to try painting. She did so well that soon her paintings were in demand and she made over a million dollars before she died at the age of one hundred and one. Undoubtedly the new mental inspiration that caused her to take up painting also gave a new life impetus to her body cells and kept her living another quarter of a century of active, useful life. Grandma Moses, as she was affectionately called by friends and the press, proved that mind can shape destiny.

I have given these two extreme examples to show you how mind sets up reflex actions of the body and sets one on the path of his destiny. You will probably never have to meet such a challenge as these two persons had in your entire life.

"A good mind possesses a kingdom," someone has said. When you start action in your mind you will create a world of your own.

2. ADJUSTING TO NATURE'S LAWS: The second realm of control has to do with adjusting to nature's laws. What you cannot change or control, you must adjust to. This is known as adaptation, and is one of the basic rules of evolution. Evolution, in the sense in

which it is used in this course of study, does *not* mean that man sprang from the lowly apes. Man was created by God and was always man, but of a lower order in his original state, and he has evolved, as we know scientifically, from the stone age, to the atomic age, through this law of adaptation.

Example: You cannot change your physical structure. Perhaps you want to be an actor, but you have a nose that is too big, a mouth that is excessively large, or feet that look like canal boats. You give up in discouragement and say, "Oh, well, I'll do some thing else," but deep within you is the urge to be an actor.

Jimmy (Schnozzola) Durante has a nose that is too big, and he adapted his talents to comedy and has made millions.

Martha Raye and Joe E. Brown were both born with large mouths, and both became famous and outstanding comedians, and, incidentally, made fortunes because of these seeming limitations. They adjusted to nature's laws.

Greta Garbo, one of our greatest stars of silent days and the early talking pictures, was considered too angular, her features were irregular and not too beautiful, her feet were too big for true beauty, and yet she became one of Hollywood's greatest stars. She too adjusted herself to nature's laws. She accepted her limitations and overcame them by persistence.

I could quote dozens of Hollywood celebrities who became famous despite their limitations and handicaps. Ernest Borgnine is short, chubby, and unprepossessing, yet he won an academy award with *Marty*. Edward G. Robinson, James Cagney, Bette Davis, Katharine Hepburn, Audrey Hepburn, Charles Laughton, Boris Karloff, and Marie Dressler certainly were no raving beauties, and yet each overcame his or her limitations by persistence, determination, and by using the power of the mind to rise above their limitations.

How You Can Be the Best of Whatever You Are: Make up your mind to be the best of whatever you are. Do not try to force nature to fit your pattern, but choose the pattern of destiny that best fits your nature. If you're too tall or too thin or too fat, adjust yourself to this fact, and then rise above it through sheer power of mind and choose the type of career you feel deep within yourself would best suit you. Nine chances out of ten you will succeed.

The story is told of a woman who saw a midget advertised in a side show of a circus. After paying her quarter to go in, she was indignant to see what appeared to be a normal-sized short man posing as the midget. She demanded her money back from the manager, saying, "Why, that man's no midget! He's at least five feet tall."

The quick-witted manager replied, "That's the remarkable thing about it, Madam. This is the tallest midget in the world!"

Be the biggest and best of whatever you are, and do not accept limitations on your mind power.

3. THE POWER OF YOUR WILL: One of the greatest weapons you possess in the arsenal of mind is the power of your human will. Will power, as used in this study, means the power of conscious and deliberate action or choice. You may exercise the power of your will in every choice you make in your life. When you choose a certain type of work, you have used your will power. If you do not like the work, or do not like the limited salary you receive, you have it within your power to exercise your will again and change that work. It may require that you study a new line of work, but it only requires that you *consciously make the choice and deliberately decide on the action you will take.* You set the wheels of action into motion with this conscious choice.

How to Exercise Your Power of Will:

A. Each day will yourself to do something that you keep putting off, like writing a letter, asking for a raise, looking for a new job or a new apartment.

B. Write down ten things that you would like to will yourself to do or be in the future. This will be a map or guide to future action.

C. Deliberately do something unpleasant because you will it, such as visiting an in-law or relative you dislike. Or go shopping with your wife, or husband, whichever the case may be. Make yourself visit three prospective clients who might be interested in your products. This applies to salesmen. In other businesses, choose some event that you do not especially like and force yourself to do it to develop and strengthen your will power.

D. Implement your will by using these three positive principles
in your thoughts and speech as much as possible:
"I will."
"I can."
"I am."
Every day, as often as possible, say, "I will succeed," "I will
be happy," "I will be rich," "I will be dynamic." Do the same
with "I can": "I can do that"; "I can be healthy"; "I can be
young"; "I can be magnetic and attractive." Then use the
I Am principle often every day: "I am now successful"; "I am
happy"; "I am young"; "I am on my way to a great destiny";
"I am loving and kind."

4. CAPITALIZE ON YOUR DESIRE AND AMBITION TO ACHIEVE: The
realm of control is implemented by a desire and ambition to
achieve a high goal. Your reflex actions will be automatically accelerated by such a mental resolve. If you aim at too low a goal,
you can never achieve a high one. But if you aim at a high goal,
you will almost certainly achieve a modest one. "When you are
aspiring to the highest place, it is honorable to reach the second
or even the third rank" (*Cicero*).

Desire means to long for something, to crave for it, and to ask
for it. You cannot achieve anything worthwhile without asking
life for it. Make your desires known to other people, enlist their
aid and support. Seek out people with similar ambitions to your
own. "Birds of a feather flock together." You must expose yourself
to the type of people who can help you achieve that which you
desire.

Using the Law of Proximity: The law of proximity works in
this respect to help you achieve your high goal in life. Proximity
means to put yourself in relationship to the persons and things
that you wish to attract.

A young man who desires to become a famous baseball player
would do well to hang out on the practice field, to meet those
who are interested in the sport, to practice the art of ball playing
in every free moment of his time. Eventually, if he has enough
ambition and skill, someone will notice his excellence and help
him achieve his goal.

You will notice that people interested in golfing form clubs and meet with people of a similar interest. Stamp collectors, boating enthusiasts, horse race players, actors, architects, mechanics, all use this law of proximity. They meet and mingle with others who are interested in the things they like. They achieve their goal because someone helps them.

You can use this same law in your life. Join a group that is interested in playwriting, if you wish to write plays. Tennessee Williams, who has made a great commercial success in the modern theater, had a ten year apprenticeship, in which he presented his formative plays in little theaters and schools, writing, perfecting, and polishing his lines, until they were ready for Broadway.

If you are interested in interior decorating, join some study group; read, study, talk, and live decorating. Subscribe to magazines that deal in this subject, until you make the contacts that can lead you to success in this field.

This is the reason why there are clubs for lawyers, doctors, dentists, optometrists, actors, authors, architects, mechanics, scientists, and artists, as well as many other groups, so they can get together and exchange useful ideas and promote their mutual interest to its fullest.

Join Some Helpful Group: Make it a point early in your career, when you have decided what it is you want to become in life, to join some helpful group that is working toward the same goal as yourself. Make friends among these people; some of them will achieve high places and will be able to help you eventually. Do not expect immediate results, for sometimes building a lifetime career can take a lifetime. If the goal is a high and worthy one, it will pay you to have patience and wait for the fulfillment of your dream. Ask people to help you, for important people usually feel flattered to have some beginner ask their support and help.

The Bible gives this law of asking in these words:

> Ask and ye shall receive.
> Seek and ye shall find.
> Knock and it shall be opened unto you.
> For everyone that asketh, receiveth.
> He that seeketh, findeth,
> And to him that knocketh it shall be opened.

If you will notice the three words, Ask, Seek, and Knock start with the letters A-S-K, again emphasizing to Ask.

5. THROUGH THE POWER OF YOUR IMAGINATION: The last principle in our realm of control is that of the power of your imagination. We have studied this elsewhere in this course, but in relation to this subject of controlling your destiny, we shall make the following points.

What you picture in your imagination is already real, so far as you are concerned. You have merely to project the inner dream to the outer world of reality by taking steps to make this picture real.

Visualization, concentration, and imagination all work together. What you visualize or see with your inner eye, and what you concentrate on, becomes the pattern that you project in your words and actions to the outer world. Concentrate on your goal, imagine the details worked out perfectly, visualize new ways of doing things, and then, with this perfect mental pattern in your mind, try to conform to this chosen destiny in everything you think, say, and do.

Climbing Your Ladder of Dreams: In your climb up the ladder of dreams, that leads to your ultimate destiny, there is a barometer which you may use to see your progress.

Those who say, "I won't" never begin on the first rung.

Those who say, "I can" are only ten percent up the ladder.

Those who say, "I don't know" are twenty percent up.

Those who say, "I wish I could" are thirty percent up.

Those who say, "What is it?" are forty percent up.

Those who say, "I suppose I should" are fifty percent up.

Those who say, "I might try" are sixty percent up.

Those who say, "I think I can" are seventy percent up.

Those who say, "I can!" are eighty precent up.

Those who say, "I will!" are ninety percent up.

Those who say, "I did" are one hundred percent up the ladder of dreams and achieve their complete destiny.

You may choose any of these rungs on that golden ladder of dreams. The choice is up to you. When you once make your choice, you will invoke the aid of your higher mind and you will be propelled in the direction of your destiny by a gravity pull of mind and body that is irresistible and which assures you of complete success.

Summary of law twelve

Mind power can help man control and shape his destiny. Mental power, the key to the creation of destiny. The five realms of control for building your future. Overcoming adversity through the power of the mind. Hollywood stars and how they overcame their handicaps and became famous and rich. The power of will, desire, and ambition for changing your life. The ladder of dreams and how to climb it for final achievement.

Law Thirteen

Mastering the Art of Commanding and Controlling Life's Forces

There are always two opposing forces in life. They might be classified as follows:

The good and the evil.
The loving and the hateful.
The friendly and the unfriendly.
The rich and the poor.
The successful and the unsuccessful.
The big and the little.
The selfish and the unselfish.
The healthy and the sick.
The dark and the light.
The attractive and the unattractive.
The happy and the miserable.
The beautiful and the ugly.
The materialistic and the spiritual.

Even in religion, we have the Satanic force opposed to the Godly power.

How man stands between opposing forces

Man stands between two opposing forces constantly in life, and it seems to be his ability to command and control these opposing forces that determines the degree to which he shall have health, happiness, and success in all his affairs.

"Wherever I have seen life, I have seen the will to power," Nietzsche said.

> power represents man's ability to take a stand
es that are negative and destructive, and to choose
which are positive and constructive. If you will
decisions you have made in your life you will see
had two choices to make. If you chose one, it
..ably led to success and achievement, but if you chose the
other, it led to defeat, despair, and disappointment. If you make
no choice and decide to beat life by remaining in a neutral zone
between two possible courses of action, this leads to inertia and
stagnation, and ultimately defeats you, much like the mule who
stood between two piles of hay: unable to decide which to eat
first, he starved to death.

Your ego determines your drive

Even your Ego has two opposing forces: those of low value or
high value, a feeling of importance or unimportance. Your Ego
determines your drive and the direction in which your decisions
are to be made in the future.

If you have been trained and educated to believe that you are
important, that you will become successful, that you have a
magnetic and charming personality, then your Ego will have a
drive in the direction of success. However, if you have lacked
education of a higher sort, if you were born in a poor family that
had no advantages of comfort or luxury, if you were told over and
over when you were a child that you were no good, that you
would never amount to anything, that you would be poor all
your life, then it is possible that your Ego-drive will be in the
direction of failure, unhappiness, and poverty all your life.

How to change your ego-drive

Can man change his Ego-drive? Yes, he can. This is where our
study of the art of commanding and controlling life's opposing
forces begins. You can build a quality of confidence in yourself
that gives you an attitude of poise and power. You can develop
the quality of confidence in other people and seek out their aid,
and undoubtedly change the direction of your destiny from a
weak, vacillating one of failure and poverty, to one of success
and wealth. "The confidence which we have in ourselves gives

birth to much of that which we have in others" (*La Roche-foucauld*).

You can work to improve your mind and the quality of your personality so that you will truly be superior. Then you will have more confidence in yourself and in others.

How to exert your will

Each day you will be called upon to make decisions in your work, in your home, in your social life. When such decisions must be made, face up to each problem squarely and force yourself to act in whatever way you think is best. Give the situation due deliberation, pro and con, and if you have any difficulty in making up your mind, sit down and write down on a sheet of paper the problem, the possible courses of action, and their possible results. Carefully examine all the possibilities and choose the one that most nearly conforms with your concept of the thing you should do. Then exercise your will power and take the necessary steps to bring about the needed action.

Avoid vacillation too long, or putting off action, for the more you vacillate, and the more you procrastinate, the weaker your power of will becomes.

The three aspects of will power

There are three aspects of will power:

1. Determination
2. Persistence
3. Patience

The moment you have made the decision to take certain action, you must invoke the determination to carry through with your decision.

The second step is persistence. After you have once made your determination to achieve something, you can only strengthen the will by never giving up. If your original idea is sound, it will ultimately be achieved.

The third step is patience. You may exert will power and feel that something should happen immediately, and then you find that nothing changes radically. You have to remember that nothing ever matures in nature overnight, except perhaps a mushroom, and it has a short lifetime. If you want to build something enduring and imperishable, you must give it time to mature and develop.

It takes time to build the success habit, just as it has taken time to build the failure habit. When you give some time each day to shaping your thoughts and actions in the mold of success, eventually you will have the success you dreamed of. When things do not seem to be shaping up the way you want them, you must re-examine your thinking and see if you have allowed negative thoughts to enter your mind. Perhaps your faith has weakened because of the length of time it takes to achieve your dream. It is then time to reaffirm that faith daily.

> Faith, mighty faith, the promise sees,
> And looks to that alone;
> Laughs at impossibilities,
> And cries it shall be done.

Scientific principles of control and command

FIRST PRINCIPLE: *Strive to be worthy of the best that life has to offer.* Life has a way of paying us exactly what we're worth. It is a sad truth, which we hate to admit, but we are generally in the position in life that we deserve or have sought out. If we are in an inferior position, perhaps it is because we have inferior talents. We can only command the better job when we are ready for it. This means, if you are displeased with your position in life, you must work to change it. You can only do it through changing your attitude towards life and towards yourself. Confucius said, "Do not worry about honors and fame; strive only to be worthy of them."

Answer These Questions Honestly:

1. Have you cultivated your mind since you left school?
2. Do you keep up on current events by reading some good daily newspaper or weekly magazine?
3. Are you enrolled in an evening course in high school or college to improve yourself?

4. Do you take advantage of your public library and the special lectures and personal development courses given by many libraries?
5. Do you attend lectures at your local Town Hall club, YMCA, or YWCA?
6. Do you learn new words and their meaning each day?
7. Have you ever written a letter to an important person asking for his aid in your career?
8. Do you try to dress your best, look your best, speak your best, and project a smiling personality?
9. Do you give your best to your present job?
10. Have you developed the art of public speaking and self-expression?

Give yourself ten points for each *Yes* answer, and you should score eighty or more to be in the excellent class. If you score less then you should be working on your mental habits and preparing yourself to be worthy of the highest rewards from life.

SECOND PRINCIPLE: *Demand the best from life and people.* When you are really worthy of the best, you can then begin to command the best from life and people. Everyone recognizes quality. You cannot fool the world. But if you think thoughts of quality and your actions show confidence, poise, and authority, it will not be long before you will be noticed by people who can help you advance.

> A moral, sensible, and well-bred man
> Will not affront me, and no other can.
> *Cowper*

You will find that quality speaks a language all its own. When you once look, act, and speak with charm, culture, and elegance, you will soon find that no person can stand in your way. Like attracts like, and you must attract persons on the same mental wave length as yourself. They will help you achieve your goal because they are aiming at the same goals as you are.

Act with Dignity and Honor: If you wish to attract the best that life has to offer, you must approach life with a sense of dignity and honor. The world recognizes quality and is indifferent to commonness and vulgarity. For a time such persons may thrive, but eventually the equalizing force of life reduces them to their right place.

Make it a point to demand respect from others. Even those closest to you should be expected to conform to your high standards and treat you with respect and dignity. A sense of personal dignity and integrity makes itself felt immediately when you contact important people. As they have built quality into their characters they instantly sense it when you raise your mental and spiritual standards to the highest and best.

THIRD PRINCIPLE: *Do not compromise with character.* In striving to win a high goal in life, you may be impressed by the fact that many unworthy persons seem to achieve a high destiny and rich rewards from life, and you may feel that this is the way you will achieve the same rewards. But do not compromise with character. Maintain your high moral standards and your sense of responsibility, even in face of general world-wide lowering of standards.

We see this universal lowering of standards in art, music, literature, and drama. We see the rise of crime and delinquency, dope addiction, alcoholism, and crimes of violence. The fact that immorality is rampant and that most people are losing their sense of morality does not make it right. You can still win the biggest rewards from life by maintaining a high personal moral code and building your life on a solid foundation of honesty, goodness, love, consideration, and generosity.

"Let us have faith that right makes might; and in that faith, let us, to the end, dare to do our duty as we understand it" (*Lincoln*).

FOURTH PRINCIPLE: *Command attention by speaking in a compelling and authoritative tone of voice.* It's amazing how people respect and obey a person who has a compelling and magnetic voice. Bruce Barton, the noted author and lecturer, tells in his study of over ten thousand men and women who have achieved outstanding success that every one of them did so through the power to command attention through the spoken word. Make it a point to study your voice and to learn how to use it intelligently to express the subtle shades of meaning you wish to convey.

There are many excellent books on this subject in the library and in book stores. Also you may enroll in free public speaking courses in high schools. The main thing about developing your voice is to study and practice reading aloud. This should be done at least one hour a day for a period of six months to a year, until you have such command of the English language that you can express yourself forcefully and dramatically.

There is hardly a field of human endeavor in which the human voice is not important. This is especially true if you are seeking a position where you are in charge of others or have to give orders to your co-workers.

Cultivate a magnetic voice: You can cultivate a magnetic voice if you practice this simple exercise: Say the sounds *Bree, Bray, Brah, Broh,* rolling the *R's* and keeping the tone on the lips as much as possible. Start at the lowest tone you are capable of making comfortably, and go up the scale saying the four words on each note until you have gone as high as you can comfortably. This exercise will tend to place your voice in the mask of the face and give you projection and magnetism. It is one of the simplest and best voice control methods I know for one who wishes to achieve a pleasant and magnetic voice. There are many other exercises which help do this also, but you should go to a competent teacher if you wish more extensive training of the voice.

Enlarge the vocabulary: It is also vitally important to enlarge your vocabulary if you wish to rise higher in almost any field. You can do this with a simple dictionary, and by learning and using only one new word a day for one year. There are also special books on vocabulary building which you may obtain in paperback editions or from your public library. Time spent in this study will pay off big dividends.

Try to speak as grammatically as possible, avoiding slovenly diction and slipshod speech. Make it a conscious habit for six months or so to build your voice and your speech patterns and then later this will become automatic and easy. People have no other way to judge you than through the way you dress and the way you speak. If you can express yourself fluently and with authority, there is no doubt but that you will attract the attention of people who can help you achieve your goal.

FIFTH PRINCIPLE: *Develop a magnetic and compelling personality by using your eyes correctly.* In trying to command and control people it is amazing how much you can do with the power of your eyes. If your gaze is unsteady, wavering, and unmagnetic, people sense your insecurity and take advantage of you. In any work where you deal with the public, or have others working under you, it is vitally important that you develop a magnetic and compelling personality by using the power of your eyes.

To be truly magnetic, your eyes should be held steady and not blink too often, when you are trying to control another person or make a sale. It is best to look between a person's eyes, rather than to try to look from one eye to another, as you can never focus on both eyes at one time, and if you try to look into someone's eyes, you will shift your eyes, giving you an evasive and, possibly, a crafty appearance.

How to Achieve the Hypnotic Eye: To control others you need the hypnotic eye. You can develop this by looking steadily at a spot on a wall or any object in your room, and keeping your gaze fixed there as long as you feel comfortable. At first you will probably blink many times, and your eyes may begin to tear, but after a few days' practice you can comfortably look at the same spot for many seconds without blinking.

When you use the hypnotic eye with other people you should attempt to look between their eyes, without blinking too often, and hold the thought in your mind, "I like you and you are going to like me."

How to Extend the Golden Line of Power: When you are trying to win control of another person, either to sell yourself to them or to sell them some object or service, mentally extend a golden line between your forehead and theirs, feeling that this line is being attached to the person's brain. Now mentally, pull that line in from the center, feeling that you are drawing that person to you magnetically. This golden line of power is a very strong personality factor, for it causes you to project your mental power to the other person, and he feels your strength, without knowing what you are doing. Almost all magnetic people subconsciously do this. You can think of this golden line as a web which you are spinning with your mind, and you attach one end of a strand to the other person's mind and pull it in. They feel a compelling urge to like you, without knowing why. In fact, few people can resist this golden line of power. It is one of the secrets that many salesmen use who are trying to make a big sale. They concentrate all the power of their minds on projecting a pleasant and magnetic quality to the other person, winning him over completely.

The late President Franklin Delano Roosevelt had this quality in his personality more strongly than any man in recent times; this, coupled with his magnetic voice, kept him in power for four terms in the Presidency.

SIXTH PRINCIPLE: *Refuse to take "no" for an answer.* You can control and command life's forces by the simple application of this Sixth Principle. Many people win out in life because they refuse ever to admit they are defeated.

There is something compelling about a person who is persistent. It shows strength of character to never admit you are beaten. People cannot help but admire such a person. This does not mean to be stubborn or obnoxious, but merely to know when you are in the right, and when you want something which is good for you and for others, and never to give up.

A Million Dollars' Worth of Persistence: An insurance salesman I know who sold over one million dollars worth of insurance in one year used this principle and made a great success. No matter if a prospective client turned him down the first or second time, he kept on, meeting the person, arranging to see him socially or in some other way, such as on a golf course, until he caught the person in a weak moment and the person bought a policy. It takes great persuasion, it's true, to be able to persist like this, but if the goal is a high one you simply cannot take the first rejection by the other person.

SEVENTH PRINCIPLE: *Control your emotions if you wish to have greater power over others.* This Principle is a very important one, for if you allow your emotions to run rampant and you lose your poise in dealing with other people, you will never be in a position to command and control people or life.

"How shall I be able to rule over others, that have not full power and command of myself?" (*Rabelais*).

What are some of the emotions you should control?

1. A quick temper and anger when someone says or does something you do not like.
2. Worry about how things are going to turn out. This emotion causes you to be uneasy and to lack command of all your mental faculties.
3. Fear generates a chemistry that others sense and resent. Make it a point not to tell people about the things you fear.
4. Greed. This is an emotion that causes the facial muscles to grow into unpleasant lines that people can read in your personality. They tend to shun a greedy person.
5. Hate. This emotion drives people away from you.
6. Impatience. People sense it when you are impatient with them or when you show irritation because of their weaknesses or lack of education, and they resent this.

EIGHTH PRINCIPLE: *Use an appeal to men's primary urges if you wish to influence them and control them*

What are man's primary urges?

1. Hunger
2. Sex
3. Money
4. Power
5. Social acceptance
6. Love
7. Recognition
8. Desire for new experiences
9. Self-preservation

Many women have discovered that old proverb, "The way to a man's heart is through his stomach." This may not be literally true, but the hunger urge is a strong one in many people. How many business deals are consummated over dinner or cocktails? You can use this simple urge to win over those who might be helpful in your own career. These urges are basic in all people and by their judicious use you may control the minds and actions of most people.

In another law where we discuss the Master Motives of life we shall go thoroughly into all of these primary urges which give you amazing control of others. The way to use this eighth principle is to write down on a card these nine primary urges and keep it handy where you can examine it for a month or two. Read it each day and apply it for that day. Each person you meet or work with will have a special response to one or more of these urges. Check the list and see which urge fits which person.

Example: Mr. J. thinks and talks and plans about nothing but money. He may want money for power, or to win social acceptance, or to have recognition for his work. Therefore he can be appealed to by using primary urges numbers three, four, five, and seven. The predominant urge is not love or sex, but money with which he can buy the things that are important to him.

In dealing with Mr. J. you would not try to win his interest talking about baseball or the latest play, but about money; how he can make more money or increase his worldly goods.

Miss G. may have number six as her primary urge, but also numbers eight and two. If you were trying to win her interest and control her, you would talk about love, marriage, children, the home, the latest romance or scandal in Hollywood or in society. You would not be able to interest such a girl with the other primary urges; although they may motivate her in some respects, they are not her dominant interests.

Summary of law thirteen

The two opposing forces in life. Man's choice determines his success or failure. The Ego-drive that gives dynamic direction to your life. Three aspects of will power: determination, persistence, and patience. The regimen for attaining honors and success through control and command of the forces of life. Demand the best from life. Act with dignity and honor. Do not compromise with character. How to build a compelling and authoritative voice and personality. Build a magnetic personality to command and control people. The golden line of power and how to weave it. Emotional control and the importance of appealing to man's nine primary urges.

Law Fourteen

Using Psychic Phenomena to Discover and Enhance Your Future

Can man ever really know his future? Are some people psychic, with the ability to predict certain events in the future? I believe the answer to these questions is "Yes." There are universal laws that govern psychic phenomena, just as there are laws that control light waves, cosmic rays, and the invisible phenomena that propel pictures and music in space, that appear on our TV screens and which we see and hear with our physical senses.

Psychic phenomena work on the same principle of atomic vibration as those which govern our ability to see color and physical objects. There is an entire invisible universe which man cannot see with his physical eye, just as there is an entire range of the spectrum, above and below man's vision, which exists but which cannot be seen by the human eye.

You can choose the events that make the future

If you adhere faithfully to the laws that govern psychic phenomena, you can certainly know the general pattern and trend of your future life. You can be guided the rest of your life to the pattern of events that you choose for your future. You can know the future because you will know how to pick the events that make up that future, either consciously or subconsciously.

Example: A man drinks too much, gets into a car, drives that car and kills someone in an accident. Was this just an accident, or was it a predetermined event which the man's subconscious mind chose to punish him for something he had done in the past?

169

There is now scientific proof that man not only shapes his future destiny with his conscious and subconscious minds, but also that he chooses the events his soul seems to need, and that he chooses the events that will discipline him and punish him, if he has erred or, as religion calls it, sinned. Also, he chooses the events that reward him if he has obeyed the mental, moral, ethical, social, and spiritual laws of the universe.

In the above hypothetical case of the drunkard who kills a man (literally true in thousands of cases, unfortunately), the person who drives that car when he is drunk has already predicted his future. Not only has he predicted it, he actually goes out and makes it come to pass! He is at one and the same time the judge, the jury, and the executioner or jailer, carrying out the predetermined act and consequent punishment, because he feels he has a psychic need for being punished.

There is sufficient proof that drinking and driving don't mix: sixty thousand dead and a million injured each year constitute that proof. Therefore, any person who deliberately gets drunk, or even drinks moderately, and gets into a car to drive, has already predicted the future that might be his.

A recent example of this type of indiscriminate action was that of a judge's son, in New York City, who drove while he was allegedly drunk, and had an accident in which five persons were killed. He was exonerated by his father's associate judges in a five minute hearing, but later action by the district attorney tried to punish him for his crime; however, the courts held that he could not be tried twice for the same offense. This does not mean that the boy will go unpunished; the universal law of Justice is at work, and the results are assured; he will be sick mentally or physically, or both, and will undoubtedly have a tragic ending—all predetermined, or predicted, if you will, by his choice of thoughts and actions that determine his future.

In fact, we can even go so far as to say that man's invention of the destructive atom bomb was the result of his mass consciousness of guilt because of wars which have killed millions, mass starvation, greed, selfishness, discrimination, and other universal crimes, making it imperative that man create the means for his future punishment and even destruction, if he persists in violating God's and nature's laws.

You can predict your future by the creative thinking processes of your own mind. By studying your past thoughts and actions you will have a pretty accurate gauge as to what your future will be.

How the human psyche knows its future

Another example of how the human psyche knows pretty much how to shape the future destiny it requires for the completion of its life function is the fact that, when a child is born to a family, they begin immediately to plan its future. They start a college fund to be sure the child will become well educated; they determine he shall be a doctor, lawyer, architect, accountant, or politician, depending on what the father's profession is; they start the shaping process of that child's mind for that particular destiny, from the very first breath he draws. Then, when that child begins the unraveling process of the future which his parents chose and predetermined, the child comes into that pattern of events that has been set for him.

How nature utilizes prediction

When we look at the cycles of nature, we can well see how nature utilizes this art of prediction or prophecy of the future. When winter comes it is difficult for us to realize that it will ever be springtime again. And yet the earth has already foreseen that phenomena of springtime. You can, even when there is snow upon the ground, predict with accuracy that there will be leaves on the trees and roses in your garden. You can predict this with as much certainty as the fact you will draw your next breath; in fact, with more certainty, because you know that this is a part of the pattern which is involved in the cosmic thinking which is a part of God's omniscience. When you once learn how to think cosmically and channel the Cosmic Mind of God, what Emerson calls the Over Soul of the universe, then you know the events of the future, not only in nature, but in your own life.

Even when the barrenness of winter seems to blight your life, you know that love will blossom and bless your life, as certainly as you prepare for the advent of spring. You will be able to predict that business success will be yours, when you have laid the foundation for success; you do this by planting the causes in your mind for the effects you want in your outer life and experiences.

Using the law of cause and effect

This is all there is to the law of cause and effect: mental action and physical reaction. This is how we are able to accurately predict the future. We put thoughts of health, happiness, success, and fulfillment into our conscious and subconscious minds, and then under this law of action and reaction these thoughts begin their process of externalizing in our lives to produce the effects we desire in our destinies.

Wilde said, "The gods we worship write their names across our faces."

In other words, the things we think, the things we desire, the type of person we are, stamps an indelible mark upon our faces and an invisible but definite mark upon our destiny. Look at the faces of your friends, and see how accurate the above is. If they are joyous, optimistic, pleasant people, their faces reflect brightness and beauty and serenity; but if they have a miasmic pall of disaster, problems, fears, worries, hatreds, and anxieties in their personalities, you can readily sense this. People tend to avoid such crepe-hangers and prophets of doom and seek out those who have a cheerful exterior and a bright expression.

The people who have such negative thoughts as described above usually have all types of problems and misfortunes. They have already set the stage for the fulfillment of a negative destiny. They have problems at home, their marriages turn out wrong, they lose their jobs, they are always broke, and their friends and relatives desert them.

Why what you are speaks loudly

Emerson said: "What you are speaks so loudly I cannot hear what you say."

This means the human psyche which reveals itself in a person's external self. A poverty of consciousness shows itself in a person's physical appearance, the slouch of his shoulders, the expression on his face. Even the way he talks reveals to the world that he is already pre-doomed to failure and misery.

Conversely, if your consciousness is rich and elevated, you will reveal to the world a success attitude that will rapidly take you to the heights.

The making of a multi-millionaire

Example: In the early part of the twentieth century, a seventeen-year-old boy named Cyrus Eaton met the late John D. Rockefeller, Sr. Rockefeller felt something psychically about the boy and offered to help him by making him an office boy in his firm in Cleveland. There was a feeling that this young man would one day be a great success. Rockefeller carefully planted his own success principles in the boy's mind and taught him the value of honesty, thrift, perseverance, and morality. Gradually Cyrus Eaton went out on his own to conquer the world. Anyone could have predicted his future with accuracy by merely observing the functioning of his mind and his outer actions. In a few years' time this man, still young, had built seven power plants for which he was offered two million dollars cash. He went on to become one of the world's richest men.

We proclaim our future destiny as definitely as though a herald went before us, trumpeting it to the world. This is done through our thoughts, words, and acts, and nothing can change that pattern which we set mentally for ourselves.

What are the laws of psychic phenomena, then?

Just as your present is the future of yesterday, so tomorrow will be the future of today. Just as the thoughts and actions of yesterday shaped today, so too the thoughts and events of today are shaping the future that you will inherit.

How the laws of psychic phenomena can help you

Study this point very carefully, for upon it will hinge your entire future destiny. The foundation you are now laying for your future work, romance, social life, financial security, and leisure time will determine what kind of future you will have. The law of cause and effect, action and reaction, must work in your life as it works in all of nature. Let us examine some of the ways in which these laws of psychic phenomena work

1. Honesty and hard work. You may see no connection between honesty and hard work and a future successful life, but there is a very real one. This is the mental cause or law which is behind all success. If you violate this law and try to build on dishonesty or laziness, you will be able to predict instantly that you will reap a future destiny shorn of success.

The story is told of the head of a Stock Exchange who had been worth millions but who went to jail for fraud. A friend of his visited him in prison one day and found him sewing a pile of burlap bags. He asked, "What are you doing, sewing?"

The former Exchange head replied, "No, reaping."

In the days when this man had a mansion on Long Island, chauffeur-driven limousines, and millions of dollars, no one would have dared predict he would one day go broke and land in jail for fraud! But this man's own psychic nature could have predicted this unfortunate destiny. He violated the laws of the universe and practiced fraud, which is dishonesty, and cheated people out of their hard-earned money. He had to pay the price with dishonor, imprisonment, loss of his fortune, and utter disgrace for his family and himself. Any astute person, knowing the basic principles under which this man operated, could have predicted accurately his disastrous future.

The Bible states this law: "They have sown the wind, and they shall reap the whirlwind."

Byron also speaks of this ability of man to know the future he shall inherit by the mental seed he plants:

> The thorns which I have reap'd are of the tree
> I planted; they have torn me and I bleed.
> I should have known what fruit would
> spring from such a seed.

Plant the right seed: reap the right crop

If you plant the right mental seed, you will reap the right crop of Destiny. The two go together, like the simple mathematical equation which states two and two make four. No matter how you try, the result can never be five.

2. As you shape your thoughts today, so you are shaping your future. Your thoughts should be shaped as follows: in the pattern of kindness and friendship—this will win friends and people will be willing to help you; in the pattern of goodness and truth—anyone who is good will inevitably be accurately judged by the world and will receive his just rewards eventually. Truth is a spiritual as well as a moral law. If you are true to your ideals, true to yourself, and tell the truth in life, you can definitely predict that you will inherit a future that will reflect health, happiness, peace, and prosperity. In psychology we know that people who habitually lie gradually become mentally and physically sick. You cannot violate this vital law of nature. Be true to yourself and your life will gradually radiate peace and happiness and fulfillment.

3. Choose the situations and people you want in your future. Then work toward taking steps to make these conditions come to pass in your life. Just as you cannot have a crop of apples until you have planted the seed first, so too you cannot have a destiny of success or happiness until you have chosen the situations and people you want to inhabit your future.

Are you associating with people of a high caliber, or do you choose people who are of low mental standards? We are judged by the world by the friends we keep. "Show me a man's friends, and I will tell you what he is," is a true saying. You must consciously choose the people and situations that you want to inhabit your future. This is predicting the future as accurately as any human being can do so.

The caterpillar weaves a cocoon and goes to sleep, only to awaken, a golden-winged butterfly. Something in that little crawling creaure's nature predicted he would be a butterfly. Know the results you want to attain. Find the dream within, then start today to take the first steps to make that dream come to pass in the outer world.

Other points about psychic phenomena

1. Psychic phenomena work best for people who practice receiving impulses from the higher mind within them. Make it a point to retire into the silence for a few moments each day,

and sit and ask for guidance as to how to solve your problems. Ask for information as to how to make more money. Direct this higher mind to give you inventions, stories, compositions in music that might make you rich.

2. If you want to project thoughts to other minds, sit quietly in the silence and hold the person's face in your mind with whom you wish to communicate. Then speak the person's name and convey your message just as you would if he were there in person. Many times you can imprint the minds of your boss, your landlord, some person you want to reach with some special message, and they will, in turn, receive your message through their own higher mind.

3. Study the pattern of your past thinking and past actions and see how they produced the things you are now doing. If you want to change this pattern and have a different future from the past, you must first change the pattern of your thinking from negative to positive. Start seeing yourself as successful and healthy and happy, and soon this pattern will express itself in your body and your environment.

4. Bear in mind the law of the harvest: "As ye sow, so shall ye reap." And be sure to sow in the field of Destiny only those thoughts and actions which you wish to come back to you in an abundant crop. Be kind, and others will respond with kindness; be loving, and you will attract love. Be generous, and you will always be provided for. Be forgiving, and you will win the admiration and respect of the world.

5. Obey the spiritual laws and you can predict that you will always attract a future destiny that is fortunate. The spiritual laws are simple, basic principles which society builds on. You cannot lie or cheat or steal. You cannot commit adultery, or steal another's husband or wife, without paying the penalty. You cannot be careless and shiftless, lazy or inefficient, without reaping the bitter crop of failure and misery. These are basic spiritual and moral laws which all the great philosophers and prophets have taught humanity. When you apply them to your own life, you can serenely sit back and await your destiny; you will already know what you will attract, for you have fol-

lowed the laws of the universe and these laws will operate inexorably to produce the destiny you have already predicted for yourself by your thoughts and actions.

Summary of law fourteen

Man can know his future through the invisible laws of psychic phenomena. The subconscious mind can be trained to choose the events that make up the future. How man punishes himself through his evil deeds. The creation of the atomic bomb for mass murder is punishment for these universal crimes perpetrated by man. The past, present, and future represent one unit in time and space. The law of sowing and reaping. The choice of destiny in shaping one's destiny. The laws under which psychic phenomena work.

Law Fifteen

How to Possess Forever the Ten Golden Keys to the Secrets of the Universe

The secrets of the universe can be yours if you once know the keys to unlock the hidden doors to universal wisdom. Great geniuses of the past used ten golden keys to unlock the doors to the hidden treasures of the universe. The secrets of the entire universe, from the building of an atom to the creation of a vast solar system such as ours, are all contained in the Cosmic Mind of God.

When you once understand this Cosmic Mind, which operates in and through you, as well as in the universe, you will become a creative genius. The laws of the invisible will obey your imperious commands, and events in your life will shape themselves to your bidding.

First, let us understand the three attributes which the Cosmic Mind possesses. They are:

1. *Omniscience:* All-knowing, all-wise.
2. *Omnipotence:* Unlimited power; all-powerful.
3. *Omnipresence:* Being present in all places at the same time.

When you once learn how to tap the power of the Cosmic Mind, you too will possess its powers of Omniscience, Omnipotence, and Omnipresence.

The realm of the absolute

It is in the realm of the absolute that this Cosmic Mind resides. When you once learn how to tap this higher power you will work in the realm of the absolute, and life will obey your commands and yield to you her most priceless possessions.

179

How to summon the magic genie within your mind

You know the story of Aladdin's Lamp, and the Magic Genie in the fairy story. When Aladdin rubbed this magic lamp, the Magic Genie appeared and carried out any order that Aladdin gave him. Strangely enough, you too possess a Magic Genie within your own higher mind, that part of you where the Cosmic Mind of God reveals the secrets that underlie the universe.

The genes within your body carry the hidden secrets of how to build a perfect human being in nine months' time. When you mate with a member of the opposite sex, these genes transmit their amazing secrets for the color of the hair, the shape and size of the body, the height, and weight of the future person; all these secrets are hidden in the invisible genes that are transmitted to the new cell which begins life.

Gregor Mendel, an Austrian geneticist, first discovered the law which bears his name. This law states that all human genes have this mystical knowledge locked up within their structure: the racial memories, the method for constructing the body and its organs, the Cosmic Blueprint of God Himself, is there within the human organism and is capable of being transmitted from one person to another.

You may tap this higher power

You may tap this higher power and possess some of the omniscience of God Himself in shaping your destiny and forming the events which you wish to make up your future. How can you tap this higher power of the Creative Mind of God? By putting your mind in tune with His Cosmic Mind, and by being in tune with the universal forces that rule all creation. The qualities of this Infinite or Cosmic Mind of God are perfection and creativity.

When you use the ten golden keys we are now studying you can open the secret doors of consciousness that give you some of God's omniscience, omnipotence, and omnipresence.

THE FIRST GOLDEN KEY: VISION

Vision means more than seeing with the physical eye and brain. It also means the ability to foresee something, as through mental acuteness. The mental images which your mind is capable of seeing also represent a form of vision.

Let us examine this quality of the Cosmic Mind in relation to the great discoveries of past history.

What if a Magic Genie had appeared to mankind a hundred years ago and said, "I shall give you the power to create the following things:

"An instrument with eyes that see through solid objects.

"Ability to project man's mind to distant places and see what is happening there.

"Wings that cause one to fly, like a bird.

"Power to see those who have been dead for years, and to hear their voices, as well as to see them in color.

"An instrument from which music and voices would issue.

"A machine that could count, add, multiply, talk, and write.

"A magic eye that could penetrate the heavens and see millions of miles into space.

"A giant eye that could cause one to see things which were invisible and unseen by the human eye.

"The ability to swim under water for hours without emerging.

"The ability to harness the power of the sun and use it to run motors."

Would not mankind have rejected such a Magic Genie as being deluded, and instantly have ordered its extinction?

Do you recognize in the above list of things the following:

The X ray: eyes that see through solid objects.

Television: projecting man's mind to distant places and seeing what happens there.

The airplane: wings that cause one to fly like a bird.

Motion pictures: the power to see those who have been dead for many years.

Radio: the instrument from which music and voices may be heard.

Adding machines, computers, teletype machines, that can count, add, multiply, talk, and write.

Telescope at Palomar: the giant eye that can penetrate the heavens and see millions of miles into space.

The electron microscope: a giant eye that can see things which are invisible.

Submarine: power to swim under water.

Solar battery: the harnessing of the power of the sun.

Expand Your Vision: Change Your World. In the moment that you expand your vision you will change the world for yourself. Actually, the outer world will *not* change, but you will change in relation to the world. You will begin to see unlimited opportunities for your good around you. You will begin to realize people are channels to wonderful opportunities, instead of being obstacles to your progress.

A philosopher once said, "Every man takes the limits of his own field of vision for the limits of the world."

Expand your vision today and begin to envison the things you would like to have, the things you want to do, the people who could help you, and then confidently proceed with your plans for the future, knowing that the unlimited horizons of your mind will be an open invitation to the great experiences of life.

THE SECOND GOLDEN KEY: DESIRE

To desire something is to long for it, to crave it, to ask for it. Desire is the emotion that is given to man to help him attract the conditions he requires to fulfill his life.

You can unlock doors to the treasures of the universe if you will use desire correctly. There is such a thing as desiring too much too soon, and this is called greed or selfishness, but when you have moderate desires, this golden key can open many wonderful doors for your future good.

It was this strong emotion of desire that caused Columbus to find new worlds through his explorations.

Henry Ford gave the world reasonable cars because of this desire to help the world. Incidentally, it enriched him personally also. When he died he left five hundred million dollars and the Ford Foundation which has given great benefits to the world.

Albert Schweitzer had a desire to heal humanity and it led to his wonderful work with the Africans in the jungles.

Always latent in every great creative act of life there is this powerful and stimulating emotion of Desire. You may not like the situations you find yourself in and you may want to change them. How can you do so with certainty that they will change? Hold a strong desire for another job, and you will be forced to take the steps that lead to this better job. Hold a desire within your mind for a home of your own, and you will eventually attract it.

Begin today to shape your thinking in the direction of your desires. You will soon find the old negative mold of lack and limitation, loneliness and misery, fear and worry, problems and anxieties, changing under the impetus of your desires into the new pattern of your Desires.

The Rubáiyát of Omar Khayyám speaks of this heart's desire in these beautiful and inspiring words:

> Ah love! could you and I with him conspire
> To grasp this sorry scheme of things entire,
> Would not we shatter it to bits—and then
> Re-mold it nearer to the heart's desire!

Your mind possesses this power of re-molding life to your heart's desire.

Do not be ashamed of your desires, whether they be for money, fame, power, social prestige, love fulfillment, or for worldly recognition of your gifts; these desires are healthy, normal, and are implanted in your human psyche because *they are possible of achievement*.

Only one warning about Desire: do not make yourself miserable by desiring too much. And be willing to be patient and wait for the fulfillment of your desires, if they happen to be a bit on the extreme side. Remember, nothing is impossible for man to achieve, if he can first conceive it.

THE THIRD GOLDEN KEY: CURIOSITY

Curiosity is an innate emotion in man, which represents a deep-seated desire to learn or know about the world in which man lives. Nature has always revealed her hidden secrets to those who possess curiosity to a high degree.

The great healing drug, penicillin, would never have been discovered if it had not been for a scientist's enormous curiosity. He observed some green mold on some bread one day, and wondered if it would have any effect on some germs he had in a test tube. He put some of the green mold into the tube, and when he looked at the tube later, and observed the germs under his microscope, he found that the green mold had killed the germs!

Burbank was curious as to what would happen if he attempted to cross-pollinate and graft certain fruits and vegetables. This form of curiosity led to thousands of experiments whereby he perfected nature's products and gave the world many new and wonderful edible foods, as well as lovely flowers.

Samuel Johnson said, "Curiosity is one of the permanent and certain characteristics of a vigorous intellect."

The moment you start asking the five questions of philosophy —What? Why? Where? When? and Who?—you are exercising the stimulating emotion of curiosity.

Ask of every situation in your present life these questions:

What is it leading me to?

Why am I doing this?

Where shall I go from here?

When can I take a progressive step forward?

Who can I find to help me advance my interests?

"The whole art of teaching is only the art of awakening the natural curiosity" (*Anatole France*).

THE FOURTH GOLDEN KEY: FAITH

One of the most potent forces for releasing your creative energies and stimulating your higher mind is Faith. It is literally a miracle-worker. When you once harness this magical power there is hardly anything in life that you cannot attain.

Faith first implies an underlying Cause at the basis of all creation. This first Cause we call God. We come into this world on a mystical journey, which we do not understand, and entirely on faith. The little child nursing at its mother's breast is born with faith in that source of its life and the power to sustain it. The child does not question this loving source of its creation. It has implicit faith that its needs will be met, and that the fountain of milk is awaiting its joyous arrival.

You must have the faith of a little child if you wish to harness the magical power of this great emotion. Believe in yourself, in your talents, in your ability to reach the top rung of the ladder of success. "Nothing in life is more wonderful than faith" William Osler said; "the one great moving force which we can neither weigh in the balance nor test in the crucible."

Faith stirs the chemistry of the body, stimulates the glands and causes the body to remain healthy, young, and vital. Have faith that the healing agency is within your body. Many people have faith in drugs and they are often helped, not by the drugs necessarily but by their *faith* in the drugs.

Many doctors know of this healing miracle of faith, and they often give a patient an injection of distilled water, telling him that it is morphine and will cause him to sleep. Cases have been noted where the patient described the feeling of numbness creeping up the legs, until finally he felt drowsy and went to sleep.

A belief in life can give you more life force.

A belief in sickness, old age, accident, and death, can often produce the conditions we believe in.

Example: French scientists experimented on a convict who had been convicted for murder and was to die anyway. He was strapped to a table and told that an artery in his arm was to be severed and he would bleed to death in a few moments' time. What the convict did not know was that only a superficial wound was made on the surface of his skin, and that warm water was poured over his arm, which he thought was blood. He believed he would die in a few moments, and he did. His mind killed him, because he *believed he was dying!*

Six patients in a ward in a South American hospital were paralyzed and had not walked for years. The hospital was located near a jungle. One summer afternoon a giant boa constrictor crawled up a tree and into the open window, and slowly made its way towards the paralyzed patients' beds. All six men jumped from their beds and ran from the ward! Their faith, galvanized by their physical danger, made them believe they could walk on muscles that hadn't been used for years, and they did!

Have faith in success, not failure.
Have faith in health, not sickness.

Have faith in happiness, not misery.
Have faith in riches, not poverty.
Have faith in friendship, not enmity.
Have faith in love, not hate.
Have faith in good, not evil.
Have faith in beauty, not ugliness.
Have faith in immortality, not death.

THE FIFTH GOLDEN KEY: INSPIRATION OF LOVE

Love is probably one of the most stimulating and energizing of all emotions. It has the power of life and death within its scope. A famous pediatrician was noted for his great success in saving the lives of sick little children. On each sick child's chart he wrote, "This child is to be taken up every hour on the hour and *loved*."

In cases of little orphaned children in hospitals it was noted that the death rate was unusually high until the doctors had the nurses pick the little children up and love them as a part of their daily routine. The deaths mysteriously stopped.

Life responds to love. Hate produces sickness and death. This is the invisible law of life. If you wish to unlock doors to the secrets of the universe, use this magical golden key of love daily.

Lincoln used the key of love to heal a sick nation, and his memory is revered in history. Love was the magic key used by Florence Nightingale in healing the soldiers on the battlefields, and this valiant woman raised nursing to a new high level of achievement through her noble example. Mme. Curie's love of her husband caused her to labor for twenty years to isolate healing radium. The inspiration of love built the Taj Mahal, as a memorial to a Ruler's wife. This is one of the loveliest of all buildings in the Far East.

Richard M. Milnes wrote of love:

> He who for love hath undergone
> The worst that can befall,
> Is happier thousandfold than one
> Who never loved at all.

Practice the art of love daily. To help heal the negative conditions of your life make it a point to practice the art of love daily.

Do not wait for some propitious moment to indulge this positive emotion. Look for occasions where you can hold a loving thought towards some friend or relative. Search each day for some person for whom you can do a loving, thoughtful act. Love is more than physical expression of the biological urge. It has many facets and forms. There is the devotion and love one has for his parents. Then there is love of your mate, your children, your relatives. This is a different degree of love, it's true, from the love you may show strangers or have for the world, but any degree of love, when it is expressed daily, will help enhance your personality and give power and drive to your mental, physical, and spiritual energies.

Do Not Hate Anyone. Make it a practice not to hate anyone, for any degree of hatred has its repercussions in your body and poisons the body cells and makes you sick. If you find yourself hating some person who has wronged you, try to forgive that person, even if you cannot love him, and release him to God for his just rewards or punishment. This then relieves you of the burden of hate, and the harmful effect of this powerful emotion on your mind and body.

Many people are in mental institutions because they allowed hate to dominate their minds. Many people have accidents because they hate some person, and this sets up a destructive reflex action which tries to destroy them. See the harmful effect of hate in a Hitler's mind! You will realize then that you cannot hate any person. In fact, if you are wise you will not even hate your job or your limited conditions in life, or the poverty which afflicts you, but you will transmute this negative emotion into a positive one of desiring to better your circumstances. This will lead you to take constructive steps to change your entire life and remove the conditions which you hate.

God Is Love. The Bible defines God as love. When you express love in your personality you will have a quality of the Divine which will make everyone who knows you admire and respect you.

The attributes of love are understanding, compassion, and forgiveness. Later, when we study the effect of the positive and negative emotions on your mind and body, you will see why you must fortify yourself with love and its attributes. "Better is a dinner of herbs where love is, than a stalled ox and hatred therewith" (Prov. XV: 17).

THE SIXTH GOLDEN KEY: KNOWLEDGE

The Chinese have a saying, "Man with education seems to always have good luck." Education is simply the accumulation of knowledge. And knowledge is the fact or state of knowing. Nature yields her greatest blessings and reveals her priceless secrets to those who have taken the time and bother to add to their knowledge, either from observation, experience, by following the precepts laid down by others, or through the study of books.

When we have knowledge, we should have wisdom, for wisdom is merely the quality of being wise through the knowledge that we have accumulated. Even the Bible speaks of the importance of getting wisdom (Prov. 4:5-9):

> Get wisdom, get understanding: forget it not; neither decline from the words of my mouth. Forsake her not, and she shall preserve thee: love her, and she shall keep thee. Exalt her, and she shall promote thee: She shall bring thee to honour, when thou dost embrace her. She shall give to thine head an ornament of grace: a crown of glory shall she deliver to thee.

Knowledge Is Power. It is not physical power that rules the world; it is mental and intellectual power. A man is worth only a few cents an hour for his labor, but for his ideas and mental concepts he can command millions. A college education can give one knowledge, but not necessarily wisdom. Wisdom only comes from experience or the application of the knowledge we have absorbed from books. When you are armed with knowledge you will have the power to choose the events of your life with wisdom, and you will be able to overcome obstacles and solve problems better.

Knowledge Applied to Vast Areas. Man's scientific knowledge spreads over a vast area of the world in which he lives. We should be aware of this so we can conduct our studies in a scientific and progressive manner, and accumulate as much knowledge as possible about the world. Following are some of the main branches of knowledge which science has explored and catalogued:

ASTRONOMY: deals with cosmic and stellar systems and their function, origin, and composition.

GEOLOGY: deals with the formation and composition of the earth and its history over millions and even billions of years.

PHYSICS: deals with the atomic structure of matter, and how energy is converted into matter and matter into energy.

PHYSIOLOGY: deals with the body, its structure and function.

PSYCHOLOGY: deals with man's mind, its operation and function.

PHILOSOPHY: deals with the accumulation of wisdom over the ages, and co-ordinates all of man's knowledge in all areas of life.

ANTHROPOLOGY: deals with the antiquity of the ages and man's origin.

ARCHEOLOGY: deals with the expanse of past history, cultures of ancient times, and the exploration of buried cities.

SOCIOLOGY: deals with man's relationship to others.

THEOLOGY: deals with religion and the nature of God.

Select Areas of Interest. No man can hope to possess all knowledge. The wise man will select those areas of knowledge in which he is interested and obtain as much information as he can on those, rather than trying to do the impossible and be brilliant in all fields of knowledge. For instance, you might be interested in psychology, philosophy, sociology, and physics, but only mildly interested in astronomy or geology or physiology. You can study the first four subjects intensively, but only take up the latter three more casually.

If your formal education is finished and you are an adult who has no desire to return to the classrooms of day schools or evening schools, there are several sources open to you where you may obtain specialized knowledge in any of the categories listed above.

The public libraries are vast repositories of man's past and present wisdom. You should belong to your local library and make frequent use of it all your life. You should study the newspapers carefully in the sections dealing with books, to discover new books which are published and which might interest you.

What Great Men Have Said of Knowledge. Following are some

statements by great men of history who have spoken glowingly of the value of wisdom and knowledge. Let their injunctions become your password to mental power.

I take all knowledge to be my province.

Bacon

For knowledge, too, is itself a power.

Bacon

To be conscious that you are ignorant is a great step to knowledge.

Disraeli

The only good is knowledge, and the only evil ignorance.

Diogenes

He who knows others is learned:
He who knows himself is wise.

Lao-Tse

And seeing ignorance is the curse of God,
Knowledge the wing wherewith we fly to heaven.

Shakespeare

Know thyself.

Socrates

Knowledge, in truth, is the great sun in the firmament.
Life and power are scattered with all its beams.

Webster

Learning is an ornament in prosperity, a refuge in adversity, and a provision in old age.

Aristotle

THE SEVENTH GOLDEN KEY: COURAGE

What courage it took for man to rise from his lowly origin in caves to the marvels of the space age where he circles the globe in eighty minutes at speeds of seventeen thousand miles per hour!

There is something divine in man's soul which causes him to aspire ever onward and upward in his evolutionary spiral from the primitive to the celestial mind.

Creative Power in Bold Action. Perhaps in your own life you would have achieved more if you had been more daring, more courageous. In a study of over ten thousand lives of great men of history I have found that fortune favors the bold!

Ovid said, "Fortune and love befriend the bold."

How true this is! You may have a magnificent idea for making more money, inventing something valuable, composing a new song, painting a great picture, or going into some big business, but your timid, fearful nature will whisper, "Who are you to think you can do anything that big!" Instantly, when you experience this type of discouragement, either from your own mind or from your friends and relatives, the inspirational and creative power of your higher mind departs, like the air from a deflated balloon.

If your higher mind gives you creative ideas of this type, do not question them, but boldly prepare yourself to take the next steps to the fulfillment of your aspirations. It is best not to tell too many people about your great ideas or dreams, for they may be inclined to laugh at them. All great geniuses had to meet this type of discouragement in the past. Seldom did anyone believe in their dream or encourage them. They had to go it alone.

Be Daring to Be Successful. A man with little talent but with daring and courage has a bigger chance of being successful than a person with great talent and little courage.

"When moral courage feels that it is in the right," said Leigh Hunt, "there is no personal daring of which it is incapable."

You can deliberately develop courage by facing up to your problems instead of evading or avoiding them. Make it a point each day from now on to do something that requires courage. Telephone for an appointment for that new job; see someone you are trying to sell an idea to. Face your boss and ask him for the raise in salary you deserve. He can do no more than say "no."

Attack and Overcome. Attack some bad habit you may have at once, and at least *try* to overcome it. The ganglia, a mass of nerve cells from which nerve impulses are transmitted from your brain to the muscles and nerves of your body, are strengthened and stimulated every time you make a mental decision to do something that requires courage. Soon, as you build mental habits of strength, decision, and action, you will find yourself becoming mentally, morally and spiritually strong enough to overcome all the negative conditions which may have been hindering your progress.

THE EIGHTH GOLDEN KEY: ACTION

All the mental resolve in the world does absolutely no good unless you are driven to some kind of action. You can dream of success for an eternity and never achieve it until and unless you are inspired enough to take physical action to achieve it.

Action is the first law of the universe. Atomic motion or action is at the heart of all creation. Duplicate this law of action in nature and you will have set your feet on that first rung of the ladder of success.

Dreams of Conquest. Many men had dreamed of conquering new worlds before Columbus, and some daring ones did make great voyages of discovery, but Columbus took bold action in enlisting the aid of Queen Isabella for his voyages of discovery, and he succeeded where others failed.

Franklin suspected that electricity was in the air about him, but until he took that first action to put a key at the end of a kite during a thunderstorm, there was no proof that this was a scientific fact.

All of Edison's many inventions and discoveries followed mental action first; then the physical form of action brought these creative ideas from the labyrinth of his mind to the outer world of reality and gave us the electric light, the phonograph, and the first movie camera.

Take That First Giant Step. Take that first giant step towards your destiny, and the other steps will all be easier.

> Let us then be up and doing,
> With a heart for any fate;
> Still achieving, still pursuing,
> Learn to labor and to wait
>
> *Longfellow*

What of that novel you've always intended to write? The first form of action is mental, the decision you want to write. The second step must be physical. Sit down and begin. How? By putting the first words down on that paper. I have found that if you just start with anything, copying words from a dictionary, writing out the alphabet, anything that starts you in the creative flow of mental action, you will begin, and then the subconscious mind takes over and finishes for you.

What of that brilliant idea you have for an invention? It seems difficult because you have not taken that first step to bring it out into the open.

What of the idea you have for a mail order business? You may not have the capital to begin now, but you can start mental action by studying your subject, looking over products that you wish to sell, reading books in the library on mail order selling. Anything that starts you in some form of action leads to the fulfillment of your original idea.

Well Begun Is Half Done. A saying, "Well begun is half done" is a truism. Do not let your mind be paralyzed by inaction or fear or by wondering if you can finish something you once start. The very momentum that you gain by starting the action will assure your carrying it through to its conclusion. One step at a time will eventually lead you to the end of the longest journey, but if you never take that first step, you will never achieve the fulfillment of your innermost dream.

THE NINTH GOLDEN KEY: PATIENCE

One of the most valuable of our golden keys to greatness and achievement is patience. It may not seem important at first glance, but if you study the lives of the great men of history carefully, you will find that every one of them had this virtue. Nothing ever matures overnight. There is a law in nature which states that everything must evolve from a central idea or germ. If you plant wheat you do not expect to reap the crop overnight. It must follow the law of nature and will only evolve and produce an abundant crop in its own time and season.

The Law of Cycles. There is a law of cycles in all nature which decrees that all forms of creation shall have their beginning, their growth, their maturity, and their end. These four successive steps must exist in all things you do in your life also. The beginning of your idea for future progress is like planting the seed; then there must be a certain time allowed for growth, for the maturity, and then the conclusion of the idea, or the flowering of it and the producing of the harvest you wish to reap. When you once start any creative action, you must school yourself in patience to await the fulfillment of your dream.

"He that can have patience can have what he will," Franklin said.

Practice acquiring this trait in your daily life. When waiting for a bus or streetcar or some friend who is late for an appointment, mentally repeat the following statement over and over to yourself: "I now exercise patience. I refuse to yield to thoughts of irritation and annoyance. All things pass, under the law of passing time. Therefore this moment will also pass. I now grow calm, poised, and peaceful. My mind is serene and no external force has the power to destroy this inner citadel of strength and patience."

THE TENTH GOLDEN KEY: DETERMINATION

With this golden key you may unlock many doors to the hidden secrets of the universe. Nature only yields her priceless treasures to those who have the ability to stick with something they have started.

A man was prospecting for gold in the Nevada desert. He found a mine and opened a small vein of gold which yielded enough for him to buy machinery to explore further. After a while the vein of gold ran out and he became so discouraged that he sold his equipment to a junk man and gave him the deed to the mine.

The junk man went on with the digging and two feet from where the former owner had given up digging, he discovered a pocket of gold that yielded forty thousand dollars. Eventually he made five million dollars from that gold mine!

Do Not Give Up Easily. Make it a point, throughout your life, not to give up easily. When you once have faith in something and you start action to bring it about, then persevere and persist until you achieve it. Your mind will tell you whether a thing is possible of achievement or not. If you really believe it, something within your mind will vibrate in tune with that belief, and your determination is all that is needed to bring your idea to complete fulfillment.

Webster said of the power of the human mind: "Mind is the great lever of all things; human thought is the process by which human ends are ultimately answered."

If you give up too soon, however, this power of your mind to express itself creatively in successful action cannot be proved. Remember your law of the harvest: plant the seed first in your mind, then give it time to germinate, then it must fulfill its cycle under the law of growth, and this is the period of time you must be determined to wait. The harvest is sweet, and well worth the time and effort expended to bring your great ideas to maturity.

Armed with Truth. You are now armed with truth, for your joyous adventure into tomorrow and all of the tomorrows to come. These golden keys represent truth in its triumphant march to goal-achievement. They can be used every day to unlock secret doors to the treasures of the universe.

During the following weeks make it a point to consciously use one or more of these golden keys in your everyday activity. *Example:* For Monday try to use two golden keys in your work and your activities. Take the first two keys, Vision and Desire. Look about you and see how you can use vision to improve the work you are doing. With vision goes imagination and visualization. Employ these tools on that day to see how many different forms of action you can begin with Vision as your guiding light.

Then on that same day use the key of Desire. Ask yourself, What do I desire most this day? Begin to analyze your desires in terms of achievement. Are you doing the things now that can lead to the fulfillment of your desires? If not, why not? Then set to work to take the first step to arouse greater desire, knowing that this key will unlock other doors to achievement. What do you desire? Money? Fame? Friends? Love? Health? Peace of Mind? Travel? Accomplishment? Recognition? Ego-expression through your creative gifts?

As you analyze each of these points, apply the key of Desire and see if it does not help you express your innermost desires in a more concrete way.

Then, on Tuesday, take Curiosity and Faith and use these golden keys all day in your activities, seeing how many things you can unfold through these two keys. Keep this up all week and practice with all ten golden keys, and keep coming back to them in the weeks ahead until you have channeled their power in every act of your life.

Summary of law fifteen

There are ten golden keys that geniuses of all ages have used for greatness. With these keys man may tap the Cosmic Mind of God in His universe. Vision needed to explore the hidden universe. Desire, the emotion that helps attract treasures and fulfillment. The five questions that stimulate the emotion of curiosity. Faith, the invisible miracle-worker. Man must practice the higher aspects of the emotion of love daily. Knowledge is power. Courage and bold action needed for overcoming. The giant step that leads to greatness. Patience and determination, the two Golden Keys that lead to achievement. Nature's law of cycles and how it works for you.

Law Sixteen

How to Create Your Own Miracles Through the Inner Power

What is a miracle? It is an event or an action that apparently contradicts known scientific laws. It is also defined in the dictionary as a remarkable thing. By this definition some of the greatest forces in the world, which you may invoke at will and duplicate, would be considered miracles.

Creative mind in itself is a miracle which science cannot even begin to understand or explain. The process by which you see and hear baffles the human mind. The ability to discern color, to interpret sounds of words or music, and to classify the millions of sense impressions you receive every day, is something so profound and mysterious that only God knows the true secret back of these miraculous forces.

How to harness this miracle power

However, even if we do not fully understand this miracle power, we may harness it to do our bidding and use it for the everyday miracles we wish to achieve.

Just as God cannot be seen in His universe, except through the evidence of His creation, so too, you may not be able to see this miracle-working power of God's creative mind, but you can harness its wonderful creativity and cause it to work especially for you and your good.

Whitman said, "The whole theory of the universe is directed unerringly to one single individual—namely You."

So far as the universe is concerned, all creation was made for you, and all God's gifts were created for you to use and enjoy.

197

When you are aware of this you can enhance your enjoyment of life a hundred percent. You can also begin to use some of these miracle powers in your own life to unfold new gifts and talents, and to give you a superior wisdom which will help you acquire possessions, power, and even great wealth.

Using the miracle of your mind

Just accept the first of these miraculous powers at face value; the miracle of your mind. Every second it performs feats that are absolutely astounding. Did you ever concentrate on just this power of your mind alone for an hour a day and try to develop it? You will be amazed at what astounding storehouses of reserve power there are within your mind.

Sit for an hour each day for the next week and concentrate on three aspects of your mental power:

1. Your imagination
2. Your memory
3. Your five senses: sight, touch, feel, smell, hearing, and taste.

Let your imagination release its various images for your personal life. Imagine yourself in work other than what you are doing. Imagine yourself writing a book, any kind of book; imagine yourself selling real estate, or insurance. Follow an imaginative pattern through from its inception to its conclusion.

Example: Look at a picture of a beautiful home in some home magazine or newspaper, and then visualize yourself owning it. See yourself living in it, entertaining your friends, furnishing its various rooms and otherwise doing the pleasurable things one associates with a home.

Another exercise for your imagination is this: look at some invention in your home—telephone, radio, TV, vacuum cleaner, refrigerator or electric iron—and try to imagine yourself inventing it originally, or improving some aspect of the present instrument. Many people have discovered or invented new things through this exercise of imagination.

Exercise for your memory

At the end of each day for one full week, run the events of your day through your mind, as one would run a movie film through a projector. Start with the time you rose in the morning. Then proceed for the full day, mirroring the main events of the day with as many details as you can recall.

Then go back over the events of your entire life and try to recall as many epochal events as you can, those events which led to major changes in your life, such as graduation from school, the time you fell in love, when you became engaged to be married, your honeymoon, the first home you lived in, the first job you got, etc. Recall as many of these main events as possible with all the details you can remember.

How to summon reserve power

By performing these mental exercises you will be working to summon reserves of mind power that lie deep within your psyche, and these will help strengthen your mind, and release creative intelligence in an orderly and systematic manner. When you need such reserves of power for any purpose in life, you will find your mind will respond quicker and more efficiently than if you have never performed such exercises. The mind is like a muscle: the more it is exercised and kept in condition, the better it responds to the demands made upon it.

Exercises for your five senses

Your enjoyment of life depends on your ability to sense with all your faculties all the subtle shades of meaning that each experience presents to you. The only contact you have with the outer world is with the five senses of touch, smell, taste, sight, hearing, and feeling. Without these man would live in a complete vacuum without ability to really know the universe in which he lives. Even Helen Keller, who was deaf, dumb, and blind, had a whole, wonderful new world opened up to her when she was able to interpret the things she could feel with her sense of touch. She says that suddenly it was as if a great golden light flamed within her and she experienced a joy in living which she had never known before. Imagine, with only the senses of touch, smell, and taste to go on, she could have such joy! Think how fortunate you are with the additional senses of sight and hearing.

To give added dimension to life, sit each day for the next week and practice for five minutes each of the five senses.

Sense of Sight: The Orientals have a system of training the student's sense of sight, and it is one of the best known to science. Look about the room with a slow, deliberate glance and see how many objects you can see in one glance. Then close your eyes and recall each object that you saw. At first you will see only a few; then gradually, as you practice, you will acquire the ability to see as many as ten or twenty. Then apply this exercise to shop windows. As you pass a store window see how many objects you can fix in your memory at one glance.

One expert, who had studied this Oriental system of concentration on the senses, could see and remember as many as one hundred objects at one single glance!

Then extend this sense of sight to other objects; for instance, a scene in nature. Look at a landscape and see its beauty and grandeur. Look at the relationship of the trees to the horizon, the highlights on the leaves, the colors and subtle shades and blendings of the various hues. Read into that landscape everything you can possibly see and hear and feel about it. You can employ all five senses in everyday life in such exercises, until your mind is so attuned to all the natural forces of the universe that you will be in complete harmony with nature and be able to use its miraculous powers more intelligently in every department of your life.

Use the same type of exercise for the sense of touch; feel various types of textured materials, with your eyes closed, and see if you can distinguish between them. Feel the luxury of silk, the smoothness of glass or porcelain, the roughness of a metal vase, the weave of an oriental rug. As you respond to these various feelings you will open complete new avenues of sensation and awareness within your mind.

Then extend this exercise to the sense of hearing and listen to beautiful music. See how many various instruments you can hear and distinguish in a symphony. Make up songs within your mind and try to hear the melody with your inner ear. Be aware of the sounds of a city at night, of morning, with the special sounds that announce an awakening city. When you go to the seashore, listen to the sound of the waves gently kissing the shore; hear the sound of a buoy bell, or a ship's whistle in the distance. Concentrate on the sense of smell in the same way and be aware of the aroma of percolating coffee, fresh baked bread, the gentle scent of perfume as someone passes you on the street. This type of practice of your mental faculties will pay rich dividends in the future.

Power of your mind greatest of all forces

Your inner life is where all the truly great powers reside. Like an iceberg which has only one-tenth of its entirety above the surface of the water, and nine-tenths submerged, so too, your mind has nine-tenths of its greatest power buried deep within your hidden psyche. Here it is that the substaining power of your subconscious and superconscious minds exist. Here it is that the seat of memory resides. Here you may tap the hidden force of divine intuition and be guided to great achievements.

Most of life's hidden forces are the most potent. For instance, steam is greater than horse power, but it is an invisible substance which seems to completely lack form or power, and yet we know that it can be harnessed to do great work. Electricity is even more potent than steam and is capable of running machines and performing miraculous tasks. Radium has many qualities that are more startling than even those of electricity, but man's mind surpasses them all, for it was through the power of man's creative mind that he was able to discover, harness, and use such things as steam, electricity, radium, and atomic power. By the application of mind power, man may use these invisible forces with astounding results and change the face of the entire world.

Implement the miracle of life

The miracle of life itself is one of the most baffling of all life's mysteries. You have it within your power to implement the life force so it flames stronger and gives you longer life and more vital energy.

To implement the miracle of life start each day with a positive affirmation that imprints power upon the cellular structure of your body. According to the latest scientific cellular theory, whatever we say with emotion and conviction imprints its quality upon the cells of the body, affecting the organs and giving us either health and vitality, or sickness, depending on the quality of the thoughts we affirm.

William James, perhaps our greatest philosopher and psychologist, said of the power of thought:

> All mental states are followed by some bodily activity of some sort. They lead to inconspicuous changes in breathing, circulation, general muscular tension and glandular or other visceral activity, even if they do not lead to conspicuous movements of the muscles in voluntary life. All states of mind, even mere thoughts and feelings are motor in their consequences.

The first thing that your thinking affects is your body. Affirm each morning this statement to imprint your life cells with more power, energy, youth, vitality, and health: *The life force now surges throughout my mind and body, giving me strength, power, energy, and perfect health. I now imprint upon every cell of my brain and body this dynamic thought:* I am LIFE—I am POWER—I am HEALTH—I am YOUNG—I am PERFECTION. I have the divine inspiration to make my life magnificent and to succeed in fulfilling my life dream.

Implement the miracle of growth

Next, in your daily practice for a period of one or more weeks, implement the miracle of growth within your mind and body. Growth is the miracle that takes a seed in the soil and perfects it and brings forth a crop in keeping with the seed. There is a law in philosophy: as within, so without. What you put into your consciousness externalizes itself in the outer circumstances of your life. Work with this Law of Growth that is in the universe and see the miracle of fulfillment blossom on your tree of life.

How to use the law of growth

1. Life is constant growth and expansion. Nature destroys that which ceases to grow and evolve. Each day add new knowledge to your mind, do new things, keep your mind youthful by being active in many fields.

2. Plant mental seed for future growth. You may not use some of the knowledge you absorb today in philosophy or psychology, such as that given in this study, but it will continue to grow and

evolve in your mind, making you stronger and producing results even years from now. Never stop planting mental seed in your garden of destiny. Absorb ideas for progress in your work, polish and perfect your personality, study public speaking so you can better express your ideas, acquire culture and social graces so you can more easily take your place with those in high places.

3. Make it a point to develop a stronger mind by building positive habits for future use. A concert pianist plays thousands of notes in a composition without once worrying about his fingering. How can he do this? Because he has spent countless hours in practicing fingering and memorizing the notes, until he has acquired the habit of playing automatically. Make it a point to build such habit patterns in your thinking and in everything you do, if you wish for more perfection and quality. Your gifts and talents will mature, if given time. Some of the great men and women in the creative arts who achieved success did it through using this principle of building positive habits.

Joseph Hergesheimer wrote for fourteen years before he sold his first story. He never stopped practicing the art of writing.

Fannie Hurst wrote for ten years and had hundreds of rejections before her first story was published.

William Inge, author of *Come Back, Little Sheba, Picnic,* and many other plays, succeeded only after practicing playwrighting for years.

Jascha Heifitz, one of the world's great violinists, practiced eight to ten hours a day for twenty years before being acclaimed as one of the most perfect technicians and one of the greatest interpretative artists of the day.

Victor Herbert, who wrote *Babes in Toyland, Ah, Sweet Mystery of Life,* and many other famous pieces of music, was forty-four before he achieved recognition. During all those years before he became famous, he was busy building habit patterns of quality, perfection, and industriousness, which later paid off with worldwide recognition.

Using the miracle of capillary attraction

One of the most mysterious forces in nature, which science cannot even begin to explain or understand, is that of capillary attraction in plants and growing things.

A seed placed in the ground seems to have the power inherent in its secret innermost self, to draw from the earth all the elements it requires for its perfect growth and evolvement. If you plant corn, wheat, appleseed, and cotton, in the same patch of soil, each will attract the elements it requires to perfect itself. There is a magnetism within the seed itself that is able to reach out and draw moisture and nourishment from the soil, the air, and the elements to cause the plant to mature and achieve the fulfillment of its destiny. Think of black soil creating white cotton, red apples, golden wheat and corn. From green grass, a cow produces white milk. These are some of the mysteries of nature which science cannot explain.

How you may duplicate this law in nature

With the power of your mind you may duplicate this law of capillary attraction and attract into your orbit of experience those persons and conditions which you need to fulfill your destiny perfectly.

You may feel inadequate and think you are isolated from the mainstream of life, and that you cannot invoke this universal law of capillary attraction, but remember that God has made provision for everything in His creation to attract what they need for its fulfillment.

See how the maple tree makes provision for its seed to find a place to grow. Nature has provided the maple seed with wings that cause it to catch a vagrant breeze and fly from the shadow of the mother tree into a sunny spot, where it can take root and grow. This is an intelligence in nature which is so great it ensures the perpetuity of the species.

Did you ever see a baby chick break out of its shell? After about twenty-one days of incubation that chick pecks with its little beak until it breaks the restraining shell and then it comes forth, a perfect chick. During its three weeks of imprisonment in the shell, the mysterious force and intelligence in nature saw to it that the chick in its embryonic stage carried its food supply with it, in the yolk and white of that egg. Anything this mysterious, that takes such care of its own, must be trusted implicitly with your destiny.

Where you are now is your supply

You may live in the midst of the desert, and yet your supply will seek you out. You may live on a farm in the midwest, and yet the law of capillary attraction will work for you to bring your right destiny to you. You know what Emerson said about the ability of man to attract his good to himself:

"If a man can write a better book, preach a better sermon, or make a better mouse-trap than his neighbor, though he builds his house in the woods the world will make a beaten path to his door."

To work this miracle of the law of capillary attraction follow this regimen:

1. Set high standards and high ideals for yourself to achieve. Do not worry about how you will achieve them; just be busy perfecting your mind, the quality of your work, the integrity of your character, the excellence of your product. Leave it to a higher power than yourself as to how you will be guided to your right place in the world. It will come, as sure as you keep working to raise your standards.

2. Find some incentive to give you the mental impetus you need to carry you to great achievement. Some have been inspired by love of their mates, families, the world, and this has given them that extra incentive they needed to achieve greatness. A desire to make money is good, but not enough; what do you want money for? If there is some concrete desire to do good with your money, it will probably come to you much quicker and easier.

3. Think of yourself as being the best of whatever it is you plan to become. Do not believe you are inferior even now, because of your limited opportunities or lack of recognition. Jim Tully, the famous author, was a hobo before he became a writer, but he was known as the King of the Hoboes.

4. Make your demands on life. Demand the best that life has to offer and do not settle for a second-rate destiny. A young man I once knew believed that he could make a success as a song writer. He learned everything he could about the business and constantly practiced the art of writing words and music. When he had written several songs he went to New York City and sought

out music publishers and record companies. Of course, he was rebuffed at every turn. He didn't give up. He cultivated secretaries in the publishing firms and record companies. He found out where the publishers lunched and made it a point to drop in casually when they were having lunch. He kept returning to the publishing firms again and again until everyone became familiar with his face. Finally his very presence became a demanding one and out of sheer desperation one of the publishers gave him an interview.

The young man came prepared. He had his demonstrated records and lead sheets of his songs ready. He played the songs and was told to come back at a later date. The appointment was a success. A decision was made to record his songs. To date he has had six songs accepted and is on the way to becoming one of our most promising younger song writers. If this young man had become discouraged along the way, if he had not made his demands on the time and attention of the publishers, he would have remained in the background all his life.

5. Have a definite goal towards which you are constantly working and change the goal to suit your needs in the years to come. If you do not have something definite towards which you are working, your efforts are apt to be spasmodic and vacillating.

In experiments with mice in a maze, scientists found that mice which were well fed and had no reason for finding their way through the maze to a place where food awaited them, did not struggle to get through the labyrinth, whereas hungry mice, who knew food was waiting for them at the end of the intricate maze, got through with greater ease.

Your goal, held constantly before your eyes, will give that spur to your ambitions which you need to meet the challenges of life and overcome the obstacles that may stand in your way.

Attaining the miracle of your divinity

The miracle of life is as nothing compared to the miracle of your true divinity. The alpha and omega of all life, the beginning and the end, are wrapped in a divine mystery which we may never fully understand. However, we may fortify ourselves in this life by the knowledge that man possesses an immortal soul, and that man is divine, created spiritually in the image and likeness of God.

Soul power is as real as mental power or physical power. To tap this hidden wellspring of divine inspiration you should practice spiritual exercises each day which give you inner strength, power, peace and poise.

Regimen for achieving spiritual power

1. Make it a point to go into silent meditation for at least half an hour each day, and meditate on the mystery of life, the nature of God, and the ultimate purpose of your own life in the scheme of things.
2. Start each day with a prayer, either the Lord's Prayer or one you make up yourself, in which you reverently talk with God, and ask Him for His Divine Blessings and guidance for that days activities. End your day with a prayer also, just before going to sleep. Thank God for the gift of life, and express your love of God.
3. Memorize the 23rd or 91st Psalm, and when you are sorely tried by life, recite these over and over until you gain your spiritual poise and peace of mind.
4. Strive to keep your mind and soul spiritually attuned to the divine laws of Good, Truth, and Love, each day. Use these three spiritual principles as your guide to better living and the building of a more perfect future.
5. Implement your faith in God each day by trying to serve humanity, and by loving God's children, as you would love God Himself. Believe in your soul's immortality, and overcome the fear of death, knowing that any intelligence which could so wisely make provision for every detail of life, and who knoweth every sparrow that falleth to earth, must certainly be trusted to have made adequate provision for your soul's continuance in an after-life.

> And when you've reached the golden summit of
>   your dreams,
> Look not back at the night you've left behind,
> For there are wondrous sights beyond the veil.

Summary of law sixteen

The miracle-working power of your creative mind. Harnessing this stupendous power for creating miracles in your life. The five senses are channels for creativity in man. Mental action leads to bodily action. Implementing the life force for better health and longer life. Use the law of growth in your personal life. Capillary attraction and how it brings fulfillment. Duplicating the laws of nature. The miracle of man's divinity. The daily regimen of living and thinking for greater spiritual power.

Law Seventeen

Channeling the Master Motives for Greater Achievement

There are six basic urges that act as master motives in compelling man to seek his destiny. When you once understand these basic urges or master motives, you may use them intelligently to give you greater impetus towards your goal. You can also use these Master Motives in understanding and controlling other people.

The six basic urges are:

1. THE LIFE URGE
2. THE HUNGER URGE
3. THE SOCIAL URGE
4. THE EGO OR POWER URGE
5. THE LOVE URGE
6. THE SPIRITUAL URGE

How to use the life urge

You can use the life urge as a master motive, and it will help you preserve your life and give you a purpose for living and achieving success.

The life urge is called self-preservation. Every living organism has this urge to live and to preserve its life. If you live for yourself alone, and do not have someone you are living and working for, this life force that preserves life grows dim. Many times, when a person has no one to love or live for, he does things that deliberately destroy him. This is known in psychosomatic medicine as the will to die. People who smoke excessively, even when they

209

know it may give them lung cancer, those who drink alcohol or take sleeping pills or other narcotics, are also indulging this will to die. They are subconsciously trying to destroy themselves for some real or fancied guilt feelings. They feel unworthy of life and are hastening their death through such immoderate and unintelligent habits.

IMPLEMENT THE WILL TO LIVE

You can implement the will to live by having something worthwhile to live for.

Here are some of the things worth living for:

1. To educate your children.
2. To protect your family and give them security.
3. To create something great to help the world.
4. To develop your gifts and talents and give them out in creative work.
5. To enjoy the companionship of other people and share with them the fruits of your thoughts and labors.

If you live just to be rich, or to become famous, you will never have as much satisfaction or completion as if you live for some definite purpose. If you wish to enjoy better health and live a long life, it is imperative that you have some big over-all goal towards which you strive. It should include one or more of the six master motives given above.

When J. P. Morgan was worth over a hundred million dollars a friend asked him why he didn't retire.

Morgan asked, "When did your father retire?"

His friend replied, "In 1908."

"And when did he die?" Morgan asked.

"In 1911," His friend said. Morgan replied, "That's the reason I don't retire."

Insurance statistics show that people who retire from their jobs begin to deteriorate mentally and physically and die within three to five years from the time of their retirement.

KEEP ACTIVE AFTER RETIRING

Even after you retire from your job in the future, keep busy doing things you enjoy, and keep your brain cells alive and active.

You will be in better health and live longer if you have such a purpose in living. You should have an avocation as well as a vocation. There should be hobbies that you can take up which keep you busy and active all your life. The brain and body cells thrive on action, as it is one of the first laws of life. Inaction and disuse cause the cells to deteriorate and lose the function for which they were created.

The hunger urge

It is obvious that the hunger urge is one of the big master motives in life. Most of man's waking hours are spent in the pursuit of money with which to buy food. This hunger urge relates to the body and its physical needs. But there are other hungers which have to do with man's intellectual needs, and with his desire for friendship, love, and companionship. These separate hunger urges will be covered in those sections of this lesson dealing with the Social Urge, the Power Urge, and the Love Urge. Man's sexual appetite is also a hunger urge, and when properly controlled can be a master motive that leads to great creative effort.

HOW TO USE THE HUNGER URGE

1. Try to control your own appetites so they do not get control of you. This is the first rule in the realm of control. When you eat or drink, or indulge any of the physical appetites, be sure to use moderation. Nothing will hurt your body if it is done in moderation. However, if the hunger urge is allowed to run wild, you will suffer from obesity, sickness, premature old age, and death.

2. You may use this hunger urge to control others for good. Do not try to influence or sell a person who is hungry. Feed him first, then make your business proposition. He will listen more readily when his hunger pains have been assuaged.

3. Be aware of the social significance of breaking bread with someone. You will note in the Bible that in most of his appearances in public, Jesus was shown eating with his disciples. There is a sense of brotherhood and unity with those who share our food. Many people who are in business know this instinctively and make some of their biggest deals at luncheons, dinners, or cock-

tail parties. When you want to bring someone closer to you, remember this point and arrange a luncheon or dinner, or cocktails with the person. You will build a sense of intimacy that you could never do in a business office.

4. As you use this hunger urge to gain control of others, be aware when someone is trying to use it to take unfair advantage of you. No contract should be signed or business deal closed under circumstances where such a person is obviously trying to ply you with drinks or an excess of food. Your will and reasoning will be lowered at such times of excesses.

The social urge

Everyone likes to be popular and well liked. The social urge is man's instinct to be gregarious and mix with his fellow mortals.

You can use the social urge as an incentive to develop a more magnetic personality and to increase your attractiveness. This social urge expresses itself as a desire to win friends and to have social acceptance.

HOW TO USE THE SOCIAL URGE

1. Let this social urge be an impetus to improve yourself mentally so that you will attract a friend with higher standards. How can you be sure that you will attract friends? There is no better formula for making friends than that given by Emerson: "If you want a friend, be a friend."

2. Develop the art of social conversation by studying voice, diction, grammar, and by reading good books and keeping up to date on current events. Choose a subject the other person is interested in, and then remember that conversation is a two-way street; do not monopolize the conversation, but give and take, by allowing the other person to participate in the discussion.

3. To expand your activities and advance your interests, remember that you live in a world of people, and most of your good will come to you through some person. Make it a point to meet as many of the right kind of people as possible. You should join some club or church group where you will be exposed to influential and important people. It is as easy to know people who are worth-

while and doing things as to waste your time on people who are shiftless and without ambition.

4. When you go on vacation, make it a point to choose a place where you can meet friends who will be valuable in the future. This does not mean you should be conniving and choose only people who are rich or important, but remember the words of the Quaker father who said to his daughter, "Daughter, marry thee not for money, but go thee where money is."

The ego or power urge

The power that motivates most people is supplied by their Egos. In psychology the Ego is defined as that part of the person's mind which makes him aware of himself. In psychoanalysis it is that part of the psyche which consciously controls the impulses of the Id. The Id, in turn, is that part of the psyche which is the source of instinctive and unconscious energy.

Most people think of the sexual nature as being the motivation for most of their acts. Certainly it plays a very big part in man's conscious and subconscious motivation, but it is not the sole determining agent in the release of instinctive and unconscious energy, as Freud once believed.

The Ego urge makes people want recognition and acceptance. The desire to have a beautiful home, a big car, a beautiful suit or dress, is the Ego urge in action. It is the thing that makes people work so hard for positions in life that represent high status.

The Ego, as used in this sense, does not mean egoism, which is selfishness and conceit. To have a personality that functions gracefully in the presence of others, it is essential that you develop the Ego or power urge.

HOW TO USE THE EGO OR POWER URGE

1. Every person instinctively desires recognition. Give this recognition to those you know. Praise them when they deserve it. Flatter your friends when they wear something new and attractive. Remember their birthdates, anniversaries, and other special events, such as Valentine's Day, Christmas, etc. Send thank-you telegrams when the occasion warrants it. How many wives have

divorced their husbands because the men forgot such important dates as anniversaries and birthdates! Not that this oversight in itself is so serious, but it is a symptom of deeper, basic character defects that makes the mate unsatisfactory in other departments of the relationship.

2. You can develop your own Ego or power urge by overcoming feelings of inferiority and inadequacy. How? By a process of self-improvement and mental development. Studying this course is evidence of the fact that you are even now building qualities of value and importance in your Ego. This type of self-improvement should continue all your life through. Study a cultural language such as French; join a dance group, where you can develop social graces; subscribe to magazines that deal with world-wide subjects and current events. Read at least an hour a day, if you can, rather than spend too much time looking at TV or movies. Such study and mental growth will improve your Ego and give you power to influence others.

3. Study your face in the mirror with various expressions on it of greed, hate, fear, worry, and other negative emotions. See how these emotions cause you to wear a mask that is unattractive and repellent?

Now change these expressions to those of hope, faith, good, love, and beauty, and see how instantly your expression changes from a negative, unattractive one, to a positive, attractive one. Add a smile to your facial expression as often as you can, and it will also add great charm to your personality. If you have defective teeth that can be corrected by dentistry, do so; it will be one of the best investments in your future good that you have ever made.

The love urge

The love urge accounts for most of man's basic drives to improve himself and the world. First, let us understand what we mean by the word "love." It can be associated with sex in marriage, but social mores demand that there be sexual expression only in marriage. This is a matter that must be dictated by each person's own conscience, as no hard and fast rule can be made in such an important area of personal relationships.

However, there can be love without sex. There is parental love, love of friends, love of country, love of one's mate in marriage, and, cosmically, love of humanity and love of God. All these forms of love can be channeled in your life and you will be greatly enriched and benefited because of this noble and powerful emotion.

HOW TO USE THE LOVE URGE

1. Love is an emotion that should be indulged daily, in the sense of the meaning we have learned above. Practice loving people who are close to you first, then extend your love to your co-workers, your boss, your landlord, and your neighbors.

When you develop a loving presence others will instantly sense it, and they will react with actions that are agreeable and friendly. Emerson said of love, "Love, and you shall be loved, for love is as mathematically just as the two sides of an algebraic equation."

2. Write down on a little filing card and carry in your purse where you can read it several times a day, these words:

"I now extend Divine Love to every person I meet today. I know they are Divine, and that God loves them, for we are all His loving children."

Also, on the same card you might write the definition for God, which is given in the Bible.

"God is love."

Then reread the New Testament, especially the part telling of the true ministry of Jesus. "A new commandment I bring unto you; that ye love one another."

3. Have a desire to share your love with some person who is close to you. A sweetheart or husband and wife, in whom you confide and who is the closest person in the world to you, will give you a greater sense of creative expression. More art, music, literature, and other forms of creative works have been done by people who loved someone than because of any other single emotion. The Taj Mahal was created in memory to the wife of one of India's great rulers.

4. Marry early in life and have a family as soon as possible. This is good advice for young people who want an incentive which will make them successful and outstanding in their fields.

Nothing releases more mental and physical energy than having your own family for whom you are working to achieve security in the future. Buy your own home, go into debt for the things you desire, such as a car and house furnishings, depending on the resourcefulness of your creative higher mind to always provide security and comfort for you and your family.

The spiritual urge

Man has a deep-seated cosmic urge within his soul to know God and to love Him more than life itself. It is the promise of immortality that lifts man above the realm of animalism and causes him to aspire to the highest pinnacles of achievement.

There are no real atheists in life, for when a man faces the unknown, in that final sleep of earth, his questing soul generally turns to the contemplation of the divine mystery, and his soul reaches out for the solace and peace that come from a belief in a higher power.

HOW TO USE THE SPIRITUAL URGE

1. Believe in God and His omniscience, omnipotence, and omnipresence, knowing that there must be some great intelligence underpinning the miracle of life.

2. Join the church of your choice and join others in worship of God, for there is a wonderful sense of security that comes from such group action in a spiritual environment.

3. Pray daily, when you start your day and when you go to bed at night, thanking God for the good things He has given you, as well as asking for guidance to a better life.

4. Have faith in the power of God to influence and direct your life. "All things are possible to him that believeth," says the Bible.

5. Practice the Ten Commandments in your daily life, and also live by the Golden Rule, "Do unto others as you would have others do unto you." Memorize the Sermon on the Mount, as this is one of the greatest sermons ever preached by Jesus, and apply the spiritual laws that it contains to your daily life.

6. Practice the spiritual virtues of love, faith, hope, charity, forgiveness, tolerance, and good, for these are the unwritten laws of spirit. It is good mental therapy to live according to these spiritual

principles, for you will know an inner sense of peace and serenity that nothing can ever disturb.

Summary of law seventeen

Six basic urges act as master motives in life: the Life Urge, the Hunger Urge, the Social Urge, the Ego or Power Urge, the Love Urge, and the Spiritual Urge. The life urge leads to self-preservation, better health and long life. The hunger urge as a means of controlling others. The social urge builds friendship with others. The power and ego urge as means of winning recognition and acceptance. Love is a creative emotion that can become one of life's dominant master motives. The spiritual urge as a means for coming closer to God and knowing cosmic security and peace of mind and soul.

Your Mystic Journey Into Future Glory

Ultimately, man reaches a point in his destiny where he has conquered the forces of life and won for himself the rich rewards and satisfying experiences for which he quests. This study of universal and mental laws, which we have undertaken together, has brought you to a point now where you can eagerly and hopefully await life's richest rewards on the mental, material, physical, and spiritual planes of consciousness.

However, you must realize, as you conclude this phase of your study with me, that material rewards and achievements are not enough in themselves. You must still continue to grow and evolve in all phases of your life and to seek out truth and wisdom in every field of future endeavor. "Man shall not live by bread alone" is a truism which applies to man's physical and material achievements. Man's eternal soul-quest for permanent values cannot end in any specific area of man's earthly experiences. It must go on continually, reflecting constant growth and evolvement mentally, physically, emotionally, and cosmically.

The beginning of a great and glorious experience

In this study of the universal and mental laws that govern and control life you have been equipped with the mental, moral, ethical, social, emotional, and spiritual values that can enrich your life and help guide you to the very pinnacles of achievement. This transitory journey through life is only the beginning of a great and glorious cosmic experience which leads man to spiritual fulfillment on this mystic journey into the future. Man can only guess as to the mystery which enshrouds the life experience. When he fully develops his consciousness he will be the recipient of divine pulsations which will help steer his ship of destiny to the harbor of self-realization and fulfillment.

Upon completion of this study and to prepare you for new and more glorious adventures in the realm of mind and spirit, let me advise you to continue your search for Truth, Knowledge, Beauty, Love, and Goodness, as a lapidary searches for precious jewels. Your growth and progress in the future will depend on how you utilize the knowledge you have gleaned from this book.

Your constant companion

Let this book be your constant companion, and renew your study of these laws and principles every few months. Then add to the spiritual treasures of your mind and soul by searching for greater wisdom and knowledge in the years ahead.

When you experience situations that might prove challenging and disturbing to your peace of mind, return to this book and refresh yourself with inspiration for living, as a weary traveler in the desert might refresh himself at an unexpected oasis. Study the contents of Law Sixteen, for instance, and once again remind yourself of the miracles you can perform through your own inner creative power.

If you find your life goal dimmed and your viewpoint restricted by problems and discouragements, refresh your mind and raise your spirits by studying once more the sixteen dynamic steps for achieving your life goal which are given under Law Five. Once again you will be given fresh impetus and inspiration to struggle upwards to your bright goal.

Stimulate your imagination anew

If you find yourself at a point in your future life where you are not demonstrating a better life, or where working conditions are not to your liking, you should turn once again to Laws Ten and Eleven, on utilizing the laws of demonstration and energizing your drive towards wealth. These Laws will once again refresh your mind and stimulate your imagination, giving new impetus to your mental and physical drive to success.

Your growth and progress should follow the laws of nature.

There must be continued evolvement of your mind; you should constantly refine your personality, idealize your thoughts, control your emotions, and spiritualize your every experience in life. You will be greatly helped in this ambitious program for future growth and expansion in every department of your life by reviewing Laws Nine and Twelve, on how to receive divine guidance for a richer, fuller life, and how to control your destiny through mind power.

There should be a continuing program of study and evolvement all your life, which will encompass all the great branches of human knowledge. Study other self-help books, such as this, and strive constantly to perfect your mind, your talents, and your personality. Knowledge is power, and when you are once fortified with this type of wisdom you will raise your level of consciousness to new and more glorious heights. Life will become easier and more beautiful as you expand the horizons of your consciousness to encompass higher levels of experience and more noble and expansive emotions.

Last of all, but perhaps most important, when you continue to keep your mind active and progressing along the lines of thought expressed in this book, you will so magnetize the brain and body cells that you will take on a more attracive personality and be able to attract into your orbit more interesting and worthwhile people who can profitably enrich your life. An active, progressive mind also stimulates the body cells with new energy and, science has now found, keeps the body younger and more healthy. Not only will you be more energetic, more youthful and vital, but your chances of living to a grand old age are enhanced enormously when you keep up a daily pattern of mental activity, study and growth.

Ultimate fulfillment can be yours

Fortified with the knowledge you now have from this study, you will come into what the ancient Indian Sanskrit called Darshan, a state of Ultimate Fulfillment of your every secret dream and aspiration. Keep your eyes on the stars and your thoughts high and you will ultimately achieve your true life goal.

Page 185